G000151989

MIDDLESBROUGH
A COMPLETE RECORD
1876 HARRY GLASPER 1989

MIDDLESBROUGH
A COMPLETE RECORD
1876 HARRY GLASPER 1989

Breedon Books Sport

First published in Great Britain by
The Breedon Books Publishing Company Limited
44 Friar Gate, Derby DE1 1DA.

© Harry Glasper 1989

All Rights Reserved. No part of this publication may be reproduced,
stored in a retrieval system, or transmitted in any form, or by any
means, electronic, mechanical, photocopying, recording or otherwise
without the prior permission in writing of the Copyright holders, nor
be otherwise circulated in any form or binding or cover other than in
which it is published and without a similar condition including this
condition being imposed on the subsequent publisher.

ISBN 0 907969 53 4

Printed by Butler and Tanner Limited, Frome.
Jacket designed by Graham Hales and printed by Arkle Print,
Northampton.

Contents

This book is dedicated to the memory of my dear father, Ernest Glasper, who supported Middlesbrough Football Club from the age of 14 until his death in March 1963, at the age of 47. Indeed, the book began with his elementary jottings in meticulous handwriting in a school exercise book which I found by chance amongst his personal effects.

Acknowledgements

The author acknowledges the following for the assistance and encouragement received in the compilation of this book: Alan Berry, John Drennan, Derek Ferguson, Colin Galloway, Harry Green, Tina Hunter, Khalid Hussein, Karen Johnson, Arthur Lancaster, Randy McCartney, Brian Mackin, John Myers, Colin Naylor, Bob Page, Ray Robertson, Kharati Singh, Roop Wanty Singh, Bill Tait, Bob Ward, Neil Watson, Pam, Joyce and Anita of Stockton Library and Larry Bruce of Middlesbrough Reference Library. To those people who contributed but who I have unintentionally missed from the list, I offer sincere apologies.

The task of compiling this history of Middlesbrough Football Club would have been almost impossible without the existence of the town's newspaper, the *Evening Gazette*, and I am indebted to the *Gazette* staff, in particular the members of its sports department, who allowed me unrestricted access to their records.

I acknowledge the special assistance given by Nigel Gibb, who offered help when time was fast running out and also checked the statistical data and advised me of errors in the work.

Long after the deadline for the delivery of this work had passed, I had to lean heavily on the editorial staff at Breedon Books to help complete the work and for this I am grateful. It is to their credit that publication of the book was not delayed too long.

Finally, but perhaps most important of all, my wife Christine kept me going with moral support and endless cups of coffee as my spirits flagged. I only hope that both she and my children, Michael, Vicki and Richard, who grew up whilst I was turning dusty pages in distant libraries, will, in later years, think that it was time well spent.

Harry Glasper
Redcar
September 1989

Photographic Acknowledgements

Photographs supplied by Colorsport, Illustrated London News Picture Library and Arthur Foreman.

Middlesbrough

T HE story of Middlesbrough Football Club runs parallel with the story of soccer in the North-East. The origin of the 'Boro club goes back to the very beginnings of the game in that part of England and Middlesbrough FC are the oldest of today's major clubs in the area. Indeed, Middlesbrough is one of the oldest names in the history of football.

Many of today's Football League clubs owe their birth either to Victorian church, chapel or works sides. Middlesbrough Football Club was born at a tripe supper in a local hotel, when a group of young men who had been playing kickabout games on the Old Archery ground in Albert Park decided to organize themselves into a properly constituted club along the lines of those springing up all over the north of England. The date of Middlesbrough's birth, conceived at that most northern of functions, is 18 February 1876.

Mr J.Greenwood was appointed to the dual post of secretary-treasurer and, although nationally the formation of the new club did not attract much interest — the stronghold of soccer in the industrial north in the 1870s was rooted firmly in Sheffield — the applications to join Middlesbrough FC came in thick and fast from local young men. The early Middlesbrough club had a problem in finding opponents and their first-ever match was played against a leading local rugby side called Tees Wanderers. The match lasted for two 20-minute periods and at the end Middlesbrough had drawn their first game 1-1. Alas, the name of that scorer of the club's first-ever goal is lost in the mists of time.

Gradually, more soccer clubs in the North-East sprang up and in 1877-8 Middlesbrough played what is thought to be their first-ever away match when they went down 1-0 at Barnard Castle on 22 December 1877. Three weeks later they scored a fine 4-0 win over older-established South Bank and on 26 January 1878, the visit of the Newcastle club, Tyne Association, drew 150 spectators to Albert Park to see the sides draw.

A month later, in Newcastle, the sides drew again — this time in a match played in four separate periods — and when first Loftus, and then Eston, were beaten at Albert Park, Middlesbrough's home attendances had reached the 200 mark. The result of this new-found success meant that the club had to change grounds. The local Parks Committee, mindful of the fact that the ever-growing number of spectators were spilling on to the pitch and damaging the turf, told Middlesbrough to find another venue for their home matches.

In March 1879, the club moved to Breckon Hill Road, where they rented a field from a Mr Kemp, charging threepence admission to help pay the rent. Small boys paid a penny and what few women chose to see the matches were let in free. An old man collected the 'gate money' in a white basin and average takings were under £3.

Middlesbrough still found matches hard to come by and it was November before the first match of 1878-9 was played, when Billy Pickstock — later to become a great Middlesbrough favourite — made his debut at South Bank. Later that month

Opposite: Wilf Mannion (left) and George Hardwick walk out for their joint benefit match.

9

Tyne were beaten 3-2 at Breckon Hill and Middlesbrough wound up their season with a win over Redcar.

The following season saw Middlesbrough move home again, this time to an old cricket field in Linthorpe Road, and 1879-80 also saw the club play their first-ever cup match when Sheffield Exchange drew 1,000 when they visited Middlesbrough for a Sheffield Cup game. Although they were easily beaten, Middlesbrough had much to be pleased about that season. Jackson Ewbank was chosen to play for a representative Sheffield Association side against a Scottish team and the club signed two fine players in Albert Borrie and Dicky Peel. Peel was a ball-playing half-back and Borrie later served Middlesbrough with distinction as an administrator.

The club's success meant that soccer was taking a real hold in the area and other teams came into being. Redcar were Middlesbrough's greatest rivals and in October 1880, some 2,500 packed Linthorpe Road to see the sides meet in a Sheffield Cup game. After a draw, Middlesbrough won the replay 3-1 and Ewbank established his personal prowess as one of the North-East's leading players with a hat-trick. Thus confirmed as a first-class side, Middlesbrough invited Scottish sides Govan and Athole to Linthorpe Road and, in the space of three days, beat both Glasgow teams.

On 5 February 1881, the Cleveland Association was formed in the Swatters Carr Hotel and in a pipe-opening representative game against Northumberland and Durham, Cleveland won 10-0 with five Middlesbrough players in their side. Redcar supplied four players to underline the superiority of the two clubs, but Middlesbrough were clearly the top side in the North-East.

They dominated the Cleveland Association Challenge Cup for the first five years of that competition's existence before making way for other teams in 1886. In October 1881, Jack Thompson made the first of many appearances for the club as a menacing right-winger and Middlesbrough scored convincing victories over all their visitors. Newcastle Rangers were hammered 8-0, Sheffield Albion 6-0 and South Bank and Tyne 4-0 each, although Glasgow Rangers Swifts won 6-2 on New Year's Day in what was to become an annual fixture.

On 10 November 1883, Middlesbrough played their first-ever FA Cup-tie when the Derbyshire mining team of Staveley travelled north and inflicted a 5-1 defeat on 'Boro in the first round of the competition. The following season, Middlesbrough did better in reaching the fourth round where they lost 5-2 to Old Etonians.

A win would have given 'Boro a bye into the last eight but, even so, the mere fact that they were now playing such teams as Old Etonians, six times FA Cup Finalists and twice winners of the trophy, meant that Middlesbrough had arrived as a force in English soccer.

Redcar, too, were also making their way and in the fifth round of the 1885-6 FA Cup, the Yorkshire rivals met at Redcar Cricket Field. Middlesbrough had beaten Grimsby Town 2-1 in the third round and then, like Redcar, received a bye into the fifth. Amid the snow and sleet of 23 January 1886, some 1,000 people saw Redcar win 2-1, but they were then knocked out 2-0 by Small Heath in the quarter-finals.

That season Middlesbrough and Redcar were also due to meet in the Cleveland Association Challenge Cup Final — Middlesbrough had won the previous four Finals against Redcar — and on 13 March 1886, over 5,000 spectators packed the Saltburn ground to see the two North-East giants draw 0-0 after extra-time. The match was stopped short of the full period when Redcar's Paul broke a leg. The replay was set for 3 April and, as their opponents were short of their two best players, Middlesbrough agreed to the Final being staged at Redcar. It made little difference as 'Boro romped home 8-1 before withdrawing from the competition.

10

Season 1885-6 was a magnificent one for Middlesbrough — that FA Cup defeat by Redcar excepted. They twice drew with Blackburn Olympic, FA Cup winners in 1883, and beat Nottingham and District 2-1. Individual players turned out for Cleveland against Northumberland with Oswald Cochrane captaining the side. Jack Thompson was a reserve in the North v South game and Albert Borrie played centre-forward for the North-East team which met the famous Corinthians on Tyne's ground.

Two seasons later, in 1887-8, 'Boro played their first game against Sunderland, who were rising stars and challenging Middlesbrough's place at the top of the North-East soccer ladder. This first-ever encounter between sides who were to become great rivals was fraught with incident. The match was in a qualifying round of the FA Cup and at half-time, Sunderland led 2-0 at Linthorpe Road. In the second-half Middlesbrough tore their way back into the game and earned a 2-2 draw before 8,000 spectators. Each club received £34 7s 9d and by the time the teams met at Newcastle Road for the replay, they knew that the winners would receive a bye into the last 16, where they would entertain the London side, Old Foresters.

This time it was Middlesbrough's turn to take a 2-0 lead and Sunderland's to fight back. The Wearsiders won 4-2, but Middlesbrough immediately protested about the professionalism of three Scotsmen in the Sunderland side. On 27 December 1887, at the North-Eastern Hotel, Darlington, an inquiry suspended the three players, booted Sunderland out of the Cup and gave their place to Middlesbrough, who gratefully went through to the quarter-finals with a 4-0 win over Old Foresters.

Even that game was soured by controversy. The London side complained about the state of the Linthorpe Road pitch, hoping for a home replay. When the FA upheld their protest but ordered the game to be replayed at Middlesbrough, Old Foresters withdrew rather than face another trip north. In the quarter-finals, Crewe Alexandra won 2-0 before 6,000 fans at Linthorpe Road. Amazingly, Middlesbrough are still waiting to play in their first FA Cup semi-final.

In 1888, the Football League was formed and that development, plus the obvious need for professional players, led to a split in Middlesbrough football. The club's officials and supporters were divided as to whether they should adopt professionalism and eventually those who wanted to pay players and stay in touch with the clubs which were now taking over the stage, broke away from the old club.

They formed a team called Ironopolis Football Company which had its headquarters at the Swatters Carr Hotel in Linthorpe Road, a stone's throw from Middlesbrough's HQ. The new club's colours were maroon and green stripes and three Middlesbrough first-teamers switched camps, being joined by players from Scottish clubs, Arthurlie and Dundee Strathmore. Ironopolis's chairman was Alfred Mattison.

The old club now knew that they had to turn professional as well, if they were to avoid becoming second-best. After a brief attempt to bring in legislation allowing players to be paid expenses while retaining their amateur status, Middlesbrough joined the professionals and, indeed, played their first game as a professional club one week before Ironopolis. On 7 December 1889, Sunderland won 3-0 at Linthorpe Road. That Saturday, Ironopolis drew 1-1 with Gainsborough Trinity before 5,000 spectators. The battle for soccer supremacy in Middlesbrough was joined.

Both teams were now members of the newly-formed Northern League. In its first season of 1889-90, the League had been won by Darlington St Augustine's before Ironopolis took the next three championships. Other clubs in the Northern League at that time were Bishop Auckland, Birtley, Darlington, Elswick Rangers, Newcastle East End, Newcastle West End, South Bank and Stockton.

Middlesbrough ('The Scabs') and Ironopolis ('The Washers' or The Nops') vied for position. Ironopolis arranged top friendlies against Preston, Everton and Sunderland at their ground — their dressing-rooms and headquarters were now at the County Hotel, Newport Road — and Middlesbrough finished runners-up in the Northern League and reached the second round of the FA Cup, where they lost 2-1 at home to Preston, who had beaten Ironopolis 6-0 in the previous round.

Although both clubs had been successful in 1891-2, officials from both camps knew that only amalgamation would be the answer to mounting a serious challenge in the Football League which was now four seasons old. On 7 May 1892, a meeting was held to discuss such a merger and it was agreed to make an application to the Football League annual meeting in Sunderland later that month, under the name of Middlesbrough & Ironopolis Football and Athletic Co Ltd.

Newcastle East End also applied, but the clubs received only one vote each and although they were later invited to form part of the new Second Division, both declined on the grounds that many of their prospective opponents would not be sufficiently attractive to warrant the increased travel.

With admission to the Football League not now an issue, the Middlesbrough clubs again went their separate ways. In the 1892-3 FA Cup, Middlesbrough were knocked out 2-1 by Wolves, the eventual Cup winners, whilst Ironopolis reached the next round before being trounced 7-0 at home to Preston after drawing 2-2 in Lancashire.

In the close season of 1893, Ironopolis made the decision to go it alone in a bid to join the Football League and when the League decided to extend the Second Division to 15 clubs, Ironopolis were in. Bootle resigned from the Second Division, Accrington failed to gain election after finishing next to the bottom of the First Division, and Ironopolis — along with Newcastle United, Rotherham United, Arsenal and Liverpool — stepped up to take their places alongside existing Second Division clubs like Walsall, Burton Swifts, Grimsby, Northwich Victoria, Lincoln City, Crewe Alexandra and Manchester City.

The first-ever Football League match in Middlesbrough took place on 2 September 1893, when Liverpool visited the Paradise Ground and won 2-0. Ironopolis lost their next two games — away to Manchester City (6-1) on 9 September and away to Burton (5-0) on 20 September — before beating Manchester City (then Ardwick) 2-0 on 23 September.

From a playing point of view, Ironopolis's only season in the Football League was not a disaster. True, they lost all but one away game, but they totalled 20 points from 28 games, which kept them out of the re-election zone. The real problems had been financial. At the end of the season Ironopolis folded, underlining the argument that if the combined sides had taken up the invitation to join the Second Division a season earlier, they would have had the undivided support of all the town's football enthusiasts. As it was, support was too fragmented to sustain two top clubs and Ironopolis's name faded, not from the Football League alone, but from the story of English soccer altogether.

Middlesbrough, meanwhile, had reverted to amateur status during Ironopolis's Football League season and the town was in exactly the same position as it had been before the breakaway club was formed. The amateur Middlesbrough now asserted themselves with the Northern League championship in 1894, 1895 and 1897 and the FA Amateur Cup in 1895 and 1898.

The Amateur Cup was inaugurated in 1893-4, when Old Carthusians became the first winners of the new trophy. The following season Middlesbrough beat Bishop Auckland, Darlington (after two drawn games) and Old Brightonians, who they hammered 8-0, before meeting the Lancaster Regiment (Portsmouth) in the semi-final at Derby. Middlesbrough won 4-0 and met Old Carthusians in the FA Amateur

Middlesbrough, winners of the FA Amateur Cup in 1894-5. Back row (left to right): J.H.Gettins, D.Wilson, S.Cooper, R.Piercy, J.Murphy. Front row: A.Nelmes, T.Morren, T.Bach, H.Alport, A.Johnson, D.Mullen.

Centre-forward J.H.Gettins, who helped Middlesbrough win the FA Amateur Cup. Gettins also turned out for Millwall Athletic and played first-class cricket for Middlesex and London County. He was once described as 'a centre-forward who is distinctly above the average. Fast as well as clever, a safe tackler and a smart shot at goal, he has all the qualifications for a really first-class player.'

13

Cup Final on 27 April 1895. The Charterhouse old boys' side took a second-half lead at Headingley before 4,000 people saw Dave Mullen level the scores and then 'Happy' Nelmes hit the winner.

At Middlesbrough railway station a band led the triumphant team to the celebrations at the Masham Hotel, kept at that time by Tom Bach, the Middlesbrough skipper. Alas, there was no trophy to present. Old Carthusians had considered the result such a formality that they had not bothered to bring the FA Amateur Cup with them. It was some days before the new winners laid hands on their prize.

This success had its drawbacks. Players were suddenly thrust into the limelight and professional clubs were soon flocking to offer terms to Middlesbrough's amateurs. Tom Morren moved to Sheffield United, where he went on to win an international cap for England, and Phil Bach did the same when he moved on to Sunderland, although he returned to give great service to Middlesbrough as chairman. Despite losing some of their best players, Middlesbrough remained a force and in 1898 they won the FA Amateur Cup again after reaching the semi-finals the previous season, where they were beaten by Royal Artillery (Portsmouth).

Middlesbrough's path to their second Final was bizarre to say the least. After beating Leadgate Park, Thornaby Utopians and Casuals, Middlesbrough faced a semi-final tie against Thornaby at Darlington. At that time there was a smallpox epidemic in the lower Teesside area and Darlington people protested strongly about supporters of two semi-finalists bringing the disease into their town. The FA arranged for the semi-final to be played in secret in the Cleveland hill village of Brotton, two miles from the sea.

Middlesbrough won this eccentric semi-final and took their place in the Amateur Cup Final against Uxbridge at the Crystal Palace. It was a hot, humid day as Middlesbrough, skippered by left-back Robert Piercy, took control of the game and won 2-1 with goals from Bishop and Kemplay. The date was 23 April 1898 and it was Middlesbrough's last cup win until their Anglo-Scottish Cup triumph 78 years later.

Middlesbrough's days in the unpaid ranks were almost over. The players were at the top of the amateur tree and there was really nothing more that they could achieve. In addition they could see that fellow players — some not nearly so talented — were making money at other clubs. The end of the old-fashioned opposition to professionalism was also in sight and Middlesbrough played only one more season as an amateur club. In the FA Cup they beat Darlington 6-2 in the qualifying competition before going out 1-0 at home to Hebburn Argyle.

Apart from the FA Cup, the only time Middlesbrough fans saw top-class professional opposition was when Middlesbrough arranged friendlies against teams like Preston, Millwall, Burnley, Spurs and Southampton, paying the visiting clubs guarantees of between £10 and £40 to visit Teesside. The breach with the people who had broken away to form Ironopolis was healed and the way was now clear for Middlesbrough to assume professional status once again. On 28 February 1899, at a meeting presided over by the club chairman, R.H.Forrester, Middlesbrough FC rejoined the ranks of the professional clubs.

'Boro's next ambition was to join the Football League and after raising 1,000 £1 shares, they applied, with the backing of Sunderland, Newcastle United and Harry Walker, North Riding FA's representative on the FA Council. The Football League annual meeting was held on 19 May 1899, at the Old Boar's Head Hotel in Manchester, and there were nine applicants for three vacant places in the Second Division. Middlesbrough received 17 votes to Blackpool's 15 (Blackpool were seeking re-election) and League football returned to Middlesbrough after a gap of five seasons. Next-to-bottom Loughborough were re-elected with 28 votes and newcomers

Chesterfield (27 votes) came in at the expense of the bottom club, Darwen, who had conceded 141 goals and won only nine points in 34 games.

Middlesbrough did just enough in their first season as a Football League club. The first game was on 2 September 1899, when they lost 3-0 at Lincoln. There followed two more defeats before Middlesbrough won their first League point with a 1-1 draw at New Brighton on 16 September. A week later they recorded their first League win by beating Grimsby Town 1-0 at Linthorpe Road. On 11 November, Middlesbrough crushed Burton Swifts 8-1 at home. Although there were several defeats at Linthorpe Road, it was their home form which kept them alive. They failed to win a single away match in finishing 14th out of 18 clubs.

Unlike Ironopolis, Middlesbrough's debut in the Football League was successful in terms of finance and they finished the season with a profit of £176. Near the end of the season they signed Newcastle United's left-winger, Willie Wardrope, to underline their arrival as a serious force in professional football under manager John Robson.

Middlesbrough's colours in those early days of the Football League were white shirts and blue shorts with a change strip of black shirts and white shorts. Even in those times, vandalism was a problem and a report to the June board meeting told of damage to the ground. The members' entrance had been broken by carthorses and it was resolved 'that horses shall not be allowed on the field in future'. Shares were offered to local tradesmen and one proprietor of a local boot and shoe firm offered 11 pairs of boots — which were gratefully accepted.

Once settled into the Football League, Middlesbrough lost little time in making their presence felt and in the 1900-01 season they shot up the table to finish in sixth place. After winning their first match of the season, 2-0 at home to Lincoln, they went down 4-0 at Newton Heath (later Manchester United) and then drew 2-2 at home to Glossop North End. On 22 September, however, Middlesbrough recorded their first-ever away win in the Football League when they beat Chesterfield 3-2.

On 9 March 1901, Middlesbrough crushed Gainsborough 9-2 at Linthorpe Road and at the end of the season they had climbed up the table and had almost doubled their gate receipts to £8,347. If 'Boro fans felt that their team was on the verge of greater things, they were not going to be disappointed. In only their third season in the Football League, Middlesbrough stormed to promotion, finishing runners-up to West Bromwich Albion and nine points clear of third club Preston North End.

From the moment they won their opening game of the season, beating Stockport County 3-1 at Edgeley Park, Middlesbrough looked set for the First Division. Only West Brom managed to win at Linthorpe Road — a 2-1 defeat for 'Boro on 12 October 1901 — and Middlesbrough's final goals for and against tallies of 90-24 were each the best of any club in the Football League. In 17 home matches, Middlesbrough dropped only three points and scored 58 goals with just seven against.

The Middlesbrough side had undergone a complete transformation. Of the old guard, only Ramsey remained at left-back. The club's half-backs in that promotion season were Dave Smith, 'Bullet' Jones and Andy Davidson — a half-back line which supporters talked about for years afterwards.

On 19 April 1902, Middlesbrough entertained Bristol City and beat them 2-0. In that game, manager John Robson gave a debut to a young goalkeeper, 18-year-old Tim Williamson. Less than 5ft 10in. tall, Williamson became known as 'Tiny' and went on to establish himself as one of the best goalkeepers of his day. When he appeared against Ireland at Ayresome Park in February 1905, he became the first player to be capped for England while playing for Middlesbrough. Williamson

15

Middlesbrough 1901-02. Back row (left to right): W.J.Gill (president), G.Pickard (director), W.Mullen (director), unknown, J.Dow, D.Smith, J.Frail, A.Davidson, J.Tennant, C.Harper (trainer), J.Cummings. Seated: W.Wardrope, J.Brearley, J.Cassidy, P.Turner. On ground: A.Jones, A.Ramsey, J.Leslie.

was capped seven times in all and there could have been no-one in the crowd for that match against Bristol City who realized that they were watching the start of an illustrious career. When he left the club in 1923, Williamson had played a record 610 games for Middlesbrough (563 League and 47 FA Cup). He is part of the Middlesbrough legend.

Season 1902-03 was not only Middlesbrough's first in the First Division. It also signalled the beginnings of their present home at Ayresome Park. Even before the season began there was tremendous interest in 'Boro's fortunes and crowds of 12-15,000 turned up to see their pre-season practice matches. On 1 September 1902, Middlesbrough played their first match in the First Division and 'Sandy' Robertson gave them the best possible start to their career in the top-flight when he scored the only goal of their match at Blackburn Rovers. One week later Robertson was on target again when he scored the only goal against Everton as Middlesbrough recorded their first home win in the First Division. The crowd at Linthorpe Road that day was around 20,000.

Middlesbrough also had their first taste of local derby games at the highest level. On 18 October 1902 they beat Newcastle United 1-0 at St James' Park. When they met Newcastle in the return at Linthorpe Road on 14 February, Middlesbrough won by the same score. The games against Sunderland, however, were a different tale. On 20 December, the Wearsiders won 1-0 at Middlesbrough and late in the season — on 18 April 1903 — Sunderland won 2-1 in a match played at Newcastle after Roker Park had been closed due to crowd trouble.

Middlesbrough finished their first season in the First Division in 13th place, seven points clear of relegated Grimsby Town. Ten of their 14 wins were at Linthorpe Road, where they scored 27 of their 41 goals. Newcastle finished on level points with 'Boro but an inferior goal average pushed them into 14th place.

In the FA Cup, Middlesbrough went out in the first round, losing 3-1 at Bristol City. Indeed, Boro's progress in the Cup had been painfully slow. After their quarter-final appearance of 1888 they had to wait 13 seasons before appearing in the last 16 again. In 1900-01 they fought through the preliminary competition for the right to meet Newcastle at Middlesbrough and won the local derby 3-1. In the next round an easy home tie with Kettering was won 5-0 and Middlesbrough fans were thinking of a semi-final place when West Brom upset their plans by winning 1-0 at Linthorpe Road.

Throughout the 1902-03 season preparations had been underway to move from Linthorpe Road to Ayresome Park. The last game played on the old ground which had served Middlesbrough so well was the 1-1 draw against Stoke on 25 April 1903. Then 'Boro moved lock, stock and barrel to their new home. Early in September 1903, Glasgow Celtic took part in the first game at Ayresome Park and were beaten 1-0. But the official opening came a few days later, on 12 September 1903 when Sunderland were the visitors for a First Division match.

Once settled into their new ground — their first League win at Ayresome Park was on 26 September 1903, when they beat Small Heath (later Birmingham City) 3-1 — Middlesbrough began to consolidate themselves in the First Division and finished a respectable tenth. In addition, 'Boro had the added bonus of a profit of £3,314 on the season.

In the FA Cup that year, they equalled their best run with a trip to the quarter-finals. In the first round proper they went to Millwall and beat the London club 2-0. 'Sandy' Brown scored both goals against a Millwall side which included Joe Gettins, who had played for 'Boro in the 1895 FA Amateur Cup Final and who was an amateur on the books of both clubs. In the second round Middlesbrough visited Preston and another two goals from Brown helped them on their way to a sensational 3-0 victory over that season's Second Division champions. It was Preston's only defeat of the season.

'Boro were in the quarter-finals for the third time in their history and when they managed a goalless draw at Manchester City there were many Middlesbrough fans who thought that 1904 might be their year. But when the sides met at Ayresome Park for the replay, the Lancashire club cruised to a 3-1 win — a big disappointment to the thousands of Teesside youngsters who had been given the Wednesday afternoon off school to watch their favourites battle for the right to meet Sheffield Wednesday in the semi-final.

All was not well in the Middlesbrough camp, despite the satisfactory performances of 1903-04, and the following season 'Boro found themselves in the relegation zone. By February 1905, they were next-to-bottom of the First Division and had not won an away game in the League for two years. The club knew that they had to do something out of the ordinary to revive the fortunes of their flagging side. Middlesbrough had already moved into the transfer market with the signing of Stockport County's centre-forward Tom Green. In the New Year they also approached Sunderland and asked the Roker Park directors about the possible transfer of forward Alf Common.

The deal took some time to set up but by the end of February, Common was a Middlesbrough player and destined to become one of the most famous names in the history of soccer, not for what he achieved in the game, but for the fact that at a transfer fee of £1,000, he became the first 'four-figure footballer'. Although it was perfectly acceptable for a club to buy players to win titles, it was considered almost immoral to spend money on avoiding relegation. And when such extravagance was shown by one of the Football League's newest clubs *The Athletic News* commented: 'As a matter of commerce, ten young recruits at £100 apiece might have paid better, and as a matter of sport, the Second Division would be more honourable than retention of place by purchase.'

17

Above and below: Action from 'Boro's FA Cup game against Tottenham Hotspur in February 1905.

Whatever the morals of the transfer, Common proved his worth immediately. On 25 February, Middlesbrough went to Bramall Lane to play Sheffield United and won 1-0, Common scoring the only goal of the game from the penalty-spot. It was 'Boro's first away win since their 3-1 victory against the same club on 7 March 1903. Middlesbrough's fortunes picked up and when they won 2-0 at Blackburn on 15 April 1905, they were safe. Even a 3-0 home defeat at the hands of Newcastle on the last day on the season could not harm them and they finished 15th.

In the FA Cup, Middlesbrough could only draw 1-1 with Tottenham Hotspur, who were then a Southern League side. In the replay at White Hart Lane, the Londoners won 1-0. Perhaps the greatest measure of 'Boro's mediocre season was the fact that their leading scorer for 1904-05 was Tom Green, the centre-forward signed midway throuh the season from Stockport. Green headed 'Boro's scorers with just four goals.

Even after relegation had been avoided the club's troubles were not over and during the course of the following season — when 'Boro again fought to avoid the drop to the Second Division — the Football Association fined the club £250 and suspended 11 of the 12 directors, including the chairman R.W.Williams, for allegedly making irregular bonus payments to players.

In 1905-06, Middlesbrough came nearer to relegation than the previous season, saved only perhaps by the Football League's decision to retain the bottom two clubs of 1904-05 — Bury and Notts County — and extend the First Division to 20 clubs. Alex Mackie, the former Sunderland boss, was now manager in place of John Robson. In the end it was Mackie's swoop into the transfer market which once again saved 'Boro's First Division status. Again the deals involving Middlesbrough were little short of sensational. In March 1906, the club amazed the football world with three signings.

Middlesbrough in 1905-06. Back row (left to right): A.McCallum (director), H.Pickard (director), D.Mullen (director), A.Barritt (director). Third row: Tinsley, Lt-Col T.G.Poole (director), T.Murray, C.Hewitt, W.Agnew, J.Frail, J.Hogg, T.F.Phillipson, S.Aitken, Dr Bryan, J.Allan. Second row: Ratherton, D.McCallum, J.Cassidy, G.Henderson, R.Williams (director), A.Jones, A.Davidson, D.Smith, W.Mackie, G.W.Allan. Front row: T.Bingley (trainer), T.Coxon, J.Bell, J.Thackeray, A.Common, T.Green, G.T.Reid, Barker, T.Coulson (assistant trainer).

The legendary Steve Bloomer — already an established England international — came from Derby County, a move which was as much a shock to his devoted fans at the Baseball Ground as it was to Ayresome Park supporters; Billy Brawn arrived from Aston Villa after winning two England caps and playing for Villa against Newcastle in the 1905 FA Cup Final; and Fred Wilcox moved from Birmingham to Ayresome Park. In addition, Middlesbrough also brought Bloomer's teammate, full-back Emor ('Jack') Ratcliffe from Derby, although he was only a makeweight which enabled Derby to obtain a more realistic fee for Bloomer under the transfer regulations then in force.

Unlike Alf Common, there was to be no story-book debut for Bloomer. He played his first game for 'Boro against First Division leaders Liverpool at Anfield on 17 March 1906 and saw his side humiliated by the Merseysiders, who were on their way to their second Championship. The last day of the season arrived with Wolves already relegated. Middlesbrough and Bury had 30 points each, Nottingham Forest 31. Bury won 3-0 at Sunderland, Forest went down 4-1 at Everton and Middlesbrough managed a 1-1 draw at Blackburn to escape the drop by virtue of a better goal-average than Forest, who joined Wolves in the Second Division.

The years leading up to the start of World War One were memorable more for the controversy surrounding the club's financial dealings than for anything Middlesbrough achieved on the field. In the FA Cup, they never progressed beyond the third round. In fact, they had to wait until 1936 for their next quarter-final appearance. In the First Division they rose to fourth in 1914, but for most of the time hovered around mid-table.

The financial problems were highlighted on 4 January 1906, when the FA suspended the club because the £250 fine imposed for irregular payments had not been paid. So that Middlesbrough could play Derby County at the Baseball Ground the following Saturday, 'Boro's new chairman, Lieutenant-Colonel T.Gibson Poole, sent his personal cheque to clear the debt and Middlesbrough duly went to Derby and drew 1-1 with a goal from Alf Common. The club also owed Stoke £155 for the transfer of Coxon and this was also settled in due course.

Middlesbrough's March 1906 transfer dealings had made the club unpopular — as had the £1,000 signing of Alf Common, who finished 1905-06 as 'Boro's leading scorer with 19 goals — and soon rumours were rife that several clubs, wishing to see Bury relegated, had assisted Middlesbrough in the purchase of Bloomer, Brawn and Wilcox. Football's ruling body could hardly ignore such accusations and in May 1906 a commission met in Manchester to examine Middlesbrough's books and question officials from Derby, Villa and Birmingham.

A later meeting at Blackburn cross-examined chairman Poole and manager Mackie and reported that 'Boro had paid Bloomer an improper bonus of £10 to re-sign for 1906-07. In addition, they said, 'Boro's books were not properly kept. Middlesbrough were fined £50 and two members of the League Management Committee would visit the club twice before the end of April 1907 — at 'Boro's expense — to ensure that the books were kept in order. By now the FA considered Middlesbrough's accounts to be in such a mess that a special commission was set up to investigate the entire financial running of the club.

The commission found, among other things, that the club chairman sometimes retained takings himself, paying the club's bills out of his personal account, and that he owed Middlesbrough £500. The chairman paid the balance into the club's bank and escaped public censure. But Alex Mackie, who had already resigned, was suspended. Steve Bloomer was also banned for two weeks.

On the field things were going just as badly and 'Boro started 1906-07 with only two points from their first eight games, losing two home games to Sheffield Wednesday

(1-3) and Manchester City (2-3). In late October, they appointed a player-manager in the shape of Andy Aitken, a Scottish international centre-half and great favourite at St James' Park. Although Middlesbrough were bottom of the First Division by Christmas, under Aitken they rallied to finish the season in 11th place, thanks mainly to the inspiring example of their new manager and the splendid Williamson in goal. Before the end of the season, Middlesbrough made another important signing when Sunderland's left-back, Jimmy Watson, arrived at Ayresome Park.

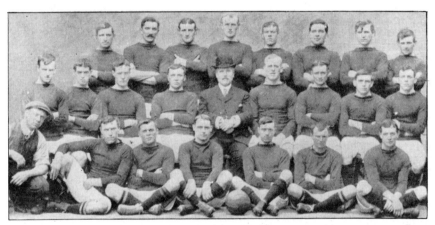

Middlesbrough during 1907-08. Back row (left to right): J.Tildsley, J.Watson, R.G.Williamson, A.A.Hasel, A.Campbell, J.Tomlin, M.Wilson, T.Dixon. Middle row: S.Aitken, J.O'Gara, W.Brawn, S.Bloomer, Lt-Col T.G.Poole VD (director), A.Common, F.Wilcox, J.Thackeray, T.Wilson. Front row: J.Bingley, W.Barker, W.Haxby, A.Aitken, R.Brown, E.Verrill, J.Harkins.

With their defence strengthened by the inclusion of Aitken, Watson and the fast-improving Williamson, Middlesbrough set out on the 1907-08 season in more confident mood and, although they again failed in the FA Cup, losing 2-0 to Notts County in the first round, they climbed up the First Division to finish in what was then their best-ever position of sixth.

'Boro were only two points behind runners-up Aston Villa and had it not been for a poor start to the season — 17 points from their first 21 games — they would have finished second to champions Manchester United. Bloomer was leading scorer with 12 League goals to add to the 18 which had seen him in first place the previous season.

In the close season, Aitken left the club for Leicester Fosse, who had just won promotion to the First Division and in 1908-09 'Boro finished in ninth place. Their FA Cup run again ended in the first round, this time at Preston.

In 1909-10, Middlesbrough found themselves at the wrong end of the table and by New Year they were second from bottom. Into the side had come George Elliott, a Sunderland-born youngster who teamed up with Steve Bloomer, Common having been tried at centre-half in a bid to plug the gap left by the departure of Aitken.

Elliott was an immediate success with the Ayresome Park fans. Like 'Tiny' Williamson he was to give great service to 'Boro and when he left in 1925, he had played 364 League and FA Cup games and scored 208 goals. When one considers that World War One robbed Elliott of four seasons, they are awesome figures indeed.

Four victories in March 1910 saved Middlesbrough from relegation. Wins over Bolton (home 5-0), Bristol City (home 2-1), Sheffield United (home 1-0) and Nottingham Forest (away 1-0) edged 'Boro to 31 points, level with Arsenal and two more than relegated Chelsea, who went down with bottom club, Bolton Wanderers.

But still there were dark clouds off the field. After the 1-1 draw with Newcastle at Ayresome Park on 9 April, the referee alleged that 'Boro and the FA Cup Finalists had come to an arrangement over the result. A joint FA-Football League inquiry reported: 'There was no proof of any arrangement between clubs of players to influence the result.' Nevertheless, Middlesbrough's name had cropped up again in connection with alleged irregularities.

The club's gate receipts were £1,000 down on the previous season and Lieutenant-Colonel Poole offered Alf Common a free transfer if he did not claim the £250 benefit which the club had promised him. Common agreed and soon the history-making footballer was on his way to Arsenal. It was ironic that the game's first four-figure footballer should be given away to save the club from financial embarrassment. Bloomer went back to Derby in September 1910 and Watson became assistant trainer before joining non-League Shildon shortly afterwards.

Despite losing three star names, Middlesbrough began 1910-11 well. Manager Andy Walker introduced a Scottish lad, Andy Jackson, at centre-half and at last the gap created by Aitken's departure was filled, although Robert Young, who had joined Everton in the close season for £1,200, had done well enough. Young Jackson's performances made him a firm favourite at Ayresome Park. But for his tragic death in World War One, he may well have become one of the game's great players.

On 17 December 1910, Middlesbrough beat Bradford City 3-2 at Ayresome Park to put themselves only a point from the top of the First Division after a superb run which had given them 23 points from their first 16 games. From that moment the side took only nine points from their remaining 22 games. What happened to halt this Boro side in its tracks? Again it was an off-the-field scandal.

This time the row centred around the visit of League leaders Sunderland on 3 December 1910. At that time the Wearsiders were the only unbeaten side in the Football League and nearly 28,000 fans packed into Middlesbrough's ground for what they saw as the match of the season. At the same time, the Middlesbrough Parliamentary election was only two days away and Lieutenant-Colonel Poole was standing as Tory candidate. Some of the 'Boro players had spoken on his behalf and, amazing though it may seem today, the result of the First Division match became tied up with the election result as the Liberals forecast a Sunderland victory.

All this may, on the face of it, seem harmless enthusiasm. But it had sinister overtones. Before the game 'Boro manager Andy Walker offered Sunderland's skipper Charlie Thomson £30 (£10 for himself and £2 for each of the other Sunderland players) to let Middlesbrough win the game, 'so as to help the chairman win the election.' Thomson told Sunderland's trainer, Billy Williams, and Williams told Mr Fred Taylor, the Wearsiders' chairman. Taylor and another Sunderland director reported the matter to the Football Association.

Even though Sunderland could not have been trying harder, Middlesbrough won the game 1-0, through a goal from outside-left Nichol. Despite the result, the 'Boro chairman lost the election by 3,749 votes and once again Middlesbrough were before a commission of inquiry. In addition, Walker was also in trouble for making an illegal approach to an Airdrieonians player. He was suspended for four weeks on that charge and the 'Boro club fined £100.

On 16 January 1911, the commission reported they were satisfied that an offer of money to influence the result had been made and both Walker and Poole were suspended permanently. Poole received little sympathy, but over 12,500 people signed a petition asking the FA to reinstate Walker, without success.

Middlesbrough's name was now bad news to both the FA and the Football League and at the club's annual meeting, the League president told shareholders that any further malpractices would result in Middlesbrough losing their place in the competition. The affair probably cost the club the First Division title because the players never recovered from the scandal and the jibes that they had tried to buy victory.

Two players seemingly unaffected by the scandal were Tim Williamson and George Elliott. Williamson won his second cap, against Ireland at Derby on 11 February 1911, thus breaking Sam Hardy's seemingly permanent hold of the position, and went on to play in six of the next seven England games. Elliott became Middlesbrough's leading goalscorer with ten goals out of Boro's total of 49. Elliott held the top 'Boro goalscoring spot for the next three seasons and for several seasons after the war.

For season 1911-12, Middlesbrough had a new set of directors and a new manager. Andy Aitken applied for his old job but the post went to Tom McIntosh, the Darlington boss. For the first few weeks of the season, the North-East took the

George Elliott maintained his consistency as Middlesbrough's most prolific goalscorer.

First Division by storm. In November, 'Boro topped the table with Newcastle second and Sunderland third. Eventually, only Newcastle finished in the top three and Middlesbrough had to be content with seventh place, one ahead of Sunderland.

Alf Common led Arsenal to a 3-1 win over 'Boro at Highbury on 16 December and when the Gunners came to Ayresome Park in February, they won again, this time 2-0. But the highlight of the season was the visit of Newcastle on 11 November. The clubs stood first and second in the table and a record 30,000 crowd packed Ayresome Park to see the 1-1 draw. It was the final confirmation that the bad old days of relegation worries and scandals were over for the time being.

The splendidly-named George Washington Elliott continued to bang home the goals — although in the last season before the shutdown for World War One, he made way for Walter Tinsley, who scored 23 League goals.

The Carr brothers joined the club around this time. Willie Carr, a centre-half and the eldest of the three, signed in November 1910; three months later, Jackie, who was to go on to make 466 first team appearances and score 78 goals, signed; later, younger brother George also pulled on a Middlesbrough shirt.

In 1912-13, 'Boro finished 16th but Williamson continued to perform wonders in goal and was now club skipper, whilst Elliott played his first game for England, against Ireland in Belfast. In that same game, incidentally, Williamson won his last cap.

'Boro's 1912-13 squad of players pictured at Ayresome Park.

In 1913-14, Middlesbrough achieved their best position in the First Division when they finished third behind Blackburn and Aston Villa. Elliott's 31 goals made him the top scorer in the First Division, despite the fact that he had missed six games, and Walter Tinsley, who came from Sunderland in December 1913, managed 19 goals in only 23 games. 'Boro had now found their goalscoring touch with 77 goals. Only champions Blackburn (with 78) hit more.

'Boro's last season before World War One saw them drop to 12th place after averaging a point a game. In their match with Oldham at Ayresome Park on 3 April 1915, 'Boro were leading 4-1 after 55 minutes when the Oldham full-back, Billy Cook, refused to leave the field after being sent off. The referee abandoned the game and the League ordered the result to stand.

The outbreak of war meant the end of many potentially illustrious football careers. Besides those players who were too old to resume when war ended in 1918, Middlesbrough lost three players killed in the fighting — Andrew Jackson, Archie Wilson and the former Celtic player, Don McLeod. Ayresome Park became a military training centre and the club closed down for the duration.

In January 1919, Middlesbrough, Newcastle and Sunderland were the mainstays of the Northern Victory League, introduced as a preliminary to the return of the Football League. 'Boro took the title, three points ahead of the Wearsiders, and the club looked forward to the first proper football since 1915.

Willie Carr had taken over from Jackson at centre-half and under Tom McIntosh — the man who guided Middlesbrough to their highest-ever First Division position in 1913-14 — 'Boro looked forward to their first game of the season in a First Division now extended to 22 clubs. Their first post-war match took place at Hillsborough on 30 August 1919, when 'Boro won 1-0 against Sheffield Wednesday, the side which finished seventh in the last season of peace.

But the intervening years had done much to change the face of football and at the end of the season, Wednesday were relegated, finishing bottom of the table, 13 points adrift of the next club, Notts County. Middlesbrough floundered after their promising start. Although George Elliott was still finding the net regularly — 31 League goals in the season — and despite the fact that Williamson was performing as well in goal as he had done almost two decades earlier, 'Boro's play lacked the consistency to make them Championship contenders. They finished 13th and were knocked out of the FA Cup in the second round, going down 1-0 at Notts County.

Willie Carr (left) and Bill Fox (right) each made over 100 League appearances for 'Boro.

For the next two seasons, 'Boro's League position maintained a steady improvement. They finished eighth in both 1920-21 and 1921-2. In the latter season, Middlesbrough had the added bonus of their Scottish international, Andrew Wilson, returning to the fold. Wilson was injured during the war and played with a glove over a paralysed hand. He went 'on loan' to Dunfermline, then playing in a 'rebel' Central League in Scotland, but 'Boro refused to transfer him and he returned to Ayresome Park in August 1921, to a hero's welcome.

Middlesbrough in 1922. Back row (left to right): W.Birrell, J.Carr. Third row: P.Donaghy, R.Pender, V.Fox, R.G.Williamson, W.Carr, G.Carr. Second row: J.Marshall, A.N.Wilson, S.Davidson, G.W.Elliott, W.Ellerington. Front row: T.Urwin, W.Murray.

Elliott moved to inside-forward to accommodate the Scottish international centre-forward and, despite his reluctance to return, Wilson repaid 'Boro with 32 goals in his first season as the side maintained eighth place in the First Division, with exactly the same number of points — 46.

Middlesbrough's forward line read: Jackie Carr, Billy Birrell (from Raith Rovers), Andy Wilson, George Elliott and Tommy Urwin. It is a front line which still rolls easily off the tongues of the most senior of today's 'Boro supporters.

A measure of Elliott's talent was the fact that on 8 April 1922, when Wilson was scoring the winning goal for Scotland against England at Birmingham, Elliott deputized at centre-forward and netted a hat-trick in the 4-2 win over Arsenal at Ayresome Park. And the following season Elliott was back as 'Boro's leading scorer with 23 goals.

But if 1922-3 was a good one for Elliott, it was a bad one for the 'Boro team who slipped to 18th place in the First Division, albeit six points clear of relegation Off the field the club lost over £7,000 and it was clear that a crisis was at hand It broke the following season.

The 1923-4 season was Middlesbrough's 18th in the First Division since winning

26

Winger Jackie Mordue (left) and goalkeeper Harry Harrison (right) were on the fringe of first-team selection during their time at Ayresome Park.

promotion in 1902. It also proved to be their last for three seasons. The side won only seven games and finished bottom of the table with 22 points — ten fewer than Chelsea, who went down with them. 'Boro won only one game away from home (a 1-0 victory at Sheffield United on 29 December) and Andy Wilson was leading scorer with only eight goals, five of which had been scored in one game against Nottingham Forest when 'Boro had a purple patch and won 5-2. Manager Jim Howie, who had replaced Tom McIntosh in 1921, left Ayresome Park early in the relegation season to be replaced by Herbert Bamlett. But the former referee could not halt the slide.

After his five goals against Forest, Wilson was transferred to Chelsea for £6,000; Tim Williamson was missing from the Middlesbrough side for the first time since 1902; and George Carr had been transferred to Leicester City, then a mid-table Second Division side. 'Boro themselves were busy in the transfer market. Bamlett

Reg Freeman, bought from Oldham Athletic by Herbert Bamlett.

brought full-backs Reg Freeman from Oldham Athletic and Alf Maitland from South Shields, and Owen Williams, Clapton Orient's English international outside-left. Williams and Freeman settled into the 'Boro side, but Maitland was soon on his way to Newcastle. A deficit in the transfer market saw 'Boro lose £8,000 on the season, making their total loss for two seasons some £15,000 and they were fined £50 for an illegal approach to a player of another club.

'Boro's first season back in the Second Division was one of consolidation and they finished 13th and scored only 36 goals, of which Owen Williams and Ian Dickson bagged seven each. At the back, their defence held out match after match to restore the balance, although when George Carr returned to Ayresome Park with Leicester City on 3 January 1925, 'Boro conceded five goals as City continued their romp towards the Second Division title. Before the season began, Tommy Urwin was transferred to Newcastle United, who were already looking to strengthen the side which had just won the FA Cup.

Season 1925-6 started off in glorious style. Beating Portsmouth 5-1 at Fratton Park on the opening day, 'Boro won 11 of their first 14 games. But the rot set in and 'Boro lost six games on the trot to finish ninth. There were individual triumphs, however. Jimmy McClelland, signed from Raith Rovers, scored a club record 38 goals (32 in the League) and in the FA Cup third round game against Leeds United at Ayresome Park he netted all the goals as 'Boro romped home 5-1. In the next round, Owen Williams had an unhappy return to his old club as Clapton Orient beat 'Boro 4-2.

The 1926-7 season opened disastrously for Middlesbrough with a 3-0 defeat at Chelsea, followed by a 2-1 reverse at Southampton two days later. When Preston went to Ayresome Park for 'Boro's first home game of the season, the Lancashire side won 2-0. A goalless draw at South Shields meant that 'Boro had started the season with only one point and one goal from four games. Yet by the end of that season, they had romped away with the Second Division championship, eight points clear of Portsmouth. Their 122 goals is a Second Division record which will surely never be beaten.

What was the reason for this transformation? It is always dangerous to attribute a side's success to one player, but consider the facts. For the fifth game of the season against Hull City, McClelland was injured and 'Boro brought in George Camsell, who had been signed from Third Division North side Durham City the previous season. Camsell finished the 1926-7 campaign as 'Boro's leading scorer with a record League 59 goals, including nine hat-tricks.

After he came into the side, 'Boro won nine out of the next ten games and from mid-November to mid-April they were unbeaten in the League. Over Christmas, Camsell scored 14 goals in four games including five at Manchester City on Christmas Day. 'Boro scored seven goals three times — against Portsmouth and Swansea at home and at Grimsby.

Camsell was just the player to exploit Middlesbrough's style. Wingers Billy Pease and Owen Williams repeatedly got round the backs of defences and slung over crosses which Camsell converted into goals; and Jackie Carr schemed away and released the ball at just the right time for the centre-forward to run on to and take through to goal. Pease was a close-season signing from Northampton and, with new goalkeeper Jimmy Mathieson from Raith Rovers also establishing himself in the illustrious boots of Williamson, the new-look 'Boro side were on the crest of the wave. Camsell would be 'Boro's leading goalscorer for each of the next ten seasons. In fact, he would become the club's greatest scorer of all-time.

Middlesbrough romped back to the First Division, although they went out in the fifth round of the FA Cup when Millwall won 3-2 at The Den. Incredible though

Middlesbrough, champions of the Second Division in 1926-7. Back row (left to right): Miller, Smith, Mathieson, Freeman, Ashman. Front row: Pease, Birrell, Camsell, Carr, Williams, Holmes.

it may seem, both Camsell and Pease (who scored a record 23 goals from the wing that season) both missed penalties.

In January 1927, Middlesbrough had suddenly decided to change their manager, even though Herbert Bamlett was in the middle of a fine run with the side. In the New Year, former Spurs manager Peter McWilliam took charge at a salary reported to be £1,500 a year — the highest in the country for a soccer manager at that time.

But disaster was just around the corner. Within one season Middlesbrough were back in the Second Division, finishing bottom of the table with the doubtful consolation of having the highest number of points — 37 — ever gained by a relegated club. Tottenham, too, went down with the same number, although they were on a foreign tour when they heard their fate.

'Boro started off reasonably well and in most seasons that number of points would have ensured a position away from the relegation zone. But there was little to choose between the teams and on the last day of the season, Middlesbrough met Sunderland at Ayresome Park. Both clubs had the same number of points. Each needed a win to be safe. The date was 5 May 1928, when nearly 42,000 fans crammed into the Middlesbrough ground. After a bright start 'Boro faded and Wright gave Sunderland a half-time lead. In the second-half Halliday and then the aptly-named Death sealed Boro's fate at 3-0.

Middlesbrough bounced back. It took them only one season to win the Second

Division title again, this time with 55 points. Camsell continued to score the goals, Pease broke the record for a winger when he had netted 105, and Bobby Bruce, from Aberdeen, and Jackie Carr, now 37, all contributed much to 'Boro's quick return. On 9 February 1929, Middlesbrough beat Wolves 8-3 at Ayresome Park and Pease scored four.

Middlesbrough's return to the First Division was not met by another disaster. The side managed to finish 16th, beating Sunderland 3-0 at Ayresome Park in November 1929 and reaching the fifth round of the FA Cup before going out 2-0 to Arsenal after wins over Chesterfield (after a replay) and Charlton (after two replays). Camsell was still finding the net and finished the season with 30 League goals.

In 1930-31, Middlesbrough finished seventh and on 18 April that season, at Blackburn, Camsell scored his 200th League goal in helping 'Boro to a 5-4 win. That score epitomised much of 'Boro's season — 98 goals for and 90 against — and they lost heavily to Aston Villa (8-1) and Leeds United (7-0).

Middlesbrough were now settled in the First Division and they finished just out of the relegation zones in 1931-2 and 1932-3. In 1933-4, came one of the most sensational games in the club's history when they met Sheffield United at Ayresome Park. Only 6,461 people turned up on a miserable, rain-sodden day, but they were rewarded with 'Boro's record win of 10-3, with Camsell netting four. In the Reserves, young Micky Fenton played well enough to warrant three first-team games that season — the first of many.

In 1934-5, Middlesbrough again found themselves in deep water when they won only ten games and finished in 20th position, missing relegation by only one point. Ralph Birkett, Arsenal's right winger, was signed in mid-March but returned to Highbury to see his old teammates crush 'Boro 8-0 on 19 April 1935. The relegation issue was not decided until the very last day of the season when goals from Yorston and Warren saw Middlesbrough draw 2-2 with Chelsea and the Ayresome Park club squeezed home. Fenton played in half the games, but Camsell missed half the season through ill health.

Things looked different for 1935-6 when 'Boro won their first two away matches — 5-0 at Preston and 7-2 at Aston Villa with Camsell scoring five. Middlesbrough continued to crack in the goals — four against League leaders Huddersfield, six against Everton and Blackburn and five against Grimsby and Sheffield Wednesday. Camsell took his season's total to 28 and 'Boro netted 84 goals in finishing 14th.

Perhaps the most controversial event of the season was the visit of champions-elect Sunderland on 28 March 1936. 'Boro thrashed them 6-0 and the Wearsiders lost Carter and Davis, both sent off. Other milestones were left-back Bobby Stuart's 100th consecutive appearance for 'Boro in November 1935 and Camsell's first England cap, against Scotland. In the FA Cup, 'Boro reached the quarter-finals for the first time since 1904. Southampton, Clapton Orient and Leicester were all beaten at home before Grimsby Town beat 'Boro 3-1 at Blundell Park to earn themselves a semi-final tie against Arsenal.

Season 1936-7 saw the emergence of a player destined to become one of the most famous in English football, when a fair-haired youngster called Wilf Mannion, who Middlesbrough had signed from local club South Bank St Peter's, arrived on the scene. Seventeen-year-old Mannion made his debut in a 2-2 draw with Portsmouth at Ayresome Park on 2 January 1937. He played once more that season, but 'Boro had already seen enough to know that they had an international in the making.

During the same season, another face appeared at Middlesbrough in the shape of full-back George Hardwick. Hardwick came from South Bank East End and he, too, was to become a Middlesbrough and England giant in the years after World War Two. Middlesbrough, with Aberdeen-born Dave Cumming now in goal, finished

Former Middlesbrough centre-forward Andy Wilson was in the headlines when he played for Chelsea against his old club in October 1930. 'Boro, without the services of George Camsell, lost 4-0. Above: Mathieson fails to stop a goal by Chelsea's Pearson.

Andy Wilson Celebrates His Return

ROUSING SUCCESS OF THE "PENSIONERS."

JACK ELKES FINDS THE SHADOWING OF JACKSON RATHER MORE THAN HE CAN MANAGE.

By REYNARD.

Chelsea 4, Middlesbrough 0.

NOT for many a day has public opinion been so completely vindicated as it was on Saturday in the changes which Chelsea made in their team to meet Middlesbrough.

Andy Wilson was given a rousing reception on his return to the side as he led his men on in the capacity of captain, and enthusiasm became boundless when, by opportunism of the sort that comes from football brains, he scored his side's first two goals.

Andy Wilson.

Another great success was Crawford, who gave a display which justified those bold people who have been saying that, despite the acquisition of Jackson, he is the best outside right the club has. With the valuable aid of Cheyne, Crawford sparkled, and cannot be left out of the team to make room for anybody.

Jackson's appearance at centre forward was interesting and to a large extent successful. Big Jack Elkes, the former 'Spur, who played at centre half for Middlesbrough, did his best to reduce Jackson to impotence, but Jackson never gave up trying, and eventually got a goal—the only one in the second half—by heading in from a corner kick beautifully taken by Crawford.

It was also Jackson who initiated the movement which led to Pearson obtaining Chelsea's third goal, so that he amply played his part. What the team selectors will do with him when Gallacher is again declared fit remains to be seen, but it would be an injustice—if there is any dispute about the right of Crawford to continue as Cheyne's partner.

Minus the services of Camsell, the Middlesbrough attack was not good enough to extend the Chelsea defence, even though Odell did not inspire too much confidence in the goal of Smith. As a matter of fact the entire Middlesbrough eleven was rather badly overplayed. Bruce was given little scope by Rodger, and the most effective forward on the visiting side was Cameron at inside left. Pease was very ordinary, and missed a great chance to score early in the second half.

ELKES UPSET.

It is to be feared that the fact of playing in direct opposition to Jackson upset the equilibrium of Elkes. Middlesbrough's two acquisitions from Cardiff City—Jennings (right full-back) and Warren (left half)—did enough to show how ill the Welsh club, from a playing point of view, can afford to part with such men, but, generally speaking, there was an absence among the visitors of the high standard of football which we have grown accustomed to expect from men wearing the colours of the Teessiders.

In the light of recent failures, Chelsea are naturally anxious to prove themselves worthy of the thunder they have been trying to steal from the Arsenal, and it must be said that their victory was no complete that real interest in the exchanges ceased for a long time before the expiration of the ninety minutes.

In other words, Middlesbrough failed to make a fight of it. Their heart had been killed by the two goals scored by their old star performer, Wilson, whose display was a great "come-back," and a reminder that he is far from being a spent force.

'Stones Scrape Through.

Clapton Knocked Out By Essex Rivals.

By DRACO.

Leytonstone 1, Clapton 0.

LEAGUE form is not regarded as a true guide to what may happen in a cup tie, but at Leytonstone on Saturday the tie, but at Leytonstone on Saturday football proved no better than could be expected from the two bottom clubs in the Isthmian League. Leytonstone, holding one point, scored the only goal, and just managed to beat Clapton, who have suffered six consecutive defeats. Victory went to the better side in a display that produced little combination and not much individual excellence.

Neither team rose to the occasion, and it must be a long time since amateur clubs of such standing have put such moderate sides in the field.

One does not like to criticise severely, but the 1,000 spectators—nearly staunch supporters of the two competing clubs to have preferred the possibilities of this F.A. Cup qualifying tie to the London Charity Cup tie at Leyton, where London Caledonians were the visitors—found little to interest them.

The result turned on a goal headed by W. A. Williams from a centre by L. Cauels.

THE DAI SPORTLIGH

By TREVOR C. WIGN

PARIS, Sunday, O

THIS to-day is a sadden-d ci
one topic of conversation
awful tragedy of the. It in
homeward bound early this
when the first whispers of the
began to circulate along the bc
The first story was that an bi
plane had crashed near Pr
was only many hours later c
truth was known. And so in
gay city is in mourning, and
find it hard to concentrate on
save this terrible affair.

HOOD AND SHADE.

MR. JEFF DICKSON has
in to tell me his plan
future. His next big fight i
will be on the night of r
when Jack Hood, the British
weight champion, will meet
Shade, the American who was
by Len Harvey last week. I of
last night that Shade still it
was entitled to the verdict
Harvey. It is true that the
of the critics thought he had

seventh in 1936-7, when Arthur Cunliffe broke Camsell's monopoly of the leading scorers position with 22 goals. Camsell netted 18.

In 1937-8, Middlesbrough finished fifth, with Micky Fenton now established. Fenton was leading scorer with 24 goals and became the fourth Middlesbrough centre-forward to play for England between the wars, when he appeared in the 1-0 defeat by Scotland at Wembley on 9 April 1938.

The following season — the last full one before World War Two — 'Boro climbed up a place to fourth, their highest in the First Division since 1913-14. Fenton was again top scorer, this time with 34 goals, but the real revelation was the young Mannion. He had come to everyone's notice the previous season but now he began to score goals and finished second-highest scorer with 14 — including four in the 9-2 win over Blackpool on 10 December 1938. Camsell played only 11 games but scored ten goals and Milne appeared on either wing with equal skill.

There was a potentially epic tussle in the fourth round of the FA Cup when 'Boro met Sunderland at Ayresome Park. A record 51,080 paid just under £4,000 and saw Middlesbrough go down 2-0. Again their Wembley hopes were sealed for another season, yet the team assembled under former Grimsby boss, Wilf Gillow, who had succeeded McWilliam in 1934, looked good enough to take the title in 1939-40. Mannion and Hardwick were coming into their own and Fenton, too, was fulfilling the rich, early promise he had shown.

In fact, Middlesbrough were next-to-the-bottom of the First Division when war was declared on 3 September 1939, having lost the opening game of the season, 2-0 at Aston Villa on 26 August, and going down 4-1 at Liverpool the following

Wilf Mannion, probably 'Boro's
greatest-ever player.

Wednesday before earning their first point with a 2-2 draw at home to Stoke on what was the second — and last — Saturday of the season.

Whether or not they would have recovered is idle speculation, but certainly Middlesbrough had potentially their finest-ever side. For the next seven years football took on a bizarre aspect with guest players and regional leagues. Both Hardwick and Mannion played in wartime internationals, as did Ralph Birkett, who turned out against Scotland in 1940-41.

Middlesbrough started the first season of peacetime football with a new manager. Wilf Gillow died in 1944 and was replaced by David Jack of 'White Horse Cup Final' fame. He scored the first goal in a Wembley Cup Final, for Bolton in 1923. Jack led 'Boro into the 1945-6 FA Cup — it was played on a two-legged basis up to and including the quarter-final — with a side containing old heads from pre-war days and youngsters who had made their way during the hostilities.

In the third round, 'Boro drew 4-4 at Leeds in the first leg before completing the job with a 7-2 win at Ayresome Park. Blackpool then took 'Boro to a third game before the Ayresome club ran out 1-0 winners in the replay. In the fifth round, Bolton won 1-0 at Burnden Park and then held on 1-1 at Ayresome Park. Middlesbrough were out of the Cup again.

In 1946-7, League football returned and 'Boro finished 11th with Mannion and Fenton each scoring 18 goals. Hardwick had blossomed into a fine player and behind him, Dave Cumming, the pre-war goalkeeper, was also performing well. Again 'Boro had a good run in the FA Cup. It started with a 1-1 draw at QPR before Rangers went down 2-1 at Middlesbrough. Then 42,250 fans saw Chesterfield beaten 2-1 in the fourth round and, although Mannion scored an own-goal to help Nottingham Forest draw 2-2 at the City Ground, the same player netted a hat-trick at Ayresome Park as Forest crashed 6-2 in the replay.

Yet again, 'Boro could not get past the quarter-final stage. A crowd of 53,500 saw Second Division Burnley draw 1-1 with an equalizer in the last ten minutes. At Turf Moor, a hotly-disputed goal by Billy Morris gave the Lancashire side a semi-final place against Liverpool. Middlesbrough's Wembley dreams were over again. At the end of the season Hardwick and Mannion played for the Great Britain side against the Rest of Europe, with Hardwick captaining the British side to a 6-1 win.

In 1947-8, 'Boro transferred McCabe to Leeds for £10,000, Dews (£7,000) and Stuart (£4,000) to Plymouth, during which time they finished 16th in the League and went out of the FA Cup in the fifth round when Derby beat them 2-1 at Ayresome Park. That day the Rams had third-choice goalkeeper Frank Payne playing what was to be his only game for them.

Mannion had been reluctant to sign for that season and in the close season of 1948, he moved his home to Oldham, intending to set up a business and play for the Third Division North side. But Oldham could not afford the £25,000 fee and Mannion would go to no other club. In January 1949, Mannion returned to Ayresome Park to find his side struggling again.

'Boro had tried to buy Jackie Milburn from Newcastle, instead settling for United's reserve-team centre-forward Andy Donaldson, for what was then a big fee of £17,000. Donaldson scored six vital goals as 'Boro avoided the drop by one point to finish in 19th place.

Mannion was playing well enough to have re-established himself in the England team but, before the start of 1949-50, 'Boro received a blow when Donaldson broke his ankle in a practice match and was soon on his way to Peterborough United, then in the Midland League.

On 27 December 1949, Middlesbrough's present ground record was set when 53,802

Wilf Martin sends Martin and Powell of Aston Villa the wrong way.

George Hardwick clears as Chelsea's Billington puts in a challenge.

'Boro's Whitaker tackles Baily of Spurs.

saw them beat Newcastle United 1-0. With Jamaican-born Lindy Delapenha, signed from Portsmouth, playing well on the wing, 'Boro climbed to ninth in the First Division. In the FA Cup, Second Division Chesterfield beat them 3-2 in the fourth round at Saltergate.

Middlesbrough headed the First Division towards the end of 1950, but a 1-0 defeat in the FA Cup at Leeds seemed to affect the players and after that they took only

Middlesbrough FC in 1949-50. Back row (left to right): R.Robinson, W.Linacre, W.Whitaker, R.Ugolini, P.McKennan, J.Gordon. Front row: A.McCrae, P.Desmond, G.Hardwick, W.Mannion, H.Bell.

35

Middlesbrough during 1952-3. Back row (left to right): Shepherdson (trainer), Russell, Robinson, Ugolini, Delapenha, Corbett, Dicks. Front row: Mochan, Mannion, Bell, Whitaker, Fitzsimons, Walker.

13 points from 19 games to finish in sixth position. Midway through the season, George Hardwick had left the club to become player-manager of Oldham Athletic. From that moment 'Boro began to falter, finishing 18th the following season and 13th in 1952-3 before the dreaded blow of relegation fell once more in 1953-4.

Walter Rowley had taken over as manager from David Jack in 1952 and the 'Boro side now contained Rolando Ugolini, Mannion and Bill Harris, who was signed from Hull City and made his debut against Chelsea on 6 March 1954. Two months later Harris was playing his first game at wing-half for Wales against Austria in Vienna.

'Boro gained only 12 points from their first 19 games. It was a start too bad to overcome and they went down with Liverpool, although five draws in a row, followed by a shock 4-2 win over champions-elect Wolves, gave them some hope of staving off the drop. But after losing 5-2 to Manchester City, Middlesbrough dropped four points in their two Easter games with Liverpool and, in the end, it was their fellow strugglers who pulled them down. Only Delapenha, with 18 goals, could look back on the season with any satisfaction.

Walter Rowley retired in the close season and his place was taken by Bob Dennison, the former Newcastle, Forest and Fulham player, who was in charge of Northampton Town. Dennison had the worst possible start. First Mannion refused to sign and, then after a 2-2 draw at Plymouth on 21 August 1954, 'Boro lost their next eight games.

It was not until 25 September, when they beat Lincoln 2-1 at Middlesbrough, that 'Boro came to terms with the Second Division. That was the start of a run of ten points from six games, including a 6-0 win against West Ham United. A week later, Middlesbrough went to Blackburn and crashed 9-0. It says much for the character of the side that they recovered to finish in 12th position.

36

Middlesbrough in 1955-6. Back row (left to right): Stonehouse, Bilcliff, Ugolini, Dicks, Robinson. Front row: Delapenha, Scott, Harris, McPherson, Fitzsimons, Mitchell.

Wilf Mannion had played his last game for Middlesbrough in their relegation season, refusing terms for the following season before being transferred to Hull City, where he played a handful of games before being suspended over some newspaper articles which appeared under his name. Eventually the greatest ball-player ever to pull on a Middlesbrough shirt disappeared into non-League soccer.

Middlesbrough now began a 20-year spell outside the First Division. Yet, on the horizon was another in the long line of great Middlesbrough centre-forwards. Brian Clough made his debut in 1955-6 and played nine games, scoring his first goal at home to Leicester on 8 October as 'Boro won 4-3. The young centre-forward took over from former Preston player, Charlie Wayman, who was injured in training. He showed a flair for goals and Dennison surely knew he had a great striker in the making.

Another player to make his debut that season was Billy Day and with Delapenha knocking home 17 goals, 'Boro finished in 14th place. The following year belonged to Clough. He scored 38 League goals as 'Boro climbed up to sixth in the Second Division, taking 15 points from their last nine games, including a 7-2 win over Huddersfield and a 6-2 win against Swansea. Peter Taylor, one day to become Clough's managerial 'twin', took over in goal from Ugolini and Wayman signed for Darlington.

For the next four seasons, Clough rattled in the goals — 40 in 1957-8, 43 in 1958-9, 39 in 1959-60 and 34 in 1960-61. He played two England matches in 1959-60 — it is still a mystery as to why he was never selected again — and scored five goals for the Football League in Belfast in September 1959.

Brian Clough jumps over Blackburn's Harry Leyland as the ball enters the net.

In that time, Middlesbrough maintained reasonable progress in the Second Division without ever looking as if they would win promotion. New players like Alan Peacock and Edwin Holliday came into the team. Peacock, an 18-year-old reserve centre-forward, came into the Middlesbrough side in December 1957, when a run of five defeats sent 'Boro plunging from third place in the table. Clough was now the inevitable target for opposing defenders and Peacock came in and took some of the weight off the prolific goalscorer's shoulders.

'Boro began the 1958-9 season in tremendous style, beating newly-promoted Brighton 9-0. Clough hit five and Peacock two as the South Coast team were destroyed. There followed a run of nine games without victory and, after trying to persuade Don Revie — a native of Middlesbrough — to join the club, Dennison went to Glasgow Celtic and brought back Willie Fernie for £17,000. But Middlesbrough could only finish 13th.

The era had also seen Middlesbrough's trainer, Harold Shepherdson, take over in that role with the England party — the start of another illustrious career. Shepherdson served his country for many years and was trainer when they won the World Cup in 1966. On 13 December 1958, Ray Yeoman made his debut in the 2-0 defeat at Hillsborough. He was still in the side 215 matches later, ending his record run when 'Boro beat Norwich 6-2 at Ayresome Park in the final game of 1962-3.

After finishing fifth in consecutive seasons in 1959-60 and 1960-61, 'Boro slipped to 12th place in 1961-2. In July 1961, Brian Clough went up the coast to Sunderland for £40,000. Never far from controversy, even in those days, Clough's departure

Middlesbrough in 1961-2. Back row (left to right): Stonehouse, Waldock, Emmerson, Million, Appleby, Chapman, Yeoman. Middle row: Fenton (assistant trainer), J.Green (secretary), Holliday, Livingstone, McNeil, Peacock, Thomson, Harris, Walker, Shepherdson (trainer), R.Dennison (manager). Front row: Kaye, Horner, Jones, Day, Burbeck, McLean.

Grimsby goalkeeper Charlie Wright punches clear to foil a 'Boro attack.

from Ayresome Park was perhaps inevitable but sad. He became Sunderland's top scorer, whilst the gap he left at Middlesbrough was never filled.

Alan Peacock took over the leading goalscoring spot with 24 League goals and followed this up with 31 in 1962-3, when Middlesbrough finished fourth. Sunderland were third and another four points for 'Boro would have seen them back in the First Division.

Yet from that moment on, the only way for 'Boro was down. Slowly they slid towards the bottom of the Second Division until in 1965-6, the unthinkable happened and Middlesbrough FC were a Third Division club. Bob Dennison had resigned in 1963 and his place was taken by Raich Carter, the former Sunderland idol.

The drop hinged on the last match of the season with 'Boro needing to draw at Ninian Park against Cardiff City, who needed both points to be safe. 'Boro converted centre-half Dickie Rooks to centre-forward and the makeshift striker responded magnificently with a hat-trick. But there was to be no *Boys' Own Comic* finish. Cardiff won 5-3 to stay up. 'Boro plunged down into Division Three. Carter had resigned just before the end of the season, his place taken by skipper Stan Anderson. It was now Anderson's job to get the side back into the Second Division.

He did so at the first attempt. 'Boro finished second in the Third Division. After the brief interlude of some World Cup matches at Middlesbrough, the team won their first match of the season at Colchester United. There followed a slump of nine League games which produced only one win and the more despondent 'Boro supporters saw their side already down into the Fourth Division.

But new signings were on the way. John O'Rourke came as a centre-forward from Luton Town, winger Dave Chadwick from Southampton and goalkeeper Willie Whigham from Falkirk. Sheffield Wednesday full-back John Hickton joined 'Boro, who were now skippered by Gordon Jones. Jones, a former apprentice, was to set a post-war record of 523 games for the club.

O'Rourke soon began to find the back of the net and with six games left, Middlesbrough were in seventh place. A thrilling win at Peterborough started a winning run which took the club to fourth place with 53 points and one game to play. On 16 May 1967, 'Boro met Oxford United at Ayresome Park before 39,683 spectators. Queen's Park Rangers were already champions, Watford were second with 54 points and Reading third with 53. Both Watford and Reading had completed their fixtures.

'Boro had to win and they did so in style, beating Oxford 4-1 to bring Second Division soccer back to Ayresome after only one season in the Third. John O'Rourke had finished the season with 27 goals and Arthur Horsfield with 22. In the FA Cup, 'Boro had the strange experience of going into the hat for the first-round draw. After hammering Chester 5-2 at Sealand Road, they went out in the very next round, 2-0 at Mansfield's Field Mill.

For Middlesbrough fans, the experience of seeing their once proud club with its long traditions, floundering for a time in the Third Division had been a traumatic one. Now they had witnessed 'Boro's first promotion triumph since they won their way to the First Division in 1929. Anderson set about strengthening the side for a concerted push towards the Second Division championship and one of his first signings was Manchester City's Irish international midfielder, Johnny Crossan, whose curious career had taken him to Ayresome Park via a controversial spell in the comparative backwaters of Irish soccer, Dutch and Belgian League football with Sparta Rotterdam and Standard Liege, Sunderland and Maine Road.

In the other direction Anderson transferred full-back Geoff Butler to Chelsea for a Middlesbrough record fee of £57,500, after Tommy Docherty's First Division side had met 'Boro in the Football League Cup. In the FA Cup there was a marathon

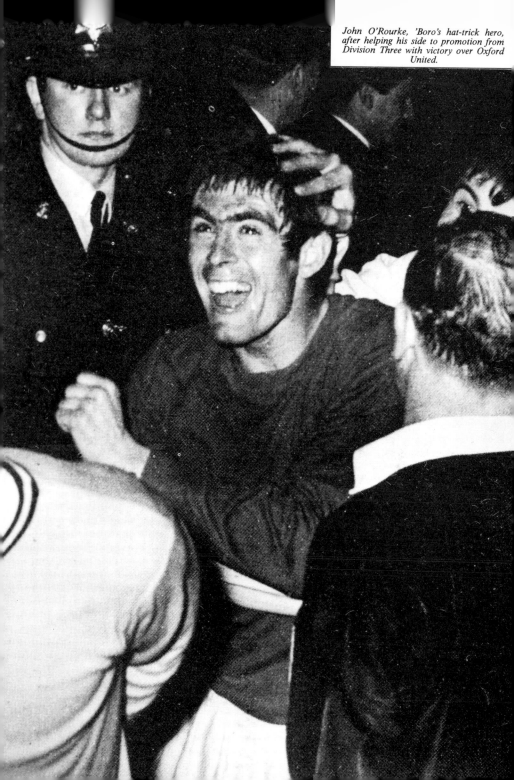

John O'Rourke, 'Boro's hat-trick hero, after helping his side to promotion from Division Three with victory over Oxford United.

third-round tie with Hull before 'Boro won the second replay at York, only to go down in the next round at Bristol City. The season ended with Middlesbrough in sixth place — a satisfactory placing after winning promotion.

The following season, 'Boro again moved up the table to finish in fourth place. Indeed, two away wins at Sheffield United and Oxford at the end of October saw 'Boro on top of the table. But a 'flu bug which hit the club in February meant the postponement of the game with Blackburn and, although they were still in second place with ten games to play, 'Boro fell away badly in the run-in to the season.

One of the real revelations of 1967-8 was the form of John Hickton, who was moved up to the attack with devastating effect. He finished top scorer with 24 goals and as 'Boro vied for the title in 1968-9, it was Hickton again who led the way with 18 goals. Hickton had played the occasional game in attack for Wednesday, but when Anderson found him a regular place up front, the powerful defender responded in fine style. Crossan played only two games in 1969-70 before moving to Belgium, but his short career at Ayresome Park had been reasonably successful.

As 'Boro finished fourth again, Anderson brought Carlisle's Hugh McIlmoyle to play alongside Hickton. Once again Middlesbrough reached the quarter-finals of the FA Cup, only to find their path to the semi-final barred. Derrick Downing and Hugh McIlmoyle gave them a third-round win over First Division West Ham; York City were removed 4-1 and then 'Boro went to their 'bogey' ground of Brunton Park, where they managed their first-ever win over Carlisle United, 2-1, thanks to goals from Hickton and Downing.

Middlesbrough now faced First Division Manchester United. The first game at Ayresome Park ended 1-1 and 'Boro fans could already see their chances of following their team into the semi-finals for the first time, receding. Sure enough, the task of beating United at Old Trafford proved too much and 'Boro went down 2-1. The two games were watched by a total of 100,000 people. Willy Maddren and David Mills made their debuts during the season. Both would become important parts of Middlesbrough's machine in the coming years.

Boro stayed in the promotion race for much of 1970-71. But their last win of the season came at home to Luton on 27 March 1971, after which a run of eight drawn games left them in seventh position and far behind promoted clubs Leicester City and Sheffield United. In the FA Cup, Middlesbrough had revenge over Manchester United, beating them in a third-round replay at Ayresome Park through McIlmoyle and Downing. In the fourth round, however, 'Boro crashed 3-0 to Everton at Goodison Park.

For 1971-2, Middlesbrough's team took on a new look. During the close season, Manchester United's former World Cup star Nobby Stiles, Newcastle's John Craggs and Mansfield's Stuart Boam were signed. Maddren and Mills, together with Laidlaw, were now regulars and Jim Platt had taken over in goal. David Armstrong was brought in for his first game.

The team was taking shape but it was not ready to make the supreme effort and had to be content with ninth place. In the FA Cup, 'Boro fought through to the fifth round with replays against Manchester City and Millwall. It was Manchester United who again stood in their way. This time it was United's turn to win a replay. After doing the difficult bit by drawing 0-0 at Old Trafford, 'Boro collapsed at home and went down 3-0.

On the opening day of the 1972-3 season, Middlesbrough beat old rivals Sunderland 2-1 at Ayresome Park with both goals coming from Malcolm Smith, who had been on the club's books as a junior. A win over Wrexham in the second round of the Football League Cup set 'Boro up for a tie with Spurs which they surrendered only after a second replay on the London club's ground.

Things looked set for another fine season, this time with the possibility of a return at last to the top flight. But 'Boro's goals tally was still worrying Anderson and in October he moved for ex-Newcastle striker, Alan Foggon, who was playing with Cardiff. Two months later, Graeme Souness, Spurs' reserve midfielder, was on his way north and Anderson said that he now had the team which could win promotion.

But there were black clouds on the horizon. In January, 'Boro suffered a shock defeat at the hands of Plymouth Argyle in the third round of the FA Cup. Stan Anderson had seen enough. He resigned his post and for the rest of the season Harold Shepherdson took charge of the side which finished in fourth place, losing only three of the last 16 games.

Middlesbrough needed a 'name' to take over and they plumped for Jackie Charlton, Leeds United's distinguished England international centre-half. Charlton made only one change. Stiles joined Charlton's brother, Bobby, at Preston and was replaced by Scottish international midfielder, Bobby Murdoch, from Celtic. For the rest of the team which he had inherited, Charlton elected to give them all a run.

What a season the 1973-4 campaign turned out to be. After winning their opening game at Portsmouth, 'Boro lost a home game to Fulham 2-0 and people began to doubt Jack Charlton's ability to get the side back into the First Division. But Charlton knew better. 'Boro remained unbeaten until the New Year. They went to the top of the table in October and stayed there for the rest of the season, ensuring promotion as early as 23 March. And with eight games of the season still to play, Middlesbrough became runaway champions of the Second Division with victory at Luton.

Middlesbrough manager Jack Charlton with some young fans.

43

David Armstrong is challenged by Reardon of Wycombe Wanderers during the FA Cup tie between the clubs.

Graeme Souness lends a helping hand as Jim Platt grabs at the ball.

In storming to the title Middlesbrough had achieved the following:
Their highest-ever number of points — 65.
A run of 20 home games without defeat.
Their longest unbeaten League run — 24 games.
Their best defensive record of 30 goals against.
The biggest-ever points margin — 15 — in the Second Division.
Every player except the goalkeeper had found himself on the score-sheet.

In their first season back in the First Division since 1953-4, Middlesbrough relied on the players who had won them promotion, plus Charlton's old Leeds teammate, full-back Terry Cooper. It was a satisfactory blend as 'Boro climbed to seventh place — a good performance from any newly-promoted side. Alan Foggon, the man brought back to the North-East, responded in the promotion season with 19 League goals, thus ending Hickton's run of six seasons as 'Boro's top scorer, and in the first season back at the top the ex-Newcastle striker finished top again, this time with 16.

Until their return to the First Division, Middlesbrough's progress in the Football League Cup — they first entered the competition in 1960-61 — was parallel in many ways with their lack of success in the FA Cup. But in 1974-5, 'Boro not only reached the sixth round of the FA Cup, they also went to the quarter-finals of the League Cup, where their old Cup adversaries Manchester United beat them 3-0 after yet another replay.

The following season 'Boro went one step further and reached the semi-finals of the League Cup. Their run started with a second-round match at Bury, where they won 2-1. There followed a good win over League Champions Derby County at the Baseball Ground; an easy fourth-round tie with Peterborough United at Ayresome Park; and a 2-0 victory at Burnley which put them into the last four against Manchester City. In the first leg on 13 January 1976, Hickton gave 'Boro a slender 1-0 lead. 'Boro fans feared that it may not be enough and they were

John Hickton under pressure from an opponent.

45

Phil Boersma of Middlesbrough and Emlyn Hughes of Liverpool.

right. Eight days later, Keegan, Oakes, Barnes and Royle sent City through to Wembley with a 4-0 win.

But Middlesbrough did win their first cup as a professional side in 1975-6. They lifted the Anglo-Scottish Cup in a two-legged Final with Second Division Fulham. After winning a qualifying competition involving Sunderland, Newcastle and Carlisle, 'Boro beat Aberdeen in the quarter-finals and Mansfield Town in the semi-final before Dave Armstrong's goal in the first leg at Ayresome Park on 26 November set them up for a goalless draw at Craven Cottage. They finished the season 13th in the League.

One again 'Boro almost reached the semi-finals of the FA Cup in 1976-7. Spurs had knocked them out of the League Cup as early as the second round, but after a scare at non-League Wimbledon — who were later to be elected to the League partly as a result of holding 'Boro to a 0-0 draw at Plough Lane — Middlesbrough put four goals each past Hereford and Arsenal to earn a quarter-final place with Liverpool at Anfield. Liverpool, though, were on their way to Wembley and goals from Keegan and Fairclough sent 'Boro spinning out again before 55,881 fans.

Another mid-table spot, 12th, was all that 'Boro could manage in the First Division and on 21 April 1977, Jack Charlton resigned after some four years at Ayresome Park. On 19 May, John Neal, after just failing to lift Wrexham into the Second Division, became the new boss of Middlesbrough. The former Hull, Swindon, Aston Villa and Southend player had steered the Welsh club to promotion from the Fourth Division in 1970 and taken them to the quarter-finals of the European Cup-winners' Cup in 1976.

In his first season at Ayresome Park, Neal saw 'Boro into 14th place and to the quarter-finals of the FA Cup once again. This time 'Boro really should have made that elusive semi-final. Their opponents in the last 16 — after eliminating Coventry, Everton and Bolton — were Second Division Orient, a side struggling in the bottom half of the table. Middlesbrough should have finished the job at Ayresome Park, but the London club held on to draw 0-0 and 'Boro faced the unenviable task of visiting Brisbane Road three days later. The Londoners' tails were up and, although Armstrong scored for Middlesbrough, goals from Kitchen and Mayo saw Orient through to the last four.

David Mills finished the season as top scorer with ten goals in the League, four in the FA Cup and two in the League Cup. The Whitby-born striker had also passed his 250th match for 'Boro. John Hickton, the defender turned striker, had his contract cancelled in April 1978. Hickton had played well over 400 games for 'Boro and in League matches alone he netted 159 goals to put him up with the great Middlesbrough strikers of yesteryear.

Boro's 1978-9 season never really got off the ground. They were knocked out of both the FA Cup and the League Cup at the first hurdles and never rose above tenth in the table, finally finishing in 12th place. The real bright spot of the season was the form of Micky Burns, who arrived at Ayresome Park via Blackpool, Newcastle and Cardiff and who finished leading scorer with 14 League goals, including four in one match against Chelsea when 'Boro hammered the soon-to-be-relegated Londoners 7-2.

Burns continued his goalscoring in 1979-80, when he scored ten as 'Boro edged back up the table to ninth place. But he was overtaken as the club's leading scorer by David Armstrong who netted 11 in the League and made his first appearance in a full England shirt when he played against Australia — the first time the countries had met in a full international. Northern Ireland's Jim Platt continued his fine run in Middlesbrough's goal, taking his League appearances to 296 by the end of the season.

Middlesbrough goalkeeper Jim Stewart punches clear from Frank Stapleton and Willie Young of Arsenal. The other 'Boro players are McAndrew, Ashcroft and Boam.

Boro's 1980-81 season was one of contrasts. The club might have reached their first-ever FA Cup semi-final when they played Wolves in the quarter-final at Ayresome Park. In the end, only the brilliance of the ever-reliable Jim Platts kept 'Boro in the game and they lost the replay to the Midlanders.

Then South African-born Craig Johnston was sold to Liverpool for £750,000 after he alleged that 'Boro's fans had ultimately driven him away from Teesside when he and the club disagreed over money. Finally, 'Boro settled the First Division championship on the last Saturday of the season when they beat contenders Ipswich 2-1 — with both goals from Jankovic — and allowed Villa through, despite the fact that they had lost at Highbury. But for Middlesbrough, a major honour still eluded them and at the season's end, John Neal became the game's latest managerial casualty.

The 1981-2 season saw former 'Boro player, Bobby Murdoch, take over as manager at Ayresome Park, but he saw two of his star players leave the club. David Armstrong was on his way to Southampton and Mark Proctor moved to Nottingham Forest.

Three players — Joe Bolton, Mick Baxter and Heine Otto — made their debuts in the first game of the season, at home to Tottenham Hotspur. Otto scored for 'Boro, but it was Spurs who won the game, 3-1.

The first victory, three games later, was at Ayresome Park against Birmingham City, Otto and David Hodgson scoring in a 2-1 win. John Craggs started the season as captain, but eventually conceded the job to Tony McAndrew.

In October, a 2-1 home victory against Plymouth Argyle in the second round of the Milk Cup was sufficient to carry Middlesbrough through the Home Park leg, which ended 0-0. The third round brought sterner opposition in the shape of Liverpool and the Merseysiders coasted through to the next round with a 4-1 victory at Anfield.

'Boro did not progress beyond the third round of the FA Cup, yet they started well enough with a goalless draw at Loftus Road, always a difficult venue for Middlesbrough, on 2 January. Bad weather meant that the much-postponed replay eventually took place on 18 January, when Rangers took the tie in extra-time, winning 3-2.

In February 1982, Middlesbrough chairman Charles Amer and his son Kevin, a director, resigned from the board, stepping aside for George Kitching to move in. The 100th Tees-Wear derby game on 3 April saw a rare victory for Middlesbrough at Roker Park, but the attendance was a disappointing 19,006.

Escape from relegation had been a mathematical possibility right up until the home game against Arsenal, but the London club sealed Middlesbrough's fate by winning 3-1 at Ayresome Park in May 1982. The penultimate game of the disappointing season brought a rare away victory, the eighth win of the season, at Vetch Field against First Division debutants Swansea City. Middlesbrough's last First Division game was against eventual champions Liverpool and 'Boro pulled off a creditable draw against the Reds.

Although only 34 League goals were scored, Middlesbrough ended the season with more points (39) than the previous season, but finished bottom of the Division. The juniors winning the Northern Intermediate League was one of the few bright spots of the campaign.

Jim Platt, the only ever-present of the season, took part in the World Cup Finals in Spain, appearing once for Northern Ireland, but Terry Cochrane, originally selected, had to withdraw from the squad through injury. Graeme Hedley, Colin Blackburn, Jeff Peters and Andy McCreesh, all players with limited League appearances, were released and at the 90th annual meeting, held in December 1982, a loss of £307,718 was reported to shareholders.

With Bobby Murdoch still in the managerial hot seat and Jim Platt as captain, Middlesbrough kicked off the 1982-3 season at Hillsborough, against Jack Charlton's Sheffield Wednesday. David Currie and Mick Kennedy made their Middlesbrough debuts as Wednesday won 3-1.

In September, Tony Mowbray made his Middlesbrough debut at outside-right in front of 27,986 (the season's highest League attendance) at St James' Park, Newcastle, where a Darren Wood goal earned 'Boro a point.

Three successive 4-1 home defeats plunged 'Boro into hot water in September. Third Division champions Burnley, Fulham (Tony Mowbray's home debut) and Grimsby Town (Ray Hankin's debut game in which he was sent off) all put four past a disheartened defence. The Middlesbrough board had little option and manager Murdoch was asked to resign. Harold Shepherdson again filled the breach until a successor could be recruited.

A Garry Macdonald goal gave 'Boro their first win of the season, against Bolton Wanderers in October. Then George Kitching relinquished the chair and Mike McCullagh stepped up with Keith Varley being named as vice-chairman.

McCullagh introduced Malcolm Allison, Murdoch's successor, to the crowd before the start of the home game against Queen's Park Rangers and goals from Nattrass (penalty) and Otto took 'Boro to a 2-1 win.

Middlesbrough's fortunes seemed to have turned the corner as Allison's first game in charge brought a precious away point against Rotherham United — but then Blackburn Rovers won 5-1 at Ayresome Park.

In January 1983, non-League Bishop Stortford proved to be bonny FA Cup fighters in forcing a 2-2 draw at Ayresome Park. A sensational Cup exit was on the cards and in the replay at the George Wilson Stadium on 11 January, Lynch put the non-league club into the lead on the stroke of half-time. David Shearer saved Middlesbrough from further embarrassment by scoring two second half goals, but it had been a close shave.

Notts County were the fourth-round visitors on 29 January, before an Ayresome Park crowd of 17,114. A first-half goal by Rankin was consolidated by a Beattie penalty in the second half and together they earned 'Boro a home tie against First Division Arsenal.

At Ayresome Park, an Otto goal helped Middlesbrough to a 1-1 draw against the Gunners but a spirited display and two goals from David Shearer were not enough to stop the Londoners winning 3-2 at Highbury.

In January, Charles Amer, who had joined the Middlesbrough board in the early 1960s, severed his long association with the club by resigning his directorship.

In early March 1983, Queen's Park Rangers, on their way to the First Division, tore Middlesbrough apart, winning 6-1 at Loftus Road. *Match of the Day* cameras showed Clive Allen securing a hat-trick, with Middlesbrough playing in borrowed bright orange shirts.

Goals from Sugrue, Hamilton and Otto saw Middlesbrough notch their first away win of 1983 at Grimsby Town, avenging the earlier reverse at Ayresome Park. And one defeat in the last six games of the season ensured that the club finished in a respectable 16th in Division Two.

A long-awaited testimonial game was played at Ayresome Park on 17 May 1983, when two of Middlesbrough's most famous sons shared a benefit. Wilf Mannion and George Hardwick, names synonymous with the club's immediate post-war period, were honoured when a Middlesbrough XI played an England XI. England starlet Paul Walsh scored two goals as 'England' won 2-1.

Jim Platt had returned to Ireland in April 1983 and with no new players in the side Middlesbrough won the opening game of 1983-4 at Fratton Park with a Heine Otto goal, despite Portsmouth protests that their goalkeeper had been fouled. The joy was short-lived, however, as Chesterfield won 1-0 at Ayresome Park in the first leg of the Milk Cup. Two important League games followed immediately. David Currie scored twice in a pulsating 2-2 home draw against Leeds United and, three days later, the season's highest home crowd saw Middlesbrough pull off a thrilling 3-2 win over Newcastle United, Currie scoring two and Gary Hamilton the third.

Otto scored the only goal in the second leg of the Milk Cup tie at Chesterfield to take the game into extra-time. With no further goals, there was a sudden-death penalty shoot-out, which Chesterfield won 5-3.

Middlesbrough's League form, meanwhile, was excellent, and they won three of the first four games. Then five successive defeats followed. The rot was checked in late October with a confidence-boosting 4-0 home win against Rotherham United and promotion-winning form returned in November with only one defeat — a 1-0 reverse at Derby.

In the home game against Cardiff City, Stephen Pears, on loan from Manchester United, made his debut as 'Boro beat the Welshmen 2-0. Only one win came in December, a 2-0 success at Hillsborough against that season's Second Division champions.

An early opportunity to avenge the previous season's FA Cup exit at Highbury came on 7 January, when Arsenal were the opposition at Ayresome Park for a third-round tie and goals from Garry Macdonald, Paul Sugrue and Mick Baxter carried Middlesbrough through.

On the last day of the month it was Bournemouth's turn to be dumped out of the Cup, two goals from Sugrue doing the job at Ayresome Park. However, a fifth-round journey to Notts County ended Middlesbrough's Wembley dreams for another season.

David Currie (left) was Middlesbrough's leading scorer in 1983-4 with 15 League goals. Paul Sugrue (right) also had a good season and was almost ever-present.

As usual, the biggest attendances of the season centred around the derby games and on 17 March at St James' Park, a crowd of 30,421 saw Newcastle United win 3-1.

With serious financial problems staring Middlesbrough in the face, Malcolm Allison was being pressured into off-loading the club's star players to keep the 'Boro afloat financially. Matters came to a head in late March 1984, when he claimed that it was 'better for the club to die than to linger slowly on its deathbed'. This statement was the kiss of death for extrovert Allison and out he went. Jack Charlton agreed to steer the club through its temporary crisis and, assisted by Willie Maddren, he stayed until the end of the season. Middlesbrough struggled through, finishing in 17th place.

Middlesbrough's 1984-5 season began at Fratton Park but, even with new boys Mick Buckley and the prodigal David Mills in Willie Maddren's side, the team could not repeat the success of 1983-4 and lost 1-0.

Middlesbrough went out of the Milk Cup on aggregate to Bradford City and then Darren Wood, one of the club's major playing assets, was transferred to Chelsea in a deal that saw cash change hands and the return of former Middlesbrough stalwart, Tony McAndrew, to the 'Boro side. The club then reached their highest League position of the season beating Manchester City 2-1 at Ayresome Park, to complete a sequence of three victories in October.

Tony Mowbray, now established in the side, was sent off at Leeds on 27 October and David Currie was dismissed in November, at home to Blackburn Rovers. Paul Sugrue joined Portsmouth on a free transfer in early December and over Christmas, 'Boro picked up three useful points at Carlisle.

The FA Cup meeting with neighbours Darlington at Ayresome Park in early January 1985 attracted a crowd of 19,084 and Middlesbrough were fortunate to escape with a 0-0 draw. The Feethams replay three days later was deservedly lost 2-1, despite a late goal from Tony McAndrew, in front of a 14,237 crowd. The

David Mills scored 14 goals to head Middlesbrough's scorers in 1984-5, but the club still finished 19th in Division Two.

victory must have been doubly sweet for the Skernesiders, for it was their first-ever success over Middlesbrough.

An abysmal sequence of the ten League games without a win had started on New Year's Day, with a 1-0 home defeat against Oxford United, the eventual Second Division champions. Middlesbrough's next victory was a 1-0 win over Sheffield United, on the day that 'Archie' Stephens signed for 'Boro.

The highest home and away attendances of Middlesbrough's season were recorded in successive games in March. The visit of Yorkshire rivals Leeds United attracted only 8,817, yet it was still the highest home 'gate'. And the following week, 'Boro played in front of a crowd of 22,399 at Maine Road against Second Division leaders Manchester City.

Needing three points to ensure a further season of Second Division football, Middlesbrough pulled off a fine 2-0 win at Gay Meadow on the last day of the season, but a double dismissal was recorded when Gary Hamilton and Peter Beagrie were sent off.

David Mills ended the 1984-5 season as the club's highest scorer on 15 goals, but again Middlesbrough floundered and this time finished in 19th place.

They released regular goalkeeper Kelham O'Hanlon, who quickly got fixed up with Rotherham United, and Mick Buckley. Heine Otto, who had scored some valuable goals for the club, turned down an extension on his contract, returning home to sign for Den Haag, a Dutch Second Division side.

On the recommendation of Jack Charlton, Middlesbrough chairman Mike McCullagh offered the vacant manager's job to Willie Maddren. The new boss named four debutants — Steve Corden, Gary Pallister, Don O'Riordan, Gary Rowell — in the side that lost 3-0 on the opening day of the 1985-6 season, at Plough Lane, Wimbledon. Defender Corden, son of director Dick Corden, broke a leg just before half-time and never played for the club again.

The Milk Cup first round paired Middlesbrough with Mansfield Town, with the first leg at Field Mill. The Stags won 2-0 and a week later, at Ayresome Park, Middlesbrough's leaky defence helped Mansfield to draw 4-4 and go through on aggregate. 'Boro, once renowned as 'bonny Cup fighters', were now getting knocked out of the competition with alarming regularity in the early rounds.

The club's luck in the Full Members' Cup, however, was holding out and a 2-0 home victory over Carlisle United in early October meant a visit to Hull City in the Northern Area semi-final.

The Elland Road fixture on 12 October is a red-letter day in the history of Middlesbrough Football Club. The game marked the debut of Bernie Slaven in the forward line. He did not score — indeed, the game ended 0-0 — but he made his mark on his home debut, against Bradford City. That day, Slavin scored the first of many goals for 'Boro, in a match that ended 1-1.

On 2 November a double sending-off occurred at Ayresome Park, in the goalless draw against Blackburn Rovers. David Currie went for a 'double-booking' and Blackburn's Northern Ireland international Noel Brotherston followed for a similar reason.

Middlesbrough's 3-2 home victory over Oldham Athletic in mid-November ended a sequence of eight League games without a win, but hopes of a Cup victory disappeared as 'Boro went out of the Full Members' Cup Northern Area semi-final, losing 3-1 at Boothferry Park.

Middlesbrough desperately needed cash but the board was split over plans to raise £1 million by a public share issue. On 2 December, chairman Mike McCullagh and director Peter Cook resigned over the matter and Alf Duffield stepped into the breach.

The highlight of the Christmas games was an excellent 2-0 victory over Sunderland at Ayresome Park. Goals from Tony Mowbray and Tony McAndrew sent the crowd of 19,701 (the highest home attendance of the season) home delighted.

The month of January saw Middlesbrough relinquish any FA Cup dreams that they may have cherished, as they tamely submitted 3-1 to Southampton at Ayresome Park in the third round.

A spell of bad weather bit deeply into the February programme and Middlesbrough played only one game during the month, another home defeat, this time against Charlton Athletic.

Willie Maddren had left the club and coach Bruce Rioch was in charge of team affairs when, in March 1986, 'Boro went down with all guns blazing at Ayresome Park, losing 2-1 to Sheffield United. Such was the team's commitment to the game that, despite the loss of three desperately-needed points, they were accorded a standing ovation as they walked off the pitch.

Bruce Rioch received a midnight call from chairman Duffield offering him the manager's job and, to the relief of Teesside fans, he accepted.

In April 1986, the club, now fighting for its very existence, had to borrow £30,000 from the Professional Footballers' Association to pay the players and things were looking very black indeed.

It was a case of *déjà vu* for the final game of the season. The venue was again at Gay Meadow and Middlesbrough needed to win to stay in the Second Division. Archie Stephens scored for 'Boro and Gary Pallister was sent off as Shrewsbury won 2-1 and down Middlesbrough went.

On 21 May 1986, the worst fears of 'Boro's fans were realized. With crippling debts, rumoured to be approaching £2 million, the club called in the Provisional Liquidator and shortly afterwards, Middlesbrough Football Club's pulse ceased to beat.

In late July 1986, the Inland Revenue took the club to court, claiming £115,156 in tax arrears and the judge issued a winding-up order. On 2 August, Bruce Rioch and 29 other non-playing staff were sacked by the Official Receiver and the gates to Ayresome Park were padlocked.

Some players decided to leave the club and were now free to do so, arranging new contracts with other clubs and duly moving on. The ones that stayed, all unpaid, became more resolute in their determination to see the thing through and, led by Bruce Rioch and coach Colin Todd, they changed in the backs of cars and trained on any piece of turf that was available.

The club reformed under the name of 'Middlesbrough Football and Athletic Company (1986) Limited' and, chaired by Colin Henderson, intended to carry on playing football, no matter what class of soccer they ended up in.

In order to continue under the auspices of the Football League, stringent rules had to be adhered to and with the first game of 1986-7, at home to Port Vale, fast approaching, frantic behind-the-scenes talks meant that the reformed club could stay in the League, provided they could fulfill the Port Vale fixture.

Hartlepool United offered Middlesbrough (no longer on the football coupons) the use of the Victoria Ground and the gracious gesture was gratefully accepted. Port Vale complained to the Football League over the intended venue, but the League overruled Vale's complaint. Hartlepool were also at home on the first day of the season, so the League sanctioned Middlesbrough's game as an evening kick-off.

Archie Stephens scored two cracking goals to put Middlesbrough into a 2-0 lead, but 'Boro had not played any pre-season practice games and Vale, a fitter and better-prepared side, forced a 2-2 draw.

Three days later, in the first round of the Littlewoods Cup, the long arm of coincidence threw Hartlepool and 'Boro together for the first competitive meeting between the two clubs. At the Victoria Ground, a crowd of 7,735 saw the sides play out a 1-1 draw with Bernie Slaven netting for 'Boro.

The next League fixture was a 2-0 win at Wigan Athletic and the players and supporters made an emotional return to Ayresome Park for the second leg of the Littlewoods Cup on 2 September. Hartlepool offered little resistance as 'Boro won 2-0 with goals form Stuart Ripley and Gary Hamilton, who also missed a penalty.

Middlesbrough recovered from their traumatic start to the season and remained unbeaten in the League until Blackpool won 3-1 at Ayresome Park on 11 October. The Seasiders were back at Ayresome Park in November, for the first round of the FA Cup, but this time a Bernie Slaven hat-trick saw Middlesbrough through to the next round.

The first local derby of the season was at Feethams against Darlington, also in November, when a goal from Stephens was enough to ensure victory for 'Boro. December yielded an excellent points return as Middlesbrough went through the month unbeaten, winning four of their five games. One of those victories was at Notts County in the second round of the FA Cup.

York City halted Middlesbrough's League progress at Bootham Crescent on New Year's Day, with an impressive 3-1 win, and further disappointment followed nine days later when Fourth Division Preston North End scored the only goal of the FA Cup third-round game at Ayresome Park.

On 7 February, 'Boro lost the services of Brian Laws when he stepped up to take a penalty against Bristol Rovers at Ayresome Park. He severely damaged his knee ligaments in his run-up and was ruled out for the rest of the season.

In April and May, seven successive wins kept Middlesbrough in the promotion frame and a point was needed at Ayresome Park in the last home match of the season to guarantee promotion to the Second Division. Wigan proved to be unyielding in defence but, more important, failed to score. At the end of the game the Ayresome Park crowd were in raptures. The 'impossible' had happened — not only were Middlesbrough FC still alive, they were back in Division Two.

Bruce Rioch returned to his old club, Aston Villa, to buy defender Dean 'Dino' Glover in the summer of 1987 and Glover made his debut at right-back at Ayresome Park against Millwall on 15 August. Archie Stephens scored for Middlesbrough as Millwall forced a 1-1 draw before a crowd of 11,471.

Glover, who quickly became a favourite at Middlesbrough because of his commitment and 'hard man' image, hit the headlines three days later at Roker Park. In the Littlewoods Cup game against Sunderland he incurred the wrath of the referee when he struck Gary Bennett and received his marching orders after only 12 minutes on the pitch. Sunderland won the match 1-0. A week later, Middlesbrough wrapped up the second leg when goals from Bernie Slaven and skipper Tony Mowbray carried the club through on aggregate.

Bradford City won 2-0 at Valley Parade on 3 October but this defeat launched Middlesbrough on a run of 14 unbeaten games which ended in a 2-0 defeat at Elland Road on 28 December before a crowd of 34,186. The match was soured by the double dismissal of 'Boro's Stuart Ripley and United's Ian Snodin in the 43rd minute.

Middlesbrough's name was paired with non-League opposition for the third round of the FA Cup and underdogs Sutton United, cheered on by the nation, almost took 'Boro's scalp. A Gary Pallister goal put 'Boro ahead after 63 minutes, before Golley's equalizer ten minutes from time meant an Ayresome Park replay.

It took a goal from Paul Kerr in extra-time of that replay to extinguish brave

Sutton's Cup dreams and earn Middlesbrough a fourth-round game against First Division Everton at Goodison Park. This time 'Boro were the underdogs and the game's two goals came either side of the interval. Graeme Sharp put the Blues ahead with almost the last kick of the half. Paul Kerr equalized almost from the second-half kick-off.

The Àyresome Park replay was a stamina-sapping cracker. Dave Watson put the Merseysiders ahead inside 66 minutes and Tony Mowbray equalized in the dying seconds of normal time. Alan Kernaghan put 'Boro ahead for the first time in the tie, after 99 minutes, but Trevor Steven equalized with the last kick of the game. A second replay took place at Everton and this time the Merseysiders took command on a blustery night, winning 2-1.

Bruce Rioch took Watford striker, Trevor Senior, to Ayresome Park and the player contributed with two goals as 'Boro crushed Sheffield United 6-0 on his home debut.

Middlesbrough needed to beat Leicester City at Ayresome Park in the last game of the season to ensure a second promotion success, but City turned 'Boro's impending celebrations into a funeral wake by winning 2-1. 'Boro's players were asking the crowd how other results had gone as they walked off the pitch and learned that Aston Villa — on the same number of points and with the same goal-difference — had achieved promotion by virtue of winning more games, leaving Middlesbrough to try for the First Division through the play-off system.

Four play-off games stood between Middlesbrough and the First Division and the first one kicked-off at Valley Parade on Sunday 15 May, against Bradford City. The match yielded three goals, all scored in a three-minute second-half spell. City went ahead after 67 minutes, then Senior scored 'Boro's equalizer two minutes later. City's captain, Stuart McCall, restored Bradford's lead within a minute and set the scene for an interesting game at Ayresome Park three days later.

A goal by Bernie Slaven took the scores level on aggregate and with no further goals the match went into 30 minutes' extra-time. Within the first minute, Gary Hamilto.. ended City's aspirations by scoring the conclusive goal.

Chelsea now stood between Middlesbrough and Division One and the first game of the play-off 'Final', at Ayresome Park, took place on Wednesday 25 May. Despite Chelsea's obvious class, Middlesbrough took the game 2-0 with goals from Trevor Senior and Bernie Slaven.

At Stamford Bridge the following Saturday, Pat Nevin was in inspiring form and set up Chelsea's goal, Gordon Durie scoring after 19 minutes. Middlesbrough's defence, with Mowbray and Pallister twin towers of resistance, thwarted every Chelsea raid and they held on to take the tie 2-1 on aggregate. Chelsea's fans, unable to take defeat with dignity, marred the afternoon with ugly scenes which were later shown on television. It was half an hour before the Middlesbrough players were allowed back on to the pitch to celebrate promotion with their fans.

For Middlesbrough's return to the First Division, manager Bruce Rioch went into the transfer market to bring Mark Brennan to Ayresome Park. Brennan was given his debut on the opening day of the 1988-9 season, at Derby where a Paul Goddard goal was enough to give the Rams victory.

'Boro also lost the next two games. Their first win eventually came on 17 September, when Gary Hamilton's goal gave them victory over Wimbledon. It was an unhappy match, however, for striker Trevor Senior, who was booed off the pitch and within a matter of days had been transferred back to Reading.

Once again, Middlesbrough were dumped out of the Littlewoods Cup by a team in the lower reaches of the Football League. Tranmere Rovers forced a draw at Ayresome Park and deservedly won the Prenton Park game 1-0.

'Boro on the end of another Cup shock! Substitute Marc North was the Grimsby hero with two fine goals. Top: North equalizes with his first kick of the game. Bottom: North's diving header gives the Mariners a place in the fourth round of the FA Cup.

Sandwiched between the Littlewoods games, Bernie Slaven and David Speedie both scored hat-tricks at Highfield Road, where 'Boro just held on to beat Coventry City 4-3. At the end of October, however, Middlesbrough suffered a humiliating 3-0 defeat at Newcastle. Three days later, Middlesbrough beat a slick Millwall side 4-2 and everyone was happy again.

Later that month, Peter Davenport agreed to sign for Middlesbrough and, although he struggled to find his scoring touch, he did have the satisfaction of netting against his old club, Manchester United, on 2 January, helping 'Boro to end a sequence of seven games without a win.

There was another shock just around the corner, however, and Fourth Division Grimsby Town lowered 'Boro's FA Cup colours at Ayresome Park. Middlesbrough went ahead but then the Mariners' substitute, Marc North, scored twice.

In March 1989, Mark Proctor was surprisingly re-signed by Middlesbrough when Rioch paid £300,000 to buy him from Sheffield Wednesday. Proctor and Mark Barham made their debuts in a 1-1 draw at Wimbledon, although for Proctor, of course, it was his second League bow for the club.

Middlesbrough were now slipping deeper into trouble and a run of 12 games without a win saw them slump into the relegation zone. Then late goals by Slaven at West Ham earned 'Boro a 2-1 win and gave rise to hopes of a climb to safety.

Yet there was still much work to be done and when Arsenal kept their League Championship hopes alive with a 1-0 win at Ayresome Park on 6 May, they also left Middlesbrough needing victory at Hillsborough in the last match of the season. But Sheffield Wednesday were also desperate for the points and they scored the only goal of the game to send Middlesbrough back to the Second Division. In the summer, 'Boro also lost one of their best players of recent times when Gary Pallister was transferred to Manchester United for £2.3 million.

The history of Middlesbrough Football Club has, like the story of all clubs, had its fair share of ups and downs. From amateur giants in the gaslit days of the last century to a First Division side that has boasted the likes of Camsell, Mannion and Hardwick, 'Boro have contributed to football's rich tapestry. After the trials and tribulations of the last few years, when the club's very existence was in doubt, their supporters will be grateful that they have a club at all. Thus, when relegation to Division Two is set within that context, it does not seem quite such a disaster. At least the 'Boro lived to fight another day.

Middlesbrough's playing staff at the start of 1989-90, when expectations were high of a quick return to the First Division. Back row (left to right): Alan Comfort, Gary Parkinson, Garry Agnew, Kevin Poole, Stephen Pears, Matthew Coddington, Peter Davenport, Michael Trotter, Mark Proctor. Middle row: Gary Hamilton, Colin Cooper, Nicky Mohan, Tony Mowbray, Paul Kerr, Stuart Ripley, Alan Kernaghan, Andrew Fletcher. Front row: Colin Todd (first-team coach), Gary Pallister (now Manchester United), Bernie Slaven, Mark Burke, Bruce Rioch (manager), Trevor Putney, Mark Brennan, Owen McGee, David Nish (reserve-team coach).

Middlesbrough's Wilf Mannion enjoys an impromptu kick-about with some local youngsters.

Jeremiah Dawkins, Middlesbrough's goalkeeper in the 1880s, often smoked a pipe when his forwards were pressing in the opponents' half. Against Ecclesfield he decided to join the forwards. His counterpart noticed that he was out of the goal and punted the ball up field to his outside-left, who tapped the ball into the empty net.

The
Ayresome Park
Story

L IKE many of today's Football League clubs, Middlesbrough have not always played at their present home. The club's earliest games were staged at the Old Archery Ground, Albert Park, before they moved to Breckon Hill Road in March 1879. A year later they were on the verge of another move, this time to Linthorpe Road, where the Middlesbrough Cricket Club played.

In 1885, when the split over professionalism gave birth to Middlesbrough Ironopolis, those who favoured the paid ranks took their new club to the Paradise Ground on nearby Milton Street, whilst the amateurs stayed at Linthorpe Road and eventually saw the Irons fold.

By the time Middlesbrough FC moved home for the last time — to Ayresome Park in 1903 — they, too, had embraced professionalism and were members of the Football League. When the new ground was officially opened in September that year, it was regarded as one of the best in the country. Work had cost £11,000 and Ayresome Park had a capacity of some 40,000 and boasted two stands. One of them, the South Stand, had been moved from Linthorpe Road. The other, the North Stand, was quite magnificent for its time and, indeed, is still used today, running along the length of the Ayresome Street side of the ground.

The stature of Middlesbrough's new home was soon recognized by the Football Association, who staged the England-Ireland game there in February 1905, the first of three full internationals to be played at Ayresome Park. The FA also chose the ground for several amateur internationals and FA Amateur Cup Finals.

Ayresome Park remained largely unaltered until 1936, when the old South Stand was pulled down and the present South Stand was built. Later improvements included the rebuilding of terracing at each end of the ground and a cover being erected over the West End, although the corners are still uncovered.

In December 1949, a record Ayresome Park crowd of 53,802 saw the game between 'Boro and Newcastle United. These, of course, were the golden days for Football League attendances and in 1947, when 52,025 crammed in for the first leg of the FA Cup sixth-round tie against Burnley, thousands more were locked out. The story goes that the Chief Constable of Middlesbrough, A.E.Edwards, stood on a wall and gave what amounted to a running commentary to the unfortunates who were missing the action first-hand.

The first proper floodlit game at Ayresome Park was staged on 16 October 1957, when Sunderland were the visitors, and nine years later the ground staged three World Cup matches, ironically at a time when 'Boro had plunged into the Third Division for the first time in the club's history. The World Cup meant further improvements and a roof was put on the East End and seating installed on the

◀ Overleaf: Aerial view of Ayresome Park taken in September 1981.

terrace there. Extra seats were also accommodated in the North and South Stand paddocks, reducing the ground capacity to 40,000.

Like every other ground in the country, following safety legislation, the capacity of Ayresome Park has been reduced still further and in 1989 it stood at 32,000, which included 10,000 seats.

One 'white elephant' which, figuratively if not literally, looms large over Ayresome Park, is the sports hall which was first erected, without planning permission according to the local council, in 1981. Middlesbrough received grants to help towards its construction and later tried to sell it to the council, who refused. Although the club use its training facilities, plans for the public to make use of it in the evenings and on Saturdays when 'Boro are playing away have come to nothing. The complicated wrangle has continued and the sports hall remains largely unused.

Postcard produced to mark the opening of Ayresome Park.

The Publishers acknowledge that some of the above information also appears in *The Football Grounds of England & Wales* by Simon Inglis (Collins Willow, 1983).

1966 World Cup Games

at Ayresome Park

ENGLAND staged the 1966 World Cup Finals and the Group Four North-East matches were originally scheduled for Roker Park, Sunderland and St James' Park, Newcastle. United were not the owners of the ground and had to have the blessing of Newcastle City Council in order to stage the matches. A dispute between both parties meant that Middlesbrough, as a Third Division side, was offered the chance to stage the games and, at the 11th hour the World Cup came to Ayresome Park in July 1966.

12 July 1966
USSR 3   **North Korea 0**
USSR: Kavazashvili; Ponomarev, Shesternev, Khurtsilava, Ostrovoskiy, Sabo, Sichinava, Chislenko, Banishevskiy, Malofeev, Khusainov.
Scorers: Malofeev 2, Banishevskiy
North Korea: Li Chan Myung; Pak Li Sup, Shin Yung Kyoo, Kang Bong Chil, Lim Loong Sun, Im Seung Hwi, Pak Seung Zin, Han Bong Zin, Pak Doo Ik, Kang Ryong Woon, Kim Seung Il.
Att: 22,568
Ref: Juan Gardeazabal (Spain)

15 July 1966
Chile 1   **North Korea 1**
Chile: Olivares; Valentini, Cruz, Figueroa, Villanueva, Prieto, Marcos, Fouilloux, Landa, Araya, Sanchez.
Scorer: Marcos (pen)
North Korea: Li Chan Myung; Pak Li Sup, Shin Yung Kyoo, Lim Zoong Sun, Oh Yoon Kyung, Pak Seung Zin, Im Seung Hwi, Han Bong Zin, Pak Doo Ik, Li Dong Woon, Kim Seung Il.
Scorer: Pak Seung Zin
Att: 15,887
Ref: Aly Kandil (United Arab Republic)

19 July 1966
Italy 0   **North Korea 1**
Italy: Albertosi; Landini, Janich, Guarneri, Facchetti, Bulgarelli, Fogli, Perani, Mazzola, Rivera, Barison.
North Korea: Li Chan Myung; Sim Zoong Sun, Shin Yung Kyoo, Ha Jung Won, Oh Yoon Kyung, Im Seung Hwi, Pak Seung Zin, Han Bong Zin, Pak Doo Ik, Kim Bong Hwan, Yang Sung Kook.
Scorer: Pak Doo Ik
Att: 18,727
Ref: Pierre Schwinte (France)

FINAL GROUP POSITIONS

	P	W	D	L	F	A	Pts
USSR	3	3	0	0	6	1	6
North Korea	3	1	1	1	2	4	3
Italy	3	1	0	2	2	2	2
Chile	3	0	1	2	2	5	1

64

Football League Representative Games

17 Feb 1912
Football League 2   **Scottish League 0**
Football League: Williamson (Middlesbrough); Crompton (Blackburn R), Pennington (WBA), Duckworth (Manchester U), Boyle (Burnley), Fay (Bolton W), Wallace (Aston V), Buchan (Sunderland), Freeman (Burnley), Holley (Sunderland), Mordue (Sunderland).
Scorers: Freeman, Mordue
Scottish League: Brownlie (Third Lanark); Blair (Clyde), McNair (Celtic), Galt (Rangers), McAndrew (Clyde), Mercer (Hearts), Brown (Celtic), Cunningham (Kilmarnock), Quinn (Celtic), McMenemy (Celtic), Bennett (Rangers).
Att: 24,149
Ref: H.S.Bamlett (Gateshead)

22 Mar 1950
Football League 3   **Scottish League 1**
Football League: Williams (Wolves); Ramsey (Spurs), Aston (Manchester U), Wright (Wolves), Franklin (Stoke C), Dickinson (Portsmouth), Hancocks (Wolves), Mannion (Middlesbrough), Mortensen (Blackpool), Baily (Spurs), Langton (Blackburn R).
Scorers: Mortensen 2, Baily
Scottish League: Brown (Rangers); Cox (Rangers), Young (Rangers), Hewitt (Partick T), Woodburn (Rangers), Evans (Celtic), Reilly (Hibs), Brown (East Fife), Bauld (Hearts), Mason (Hibs), Smith (Hibs).
Scorer: Young (pen)
Att: 39,352
Ref: H.Holt (Rochdale)

20 Mar 1968
Football League 2   **Scottish League 0**
Football League: Stepney (Manchester U); K.Newton (Blackburn R), Knowles (Spurs), Stiles (Manchester U), Labone (Everton), Moore (West Ham), Ball (Everton), Hunt (Liverpool), R.Charlton (Manchester U), Hurst (West Ham), Peters (West Ham).
Scorers: Hunt, Newton
Scottish League: McCloy (Motherwell); Callaghan (Dunfermline), Gemmell (Celtic), Greig (Rangers), McKinnon (Rangers), D Smith (Rangers), Johnstone (Celtic), Murdoch

(Celtic), Stein (Rangers), Lennox (Celtic), Hughes (Celtic), J.Smith (Aberdeen).
Att: 34,190
Ref: J.E.Carr (Sheffield)

15 Mar 1972
Football League 3   **Scottish League 2**
Football League: Clemence (Liverpool); Lawler (Liverpool), Nish (Leicester C), Doyle (Manchester C), Blockley (Arsenal), Moore (West Ham), Hughes (Liverpool), Macdonald (Newcastle U), Currie (Sheffield U), Hurst (West Ham), Wagstaffe (Wolves).
Scorers: Currie 2, Doyle
Scottish League: Hunter (Kilmarnock); Brownlie (Hibs), Forsyth (Partick T), Jardine (Rangers)[Graham (Aberdeen)], Connelly (Celtic), Blackley (Hibs), McQuade (Partick T), Phillips (Dundee), Stein (Rangers), Hay (Celtic), Ford (Hearts).
Scorer: Stein 2
Att: 19,996
Ref: P.Partridge (Middlesbrough)

UEFA Youth Tournament

5 Oct 1983
England Under-16 3   **Scotland Under-16 1**
England: Digby (Manchester U); Ratcliffe (Manchester U), Crane (Ipswich T), Keen (West Ham), Adams (Arsenal), Anderson (Coventry C), Carr (Blackburn R), Moulden (Manchester C), Beckford (Manchester C), Beresford (Manchester C), Kilner (Burnley).
Scorers: Beckford, Moulden, Carr
Scotland: Donaldson (Dundee U); Traynor (Celtic), McGee (Celtic), Robertson (Aberdeen), Riddell (Aberdeen)[McLeod (Dundee U)], Winnie (St Mirren), Shepherd (Celtic), Ferguson (Rangers), Gray (Aberdeen), Miller (Aberdeen), Wright (Aberdeen)[Fraser (Celtic)].
Scorer: Winnie
Att: 929

Full England International Matches

Played at
Ayresome Park

25 Feb 1905
England 1   **Ireland 1**
England: Williamson (Middlesbrough); Balmer (Everton), Carr (Newcastle U), Wolstenholme (Everton), Roberts(Manchester U), Leake (Aston V), Bond (Preston NE), Bloomer (Derby C), Woodward (Tottenham H), Harris (Corinthians), Booth (Manchester C).
Scorer: Bloomer
Ireland: Scott (Linfield); McCracken (Newcastle U), McCartney (Everton), Darling (Linfield), Connor (Belfast C), Nicholl (Belfast C), Sloan (Bohemians), Sheridan (Stoke), Murphy (QPR), Shanks (Brentford), Kirwan (Tottenham H).
Scorer: Williamson (own-goal)
Att: 24,000
Referee: T.Robertson (Scotland)

14 Feb 1914
England 0   **Ireland 3**
England: Hardy (Aston V); Crompton (Blackburn R), Pennington (WBA), Cuggy (Sunderland), Buckley (Derby C), Watson (Burnley), Wallace (Aston V), Shea (Blackburn R), Elliott (Middlesbrough), Latheron (Blackburn R), Martin (Sunderland).
Ireland: McKee (Belfast C); McConnell (Bohemians), Craig (Morton), Hampton (Bradford C), O'Connell (Hull C), Hammill (Manchester C), Rollo (Linfield), Young (Linfield), Gillespie (Sheffield U), Lacey (Liverpool), Thompson (Clyde).
Scorers: Gillespie, Lacey (2)
Att: 24,000
Referee: A.Jackson (Scotland)

Steve Bloomer, later to join 'Boro, scored England's goal at Ayresome Park in 1905.

17 Nov 1937
England 2   **Wales 1**
England: Woodley (Chelsea); Sproston (Leeds U), Barkas (Manchester C), Crayston (Arsenal), Cullis (Wolves), Copping (Arsenal), Matthews (Stoke C), Hall (Tottenham H), Mills (Chelsea), Goulden (West Ham U), Brook (Manchester C)
Scorers: Hall, Matthews.
Wales: Gray (Chester); Turner (Charlton A), Hughes (Birmingham), Murphy (West Brom), Hanford (Sheffield W), Richards (Brentford), L.Jones (Coventry C), Perry (Doncaster R), B.Jones (Wolves), Morris (Birmingham).
Scorer: Perry
Att: 30,500
Referee: W.E.Webb (Scotland)

66

AMATEUR CUP FINALS PLAYED AT MIDDLESBROUGH

1898-1899	Stockton	1	Harwich & Parkeston	0
1911-1912	Stockton	0	Eston United	0
	Stockton	1	Eston United	0
1920-1921	Bishop Auckland	4	Swindon Victoria	2
1921-1922	Bishop Auckland	5	South Bank	2
1927-1928	Leyton	3	Cockfield	2
1934-1935	Bishop Auckland	0	Wimbledon	0
1953-1954	Crook Town	1	Bishop Auckland	0
1955-1956	Bishop Auckland	4	Corinthian Casuals	1
1961-1962	Crook Town	4	Hounslow Town	0

ENGLAND TRIAL GAMES PLAYED AT AYRESOME PARK

Wednesday, 8 Feb 1928

England 8

England: Brown (Sheffield W); Goodall (Huddersfield T), Osborne (Leicester C), Edwards (Leeds U), Kean (Sheffield W), Bishop (Leicester C), Hulme (Arsenal), Kelly (Huddersfield T), Dean (Everton), J.Carr (Middlesbrough), W.H.Smith (Huddersfield T).
Scorers: Dean 5, W.H.Smith, Hulme 2
Referee: A.Josephs

Rest 3

Rest: Hufton (West Ham U); Finch (West Bromwich A), Silcock (Manchester U), Andrews (Sunderland), Matthews (Sheffield U), Storer (Derby C), Burton (Burnley), Hine (Leicester C), Camsell (Middlesbrough), Stephenson (Derby C), Tunstall (Sheffield U).
Scorers: Tunstall, Hine, Camsell.
Attendance: 18,000

OTHER REPRESENTATIVE GAMES PLAYED AT AYRESOME PARK

Amateur Internationals		**Youth Internationals**	
27 Jan 1923	England 4 Wales 4	6 Feb 1954	England 2 Scotland 11
15 May 1951	England 2 Norway 1	22 Feb 1964	England 1 Scotland 1
10 May 1963	England 0 West Germany 1		

67

Attendances at
Ayresome Park

Although the Football League has been in existence since 1888, exact attendances for all League clubs are complete and available only from season 1925-6, so for Middlesbrough the previous 22 seasons' attendances remain incomplete and where attendances have been unearthed, the majority found are contemporary newspaper approximations.

Exhaustive scrutiny of Middlesbrough's home and away attendances since 1925-6 brought many discrepancies to light, the prime example being the record attendance for Ayresome Park. For almost 40 years, all sources quoted the record as 53,596 for the game against Newcastle United on 27 December 1949 but Football League figures revealed a higher figure of 53,802, a difference of 206. Many such discrepancies exist so all attendances quoted in this book are taken from the official attendance figures records held by the Football League and must, therefore be taken as the correct ones.

Attendances over 40,000 at Ayresome Park

DIVISION ONE
27 Dec 1949	Newcastle U	W 1-0	53,802
14 Oct 1950	Sunderland	D 1-1	52,764

FA CUP SIXTH ROUND
1 Mar 1947	Burnley	D 1-1	52,025

FA CUP FOURTH ROUND
21 Jan 1939	Sunderland	L 0-2	51,080

FA CUP THIRD ROUND REPLAY
11 Jan 1950	Aston Villa	D 0-0	49,850

DIVISION ONE
23 Sep 1950	Manchester U	L 1-2	48,051
31 Aug 1949	Blackpool	W 2-0	47,870

DIVISION TWO
10 Oct 1959	Sunderland	D 1-1	47,297

DIVISION ONE
12 Mar 1938	Arsenal	W 2-1	46,747
11 Mar 1950	Manchester U	L 2-3	46,702
9 Sep 1950	Arsenal	W 2-1	46,119
1 Jan 1938	Sunderland	W 2-1	45,854
26 Dec 1946	Leeds U	W 3-0	45,336

DIVISION TWO
27 Dec 1954	Leeds U	W 1-0	45,271

DIVISION ONE
6 Dec 1947	Sunderland	D 2-2	45,145
30 Oct 1948	Blackpool	W 1-0	44,780
27 Mar 1937	Arsenal	D 1-1	44,523
29 Aug 1951	Manchester U	L 1-4	44,434
10 Apr 1950	Sunderland	W 2-0	44,260
5 Oct 1946	Chelsea	W 3-2	44,082
18 Apr 1949	Newcastle U	W 3-2	44,037
18 Aug 1951	Tottenham H	W 2-1	44,004

DIVISION TWO
26 Oct 1963	Sunderland	W 2-0	43,905
27 Dec 1926	Manchester C	W 2-1	43,754

FA CUP FIFTH ROUND
7 Feb 1948	Derby C	L 1-2	43,708

DIVISION ONE
7 Sep 1946	Stoke C	W 5-4	43,685

DIVISION TWO
15 Dec 1962	Sunderland	D 3-3	43,509

DIVISION ONE
27 Dec 1948	Sunderland	D 0-0	43,455

DIVISION TWO
3 Sep 1958	Sheffield U	D 0-0	42,866

FA CUP FOURTH ROUND
26 Jan 1957	Aston Villa	L 2-3	42,396

FA CUP FOURTH ROUND REPLAY
25 Jan 1947	Chesterfield	W 2-1	42,250

FA CUP FIFTH ROUND
15 Feb 1936	Leicester C	W 2-1	42,214

DIVISION ONE
27 Aug 1952	Cardiff C	W 3-0	42,159
15 Feb 1930	Arsenal	L 0-2	42,073
5 May 1928	Sunderland	L 0-3	41,997
3 Sep 1949	Portsmouth	L 1-5	41,974
20 Aug 1949	Everton	L 0-1	41,722
26 Aug 1950	Chelsea	W 3-0	41,573

FA CUP FOURTH ROUND
6 Feb 1952	Doncaster R	L 1-4	41,560

DIVISION ONE

23 Aug 1950	Everton	W 4-0	41,478
25 Dec 1950	Newcastle U	W 2-1	41,318
28 Dec 1946	Aston Villa	L 1-2	41,299
14 Jan 1950	Wolves	W 2-0	41,155
4 Oct 1947	Liverpool	W 3-1	41,140

FA CUP FIFTH ROUND

21 Feb 1970	Manchester U	D 1-1	41,000

FA CUP THIRD ROUND REPLAY

17 Jan 1934	Sunderland	L 1-2	40,882

DIVISION ONE

26 Dec 1929	Newcastle U	D 2-2	40,538
25 Oct 1950	Blackpool	W 4-3	40,487
27 Apr 1949	Stoke C	D 1-1	40,329
21 Sep 1946	Preston NE	W 2-0	40,317
9 Nov 1946	Sunderland	L 1-3	40,219

FA CUP THIRD ROUND REPLAY

5 Jan 1971	Manchester U	W 2-1	40,040

Away Games in which Middlesbrough have played in front of 50,000 plus crowds.

DIVISION ONE

14 Sep 1946	Manchester U	L 0-1	65,279
15 Apr 1949	Newcastle U	L 0-1	64,381

FA CUP FIFTH ROUND REPLAY

25 Feb 1970	Manchester U	L 1-2	63,418

DIVISION ONE

13 Jan 1950	Arsenal	L 1-3	63,038
7 Apr 1950	Sunderland	L 0-2	62,487
26 Dec 1949	Newcastle U	W 1-0	61,184
2 Dec 1950	Tottenham H	D 3-3	61,148
21 Aug 1948	Chelsea	L 0-1	60,981
18 Feb 1950	Manchester C	W 1-0	59,714
23 Nov 1935	Sunderland	L 1-2	58,902
27 Mar 1976	Manchester U	L 0-3	58,527
11 Apr 1952	Newcastle U	W 2-0	59,364
3 Mar 1950	Sunderland	L 1-2	57,958
23 Oct 1948	Liverpool	L 0-4	57,561
26 Mar 1948	Arsenal	L 0-7	57,557

DIVISION TWO

4 Sep 1963	Newcastle U	L 0-2	56,918

DIVISION ONE

28 Aug 1937	Sunderland	L 1-3	56,717
18 Sep 1976	Manchester U	L 0-2	56,712
26 Dec 1936	Manchester C	L 1-2	56,227

FA CUP SIXTH ROUND

19 Mar 1977	Liverpool	L 0-2	55,881

FA CUP FIFTH ROUND

18 Feb 1928	Huddersfield	L 0-4	55,200

FA CUP FOURTH ROUND

23 Jan 1971	Everton	L 0-3	54,875

DIVISION TWO

28 Dec 1964	Newcastle U	L 1-2	54,750

DIVISION ONE

16 Aug 1980	Manchester U	L 0-3	54,394

FA CUP FIFTH ROUND

26 Feb 1972	Manchester U	D 0-0	53,850

DIVISION TWO

11 Feb 1961	Sunderland	L 0-2	53,254

DIVISION ONE

12 Oct 1974	Liverpool	L 0-2	52,590
24 Apr 1948	Sunderland	L 0-3	51,581
9 Apr 1949	Arsenal	D 1-1	51,540
3 Sep 1952	Cardiff C	D 1-1	51,512
1 Sep 1979	Manchester U	L 1-2	51,015
22 Mar 1952	Arsenal	L 1-3	50,979
10 Sep 1949	Wolves	L 1-3	50,424

Aggregate Attendances
(1925-89)

Season	Games	HOME Aggregate	HOME Average	AWAY Aggregate	AWAY Average
		DIVISION TWO			
1925-26	42	278,442	13,259	304,344	14,493
1926-27	42	458,563	21,836	351,782	16,752
		DIVISION ONE			
1927-28	42	475,335	22,635	525,584	25,028
		DIVISION TWO			
1928-29	42	393,201	18,724	369,200	17,581
		DIVISION ONE			
1929-30	42	402,604	19,172	461,047	21,955
1930-31	42	354,025	16,858	421,568	20,075
1931-32	42	291,696	13,890	425,502	20,262
1932-33	42	255,290	12,157	327,769	15,608
1933-34	42	265,322	12,634	431,041	20,526
1934-35	42	301,906	14,376	435,557	20,741
1935-36	42	394,198	18,771	470,708	22,415
1936-37	42	470,194	22,390	521,006	24,810
1937-38	42	509,469	24,260	488,904	23,281
1938-39	42	444,945	21,188	485,805	23,134
1946-47	42	754,143	35,912	682,203	32,486
1947-48	42	711,912	35,901	752,903	35,853
1948-49	42	720,141	34,292	811,226	38,630
1949-50	42	743,541	35,407	723,668	34,460
1950-51	42	758,579	36,123	811,226	38,630
1951-52	42	604,279	28,775	691,428	32,925
1952-53	42	568,608	27,077	675,160	32,151
1953-54	42	567,037	27,002	614,931	29,282
		DIVISION TWO			
1954-55	42	443,272	21,108	409,955	19,522
1955-56	42	375,191	17,866	395,782	18,847
1956-57	42	443,657	21,127	380,371	18,113
1957-58	42	512,358	24,398	396,618	18,887
1958-59	42	522,401	24,876	422,625	20,125
1959-60	42	536,554	25,550	410,535	19,549
1960-61	42	333,038	15,859	373,517	17,787
1961-62	42	332,011	15,810	318,225	15,154
1962-63	42	347,094	16,528	365,541	17,407
1963-64	42	394,512	18,786	338,157	16,103
1964-65	42	306,855	14,612	361,245	17,202
1965-66	42	282,452	13,450	285,238	13,583
		DIVISION THREE			
1966-67	46	380,321	16,540	188,285	8,186
		DIVISION TWO			
1967-68	42	397,027	18,906	330,685	15,747
1968-69	42	442,332	21,063	373,647	17,793

Season	Games	HOME Aggregate	Average	AWAY Aggregate	Average
1969-70	42	416,966	19,856	330,013	15,715
1970-71	42	389,224	18,534	332,213	15,820
1971-72	42	376,794	17,943	306,651	14,602
1972-73	42	218,774	10,418	244,469	11,641
1973-74	42	472,459	22,498	359,962	17,141

DIVISION ONE

Season	Games	HOME Aggregate	Average	AWAY Aggregate	Average
1974-75	42	600,696	28,605	574,823	27,372
1975-76	42	487,687	23,223	558,954	28,617
1976-77	42	451,074	21,480	548,650	26,126
1977-78	42	417,349	19,874	538,496	25,643
1978-79	42	387,648	18,459	496,425	23,639
1979-80	42	393,522	18,739	476,216	22,677
1980-81	42	345,076	16,432	463,676	22,080
1981-82	42	281,668	13,413	386,764	18,417

DIVISION TWO

Season	Games	HOME Aggregate	Average	AWAY Aggregate	Average
1982-83	42	210,380	10,018	218,726	10,416
1983-84	42	177,930	8,473	220,776	10,513
1984-85	42	107,827	5,135	157,808	7,515
1985-86	42	131,400	6,257	149,287	7,109

DIVISION THREE

Season	Games	HOME Aggregate	Average	AWAY Aggregate	Average
1986-87	46	234,010	10,174	134,498	5,848

DIVISION TWO

Season	Games	HOME Aggregate	Average	AWAY Aggregate	Average
1987-88	44	319,621	14,528	236,651	10,757

DIVISION ONE

Season	Games	HOME Aggregate	Average	AWAY Aggregate	Average
1988-89	38	379,989	19,999	370,399	19,495

The discord between Middlesbrough Football Club and Jock Marshall came to a head in June 1923, when the player reported the club's activities to the football authorities. At the subsequent hearing, the Football League Management Committee heard both parties' evidence and came to the conclusion that Middlesbrough's errors when re-signing Jock Marshall were serious enough to warrant a £100 fine. The offences of which the club had been found guilty were:

1. Promising a benefit match to the player in contravention of Football League rules (only the Football League Management Committee could sanction a player's benefit.)
2. The player, at the instigation of his club, had signed a contractual agreement for a period longer than the rules allowed.

The Committee imposed a £50 fine on the club for each offence, and Marshall's transfer fee was reduced to £2,000.

Middlesbrough
Managers

John Robson
May 1899 to May 1905

JOHN Robson was born at Gainford in Durham and, as a young boy, moved with his family to Middlesbrough. He played in goal for Middlesbrough Swifts, the club's reserve side, and when the 'Boro sampled professionalism, the Swifts team retained its amateur status. Robson's natural flair for administrative matters surfaced and he became secretary of the Swifts' committee soon afterwards. When Middlesbrough reverted to amateur status he became assistant secretary to Albert Borrie.

In May 1899, Middlesbrough Football and Athletic Club Limited successfully applied to join the Football League as a Second Division side and, at the club's annual general meeting convened shortly after, a bombshell was dropped when it was announced that 'Boro secretary Herbert W. Winney, a schoolteacher, had regretfully offered his resignation because of health reasons. So, with League football only three months away, the club turned to Robson in a moment of crisis.

He reluctantly accepted the position of secretary-manager at a salary of £156 per annum. Apparently one of the conditions of his appointment was that, as an economy measure, he was not to accompany the team to away games. His response was magnificent and in the space of three months he moulded the Northern League club into a side ready for the Second Division.

John Robson was left untarnished by the irregular payments to players scandal which shook the football world in 1905. He had the foresight to have a document signed by the club chairman, totally absolving him of any dubious involvement in the unsavoury episode.

Robson ran a tobacconist's shop in Wilson Street for a while, but the urge to return to football proved too strong and, after 17 years with the Middlesbrough club, he moved south to become Crystal Palace manager for the start of the 1905-06 season, where he stayed for two seasons. Such was the esteem that his old club and its grateful supporters held for Robson, at a 'smoker evening' held in his honour, he was presented with a handsome gold watch and chain, whilst Mrs Robson received a silver tea service and both were assured of the good wishes of the townspeople.

He took charge of team duties at Manchester United on 28 December 1914, whom he joined from Brighton. When John Chapman became United team manager in 1916, Robson became his assistant. Ill health had dogged Robson, eventually forcing his early retirement in October 1921. A heavy cold led to pneumonia which claimed his life on 11 January 1922.

Middlesbrough, along with the rest of the football world, paid its final respects to a loyal friend and servant at his funeral. On the practical side, Manchester United staged a benefit game for his widow and family when Jackie Carr, 'Boro's England international, represented John Robson's old club.

Alex Mackie
June 1905 to May 1906

ALEX Mackie was born in 1870, in Banffshire, and played his early football for Aberdeen and then joined Glasgow Association before becoming club secretary at Inverness.

Mackie then spent seven seasons at Sunderland as player-manager in one of the Wearsiders' most productive playing periods, although his involvement in the 'Andy McCombie Scandal' brought him a suspension imposed by the Football Association.

He was one of 70 applicants for the Middlesbrough job vacated by John Robson and his achievements at Roker Park convinced the 'Boro board that he was the man for the job, which he took on in the summer of 1905.

Whilst Robson had shown perspicacity in securing a letter of absolution in the irregular payments scandal, Mackie had failed to insure himself in a likewise manner and, for his part in the incident, he received a ban forbidding him from any active participation in football. He was, however, already disillusioned with the game and its ruling body and pre-empted the ban by voluntarily severing his interests in football. He took over the Star and Garter Hotel in Marton Road, Middlesbrough, in June 1906.

Andy Aitken
October 1906 to February 1909

ANDY Aitken's first job was as a grocer's assistant, but he later admitted that, more often than not, when he should have been delivering groceries he was kicking a football around a field. He became apprenticed to a trade and played as a forward for his local side, Elmbank. After a couple of seasons, he moved to Ayr Parkhouse, where he stayed for one season. He was 17 when Manchester United and Preston North End showed a positive interest in him, but he decided to finish his apprenticeship in Scotland.

Newcastle United made the first firm offer after his appenticeship was completed and, in July 1895, he became an adopted Geordie, signing for the Magpies as an inside-forward. His first full Scotland cap came in 1901-02 and he made over 300 appearances in a Newcastle career that lasted 11 years and took in two FA Cup Finals and a League Championship, although he was to miss their greatest days of the later 1900s.

At the age of 30, Aitken joined 'Boro on 31 October 1906, as the club's first player-manager. The transfer deal cost Middlesbrough £500. Within a fortnight of joining his new club, he was also appointed secretary and his brilliance as a pivotal defender for 'Boro won him a further three international caps.

Aitken later said that the Middlesbrough job had given him the most satisfaction in his career, but that there was one particular person at Ayresome Park with whom he could not get on. He diplomatically refused to disclose that person's identity, but the clash of personalities forced him to leave and he joined Leicester Fosse as player-manager in February 1909.

Again he was chosen to play for his country, eventually taking his total of Scottish caps to 14 caps. After two and a half seasons at Leicester, Aitken returned to his native Scotland to play for Dundee in May 1911 and then turned out for Kilmarnock before a groin injury ended his playing career.

Shortly afterwards he managed Gateshead Town for a spell, then became a licensee and acted as a scout for Arsenal in the 1930s. He once said that he was never fast and felt that his best work was done as a centre-half, his playing strength being the effective use of his head to clear the ball. He was born at Ayr in 1877 and died on Tyneside in 1955.

Andy Walker
June 1910 to January 1911

FOLLOWING the departure of Andy Aitken to Leicester Fosse, the Middlesbrough board approached Airdrie manager Andy Walker and he accepted the job on 27 June 1910. Soon afterwards, however, Walker was in trouble for illegally approaching an Airdrie player to induce him to sign for Middlesbrough. The manager was suspended for four weeks and the 'Boro club was fined £100.

In December 1910, Middlesbrough chairman Thomas Gibson-Poole, the local Tory Parliamentary candidate, thought that if Middlesbrough beat Sunderland in the 'derby' game at Ayresome Park two days before the election, it would enhance his chances of becoming an MP for the town. Before the game, Andy Walker offered Sunderland skipper Charlie Thomson £30 to 'throw' the match, but Thomson reported the matter to his chairman, Fred Taylor, who promptly notified the FA. Jimmy Nichol ensured a Middlesbrough victory, but Gibson-Poole lost the election by over 3,000 votes.

On 16 January 1911, an FA Commission decided that money had been offered and Walker and Gibson-Poole were permanently suspended from football. Certain factions believed that the manager had simply been used as the pawn of a scheming chairman and, bearing this in mind, the FA should view his case sympathetically. A petition containing 12,500 signatures was presented to the FA for Walker's reinstatement, but without success.

Tom McIntosh
August 1911 to December 1919

TOM McIntosh began his career as a right-half with Darlington in 1895. In July 1902, the Darlington board offered him the secretary's job at Feethams and he began his association with football administration which was to last for more than 20 years.

The bribery scandal of 1910-11 saw the suspension of secretary-manager Andy Walker and chairman Thomas Gibson-Poole. Phil Bach, the new chairman, was given the task of reforming the Middlesbrough board of directors and McIntosh accepted the post of 'Boro secretary-manager on 1 August 1911.

He was at Ayresome Park to see the club achieve its highest League placing of third in Division One in 1913-14 but, with a potential League Championship-winning team shaping under his guidance, his plans were abruptly shelved with the outbreak of World War One, although the League continued until the end of 1914-15.

Middlesbrough released their players and closed down, whilst Ayresome Park was used by the Army as a storage depot. At the start of the war in August 1914, McIntosh had joined the Teesside Pioneers and later saw active service as a sergeant in France.

At the beginning of 1919, the war over, he guided Middlesbrough to the Northern Victory League title and prepared the club for 'normal' football, with Herbert Glasper now acting as secretary. In December that year, however, Everton offered McIntosh the opportunity to steer the Goodison side into the 1920s and he left with the full blessing of the Middlesbrough board. Tom McIntosh died, aged 56, on 29 October 1935.

Jimmy Howie
April 1920 to July 1923

JIMMY Howie, who was born at Galston, Ayrshire, on 19 March 1878, became the second ex-Newcastle United player to become manager of Middlesbrough, when he succeeded Tommy McIntosh in April 1920.

His playing career began with his home-town club, Galston Athletic, and he moved to Kilmarnock in 1899 before travelling south to play for Kettering Town. In 1902 he was transferred to Bristol Rovers, but his career really took off upon his arrival at Newcastle United in May 1903.

At St James' Park he won League Championship medals in 1905, 1907 and 1909, although Newcastle's failure to win the FA Cup Final in 1905, 1906 and 1908 (he scored a goal against Wolves that year) meant runners-up medals for 'Gentleman Jim'. In 1910, he finally gained a winners' medal when Newcastle needed a replay at Everton to beat Barnsley 2-0. By the time his Newcastle United career ended in December 1910, with a £675 transfer to ambitious non-League Huddersfield Town, he had clocked up 198 League appearances, 67 goals and three full Scotland caps, mainly as an attacking inside-forward.

In November 1913, with his League career behind him, he successfully applied for the job of manager at Queen's Park Rangers, then in the Southern League. He was named as Tommy McIntosh's successor in April 1920, and stayed at Ayresome Park until July 1923. He later became a tobacconist in the London area and died in January 1963.

Herbert Bamlett
August 1923 to March 1927

WHEN 32-year-old Herbert Bamlett took charge of the 1914 FA Cup Final between Burnley and Liverpool, he became the youngest man to referee the Cup Final. For Bamlett, who was born at Gateshead on 1 March 1882, it was his last game as a referee and the following month he took over as manager of Oldham Athletic.

Those were difficult times and within a few weeks of his appointment at Boundary Park, war broke out. However, despite the problems of finding a regular team, Bamlett steered Oldham to what is still their best-ever League position of runners-up in Division One, a considerable feat in the face of selection problems and severe financial restrictions.

Called up for military service in 1916, Bamlett was demobbed in 1919 and set about re-building the team for the first peacetime season. After two indifferent seasons, though,

76

he left for Wigan Borough, becoming manager for their first two seasons in the new Third Division North.

Wigan finished 17th and then fifth and on 12 August 1923, Bamlett was appointed manager of Middlesbrough. With the inevitable retirement of Tim Williamson and the ageing George Elliott's loss of form, he saw his new club relegated to Division Two — 'Boro's first-ever taste of relegation — at the end of his first season in charge at Ayresome Park.

The Middlesbrough board did not, as expected, sack him and their faith in his potential was realized two seasons later, in the club's golden jubilee year. A disastrous start to that eventful 1926-7 season saw the team lose the opening three games, before the first point was wrested in a bruising game at South Shields. Injuries to Maurice Webster and Jimmy McClelland prompted Bamlett to try Walter Holmes at centre-half, whilst one of the directors suggested playing young George Camsell at centre-forward for the home game against Hull City.

The team went on to win their next six matches, scoring 16 goals with Camsell bagging seven of them. Middlesbrough quickly became the talk of the country as they rattled in goal after goal. They scored 122 goals, still a Second Division record, and Camsell's personal tally was a record 59 as 'Boro steam-rolled their way out of Division Two.

Herbert Bamlett, though, was not at Ayresome Park to see the culmination of that triumphant season. Three years earlier the 'Boro board had kept him on after relegation. Now, on the brink of promotion, they dismissed him.

He became manager of Manchester United and the opening game of the 1927-8 season saw his old team take on his new side at Old Trafford. Bamlett must have been extremely satisfied when United ran out 3-0 winners. He stayed at Old Trafford for four seasons, until United suffered relegation at the end of 1930-31, conceding 115 goals along the way.

Peter McWilliam
April 1927 to March 1934

PETER McWilliam was born in Inverness in 1882 and played for Inverness Thistle in 1899 before signing for Newcastle United in August 1902. He was nicknamed 'Pat' by his teammates at St James' Park and 'Peter the Great' by his adoring Geordie fans. A contemporary pen-picture of the likeable Scot described him as 'popularly believed to possess India-rubber legs . . .he developed a body wriggle that was annoyingly deceptive'. Football folklore records that he was so relaxed before a game that he would occasionally take a half-hour nap before the kick-off but, as a manager, he was sometimes so nervous that he could not bear to watch his team in action.

His League and Cup successes were identical to his friend and Newcastle teammate Jimmy Howie, even matching Howie on 198 League appearances for United. He won eight full Scottish caps whilst on Tyneside, but a knee injury suffered against Wales ended his playing career in 1911.

McWilliam made a successful transition from player to manager with Tottenham

Hotspur, whom he joined in 1912. His team experienced relegation to the Second Division at the end of 1914-15, before war intervened, but in 1920 promotion was achieved with a remarkable 70 points (a Second Division record in the days of two points for a win). McWilliam's team were triumphant in winning the FA Cup in 1921, beating Wolves 1-0 in the Final, and he was Tottenham's longest-serving manager until Bill Nicholson.

The Middlesbrough board had made several furtive attempts to wrench McWilliam from Spurs three years earlier, but had failed at every attempt. His eventual 'appointment' as Middlesbrough manager broke in the Press in early January 1927, but was initially strenuously denied by the Tottenham board. He was on a salary of £850 per annum at Spurs and later admitted that he would have stayed at White Hart Lane 'if Spurs had offered another £3 a week'.

Middlesbrough had no such reservations about paying the man they wanted and offered him £1,500 a year, then a phenomenal sum for a manager, and he moved north. His wife hailed from Redcar and she probably played an influential part in his decision to accept the post at Ayresome Park.

McWilliam was to be given total control in team selection without any interference from the board, but he never won the hearts of the Middlesbrough public whose sympathy lay with Herbert Bamlett. His time at the club was very much an up and down period. He enjoyed the tail-end of promotion in 1927 but the following season 'Boro dropped back into Division Two. In 1928-9, with McWilliam still at the helm, they won the Second Division title again.

McWilliam kept them in Division One until his dismissal in March 1934 and he then had a spell as chief scout for Arsenal before he made a sentimental return to manage Tottenham Hotspur in 1938. He remained at White Hart Lane for little more than a year, although in that short time he began to promote the famous Northfleet nursery which was to produce so many fine players for Tottenham.

Peter McWilliam returned to the North-East but, when the war was over, he decided he was too old to remain in football. He died at his home in Corporation Road, Redcar, on 1 October 1951, aged 72 and was buried at nearby Kirkleatham cemetery. Representatives from all his former clubs attended his funeral.

Wilf Gillow
March 1934 to March 1944

WILF Gillow was born in Peston on 8 July 1892 and first played for Lancaster Town in the West Lancashire League when he was 15. He was on Preston's books without making a League appearance and then signed for Fleetwood before moving to Blackpool in 1912. He made 26 League appearances for the Seasiders and then returned to Deepdale, where he played three League games before joining the Army upon the outbreak of World War One.

Gillow played briefly for Preston in 1918-19 and then made another four League appearances in the first proper peacetime season before signing for Grimsby Town in February 1920. He played 80 games for them, mostly at right-half, and then rejoined Fleetwood, only to return to Grimsby in 1923. A year later he became player-manager of the Mariners and older Grimsby supporters rate him amongst the top three Town managers of all time.

Under Gillow the Blundell Park club achieved promotion to Division One in May 1929, for the first time in 26 seasons, and when Middlesbrough and Grimsby met at Ayresome Park in the final game of that season, both clubs were already assured of promotion, but 'Boro pipped the Mariners to the Second Division championship.

Town's flirtation with First Division football was brief and within two seasons they were back in the Second Division. In April 1932, Wilf Gillow relinquished the manager's job and left football management until March 1934, when he replaced Peter McWilliam at 'Boro. The Ayresome club just escaped relegation in his first season, but every season after that showed an improvement.

The quietly spoken pipe-smoker was much respected by players and fans alike and, under his guidance, Middlesbrough finished fourth at the end of season 1938-9. Many thought that, with the emergence of bright young stars like Wilf Mannion, Micky Fenton, George Hardwick and the older heads of Bobby Stuart, George Camsell, Billy Forrest, the elusive League Championship was only a season or two away.

War spoiled that dream, but football was allowed to continue on a regional basis. Gillow, too old for active service, worked in Middlesbrough Council treasurer's department during the day, serving as 'Boro manager on a part-time basis at evenings and weekends. He died in his early 50s, on 11 March 1944 in a County Durham Hospital after complications set in following an operation. He is buried in Thornaby cemetery.

Gillow, incidentally, was also a good cricketer and he turned out for Middlesbrough CC in the North Yorkshire and South Durham League until well into his 40s. An earlier spell on the Lancashire groundstaff had seen him field as a substitute for England against Australia at Old Trafford.

David Jack
November 1944 to April 1952

DAVID Jack was born on 3 April 1899, in Bolton where his father, Bob Jack, was playing for the Trotters. When Bob Jack became manager of Plymouth Argyle in 1910, young David also went south and eventually signed for Argyle (after playing in Southend junior football when his father had a spell as manager there). During World War One he guested for Chelsea whilst on leave from the Royal Navy and played in the Home Park club's final Southern League season of 1920-21.

After only 14 Football League appearances for Plymouth, Jack was transferred to Bolton Wanderers in December 1920, for £3,500 (a record for both clubs). He has a permanent spot in the football history books as the first player to score a goal in a Wembley Cup Final. Indeed, he scored both goals when Bolton beat West Ham 2-0 in that historic 1923 game.

He also played for Bolton in the 1926 Final before being transferred to Arsenal for a record fee of £10,340 in October 1928. He had five successful seasons at Highbury and played in the 1930 and 1932 FA Cup Finals for the Gunners, won three League Championship medals (1930-31, 1932-3 and 1933-4) and won a total of nine England caps with Bolton and Arsenal. At the end of a playing career during which he became known as the 'prince of centre-forward', he had scored well over 250 goals in just over 500 games.

His first position as a League club manager was with Southend United in May 1934, a post he held until 1940. On the untimely death of Wilf Gillow he relinquished his job as manager of Sunderland Greyhound Stadium to become manager at Ayresome Park on 1 November 1944, when 'Boro was playing wartime League North football.

The 1950-51 season was David Jack's best with Middlesbrough. 'Boro and Spurs were vying with each other at the top of the First Division but injuries and loss of form saw the Ayresome club slip away after Christmas and eventually they finished sixth. One criticism of pipe-smoking David Jack was that he was too 'relaxed' and lacked the forceful personality needed to motivate his players.

He resigned his position as manager in April 1952 and, disillusioned, he left the game to become a publican in Islington, London. He soon discovered, however, that the game meant too much to him and he needed little persuasion to return to management with League of Ireland club Shelbourne, in August 1953. He stayed there until April 1955 and then took a job with the Air Ministry. He died in St Thomas' Hospital, London, on 10 September 1958.

Walter Rowley
June 1952 to February 1954

WALTER Rowley spent all his working life in football, including 38 years with Bolton Wanderers, as a half-back, coach and manager. He was born at Little Hulton in 1891 and spent two years with Oldham Athletic Reserves before signing for the Trotters in August 1912, aged 21.

Rowley missed the 1923 Cup Final because he had only just finished a six-week suspension and in May 1925 he was forced to retire through injury and was appointed coach to Bolton's reserve team. In August 1944 he became secretary-manager at Burnden Park and at the end of his first season in charge, Bolton won the Football League War Cup. In his second they reached the FA Cup semi-finals. Ill health forced him to resign in October 1950 and Bolton made him a life member of the club.

Fully recovered, he succeeded David Jack as Middlesbrough manager in June 1952. 'Boro finished 13th in his first full season as manager, but worse was to come the following season. It was a frustrating time for Rowley. The team were struggling in the relegation zone and his doctors advised him to undergo hospital treatment for a stomach ulcer. On 3 February 1954, before entering hospital, he proffered his written resignation, stating that a football club fighting for survival in the First Division should have a fully fit man at the helm.

On 10 March, the Middlesbrough board announced that they had reluctantly parted company with their manager but, by then, Rowley had recovered sufficiently to withdraw his resignation.

'Boro's directors, though, had begun to canvas for a new manager and, although their first choice, Alec Stock of Leyton Orient, eventually turned down their offer because his wife did not wish to leave London, there was now no place for Walter Rowley in the board's plans. He spent three seasons as manager of Shrewsbury Town before leaving football in 1957.

Bob Dennison
July 1954 to January 1963

BOB Dennison was born in Amble, a village on the Northumbrian coast, on 6 March 1912. He played junior football for Radcliffe United before joining Newcastle United as an inside-left in May 1929, but his appearances in the famous black and white striped shirt were restricted to 11 League games in five seasons because, in his own words, he was 'just an ordinary player'.

In May 1934 Dennison was transferred to Nottingham Forest but, a year later, moved to Fulham. At Craven Cottage he was converted to centre-half and during the war guested for Northampton Town after working in the timber business in that town. Dennison eventually signed for the Cobblers and was appointed their manager in 1948.

In July 1954, Northampton released him from his contract and he joined Middlesbrough for the start of the club's first season back in the Second Division. He assumed the secretarial duties at Ayresome Park from August 1955 until the arrival of Harry Green in 1961.

Bob Dennison spent nine eventful years as Middlesbrough manager as, season after season, the club narrowly missed out on promotion, even with Brian Clough, Alan Peacock, Billy Day and Eddie Holliday in the team. It was Dennison who 'discovered' Clough and who also took Peter Taylor to Ayresome Park, thus bringing together the men who would later form one of the most famous and successful managerial partnerships in football.

On 10 January 1963 Dennison was told that his contract, which still had 19 months to run, would be terminated forthwith. The board issued a Press statement to the effect that the parting was by mutual consent, but Dennison subsequently took the club to the High Court, where he won damages of £3,200 for 'unfair dismissal'.

Undaunted, in December 1963 he went into non-League management with Southern League Hereford United and later served Coventry City, as chief scout from December 1967 and then as assistant manager from December 1968. He was caretaker manager at Highfield Road for a brief spell in 1972, between the reigns of Noel Cantwell and Gordon Milne, before retiring in 1978. Today, he lives in Kent and is still involved with Coventry, scouting for them on a part-time basis.

Raich Carter
January 1953 to February 1966

RAICH Carter — real name Horatio Stratton Carter — was born the son of a professional footballer on 21 December 1913, in Sunderland. He was a natural sportsman and a prolific scorer in junior football with Hendon Boys' School, Whitburn St Mary's, Sunderland Forge and Esh Winning, before collecting England Schoolboy honours in 1927.

He had trials with Leicester City but was turned down as being 'too small'. Sunderland, his home-town club, realized his potential, however, and his career blossomed at Roker Park. By the time he was 24, Carter had won every major honour then open to a footballer — England caps, League Championship and FA Cup winners' medals. During the war he joined, first the fire brigade, then the RAF. It was whilst at RAF Loughborough that he teamed up with another great inside-forward of the day, Peter Doherty, and the two of them guested for Derby County and helped the Rams win the FA Cup in 1945-6.

By then Carter had joined Derby officially and he stayed with them until April 1948, when he signed for Hull City as player-assistant manager. He was a naturally left-footed player who was renowned for his ability to split defences with unerringly accurate passes. His style made him appear slow, but he could quickly switch into top gear and leave opponents standing. He was also a fine cricketer who played for Minor Counties side, Durham, and made three first-class appearances for Derbyshire in 1946.

Carter became manager at Boothferry Road and helped Hull win the Third Division North title in 1948-9. He retired as manager in September 1951 and as a player in 1952, although he played for Cork Athletic in the League of Ireland from January to May 1953, when he took over from Major Frank Buckley as manager of Leeds United. Five years earlier he had taken over from Buckley at Hull.

Carter shrewdly guided the Yorkshire club back into the First Division in 1956, having built his team around the brilliant John Charles, but was surprisingly sacked on 10 May 1958, after Leeds had slipped to 17th place in Division One and his contract was up for renewal. He re-emerged as Mansfield Town manager in February 1960 and laid the foundations for the Stags' return to Division Three before turning his attentions to Ayresome Park in mid-January 1963.

Carter's days at Middlesbrough were the least successful of his football career. 'Boro went to the brink of relegation to Division Three for the first time in their history and he was dismissed on 12 February 1966, with Harold Shepherdson in the role of caretaker manager, selecting the team until a successor could be appointed. Carter became a sports department manager at a large Hull store and todays lives in retirement at Willerby on North Humberside.

Stan Anderson
April 1966 to January 1973

STAN Anderson, who was born in Horden on 27 February 1934, had a trial for Middlesbrough, but manager David Jack turned him away because he felt that the club had an abundance of wing-halves. Anderson signed for Horden Colliery Welfare and took a job as an apprentice plumber.

In 1949, however, Sunderland came knocking on his door and he signed junior forms for the Wearsiders. His First Division debut came three seasons later, in 1952-3, when he quickly impressed as a stylish wing-half but took the precaution of playing part-time football and keeping on with his trade until his 19th birthday.

His stylish displays caught the eyes of the England selectors and Anderson won four Under-23 caps and two full caps during his stay at Roker. Then, to the surprise of Sunderland supporters, he was sold to Second Division Newcastle United for £30,000 in November 1963, after clocking up 402 League appearances for the Wearsiders.

Anderson captained the Magpies to the Second Division championship in 1964-5, but another surprise was on the way and in November 1965, he accepted the position of player-coach with 'Boro, the first such appointment in Middlesbrough's history. His new club, managed by Raich Carter, were attempting to avoid the drop to Division Three and within a short time he became the first player to have captained all three of the North-East's major clubs.

Stan Anderson accepted the job of manager in April 1966, but could not help Middlesbrough avoid relegation. After an indifferent start, however, he led the side to promotion in his first full season as boss, when 'Boro ensured promotion in the last game, at home to Oxford United.

On 25 January 1973, however, following a 1-0 FA Cup defeat at Plymouth, Anderson, a taciturn, deep-thinking man, resigned, despite the directors' attempts to persuade him to change his mind. He was adamant that he was not the man to take the club into the First Division.

As when Raich Carter left the club, Harold Shepherdson looked after team selection until the end of the season. By August 1973, Anderson was named as manager of Greek club, AEK Athens. He later managed Panathinaikos, but returned to England in September 1974, to become assistant manager of Queen's Park Rangers.

In February 1975, he took over from Maurice Setters as manager of Doncaster Rovers and joined Bolton Wanderers in November 1978 as assistant manager to Ian Greaves. He succeeded Greaves as manager in February 1980, but again was unable to prevent relegation, this time from Division One. Despite being allowed to strengthen the Trotters' squad, Anderson could not provide an improvement in results the following season and in May 1981 he was sacked with two years of his contract still to run.

Jack Charlton OBE
May 1973 to April 1977

JACK Charlton was born at Ashington, Northumberland, on 8 May 1935. His was a footballing family (he is related to the Milburns) and he followed his brother Bobby into League football, joining Leeds United straight from school.

His uncle, Jim Milburn, then a Leeds full-back, recommended Jack to the Yorkshire club. His made his League debut in April 1953, against Doncaster Rovers, and went on to notch up a record 629 League games for Leeds, spending almost two decades with United.

Middlesbrough-born Don Revie became Leeds' manager in 1961 and within two seasons had moulded Jack Charlton into a commanding centre-half. Leeds returned to Division One and Jack Charlton shared in all their great domestic and European triumphs of the late 1960s and early '70s. He won 35 full England caps and was in the side which lifted the World Cup in 1966. A year later, he succeeded his more famous brother as the Footballer of the Year.

On his retirement in 1973, Jack Charlton expressed an interest in League management and was offered the job at Middlesbrough. He accepted the post on 7 May 1973, saying that he would not stay longer than four years in the job. The pre-season tour of Scotland proved to be the ideal scenario for the new manager to get to know the strengths and weaknesses of his playing staff and the players knew from the start that Charlton was the boss.

The manager and the team got off to a flying start, winning all three friendlies. His managerial League baptism also proved to be a successful one, a 1-0 victory at Fratton Park against promotion hopefuls Portsmouth. The first home game was against Fulham but the Cottagers won 2-0. At the final whistle, Jack Charlton was heard to comment, "Unbelievable . . .they'll do it my way now!" And they did.

His first managerial master-stroke was persuading Celtic legend Bobby Murdoch to come to Ayresome Park on a free transfer. The Scot proved to be the missing link that had eluded Stan Anderson for so long.

Charlton took a team, basically the side built by Anderson, blended the experience of Murdoch and piloted the club into Division One in his first season. Once back in the top flight, the quality of the team was emphasized by the impressive final placing of sixth — all done without further recourse to the transfer market.

The transition from successful player to successful manager was instantaneous and Charlton was voted Bell's Manager of the Year for his achievements at Ayresome Park. Yet the first Second Division manager to lift the title was unwilling to accept any contract from the Middlesbrough board.

On 12 November 1974, Jack Charlton had an important date in a London — an 11am appointment at Buckingham Palace to receive his OBE. Later that day he was at Anfield for a League Cup tie and diplomatically refused to comment on which occasion gave him more satisfaction, for his team beat Liverpool 1-0.

In 1976 he steered the club to within 90 minutes of the League Cup Final. It would have been the first Wembley appearance in 'Boro's history, but in the semi-final second-leg, Manchester City won 4-0 at Maine Road and 4-1 on aggregate.

True to his word, Charlton resigned as 'Boro manager at the end of April 1977, saying that after 26 years in football and with his financial security guaranteed, it was about time he had a rest and was looking forward to some fishing, hunting and shooting, some after-dinner speaking and to spending more time with his family.

Yet he was back in managerial harness in late 1977, when he took on the task of rebuilding Third Division Sheffield Wednesday after the departure of Len Ashurst. Again he stipulated that his stay would not be long-term. Within two seasons, the Owls were back in Division Two and in 1982 they missed promotion to the First Division by only one point. He left Wednesday, as promised, in 1983, having laid the foundation for his successor, Howard Wilkinson, to lead Wednesday back into Division One in his first season as Owls' manager.

Shortly afterwards, Charlton became manager of Newcastle United but spent only one mediocre season on Tyneside, quitting after he was booed by the Geordie supporters during a pre-season friendly game. Appointed team manager of the Republic of Ireland, he received much public acclaim in June 1988, when he engineered Eire's famous 1-0 victory over England in the European Championships.

John Neal
May 1977 to July 1981

JOHN Neal, regarded as one of the quiet men in football, was born on 3 April 1932, in Silksworth, County Durham, and supported Sunderland as a boy. He progressed from junior football with Silksworth Juniors to Hull City, signing for the Tigers, then managed by Raich Carter, in August 1949. Despite several seasons on Humberside, Neal played in only 60 League games and in July 1956 he dropped into non-League soccer with King's Lynn.

In July 1957 he was back in League football with Swindon Town and was a regular full-back at the County Ground until Joe Mercer took him to Villa Park in August 1959. He enjoyed most success as a player there. Aston Villa had been relegated to Division Two at the end of 1958-9, but returned immediately as Second Division champions. Neal added a League Cup winners' medal in 1961, when Villa became the first team to win the trophy, beating Rotherham United in a two-legged Final.

A move to Southend United in November 1962 saw Neal spend almost three seasons with the Shrimpers, making over 100 League appearances until, in 1965, he decided to try League management and successfully applied for the vacant manager's job at Fourth Division Wrexham.

He did well at the Racecourse Ground, taking the Welsh club into the Third Division and to the quarter-finals of the European Cup-winners' Cup. When he moved to Ayresome Park on 19 May 1977, he left behind a strong side which soon went on to win promotion to Division Two for the first time in Wrexham's history.

John Neal caught up with his new club in Australia, on their world tour. Those who thought that he would walk in the shadow of Jack Charlton were quickly silenced with his comment: "I have my own style, my own beliefs and my own principles."

He instilled an attacking flair into the team, but came in for strong criticism when he methodically dismantled the nucleus of Jack Charlton's side. His list of departures included Graeme Souness to Liverpool, David Mills to West Brom, Stuart Boam to Newcastle and Stan Cummins to Sunderland.

The players he brought to Ayresome included Billy Ashcroft (from his old club Wrexham), Welsh international John Mahoney, Micky Burns, Terry Cochrane, Bosco Jankovic, goalkeeper Jim Stewart and club record buy Irving Nattrass from Newcastle United.

Neal left Middlesbrough in the summer of 1981, after disagreeing with the club's decision to sell Craig Johnston to Liverpool, and was snapped up by Chelsea chairman Ken Bates, who saw him as the man to replace Geoff Hurst at Stamford Bridge. Neal soon returned to Teesside, but only to lure 'Boro favourite Tony McAndrew to Chelsea.

Neal took the Londoners back to Division One at the end of 1983-4, but his health was not robust after heart surgery and in 1986 he was replaced by long-serving Chelsea player John Hollins.

Bobby Murdoch
June 1981 to October 1982

BOBBY Murdoch was one of Scotland's most influential post-war players and spent 14 good years at Celtic where he shared in seven consecutive League Championship wins as well as success in the Scottish FA Cup and League Cup. In addition, Murdoch was capped 12 times for Scotland and was voted Scotland's Player of the Year in 1969, two years after he was a member of the Celtic team which became the first British club to win the European Cup.

At the beginning of the 1973-4 season, one of Jack Charlton's first jobs as 'Boro manager was to persuade Bobby Murdoch to join him at Ayresome Park. Murdoch made his debut in a Middlesbrough shirt at Halifax in a North Midlands League game in September 1973. His League debut followed soon afterwards and he marked his first appearance with a superb goal against Bristol City.

Murdoch, who was born in Bothwell, Lanarkshire, on 17 August 1944 and began with Cambuslang Rangers, had forged his reputation as an attacking inside-forward and, although not as mobile as in his Parkhead days, he nevertheless proved an effective signing for 'Boro. His vision in the midfield helped take the Ayresome club back to Division One in his first season with 'Boro.

In 1975, his first-team playing days over, Murdoch was appointed youth-team coach at Middlesbrough and when John Neal left Ayresome Park in the summer of 1981, the former Celtic man took over the side, even though he had no previous managerial experience.

He was unfortuate to become manager at a time when 'Boro were suffering from the loss of several fine players. Mark Procter, Craig Johnston and David Armstrong had all left the club and the team was not strong enough to survive in the top flight.

After relegation at the end of Murdoch's first season as manager, many people thought he would be dismissed. In fact, he held the job until early the following season but could not survive a dreadful 'Boro performance against Grimsby Town at Ayresome Park in September 1982. The Mariners won 4-1 and Murdoch was soon on his way. For the fourth time in his 45-year career at Middlesbrough, Harold Shepherdson took over as caretaker manager whilst the board looked around for a more permanent successor to Murdoch.

Malcolm Allison
October 1982 to March 1984

MALCOLM Allison is one of the most colourful characters to emerge in post-war football. The flamboyant manager, with his fedora hat, cigar and champagne in hand, livened many a Press conference at the peak of his managerial career, whilst his personal life sometimes put him on the front pages, rather than the sports pages, of the national newspapers.

Indeed, his image as a manager has overshadowed the fact that Allison was a fine centre-half in his playing days. He was born at Dartford on 5 September 1927 and his first League club was Charlton Athletic, for whom he signed in 1944. He made only two League appearances for Charlton but his career took off after he joined West Ham United in February 1951. By the time he was forced to retire in 1958 because of a serious illness — he had a lung removed after contracting tuberculosis — Allison had made 238 League appearances for the Hammers.

He had been a member of a fine West Ham team, several of whose members later became prominent coaches and managers, and Allison also took up coaching after his playing days had ended. He worked with the Cambridge University side, then in Toronto and with Southern League Bath City before entering Football League management with Plymouth Argyle in 1964.

In his one season at Home Park, Allison took Argyle to the semi-final of the Football League Cup — admittedly, then a lack-lustre competition — but their League form was patchy and before the campaign was over, he was at loggerheads with the directors over team selection and left.

In July 1965, he joined Joe Mercer at Maine Road and the two men took Manchester City to some of that club's greatest successes. By 1972, though, Allison felt that his contribution was such that he deserved more than the title of assistant manager. Mercer left to manage Coventry City and Allison had his wish. Before the end of his first season, however, he was off to manage Crystal Palace, saying that he could no longer motivate the City players.

There followed another spell at Plymouth and then periods coaching in Istanbul and in North America before he returned to Maine Road in July 1979. Despite spending huge sums of money on players, there was no return to the glory days and early in the 1980-81 season both Allison and general manager Tony Book were dismissed.

Again Allison was on his travels. He returned to Crystal Palace briefly and worked as an advisor to non-League Yeovil Town before Sporting Lisbon offered him a job. Allison repaid them by taking Sporting to the Portuguese League and Cup double before being controversially sacked in July 1982.

Three months later he broke a pledge never to return to Football League management by signing a two-year contract with Middlesbrough. Teesside's football fans, starved of success, looked upon the appointment of this colourful character as the arrival of a 'Messiah', who would lead their club from the wilderness of the Second Division.

They warmed to him still further when 'Boro beat table-topping QPR, but there was no money to buy new players and the club was limping along on meagre attendances. When he did sign a player — former England man Kevin Beattie, who came from Colchester United in November 1982 — bad luck followed. Beattie was injured after only two games and sidelined until January.

In his first season, Allison saw Middlesbrough finish in 16th place and reach the last 16 of the FA Cup. He showed himself determined to hang on to young talent by signing Stephen Bell on a four-year contract.

Allison also signed a new contract, for two years from March 1983, but the club was being sucked into the maelstrom of financial disaster and he was coming under intense pressure to sell the best players. His response was typically controversial — "It's better for the club to die than linger on" — and on 28 March 1984 he was dismissed, the gap between directors and manager now too wide to overcome.

He later worked in such diverse places as Willington, County Durham, and Kuwait. In the summer of 1989, Malcolm Allison was back in the news again, this time as manager of GM Vauxhall Conference club, Fisher Athletic.

Willie Maddren
June 1984 to February 1986

WILLE Maddren, who was born at Haverton Hill on 11 January 1951, had an unlucky start to his football career. He was playing for Port Clarence Juniors and broke his ankle just two days before he was due to have a trial with Leeds United. Leeds never followed up his progress and that was to Middlesbrough's good fortune, for Maddren went on to become one of the club's finest players.

He was recommended to 'Boro by local scout Freddie Barnes and signed professional forms in June 1968, at the same time as David Mills. He made his League debut as a forward in the last home game of that season, against Bury at Ayresome Park, but had been on the pitch for only ten minutes when he broke his nose. Maddren soon returned to the fray and scored a goal, but his heroics were in vain as 'Boro eventually went down 3-2.

He was voted Player of the Year by Middlesbrough supporters in 1971 and proved his versatility by appearing in seven different positions. It was as a central defender, though, that he made real progress. After Bill Gates broke his jaw in an FA Cup game at Old Trafford, Maddren stepped up and established himself.

His emergence as a defender of the highest quality coincided with the signing of Stuart Boam. The two forged a marvellous understanding and, although the selectors ignored Boam, Maddren was rewarded with five England Under-23 caps.

His playing career, during which he made over 300 appearances for 'Boro, ended after a serious injury to his right knee in 1977. After a spell as coach at Hartlepool United, he returned to Ayresome Park as a coach and physiotherapist. He came back on the recommendation of Jack Charlton, who was at Ayresome for a short spell following the dismissal of Malcolm Allison.

The fans wanted Charlton to stay but he was adamant that the arrangement should be only short-term. Chairman Mike McCullagh offered Maddren the manager's job and the former 'Boro player took it on, commenting that the task of resurrecting the club's playing fortunes would take at least three years' hard work.

David Mills returned and ended the 1983-4 season as 'Boro's top scorer, but things were far from rosy. Middlesbrough were already £1.2 million in debt and the chances of rebuilding the team with quality players were negligible. Mills was injured the following season but Maddren resisted pressure to blood youngsters at this traumatic time in 'Boro's history.

In October 1985, he threatened to resign but stayed on. Early in 1986, Maddren appointed Bruce Rioch as coach. In February, the manager was sacked and Rioch took over.

Willie Maddren now runs two successful sports outfitters shops, in Stockton and Coulby Newham, but he has never returned to the ground that he graced with so many superlative displays for nine years.

Bruce Rioch
February 1986 to date

BRUCE Rioch, the son of a Scottish RSM, was born in Aldershot on 6 September 1947 and was brought up in Luton. He joined the Hatters on leaving school and became a professional in September 1964.

Luton were relegated to the Fourth Division for the first time in 1965, but Rioch's goals helped them to the Fourth Division title in 1968 and Tommy Docherty parted with £100,000, a record for a Third Division player, to take him to Second Division Aston Villa in July 1969. Again, Rioch experienced relegation when Villa slipped into the Third Division for the first time in their long history.

Rioch, an aggressive, attacking wing-half, was prone to cartilage trouble throughout his playing career, having cartilages removed from both knees during 1971-2. But he made a remarkable recovery and played an active part in Villa winning the Third Division championship and reaching the Football League Cup Final the same season.

Dave Mackay paid £200,000 to take him to Derby County in February 1974 and Rioch was ever-present in the Rams' League Championship side of 1974-5, ending the season as Derby's leading scorer. The first of his 24 full Scotland caps came in Glasgow in May 1975, against Portugal.

Rioch was on the move again in December 1976, this time to Everton, but was back at the Baseball Ground after only 11 months on Merseyside. He had two loan spells whilst on Derby's books, with Birmingham City and Sheffield United.

The highlight of his playing career was his captaincy of Scotland in the 1978 World Cup Finals in Argentina, when he created history by becoming the first English-born player to skipper the Scots.

He played with Seattle Sounders in the North American Soccer League before returning to England on a free transfer in October 1980. He joined Fourth Division Torquay United, progressing from player to coach and ultimately replaced manager Frank O'Farrell in July 1982.

Rioch joined Middlesbrough as first-team coach in January 1986, but on the departure of Willie Maddren the following month, chairman Alf Duffield offered Bruce the job, although it was too late to stop the club's slide into the Third Division.

'Boro's spluttering demise in the summer of 1986 meant that the non-playing staff, which numbered 30 including Rioch and coach Colin Todd, lost their jobs as the gates were closed at Ayresome Park. But Rioch and Todd stayed on, even more determined to see the job through.

A dramatic last-minute reprieve saw a new Middlesbrough club rise from the ashes of liquidation and Bruce Rioch, who had turned down the opportunity to move to a First Division club that summer, steered 'Boro back to the Second Division. He became the first Middlesbrough manager to take the club to two successive promotion successes, even though the route back to the First Division was via the exciting play-offs against Bradford City and Chelsea in May 1988.

For a man who has worked so hard for success and who has achieved so much personal glory in his football career, relegation at the end of the 1988-9 season must have been a bitter pill to swallow. Bruce Rioch, however, is still regarded as one of British football's progressive, bright young managers. The footballing public of Middlesbrough certainly owe him a great debt of gratitude.

Bruce Rioch picks up another award as manager of Middlesbrough.

91

'Boro Stars

DAVID ARMSTRONG

Midfielder David Armstrong, who was born at Durham City on Boxing Day 1954, began his long association with Middlesbrough when he was only nine. George Wardle brought him from his native city and 'Boro watched the lad develop into an England Schoolboy international. He signed as an amateur in September 1968, became an apprentice in June 1970 and a full-time professional on New Year's Eve 1971. A natural left-sided midfielder, Armstrong made his first-team debut as a 17-year-old substitute against Queen's Park Rangers in March 1972. He won England Under-23 and 'B' international caps and gained full recognition against Australia in May 1980. Middlesbrough manager Jack Charlton called him his 'little gem' and he was only 25 when 'Boro awarded him a testimonial match in October 1980, against the club's 1973-4 promotion-winning team. He is the current holder of Middlesbrough's consecutive appearances record (356 League and Cup games). In the 1981 close season, Armstrong was transferred to Southampton for a record £600,000 and went on to win three further full England caps. After 222 League games for the Saints, he ended his playing career with Bournemouth and is currently a soft-drinks salesman on the South Coast, although desperately keen to get into football management.

	LEAGUE		FA CUP		FL CUP		TOTAL	
	App	Gls	App	Gls	App	Gls	App	Gls
1971-72	5/1	0	0	0	0	0	5/1	0
1972-73	19/1	1	0	0	1/1	0	20/2	1
1973-74	42	5	2	1	3	0	47	6
1974-75	42	5	6	1	5	1	53	7
1975-76	42	6	2	0	6	1	50	7
1976-77	42	8	5	4	1	0	48	12
1977-78	42	6	5	1	4	2	51	9
1978-79	42	11	2	0	2	0	46	11
1979-80	42	11	3	1	3	2	48	14
1980-81	39	6	4	0	2	0	45	6
	357/2	59	29	8	27/1	6	413/3	73

Staindrop-born Don Ashman, a cool, unruffled half-back, worked as a coal-miner and played part-time football for Cockfield Albion. Middlesbrough manager Herbert Bamlett brought him to Ayresome Park on 5 May 1924, for a £10 fee and a guaranteed friendly match at Cockfield's ground. Ashman was soon pushed into Middlesbrough's reserve team in the North-Eastern League and made his first-team debut six months later, at Coventry City on 1 November 1924. He was an established member of the promotion winning sides of 1926-7 and 1928-9, clocking up 174 League and Cup games before his £500 transfer to Queen's Park Rangers in May 1932. He returned to the North-East to play for Darlington before the outbreak of World War Two.

	LEAGUE		FA CUP		TOTAL	
	App	Gls	App	Gls	App	Gls
1924-25	13	0	0	0	13	0
1925-26	35	0	1	0	36	0
1926-27	41	1	3	0	44	1
1927-28	15	1	2	0	17	1
1928-29	3	0	1	0	4	0
1929-30	31	0	6	0	37	0
1930-31	4	0	0	0	4	0
1931-32	18	0	1	0	19	0
	160	2	14	0	174	2

DON ASHMAN

When Middlesbrough manager Peter McWilliam went to Scotland on a scouting mission and found the game he intended to watch had been cancelled, he switched to another match and discovered Bob Baxter. A coal-miner, Baxter was playing for Bruntonian Juniors and supplemented his wages by running a dance band in the evenings. 'Boro took him away from all that and he made his League debut in October 1932, at inside-left against Birmingham at St Andrew's. In November 1935, after centre-half and captain Tom Griffiths was transferred to Aston Villa, Baxter was tried at pivot and held the position until the outbreak of war, winning three Scottish caps. He was a constructive player, but was sometimes inclined to overdo the fancy stuff. During his Middlesbrough career he played in nine different first-team positions and was rated by many as the club's best-ever captain. At the outbreak of war he returned to Scotland and resumed his occupation as a miner. He also ran a newsagent's and tobacconist's shop and guested for Hibs and Hearts. Released by Middlesbrough in August 1945, he was transferred to Hearts. Baxter later managed Leith Athletic and Edinburgh Monarchs speedway team. He now lives in retirement in Billingham.

BOB BAXTER

	LEAGUE		FA CUP		TOTAL	
	App	Gls	App	Gls	App	Gls
1932-33	25	5	4	1	29	6
1933-34	36	6	2	0	38	6
1934-35	39	6	1	0	40	6
1935-36	39	2	4	0	43	2
1936-37	37	0	1	0	38	0
1937-38	38	0	3	0	41	0
1938-39	33	0	4	0	37	0
	247	19	19	1	266	20

Harry Bell was spotted by Sunderland whilst playing junior football with Hylton Colliery and signed amateur forms for his home-town club in 1943. Bell, who was born in Sunderland on 14 October 1924, remained at Roker Park until his transfer to Middlesbrough in September 1945. It was David Jack who noticed Bell, when Jack was manager of Sunderland Greyhound Stadium and Bell was playing in a five-a-side competition there. Bell was signed as a full-time professional at Ayresome Park and his fee set at £1,250. He arrived there as an inside-forward, but was switched to right-half as an emergency measure and became an immediate success in his new position. Bell proved a brave performer and this was highlighted during a game at Huddersfield in November 1948, when he broke his nose early on but continued to the final whistle. In September 1955, after over 300 League and Cup appearances for 'Boro, he moved to Darlington and spent one season as a full-timer and four as a part-timer at Feethams. Bell, who was also a professional cricketer with Middlesbrough and Crook, now lives in Gosforth and has a top job with Tetley Breweries.

HARRY BELL

	LEAGUE		FA CUP		TOTAL	
	App	Gls	App	Gls	App	Gls
1945-46	-	-	7	0	7	0
1946-47	31	0	4	0	35	0
1947-48	36	0	3	0	39	0
1948-49	30	0	1	0	31	0
1949-50	34	2	4	0	38	2
1950-51	42	2	1	0	43	2
1951-52	38	2	3	1	41	3
1952-53	37	3	0	0	37	3
1953-54	35	0	2	0	37	0
1954-55	7	0	0	0	7	0
	290	9	25	1	315	10

RALPH BIRKETT

Speedy winger Ralph Birkett, the son of a Middlesbrough man, was born in Ashford, Kent, on 9 January 1912 and first played junior football with his local side, Dartmouth United, while he followed employment as a clerk. In August 1929, Birkett signed for Torquay United, spending almost four seasons at Plainmoor and scoring 15 goals in 95 appearances. In March 1933, he moved into the big time with a £2,000 transfer to First Division Arsenal. However, Arsenal's resources were hugely talented and he made only 19 appearances, scoring seven goals, in two years at Highbury. In March 1935 he moved to Middlesbrough for £5,900 and made an immediate impact, his four goals in seven League games helping keep 'Boro in the First Division. In October 1935, Birkett was capped for England against France but missed the game against Germany two months later due to a pulled leg muscle. Back to full fitness, he finished the season with 21 goals. Teesside fans were dismayed when Middlesbrough agreed to sell the popular Birkett to Second Division Newcastle United in July 1938, for £6,000. One year later, his football career was drastically curtailed by the outbreak of war. He became an Army PT instructor and served in India.

	LEAGUE		FA CUP		TOTAL	
	App	Gls	App	Gls	App	Gls
1934-35	7	4	0	0	7	4
1935-36	36	22	4	0	40	22
1936-37	28	7	1	1	29	8
1937-38	22	2	3	0	25	2
	93	35	8	1	101	36

94

Considering his experiences during World War One, Billy Birrell did well to enjoy such a successful football career when peace was restored. In 1915, whilst serving with the Black Watch, he suffered a foot injury soon after arriving in France. And in 1918, shortly before the Armistice was signed, he was captured and spent the remaining weeks of the war as a PoW. After the war he played for Raith Rovers, but decided that his future would be brighter on the other side of the world. In January 1921, he had completed his plans to emigrate to America when Middlesbrough stepped in with an offer of £2,100. 'Boro manager Jimmy Howie saw Birrell as a replacement for Jackie Mordue, but little did Howie realize that his new signing would become one of Middlesbrough's most influential midfield generals. In his early days at Ayresome Park, Birrell was still troubled by his war wound but the injury cleared up after a period of rest. He was one of Middlesbrough's shrewdest captains and skippered the side which stormed out of the Second Division in 1926-7. He owned a cafe near the ground but found that his long-term interests lay in football and was keen to try League management. The Middlesbrough board reluctantly agreed to release him if a job came up and in November 1927, Birrell returned to Raith Rovers as player-manager, with full-back Syd Jarvis travelling south in an exchange deal. Birrell became secretary-manager of Third Division South club Bournemouth in 1930, staying five seasons at Dean Court before accepting the manager's job at QPR in 1935. By the outbreak of World War Two, he was managing Chelsea, linking up with his old Middlesbrough colleague, Stewart Davidson, who was assistant manager. They led Chelsea to two wartime

BILLY BIRRELL

Cup Finals. Billy Birrell retired as manager in 1952 and died in November 1968.

	LEAGUE		FA CUP		TOTAL	
	App	Gls	App	Gls	App	Gls
1920-21	14	2	0	0	14	2
1921-22	35	9	1	0	36	9
1922-23	38	9	3	1	41	10
1923-24	21	2	0	0	21	2
1924-25	27	3	1	0	28	3
1925-26	42	17	2	1	44	18
1926-27	41	16	3	2	44	18
1927-28	7	1	0	0	7	1
	225	59	10	4	235	63

STEVE BLOOMER

Middlesbrough caused quite a stir when they signed Derby County's prolific goalscorer Steve Bloomer in March 1906. Bloomer was an established England international and the Derby fans were incensed that their great favourite had been sold. In fact, Bloomer's debut for his new club was something of a disaster, for 'Boro went down 6-1 at Liverpool. But by the end of his time at Ayresome Park, he had made a valuable contribution to 'Boro's First Division survival and scored over 60 League and Cup goals for the club. Born at Cradley Heath on 20 January 1874, Bloomer began with Derby Swifts and Tutbury Hawthorn before signing for the Rams in April 1892. He soon established himself as a goalscorer, knocking them in from all angles, from close range and from long distance. He was Derby's leading scorer in 14 seasons (altogether he scored 332 League and Cup goals in 525 games for them) and won 23 caps with his two clubs. One contemporary critic said he was 'as slippery as an eel and much given to dealing electric shocks to goalkeepers'. He returned to Derby in September 1910, after a chance meeting with Rams manager Jimmy Methven on a railway station, and skippered his old club to promotion from Division Two in 1911-12. In 1914 he went to coach in Germany and was caught up in World War One, being interned for the duration. After the war he coached at Derby and in Spain before returning to the Baseball Ground as a general assistant. Bloomer's health had been failing for some years and in 1938 he was sent on a cruise. In April, three weeks after returning, he died and was buried in Nottingham Road cemetery, Derby.

	LEAGUE		FA CUP		TOTAL	
	App	Gls	App	Gls	App	Gls
1905-06	9	6	0	0	9	6
1906-07	34	18	2	2	36	20
1907-08	34	12	1	0	35	12
1908-09	28	14	0	0	28	14
1909-10	20	9	2	1	22	10
	125	59	5	3	130	62

Stuart Boam was born at Kirkby-in-Ashfield on 28 January 1948 and played his early football for Kirkby Boys' Club. He signed for Mansfield Town in July 1966 and over the next four seasons missed only ten matches for the Stags. A commanding centre-half, Boam made over 170 appearances — 162 of them consecutively — for Mansfield. When 'Boro manager Stan Anderson signed Boam in May 1971, he had to part with a reported £50,000 for the Mansfield skipper. Both Boam and Nobby Stiles, the man he was to replace as team captain, made their 'Boro debuts in August 1971, at Portsmouth. Boam was appointed captain on the arrival of new manager Jack Charlton in the summer of 1973, although in Charlton's early days at Ayresome Park, the player was not happy with the manager's forthright criticism of his style. Boam settled down, however, and developed an almost 'telepathic' understanding with Willie Maddren that confounded many opposing forwards. Boam captained the First Division promotion side but, unlike Maddren, did not win international honours. After almost 400 games for Middlesbrough he moved to Newcastle United in August 1979, for £100,000, and made 69 League appearances for the Magpies before returning to

Mansfield as player-manager in July 1981. Towards the end of his League career he played some games for Fourth Division Hartlepool United, before a spell as player-manager at Guisborough Town in August 1983.

STUART BOAM

	LEAGUE		FA CUP		FL CUP		TOTAL	
	App	Gls	App	Gls	App	Gls	App	Gls
1971-72	38	0	6	0	2	0	46	0
1972-73	40	2	1	0	4	0	45	2
1973-74	42	4	2	0	3	0	47	4
1974-75	42	1	6	0	5	0	53	1
1975-76	39	3	2	0	6	1	47	4
1976-77	42	1	5	0	1	0	48	1
1977-78	39	2	5	0	4	1	48	3
1978-79	40	1	2	0	2	0	44	1
	322	14	29	0	27	2	378	16

BILLY BRAWN

Few players can have been so aptly named as Billy Brawn, who, despite being an outside-right, stood over 6ft 1in tall and tipped the scales at well over 13st. Brawn's Middlesbrough career was relatively brief — he joined them from Aston Villa in March 1906 and was transferred to Chelsea in November 1907 — but he was one of the leading players of the day. Born at Wellingborough on 1 August 1878, Brawn played for Wellingborough Town and Northampton Town before entering League football with Sheffield United in January 1900. He moved to Villa Park in December 1901 and, although injured on his debut, he recovered to enjoy a fine career in the Midlands. Brawn won an FA Cup medal in 1905 and two England caps before signing for 'Boro. He made his debut against his old club, Sheffield United, and helped 'Boro preserve their First Division status that season. After Chelsea he played for Brentford and ran a pub in that area after hanging up his boots. From July 1919 until June 1921, he acted as an advisor to Brentford, who were regrouping after the war.

	LEAGUE		FA CUP		TOTAL	
	App	Gls	App	Gls	App	Gls
1905-06	8	1	0	0	8	1
1906-07	37	4	2	1	39	5
1907-08	11	0	0	0	11	0
	56	5	2	1	58	6

Billy Brown was working as a miner and playing football as a part-timer with West Stanley, where he was born, when Middlesbrough manager Peter McWilliam paid a £225 fee to sign the young wing-half in December 1928. McWilliam guaranteed the West Stanley club a further £100 when Brown had made 12 first-team appearances but after three years, with their former player still waiting to make his League debut, West Stanley must have thought they would never receive their money. However, after finally making his bow against Leicester City in August 1931, Brown went on to make 273 League and Cup appearances and Middlesbrough certainly had good value for their modest outlay. Although primarily a right-half, Brown did extremely well at right-back after being switched there when Jack Jennings was injured. During World War Two, the former miner guested for Watford and, after being released by Middlesbrough at the end of the 1945-6 season, he made 80 League appearances for Hartlepools United in the Third Division North before retiring in 1948.

	LEAGUE		FA CUP		TOTAL	
	App	Gls	App	Gls	App	Gls
1931-32	9	0	0	0	9	0
1932-33	30	1	4	0	34	1
1933-34	39	0	2	0	41	0
1934-35	35	0	1	0	36	0
1935-36	41	0	4	0	45	0
1936-37	39	0	1	0	40	0
1937-38	29	1	1	0	30	1
1938-39	34	0	4	0	38	0
1945-46	-	-	1	0	1	0
	256	2	18	0	274	2

BILLY BROWN

BOBBY BRUCE

Bobby Bruce, was born in Paisley on 29 January 1906 and played for St Anthony's (Glasgow) before signing for Aberdeen in the 1924 close season. Bruce, who stood only 5ft 6in tall, was equally at home at centre or inside-forward and proved an elusive opponent who could pass the ball accurately, even when running at top speed. Despite his youth, Bruce quickly became a regular Dons first-teamer. He toured South Africa with Aberdeen in 1927 and, just before joining Middles-

brough for £4,500 in January 1928, he created history by becoming the first player to score a hat-trick in a Scottish Cup tie and still finish on the losing side. He made his 'Boro debut in a 5-2 defeat at Burnden Park and was a member of the Middlesbrough side which won the Second Division championship the following season. In April 1930, Bruce asked for a transfer after being barracked by a section of the Ayresome Park crowd, but manager Peter McWilliam refused the request. One of Bruce's faults, which riled the crowd so much, was that he sometimes liked to try long-range shots rather than pass to a better-placed colleague. He was described as 'consistently inconsistent' and the crowd never took to his style of play. Despite this, he was capped against Austria in November 1933. After seven seasons on Teesside, Bruce was transferred to Sheffield Wednesday in October 1935 for £2,500. He made only five League appearances for the Owls before signing for non-League Ipswich Town in July 1936 and ended his career with Mossley, whom he joined in the close season of 1938.

	LEAGUE		FA CUP		TOTAL	
	App	Gls	App	Gls	App	Gls
1927-28	12	4	0	0	12	4
1928-29	35	11	2	0	37	11
1929-30	36	12	6	4	42	16
1930-31	27	9	2	0	29	9
1931-32	35	12	1	1	36	13
1932-33	35	5	3	2	38	7
1933-34	35	8	2	0	37	8
1934-35	22	3	0	0	22	3
	237	64	16	7	253	71

Micky Burns was born in Preston on 21 December 1946 and began his football career as an amateur with Chorley. He joined Skelmersdale United and won an FA Amateur Cup runners-up medal with them in 1967 as well as being capped for the England Amateur side. Burns turned professional with Blackpool in May 1969 and made a scoring League debut against Portsmouth the following August. His goals helped the Seasiders back to the First Division that season, but relegation followed at the end of the 1970-71 campaign. In July 1974, Newcastle United paid £166,000 for the former schoolteacher, who has a degree in economics from Manchester University, and he ended that season with a Texaco Cup winners' medal. Burns and Irving Nattrass were in the Newcastle team that lost to Manchester City in the 1976 League Cup Final. He left St James' Park in August 1979, after over 150 appearances, and became player-coach at Cardiff City. Burns could not settle in Wales, however, and two months later he moved to Middlesbrough for £72,000, the same figure that Cardiff had paid for him. He scored on his debut for 'Boro, at Old Trafford in October, but missed some of the season because of a back injury. When his playing career ended, Burns coached the juniors at Ayresome Park but, working without a contract, he was sacked in November 1982, as part of the club's economy drive. He is currently involved in a YTS football training scheme in Darlington.

MICKY BURNS

	LEAGUE		FA CUP		FL CUP		TOTAL	
	App	Gls	App	Gls	App	Gls	App	Gls
1978-79	31	14	2	0	0	0	33	14
1979-80	23/1	10	0/1	0	3	0	26/2	10
1980-81	4/2	0	0	0	0	0	4/2	0
	58/3	24	2/1	0	3	0	63/4	24

GEORGE CAMSELL

Centre-forward George Camsell will always be remembered as the man who scored a record 59 League goals when Middlesbrough stormed away with the Second Division championship in 1926-7, a figure which stands second only to Dixie Dean's 60 for Everton the following season. Camsell was born at Framwellgate Moor, County Durham, on 27 November 1902 and made 21 Third Division North appearances for Durham City before joining Middlesbrough in October 1925, for £600. In his early days he was an outside-left but made little impression and might have joined Barnsley for £200, but the Colliers found it difficult to raise the money.

Camsell's career as a centre-forward at Ayresome Park took off after he came into the side for the fifth game of 1926-7, when 'Boro were struggling after a disastrous start. Middlesbrough won nine of their next ten games and by the end of the season they were back in Division One and Camsell had his astonishing record. He was a brave, two-footed centre-forward and it is surprising that he won only nine full England caps, especially as he responded with 18 goals in those international appearances. He possessed excellent ball-control and would try a shot from any angle if he could see a half-chance. In a long line of great 'Boro centre-forwards — Common, Elliott and Clough to name but three — George Camsell surely stands at the top of the list. He won a second Division Two championship medal with 'Boro in 1928-9 and also represented the Football League. Camsell retired during World War Two and between 1944 and 1963 served Middlesbrough as chief scout, coach and assistant secretary respectively. He died, after a long illness, in Middlesbrough General Hospital on 7 March 1966.

	LEAGUE		FA CUP		TOTAL	
	App	Gls	App	Gls	App	Gls
1925-26	4	3	0	0	4	3
1926-27	37	59	3	4	40	63
1927-28	40	33	3	4	43	36 ·
1928-29	40	30	3	3	43	33˙
1929-30	34	29	4	2	38	31
1930-31	37	32	2	0	39	32
1931-32	37	20	2	0	39	20
1932-33	31	17	4	1	35	18
1933-34	36	23	2	1	38	24
1934-35	26	14	2	0	28	14
1035-36	38	28	4	4	42	32
1936-37	23	18	1	0	24	18
1937-38	24	9	3	1	27	10
1938-39	11	10	2	0	13	10
	418	325	35	20	453	345

who weighed only 9st, had his jersey and shorts 'tightened' with safety pins for the big occasion. During World War One he served in the Royal Engineers and in the first post-war season he was capped by England against Ireland. Injured in his second, and last, international, against Wales in 1923, he contracted pneumonia later that year but recovered and was a key figure in 'Boro's two Second Division titles of the 1920s. In 1929, after 19 years at 'Boro, he moved to Blackpool for £500 and helped the Seasiders win promotion to Division One in 1930. A year later he became player-coach of Hartlepools United and managed them from 1932 to 1935. Carr also managed Tranmere Rovers and Darlington before World War Two. During the war he worked at Head Wrightson, but died suddenly on 10 May 1942 and is buried in Normanby cemetery.

JACKIE CARR

John 'Jackie' Carr was the most famous of five footballing brothers, four of whom played League soccer. Born at South Bank on 26 November 1891, he was playing for South Bank East End when Sunderland rejected him as being too small. In 1910, South Bank reached the FA Amateur Cup Final and Jackie Carr, with brothers Harry and Willie, were in their team which lost to Royal Marine Light Infantry at Bishop Auckland. Jackie, a tee-totaller and non-smoker, joined Middlesbrough in 1910. Offered £3 per week, he said he could earn more by following his trade as a gas-fitter. 'Boro upped his wages by 10s (50p) and he signed. Carr scored twice on his debut, against Nottingham Forest at Ayresome Park in January 1911, although that was the only game he played that season. Local folklore has it that Carr,

	LEAGUE		FA CUP		TOTAL	
	App	Gls	App	Gls	App	Gls
1910-11	1	2	0	0	1	2
1911-12	4	1	0	0	4	1
1912-13	30	16	4	3	34	19
1913-14	30	11	1	0	31	11
1914-15	33	9	2	3	35	12
1919-20	37	2	2	0	39	2
1920-21	38	4	1	0	39	4
1921-22	28	2	1	0	29	2
1922-23	24	2	3	0	27	2
1923-24	24	3	0	0	24	3
1924-25	31	1	1	0	32	1
1925-26	29	6	2	0	31	6
1926-27	35	6	3	0	38	6
1927-28	32	6	3	0	35	6
1928-29	29	1	3	0	32	1
1929-30	16	3	2	0	18	3
	421	75	28	6	449	81

One of the four Carr brothers to play League football for Middlesbrough, George Carr was the only one not to begin his career with South Bank. Mostly an inside-forward, he signed for Bradford in 1916 and when 'Boro tried to tempt him from Park Avenue, it was rumoured that he would not consider the matter until they awarded his brothers, Jackie and Willie, benefit games. Only the Football League could sanction such

GEORGE CARR

games and George eventually signed for 'Boro in June 1919. Jackie and Willie got their reward in April 1922, when they shared a £650 benefit game with Andy Wilson. George Carr's time at Ayresome Park was not a particularly happy period of his career and he was often barracked by the crowd. In March 1924 he moved to Leicester City for £2,300 and spent 11 happy years at Filbert Street, three as captain. He won a Second Division championship medal in his first season, missing only one game. Despite breaking a leg against Leeds United in 1925, he recovered and ended his League career with a move to Stockport County in 1932. Carr later played for Nuneaton Town and spent seven years as manager of Cheltenham Town before returning to Teesside as a Leicester City scout. He managed the Black Lion Hotel in North Ormesby for a spell and coached South Bank in the late 1940s.

	LEAGUE		FA CUP		TOTAL	
	App	Gls	App	Gls	App	Gls
1919-20	15	2	2	0	17	2
1920-21	5	2	0	0	5	2
1921-22	28	15	0	0	28	15
1922-23	13	4	1	0	14	4
1923-24	6	0	0	0	6	0
	67	23	3	0	70	23

Brian Clough made his name in two very distinct phases of his career, first as a goalscoring centre-forward with Middlesbrough and Sunderland, then as one of the game's most successful post-war managers. Clough was born in Grove Hill, Middlesbrough, on 21 March 1935, one of nine children. He worked as a clerk with ICI and played for Billingham Synthonia and Great Broughton before joining Middlesbrough as an amateur in November 1951. Clough, 'oozing confidence to shoot from every angle,' became a full-time professional in May 1952 and made his League debut in September 1955, against Barnsley, when 'Boro were in the middle of an injury crisis. Despite an impressive season, he put in the first of many transfer requests, but manager Bob Dennison turned them all down flat. Despite being the Second Division's leading scorer for three seasons in a row, Clough could not help Middlesbrough to promotion, but his tally of 254 goals in 271 games for 'Boro and Sunderland is still a post-war record. It was strange that he was capped only twice for England, though he failed to score on either occasion. In November 1959 came the infamous 'round robin' incident when nine of his teammates signed a petition asking for Clough to be relieved of the captaincy. Again, a transfer request was denied. In July 1961, however, Clough finally left Ayresome Park for Sunderland, although the £45,000 move upset many 'Boro fans. In two seasons with Second Division Sunderland he scored 53 goals, before an injury suffered against Bury on Boxing Day 1962 virtually ended his playing career. After a spell on Sunderland's coaching staff, Clough became manager of Hartlepool United. He rejuvenated that club before taking Derby County from Division Two to League Champions, with his old 'Boro colleague Peter Taylor as his assistant. There followed a spell at Brighton and 44 unhappy days as manager of Leeds United before Clough took over Nottingham Forest and guided them from the Second Division to European Cup winners. He was the first British manager to pay £1 million for a player — Trevor Francis — and has taken Forest to two League Cup Final successes as well as their League Championship and European victories.

BRIAN CLOUGH

	LEAGUE		FA CUP		FL CUP		TOTAL	
	App	Gls	App	Gls	App	Gls	App	Gls
1955-56	9	3	0	0	-	-	9	3
1956-57	41	38	3	2	-	-	44	40
1957-58	40	40	2	2	-	-	42	42
1958-59	42	43	1	0	-	-	43	43
1959-60	41	39	1	1	-	-	42	40
1960-61	40	34	1	0	1	2	42	36
	213	197	8	5	1	2	222	204

Middlesbrough line-up in 1956-7, Brian Clough's first full season in the League side. Back row (left to right): Robinson, Bilcliff, Harris, Taylor, Clough, Fitzsimons. Front: Delapenha, Scott, Lawrie, Dicks, Stonehouse.

100

football for Derry City in the Irish League. At the age of 17 he had a trial with Nottingham Forest but failed to impress and, two years later, suffered a similar rejection by Everton. He was laying electric cables and supplementing his wages by playing for another Irish League club, Linfield, when the Linfield boss, Bertie Peacock, switched Cochrane from his usual midfield position to the wing. Thereafter, Cochrane's fortunes improved and his form so impressed Burnley that the Turf Moor club paid £38,000 for his signature in October 1976. After 67 League appearances (13 goals) for the Clarets, he was transferred to Middlesbrough in October 1978, when manager John Neal paid a club record fee of £238,000. Neal rated Cochrane as one of the top wingers in the League and he showed great form at Ayresome Park, teasing and tormenting defenders with his tricky ball skills. In October 1983, he moved to Gillingham and later played for Millwall and Hartlepool on a non-contract basis before helping Billingham Synthonia to win the Northern League title in 1988-9. Cochrane won 19 of his 26 Northern Ireland caps when he was with 'Boro.

TERRY COCHRANE

Terry Cochrane was born in Killyleagh, Northern Ireland, on 23 January 1953 and became a labourer in a tannery when he left school, playing part-time

	LEAGUE		FA CUP		FL CUP		TOTAL	
	App	Gls	App	Gls	App	Gls	App	Gls
1978-79	18/1	3	2	0	0	0	20/1	3
1979-80	25/4	1	3	2	0	0	28/4	3
1980-81	24	1	5	2	0	0	29	3
1981-82	22/3	1	2	0	3	0	27/3	1
1982-83	7/7	1	0	0	2	1	9/7	2
	96/15	7	12	4	5	1	113/15	12

Alf Common will always be known as the first footballer to be transferred for a four-figure fee, when he moved from Sunderland to Middlesbrough for £1,000 in February 1905. Common, who was born in Millfield, Sunderland, played for South Hylton Juniors and Jarrow before joining the Wearsiders. In 1901 he was transferred to Sheffield United for £325 and won an FA Cup-winners' medal with the Blades in 1902 and two England caps in 1903-04. In the 1904 close season he returned to Sunderland, joining the Roker club for a record fee of £520. Seven months later, Middlesbrough broke the transfer record by paying Sunderland what was then the remarkable sum of £1,000 for Common's signature. 'Boro were denounced for 'buying' their way out of the relegation zone and a transfer-fee limit was enforced. Common, meanwhile, scored a penalty at Bramall Lane to help Middlesbrough achieve their first away win for two years. Capped again whilst with 'Boro, Common was an aggressive forward, once described as 'brawny and full of stamina'. He weighed around 13st, yet was deceptively quick. He lost the Middlesbrough captaincy in September 1907 and was fined £10 by the club for

ALF COMMON

'drunkenness and violent behaviour'. In August 1910, Common moved to Woolwich Arsenal for £100 before being transferred to Preston in December 1912. He won a Second Division championship medal with Preston and later took a pub in Darlington. Common retired in 1943 and died in the town on 3 April 1946.

	LEAGUE		FA CUP		TOTAL	
	App	Gls	App	Gls	App	Gls
1904-05	10	4	0	0	10	4
1905-06	36	19	5	5	41	24
1906-07	29	12	2	1	31	13
1907-08	34	9	1	0	35	9
1908-09	33	10	1	0	34	10
1909-10	26	4	1	1	27	5
	168	58	10	7	178	65

Colin Cooper, born in Middlesbrough on 28 February 1967, is a former apprentice who joined 'Boro on the YTS scheme. As a schoolboy he played for Kelloe Under-11s and Bishop Auckland Boys and had trials at Ayresome Park as well as for Newcastle United and Crystal Palace, but it was Middlesbrough who won the race for his signature. Since making his first-team debut in the 1985-6 season, Cooper has given some impressive performances as the club's regular left-back, although he is a naturally right-footed player. Winner of three Barclay's Young Eagle of the Month awards, he has been capped several times by England Under-21s and played for his country in the first-leg of the European Championship semi-final in France. Cooper missed the last three games of Middlesbrough's 1988-9 season — when the team was struggling, unsuccessfully, to avoid relegation — because of stress fractures to his right foot, a problem which had started the previous October.

COLIN COOPER

	LEAGUE		FA CUP		FL CUP		TOTAL	
	App	Gls	App	Gls	App	Gls	App	Gls
1985-86	9/2	0	0	0	0	0	9/2	0
1986-87	46	0	3	0	4	0	53	0
1987-88†	43	2	5	0	4	0	52	2
1988-89	35	2	1	0	2	0	38	2
	133/2	4	9	0	10	0	152/2	4

†Also made three play-off appearances

TERRY COOPER

Castleford-born Terry Cooper was an attacking left winger as a schoolboy and played for Ferrybridge Amateurs whilst he served his apprenticeship as a colliery fitter. He failed to impress in a trial at Wolves before joining Leeds United as a 16-year-old apprentice. He signed full-time professional forms in July 1962 and it was Don Revie who converted him into an attacking full-back. Cooper played a great part in Leeds' success story. He won the first of 20 full caps in 1969 and was one of England's stars in the 1970 Mexico World Cup Finals. In April 1972, he broke a leg but returned to action and won another cap. Cooper made 350 appearances for Leeds and scored 11 goals, including the winner in the 1967 League Cup Final. He joined his former Leeds teammate, Jack Charlton, at Middlesbrough in March 1975, for £50,000, but things turned sour when he refused to accompany the club on their Norwegian tour in 1978. 'Boro suspended him and he asked to go on the transfer list with a year of his contract still to run. Cooper joined another Leeds United old boy, Norman Hunter, at Bristol City but stayed only one season before moving to Bristol Rovers, first as a player, then as player-manager. Controversially dismissed from Eastville, Cooper teamed up with Billy Bremner, yet another ex-Leeds player, at Doncaster before returning to Bristol City as player-manager. Cooper guided City to two Wembley appearances in Freight/Rover Trophy Finals. He joined the board at Ashton Gate (he was English football's first player-director) but eventually left the club and in 1989 was managing Exeter City.

	LEAGUE		FA CUP		FL CUP		TOTAL	
	App	Gls	App	Gls	App	Gls	App	Gls
1974-75	9	0	0	0	0	0	9	0
1975-76	40	1	2	0	6	0	48	1
1976-77	40	0	5	0	1	0	46	0
1977-78	16	0	0	0	4	0	20	0
	105	1	7	0	11	0	123	1

Stan Anderson returned to his former club, Newcastle United, to bring stocky John Craggs to Ayresome Park in August 1971 for £60,000, a sizeable fee for a player who was not even a regular in United's senior side. Craggs, a former England Youth international, joined United in December 1965 but found his progress checked by the consistency of the brilliant David Craig, who limited Craggs to 50 appearances in six years at St James' Park. When Jack Charlton took over as

'Boro manager he called Craggs 'the best attacking right-back in the business'. He was, indeed, a polished defender who liked to make penetrative, overlapping runs into the opponents' half and, as a result, he scored some spectacular goals for 'Boro. One critic described him as playing 'with a calm assurance, indulging in delightful precision passing'. He was called 'Ted' by his teammates after someone spotted a letter arrive at the club addressed to him and quoting his full name of John Edward Craggs. A keen sportsman, he plays golf, cricket, table-tennis and snooker and is also an accomplished guitarist. With over 400 League appearances to his credit, he was awarded a benefit game against his old club, Newcastle United, before returning to St James' Park on a free transfer in the summer of 1982. In December 1988, after a spell with Darlington, he teamed up again with his old Newcastle teammate, Bobby Moncur, the manager of Hartlepool United. Craggs went to the Victoria Ground as youth-team coach.

JOHN CRAGGS

	LEAGUE		FA CUP		FL CUP		TOTAL	
	App	Gls	App	Gls	App	Gls	App	Gls
1971-72	38	2	6	0	2	1	46	3
1972-73	41	1	1	0	4	0	46	1
1973-74	39	3	2	0	3	0	44	3
1974-75	41	1	6	0	4	0	51	1
1975-76	36	1	2	0	6	0	44	1
1976-77	42	1	5	0	1	0	48	1
1977-78	37	2	5	0	2	0	44	2
1978-79	41	0	2	0	2	0	45	0
1979-80	42	1	3	0	3	0	48	1
1980-81	28/1	0	1	0	2	0	31/1	0
1981-82	23	0	0	0	2	0	25	0
	408/1	12	33	0	31	1	472/1	13

Johnny Crossan first caught the headlines when he was alleged to have been paid whilst an amateur with Irish League club, Coleraine. Peter Doherty brought him to England to sign for Bristol City, but when his registration forms were sent to the Football League for approval, they were refused and Crossan returned to his Londonderry home — he was born there on 29 November 1938 — and was later banned from playing football in England. Determined to seek a higher grade of soccer, Crossan signed for the Dutch club, Sparta Rotterdam, and later played Belgian League football with Standard Liege, for whom he also appeared in the European Cup. The Football League ban was eventually lifted and in October 1962, Crossan signed for Sunderland, for £27,000. He was in the side which clinched promotion to Division One for the Wearsiders in 1964 and in January 1965, Manchester City paid £40,000 for his midfield skills. He skippered City back to the First Division but, after one season in the top flight, he found his place threatened by Bell and Young. City sold him to Middlesbrough for £35,000 — 'Boro's record fee — in August 1967. During 1968-9 he suffered so badly from insomnia that he received hospital treatment and later had major abdominal surgery, so his stay at Ayresome Park was not altogether successful. Winner of 24 Northern Ireland caps, Crossan was released by 'Boro at the end of the 1969-70 season and returned to Belgium to play for Tongren FC.

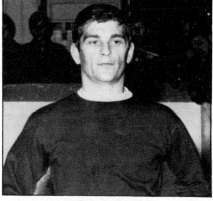

JOHNNY CROSSAN

	LEAGUE		FA CUP		FL CUP		TOTAL	
	App	Gls	App	Gls	App	Gls	App	Gls
1967-68	32	4	5	1	2	0	39	5
1968-69	22	3	0	0	0	0	22	3
1969-70	0/2	0	0	0	0	0	0/2	0
	54/2	7	5	1	2	0	61/2	8

Early in the 1936-7 season, Middlesbrough tried to buy Grimsby Town goalkeeper Jim Tweedy as a replacement for Fred Gibson, but Tweedy was happy to stay at Blundell Park. 'Boro switched their attentions to Arbroath's Dave Cumming, who signed for the Ayresome club in October. Cumming, who was born on 6 May 1910, started in junior football with Hall Russell in his home town and joined Aberdeen in 1929. He spent four seasons at Pittodrie before going to Arbroath on a free transfer. He enjoyed immediate success at Gayfield Park and Middlesbrough had to pay £3,000 to sign him, which made Cumming the most expensive goalkeeper to leave Scotland. Cumming and Tom Cochrane, newly transferred from Leeds United, made their debuts in a 3-3 draw against Liverpool at Ayresome Park. Cumming soon adapted to the English game and was capped for Scotland against England in 1938. He won several wartime caps and was the only 'Boro player to guest for Newcastle United. In December 1947, he was sent-off for striking Arsenal's Leslie Compton. Cumming handed his jersey to Johnny Spuhler and walked off before the referee could dismiss him. He played his last game, at home to Blackpool, that month when he dislocated a kneecap.

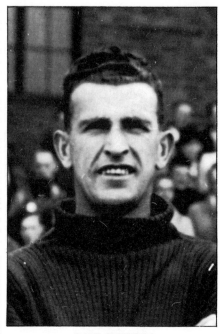

	LEAGUE		FA CUP		TOTAL	
	App	Gls	App	Gls	App	Gls
1936-37	32	0	1	0	33	0
1937-38	28	0	3	0	31	0
1938-39	38	0	4	0	42	0
1945-46	-	-	7	0	7	0
1946-47	37	0	7	0	44	0
	135	0	22	0	157	0

DAVE CUMMING

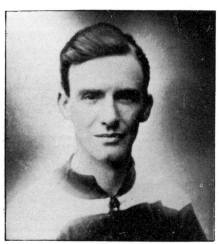

STEWART DAVIDSON

Stewart Davidson, who was born in Aberdeen on 1 June 1889, was a legal clerk by profession. He first played for Aberdeen Shamrocks and was signed by Middlesbrough manager Tom McIntosh from Aberdeen on 17 April 1913, for £675. Davidson made his 'Boro debut at right-half — the position in which he played most of his games for the club — on 6 May 1913, against Manchester City at Hyde Road. During World War One he guested for Chelsea before joining up. Although wounded in action, he was able to resume his football career when the war ended in 1918 and took over as club captain from George Elliott in 1920. His loyal service to Middlesbrough was rewarded with a benefit match against Derby County on 20 November 1920. He was capped for Scotland against England in 1921 but in May 1923, 'Boro felt they could release him. Davidson appealed against the £500 fee which the club wanted and the Football League reduced it to £250. His former club, Aberdeen, stepped in and Stewart returned home. He was later player-manager of Forress Mechanics and coached for the Kent County FA before joining his former Middlesbrough colleague, Billy Birrell, who was then manager at Chelsea. Davidson remained as assistant manager at Stamford Bridge until his retirement in July 1957. He died on Boxing Day 1960.

	LEAGUE		FA CUP		TOTAL	
	App	Gls	App	Gls	App	Gls
1913-14	30	1	1	0	31	1
1914-15	36	0	1	0	37	0
1919-20	42	1	2	0	44	1
1920-21	37	0	1	0	38	0
1921-22	41	2	1	0	42	2
1922-23	22	0	2	0	24	0
	208	4	8	0	216	4

BILLY DAY

Germany with the Army on National Service, manager Bob Dennison considered him so vital a member of the team that he arranged for the club to pay for Day to be flown home home for matches every week. After making over 100 League appearances for 'Boro, Day had the misfortune to break his leg in a practice match at the club's training ground in Hutton Road. Eager to get back into action, his return to League duty was a little premature and he did not allow the leg sufficient time to heal. Dennison eventually agreed to his transfer request and Newcastle United paid £12,000 for Day in March 1962. He scored on his League debut for the Magpies, at home to Scunthorpe United, but it was his only League goal for them. Still dogged by leg trouble, he moved to Peterborough United in April 1963. However, after only 17 League games for Posh he signed for Cambridge United, then in the Southern League. He recovered his form, but a bout of pneumonia ended his playing career and, at the age of 29, he returned to Teesside and became a successful bookmaker.

Billy Day, who was born in Middlesbrough on 27 December 1936, was an amateur with Sheffield Wednesday but made no first-team appearances for the Owls before signing professional forms for 'Boro in May 1955. Day, who had been playing for South Bank Juniors, made his League debut at outside-right against Leicester City on 8 October 1955 and went on to serve Middlesbrough well for over a century· of Football League games. When he was posted to

	LEAGUE		FA CUP		FL CUP		TOTAL	
	App	Gls	App	Gls	App	Gls	App	Gls
1955-56	25	6	0	0	-	-	25	6
1956-57	17	1	2	1	-	-	19	2
1957-58	18	2	2	1	-	-	20	3
1958-59	14	1	1	0	-	-	15	1
1959-60	19	5	0	0	-	-	19	5
1960-61	9	0	0	0	0	0	9	0
1961-62	18	3	4	0	2	1	24	4
	120	18	9	2	2	1	131	21

Lindy Delapenha was one of those footballers whose name was always being misspelt, but the player himself confirms the above as the correct version. Delapenha, whose first name was really Lloyd, was born in Jamaica on 25 May 1927 and, after being demobbed from the RAF, he had a trial with Arsenal. He did not impress the Highbury management, however, and in April 1948 was allowed to move to Portsmouth. At that time Pompey had probably the best side in their history and Delapenha was restricted to only seven League appearances. In April 1950, Portsmouth were happy to let him go to Middlesbrough and it was at Ayresome Park that his career really took off. As a fast, clever and powerful winger or inside-forward, playing in the same front line as Wilf Mannion, he soon impressed. He was Middlesbrough's leading scorer in 1952-3, 1953-4 and 1955-6 and his sturdy physique — he was a stocky 5ft 7in tall — made him particularly effective in the rough and tumble around the penalty area. He enjoyed a good strike rate for 'Boro — he

LINDY DELAPENHA

was also something of a penalty expert — before joining Mansfield Town in June 1958 and he also gave the Stags good service with 27 goals in 115 League appearances before retiring from League soccer in 1960. He later played for Burton Albion and Heanor Town before returning to Jamaica and now holds a senior position with the sports department of the Jamaican Broadcasting Corporation.

	LEAGUE		FA CUP		TOTAL	
	App	Gls	App	Gls	App	Gls
1949-50	1	0	0	0	1	0
1950-51	40	8	1	0	41	8
1951-52	33	15	3	2	36	17
1952-53	30	9	0	0	30	9
1953-54	40	18	2	0	42	18
1954-55	38	15	1	0	39	15
1955-56	35	17	2	1	37	18
1956-57	26	8	1	0	27	8
1957-58	17	0	0	0	17	0
	260	90	10	3	270	93

Ronnie Dicks was once described as 'a barrel-chested 90-minute footballer'. Born in Kennington on 13 April 1924, Dicks first played for Dulwich Hamlet and signed as an amateur for Middlesbrough in April 1943, whilst doing military service on Teesside. A month later he became a professional and played his early games for the club as a winger. Despite making many wartime appearances, he had to wait until August 1947 — the second season after the resumption of the League — for his senior debut in peacetime. He impressed in that first game, against Manchester United at Ayresome Park, and it was the start of an illustrious career with 'Boro. He developed into something of a utility player — David Jack called him, 'The Handyman of Ayresome Park' — but settled down at wing-half or full-back. A long throw-in specialist, he had 'speed,

	LEAGUE		FA CUP		TOTAL	
	App	Gls	App	Gls	App	Gls
1947-48	22	2	1	0	23	2
1948-49	19	2	0	0	19	2
1949-50	22	0	4	0	26	0
1950-51	35	1	1	0	36	1
1951-52	27	0	3	0	30	0
1952-53	10	0	1	0	11	0
1953-54	32	0	2	0	34	0
1954-55	39	2	1	0	40	2
1955-56	36	0	2	0	38	0
1956-57	41	2	3	0	44	2
1957-58	25	1	0	0	25	1
1958-59	8	0	0	0	8	0
	316	10	18	0	334	10

RONNIE DICKS

a deceptive swerve and the ability to kick with either foot'. He did chase the ball but preferred to 'loiter' until it came his way. A chipped ankle-bone against Derby in 1949-50 kept him out for a month and an Achilles tendon injury later cost him a place in the Football League side. Yet another injury saw Dicks miss an England 'B' cap. He retired in 1958 and still lives in Middlesbrough. Younger brother, Alan, played League football for Chelsea, Southend and Brighton and managed Bristol City.

DERRICK DOWNING

Derrick Downing was born in Doncaster on 3 November 1945 and worked as a clerk after leaving school. He played some games at junior and reserve level for Doncaster Rovers before signing for Frickley Colliery and then joining Middlesbrough, where Raich Carter was manager, in February 1965. Downing had plenty of success as a forward with 'Boro and also made something of a name for himself as a long throw-in expert. He could reach the far post with the ball when taking throw-ins and also scored several goals with brave, diving headers. A prime example of this was the one he netted against West Ham in the FA Cup in 1970. In May 1972, Downing found himself surplus to manager Stan Anderson's requirements and was transferred to Orient. He made exactly 100 full League appearances for the Brisbane Road club, who converted him to full-back. In July 1975 he returned to his native Yorkshire to play for York City (47 League appearances and two goals) before ending his career with Hartlepool United, whom he joined in July 1977. He made 40 League appearances and scored four goals for United.

	LEAGUE		FA CUP		FL CUP		TOTAL	
	App	Gls	App	Gls	App	Gls	App	Gls
1965-66	13	2	0	0	0	0	13	2
1966-67	33	8	3	1	0	0	36	9
1967-68	7	0	4	1	0	0	11	1
1968-69	30/3	9	1/1	0	1	0	32/4	9
1969-70	32/2	5	5	2	0	0	37/2	7
1970-71	32/2	11	3	1	2	1	37/2	13
1971-72	26/3	4	6	2	2	1	34/3	7
	173/10	39	22/1	7	5	2	200/11	48

George Washington Elliott, one of a long line of Middlesbrough international centre-forwards, was born at Sunderland in 1889, the son of a seafaring captain. His father later set up in Middlesbrough with a tugboat company and, later still, managed the American Oil Company in the town. Young George was a brilliant student at Middlesbrough High School but, although his family wanted him to go to Cambridge University, the boy was a compulsive sportsman (he boxed under an assumed name) and after playing for Redcar Crusaders, he helped South Bank win the Northern League title in 1908. Late on 3 May 1909, Elliott was awakened from his bed and signed for Middlesbrough in a nearby hotel. He played his first few games for 'Boro as an inside-right. The first of three full England caps came in 1913-14, against Ireland at Ayresome Park, and that season his 31 goals made him Division One's leading scorer. He still holds

GEORGE ELLIOTT

	LEAGUE		FA CUP		TOTAL	
	App	Gls	App	Gls	App	Gls
1909-10	15	4	1	0	16	4
1910-11	25	10	4	0	29	10
1911-12	35	17	4	2	39	19
1912-13	33	22	4	3	37	25
1913-14	32	31	1	0	33	31
1914-15	29	14	2	3	31	17
1919-20	38	31	2	2	40	33
1920-21	36	26	1	0	37	26
1921-22	26	13	1	0	27	13
1922-23	33	23	0	0	33	23
1923-24	25	7	1	0	26	7
1923-24	17	5	0	0	17	5
	344	203	21	10	365	213

the club record for most goals in a single game (11 for the Reserves in a 14-1 win over Houghton Rovers) and during World War One he guested for Bradford, Fulham and Celtic. Starting in 1910-11, Elliott was 'Boro's leading scorer in seven out of nine peacetime seasons. His last appearance was at Southampton in 1924-5 after which, despite offers from Sunderland and Newcastle, he retired. George Elliott resumed his job as a cargo superintendent at Middlesbrough docks. He died, aged 59, in Middlesbrough General Hospital in November 1948 and is buried in Acklam cemetery.

Micky Fenton, who possessed a 'powerful shot with both feet' and was 'a very strong header of the ball', was born at Portrack, Stockton, on 30 October 1913 and Middlesbrough was his only professional club. He first played for Princess Street Juniors, then moved to South Bank East End. Offered a month's trial with Wolves, he returned after one day. Fenton signed professional forms for Middlesbrough in March 1933, making a scoring debut in 'Boro's 4-0 home win against

Blackburn Rovers. One of his weaknesses was that he was 'guilty of fiddling with the ball' in the opponents' penalty area and, when confronted with too much to do, he would try a shot instead of passing. He played once for England, against Scotland in 1938, and toured South Africa with the FA in 1939. During the war, Fenton served in the RAF and played in one unofficial international before resuming normal football in August 1946, when he was 33. Two months later, Everton manager Theo Kelly tried to sign Fenton as the replacement for Tommy Lawton, who had been transferred to Chelsea. The Middlesbrough team left for Derby and manager David Jack fuelled speculation that Fenton was about to leave by dropping him and playing Alex Linwood at centre-forward. Bill Kelly, 'Boro's chairman, said that the player should decide and Fenton remained at Ayresome Park.

MICKY FENTON

	LEAGUE		FA CUP		TOTAL	
	App	Gls	App	Gls	App	Gls
1932-33	1	1	0	0	1	1
1933-34	3	0	0	0	3	0
1934-35	21	8	1	0	22	8
1935-36	6	0	3	0	9	0
1936-37	35	22	1	0	36	22
1937-38	36	24	3	2	39	26
1938-39	33	34	4	1	37	35
1945-46	0	0	7	7	7	7
1946-47	40	18	7	5	47	23
1947-48	40	28	2	0	42	28
1948-49	24	12	1	0	25	12
1949-50	1	0	0	0	1	0
	240	147	29	15	269	162

Arthur Fitzsimons and Peter Desmond hit the football headlines in September 1949, when they played for the Republic of Ireland against Finland in a World Cup qualifying game in Dublin, even though they had still to make their first-team debuts for Middlesbrough. Four months earlier, 'Boro manager David Jack had signed both players from Irish club Shelbourne, paying £18,000 for Fitzsimons. Yet, even after winning his first cap, Fitzsimons had to wait a further eight months before making his League debut. After that first appearance, against West Brom at The Hawthorns, he went on to play well over 200 League and Cup games for the club and won 25 caps altogether as a Middlesbrough player. He was born in Dublin on 16 December 1929 and had played for the League of Ireland before joining 'Boro. An inside-forward, he would often jink around two or three defenders in the penalty area before sometimes skying the ball over the bar. It is alleged that on one occasion, an exasperated Brian Clough told him: "You make the bloody goals — I'll do the scoring." Fitzsimons moved to Lincoln City in March 1959 and made seven League appearances, winning his last cap, before a transfer to Mansfield Town at the beginning of the 1959-60 season. He retired in 1961, after 61 League games for the Stags. Fitzsimons later coached the League of Ireland representative side.

ARTHUR FITZSIMONS

	LEAGUE		FA CUP		TOTAL	
	App	Gls	App	Gls	App	Gls
1949-50	3	0	0	0	3	0
1950-51	6	0	0	0	6	0
1951-52	16	3	1	0	17	3
1952-53	35	11	1	1	36	12
1953-54	17	3	0	0	17	3
1954-55	38	5	1	0	39	5
1955-56	40	14	2	0	42	14
1956-57	36	9	3	1	39	10
1957-58	22	4	0	0	22	4
1958-59	10	0	0	0	10	0
	223	49	8	2	231	51

Alan Foggon was born in West Pelton, County Durham, on 23 February 1950. A former England Youth international, he signed for Newcastle United in November 1967 and played a major part in their Fairs Cup win in 1969, scoring a spectacular goal in the second leg of the Final against Újpest Dózsa. Foggon made 54 League appearances for Newcastle, scoring 13 goals, before being transferred to Cardiff City in August 1971. Cardiff were fighting to avoid relegation to the Third Division and he played only 14 times for them before signing for Middlesbrough in October 1972, for £10,000, after a week's wrangling between the clubs. He returned to the North-East under a three-week suspension, but soon proved his worth. Foggon ended the 1973-4 promotion season as 'Boro's leading scorer with 19 League goals, many of them coming as a result of his deceptive turn of speed. He was a lethal finisher, bursting through from deep positions. During the club's 1975 world tour, Foggon asked for a transfer, claiming that he did not fit in with 'Boro's style. Manchester United manager Tommy Docherty flew to Montreal to see Foggon play for Hartford Bi-Centennials in the NASL and the player joined United for £27,000. By September 1976, however, he was with Sunderland. After only seven League games for the Wearsiders he moved to Southend in June 1977, but returned to the North-East for a loan spell with Hartlepool before going to non-League Consett in August 1978.

ALAN FOGGON

	LEAGUE		FA CUP		FL CUP		TOTAL	
	App	Gls	App	Gls	App	Gls	App	Gls
1972-73	12/3	7	1	0	0	0	13/3	7
1973-74	41	19	2	0	3	1	46	20
1974-75	41	16	6	2	5	0	52	18
1975-76	11/7	3	1/1	0	1/1	1	13/9	4
	105/10	45	10/1	2	9/1	2	124/12	49

Billy Forrest, the eldest of seven brothers and three sisters, played his early football for Haddington and Musselborough Juniors, then turned out for Edinburgh St Bernard's. Middlesbrough were one of several clubs alerted to his potential and in March 1929, 'Boro manager Peter McWilliam met Forrest, who was a cooper by trade, and his father in the North British Hotel, Edinburgh, where the young player signed for the Ayresome Park club. He made his debut as a left-half against Manchester United in January 1930 and played most of his games for 'Boro in that position. McWilliam later asked Forrest's opinion of a youngster called Bob Baxter, who had just scored five goals in a Scottish junior game, and Forrest played an active part in Baxter signing for Middlesbrough. The two Scots became firm friends and married sisters, Forrest 'eloping' to Gretna Green to be wed. When he retired in 1945, Billy Forrest coached the juniors at

BILLY FORREST

	LEAGUE		FA CUP		TOTAL	
	App	Gls	App	Gls	App	Gls
1929-30	10	0	3	0	13	0
1930-31	40	1	2	0	42	1
1931-32	32	1	2	0	34	1
1932-33	39	0	4	0	43	0
1933-34	15	0	1	0	16	0
1934-35	24	1	2	0	26	1
1935-36	32	0	4	1	36	1
1936-37	38	0	1	0	39	0
1937-38	40	3	3	0	43	3
1938-39	37	1	4	0	41	1
	307	7	26	1	333	8

Middlesbrough until his appointment as Darlington manager. He left the Skernesiders at the end of the 1949-50 season and later ran the Station Hotel, Billingham. In 1956, he was partially paralysed as the result of an accident which led to his early death.

Reg Freeman, a native of Birkenhead, was starring as a full-back with Northern Nomads, one of the leading amateur clubs of the day, at the end of World War One. He joined First Division Oldham Athletic in 1920, becoming captain of the side during the 1922-3 season, and his sterling displays saw him play in an England trial. He was also named as reserve for the Football League against the League of Ireland. Middlesbrough paid £3,600 for Freeman in May 1923 and he proved to be an excellent purchase. In a Middlesbrough career that spanned seven seasons — which included two Second Division championships — he was a key figure. Freeman was transferred to Rotherham United on 5 September 1930, for £150, and was appointed player-manager at Millmoor in January 1934. He had no money to buy experienced players but moulded untried youngsters into a team which took Rotherham to the League North Third Division championship during the war. In May 1951, the Millers clinched promotion from the Third Division North with seven points to spare. Freeman later managed Sheffield United, signing a five-year contract in August 1952, but after an illness lasting several months he died on 4 August 1955.

REG FREEMAN

	LEAGUE		FA CUP		TOTAL	
	App	Gls	App	Gls	App	Gls
1923-24	40	0	1	0	41	0
1924-25	33	0	1	0	34	0
1925-26	39	0	2	0	41	0
1926-27	29	0	2	0	31	0
1927-28	4	0	0	0	4	0
1928-29	28	0	2	0	30	0
1929-30	6	0	0	0	6	0
	179	0	8	0	187	0

Bill Gates, was born at Ferryhill on 8 May 1944 and captained England Youth before joining Middlesbrough as an amateur in October 1959. He made headlines by playing for 'Boro's first team when he was a 16-year-old and still at Spennymoor Grammar School, but was initially torn between professional football and following a career as an accountant. Football won, although he continued his studies, and he made his debut against Swansea Town in 1961 before turning professional later that year. During his 13-year stay with Middlesbrough, he experienced some fluctuating fortunes, sometimes winning a place only when other players were injured. Nevertheless, he made over 300 appearances, mostly at centre-half, although he could play in a number of other positions. Gates suffered a double fracture of his jaw during a League Cup tie against Manchester United, but recovered to maintain his 'tough guy' image. He enjoyed a testimonial game against League Champions Leeds United in May 1974, when over 30,000 fans came to support him, and in July that year he was released. He played cricket for Normanby Hall and went into business after his retirement from football, concentrating on running his sports outfitting shops, the sale of which in 1989 made him a wealthy man.

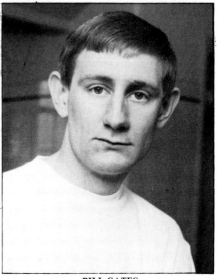

	LEAGUE		FA CUP		FL CUP		TOTAL	
	App	Gls	App	Gls	App	Gls	App	Gls
1961-62	14	0	0	0	1	0	15	0
1962-63	2	0	0	0	2	0	4	0
1963-64	14	3	0	0	0	0	14	3
1964-65	29	0	3	0	0	0	32	0
1965-66	28	0	1	0	3	0	32	0
1966-67	25/2	1	2/1	0	2	0	29/3	1
1967-68	20	0	5	0	1	0	26	0
1968-69	17/1	2	2	0	1	0	20/1	2
1969-70	31	1	5	0	1	0	37	1
1970-71	38/1	0	3	0	1	0	42/1	0
1971-72	26	2	5	0	2	0	33	2
1972-73	32/1	3	0	0	3	0	35/1	3
1973-74	1/1	0	0/1	0	1	0	2/2	0
	277/6	12	26/2	0	18	0	321/8	12

BILL GATES

Jimmy Gordon began his career with Wishaw Juniors — he was born at Fauldhouse on 23 October 1915 — and broke into the Football League with Newcastle United, for whom he signed in April 1935. Gordon, a hard-tackling, constructive right-half, made 132 League appearances for the Magpies before his transfer to Middlesbrough in November 1945. Like so many players of his generation, Gordon lost valuable years of his career to the war, but Newcastle certainly made a mistake in releasing him, even though one of their directors called him 'only a 20-minute footballer'. His move to 'Boro extended Gordon's career by nine years and he gave the club wonderful service as a tenacious, ball-player who commanded the midfield. In the early 1960s he was given charge of Middlesbrough's junior side before joining Blackburn Rovers as the Ewood Park club's reserve-team trainer. When Brian Clough and Peter Taylor took over at Derby County, they remembered Gordon, who was the Rams's trainer when they won the League Championship in 1972. Gordon later shared in Nottingham Forest's European Cup success — again with Clough and Taylor — and he was allowed to lead Forest out at Wembley for a League Cup Final. He now lives in retirement on Teesside and is an occasional spectator at Ayresome Park.

JIMMY GORDON

	LEAGUE		FA CUP		TOTAL	
	App	Gls	App	Gls	App	Gls
1945-46	-	-	6	1	6	1
1946-47	36	1	7	0	43	1
1947-48	35	0	3	0	38	0
1948-49	38	1	1	0	39	1
1949-50	38	1	4	0	42	1
1950-51	34	0	1	0	35	0
1951-52	30	0	0	0	30	0
1952-53	10	0	0	0	10	0
1953-54	10	0	0	0	10	0
	231	3	22	1	253	4

Welsh international centre-half Tom Griffiths was born in Wrexham in 1902 and joined his local League club in 1922. In 1929 he moved to Everton and spent five seasons at Goodison as a playing contemporary of Dixie Dean, although he managed only 78 League and Cup appearances for the Merseysiders. In December 1931, Griffiths joined Bolton Wanderers for a transfer fee of more than £5,500, but the following season Bolton were relegated from Division One. 'Boro manager Peter McWilliam persuaded the Trotters to part with Griffiths for £4,500 in May 1933. His move to Ayresome Park saw him embark upon the best period of his career and 50 years later, there are still those who regard Tom Griffiths as the best centre-half to have played for the club. When he challenged for a ball he seemed to 'hang in the air a little longer than his opponent' and he 'rarely failed in a tackle'. One weakness, though, was poor distribution of the ball. After injury to regular full-back Jack Jennings, Griffiths played right-back for six games and won rave reviews. In November 1935, Aston Villa — who were spending heavily in a bid to avoid relegation — signed Griffiths for nearly £6,000. But Villa still went down and he was thus relegated with three different clubs in seven seasons (he was in the Everton side which

TOM GRIFFITHS

	LEAGUE		FA CUP		TOTAL	
	App	Gls	App	Gls	App	Gls
1932-33	13	1	0	0	13	1
1933-34	40	0	2	0	42	0
1934-35	29	0	2	0	31	0
1935-36	6	0	0	0	6	0
	88	1	4	0	92	1

dropped into Division Two in 1929-30). Towards the end of his playing days, the former Welsh international skipper — he was capped 21 times altogether — joined Wrexham as player-coach and became a publican in the town. An accomplished celloist, he was later appointed a director at the Racecourse Ground and died in Wrexham on Christmas Day 1981.

scout recommended Hamilton for a day's trial at Ayresome Park in 1981 and he was asked to return for a fortnight's trial period before 'Boro signed him as an apprentice professional in January 1982. Malcolm Allison gave him his first chance of League football, against Bolton Wanderers and he became a full-time professional in May 1983. The following year, Hamilton toured Russia with the Scotland Youth side and went on to win seven caps altogether. He had a brief spell on the transfer list in May 1986 and when Middlesbrough dropped into the Third Division, Charlton Athletic offered him a two-year contract, but he decided to ride out 'Boro's troubles. Although only 23 at the start of the 1989-90 season, Hamilton had already made over 250 first-team appearances for Middlesbrough, even though he has suffered some troublesome injuries in the last two seasons. At the end of 1988-9, for instance, he missed some games because of an operation on his right knee.

GARY HAMILTON

Winger Gary Hamilton, who was born in Glasgow on 27 December 1965, attended All Saints' School in that city and played for the Eastercraigs youth team, the side which produced Tony McAndrew and Everton's Graeme Sharp. Middlesbrough's Scottish

	LEAGUE		FA CUP		FL CUP		TOTAL	
	App	Gls	App	Gls	App	Gls	App	Gls
1982-83	8/1	2	0	0	0	0	8/1	2
1983-84	26/5	3	3	0	0	0	29/5	3
1984-85	34/2	0	2	0	2	0	38/2	0
1985-86	33	4	1	0	1	0	35	4
1986-87	41/2	7	2	1	4	1	47/2	9
1987-88†	40/1	6	5	0	4	0	49/1	6
1988-89	35/1	3	1	0	2	0	38/1	3
	217/12	25	14	1	13	1	244/12	27
†Also made four play-off appearances								

George Hardwick was one of the game's best-known post-war players. Capped 13 times for England and captain of the Great Britain side which met the Rest of Europe in 1947, Hardwick was a fine left-back who served Middlesbrough in the years immediately after World War Two. He was born in Saltburn on 2 February 1920, into a footballing family, for his grandfather, Frank Hardwick, had played for Middlesbrough Ironopolis in the early 1890s. George first played for South Bank East End Juniors and when he left school he began work as a costing clerk with Dorman Long. He signed amateur forms for Middlesbrough in October 1935 and became a full-time professional in April 1937. Arsenal and Rangers had also shown an interest, but young Hardwick's sole ambition was to play for 'Boro. He scored a goal in the first minute of his debut game, at home to Bolton in December 1937, but made only a handful of appearances before the outbreak of war, during which he served as a sergeant in RAF Bomber Command. He appeared in two wartime Wembley Cup Finals as a Chelsea guest and recovered from injuries to both legs, suffered during an air-raid on his RAF base on the Isle of Sheppey, to play in 17 wartime internationals. He skippered England in every one of his full internationals. In November 1950 he joined Oldham Athletic as player-manager for £15,000 (after turning down a player-coach's job with Everton). He took Oldham into Division Two but they dropped back into Division Three North and in April 1956 he quit after Oldham had slumped still further and there was no money to strengthen the team. Later, Hardwick worked as a coach to the US Seventh Army's soccer team in Stuttgart and with PSV Eindhoven and the Dutch FA. From August 1961 to November 1963 he was youth-team coach at Ayresome Park. In November 1964 he took over as Sunderland manager but was ousted after only 169 days at Roker, having helped the Wearsiders achieve their highest post-war League position. From 1968 to 1979 he managed Gateshead. In May 1983, Middlesbrough finally gave Hardwick and Wilf Mannion a joint testimonial.

GEORGE HARDWICK

| | LEAGUE | | FA CUP | | TOTAL | |
	App	Gls	App	Gls	App	Gls
1937-38	8	0	2	0	10	0
1945-46	-	-	7	2	7	2
1946-47	33	1	7	0	40	1
1947-48	30	1	3	0	33	1
1948-49	39	2	1	0	40	2
1949-50	22	0	3	0	25	0
1950-51	11	1	0	0	11	1
	143	5	23	2	166	7

On 8 January 1949, Middlesbrough skipper George Hardwick won the toss when 'Boro met Brentford in an FA Cup tie at Griffin Park and decided which way his team would play. However, Middlesbrough centre-forward Micky Fenton kicked-off and the game was in progress before anyone noticed the error. To make amends, the Bees kicked-off the second half.

Wing-half Bill Harris was on the books of Swansea Town — he was born in that town on 31 October 1928 — but was released by the Welsh club after completing his National Service. Anxious to stay in football, he tried his luck with Llanelli and shone well enough in the Southern League to attract the attention of Hull City, who signed him for £2,000 in March 1950. The Tigers agreed to pay Llanelli an extra £250 if Harris won international honours and they eventually had to pay up, although by then Harris had moved to Middlesbrough. He made 145 League and Cup appearances for Hull before joining 'Boro for £15,000 in March 1954 and it was at Ayresome Park

that he was converted to inside-forward. Middlesbrough were soon relegated but, as a cultured Second Division performer, Harris won six full caps. In March 1965 he was transferred to Bradford City and was manager at Valley Parade before returning to the North-East to manage Stockton FC.

BILL HARRIS

	LEAGUE		FA CUP		FL CUP		TOTAL	
	App	Gls	App	Gls	App	Gls	App	Gls
1953-54	9	1	0	0	-	-	9	1
1954-55	41	1	1	0	-	-	42	1
1955-56	42	1	2	0	-	-	44	1
1956-57	42	8	3	1	-	-	45	9
1957-58	39	3	2	0	-	-	41	3
1958-59	36	7	1	0	-	-	37	7
1959-60	35	11	1	0	-	-	36	11
1960-61	31	7	0	0	1	0	32	7
1961-62	30	14	4	1	0	0	34	15
1962-63	15	2	0	0	1	0	16	2
1963-64	34	11	0	0	1	1	35	12
1964-65	6	3	0	0	1	0	7	3
	360	69	14	2	4	1	378	72

John Hickton was born in Birmingham but moved with his family to Chesterfield as a boy and signed for Sheffield Wednesday in January 1962. He scored eight goals from centre-forward in an FA Youth Cup game, but it was at left-back that he made his League debut, against Aston Villa in March 1964. Hickton began to score regularly in the Central League and was promoted to the first-team forward line when Wednesday were having problems up front. He responded with 21 goals in 52 appearances — he scored a hat-trick of headers against Arsenal in 1965-6 — but eventually lost his place to Jim McCalliog — he might have played at centre-half for Wednesday against Everton in the 1966 FA Cup Final. Vic Mobley had

JOHN HICKTON

been injured in the semi-final and Hickton deputized for five games, but conceded his place to Sam Ellis for the Wembley game. The Sheffield club sold him to Middlesbrough for £20,000 in September 1966 and lived to regret their decision. Hickton was 'Boro's leading scorer for six consecutive seasons and headed the Second Division scoring list three times. In 1974, he scored 'Boro's first goal in Division One for almost 21 years and then began the second phase of his Middlesbrough career, becoming a 'target man' rather than an out and out scorer. By the time he announced his intention to retire at the end of 1976-7, he had been loaned to Hull City in January and his appearances in a Middlesbrough shirt were diminishing as he played only the occasional game as a utility man. In his testimonial game, against Sunderland in April 1977, he scored three goals in a 6-1 win for Middlesbrough and ended his League career with over 200 League goals in 500-plus games. Hickton later broke a leg playing in the NASL for Fort Lauderdale and then turned down a chance to return to League soccer with Hartlepool United. He played for Whitby Town in September 1979 before finally hanging up his boots.

	LEAGUE		FA CUP		FL CUP		TOTAL	
	App	Gls	App	Gls	App	Gls	App	Gls
1966-67	40	15	5	2	0	0	45	17
1967-68	42	24	5	1	3	4	50	29
1968-69	34/3	18	2	0	1	0	37/3	18
1969-70	42	24	5	4	1	0	48	28
1970-71	41	25	3	0	2	2	46	27
1971-72	39/1	12	6	3	2	1	47/1	16
1972-73	36/2	13	1	0	4	2	41/2	15
1973-74	40	11	2	0	2	0	44	11
1974-75	39	8	6	2	5	1	50	11
1975-76	35/1	9	2	1	6	3	43/1	13
1976-77	4/5	0	0	0	0/1	0	4/6	0
1977-78	3/8	0	0	0	0/3	0	4/11	0
	395/20	159	37	13	26/4	13	458/24	185

David Hodgson, the son of a former Northern League footballer, was born in Gateshead on 6 August 1960. He had trials with Ipswich Town, Bolton Wanderers and Sheffield Wednesday, but opted for Middlesbrough and signed apprentice forms on his 16th birthday. He was playing for 'Boro's reserve side when he was 17 and made an occasional substitute appearance in the first team before establishing himself in 1978-9, although he missed some games late in the season due to a broken toe. When he was out of action, Hodgson would delight the Holgate End crowd by standing with them to watch the team. He netted a marvellous hat-trick against Spurs in December 1980, when Middlesbrough won 4-1, and although he did not score as many goals as was perhaps expected of him, he used his speed to get past defenders and set up chances for others. In 1981, Hodgson won the first of six England Under-21 caps with Middlesbrough, but in August 1982 he followed in the footsteps of Graeme Souness and Craig Johnston, joining Liverpool for £450,000. After only 28 League appearances for the Merseysiders, however, Hodgson returned to the North-East in a £125,000 transfer to Sunderland. Norwich City signed him, also for £125,000, in July 1986, but his first-team opportunities were even more restricted at Carrow Road and he was loaned to Middlesbrough in February 1987. Alas, his old sparkle was missing and his second spell was marred by being sent off against Bristol City (he had earlier been dismissed against Manchester City in 1980). After an unhappy spell with the Spanish club, Jerez, Hodgson returned to the Football League with Sheffield Wednesday in July 1988. In 1989 he was the subject of a £25,000 bid from Japanese club, Mazda.

DAVID HODGSON

	LEAGUE		FA CUP		FL CUP		TOTAL	
	App	Gls	App	Gls	App	Gls	App	Gls
1978-79	13/6	1	0	0	0	0	13/6	1
1979-80	40	7	3	1	3	0	46	8
1980-81	32	5	4	3	2	0	38	8
1981-82	31/3	3	2	0	1	0	34/3	3
1986-87	2	0	0	0	0	0	2	0
	118/9	16	9	4	6	0	133/9	20

Outside-left Eddie Holliday was a key member of Middlesbrough's explosive attack of the late 1950s, when Billy Day, Brian Clough and Alan Peacock wrought havoc amongst Second Division defences. Holliday, who was born near Barnsley on 7 June 1939, joined Middlesbrough in June 1956. He was a fast, tidy winger whose ability to send over hard, accurate crosses brought a hatful of goals for his colleagues and earned him three full England caps as well as Under-23 and Football League representative appearances. In March 1962, Holliday was transferred to Sheffield Wednesday, but after only 55 League appearances for the Owls he rejoined 'Boro in the close season of 1965. Holliday never recaptured the heights of his first spell at Ayresome Park and in the summer of 1966 he went into the Southern League with Hereford United. He returned to League soccer with Workington in February 1968, for whom he made 56 League appearances, and Peterborough United in the close season of 1969. He managed only 16 League games for Peterborough before retiring in 1970 after breaking a leg. His uncle, Colin Grainger, played for Sheffield United and England.

EDDIE HOLLIDAY

	LEAGUE		FA CUP		FL CUP		TOTAL	
	App	Gls	App	Gls	App	Gls	App	Gls
1957-58	22	1	2	1	-	-	24	2
1958-59	29	4	0	0	-	-	29	4
1959-60	41	8	1	0	-	-	42	8
1960-61	17	1	0	0	1	0	18	1
1961-62	25	3	3	2	2	1	30	6
1965-66	23	4	0	0	3	0	26	4
	157	21	6	3	6	1	169	25

114

Walter 'Squire' Holmes played his early football as an outside-right, establishing a record of 38 goals for Bede College, where he was training to be a teacher. He became a schoolmaster in 1912 and in the 1913-14 football season helped Willington Athletic, his home-town club, to win the Northern League championship. Holmes signed amateur forms for 'Boro in October 1912 and became a professional in April 1914, although the club allowed him to continue as a teacher. During World War One he saw active service in France as an RAMC officer and recovered from bronchial pneumonia to continue his football career. He became a schoolmaster in Middlesbrough in 1921, the same year that he was awarded a benefit by the club. Given a free transfer at the end of 1927-8, Holmes served Darlington for a further season until his retirement

WALTER HOLMES

in 1929. In the late 1940s he was headmaster of South End School in Middlesbrough. A teetotaller and a Methodist lay preacher, he always considered football an 'interesting sideline'. Until his death in the summer of 1978, he was a regular spectator at Ayresome Park, along with Maurice Webster, his old friend and playing colleague of the 1920s.

| | LEAGUE | | FA CUP | | TOTAL | |
	App	Gls	App	Gls	App	Gls
1914-15	10	0	0	0	10	0
1919-20	15	0	1	0	16	0
1920-21	40	0	1	0	41	0
1921-22	9	0	0	0	9	0
1922-23	19	0	2	0	21	0
1923-24	19	0	0	0	19	0
1924-25	22	0	1	0	23	0
1925-26	26	1	2	0	28	1
1926-27	7	0	0	0	7	0
	167	1	7	0	174	1

BILLY HORNER

Billy Horner was once described as 'a no-nonsense, stylish wing-half'. He was born in Middlesbrough on 7 September 1942 and joined 'Boro's groundstaff in 1957, becoming a full-time professional in the autumn of 1959. He made his League debut at left-half against Leyton Orient at Brisbane Road in March 1961. Horner served 'Boro in over 200 League and Cup appearances before being transferred to Darlington in June 1969. Many supporters thought that 'Boro manager Stan Anderson had made a mistake in allowing Horner to leave Ayresome Park, for it appeared that the player had several good years still ahead of him. He spent five years at Feethams, making a further 200-plus appearances and then managing Darlington for a while. In 1976 he began a seven-year association with Hartle-pool and was voted Fourth Division Manager of the Month in January 1980. After leaving the Victoria Ground in 1983, he had a spell as coach with York City before returning to Hartlepool for a second time in 1984. In September 1986, however, he went the way of all 'Pool managers and paid for a continued lack of success by losing his job.

| | LEAGUE | | FA CUP | | FL CUP | | TOTAL | |
	App	Gls	App	Gls	App	Gls	App	Gls
1960-61	4	0	0	0	0	0	4	0
1961-62	12	0	0	0	3	0	15	0
1962-63	25	3	3	0	1	0	29	3
1963-64	27	1	1	0	1	0	29	1
1964-65	23	3	4	0	1	0	28	3
1965-66	24/1	2	0	0	3	1	27/1	3
1966-67	42	2	5	0	1	0	48	2
1967-68	26/2	0	4	0	2/1	0	32/3	0
1968-69	1	0	0	0	0	0	1	0
	184/3	11	17	0	12/1	1	213/4	12

Full-back Jack Jennings was a railway fireman before becoming a professional footballer. He started with Wigan Borough before joining Cardiff City and toured Canada with the FA party in 1926. Jennings hit the football headlines when he was one of three Cardiff players transferred to Middlesbrough in January 1930. Chairman Phil Bach and manager Peter McWilliam travelled to Ninian Park and after making an offer for Jennings, they were told that goalkeeper Joe Hillier and reserve winger Fred Warren were also available. A fee of £850 secured all three and each player made a firm contribution to Middlesbrough's team. Jennings made his debut at Filbert Street in a 4-1 defeat at Leicester City on 1 February 1930. He overcame a cartilage operation whilst he was at Middlesbrough to become club captain, a job he held until the arrival of Tom Griffiths. In February 1934 he was named as 12th man for the Football League team to play the Scottish League at Ibrox. His goals tally was

exceptionally high for a defender because he was 'Boro's regular penalty-taker, half of his ten goals coming from the spot. In September 1936 he was transferred to Preston North End and ended his career at Northampton Town, where he became trainer. In January 1949, he was appointed trainer to the England Amateur international team. During his time with the Cobblers, his manager at Northampton was future Middlesbrough boss, Bob Dennison.

JOHN JENNINGS

	LEAGUE		FA CUP		TOTAL	
	App	Gls	App	Gls	App	Gls
1929-30	16	1	0	0	16	1
1930-31	42	3	2	0	44	3
1931-32	18	1	0	0	18	1
1932-33	36	1	4	0	40	1
1933-34	39	3	2	0	41	3
1934-35	35	1	2	0	37	1
1935-36	8	0	0	0	8	0
1936-37	1	0	0	0	1	0
	195	10	10	0	205	10

Craig Johnston was born in Johannesburg on 8 December 1960, but lived most of his life in Australia, where he first saw Middlesbrough play. 'Boro were in New South Wales during their 1975 world tour, and Johnston, keen to break into League football, later wrote to Middlesbrough for a trial, along with Manchester United, Chelsea, Bolton and Fulham. 'Boro were the first to reply but, after paying his own air-fare to England, he was rejected and returned home. The following year, however, his persistence paid off and when he repeated the journey, Middlesbrough were sufficiently impressed to sign him on. Johnston, a ball-winning midfielder who likes to move forward for a crack at goal, worked hard and damaged a pelvis in his bid to reach peak fitness. He was qualified to play international football for Australia, England and Scotland but chose England and was rewarded with two Under-21 appearances. He followed Graeme Souness to Liverpool in April 1981, for a reputed £580,000 fee, and shared in some of the Merseysiders' greatest triumphs in Europe and at home. However, in 1988, with a year of his contract still to run, he caused quite a stir by announcing his retirement because of family problems. Johnston returned to Australia, where he now works as a sports journalist. In 1989 he was on Merseyside helping to comfort the families of Hillsborough victims.

CRAIG JOHNSTON

	LEAGUE		FA CUP		FL CUP		TOTAL	
	App	Gls	App	Gls	App	Gls	App	Gls
1977-78	4/1	1	1/2	0	0	0	5/3	1
1978-79	1/1	0	0	0	0/2	0	1/3	0
1979-80	29/1	5	0	0	3	0	32/1	5
1980-81	27	10	4	0	1	0	32	10
	61/3	16	5/2	0	4/2	0	70/7	16

Since World War Two, no player has made more appearances for Middlesbrough than full-back Gordon Jones. Born at Sedgefield on 6 March 1943, he signed amateur forms for 'Boro in August 1958 and became a full-time professional in March 1960. Jones made his first appearance in January 1961, against Southampton when he travelled as 12th man. Some 20 minutes before the kick-off, Jones was told that he was to make his debut as 'Boro had decided not to risk Derek Stonehouse, who had been taken ill overnight. His first appearance came at right-back, but when the regular left-back, Mick McNeil, was transferred to Ipswich, Jones switched over to replace him. Within weeks he had won the first of nine England Under-23 caps and he was later considered to have a chance of making the 1966 World Cup squad, although Ray Wilson claimed the position before him. Jones had been chosen for the imminent Under-23 tour, but a cracked left fibula ruled him out. He made a full recovery and took over the captaincy when Ian

Gibson left. Jones skippered 'Boro to promotion from Division Three in 1967 and two years later he was awarded a testimonial. In February 1973, after 12 years with Middlesbrough, he was transferred to Darlington, for whom he made 85 League appearances. He later played for Crook Town on a tour of India and is now a successful Teesside businessman.

GORDON JONES

	LEAGUE		FA CUP		FL CUP		TOTAL	
	App	Gls	App	Gls	App	Gls	App	Gls
1960-61	17	0	0	0	1	0	18	0
1961-62	38	0	4	0	2	0	44	0
1962-63	36	0	3	0	2	0	41	0
1963-64	29	1	1	0	2	0	32	1
1964-65	41	1	4	0	1	0	46	1
1965-66	42	0	1	0	3	0	46	0
1966-67	40/2	1	5	0	2	0	47/2	1
1967-68	41	1	5	0	3	0	49	1
1968-69	38	0	2	0	1	0	41	0
1969-70	42	0	5	0	1	0	48	0
1970-71	41	0	3	0	2	1	46	1
1971-72	34	0	6	0	2	0	42	0
1972-73	18/3	0	1	0	4	0	23/3	0
	457/5	4	40	0	26	1	523/5	5

ARTHUR KAYE

At only 5ft 3½ins tall, Arthur Kaye was one of the smallest players in the Football League. Born in Barnsley on 9 May 1933, he played for England Schoolboys before joining Barnsley straight from school and signed professional forms for the Oakwell club in May 1950, on his 17th birthday. Despite the fact that Barnsley were by no means one of the game's 'glamour' clubs, he was soon capped by England Under-23s and played for the Football League. After 265 appearances for the Colliers, Kaye moved to Blackpool in May 1959, as an eventual replacement for the legendary Stanley Matthews. But Matthews just kept going and Kaye was restricted to only 38 League appearances for the Seasiders. He arrived at Middlesbrough in November 1960, for £10,000, and quickly recovered the form he had shown at Barnsley. In five years with 'Boro he was a regular goalscorer until his final move, to Colchester United in June 1965. They had just been relegated to Division Four and Kaye stayed at Layer Road for a season and a half, making 49 League appearances.

	LEAGUE		FA CUP		FL CUP		TOTAL	
	App	Gls	App	Gls	App	Gls	App	Gls
1960-61	20	3	1	0	0	0	21	3
1961-62	36	7	4	1	3	2	43	10
1962-63	40	14	3	1	2	0	45	15
1963-64	36	8	1	1	2	0	39	9
1964-65	32	6	4	1	1	0	37	7
	164	38	13	4	8	2	185	44

117

Cyril Knowles, a strong, attacking defender, played for South Elmshall District Boys before becoming a miner at Fitzwilliam, where he was born on 13 July 1944. He turned out for Monckton Colliery Welfare and had spells as a junior with both Manchester United and Wolves, where his brother, Peter, was on the books. After writing to Harold Shepherdson, asking for a trial with Middlesbrough, he was taken on as an amateur, but was on the point of leaving when Bob Dennison offered him professional terms in October 1962. The following April he made his League debut at Derby. Knowles made nearly all his 'Boro appearances at right-back, although he preferred left-back. In May 1964, Bill Nicholson signed him for Spurs for around £45,000 and whilst at White Hart Lane, Knowles won six England Under-23 caps and four full caps, making over 500 first-team appearances before retiring in 1975 with FA Cup, League Cup and UEFA Cup-winners' medals to his name. He also became something of a cult figure as the subject of the song *Nice One, Cyril*, which became a national catch-phrase. Knowles became Billy Bremner's assistant at Doncaster Rovers before Bobby Murdoch, who Knowles had met on a coaching course, appointed him Middlesbrough's reserve-team trainer-coach in 1981. He managed Darlington from May 1983 until May 1987, when he took over at Torquay United.

CYRIL KNOWLES

| | LEAGUE | | FA CUP | | FL CUP | | TOTAL | |
	App	Gls	App	Gls	App	Gls	App	Gls
1962-63	9	0	0	0	0	0	9	0
1963-64	28	0	1	0	1	0	30	0
	37	0	1	0	1	0	39	0

The following August he was Bell's Manager of the Month and took Torquay to the 1988-9 Sherpa Van Trophy Final at Wembley. But he parted company with the club in October 1989.

Brian Laws was born in Wallsend on 14 October 1961 and played for Wallsend Boys' Club before joining First Division Burnley as an apprentice. He stayed at Turf Moor for six seasons and saw the Clarets drop down two divisions before helping them win back their Second Division place. After John Bond replaced Brian Miller as Burnley manager, Laws was transferred to Huddersfield Town in 1984 for £10,000, after making more than 120 League appearances for the Turf Moor club. 'Boro boss Willie Maddren took him to Ayresome Park in March 1985 for £30,000 and he scored some spectacular goals with long-range shots from midfield. His 1986-7 season ended prematurely when he injured knee ligaments at home to Bristol Rovers in March and, at one stage, there was concern that his career might be over. But he recovered and earned a first-team recall in October 1987. Brian Clough took him to Nottingham Forest in the summer of 1988, when his fee was fixed at £120,000 by a Football League tribunal. At the City Ground, Laws took a little while to break through into the first team but won Littlewoods Cup and Simod Cup-winners' medals, although his own-goal helped Liverpool to an FA Cup Final place and cost Forest the chance of recording a Wembley treble.

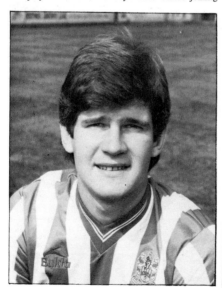

BRIAN LAWS

| | LEAGUE | | FA CUP | | FL CUP | | TOTAL | |
	App	Gls	App	Gls	App	Gls	App	Gls
1984-85	11	1	0	0	0	0	11	1
1985-86	42	2	1	0	2	0	45	2
1986-87	26	8	3	0	4	2	33	10
1987-88†	24/5	1	4/1	0	0/1	0	28/7	1
	103/5	12	8/1	0	6/1	2	117/7	14

†Also made three play-off appearances and scored one goal

Tony McAndrew was born at Lanark on 11 April 1956 and won Scottish Youth international honours after joining Middlesbrough in July 1971. He made his first-team debut in November 1973, deputizing for the injured Graeme Souness against Luton Town. It was McAndrew's solitary appearance in that record-breaking season. He scored the only hat-trick of his League career against Sheffield United in the last home game of 1975-6, his only other hat-trick being in the North Riding Senior Cup Final against South Bank. In 1976, he played for Vancouver Whitecaps in the North American Soccer League. In his own words, he was 'a naturally aggressive player'. Manager John Neal handed him the captaincy when Stuart Boam was transferred to Newcastle United in August 1979. In 1982, McAndrew rejected the contract offered by Middlesbrough and in the August of his testimonial season he joined Chelsea, who were now managed by Neal. 'Boro asked for £300,000 but the fee decided by a Football League tribunal was £92,500. Willie Maddren took him back to Teesside in September 1984 and he bolstered the defence for another two seasons, playing his last season as the club slipped into the Third Division. He looked after the juniors in March 1986, but took up an appointment as a brewery representative before the year ended, playing part-time football with Willington. He made a surprise return to League football with Hartlepool in March 1989, staying at the Victoria Ground until the end of the season. He is now on the staff at Darlington, coaching the YTS boys.

TONY McANDREW

	LEAGUE		FA CUP		FL CUP		TOTAL	
	App	Gls	App	Gls	App	Gls	App	Gls
1973-74	1	0	0	0	0	0	1	0
1974-75	1	0	0	0	0	0	1	0
1975-76	12	3	1	0	0/2	0	13/2	3
1976-77	38/1	1	3/1	0	1	1	42/2	2
1977-78	41	0	4	1	4	0	49	1
1978-79	38	1	2	0	1	0	41	1
1979-80	39	1	3	0	3	0	45	1
1980-81	36/1	3	5	0	1	0	42/1	3
1981-82	39	4	2	0	3	0	44	4
1984-85	32	0	2	1	0	0	34	1
1985-86	34	2	1	0	2	0	37	2
	311/2	15	23/1	2	15/2	1	349/5	18

JIMMY McCLELLAND

Dysart-born Jimmy McClelland was an old-fashioned, centre-forward who liked nothing better than to run with the ball. Long-legged, fair-haired McClelland played for Raith Rovers before his transfer to Southend United just before World War One. Middlesbrough manager Herbert Bamlett took McClelland to Ayresome Park in March 1925, in a player exchange which saw Morris Hick go to Southend. He scored all Middlesbrough's goals in their 5-1 FA Cup victory over Leeds United in January 1926 and was chaired off the pitch by his colleagues at the end of that marvellous feat. He had another reason to remember that day, for his son Charles, who played post-war football for Blackburn Rovers, was born. In the same season, McClelland established a new individual club scoring record of 32 goals, beating George Elliott's 31, although Elliott's were in the First Division. In September 1926, McClelland was injured in a bruising game against South Shields and for the next game, George Camsell took his place and began his magnificent career in earnest. McClelland returned to the team later that season but was now mostly a reserve (he was a prolific scorer for 'Boro's second string). In March 1928 he was happy to agree to a transfer to Bolton Wanderers, where he won an FA Cup-winners' medal in 1929.

	LEAGUE		FA CUP		TOTAL	
	App	Gls	App	Gls	App	Gls
1924-25	4	1	0	0	4	1
1925-26	38	32	2	6	40	38
1926-27	20	5	0	0	20	5
1927-28	19	4	2	0	21	4
	81	42	4	6	85	48

Alex McCrae played for Haddington Juniors before signing for Heart of Midlothian in 1941. He joined Charlton Athletic in May 1947, for a reported fee of £7,500, but his style did not fit in at The Valley and he made only 43 League appearances for the London club. McCrae turned down the chance of joining Sheffield United, a few days before Middlesbrough stepped in with an offer of £10,000 in October 1948. In his early days at Ayresome Park he could not find his best form and after a few games he was dropped from the side. He won back his place after some sterling displays for the Reserves in the North-Eastern League. McCrae, who was born in Stoneyburn on 2 January 1920, was described as 'a natural left-footed player with a lethal shot' and favoured 'the short, ground pass'. He also possessed 'quick acceleration and will play anywhere in the forward line but inside-left is his favourite position'. After three years at Ayresome Park, McCrae was transferred to Falkirk in March 1953 and became player-coach of Ballymena United in

September 1957. He returned to Scotland as manager of Stirling Albion in January 1960. Within two months, however, he was back at Falkirk, where he stayed until April 1965. In November 1966, he was appointed a Middlesbrough scout in Scotland.

ALEX McCRAE

	LEAGUE		FA CUP		TOTAL	
	App	Gls	App	Gls	App	Gls
1948-49	20	2	0	0	20	2
1949-50	36	14	4	2	40	16
1950-51	32	21	1	0	33	21
1951-52	24	6	2	0	26	6
1952-53	10	4	1	0	11	4
	122	47	8	2	130	49

ERIC McMORDIE

Alexander McMordie, always known as Eric, was born in Belfast on 12 August 1946 and played local soccer before having a trial with Manchester United — at the same time as George Best — when he was 15. Homesick, both lads went back to Ulster and, although Sir Matt Busby asked both to return to Old Trafford, only Best obliged, whilst McMordie turned out as an amateur with the Dundela club. When McMordie was

18, Middlesbrough's Irish-based scout, Matt Willis, recommended him to 'Boro manager Raich Carter. In 1964, McMordie was signed as a professional and made his debut, as an inside-forward, during the club's relegation season of 1965-6. The team bounced back into the Second Division, but he made less than 20 appearances and in 1967-8, although he started the season in the team, he did not establish himself as a regular until December. First selected for Northern Ireland for a match against Israel, his international debut was delayed when the Israelis asked for a late postponement. The first of 21 full caps eventually came against Israel in Jaffa in September 1968. In 1972-3, he lost his place in Middlesbrough's team due to a stomach complaint. When Jack Charlton arrived during the summer of 1973, the new manager was not impressed by McMordie's style and the Irishman made only seven appearances in 'Boro's successful promotion push of 1973-4. He was loaned to Sheffield Wednesday in October 1974 but, despite six goals in nine League games, nothing permanent came from his stay at Hillsborough. He signed for York City in May 1975, then Hartlepool United in December 1976, playing almost 50 games for each club. McMordie quit the game in 1977 and is now in business on Teesside.

	LEAGUE		FA CUP		FL CUP		TOTAL	
	App	Gls	App	Gls	App	Gls	App	Gls
1965-66	17	4	1	0	3	1	21	5
1966-67	19	0	3	0	0	0	22	0
1967-68	29/1	1	0/1	0	1	1	30/2	2
1968-69	39	6	2	0	1	0	42	6
1969-70	28/4	3	4	1	1	0	33/4	4
1970-71	30/3	1	3	0	1	0	34/3	1
1971-72	36/1	3	6	0	0	0	42/1	3
1972-73	26	4	1	0	4	0	31	4
1973-74	7/1	0	0	0	0	0	7/1	0
	231/10	22	20/1	1	11	2	262/11	25

Mick McNeil, who was born in Middlesbrough on 7 February 1940, played inside-left for Middlesbrough Boys. After leaving school he turned out for the works' team of Cargo Fleet, where he was studying to be an analytical chemist. Jimmy Gordon, who was then 'Boro's coach, spotted his potential and McNeil signed professional forms for the club in May 1957. His League debut was at left-half against Brighton, but he lost his place upon the arrival of Ray Yeoman from Northampton Town. Bill Harris was switched to right-half to accommodate Yeoman and McNeil went back to the Reserves. Injury to centre-half Bryan Phillips earned him a brief recall before he established himself at full-back, the position in which he would be capped for England. Picked for an FA XI against the Army at Newcastle, McNeil followed this up with Under-23 caps. He made an impressive debut against France

MICK McNEIL

	LEAGUE		FA CUP		FL CUP		TOTAL	
	App	Gls	App	Gls	App	Gls	App	Gls
1958-59	7	0	0	0	-	-	7	0
1959-60	42	0	1	0	-	-	43	0
1960-61	39	1	1	0	1	0	41	1
1961-62	38	1	4	0	3	0	45	1
1962-63	32	1	3	0	1	0	36	1
1963-64	20	0	0	0	1	0	21	0
	178	3	9	0	6	0	193	3

at Roker Park and then went on tour to East Germany, Israel and Poland. He was a forceful defender who could carry the ball through to set up attacks and his gritty displays earned him his full England debut in Belfast. Eight further full caps quickly followed. McNeil moved to Ipswich Town in July 1964 and was in the Suffolk club's side which won promotion to Division One in 1968. He retired in 1971 to run a successful sports outfitting business in Suffolk.

WILF MANNION

Wilf Mannion is undoubtedly the most famous player in the history of Middlesbrough Football Club. Born at South Bank on 16 May 1918, Mannion played in the Teesside League with South Bank St Peter's before signing for 'Boro in September 1936. During the war he served in the Auxiliary Fire Service before being called up for military service and it was in 1941 that he played his first game in an England shirt, against Scotland in an unofficial international. Demobbed in 1946, Wilf Mannion went on to become one of the finest inside-forwards of the post-war period. In the days of Carter, Hagan and Shackleton, many critics reckoned that Mannion, the 'Golden Boy' of football, was the best. He had a marvellous sense of anticipation and one contemporary description called him 'a ball-playing genius with a classic body-swerve, who has the ability to work in a confined area'. Altogether he won 26 full England caps and scored twice for Great

Britain when they beat the Rest of Europe 6-1 in 1947. At the start of 1947-8 he refused to re-sign for 'Boro and made plans to move to Oldham, to go into business there and play for Oldham Athletic. Middlesbrough, realizing Mannion's determination, agreed but placed a £25,000 transfer fee on his head. Oldham could find only £15,000 and the player eventually returned to help 'Boro avoid relegation. He retired after Middlesbrough eventually dropped into Division Two at the end of 1953-4 but was persuaded to return to League football with Hull City. Hull paid £5,000 for Mannion's signature and when he made his debut on Boxing Day 1954, the Boothferry Park attendance doubled from the average figure to nearly 40,000. He spent only one season at Hull and, during that time, trouble was brewing over newspaper articles he had written during his 'retirement'. The Football League ordered him to explain stories of alleged illegal payments to players but Mannion declined and in June 1955 the League suspended him until he complied. Instead, Mannion went to play for non-League Poole Town and later turned out for King's Lynn, Haverhill Rovers and Earlstown until his final retirement in 1962.

	LEAGUE		FA CUP		TOTAL	
	App	Gls	App	Gls	App	Gls
1936-37	2	0	0	0	2	0
1937-38	22	4	3	1	25	5
1938-39	38	14	4	0	42	14
1946-47	37	18	7	5	44	23
1947-48	35	1	3	1	38	2
1948-49	17	4	0	0	17	4
1949-50	38	6	3	1	41	7
1950-51	35	14	1	0	36	14
1951-52	39	11	3	2	42	13
1952-53	41	18	1	0	42	18
1953-54	37	9	2	1	39	10
	341	99	27	11	368	110

Immediately after World War One, John Marshall — he was always known as Jock — was hailed as 'the best right-back in the world'. He first played for Shettleston and signed for Middlesbrough from St Mirren in November 1919 for a fee of £1,800. He was also known as the 'ferro-concrete back' and was certainly a tough character. It was alleged that he could kick the ball almost the length of the field, without taking a run at it. In 1922, with six full Scottish caps to his name (and one Victory international appearance), he asked for a transfer but 'Boro would not release him and he was suspended by the Football League after taking part in a five-a-side game in Scotland. Towards the end of 1922-3, he was also suspended by the club for leaving the district without permission when he returned to Scotland. The suspension was eventually lifted but the rift between club and player was too great and he was finally given a transfer in April 1923. After declining to join Preston North End, Marshall opted for Llanelly and became the only player this century to win a Scottish cap whilst with a non-League club. He later set up in business in New York and in 1926 was playing for Belmont FC.

	LEAGUE		FA CUP		TOTAL	
	App	Gls	App	Gls	App	Gls
1919-20	24	0	2	0	26	0
1920-21	36	0	1	0	37	0
1921-22	33	0	1	0	34	0
1922-23	23	0	1	0	24	0
	116	0	5	0	121	0

JOCK MARSHALL

JACK MARTIN

Fair-haired Sunderland-born Jack Martin had trials at Portsmouth but was turned down by the Fratton Park club. Despite this set-back, he pursued his ambition to become a professional footballer and was turning out for Horden Colliery Welfare as a 'natural ball-playing wing-half' when Middlesbrough manager Peter McWilliam spotted his potential. McWilliam signed Martin in March 1932, giving the Horden club a £10 donation. The player had to wait a year for his League debut for 'Boro, playing in a 4-0 home victory over Blackburn Rovers on 6 May 1933, a game which also heralded the debut of Micky Fenton. Martin was a first-team regular until the outbreak of war in September 1939 and was one of the mainstays of a makeshift 'Boro team during the days of wartime regional football. He was injured at Bradford on 28 October 1944 and took almost a year to recover. In September 1945 he had to undergo an operation on his knee and was then unfortunate enough to tear a leg muscle. Fully recovered, however, Martin was re-signed as a professional in October that year, but was freed at the end of the season, when he was 33. He later became trainer of Huddersfield Town and then Doncaster Rovers.

	LEAGUE		FA CUP		TOTAL	
	App	Gls	App	Gls	App	Gls
1932-33	1	0	0	0	1	0
1933-34	32	0	2	0	34	0
1934-35	16	1	0	0	16	1
1935-36	34	1	2	0	36	1
1936-37	25	0	1	1	26	1
1937-38	16	0	2	0	18	0
1938-39	5	0	1	0	6	0
	129	3	8	0	137	3

Methil-born goalkeeper Jimmy Mathieson was playing for Raith Rovers when he was recommended to Middlesbrough by Peter McWilliam, before McWilliam became manager at Ayresome Park. The Middlesbrough board took Mathieson on without even seeing him play, signing him for £1,200 in June 1926, and he proved to be good value. In the next five years he missed only seven games after making his League debut at Stamford Bridge in August 1926, a game which Chelsea won 3-0. Mathieson was 'Boro's regular goalkeeper as Middlesbrough experienced promotion, relegation and promotion in successive seasons. In the early 1930s, Third Division Brentford swooped for several Middlesbrough players — Johnny Holliday, Bill Scott, Ernie Muttitt etc — and Mathieson was one of those to go to Griffin Park when he joined the Bees in May 1934. Brentford, with several former 'Boro players in their side, won promotion to the First Division and remained there for many seasons. Mathieson, meanwhile, returned to Scotland and signed for Queen of the South.

JIMMY MATHIESON

	LEAGUE		FA CUP		TOTAL	
	App	Gls	App	Gls	App	Gls
1926-27	42	0	3	0	45	0
1927-28	42	0	3	0	45	0
1928-29	40	0	3	0	43	0
1929-30	41	0	6	0	47	0
1930-31	38	0	2	0	40	0
1931-32	30	0	2	0	32	0
1932-33	12	0	0	0	12	0
	245	0	19	0	264	0

DAVID MILLS

David Mills was born in Whitby on 6 December 1951 but was brought up in Thornaby. An England Schoolboy international, he attracted several clubs, including Hull City, Stoke City, Manchester United, Burnley and Middlesbrough, but a back injury kept him out of football for almost a year. Fully recovered, he signed for Middlesbrough in July 1968, joining the club at the same time as Willie Maddren. His first-team debut was as a substitute towards the close of 1968-9 and he scored on his full debut, at Swindon in 1969-70. Capped eight times by England Under-23s, he first came to the attention of the selectors during

'Boro's 1973-4 Second Division championship season, when he showed his flair as a speedy forward. In December 1976, Mills asked for a move and was transfer-listed at £200,000. He remained at the club for a further two years before becoming Britain's first half-million pound footballer on his transfer to West Brom in January 1979. He scored on his first full appearance for Albion but, despite the huge sum invested in him, he was not given many opportunities to prove himself at The Hawthorns and was loaned to Newcastle United. Sheffield Wednesday paid only £30,000 for Mills, but he stayed only briefly at Hillsborough, before returning to Newcastle on a permanent transfer. In June 1984, Willie Maddren re-signed him for 'Boro on a free transfer and he stayed for one season, finishing top scorer with 14 goals. After coaching Middlesbrough's juniors, Mills went to play for Northern League Whitby Town. He was seriously injured in a car crash on Tyneside, which claimed the life of his father. Now recovered, David Mills works as a representative for a printing firm.

	LEAGUE		FA CUP		FL CUP		TOTAL	
	App	Gls	App	Gls	App	Gls	App	Gls
1968-69	0/1	0	0	0	0	0	0/1	0
1969-70	1/4	2	0	0	0	0	1/4	2
1970-71	10/9	1	0	0	0/1	0	10/10	1
1971-72	25/2	8	6	1	0	0	31/2	9
1972-73	37	5	1	0	4	2	42	7
1973-74	38/1	11	2	1	1	0	41/1	12
1974-75	36	8	6	1	3	2	45	11
1975-76	38	10	2	0	6	2	46	12
1976-77	41/1	15	5	3	1	0	47/1	18
1977-78	35	10	5	4	4	2	44	16
1978-79	17	6	0	0	2	0	19	6
1984-85	31/1	14	2	0	2	0	35/1	14
	309/19	90	29	10	23/1	8	361/20	108

It was Scottish international inside-forward Billy Steele who unearthed the talent of Neil Mochan. Mochan, who was born at Larbert, Stirlingshire, on 6 April 1927, was turning out for a junior club called Dunipace Thistle when Steele was playing for Morton. Small, but solidly built, Mochan had superb ball-control and possessed a snap shot which often surprised goalkeepers. He joined Morton in April 1944 and 'Boro paid £14,000 for his signature in May 1951. He played for the club against Partizan Belgrade in that year's Festival of Britain match, but made only 38 League appearances before being transferred to Celtic in May 1953 for £8,000. Despite his relatively few appearances for 'Boro, he had a good strike rate of 14 goals. He won three full Scottish caps, against Norway, Austria and Hungary in 1954, and one 'B' cap, as well as lifting Scottish League, Scottish Cup and Scottish League Cup winners' medals at Parkhead. He was something of a utility player at Parkhead and even played at left-back before moving to Dundee United in November 1963. He later played for Raith Rovers and was Celtic's trainer when they won the European Cup in 1967.

NEIL MOCHAN

	LEAGUE		FA CUP		TOTAL	
	App	Gls	App	Gls	App	Gls
1951-52	29	12	1	0	30	12
1952-53	9	2	0	0	9	2
	38	14	1	0	39	14

TONY MOWBRAY

Tony Mowbray was born at Saltburn on 22 November 1963 and as a boy he stood on the Holgate End at Ayresome Park and cheered his hero, John Hickton. Mowbray captained the Langbaurgh and Cleveland Under-15 sides, when Steve Smelt was in charge of the team, and also turned out for Grangetown Boys, Nunthorpe Athletic and Guisborough Town as well as playing rugby for his school. In 1978, his most cherished dream came true when he signed schoolboy forms for Middlesbrough and two years later he became an apprentice. The youngster had enjoyed a fine career as a schoolboy and was called up for an England trial, but broke a leg in the first practice game. Mowbray, a 6ft 1in tall central defender, made his League debut for 'Boro in September 1982, in a 1-1 draw at St James' Park, and since then has shared in all of Middlesbrough's ups and downs. In the summer of 1989 he received international recognition when he was chosen for the England 'B' tour, along with his Middlesbrough colleague, Gary Pallister. Mowbray played in all three games, against Switzerland, Norway and Iceland.

	LEAGUE		FA CUP		FL CUP		TOTAL	
	App	Gls	App	Gls	App	Gls	App	Gls
1982-83	25/1	0	3	0	2	0	30/1	0
1983-84	33/2	1	3	0	0/1	0	36/3	1
1984-85	40	3	2	0	2	0	44	3
1985-86	35	4	0	0	2	0	37	4
1986-87	46	7	3	0	4	0	53	7
1987-88†	44	3	5	1	4	1	53	5
1988-89	37	3	1	0	2	0	40	3
	260/3	21	17	1	16/1	1	293/4	23

†Also made four play-off appearances.

Fishburn-born Irving Nattrass joined Newcastle United as an apprentice and became a full-time professional in July 1970, his first-team debut coming as a substitute against Derby County in March 1971. The highlight of his career at St James' Park was a Wembley appearance in the 1976 League Cup Final, when United lost to Manchester City. While at Newcastle, Nattrass missed out on several England Under-23 caps, due to injury, and was also forced to miss England's trip to South America in 1977, when he might have won a full cap. He also missed out on United's run to the 1974 FA Cup Final, due to a knee-ligament injury. When Newcastle lost their First Division status in 1979, Nattrass wanted to stay in the top flight and an independent tribunal fixed his fee at £475,000, still a 'Boro club record. An Achilles tendon injury delayed his debut and in the following six months he suffered three hair-line fractures of the leg. Despite all this, Nattrass still managed almost 200 League and Cup games in six years with Middlesbrough and played in nine different positions for the club.

	LEAGUE		FA CUP		FL CUP		TOTAL	
	App	Gls	App	Gls	App	Gls	App	Gls
1979-80	10/3	0	0	0	1	0	11/3	0
1980-81	29/2	1	5	0	2	0	36/2	1
1981-82	27	0	2	0	2	0	31	0
1982-83	29	1	5	0	1/1	0	35/1	1
1983-84	42	0	3	0	2	0	47	0
1984-85	30	0	2	0	2	0	34	0
1985-86	19	0	1	0	0	0	20	0
	186/5	2	18	0	10/1	0	214/6	2

IRVING NATTRASS

MEL NURSE

Centre-half Mel Nurse was born in Swansea on 11 October 1937 and won Welsh Schoolboy international honours. Linked to Swansea Town via the juniors, he signed professional forms for the Swans in June 1955. Nurse spent seven years at Vetch Field, during which time he won two Welsh Under-23 caps, five full caps and played in over 150 League games. Middlesbrough paid £25,000 for the 6ft, 13st defender in September 1962 and Nurse made his debut in a 4-3 victory at Grimsby Town. He 'added stability to any defence and instilled confidence amongst his fellow defenders'. Seven full Welsh caps followed whilst with Middlesbrough and as a commanding figure in the defence he was soon appointed 'Boro skipper. One of his biggest regrets must have been scoring the goal which sent his previous club, Swansea, crashing into Division Three. His wife wanted to return nearer to Wales and in August 1965 he was transferred to Swindon Town for £15,000. Nurse renewed his association with Swansea in June 1968 and in 1970 he went into non-League football with the Suffolk club, Bury, before finishing his career with Merthyr Tydfil, for whom he was playing when he suffered a broken leg.

	LEAGUE		FA CUP		FL CUP		TOTAL	
	App	Gls	App	Gls	App	Gls	App	Gls
1962-63	32	0	3	0	0	0	35	0
1963-64	37	1	1	0	2	0	40	1
1964-65	41	6	4	1	1	0	46	7
1965-66	3	1	0	0	0	0	3	1
	113	8	8	1	3	0	124	9

Bryan 'Taffy' Orritt was born in the small Welsh village of Cwm-Y-Glo on 22 February 1937 and was one of the few Welsh-speaking players in the Football League. As a boy he attended Caernarfon Grammar School and his first club was the one with the longest name in the game, now shortened to Llanfair PG FC. At the age of 17 he was playing for Bangor in the Cheshire League and was twice chosen as reserve for the Welsh international youth team. Orritt turned professional with Birmingham City in January 1956 and went on to make exactly 100 League appearances for them. He won three Welsh Under-23 caps, played for the Army during his National Service and appeared for Birmingham in the 1960 and 1961 Inter-Cities Fairs Cup Finals. He was serving a seven-day suspension, following an incident whilst playing for Birmingham City Reserves, when he was transferred to Middlesbrough on 1 March 1962. Orrittt was Middlesbrough's first playing substitute, perhaps a fitting honour for a utility man who played in all 11 positions for the club. He emigrated to South Africa to play for Johannesburg and still lives in that country, although he is a frequent visitor to Britain.

	LEAGUE		FA CUP		FL CUP		TOTAL	
	App	Gls	App	Gls	App	Gls	App	Gls
1961-62	12	3	0	0	0	0	12	3
1962-63	35	8	3	1	2	0	40	9
1963-64	37	6	1	0	2	0	40	6
1964-65	22	2	0	0	1	0	23	2
1965-66	9/3	3	0	0	1	0	10/3	3
	115/3	22	4	1	6	0	125/3	23

BRYAN ORRITT

HEINE OTTO

Heine Otto, who was born in the Netherlands on 24 August 1954, worked for his father-in-law in the gold business, and then in a whisky distillery before becoming a professional footballer. Otto played for Twente Enschede, replacing Arnold Muhren who had left for Ipswich Town. Capped several times for Holland Under-23s, Otto won one full cap, playing the last 20 minutes of a game against Yugoslavia after coming on as a substitute. In the summer of 1981, he played in three friendly games for Middlesbrough with a view to a permanent transfer and impressed 'Boro manager Bobby Murdoch enough to be signed on a two-year contract in August that year. He made a scoring debut in the Football League, against Spurs at Ayresome Park, although 'Boro lost 3-1. A midfielder-cum-striker, Otto was the club's top scorer with a meagre five goals when 'Boro dropped into the Second Division in 1982. He turned down an extension of his existing contract in May 1985 and returned to Holland the following month, to play for Den Haag, a Dutch Second Division side.

	LEAGUE		FA CUP		FL CUP		TOTAL	
	App	Gls	App	Gls	App	Gls	App	Gls
1981-82	40	4	2	1	3	0	45	5
1982-83	40/2	9	5	1	2	1	47/2	11
1983-84	42	7	3	0	2	1	47	8
1984-85	41/1	4	2	0	2	0	45/1	4
	163/3	24	12	2	9	2	184/3	28

Gary Pallister, who was born in Ramsgate on 30 June 1965, was a fine all-round schoolboy sportsman, who played basketball for Cleveland and cricket for Stockton. Football, though, was his first love and he signed as a junior for Billingham Town in the Northern League. He went to Middlesbrough for a trial when Malcolm Allison was manager but played only one Central League game before being released. Willie Maddren, 'Boro's coach at the time and Allison's eventual successor, kept in touch with his progress and a year later, Pallister, now a stronger, fitter player rejoined Middlesbrough. Richard Corden, a local businessman and later a Middlesbrough director, paid Pallister's wages for a year during Middlesbrough's financial crisis, affording the club the opportunity to hang on to the tall defender. Early in his career, he made seven League appearances on loan to Darlington. Pallister was the first player from Division Two to be chosen by Bobby Robson for the full England squad, but Bruce Rioch pulled him out of the party in order to prepare for the play-off games. He eventually won his first full England cap in March 1988, against Hungary. After Middlesbrough dropped into Division Two,

GARY PALLISTER

	LEAGUE		FA CUP		FL CUP		TOTAL	
	App	Gls	App	Gls	App	Gls	App	Gls
1985-86	28	0	1	0	1	0	30	0
1986-87	44	1	3	0	3	0	50	1
1987-88†	44	3	5	1	4	0	53	4
1988-89	37	1	1	0	2	0	40	1
	153	5	10	1	10	0	173	6

†Also made four play-off appearances

speculation increased as to whether they could hold on to such a talented player. He ended the 1988-9 season on England's 'B' tour, with Middlesbrough skipper Tony Mowbray, before Manchester United paid £2.3m for his signature.

Gary Parkinson was born at Thornaby on 10 January 1981 and played for St Patrick's School and graduated to the Cleveland and Stockton Boys teams before joining Everton as an apprentice. The youngster soon became homesick on Merseyside and returned home within three weeks of arriving at Goodison. In 1983-4, however, he was given a second chance of League football when he joined Middlesbrough as an apprentice on the Youth Training Scheme. He soon fitted in and was a key figure in the Reserves' successful bid to win promotion to the First Division of the Central League. Parkinson made his Football League debut as a raw recruit in the 'off-on' game against Port Vale at Hartlepool's Victoria Ground, at the start of 'Boro's Third Division championship-winning season. He made a major contribution to that success and in 1987-8 regained his place, after being suspended, to play another vital role in another Middlesbrough promotion. In January 1989 he missed two games through injury and was then dropped for the Coventry game. He recovered from a knee injury in March to return to the team and became the regular penalty-taker. Still learning his trade, Parkinson should benefit by having skipper Tony Mowbray alongside him in defence.

GARY PARKINSON

	LEAGUE		FA CUP		FL CUP		TOTAL	
	App	Gls	App	Gls	App	Gls	App	Gls
1986-87	46	0	3	0	4	0	53	0
1987-88†	35/3	0	5	0	4	0	44/3	0
1988-89	36	2	0	0	2	0	38	2
	117/3	2	8	0	10	0	135/3	2

†Also made four play-off appearances.

Alan Peacock, 6ft tall and an immaculate header of a football, was born in North Ormesby on 29 October 1937 and attended Lawson Street School. He signed professional forms for Middlesbrough in November 1954 but did not make his League debut until a year later — the same season as Brian Clough's first game — in a 7-2 defeat at Bristol Rovers. Awarded England Youth honours in 1956, Peacock starred at inside-left for three seasons (National Service interrupting his career) and then formed a twin spearhead with goalscoring sensation, Clough. Their partnership produced many goals but the two players did not get on well with each other. After Clough's departure to Sunderland, Peacock was switched to centre-forward and the move proved so successful that he was chosen for England's 1962 World Cup party. Selected to play against Austria, he suffered a fractured cheekbone only 90 seconds into the derby game at Roker Park in March 1962. The injury jinx continued when he damaged his knee before joining the World Cup party but he succeeded in making his full England debut in the World Cup Finals in Chile. In December 1963, Peacock

ALAN PEACOCK

	LEAGUE		FA CUP		FL CUP		TOTAL	
	App	Gls	App	Gls	App	Gls	App	Gls
1955-56	6	2	0	0	0	0	6	2
1956-57	4	1	0	0	0	0	4	1
1957-58	22	15	2	2	0	0	24	17
1958-59	34	19	1	0	0	0	35	19
1959-60	35	13	1	0	0	0	36	13
1960-61	34	15	1	0	1	1	36	16
1961-62	34	24	4	4	3	4	41	32
1962-63	40	31	3	2	1	0	44	33
1963-64	9	5	1	0	2	3	12	8
	218	125	13	8	7	8	238	141

lost his 'Boro place through injury but was fit enough to join Leeds United in February 1964, for £55,000. With Leeds he won a Division Two championship medal, played in the 1965 FA Cup Final and won two more caps. A move to Plymouth followed in November 1967, but a troublesome knee injury forced his retirement in March 1968. He returned to Teesside, became a successful businessman and now lives in Carlton.

STEPHEN PEARS

Goalkeeper Stephen Pears was born at Brandon on 22 January 1962 and played schoolboy football for Ushaw Moor. He had trials with Middlesbrough before joining Manchester United as a 14-year-old on associate schoolboy forms and spent nine years at Old Trafford, where he was understudy to England goalkeeper Gary Bailey. Pears won his first-team chance at Old Trafford when Bailey broke a finger in training, but opportunities were few and in November 1983, Malcolm Allison took him to Second Division Middlesbrough on a month's loan. An appeal was made to raise the £80,000 to make the transfer permanent, but the target was not reached and Pears returned to United and was offered a two-year contract. Willie Maddren eventually secured Pears for 'Boro in June 1985 but his fine displays could not prevent the club falling into Division Three. Pears, though, was one of the mainstays of Middlesbrough's fight-back before injury and loss of form saw him lose his place to Kevin Poole. Pears ended the 1988-9 season out of the team after a hernia operation but signed a new three-year contract in July 1989. He also runs a successful landscaping business.

	LEAGUE		FA CUP		FL CUP		TOTAL	
	App	Gls	App	Gls	App	Gls	App	Gls
1983-84	12	0	2	0	0	0	14	0
1985-86	38	0	1	0	2	0	41	0
1986-87	46	0	3	0	4	0	53	0
1987-88†	43	0	4	0	4	0	51	0
1988-89	26	0	1	0	2	0	29	0
	165	0	11	0	12	0	188	0
†Also made four play-off appearances								

Billy Pease served with the Royal Northumberland Fusiliers in World War One, then joined Leeds City, his home-town club, as an amateur. After City were expelled from the Football League in October 1919, Pease signed for Northampton Town, who gained entry into the newly-formed Third Division in 1920. He was a speedy winger who could run hard with the ball before surprising opponents by cutting inside to try a shot at goal. Middlesbrough manager Herbert Bamlett bought his services for £2,000 on 18 May 1926 and Pease made his debut at outside-right on the opening day of the new season in Middlesbrough's 3-0 defeat at Stamford Bridge. During the Second Division championship-winning season of 1926-7, he confided in his pal, Jacky Carr, telling him that he had a date with a girl and would like to get away from the game early, so he would feign injury. Sure enough, during the game against South Shields, Pease was helped off the field — but he had broken his collarbone and was out for the rest of the season. As a Second Division player he was capped for England against Wales in February 1927 and he toured South Africa with the FA team in 1929. Transferred to Luton Town in June

BILLY PEASE

	LEAGUE		FA CUP		TOTAL	
	App	Gls	App	Gls	App	Gls
1926-27	30	23	3	2	33	25
1927-28	41	19	2	0	43	19
1928-29	35	27	3	1	38	28
1929-30	39	12	6	0	45	12
1930-31	34	12	1	0	35	12
1931-32	32	5	2	0	34	5
1932-33	10	1	0	0	10	1
	221	99	17	3	238	102

1933 for £500, he became a publican in Middlesbrough after his retirement from the game, then worked at nearby ICI Wilton in the late 1940s and coached Redcar Albion in his spare time. Billy Pease was 56 when he died on 2 October 1955 and is buried in Redcar cemetery.

Fred Pentland was born in Wolverhampton on 18 September 1883 and played for Avondale Juniors before graduating to the Football League with Small Heath (later Birmingham City) in August 1900. He moved to Blackpool in 1903 before returning to First Division football with Blackburn Rovers the same year. He moved to Brentford in May 1906, but only a year later he found himself at Queen's Park Rangers, then a force in the Southern League. Pentland joined 'Boro towards the end of the 1907-08 season, for £350, a record receipt for QPR. He won five England caps during his stay at Middlesbrough, the last three coming during a tour of Hungary and Austria. He moved to Halifax early in February 1913, before joining Stoke in the same year. He was coaching in Germany when World War One broke out in August 1914 and was interned for the duration, along with another former Middlesbrough player, Steve Bloomer. A telegram received in England via the Netherlands FA stated that he was allowed to 'go about as he likes, but he cannot leave Germany'. After the war, he coached in France and then spent 15 years in Spain, coaching Athletic Bilbao until the outbreak of the Civil War in 1936. On his return to England he joined the coaching staff at Brentford, then managed Barrow from January 1938 until World War Two was declared in September 1939.

FRED PENTLAND

	LEAGUE		FA CUP		TOTAL	
	App	Gls	App	Gls	App	Gls
1908-09	28	2	1	0	29	2
1909-10	33	2	1	0	34	2
1910-11	30	7	2	0	32	7
	91	11	4	0	95	11

Jim Platt comes from a footballing family. His father played for Ballymena United and his brother, John, was with Cliftonville. Jim, who was born at Ballymoney on 26 January 1952, was a wing-half at school but had turned to goalkeeping by the time he was 16 and playing for Ballymena. He had a three-week trial at Liverpool but the Reds had just signed Ray Clemence from Scunthorpe United. Platt won Irish Amateur caps and an Irish FA Cup runners-up medal before joining Middlesbrough for £7,000 in May 1970. After ten League appearances, 'Boro had to give Ballymena a further £3,000 but Platt soon established himself as one of the best post-war goalkeepers to come from Ireland. He displaced out-of-form Willie Whigham, making his League debut in a 1-0 home victory over Blackpool, and overcame homesickness to make the position his own for almost eight seasons. In 1971-2 he was voted 'Boro's Player of the Year. He was almost ever-present in the Middlesbrough side that won the 1973-4 Second Division championship. When promotion was assured, Jack Charlton blooded Pat Cuff, who had waited patiently for six years for his first chance. The first of 20 Northern Ireland caps won with Middlesbrough came in March 1976, when he came on as substitute against Israel in Tel Aviv. After a much-publicized row with Jack Charlton over tactics, Platt eventually lost his place and with the arrival of Jim Stewart from Kilmarnock in May 1978, he must have thought his first-team days were numbered. Stewart was the regular 'keeper for the start of 1978-9 and Platt did not return to the side until the following March. In August he was loaned to Billy Horner's Fourth Division Hartlepool United, playing 13 League games. He had a further loan spell in November, with Cardiff. Platt was unfortunate to have played at the same time as Pat Jennings and Willie McFaul but he was in goal in 1980 when Northern Ireland clinched the Home International Championship for the first time since 1914. Back in the Middlesbrough side, he was voted the North-East's Player of the Year for 1980-81 and was awarded a testimonial game against Sunderland in September 1981. Alas, things had turned sour between the player and club towards the end of the season, but his transfer request was turned down by the Middlesbrough board. He played once in the 1982 World Cup Finals in Spain and with Middlesbrough back in Division Two, was named club captain for his last full season of 1982-3. Kelham O'Hanlon replaced Platt in the Middlesbrough goal and he was appointed junior coach, but in August 1983 he returned to Ballymena United on a three-year contract as part-time player-manager. He runs a printing business in Belfast and is an occasional visitor to Ayresome Park.

JIM PLATT

	LEAGUE		FA CUP		FL CUP		TOTAL	
	App	Gls	App	Gls	App	Gls	App	Gls
1971-72	33	0	6	0	0	0	39	0
1972-73	42	0	1	0	4	0	47	0
1973-74	40	0	2	0	3	0	45	0
1974-75	42	0	6	0	5	0	53	0
1975-76	41	0	2	0	6	0	49	0
1976-77	24	0	0	0	1	0	25	0
1977-78	22	0	5	0	4	0	31	0
1978-79	15	0	0	0	0	0	15	0
1979-80	37	0	3	0	3	0	43	0
1980-81	40	0	5	0	2	0	47	0
1981-82	42	0	2	0	3	0	47	0
1982-83	23	0	2	0	2	0	27	0
	401	0	34	0	33	0	468	0

Mark Proctor, born in Middlesbrough on 30 January 1961, played for St Gabriel's and then St Anthony's Schools before having a trial with Leeds United when he was 14. Homesick, he returned to Teesside after only three days at Elland Road and signed for Middlesbrough on associate schoolboy forms in August 1975, playing some games for Nunthorpe Athletic along the way. Proctor captained the England Youth side in an international tournament in Las Palmas before becoming a full-time professional with 'Boro in September 1978. The first of his two England Under-21 caps as a Middlesbrough player came as substitute against the Republic of Ireland at Anfield in March 1981. After a further cap, against Switzerland in May, he signed for Nottingham Forest for £440,000 in August 1981. As a Forest player, he won two more Under-21 caps and was loaned to Sunderland, playing five League games before the Wearsiders signed him permanently. He made more than 120 League appearances for the Roker club before First Division Sheffield Wednesday paid £275,000 for his signature during the 1987-8 season. After 59 League appearances

MARK PROCTOR

	LEAGUE		FA CUP		FL CUP		TOTAL	
	App	Gls	App	Gls	App	Gls	App	Gls
1978-79	31/2	9	2	0	2	0	35/2	9
1979-80	38	2	3	0	2	0	43	2
1980-81	38	1	5	1	2	1	45	3
1988-89	10	0	0	0	0	0	10	0
	117/2	12	10	1	6	1	133/2	14

for the Owls, Proctor made a surprise return to Middlesbrough for £300,000, but, despite some stylish displays in midfield, he arrived too late to save 'Boro from relegation.

STUART RIPLEY

Stuart Ripley's first honour in football came when he was a member of the Middlesbrough Boys team that shared the English Schools FA Trophy with Sunderland. He was born at Middlesbrough on 20 November 1967 and had trials with Manchester City and Chelsea before joining his home-town club as an apprentice professional. Ripley was with the England Youth team in China when he heard of Middlesbrough's relegation to the Third Division and then played games on loan to Bolton Wanderers — he scored on his debut for the Trotters — before making his first appearance in 'Boro's League side. He really established himself at Ayresome Park during the 1986-7 season and in April 1988 scored the first League hat-trick of his career when Middlesbrough hammered Sheffield United 6-0 at Ayresome Park. His six goals in as many games at the close of that season did much to push 'Boro to the brink of the First Division. To date he has won seven Under-21 caps and there has been Press speculation that he will move to another club in the wake of Middlesbrough's relegation in 1989. Many supporters rated Ripley as 'Boro's most improved player in 1988-9 and felt that a quick return to Division One would see him win a full cap.

	LEAGUE		FA CUP		FL CUP		TOTAL	
	App	Gls	App	Gls	App	Gls	App	Gls
1984-85	0/1	0	0	0	0	0	0/1	0
1985-86	7/1	0	0	0	1	0	8/1	0
1986-87	43/1	4	3	0	4	2	50/1	6
1987-88†	40/3	8	4	1	4	0	48/3	9
1988-89	36	4	1	0	2	0	39	4
	126/6	16	8	1	11	2	145/6	19

†Also made four play-off appearances

Reliable, stylish Richard 'Dicky' Robinson was spotted by 'Boro manager David Jack playing football with his local side, Marsden Juniors, in the Sunderland district and was looked upon as a promising forward. Robinson, who was born at Whitburn on 19 February 1927, worked down the mines as a 'Bevin Boy' in Dunfermline during the war and guested for Dunfermline Athletic. He signed for Middlesbrough, aged 18, on 9 April 1945 and played at right-back in the club's first post-war League game, on 31 August 1946 at Villa Park, when a Wilf Mannion goal won 'Boro maximum points. Robinson's outstanding displays over the next four years earned him Football League representative honours and he also went on tour with an FA party. Alas, he lost confidence after a string of niggling injuries and a badly pulled muscle, suffered at White Hart Lane in December 1951, kept

DICKY ROBINSON

	LEAGUE		FA CUP		TOTAL	
	App	Gls	App	Gls	App	Gls
1945-46	-	-	7	0	7	0
1946-47	40	0	7	0	47	0
1947-48	35	0	3	0	38	0
1948-49	41	0	1	0	42	0
1949-50	28	0	0	0	28	0
1950-51	33	0	1	0	34	0
1951-52	20	0	0	0	20	0
1952-53	24	0	0	0	24	0
1953-54	30	0	2	0	32	0
1954-55	33	0	0	0	33	0
1955-56	30	0	2	0	32	0
1956-57	39	1	3	0	42	1
1957-58	23	0	0	0	23	0
1958-59	14	0	0	0	14	0
	390	1	26	0	416	1

him out for the rest of that season. Although most of his games were at full-back, he was also tried at centre-half and, occasionally, in the forward line. In June 1959, at the age of 32, he was transferred to Barrow, then a Football League club. He spent three full seasons at Holker Street before retiring in 1962 with over 500 League games to his credit.

Centre-half Dicky Rooks was born at Sunderland on 29 May 1940 and for many seasons was understudy to Charlie Hurley at Roker Park, his appearances restricted to 34 League games. Desperate for regular first-team football, he agreed to a £17,000 transfer to Ayresome Park in late August 1965. Raich Carter saw Rooks as the natural successor to Mel Nurse, following the Welshman's transfer to Swindon Town. Rooks made his debut at Huddersfield Town on 28 August 1965, but it was hardly a happy start as Middlesbrough were hammered 6-0. Although he wore the number-five shirt, he played at centre-forward and scored a memorable hat-trick (one goal from the penalty-spot) in 'Boro's dramatic 5-3 defeat at Cardiff City which sent the club plummeting to Division Three. In July 1966, he asked for a transfer but stayed as 'Boro clawed their way back to Division Two, when he competed with Bill Gates for the centre-half spot. He was extremely disappointed when Stan Anderson dropped him for the home game against Bury in 1968-9, which cost him the chance of being an ever-present that season. A £17,000 move to Bristol City in June 1969 caused great consternation amongst Middlesbrough fans but Anderson felt that he had a natural replacement in utility player Gates. Rooks joined Scunthorpe United as manager in 1974 and stayed two seasons at the Old Show Ground. He later had a spell at Willington as player-coach.

DICKY ROOKS

	LEAGUE		FA CUP		FL CUP		TOTAL	
	App	Gls	App	Gls	App	Gls	App	Gls
1965-66	37	8	1	0	3	0	41	8
1966-67	26	1	4	0	0	0	30	1
1967-68	33	3	0	0	3	0	36	3
1968-69	40	2	2	0	1	0	43	2
	136	14	7	0	7	0	150	14

Trevor Senior wrote to Bristol City as an aspiring 15-year-old but was played out of position when he had a trial at Ashton Gate and was not kept on. Senior, who was born at Dorchester on 28 November 1961, went into non-league football with Dorchester Town before Portsmouth snapped him up for £35,000, in December 1981. He made only 11 League appearances at Fratton Park, scoring two goals, but had more success in a loan spell at Aldershot, where he scored seven goals in ten games. Reading manager Maurice Evans spotted Senior's potential and paid £30,000 for him in August 1983. At Elm Park, Senior quickly found his scoring touch and netted 123 goals in 186 League and Cup appearances. Desperate to play in a higher division, he was on the transfer list for eight months before Watford gave him a chance in the First Division. Senior moved to Vicarage Road in October 1987, for £325,000, but the dream turned sour and he managed only one goal for them in the top flight. In late March 1988, Middlesbrough stepped in with a £200,000 offer and the 6ft 1in striker signed on the eve of the transfer deadline. He made his debut two weeks later, in a 1-1 draw against Birmingham City, and scored twice in a 6-0 home defeat of Sheffield United, but his goals against Bradford City and Chelsea in the play-off games proved the most important in 'Boro's successful bid to reach Division One. Back in the First Division, he

TREVOR SENIOR

	LEAGUE		FA CUP		FL CUP		TOTAL	
	App	Gls	App	Gls	App	Gls	App	Gls
1987-88†	5/1	2	0	0	0	0	5/1	2
1988-89	4	0	0	0	1	0	5	0
	9/1	2	0	0	1	0	10/1	2

†Also made four play-off appearances and scored two goals.

again failed to score regularly. Booed off the pitch after being substituted in one game, Senior was transfer-listed. Reading, by now in the Third Division, bought him and he resumed his goalscoring habits at Elm Park.

HAROLD SHEPHERDSON MBE

Harold Shepherdson became best-known as England's trainer and held that position when the World Cup was won in 1966, but he also gave great service to Middlesbrough for almost 50 years. He was born in

the town on 28 October 1918 and played football and cricket for Middlesbrough Boys and Yorkshire Boys. He signed as an amateur for 'Boro in 1932 and became a full-time professional four years later. First-team opportunities were hard to come by, however, because of the wealth of talent at Ayresome Park. During the war, Shepherdson served as an Army PTI staff sergeant and made the occasional appearance for 'Boro in the regional leagues. He was transferred to Southend United in May 1947 but before he made his League debut he suffered a knee injury which ended his playing career. Charlie Cole, 'Boro's trainer, recommended him for the post of assistant trainer at Middlesbrough and in 1949, Shepherdson was promoted after Tom Mayson, Cole's successor, had retired. He became England's trainer in 1957 and served under Walter Winterbottom and Sir Alf Ramsey. Awarded the MBE in 1969, Shepherdson served four periods as caretaker manager of 'Boro. In May 1973 he was awarded a testimonial by the FA and he retired in October 1983, when he was Middlesbrough's chief executive (football) and covered football for BBC Radio Cleveland.

	LEAGUE		FA CUP		TOTAL	
	App	Gls	App	Gls	App	Gls
1936-37	1	0	0	0	1	0
1937-38	4	0	0	0	4	0
1938-39	9	0	0	0	9	0
1946-47	3	0	0	0	3	0
	17	0	0	0	17	0

Bernie Slaven, who was born in Paisley on 13 November 1960, is affectionately known as 'The Wolfman' by colleagues and supporters. A non-smoker and teetotaller, Slaven played for Morton, Airdrie, Queen of South and Albion Rovers and enjoyed his biggest success with Albion, completing the 1984-5 season as Scotland's top scorer with 31 goals, which won him the Golden Shot Trophy. Despite this, he spent that summer in dispute with his club, refusing to re-sign, and did not play competitive football for three months. In a desperate bid to salvage his career, he wrote to every English First and Second Division club, asking for a trial. Slaven was a part-time gardener on a short-term contract with Glasgow Corporation and playing part-time football when 'Boro boss, Willie Maddren, offered him a trial at Ayresome Park. In October 1985, Maddren signed Slaven, at a £15,000 bargain price, with a further £10,000 to be paid to Albion Rovers after a certain number of first-team appearances. It later transpired that Maddren had moved at just the right time, for Leeds United were showing an interest in the player. Maddren agreed to buy Slaven without club chairman Alf Duffield's approval, but when Duffield saw Slaven play, he was

soon won over. Slaven became a favourite, scoring on his home debut against Bradford City. He experienced relegation in his first full season and almost returned to Scotland amidst the trauma of the club's bankruptcy. Happily, he remained to help 'Boro back and proved he could thrive in the First Division, his 18 goals making him the club's leading scorer for the third successive season. A temporary loss of form in 1988-9 saw him dropped but in the close season he signed a three-year contract, ending rumours that he was about to join Celtic.

BERNIE SLAVEN

	LEAGUE		FA CUP		FL CUP		TOTAL	
	App	Gls	App	Gls	App	Gls	App	Gls
1985-86	32	8	1	0	0	0	33	8
1986-87	46	17	3	3	4	1	53	21
1987-88†	44	21	5	0	4	1	53	22
1988-89	36/1	15	1	1	2	0	39/1	16
	158/1	61	10	4	10	2	178/1	67

†Also made four play-off appearances and scored two goals

GRAEME SOUNESS

Graeme Souness, an elegant player with a lethal shot, was born in Edinburgh on 6 May 1953, the son of a glazier. A Scottish Schoolboy and Youth international, he signed apprentice forms for Spurs in 1969 and became a professional the following year. He was a member of the Tottenham side which won the FA Youth Cup but was homesick and returned

to Scotland. He went back, but was unable to make much impression as there was fierce competition for places at White Hart Lane. In December 1972, Souness became one of Stan Anderson's last signings for Middlesbrough, joining the club for £32,000. Capped by Scotland Under-23's in his first full season in the Middlesbrough side, he was a member of the Second Division promotion team and, with 'Boro back in Division One, he won his first full cap. His 'skilful, silky style' disguised the aggression that was always just under the surface and he had a gritty determination to win. A club record receipt of £352,000 took him to Liverpool in 1978 and he spent seven seasons at Anfield, sharing in some great domestic and European triumphs and captaining both club and country. In June 1984, after making more than 350 first-team appearances for the Reds, he was transferred to Sampdoria for a reputed £600,000 fee. Souness later returned to Britain to resurrect the flagging fortunes of Glasgow Rangers, replacing Jock Wallace at Ibrox. As player-manager of a side which contained several English-born players, Souness took Rangers to several honours and became Britain's first player-manager-director, when he bought a stake in the Ibrox club.

	LEAGUE		FA CUP		FL CUP		TOTAL	
	App	Gls	App	Gls	App	Gls	App	Gls
1972-73	11	0	1	0	0	0	12	0
1973-74	34/1	7	2	0	2	0	38/1	7
1974-75	38	7	5	0	4	0	47	7
1975-76	34/1	3	0	0	5	0	39/1	3
1976-77	38	2	5	1	1	0	44	3
1977-78	19	3	0	0	3	0	22	3
	174/2	22	13	1	15	0	202/2	23

Frank Spraggon was born at Marley Hill on 27 October 1945 and joined Middlesbrough in 1962, when Bob Dennison was in charge. He signed professional forms in November that year and progressed through the junior and reserve ranks before making his first-team debut in a League Cup tie against Bradford in October 1963. Spraggon went on to become Middlesbrough's regular left-half for several seasons, although a cartilage operation and then trouble with blurred vision combined to keep him out of the game for seven months of the 1971-2 season. With the emergence of Willie Maddren in the number-six position, Spraggon made a successful switch to left-back. He was not a flamboyant player but could always be relied upon to give 100 per cent. After a testimonial game against Dinamo Zagreb in 1975, Spraggon went to play for Minnesota Kicks in the North American Soccer League and made

	LEAGUE		FA CUP		FL CUP		TOTAL	
	App	Gls	App	Gls	App	Gls	App	Gls
1963-64	5	0	0	0	1	0	6	0
1964-65	7	0	0	0	0	0	7	0
1965-66	5/1	0	0	0	0	0	5/1	0
1966-67	1	0	0	0	0	0	1	0
1967-68	32	0	5	0	2	0	39	0
1968-69	38	0	2	0	0	0	40	0
1969-70	37	1	5	0	1	0	43	1
1970-71	26	0	3	0	2	0	31	0
1971-72	14	1	0	0	0	0	14	1
1972-73	33/1	0	0	0	4	0	37/1	0
1973-74	39	1	2	0	3	0	44	1
1974-75	31	0	6	0	4	0	41	0
1975-76	9/1	0	0	0	1/1	0	10/2	0
	277/3	4	23	0	18	0	318/4	3

FRANK SPRAGGON

24 appearances for them in the summer of 1976. He returned to England and signed for Hartlepool but, after only one League appearance for them, he was forced to retire in December 1976 because of a knee injury.

Johnny Spuhler, born in Sunderland on 18 September 1917, won England Schoolboy honours in 1931 and was taken on as an office boy at Roker Park after he left school. After a while he decided to become a joiner but then Sunderland offered him professional terms and he signed for the Wearsiders in September 1943. During World War Two he guested for Middlesbrough and manager David Jack persuaded him to sign for 'Boro in October 1945, for £1,750. Quickly nicknamed 'Sulpher' by his teammates, he was playing well enough at one time to keep Andy Donaldson, an £18,000 centre-forward, out of the team. Not renowned for intricate ball-skills, Spuhler was most effective when he sprinted into good positions and he was also a fine header of the ball. Occasionally he would drift into offside positions, much to the annoyance of 'Boro's fans. In 1950, he broke his nose against Blackpool but played for several more games before agreeing to go into hospital. In 1954, after 'Boro were relegated, he joined Darlington for £1,000 and by 1956 was player-manager of Spennymoor United. He then had a spell as Shrewsbury Town manager and was full-time coach to Stockton FC but lost the job through economic cut-backs. For eight years he ran a Post Office at Yarm and now lives in Barnard Castle.

JOHNNY SPUHLER

	LEAGUE		FA CUP		TOTAL	
	App	Gls	App	Gls	App	Gls
1945-46	-	-	7	3	7	3
1946-47	32	10	7	4	39	14
1947-48	35	11	3	2	38	13
1948-49	31	6	1	1	32	7
1949-50	20	4	2	1	22	5
1950-51	35	13	1	0	36	13
1951-52	25	7	2	0	27	7
1952-53	19	10	0	0	19	10
1953-54	19	8	2	1	21	9
	216	69	25	12	241	81

135

Norbert 'Nobby' Stiles was born in Collyhurst, Manchester, on 18 May 1942, the son of a football-mad undertaker. Stiles captained Manchester Boys and played for England Schoolboys in 1957, joining the Old Trafford groundstaff shortly after leaving school. The Munich air disaster of February 1958 thrust him into United's reserve side, but he did not secure a regular first-team place until the 1964-5 season. But what a season that was for Nobby Stiles. He won a League Championship medal and made his full England debut against Scotland at Wembley in April 1965. His was a star of England's 1966 World Cup Final win — who will ever forget his toothless grin as he danced around Wembley? — and altogether he gained 28 full caps and travelled with the 1970 squad to the World Cup Finals in Mexico. He picked up another League Championship medal and a European Cup-winners' medal in 1968 and after 14 years at Old Trafford, he was transferred to Middlesbrough in May 1971 for a nominal £20,000 fee. Immediately appointed captain by Stan Anderson, injuries and loss of form restricted his appearances in a Middlesbrough shirt. Not fitting into Jack Charlton's plans, he joined Bobby Charlton's Preston North End as player-coach and was manager when they won promotion to Division Two in 1977. He assisted Johnny Giles at Vancouver White-caps and was in charge of West Bromwich Albion's youth team until his dismissal at the end of 1988-9.

NOBBY STILES

Manchester United stepped in with an offer for Stiles to help Brian Kidd coach the youngsters at Old Trafford.

	LEAGUE		FA CUP		FL CUP		TOTAL	
	App	Gls	App	Gls	App	Gls	App	Gls
1971-72	25	1	6	0	2	0	33	1
1972-73	32	1	1	0	3	0	36	1
	57	2	7	0	5	0	69	2

BOBBY STUART

Full-back Bobby Stuart started his football at Victoria Road School, Middlesbrough, before joining South Bank Juniors. He won an England Schoolboy cap and was signed on amateur forms with Middlesbrough in 1928, when Peter McWilliam was manager. Director John Pallister found Stuart a job as a motor mechanic in his Oxford Road garage before he signed professional forms on 7 January 1931. The player suffered a dislocation of the shoulder in his first game in 'Boro's reserve team, but made a quick recovery. He held the unenviable record of conceding five own-goals in a Middlesbrough shirt. Stuart saw RAF service in Iceland in World War Two but still managed to skipper Middlesbrough for much of the wartime period. On 28 October 1947, David Jack transferred Stuart and striker George Dews to Second Division Plymouth Argyle for a combined fee reported to be £11,000. Stuart had asked for a transfer in March 1947, because George Hardwick had recovered his fitness and the younger Dicky Robinson was waiting in the wings. He coached Whitby in 1951, but an accident in 1953 ended his active participation in football. Stuart died in hospital on 25 August 1987.

	LEAGUE		FA CUP		TOTAL	
	App	Gls	App	Gls	App	Gls
1931-32	2	0	0	0	2	0
1932-33	7	0	2	0	9	0
1933-34	39	1	2	0	41	1
1934-35	40	1	2	0	42	1
1935-36	38	0	2	0	40	0
1936-37	42	0	1	0	43	0
1937-38	32	0	1	0	33	0
1938-39	16	0	4	0	20	0
1945-46	-	-	2	0	2	0
1946-47	20	0	5	0	25	0
1947-48	11	0	0	0	11	0
	247	2	21	0	268	2

Peter Taylor is perhaps best known as Brian Clough's managerial partner at Derby County and Nottingham Forest in the late 1960s and 1970s. But Taylor also enjoyed a good career as a goalkeeper, primarily with Middlesbrough. He was born at Nottingham on 2 July 1928 and was on Forest's books as an amateur before signing for Coventry City in May 1946. After 86 League appearances for the Highfield Road club, Taylor was signed by Middlesbrough in August 1955 and eventually replaced Rolando Ugolini as 'Boro's first-choice 'keeper. At Ayresome Park he became a close friend of Clough and that partnership later took both Derby and Forest to League Championship wins. In June 1961, Taylor was transferred to Port Vale but played only one League game for them before retiring. He became manager of Southern League Burton Albion, whilst teaching PE on a part-time basis at a local school, and then rejoined Clough at Hartlepool United, where the former 'Boro centre-forward was manager. The pair moved to Derby in 1967 but in 1974, after Derby had enjoyed the greatest success in their history, both men resigned amidst huge controversy. They continued their partnership at Brighton, but when Clough was tempted to Leeds,

Taylor stayed at the Goldstone Ground. He joined up with Clough again at Nottingham and shared in the Reds' European Cup triumphs before an acrimonious split with Clough. Taylor later returned to Derby as manager, but when the Rams were on their way to Division Three, he was dismissed. He now lives in retirement near Nottingham.

PETER TAYLOR

	LEAGUE		FA CUP		TOTAL	
	App	Gls	App	Gls	App	Gls
1955-56	6	0	0	0	6	0
1956-57	38	0	3	0	41	0
1957-58	32	0	2	0	34	0
1958-59	30	0	0	0	30	0
1959-60	34	0	1	0	35	0
	140	0	6	0	146	0

ROLANDO UGOLINI

Rolando Ugolini, nicknamed 'Ugo' upon his entry into League football, was born in Lucca, home of Italy's olive oil industry, in June 1924. In 1925 his family moved to Scotland and he became a naturalized Briton. With his Glasgow background it is no surprise that he speaks with a pronounced Scottish accent. Ugolini earned a big reputation in junior football and was on Hearts' books before being snapped up by Celtic in April 1944, although the form of Scottish international Willie Miller kept 'Ugo' out of the first team. The young reserve 'keeper turned down a move to Chelsea, but in May 1948 he was ready to join 'Boro for £7,000 and soon established himself as first choice, despite

conceding seven goals on his first appearance, in a pre-season practice game. The following week's programme notes gave this summary on Ugolini's League debut at Stamford Bridge: 'This lithe young man, who possesses all the acrobatics of the Continental 'keeper plus the reliability associated with those who play for British teams'. Ugolini could send a dead ball well into his opponents' half, his handling was safe and he liked to keep the game flowing. Known as 'Rolando the Cat', he was a great character — a bit like today's Bruce Grobbelaar — and was 'Boro's regular goalkeeper for almost nine years, helping them finish sixth in Division One in 1950-51. Eventually he was replaced by Peter Taylor for the last game of 1955-6, at Doncaster. He spent the whole of the following season in the Reserves and in June 1957, aged 33, was transferred to Third Division Wrexham. He spent two seasons in their first team before leaving English football in 1959 with over 400 League appearances to his credit. He later played for Dundee United and now owns a string of betting shops.

	LEAGUE		FA CUP		TOTAL	
	App	Gls	App	Gls	App	Gls
1948-49	39	0	1	0	40	0
1949-50	41	0	4	0	45	0
1950-51	42	0	1	0	43	0
1951-52	41	0	3	0	44	0
1952-53	41	0	1	0	42	0
1953-54	42	0	2	0	44	0
1954-55	38	0	1	0	39	0
1955-56	36	0	2	0	38	0
	320	0	15	0	335	0

Tommy Urwin played for all three big North-East clubs and was awarded benefit games with all of them. He starred for England Schoolboys in 1910 and his first tentative steps in senior football were with Fulwell, then Lambton Star and Shildon in 1913, as he collected County Durham representative honours along the way. He signed for Middlesbrough as an amateur in February 1914, then professional in May, and made his League debut at outside-left against Sunderland in January 1915. He was awarded his Middlesbrough benefit during 1921-2 and toured with the England party, winning two full caps against Sweden in May 1923. Urwin would not accept the terms offered by Middlesbrough when the club suffered their first relegation at the end of 1923-4 and he signed for Newcastle United in August 1924. When 'Boro won the Second Division championship in 1927, Newcastle United clinched the League Championship. With Newcastle he earned Football League representative honours in 1927. In February 1930, Urwin moved to Sunderland, where he ended his League career in 1936 and took up a position as youth-team coach. In 1948

TOMMY URWIN

	LEAGUE		FA CUP		TOTAL	
	App	Gls	App	Gls	App	Gls
1914-15	7	1	0	0	7	1
1919-20	39	3	2	0	41	3
1920-21	39	3	1	0	40	3
1921-22	37	5	1	0	38	5
1922-23	37	2	3	0	40	2
1923-24	33	0	1	0	34	0
	192	14	8	0	200	14

he was acting as a scout for the club and working as an accountant at Sunderland Royal Infirmary. He once owned a tailor's shop in that town.

Geoff Walker was a speedy winger whose fierce shots from the wing and hard, dangerous centres terrorized opposing defences. He was born in Bradford on 29 September 1926 and during World War Two he played for Bradford in the regional league. Middlesbrough manager David Jack signed Walker from Park Avenue in June 1946, in time for the first peacetime Football League season, and he went on to score over 50 goals for the club in League football. In February 1949, Walker asked for a transfer but came off the list when no other club showed an interest. It was not until December 1954, with Middlesbrough now a Second Division side, that he finally moved from Ayresome Park, joining Doncaster Rovers who were also in Division Two. In almost two seasons at Belle Vue, Walker made 84 League appearances and scored 15 goals. In 1957 he moved back to his home town, this time to sign for Bradford City, but made only two League appearances for them. In August 1963, aged 36, he was playing for Clacton Town in the Southern League and was a sports master at a nearby public school.

GEOFF WALKER

	LEAGUE		FA CUP		TOTAL	
	App	Gls	App	Gls	App	Gls
1946-47	41	8	6	1	47	9
1947-48	35	11	3	0	38	11
1948-49	30	3	1	1	31	4
1949-50	22	6	4	1	26	7
1950-51	29	7	1	0	30	7
1951-52	27	7	2	0	29	7
1952-53	31	4	1	0	32	4
1953-54	21	3	1	0	22	3
1954-55	4	1	0	0	4	1
	240	50	19	3	259	53

John Walker played junior football as an outside-left in Beith, where he was born, but switched to left-back when kicking about in a makeshift game during a dinner-break when he was a factory worker. After moving to Burnbank Athletic, he was spotted by Raith Rovers and signed for the Scottish Second Division club. Dogged by a persistent leg injury and concerned that the attentions of the Raith trainer were not improving matters, he sought the advice of the Celtic trainer, who advised complete rest. Raith found out about his visit and suspended him. Walker swore that he would never play for Rovers again and returned to Beith. When he was fit again, Rangers signed him for £60 in the 1905-06 season but in the close season of 1907 he switched to Southern League Swindon Town. In 1911, he won the first of nine caps for Scotland, and toured Argentina with Swindon, who had just won the Southern League championship. In 1913, Middlesbrough manager Tommy McIntosh paid £1,000 to sign the man who was regarded as the best full-back in the Southern League and Walker served

JOHN WALKER

	LEAGUE		FA CUP		TOTAL	
	App	Gls	App	Gls	App	Gls
1913-14	37	0	1	0	38	0
1914-15	33	0	1	0	34	0
1919-20	34	0	1	0	35	0
1920-21	2	0	0	0	2	0
	106	0	3	0	109	0

'Boro either side of World War Two. He was transferred to Reading in 1921 and retired from the game a year later. He later ran a fish shop in Swindon for some years.

JIMMY WATSON

Jimmy Watson was born on 4 October 1877 and started his football career with Burnbank, a Lanarkshire junior side. He declined an offer from Hearts, on the grounds that Edinburgh was too far from his native Motherwell, and then failed to impress in two trial games at Sheffield United. Eventually he signed for Clyde and his displays at full-back quickly brought him to the attention of Sunderland, where he spent eight successful seasons, winning a League Championship medal in 1902 and four full Scotland caps, against England (three games) and Wales. His transfer to Middlesbrough came towards the close of the 1906-07 season and he was ever-present the following season. In 1909 he won two further caps, against England and Ireland, and the following year was appointed 'Boro's assistant trainer for a spell before ending his career with Shildon. He managed the Leviathan Hotel in Sussex Street, Middlesbrough, before emigrating to Canada and in the 1920s was coaching in that country. Watson had the nickname of 'Daddy Long Legs' because he 'threw' his legs and arms all over the place in his relentless pursuit of an opponent. He was instantly recognizable in team photographs because of his dark hair, parted down the middle and his 'circus strongman' moustache.

	LEAGUE		FA CUP		TOTAL	
	App	Gls	App	Gls	App	Gls
1906-07	3	0	0	0	3	0
1907-08	38	0	1	0	39	0
1908-09	27	0	1	0	28	0
1909-10	35	0	2	0	37	0
	103	0	4	0	107	0

Centre-forward Charlie Wayman was a natural goal-scorer who did well for all his clubs. Born at Bishop Auckland on 16 May 1921, Wayman worked as a miner and played for Spennymoor United before signing for Newcastle United in September 1941. He scored four of Newcastle's goals in their 13-0 Second Division rout of Newport County in 1946-7, but the headlines centred on United's debutant Len Shackleton, who rattled in six goals against the Welsh side. After scoring 32 goals in 47 League games, Wayman was allowed to move to Southampton (the team against whom he had scored an FA Cup hat-trick the previous season) in October 1947. He led the Saints' attack for three memorable seasons, scoring 73 goals in 100 League games. His wife could not settle in the area, however, and in September 1950 he moved to Preston. Wayman continued his spectacular scoring for the Deepdale club with 104 goals in 157 League games. He also netted one of Preston's goals in the 1954 FA Cup Final. Bob Dennison paid £8,000 to take Wayman to Ayresome Park in September 1954 and his goals played a vital part in keeping 'Boro in the Second Division. He spent two seasons at Middlesbrough before moving to Darlington in December 1956, at the age of 35, before a knee injury ended his League career in March 1958. He later became a brewery representative in Bishop Auckland.

CHARLIE WAYMAN

	LEAGUE		FA CUP		TOTAL	
	App	Gls	App	Gls	App	Gls
1954-55	32	16	1	1	33	17
1955-56	23	15	2	1	25	16
	55	31	3	2	58	33

Blackpool-born Maurice Webster played local football in the South Shore & District Wednesday League. He enlisted in the 4th Duke of Wellington's Regiment at the tender age of 17 and saw service in France during World War One. After the war he joined Lytham in the West Lancashire League and then turned out for Fleetwood in the Lancashire Combination. Webster declined the chance to join Blackburn Rovers, after trial games in the Central League, before signing professional forms for Stalybridge Celtic in 1921. Less than a season later, Middlesbrough manager, James Howie, persuaded Stalybridge, then in their brief career in the Football League, to part with Webster for £1,500 and he signed on 27 March 1922. Howie just beat Liverpool manager David Ashworth for Webster's signature and the player made his 'Boro debut in a reserve game at Workington the following week His Football League debut came at Huddersfield on 1 May 1922. Webster played in an England trial match at Liverpool and was given the task of marking his Middlesbrough colleague, George Camsell. He did so with distinction (his side won 6-1) and gained three England caps in 1930, the first against Scotland in April. He was selected for the England summer tour and played in Vienna and Berlin, where he had the misfortune to break his nose. Webster was transferred to Carlisle United on 6 June 1935 and in his 13th game for the Cumbrian side he broke his right leg. He remained at Brunton Park as trainer until war broke out and was trainer, coach and groundsman at Stockton FC from 1948 until 1954. He also worked at Dorman Long's Port Clarence Works and was a regular spectator at Ayresome Park, right up to his death early in 1978.

MAURICE WEBSTER

	LEAGUE		FA CUP		TOTAL	
	App	Gls	App	Gls	App	Gls
1921-22	1	0	0	0	1	0
1922-23	23	0	3	0	26	0
1923-24	32	0	1	0	33	0
1924-25	37	0	0	0	37	0
1925-26	38	1	2	0	40	1
1926-27	5	0	0	0	5	0
1927-28	5	0	0	0	5	0
1928-29	25	0	2	0	27	0
1929-30	34	1	6	0	40	1
1930-31	14	1	0	0	14	1
1931-32	31	0	2	0	33	0
1932-33	16	0	3	0	19	0
1933-34	1	0	0	0	1	0
	262	3	19	0	281	3

Goalkeeper Willie Whigham was born at Airdrie on 9 October 1939 and was a qualified motor mechanic when former Middlesbrough player, Alex McCrae, signed him for Falkirk. Whigham helped Falkirk to promotion from the Scottish First Division in 1961 and missed only a handful of games in his five seasons at Brockville Park. In October 1966, Middlesbrough manager Stan Anderson paid a bargain £10,000 for Whigham, who went straight into the first team against Watford. Gordon Jones, 'Boro's skipper during that 1966-7 promotion campaign, insisted later that the side would not have gone up without Whigham as their goalkeeper. Yet he was erratic, often playing a 'blinder' one week and letting in a 'soft' goal the next. Always considered something of a rebel, Whigham missed 14 games in 1968-9 because he was dissatisfied with his basic wage and put in a transfer request. He later withdrew it after being offered better terms while he played without a contract. He was dropped after a 4-1 defeat at Sunderland — Jim Platt replaced him

— and he moved to Dumbarton. In the summer of 1974 he joined Darlington but made only four League appearances for them.

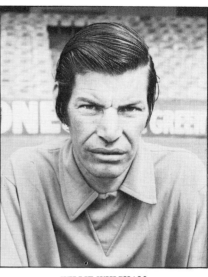

WILLIE WHIGHAM

	LEAGUE		FA CUP		FL CUP		TOTAL	
	App	Gls	App	Gls	App	Gls	App	Gls
1966-67	35	0	4	0	0	0	39	0
1967-68	32	0	5	0	1	0	38	0
1968-69	41	0	0	0	1	0	42	0
1969-70	28	0	5	0	0	0	33	0
1970-71	42	0	3	0	2	0	47	0
1971-72	9	0	0	0	2	0	11	0
	187	0	17	0	6	0	210	0

BILLY WHITAKER

In April 1942, centre-half Billy Whitaker, who was once described as 'pale-faced and possessor of a lolloping run', was a Bevin Boy down the pit when he signed amateur forms for Chesterfield. Whitaker, who was born in Chesterfield on 7 October 1923, became a professional in the summer of 1942 and soon made his first-team debut in the wartime regional league. He had played in 13 post-war League games when Middlesbrough stepped in to sign him in June 1947, for £9,500, and he went straight into 'Boro's League side. In mid-October 1949, he asked for a transfer after losing his place to Tom Blenkinsop, but regained his first-team position before anything could develop. Whitaker went on to captain Middlesbrough before losing his place again, this time because of an injury to his knee ligaments. Indeed, throughout his career he had been dogged by knee trouble and it was a cartilage problem that ended his playing days in 1954. Whitaker, who appeared for the Football League representative team at the height of his career, returned to working down the coal-mines.

	LEAGUE		FA CUP		TOTAL	
	App	Gls	App	Gls	App	Gls
1947-48	37	0	0	0	37	0
1948-49	30	0	1	0	31	0
1949-50	29	1	4	0	33	1
1950-51	32	0	1	0	33	0
1951-52	29	0	0	0	29	0
1952-53	17	0	0	0	17	0
1953-54	0	0	0	0	0	0
1954-55	3	0	1	0	4	0
	177	1	7	0	184	0

Owen Williams was born in Ryhope and was once on Sunderland's books, but was allowed to leave the area and signed for Manchester United. Things did not work out for him in Manchester, either, and he returned to the North-East to play non-League football for Easington Colliery Welfare. At the end of World War One, Clapton Orient showed an interest in him and that was the beginning of a successful League career. Williams spent five good years with Orient, making over 160 appearances before being transferred to Middlesbrough in February 1924. He made his debut for 'Boro, against West Bromwich Albion, three days later, but at the end of the season found himself in Division Two as Middlesbrough were relegated. He was, though, a member of the famous forward line – Birrell, Pease, Camsell, Jack Carr and Williams – which took 'Boro to the championship in 1926-7. At

the end of 1929-30, after another relegation and promotion for the club, he was placed on the transfer list and signed for Southend United in August 1930, for £250.

OWEN WILLIAMS

	LEAGUE		FA CUP		TOTAL	
	App	Gls	App	Gls	App	Gls
1923-24	13	0	0	0	13	0
1924-25	30	7	0	0	30	7
1925-26	33	8	2	0	35	8
1926-27	38	9	3	2	41	11
1927-28	31	5	3	0	34	5
1928-29	33	9	2	2	35	11
1929-30	6	2	0	0	6	2
	184	40	10	4	194	44

TIM WILLIAMSON

Reginald Garnet Williamson, known as 'Tim' throughout his life, was born at North Ormesby on 6 June 1884. His early football career was spent with Coatham Grammar School, Redcar Juniors and Redcar Crusaders before he kept goal as a 17-year-old for Middlesbrough in a friendly against Cliftonville. 'Boro wanted to sign him as a professional but he agreed only after they allowed him to continue his interest in becoming a qualified draughtsman. Williamson's first competitive game for the club was against Crook Town in the Northern Alliance on New Year's Day 1902. His League debut came against Bristol City at Linthorpe Road on 19 April that year — the first of 610 League and Cup appearances which stands as a

club record to this day. After initially understudying Scottish international Rab Macfarlane, he gained a regular place in 1903-04 and never looked back. The first of seven full England caps came in February 1905 in the first international to be played at Ayresome Park (he scored an own-goal for Ireland) but his second appearance was delayed for six years, due to the brilliance of Sam Hardy. A reserved occupation meant that Williamson was exempt from military service in World War One but later, the Football League refused to sanction his benefit on the grounds that those war years did not contribute towards his Middlesbrough service. He retired at the end of 1922-3 but continued to keep goal for a works team. Not interested in watching football, he spent his free time playing golf and taking his sporting gun to Teessmouth. On 1 August 1943, Tim Williamson died at North Ormesby Hospital, after an operation, and is buried in Cotham Churchyard.

	LEAGUE		FA CUP		TOTAL	
	App	Gls	App	Gls	App	Gls
1901-02	2	0	0	0	2	0
1902-03	16	0	0	0	16	0
1903-04	34	0	4	0	38	0
1904-05	33	0	2	0	35	0
1905-06	34	0	5	0	39	0
1906-07	38	0	2	0	40	0
1907-08	37	0	1	0	38	0
1908-09	38	0	1	0	39	0
1909-10	38	1	2	0	40	1
1910-11	36	1	4	0	40	1
1911-12	36	0	4	0	40	0
1912-13	37	0	4	0	41	0
1913-14	29	0	1	0	30	0
1914-15	20	0	2	0	22	0
1919-20	37	0	2	0	39	0
1920-21	42	0	1	0	43	0
1921-22	26	0	1	0	27	0
1922-23	30	0	3	0	33	0
	563	2	39	0	602	2

At Christmas 1913, Andy Wilson played for Cambuslang, a Glasgow junior team, in a friendly at Roker Park against Sunderland Reserves. After the game Middlesbrough chairman Phil Bach offered Wilson £10 to sign for 'Boro and the player agreed, although he returned to Scotland that day. On 20 February 1914, manager Tommy McIntosh travelled north and completed the formalities, Wilson joining 'Boro for the maximum wage of £4 per week. He played a full season with his new club before enlisting in the 6th Highland Light Infantry in August 1915. Posted to France with the 16th Royal Scots, he lost his lance-corporal's stripe at Arras in what he described as 'a disagreement' with another soldier. It was at Arras, early in 1918, that a shell fragment shattered his left hand. 'Boro still held his Football League registration but, after being invalided home, he was allowed to play for Hearts and also scored four goals for Scotland in two Victory international wins over England and Ireland. He won his first six full caps whilst with Dunfermline Athletic in the 'rebel' Scottish Central League (for whom he netted 104 goals in two seasons) and was a prolific scorer for Scotland on a goodwill tour of North America, before rejoining Middlesbrough in August 1921. Wilson was the leading First Division scorer in 1921-2 and in late November 1923 he moved to Chelsea for a record £6,000. At the end of that season Chelsea and 'Boro were relegated and Wilson was leading scorer for both clubs. He became a favourite at Stamford Bridge and later played for QPR and in France before managing Clacton Town, Walsall and Gravesend & Northfleet. His son, Jimmy, played for Chelsea in the 1950s.

ANDY WILSON

	LEAGUE		FA CUP		TOTAL	
	App	Gls	App	Gls	App	Gls
1914-15	9	5	0	0	9	5
1921-22	35	32	1	0	36	32
1922-23	29	11	3	1	32	12
1923-24	13	8	0	0	13	8
	86	56	4	1	90	57

Ramon Yeoman, who was known as 'Ray' throughout his football career, was born in Perth on 13 May 1934 and played for St Johnstone before moving to Northampton Town in September 1953. Bob Dennison was then managing the Cobblers and he was impressed by Yeoman, an inside-forward who was described as having 'an honest style . . .a player of integrity, dedication and determination'. Dennison moved to Middlesbrough in 1954 but it was some years later, in November 1958, that he signed Yeoman for a second time. Yeoman had been converted to wing-half at the County Ground and had made 168 League appearances before moving to 'Boro for £3,750. He went into the Reserves before making his Football League debut in a 2-0 defeat at Hillsborough in December 1958. That was the start of a fine career at Ayresome Park and in May 1963 Yeoman ended a remarkable spell of 207 consecutive League and Cup appearances. In June 1964, aged 30, he was transferred to Darlington and made 103 League appearances for them before being appointed manager in 1968. He left Feethams in 1970 and joined Sunderland as youth-team manager that summer. Now in business on Teesside, Ray Yeoman is a frequent visitor to Ayresome Park in his capacity as a scout for Everton.

RAY YEOMAN

	LEAGUE		FA CUP		FL CUP		TOTAL	
	App	Gls	App	Gls	App	Gls	App	Gls
1958-59	22	0	1	0	-	-	23	0
1959-60	42	1	1	0	-	-	43	1
1960-61	42	2	1	0	1	0	44	2
1961-62	42	0	4	0	3	0	49	0
1962-63	42	0	3	0	3	0	48	0
1963-64	20	0	0	0	0	0	20	0
	210	3	10	0	7	0	227	3

Diminutive Benny Yorston — he stood only 5ft 5in tall — was Middlesbrough's pocket-sized dynamo of a centre-forward who served the club in the years leading up to World War Two. Born at Nigg, Aberdeen, on 14 October 1905, the son of a trawler skipper, Yorston played junior football with Mugiemoss whilst working as an office boy for Aberdeen. After a few games in the Dons' third team, Yorston was allowed to sign for Richmond. He later played for Montrose, where he was capped as a Scottish junior international, before Aberdeen took him on again. He first showed his paces on Aberdeen's 1927 tour of South Africa and responded with goals galore. In 1929-30 he set a still unbeaten club record with 38 goals and was capped by Scotland in 1931. In January 1932, Sunderland snapped him up for £2,000 and in March 1934 he moved to Middlesbrough for £1,184. 'Boro wanted Raich Carter, but the Wearsiders offered 29-year-old Yorston instead. A broken leg at Blackpool in December 1937 checked his progress but he recovered to play regularly until war was declared. He joined the Army Physical Training Corps in 1940 and ended his playing days during the war. Yorston served Bury, then Barnsley, as chief scout after the war before going into business in South Kensington, London, where he let flats. In November 1977, he died at his London home, aged 72.

BENNY YORSTON

	LEAGUE		FA CUP		TOTAL	
	App	Gls	App	Gls	App	Gls
1947-48	37	0	0	0	37	0
1948-49	30	0	1	0	31	0
1949-50	29	1	4	0	33	1
1950-51	32	0	1	0	33	0
1951-52	29	0	0	0	29	0
1952-53	17	0	0	0	17	0
1954-55	3	0	1	0	4	0
	177	1	7	0	184	1

Middlesbrough line-up of the 1930s. Back row (left to right): Brown, Jennings, Hillier, Baxter, Warren, Martin. Front: Chadwick, Yorston, Griffiths, Stuart, Bruce. Inset: Forrest (left) and Coleman (right).

Middlesbrough 2   Sunderland 3

THE first game played at Ayresome Park was on Saturday, 5 September 1903, Glasgow Celtic providing the attractive Scottish opposition in a friendly game as a pipe-opener to the imminent 1903-04 season. Ayresome Park itself was designed by Scottish architect Archibald Leitch who had built many football grounds. New boy Willie White scored the only goal of the game in front of 7,000 spectators, who were more interested in giving the new ground the critical once over. Although the builders toiled many long hours to complete the outstanding work, parts of the new North Stand were not finished and were therefore closed to the public for the opening day ceremony. The old wooden stand was transported, plank for plank and nail for nail from the old Linthorpe Road ground to its new home opposite the newly-constructed North Stand.

James Clifton Robinson, president and managing director of Imperial Tramways, and also a shareholder of the club, performed the official opening ceremony of Ayresome Park on Saturday, 12 September 1903 to coincide with Middlesbrough's first home game of the new season against neighbours Sunderland. Local MPs Pike Pease and Herbert Samuel, ever keen to make their presence felt in the community, led the procession of local dignatories as Mr Robinson was handed a golden key to perform the event.

The opening ceremony was a brief affair, Mr Robinson said a few auspicious words, wishing the club good fortune in its new location and turned the key, unlocking the huge gates. Club chairman R.W.Williams hoisted the Union Jack, and the attendant band played the National Anthem, the eager crowd of 30,000 paid almost £908 at the turnstile, and the impressive new ground and enclosure was open to the paying public.

Middlesbrough's first-half display was irrepressible and Sunderland's Scottish international full-backs Andy McCombie and Jimmy Watson were sorely pressed to stop the Middlesbrough forwards attack on goal. The inevitable happened four minutes before the half-time whistle when Joe Cassidy, Middlesbrough's captain, became the first man to score at Ayresome Park, putting the ball into the net from a scrimmage.

Sunderland revved up the pace at the start of the second half and Gemmell equalized from Bridgett's pass early on but within 30 seconds Brown had restored Middlesbrough's one-goal lead. Hogg equalized for Sunderland and Robinson ensured two points for the Roker brigade before the final whistle to spoil Middlesbrough's party.

Middlesbrough: Williamson; Hogg, Blackett, D.W.Smith, A.Jones, Davidson, E.Gettins, White, A.Brown, Cassidy, Atherton.
Sunderland: Doig; Watson, McCombie, Jackson, McAllister, Farquhar, Bridgett, Gemmell, Hogg, Robinson, Craggs.

Attendance: 30,000

It is generally accepted that Middlesbrough were the first club to use half-time score-boards, later common on every League ground, although today largely replaced by electric score-boards and public-address systems. The first-ever, using hand-cranks and pullies, was erected at Middlesbrough for the start of the 1902-03 season. The first half-time score it displayed showed that Middlesbrough were winning 1-0 at Blackburn Rovers on 1 September 1902.

Middlesbrough line-up in front of goal before a match at Ayresome Park in 1905. From left to right: S.Aitken, W.Agnew, R.Atherton, J.Thackeray, A.Brown, B.Williamson, A.Jones, J.Blackett, R.Page, J.Bell, E.Gettins.

Match to Remember 2   25 February 1905

Sheffield United 0   Middlesbrough 1

BY February 1905 Middlesbrough had gone almost two years without registering a victory away from home. That last victory was at Bramall Lane against Sheffield United when 'Boro won 3-1 on 7 March 1903, the club's initial season in the First Division. The Blades had won the first encounter of the current season 1-0 at Ayresome Park the previous October.

United's Donnelly broke through towards the close of the first half, but was unlucky enough to see his shot graze the bar with Jimmy Frail stranded. Further drama quickly followed when a penalty was awarded to United as Bill Agnew fouled danger man Donnelly in the area, but Brown's spot-kick was sent spiralling high over the bar.

Early in the second half Jimmy Thackeray was soon off on one of his sprinting runs and as he glided between defenders Albert Groves (later to play for 'Boro) and Johnson he was tripped — penalty to Middlesbrough. Alf Common, once the pride of the city of steel, took the kick and put 'Boro ahead three minutes into the half. With grim determination the 'Boro defended stubbornly and when the final whistle blew, all the team 'cheered heartily'. The Press Association's report indicated that 'the Middlesbrough defence held out splendidly and the visitors won a well deserved victory'.

The Middlesbrough *North Eastern Daily Gazette's* sports editor 'Old Bird' had left a display poster secreted in his office drawer for so many weary months waiting for this eventful day. Two thousand 'Boro fans cheered and hats were joyously thrown heavenward as the poster was pinned up outside the *Gazette* offices later that night. The two brief words it displayed summed up the crowd's relief succinctly — 'AT LAST!'

Sheffield United: Lievesley; Groves, Priest, Johnson, Wilkinson, Needham, Lang, Donnelly, Brown, Drake, Lipsham.
Middlesbrough: Frail; McCallum, Agnew, S.Aitken, Jones, Cassidy, Davies, Common, Green, Atherton, Thackeray.

Attendance: 10,000

Middlesbrough 4   Oldham Athletic 1

OLDHAM Athletic were first promoted to Division One at the end of the 1909-10 season and were pressing for the League Championship in season 1914-15 when the clubs first met at Boundary Park on 28 November 1914. Middlesbrough were routed as Oldham turned on the style and ran out 5-1 winners, Jackie Carr scoring 'Boro's solitary goal.

Revenge was uppermost in Middlesbrough's mind when the return fixture was enacted at Ayresome Park on 3 April 1915, no one realizing the historic footballing precedent that was about to be witnessed. 'Boro went into the lead as early as the first minute through Walter Tinsley and on ten minutes the potential champions were reeling when Tommy Urwin beat Matthews to make the score 2-0. On 20 minutes Oldham took umbrage when referee Mr H.Smith of Nottingham refused to award a penalty, waved play on and Tom Storey broke away and set up a scoring chance for Tinsley, who clinically finished the move to put the game beyond Athletic's reach. Oldham took great indignation at Middlesbrough's scoring audacity and immediately adopted unsporting tactics. The ball was kicked off the centre-spot three times before the referee warned several Oldham players regarding their conduct. Oldham settled down again to try and play themselves back into the game, and things looked hopeful when Kemp pulled a goal back.

Bill Cook, the Oldham full-back was judged to have fouled Carr in the penalty area. Cook protested his innocence but the referee would not waive from his penalty decision and Tinsley calmly scored from the kick. Carr had won his club many penalties by verbally goading an opposing defender into committing a foul, and this appears to have been the case in this incident. Shortly after, on 55 minutes, Cook up-ended Carr and Mr Smith ordered the offending full-back to leave the field. Obviously feeling badly done by, the player refused point-blank to leave the pitch. Charlie Roberts, Oldham's captain, and one-time chairman of the Players' Union, played his part in attempting to get Cook to leave the field, but the player remained adamant that he was going to remain on the pitch.

The referee, with his options fast running out, then gave Cook a final ultimatum, one minute to leave the field. Again the player refused to leave, so the referee walked off the pitch, and with no official to control the game the match was abandoned when both teams followed the referee to the dressing-rooms.

Oldham played Cook in League games following the Ayresome Park incident but, following an FA inquiry, he was suspended from 16 April 1915 to 30 April 1916. The score of 4-1 at the time of the abandonment was ordered to stand.

Middlesbrough: Davies; Holmes, J.Walker, Davidson, A.Jackson, Malcolm, Storey, J.Carr, Wilson, Tinsley, Urwin.
Oldham Athletic: Matthews; Hodson, Cook, Moffat, Roberts, Wilson, Tummon, Pilkinton, Gee, Kemp, Walters.

Attendance: 5,000

In 1913-14, Middlesbrough received Football League permission to tour overseas on the strict understanding that players did not receive more than five shillings (25p) per day pocket money.

Hull City 5   Middlesbrough 0

THE first competitive clash between Hull City and Middlesbrough was this first-round FA Cup tie and 'Boro, a long-established First Division side, fielded a full-strength team. Tim Williamson, at 38 Middlesbrough's veteran goalkeeper of 21 years, had Scottish international full-back Jock Marshall in front of him. 'Boro's forward line included free-scoring Scottish international Andy Wilson and England forwards George Elliott, Jackie Carr and Tommy Urwin.

'Boro had just suffered a demoralizing 6-0 defeat at Sheffield United, but were still strongly tipped to brush aside Hull City's efforts. The 'Boro party were entertained the night before the match by watching the pantomime *Babes In The Wood* at a popular Middlesbrough theatre.

The Middlesbrough fans who made the journey to Hull witnessed a 5-0 drubbing and many a cynical reference was made to the previous night's pantomime and, for a short while, the Middlesbrough side was named the 'Babes in the Wood' team.

'Boro followed the club's usual pattern of not going away to prepare for the game but Hull City had spent some days at Ilkley. An early foretaste of things to come was when Flood hit an upright and Mills' shot hit the bar.

Middlesbrough's tactics were to leave Andy Wilson as their only forward up in attack and all passes were aimed at him, but centre-half Lodge stifled Wilson's attempts to pressure Mercer.

The first goal came on 40 minutes and five City players were involved in the build-up to the goal which was converted by Crawford, who sent the crowd into raptures. Eight minutes after half-time, Hughes provided the pass from which Coverdale scored Hull's second goal. Mills scored the third on 74 minutes and with five minutes of the game remaining, Bleakley netted. Then Mills' shot rebounded off Williamson and there was Coverdale to lob the ball back into the net to complete a famous victory for the Tigers and an infamous defeat for Middlesbrough.

Shortly after this ignominious Cup exit the following anonymous poem appeared in the Middlesbrough Press:

> *'Oh! poor, departed, dead eleven;*
> *May God bless every soul.*
> *For though you've find a resting place,*
> *You couldn't find the goal!'*

Hull City: Mercer; Lodge, Bell, Collier, Gilhooley, Bleakley, Crawford, Coverdale, Mills, Flood, Hughes.
Middlesbrough: Williamson; Marshall, Fox, Davidson, Ellerington, Pender, J.Carr, Birrell, Wilson, Elliott, Urwin.

Attendance: 23,000

Bill Ellerington (left) and Bob Pender (right).

Middlesbrough 0   Sunderland 3

SO important was this match, the final game of 1927-8 season, to the bottom half-dozen clubs in the First Division that Mr R.Bowie of Newcastle, the appointed referee, was replaced by Mr T.G.Bryan of Willenhall, who had refereed that season's FA Cup Final.

Both Middlesbrough and Sunderland were perilously entrenched at the foot of the table, but before the start of the game a draw would have been sufficient to ensure First Division football stayed at Ayresome Park. With Sunderland the victory was essential, anything less than two points would have meant certain relegation. Tottenham Hotspur, in 18th place, had completed their fixtures and had embarked on a Continental tour.

Middlesbrough made only one team change, Welsh international Owen Williams replacing Bill Millar on 'Boro's left wing, whilst Albert McInroy returned in goal for the Roker men. An estimated 10,000 travelled from Wearside anticipating a rare battle for First Division survival.

Against the run of play, Sunderland went into a 13th minute lead when Halliday and Wright combined, to split the 'Boro defence. Wright darted between the two backs and pushed the ball past Jimmy Mathieson. Middlesbrough had only themselves to blame and should have had a comfortable lead but were let down by poor finishing, especially by George Camsell.

Ten minutes into the second half Mathieson lost possession of the ball and, with Syd Jarvis and 'Jock' Smith on the ground, David Halliday almost walked the ball into the empty net. An element of luck was attached to the scoring of the game's final goal, when Billy Death broke away and tested Mathieson with a fierce shot from a difficult angle. Mathieson had the ball comfortably covered, but it struck Smith and was viciously deflected out of the 'keeper's despairing reach into the net. An eerie silence greeted the end of the game, even the joyous Sunderland fans realized the gravity of Middlesbrough's plight. Never before had a club been relegated with as many points as 'Boro's 37, but poor Tottenham (all the other results had gone against them) learned of their fate whilst abroad. Peter McWilliam, 'Boro's manager, watched as his current club and his previous club toppled from the First Division.

Middlesbrough: Mathieson; Jarvis, Smith, Miller, Ferguson, Peacock, Pease, J.Carr, Camsell, Bruce, O.Williams.
Sunderland: McInroy; Murray, England, Clunas, Allan, Andrews, G.Robinson, Halliday, Wright, Hargreaves, Death.

Attendance: 41,997

As a young boy, George Camsell was playing in a Sunday football match with some miners, when his local vicar gave him a ticking off for playing soccer on the Sabbath. He ended his long sermon by asking George what his father would say if he was told that his son was playing football. George replied: "You'd better ask him yourself – he's in goal for us."

Middlesbrough's line-up during their 1928-9 promotion-winning season. Back row (left to right, players only): Miller, Jarvis, Mathieson, Freeman, Peacock. Front row: Pease, Carr, Camsell, Bruce, Williams, Ferguson.

Match to Remember 6   4 May 1929

Middlesbrough 3   Grimsby Town 0

BOTH Grimsby Town, managed by Wilf Gillow, and Middlesbrough were assured of promotion to Division One, but the winners of the game would take the Second Division championship shield waiting in the North stand. The League table showed on the morning of the game that both teams had played 41 games and both had 53 points, but Middlesbrough's slightly better goal average placed them first. A draw would be sufficient for Boro and Grimsby needed to win, what a game was in prospect.

A superb performance by Jimmy Mathieson in 'Boro's goal denied shots from Prior, Coleman and Coglin in quick succession. On the half-hour 'Boro finally broke away and scored the opening goal. It started on the right wing with Charlie Ferguson finding George Emmerson, and the young reserve player fed George Camsell who rammed the ball into the back of the net.

Grimsby seemed a different side after the break, having expended so much first-half energy attempting to break down 'Boro's resolute defence, and fine defensive work by full-backs 'Jock' Smith and Reg Freeman further denied the Town forwards.

With five minutes to go Camsell headed 'Boro's decisive, second goal and Tommy Poskett, Town's debutant goalie made a blunder in the dying seconds of the game, allowing Owen Williams the opportunity to score from the wing.

Charles E.Sutcliffe, vice-president of the Football League, presented the Second Division Shield to 'Boro skipper Jack Peacock, congratulating both sides for playing 'Good, clean attractive football'.

Middlesbrough: Mathieson; Freeman, J.Smith, Miller, Ferguson, Peacock, Emmerson, J.Carr, Camsell, Bruce, O.Williams.
Grimsby Town: Poskett; C.Wilson, Jacobson, Priestley, Wrack, Calderwood, Prior, Bestall, Coleman, Coglin, Wright.

Attendance: 36,503

Newcastle United 0   Middlesbrough 5

PETER McWilliam, Middlesbrough's manager, was not at St James' Park to watch his boys beat Newcastle United on St Valentine's Day, 1931. No official reason was given for McWilliam's absence, but it was widely rumoured that he would sometimes feel physically sick before an important game and so stayed away.

Billy Pease passed a fitness test and so 'Boro kept an unchanged side from the team that drew 2-2 with newly-promoted Chelsea the week before.

The first goal came after 11 minutes after Johnny McKay found Pease, who put over a low centre. George Camsell and United defender Fairhurst both missed the ball, but Welshman Freddy Warren made it 1-0, evading a strong challenge from Jimmy Nelson.

After 38 minutes Kenny Cameron received the ball direct from a throw-in. United full-back Nelson slipped at the critical moment, and Cameron moved in for the kill, scoring with a rising shot.

Syd Jarvis, 'Boro's left-back, dropped the ball perfectly on Pease's toe and his shot hit the underside of the crossbar. Camsell, following up, pounced to smash goal number-three past Albert McInroy without a Newcastle player touching the ball.

Three minutes later 'Boro were four-up when Pease took a free-kick, passing to Camsell, whose fierce shot was pushed out by McInroy, McKay moving in to score.

Five minutes from time the Pease-Camsell combination clicked into gear again. From Pease's centre Camsell hooked the ball past McInroy to complete the scoring and guarantee a well-deserved double over the Geordies.

The Press reported that Middlesbrough had: 'extra speed in tackling' and: 'splendid ball distribution', and were: 'meritorious winners'.

Newcastle United: McInroy; Nelson, Fairhurst, Naylor, Davidson, Weaver, Boyd, Bedford, Hutchinson, Starling, Wilkinson.
Middlesbrough: Mathieson; Jennings, Jarvis, Macfarlane, Elkes, Forrest, Pease, McKay, Camsell, Cameron, Warren.

Attendance: 31,945

George Camsell scored twice as Middlesbrough humiliated Newcastle before nearly 32,000 fans at St James' Park.

Middlesbrough 10   Sheffield United 3

MIDDLESBROUGH were unchanged for the seventh consecutive match, having won the last four home games (the 'Boro forwards scoring six in the last home game against Stoke City), and Sheffield United were expected to offer little resistance to 'Boro's in-form forward line. United were experiencing some difficulty adjusting to the recent departure of Jimmy Dunne to Arsenal for a club record fee, but the side was strengthened by the timely return of captain George Green, after injury. Wintry conditions restricted the crowd to just over 6,000 at the kick-off, the lowest of the season, so far.

The 10-3 score implied that United were a bad side, but that was not the case and, in fact, they scored first. The game had only been in progress for three minutes when Baines tried a 25-yard shot, which was deflected into the net by courtesy of the underside of the crossbar. On 22 minutes George Camsell (who had registered his 250th League goal in the 4-1 home win over Liverpool a month before), scored the first of his four goals, and many of those present rated the goal as one of the best he had ever scored. He duped and jinked his way past four United defenders before unleashing an unstoppable shot that gave Smith no possible chance of saving the ball. Charlie Ferguson, in his first season with 'Boro, scored the second two minutes later, justifying the directors' persistence at playing him when he was out of form.

Further goals form Camsell (31mins) and Freddy Warren (34), gave Middlesbrough an unassailable 4-1 lead. On 41 minutes Bobby Bruce and Pickering scored for their respective sides to make the score 5-2, and the half ended with Bruce scoring his second and Middlesbrough's sixth goal.

Ten minutes into the second half Camsell completed his hat-trick before Bob Baxter, playing at inside-left in those days, scored his first goal for the club on the hour. Baines scored United's third goal in the 71st minute before a Bruce penalty 11 minutes later (his hat-trick) made it 9-3. The game's final goal, the 13th and a record aggregate score for Middlesbrough, was fittingly scored by Camsell two minutes from time.

The 'Boro forwards revelled in the mud and rain, and full credit was given to a United side who never gave up, making a game of it right up until the final whistle. One complaint received from the press-box after the game, was that the goals came too thick and fast for them to keep in touch with the events.

Camsell's performance emphasized, that arguably he was the best centre-forward currently playing in the country and his contribution in this game was enough to merit a return to the England forward line for the game against France in December 1933.

Sheffield United's leaky defence, 101 goals conceded in 42 League games, cost the Yorkshire club its First Division status and they were relegated at the end of the season with Newcastle United.

Middlesbrough: Gibson; Jennings, Stuart, Brown, Griffiths, Martin, Ferguson, Bruce, Camsell, Baxter, Warren.
Sheffield United: Smith; Robinson, Hooper, E.Jackson, Holmes, Green, Oxley, Killoury, Baines, Pickering, Williams.

Attendance: 6,461

In 1931, Sheffield United travelled by train to fulfill a League fixture at Ayresome Park. In error they failed to change trains at Stockton and ended up at Sunderland station. The United team was ferried back to Middlesbrough in taxies and the match kicked-off 20 minutes late.

Middlesbrough 6   Sunderland 0

IN late March 1936 Sunderland were League leaders, six points clear of second-placed Derby County, but had been spluttering of late having gone four games without a win. Members of the Scottish FA selection committee came to Ayresome Park to assess three Sunderland players, Hastings, Connor and Gallacher with a view to international selection, but must have left the game more impressed with 'Boro's Scottish duo, Bob Baxter and Benny Yorston.

After 16 minutes 'Boro forged into the lead through an Arthur Cunliffe goal when he cut in from the left to beat Matt Middleton. Middleton, who starred for the 'Boro as a guest player during the wartime Regional games, was again beaten, this time by Ralph Birkett who broke through on the half-hour to make it 2-0.

George Camsell scored his customary goal three minutes into the second period and ten minutes later Yorston, 'Boro's pocket dynamo, was entrusted with a penalty-kick, and it must have been an enjoyable moment for him when the ball smacked into the net, to score against the club that had discarded him earlier in his career. On 70 minutes Norman Higham, playing in only his second game for Middlesbrough, scored the fifth.

With the match at the three-quarter stage an unsavoury incident led to the dismissal of two of Sunderland's star players. Billy Brown, 'Boro's right-back, received a nasty kick from Raich Carter, and with the Sunderland star pleading innocence, experienced referee Bert Fogg of Bolton ordered Carter from the field. Baxter, the 'Boro captain, attempted to defuse the situation but the referee remained adamant that Carter must go. Brown had to leave the field for treatment but later returned to complete the game.

Within a minute, Davis, Carter's wing partner, said something that did not meet with Mr Fogg's critical approval and joined his teammate in the dressing-room.

Higham completed the rout three minutes from time with his second and Middlesbrough's final goal. The dismissals in no way affected the outcome of the game, for 'Boro were leading 5-0 before the double sending-off, and as the contemporary Press reported: 'Sunderland were not beaten, they were thrashed'.

It was Middlesbrough's first victory over Sunderland in five seasons, and the 6-0 defeat was to be Sunderland's heaviest of the season, whilst it was 'Boro's most decisive victory. The Roker Park club held on to clinch the Championship at the end of the season, beating Derby County by eight points.

At the subsequent FA inquiry at Darlington, Raich Carter was still insisting that the kick that Brown received was accidental, but he was found guilty and received a seven-day suspension. Davis received a 12-day suspension and a five guinea (£5.25) fine.

Middlesbrough: Gibson; Brown, Stuart, Martin, Baxter, Forrest, Birkett, Higham, Camsell, Yorston, Cunliffe.
Sunderland: Middleton; Murray, Hall, Thomson, Johnston, Hastings, Davis, Carter, Gurney, Gallacher, Connor.

Attendance: 29,990

When Brentford full-back Duncan McKenzie agreed to be transferred to Middlesbrough in 1938, the club agreed to pay the player's removal bill which amounted to £17.

Micky Fenton (left) and Billy Forrest (right) played well but could not stop York gaining a surprise FA Cup victory.

Match to Remember 10   12 February 1938

York City 1   Middlesbrough 0

MIDDLESBROUGH had been lucky enough to steer clear of First Division opponents in the 1937-8 FA Cup campaign. Two goals by Micky Fenton, one a penalty, carried the club through the third round against Second Division Stockport County at Ayresome Park. The fourth-round draw meant a trip to the City Ground, Nottingham, where goals from Wilf Mannion, George Camsell and Jacky Milne ensured a 3-1 victory over Second Division Forest.

Third Division North York City, 3-2 home conquerors of West Bromwich Albion in the fourth round, were the next opponents and York's name was first out of the hat so 'Boro had to travel to Bootham Crescent for the fifth-round tie on 12 February 1938. Such was the Cup fever running high through the town, that 'Boro manager Wilf Gillow smuggled his players on to the 10.15am train via the Parcels Office and on to a reserved carriage away from the well-meaning but overzealous fans. It was estimated that 10,000 'Boro fans were to converge on the historic city of York via 11 excursion trains. Through an open window of the moving train captain Bob Baxter was handed a bunch of lucky white heather tied up with blue and white ('Boro's colours that day) ribbons.

The national sporting Press gave the Third Division underdogs no hope against their First Division opponents and cruelly nicknamed the side the '£50 team'. The bookies were quoting lengthy odds of 150-1 for York to reach the last eight of the competition.

A crowd of 23,860 paid receipts of £2,193 and referee J.E.Williams of Bolton blew for the start of the match that was to be played throughout in a blustery wind. The game's only goal came on 51 minutes. Earl collected the ball and centred to inside-left Comrie and he passed to Peter Spooner who tried a speculative shot. The ball, assisted by the wind, dipped under the bar and into the net. Sensationally, York held out to finish the game 1-0 winners. Dave Cumming, 'Boro's unlucky 'keeper, admitted after the game that, in all honesty he had the ball totally covered, but a sudden gust of wind must have helped the ball into the net.

York City: Wharton; Pinder, Barrett, Duckworth, Wass, Hathaway, Earl, Hughes, Baines, Comrie, Spooner.
Middlesbrough: Cumming; Laking, Stuart, Martin, Baxter, Forrest, Birkett, Fenton, Camsell, Mannion, Milne.

Attendance: 23,860

Burnley 1   Middlesbrough 0

FIRST Division Middlesbrough and Second Division Burnley both needed home replays to dispose of their respective fifth round FA Cup opponents. Middlesbrough beating Nottingham Forest 6-2 at Ayresome Park whilst, at Turf Moor, Burnley put three past Luton Town without reply.

A record crowd of 53,025 was shoe-horned into Ayresome Park on Saturday, 1 March 1947, to see the sixth round game between Middlesbrough and Burnley. The club's first semi-final joyously loomed with seven minutes of the game remaining, a Geoff Walker goal giving Middlesbrough a tenuous lead. Micky Fenton scored a second, but the referee, spotting the linesman frantically waving Johnny Spuhler offside, disallowed the goal. Burnley broke away and instantly equalized, forcing a replay at Turf Moor the following Tuesday afternoon.

The start of the game was delayed by some 40 minutes to allow the huge crowd sufficient time to filter through the entrance gates. It was originally scheduled to kick off at 2.15pm, but referee Arthur Ellis's late pitch inspection and subsequent decision that the game could go ahead meant that the gates were opened as late as 1.30pm and the crowd of 49,244 was not to be disappointed. Willing hands wielded shovels and pickaxes to clear the reluctant snow and ice from the pitch and when the game eventually kicked off at 2.55pm, it was a fine, sunny, but cold afternoon. The Liverpool team were in the stand to watch the game, for they were to play the winners in the Semi-Final. If 'Boro won the replay, the match against Liverpool was to take place at Leeds, but if Burnley won the match the venue was to be at Blackburn Rovers' Ewood Park.

A strained groin muscle meant that Geoff Walker failed a strenuous pre-match fitness test and George Dews formed a left-wing partnership with Alec Linwood, who had not played a first-team game since New Year's day. Burnley, with no injury worries, were unchanged and took to the pitch wearing their familiar claret shirts and white shorts. Middlesbrough wore the club's alternative away strip of white shirts and black shorts.

'Boro full-back Dicky Robinson impeded Peter Kippax, and the England Amateur international took the resultant free-kick himself. Dave Cumming clasped the ball to his chest but, in the hectic goalmouth mêlée he lost the ball and fell injured to the ground. Ray Harrison appeared to scoop the ball with his hand into the path of Burnley's inside-right Billy Morris, who drove the ball into the net with George Hardwick and Dicky Robinson looking on as helpless spectators. Referee Arthur Ellis (later of *It's A Knockout* television fame), after consultation with his linesman, said the goal stood, despite 'Boro's vehement protests over the handling incident.

Burnley: Strong; Woodruff, Mather, Attwell, A.Brown, Bray, Chew, Morris, Harrison, Potts, Kippax.
Middlesbrough: Cumming; Robinson, Hardwick, Bell, McCabe, Gordon, Spuhler, Mannion, Fenton, Linwood, Dews.

Attendance: 49,244

Bolton Wanderers arrived at Middlesbrough railway station on their way to play in a First Division game at Ayresome Park in the late 1940s. When the playing kit was unloaded from the train it was found that the players' shinguards had been left at Burnden Park. Bill Ridding, Bolton's trainer and later manager, walked over to the station bookstall and bought 22 paperback romantic novels which were put to good use as replacements for the missing equipment.

Middlesbrough 1   Doncaster Rovers 4

THE FA Cup fourth-round tie between Middlesbrough and Second Division Doncaster Rovers was originally scheduled for Saturday, 6 February 1952, but 16° of heavy frost meant the inevitable postponement of the game until the following Wednesday afternoon. Gateshead v West Bromwich was the only other fourth-round tie to be postponed that afternoon.

In the early hours of the morning of the game, King George VI died of a coronary thrombosis at Sandringham, and a minute's respectful silence was paid by the crowd of 41,560 which included ex-'Boro favourite George Hardwick, watching his old team from the stand. A fifth-round match against Portsmouth was the prize awaiting the winner of the game.

Full-back Ray Barnard, doing his Army National Service near York, was released by his commanding officer to take part in the game, but he and Bobby Corbett failed to control Rovers' forwards, the occasion proving too much for both players. Things looked to be auguring well for 'Boro when Johnny Spuhler's first-minute shot just whizzed the wrong side of the upright, but Doncaster Rovers stunned the crowd by cruising into a 3-0 lead within 23 minutes. John Lawlor scored the first goal as early as the seventh minute, the ball just going into the net off the post. The same player made it 2-0 15 minutes later when the ball found him unmarked and he easily beat Rolando Ugolini. Ray Harrison scored the third after 23 minutes when Eddie Russell's failure to clear the ball gift-wrapped his scoring chance. Herbert Tindill's goal after 72 minutes came when he broke clear through the defence and blasted the ball past Ugolini.

'Boro had failed abysmally at corner-kicks, the kicker invariably putting the ball directly out of play, and it took half-back Harry Bell to show his forwards how to score when he netted 'Boro's only goal in the last minute. If only Peter Doherty had played in a Middlesbrough shirt things might have been so different. Doherty, an experienced Northern Ireland inside-forward, was nudging 40 but he used his footballing brain to compensate for the loss of speed, and let the other Rovers players do the legwork.

So once again Middlesbrough were humiliated by a side from the lower divisions of the Football League, for the fourth consecutive season, and many supporters rated it as the club's worst Cup defeat since Watford's 1-0 penalty win at Ayresome Park in season 1923-4.

Middlesbrough: Ugolini; Barnard, Corbett, Bell, Russell, Mulholland, Delapenha, Mannion, Spuhler, McCrae, Dicks.
Doncaster Rovers: Hardwick; Rouse, Graham, Jones, Patterson, Miller, Tindill, Lawlor, Harrison, Doherty, Calverley.

Attendance: 41,560

Jackie Carr, a Middlesbrough player for over 18 years, once asked for a transfer after a row concerning a £3 12s rail pass. Before World War One, the club had paid the rail fare to and from his Redcar home to Middlesbrough, but decided after the war to stop the practice. Jackie took exception to the loss of his free rail travel and immediately asked for a move. The club backed down and reinstated the pass. Carr was so much part of the Middlesbrough club, that he even named his home, 'Ayresome House'.

Cardiff City 5   Middlesbrough 3

THE Cardiff City v Middlesbrough game in early May 1966 was a vital fixture for both teams, but more so for Middlesbrough than the Welsh side. The game would decide who accompanied Leyton Orient into Division Three. Manager Jimmy Scoular's Cardiff City side had eased their problems with a 2-1 victory over Crystal Palace.

The equation looked like this — if Middlesbrough won, whatever the score, Second Division survival was assured, for at least another season. If Middlesbrough were beaten, no matter what the score, they were doomed, for 'Boro's goal average was vastly inferior to that of their two rivals, Cardiff and Bury.

The initial injury worries about captain Ian Gibson, who had pulled a hamstring early in the 1-2 defeat at Coventry, were dispelled when he passed a rigorous fitness test, but manager Stan Anderson would not name his side until he had inspected the Ninian Park pitch. The Middlesbrough team flew to Cardiff for the most important game in the club's history.

On eight minutes a corner was awarded to Middlesbrough and central defender Dicky Rooks rose above all others to power a header past Dilwyn John, Cardiff's Welsh Under-23 'keeper. Cardiff got back in the game with an equalizer. On 28 minutes Skipper Gibson conceded an unnecessary penalty, when his side were leading 2-1. Back in defence, he was pushed in the back as he was challenging for possession and his hand touched the ball and a 'stupid' penalty was conceded.

The last goal, to Cardiff, came on 89 minutes from a free-kick and the 12,935 Ninian Park crowd burst into rapturous song as only Welshmen can, grateful that the team that had represented the town of Middlesbrough had not offered sterner resistance. The spectrum of joy and sorrow was evident as the two teams walked off the pitch. The public address system crackled as the announcer wished 'Middlesbrough a speedy return to Division Two'.

The 'pantomine' (as one Press report aptly described the game) contained two 'stupid' penalties, a hat-trick from a central defender, Dicky Rooks scored two as a centre-half, and one as a centre-forward. 'Middlesbrough', the report went on 'took the lead, lost it, regained it and it went on and on . . .'. Silence greeted every 'Boro score, whilst cheers rang out for every Cardiff success.

On such an important night for Middlesbrough Football Club the team failed abjectly and deserved its fate of relegation to the unknown territory of Division Three.

Cardiff City: John; Coldrick, Carver, Williams, Murray, Hole, Farrell, Feguson, Andrews, King, Lewis.
Middlesbrough: Appleby; R.A.Smith, Spraggon, Horner, Rooks, Davidson, Downing, Gibson, Irvine, McMordie, Jones.

Attendance: 12,935

In May 1963, Arthur Lightening, Middlesbrough's goalkeeper, was given permission to go home to South Africa to attend his brother's wedding. He never returned.

West Bromwich Albion 0   Middlesbrough 4

WEST Brom's manager, Don Howe, made only one change for the important Second Division clash at The Hawthorns on 16 March 1974 — Scottish international Asa Hartford returned after injury, replacing Alan Merrick. Jack Charlton's table-toppers were unchanged, fielding the side that had pushed the club to the brink of First Division football, nine points ahead (two points for a win then) of nearest rivals, Luton Town.

Alan Foggon was the first Middlesbrough player to get his name on the score-sheet, after 32 minutes. David Mills attempted to use his speed to break clear of the pursuing defenders, but one of them managed to get in a tackle. The loose ball conveniently fell at Bobby Murdoch's feet. His astute centre found Foggon, who slammed the ball past Peter Latchford for his 15th goal of the season.

After 62 minutes John Hickton was loitering on the Throstles' left wing and with no apparent danger, he cut in across the face of the goal, then first-timed it past Latchford to put 'Boro 2-0 up. Before West Brom could restart the game Don Howe brought Gordon Nisbet off, replacing him with Dave Shaw. The best goal of the game came 15 minutes later when 'Boro's midfield starlet, Graeme Souness, burst through the middle, pulling the West Brom defenders out of position. He pushed the ball out to Hickton on the wing, and the defence chased after 'Hicky' leaving Souness space and time to run into the penalty area. Hickton quickly returned the ball to the young Scot, who had time to finish off the move to make it 3-0 to 'Boro.

With time running out, Hickton caught the defence flat-footed and ran past centre-half John Wile with consummate ease, into the penalty box. Wile lost his cool and brought 'Big John' crashing down, leaving referee Gordon Kew little option but to reward 'Boro with a penalty. The big man took the kick himself and crashed the ball past Latchford.

West Bromwich Albion: Latchford; Nisbet(Shaw, 65mins), R.Wilson, Cantello, Wile, A.Robertson, W.Johnston, A.Brown, Astle, Hartford, Glover.
Middlesbrough: Platt; Craggs, Spraggon, Souness, Boam, Maddren, Murdoch, Mills, Hickton, Foggon, Armstrong.

Attendance: 24,178

There are two instances of fathers and sons playing for Middlesbrough. Billy Fox was a star in 'Boro's pre-League days in the 1880s and his son, Victor, played for the club in the 1920s. Billy ran a sports shop in the town and coached 'Boro's juniors when Victor was at the club. Victor, who was also an accomplished cricketer, signed for Middlesbrough on 23 May 1919 and, after 100 League appearances, was transferred to Wolverhampton Wanderers in October 1924 before ending his playing days at Newport County. He also played 163 first-class games for Worcestershire CCC between 1923 and 1932. He died in Withington, Manchester, on 17 February 1947.

Jim Gallagher was a full-back, born in Dipton, who made only one League appearance for Middlesbrough in 1920 before his transfer to Millwall in the summer of 1921. His son Donald Elliott Gallagher (the family is related to Middlesbrough and England centre-forward George Elliott) played some games for Middlesbrough in wartime football.

Swansea City 0   Middlesbrough 5

BBC Television's *Match Of The Day* cameras covered the FA Cup third-round tie between Second Division Swansea City and First Division Middlesbrough at the Vetch Field on Saturday, 3 January 1981.

Middlesbrough manager John Neal, back in Wales where he had enjoyed European success with Wrexham, had selection problems. Craig Johnston had failed a fitness test and defender Mike Angus was drafted in at the last minute. David Armstrong had not recovered from a troublesome knee injury, utility player Tony McAndrew getting a chance.

Although Swansea were creating more first-half chances, it was Middlesbrough who scored first, against the run of play after 42 minutes. Terry Cochrane sent over a corner to John Craggs, who crossed to Liverpudlian Billy Ashcroft at the far post, and in it went! More misery followed for Swansea before the interval, when McAndrew and David Hodgson set up a ball for Angus to sweep home, his first senior goal for his club.

David Giles was a second-half replacement for Jeremy Charles and he thought he had equalized when he swept the ball into the net on 57 minutes, but the referee had already blown for offside. Middlesbrough continued to block everything Swansea threw at them, then Craggs was booked for a late tackle on Giles.

On 69 minutes, McAndrew's through ball reached Hodgson, who steamed for goal shaking off two defenders on the way. He shrewdly pulled the 'keeper, Welsh international David Stewart, out of positon, and scored. Within two minutes Middlesbrough were 4-0 up with the most spectacular goal of the game. Hodgson's ball was met by Cochrane who, in one swift flowing movement, sent the ball dipping just under the crossbar with an overhead bicycle-kick.

The game's final goal came ten minutes from time, when speedy Mark Proctor nipped past two defenders, and he set up a perfect ball for his pal Hodgson, who took the ball around the 'keeper to conclude the scoring.

Consolation came at the season's end for City as John Toshack, Swans manager since 1978, took the club into Division One.

Swansea City: Stewart; Attley, Hadziabdic, Rushbury, Stevenson, Phillips, Mahoney, James, Curtis, Charles(Giles), Robinson.
Middlesbrough: Platt; Craggs, Bailey, Angus, Ashcroft, Nattrass, Cochrane, Proctor, Shearer, Hodgson, McAndrew.

Attendance: 18,015

Middlesbrough's first official mascot was Andrew Gaun, who took to the field with the team against Bristol City on 11 May 1968.

The first Scottish side to visit Middlesbrough was Govan, who arrived at the Linthorpe Road ground on 8 January 1887. Jack Summerson, a Middlesbrough player, guested for Govan, who went down 3-1.

Wolves 3   Middlesbrough 1

'BORO'S army of travelling fans proceeded to the Midlands and increased the attendance to 40,524 for the FA Cup sixth round replay against Wolverhampton Wanderers. Jubilant Wolves had forced a 1-1 draw at Ayresome Park three days before, and were ready to face John Neal's young team. Keith Burkinshaw, boss of Tottenham Hotspur was in the Molineux directors' box to actively assess the game — his team were to play the ultimate winners of the tie.

As expected the 'Boro defence took an early battering from the Wolves forwards but 'Boro's Bosko Jankovic had the ball in the Wolves net after five minutes. His joy was, however, short-lived when referee Ron Challis disallowed the goal for offside. On 11 minutes Wolves' persistent bombardment of 'Boro's rearguard paid off when Ian Bailey conceded a free-kick on the edge of 'Boro's penalty area as he fouled Wayne Clarke. Kenny Hibbitt's free-kick brought out a superlative save from Jim Platt, but he failed to gather the shot, only managing to push the ball on to the upright. The ball spun off the post and Mel Eves knelt down to head the ball back and into the net.

John Neal's half-time pep talk made sure 'Boro were making more of a fight of it in the second half and as commitment from both sides increased, Terry Cochrane and Derek Parkin were both booked for a flare-up on the hour. Ten minutes later 'Boro forced themselves back into the game when David Hodgson's header set up Jankovic, standing on the byline, with an opportunity to do something positive. Seeing Hodgson clear and in a more advantageous position than himself, he returned the ball and Hodgson headed the equalizer past Paul Bradshaw.

Seven minutes into extra-time a bad error by Irving Nattrass put Wolves back in the driving seat. The full-back's throw-in was dispatched directly to an old-gold shirt. Before a Middlesbrough player could recover the situation Willie Carr's pass found Andy Gray and his simple cross into the path of John Richards restored Wolves' tenuous lead.

Two minutes from the end of extra-time a long ball was kicked down the middle of the field. Both Billy Ashcroft and Bailey decided that the other was going to clear the ball, and Sunderland-born Norman Bell seized the opportunity to put the game out of 'Boro's reach.

A tearful Hodgson walked off the pitch, knowing that 'Boro should have clinched the game in the second half. He was not to know that the game was to be hailed as a watershed in the history of the club, for the talented young team was shortly to break up, manager John Neal was to leave the club and 'Boro were bound for the Second Division at the end of 1981-2 season.

Wolverhampton Wanderers: Bradshaw; Palmer, Parkin, W.Clarke(Bell, 79mins), McAlle, Berry, Hibbitt, Carr, Gray, Richards, Eves.
Middlesbrough: Platt; Nattrass, Bailey, Johnston, Ashcroft, McAndrew, Cochrane (Shearer, 105mins), Proctor, Hodgson, Jankovic, Armstrong.

Attendance: 40,524

Middlesbrough FC opened their doors to the public on 26 July 1981 and 21,000 people took the opportunity to see how the club worked behind the scenes.

Terry Cochrane, who made over 100 League and Cup appearances for Middlesbrough and won 26 Northern Ireland caps.

Middlesbrough in the Football League 1899-1989

	P	W	D	HOME L	F	A	W	D	AWAY L	F	A	Pts	Pos
				DIVISION TWO									
1899-1900	34	8	4	5	28	15	0	4	13	11	54	24	14th
1900-01	34	11	4	2	38	13	4	3	10	12	27	37	6th
1901-02	34	15	1	1	58	7	8	4	5	32	17	51	2nd
				DIVISION ONE									
1902-03	34	10	3	4	27	16	4	2	11	16	34	32	13th
1903-04	34	9	3	5	30	17	0	9	8	16	30	30	10th
1904-05	34	7	3	7	21	24	2	5	10	15	32	26	15th
1905-06	38	10	4	5	41	23	0	7	12	15	48	31	18th
1906-07	38	11	2	6	33	21	4	4	11	23	42	36	11th
1907-08	38	12	2	5	32	16	5	5	9	22	29	41	6th
1908-09	38	11	2	6	38	21	3	7	9	21	32	37	9th
1909-10	38	8	4	7	34	36	3	5	11	22	37	37	17th
1910-11	38	9	5	5	31	21	2	5	12	18	42	32	16th
1911-12	38	11	6	2	35	17	5	2	12	21	28	40	7th
1912-13	38	6	9	4	29	22	5	1	13	26	47	32	16th
1913-14	38	14	2	3	55	20	5	3	11	22	40	43	3rd
1914-15	38	10	6	3	42	24	3	6	10	20	50	38	12th
1919-20	42	10	5	6	35	23	5	5	11	26	42	40	13th
1920-21	42	10	6	5	29	21	7	6	8	24	32	46	8th
1921-22	42	12	6	3	46	19	4	8	9	33	50	46	8th
1922-23	42	11	4	6	41	25	2	6	13	16	38	36	18th
1923-24	42	6	4	11	23	23	1	4	16	14	37	22	22nd
				DIVISION TWO									
1924-25	42	6	10	5	22	21	4	9	8	14	23	39	13th
1925-26	42	14	1	6	56	28	7	1	13	21	40	44	9th
1926-27	42	18	2	1	78	23	9	6	6	44	37	62	1st
				DIVISION ONE									
1927-28	42	7	9	5	46	35	4	6	11	35	53	37	22nd
				DIVISION TWO									
1928-29	42	14	4	3	54	22	8	7	6	38	35	55	1st
				DIVISION ONE									
1929-30	42	11	3	7	48	31	5	3	13	34	53	38	16th
1930-31	42	13	5	3	57	28	6	3	12	41	62	46	7th
1931-32	42	11	3	7	37	29	3	6	12	23	54	38	18th
1932-33	42	8	5	8	35	33	6	4	11	28	40	37	17th
1933-34	42	13	3	5	51	26	3	4	14	17	51	39	16th
1934-35	42	8	9	4	38	29	2	5	14	32	61	34	20th
1935-36	42	12	6	3	56	23	3	4	14	28	47	40	14th
1936-37	42	14	6	1	49	22	5	2	14	25	49	46	7th
1937-38	42	12	4	5	40	26	7	4	10	32	39	46	5th
1938-39	42	13	6	2	64	27	7	3	11	29	47	49	4th
1946-47	42	11	3	7	46	32	6	5	10	27	36	42	11th

	P		HOME					AWAY					
	P	W	D	L	F	A	W	D	L	F	A	Pts	Pos
DIVISION ONE													
1947-48	42	8	7	6	37	27	6	2	13	34	46	37	16th
1948-49	42	10	6	5	37	23	1	6	14	9	34	34	19th
1949-50	42	14	2	5	37	18	6	5	10	22	30	47	9th
1950-51	42	12	7	2	51	25	6	4	11	25	40	47	6th
1951-52	42	12	4	5	37	25	3	2	16	27	63	36	18th
1952-53	42	12	5	4	46	27	2	6	13	24	50	39	13th
1953-54	42	6	6	9	29	35	4	4	13	31	56	30	21st
DIVISION TWO													
1954-55	42	13	1	7	48	31	5	5	11	25	51	42	12th
1955-56	42	11	4	6	46	31	5	4	12	30	47	40	14th
1956-57	42	12	5	4	51	29	7	5	9	33	31	48	6th
1957-58	42	13	3	5	52	29	6	4	11	31	45	45	7th
1958-59	42	9	7	5	51	26	6	3	12	36	45	40	13th
1959-60	42	14	5	2	56	21	5	5	11	34	43	48	5th
1960-61	42	13	6	2	44	20	5	6	10	39	54	48	5th
1961-62	42	11	3	7	45	29	5	4	12	31	43	39	12th
1962-63	42	12	4	5	48	35	8	5	8	38	50	49	4th
1963-64	42	14	4	3	47	16	1	7	13	20	36	41	10th
1964-65	42	8	5	8	40	31	5	4	12	30	45	35	17th
1965-66	42	8	8	5	36	28	2	5	14	22	58	33	21st
DIVISION THREE													
1966-67	42	16	3	4	51	20	7	6	10	36	44	55	2nd
DIVISION TWO													
1967-68	42	10	7	4	39	19	7	5	9	21	35	46	6th
1968-69	42	13	7	1	36	13	6	4	11	22	36	49	4th
1969-70	42	15	4	2	36	14	5	6	10	19	31	50	4th
1970-71	42	13	6	2	37	16	4	8	9	23	27	48	7th
1971-72	42	16	4	1	31	11	3	4	14	19	37	46	9th
1972-73	42	12	6	3	29	15	5	7	9	17	28	47	4th
1973-74	42	16	4	1	40	8	11	7	3	37	22	65	1st
DIVISION ONE													
1974-75	42	11	7	3	33	14	7	5	9	21	26	48	7th
1975-76	42	9	7	5	23	11	6	3	12	23	34	40	13th
1976-77	42	11	6	4	25	14	3	7	11	15	31	41	12th
1977-78	42	8	8	5	25	19	4	7	10	17	35	39	14th
1978-79	42	10	5	6	33	21	5	5	11	24	29	40	12th
1979-80	42	11	7	3	31	14	5	5	11	19	30	44	9th
1980-81	42	14	4	3	38	16	2	1	18	15	45	37	14th
1981-82	42	5	9	7	20	24	3	6	12	14	28	39	22nd
DIVISION TWO													
1982-83	42	8	7	6	27	29	3	8	10	19	58	48	16th
1983-84	42	9	8	4	26	18	3	5	13	15	29	49	17th
1984-85	42	6	8	7	22	26	4	2	15	19	31	40	19th
1985-86	42	8	6	7	26	23	4	3	14	18	30	45	21st
DIVISION THREE													
1986-87	46	16	5	2	38	11	12	5	6	29	19	94	2nd
DIVISION TWO													
1987-88	44	15	4	3	47	16	7	8	7	19	20	78	3rd
DIVISION ONE													
1988-89	38	6	7	6	28	30	3	5	11	16	31	39	18th

163

1899-1900

Manager: John Robson

#	Month	Date		Opponent	Result	Scorers	Att.
1	Sep	2	(a)	Lincoln C	L 0-3		
2		4	(a)	Port Vale	L 1-3	Page	1,800
3		9	(h)	Small Heath	L 1-3	M.Murphy	10,000
4		16	(a)	New Brighton	D 1-1	Eglington	
5		23	(h)	Grimsby T	W 1-0	Eglington	
6		30	(a)	W Arsenal	L 0-3		5,000
7	Oct	7	(h)	Barnsley	W 3-0	Longstaffe, Lamb 2	
8		14	(a)	Leicester F	L 1-4	Lamb	
9		21	(h)	Luton T	D 0-0		
10	Nov	4	(h)	Walsall	D 1-1	Lamb	
11		11	(h)	Burton S	W 8-1	J.Murphy 3, Longstaffe, Pugh 2, Reid 2	
12		25	(h)	Gainsborough T	D 0-0		6,000
13	Dec	2	(a)	Bolton W	L 0-3		3,156
14		9	(h)	Loughborough T	W 3-0	Raisbeck, M.Murphy, J.Murphy	3,000
15		16	(a)	Newton Heath	L 1-2	Reid	4,000
16		23	(h)	Sheffield W	L 1-2	Reid	
17		30	(h)	Lincoln C	D 1-1	J.Murphy	6,000
18	Jan	6	(a)	Small Heath	L 1-5	Pratt	
19		13	(h)	New Brighton	W 5-2	Page, Longstaffe, Lamb 2, Pugh	4,000
20		20	(a)	Grimsby T	L 0-2		4,000
21		27	(a)	Chesterfield	L 1-7	Pugh	1,000
22	Feb	3	(h)	W Arsenal	W 1-0	Pugh	5,000
23		10	(a)	Barnsley	L 2-5	Reid, H.Piercy	
24		17	(h)	Leicester F	L 0-1		8,000
25		24	(a)	Luton T	D 1-1	Osborne	1,000
26	Mar	3	(h)	Port Vale	W 1-0	Pugh	
27		10	(a)	Walsall	D 1-1	Pugh	1,000
28		17	(a)	Burton S	L 0-5		
29		24	(h)	Chesterfield	L 0-1		5,000
30		31	(a)	Gainsborough T	L 0-5		
31	Apr	7	(h)	Bolton W	L 0-3		8,000
32		14	(a)	Loughborough T	D 1-1	Niblo	500
33		21	(h)	Newton Heath	W 2-0	Niblo, Osborne	8,000
34		28	(a)	Sheffield W	L 0-3		3,000

FINAL LEAGUE POSITION: 14th in Division Two

Appearances
Goals

FA Cup

	Month	Date		Opponent	Result	Scorers	Att.
Q1	Oct	28	(h)	Jarrow	L 1-2	Eglington	

Appearances
Goals

Appearance / line-up grid (values are shirt/position numbers; final column is the match number).

Smith EG*	Shaw TW*	Ramsey A*	Allport HG*	McNally J*	McCracken JP*	Wanless R*	Longstaffe G*	Gettins JH*	Page R*	Pugh CE*	Osborne F*	Hughes M*	Redfern J*	Callaghan J*	Murphy M*	Bell FW*	Pratt R*	Eglington R*	Stott J*	Lamb TJ*	Piercy FR*	Gray R*	Raisbeck L*	Clark E*	Reid G*	Murphy J*	Cowan J*	McCorquodale D*	Jones J*	Piercy HR*	Buckley S*	Madden G*	Evans RW*	Linton T*	Clark J*	Ostler J*	Niblo TB*	Wardrope W*	No.
1	2	3	4	5	6	7	8	9	10	11																													1
1	2	3	4	5	6	8	7		10	11	9																												2
	2	3	4		5	7		9		11		1	6	8	10																								3
	2	3	4		5	7				11		1		8		6	9	10																					4
	2	3	4		5	7				11		1					9	10	6	8																			5
	2	3	4		5	7				11		1	6				9	10		8																			6
1	2	3	4		5	7				11					6		9	10		8																			7
1	2	3	4		5	7				11							9		8	6	10																		8
1	2	3	4		5	7				11	9						8			10	6																		9
1	2	3	4		5	7	8			11							10			9	6																		10
1		3	4		6		7			11							8		5	2	9	10																	11
1		3	4		6		7			11							8		5		9	10	2																12
		3	4		6		7			11	1						8		5		9	10	2																13
		3	4		6		7			11	1		10				8		5		9		2																14
		3	4		6					11	1		10				8		5		9		2	7															15
		3	4		6					11	1		10				8		5		9		2	7															16
					6	7				11	1		10				8		5		9	10	2		3	4													17
	2					7			6		1		10				8		5		9	11	3		4														18
		4	3		7		6	11		1			10				8		5		9		2																19
		4	3		7		6	11		1			10				8		5		9		2																20
		4	3		7		6	11		1			10				8		5				2						9										21
		4	2		7		6	11		1							8				9							3	5	10									22
	3	4	2		8		6	10		1							7				9							5	11										23
	2	4	3		7			11	8	1							5				9				6				10										24
	3	4	2					11	8	1							7	8	5						6				10	9									25
	3	4	2	7				11	8	1						10					6				5				9										26
	3	4	2	7				10	11	8	1										5				6				9										27
	3	4	2	7				10	11	8	1										5				6				9										28
	3	4	2	7				11	8	1									10		5				6				9										29
	3	4	5					11	8	1					10			7			6		9		2														30
	3	4	5			9	6	10	1										7						11	2								8					31
	3	4	6			10	11	8	1	7																2										5	9		32
1	2	4	3			6	11	8							10														2							5	9	7	33
1	3	4			6	11	7								10														2							5	9	8	34
10	12	27	31	2	33	10	19	3	14	31	12	24	3	2	2	1	16	5	1	23	1	3	19	1	15	6	17	2	2	8	1	3	2	4	1	3	3	2	
							3		2	7	2				2			1	2		6		1		5	5						1					2		

Smith EG*	Shaw TW*	Ramsey A*	Allport HG*	McNally J*	McCracken JP*	Wanless R*	Longstaffe G*	Gettins JH*	Page R*	Pugh CE*	Osborne F*	Hughes M*	Redfern J*	Callaghan J*	Murphy M*	Bell FW*	Pratt R*	Eglington R*	Stott J*	Lamb TJ*	Piercy FR*	Gray R*	Raisbeck L*	Clark E*	Reid G*	Murphy J*	Cowan J*	McCorquodale D*	Jones J*	Piercy HR*	Buckley S*	Madden G*	Evans RW*	Linton T*	Clark J*	Ostler J*	Niblo TB*	Wardrope W*	
	2	3	4		5		7			11		1					9	10		8	6																		Q1
	1	1	1		1		1			1		1					1	1		1	1																		
																	1																						

1900-01

Manager: John Robson

1	Sep	1	(h)	Lincoln C	W	2-0	Wardrope, A.Robertson	11,000
2		8	(a)	Newton Heath	L	0-4		5,500
3		15	(h)	Glossop	D	2-2	Moran, A.Robertson	12,000
4		22	(a)	Chesterfield	W	3-2	John Brown 2 (1 pen), Moran	4,000
5		29	(a)	Burnley	L	0-2		
6	Oct	6	(h)	Port Vale	W	4-0	A.Robertson, Wardrope 2, John Brown	8,000
7		13	(a)	Leicester F	L	0-1		5,000
8		20	(h)	New Brighton	W	2-1	John Brown (pen), Wardrope	8,500
9		27	(a)	Gainsborough T	D	1-1	Wardrope	2,000
10	Nov	10	(a)	Burton S	D	0-0		5,000
11		24	(a)	W Arsenal	L	0-1		8,000
12	Dec	1	(h)	Blackpool	W	3-1	Moran, Wardrope, Higgins	10,000
13		15	(h)	Small Heath	L	0-1		12,000
14		22	(a)	Grimsby T	L	0-2		8,000
15		26	(h)	Barnsley	W	3-0	A.Robertson 2, Moran	8,000
16		29	(a)	Lincoln C	W	2-1	A.Robertson, J.H.Gettins	5,000
17	Jan	1	(h)	Newton Heath	L	1-2	Wardrope	12,000
18		12	(a)	Glossop	L	0-2		4,000
19		19	(h)	Chesterfield	W	2-0	Moran, D.W.Smith*	8,000
20	Feb	16	(h)	Leicester F	W	2-1	Wardrope 2	8,000
21	Mar	2	(h)	Gainsborough T	W	9-2	Wilkie 5, Davidson, A.Robertson, McCowie 2	6,000
22		9	(h)	Walsall	W	2-1	McCowie, Wilkie	8,000
23		11	(a)	Port Vale	W	2-0	A.Robertson, Davidson	4,000
24		14	(a)	Barnsley	L	1-3	Wardrope	
25		16	(h)	Burton S	W	3-1	McCowie 2, D.W.Smith (pen)	
26		25	(a)	New Brighton	L	1-3	Goldie (og)	
27		30	(h)	W Arsenal	D	1-1	A.Robertson	6,000
28	Apr	5	(a)	Stockport C	W	1-0	Wilkie	4,000
29		6	(a)	Blackpool	L	0-3		2,000
30		9	(h)	Burnley	D	0-0		6,000
31		13	(h)	Stockport C	W	2-0	John Brown, Wilkie	
32		20	(a)	Small Heath	L	1-2	Wardrope	8,000
33		22	(a)	Walsall	D	0-0		1,000
34		27	(h)	Grimsby T	D	0-0		6,000

FINAL LEAGUE POSITION: 6th in Division Two   Appearances

*Some sources credit own-goal, but club credit D.W.Smith.   Goals

FA Cup

Q1	Nov	3	(h)	Willington A	D	3-3	John Brown, Wardrope, Higgins	6,000
R		7	(a)	Willington A	D	0-0		2,000
2R		12	(h)	Willington A	W	8-0	Moran, Carrick 2, Wardrope, A.Robertson 2, Higgins 2	4,000
Q2		17	(h)	Jarrow	W	3-0	Carrick 2, A.Robertson	8,000
Q3	Dec	8	(h)	Bishop Auckland	W	4-0	John Brown 4	9,000
1	Jan	5	(a)	Grimsby T	W	1-0	Wilkie	8,000
2	Feb	9	(h)	Newcastle U	W	3-1	A.Robertson, McCowie, Wardrope	16,000
3		23	(h)	Kettering T	W	5-0	McCowie, Wilkie, A.Robertson 3	12,000
4	Mar	23	(h)	West Brom A	L	0-1		20,000

Appearances

Goals

166

Appearances grid (numbers indicate shirt/position number worn by each player in each match). Columns are players; rows are matches.

Frail J*	Dow MJ*	Ramsay A	Millar J	Higgins W*	Davidson A*	Moran M*	Wardrope W	Robertson A	Wilkie J*	Brown James*	Brown John*	McCowie A*	Eckford J*	Carrick C*	Jones J	Doig T*	Hodgson G*	Smith DW*	Gettins JH	Macfarlane T*	Thompson A*	McNally J	Cochrane M*	Brearley J*	No.
1	2	3	4	5	6	7	8	9	10	11															1
1	2	3	4	5	6	7	8	9	10		11														2
1	2	3	4	5	6	7	11	9	10		8														3
1	2	3	4	5	6	7	11	9	10		8														4
1	2	3	4		6	7	11	9	10	5	8														5
1	2	3	4	5	6	7	11	9	10		8														6
1	2	3	4	5	6	7	11	9	10		8														7
1	2	3	4	5	6	7	11	9	10		8														8
1	2	3	4	5	6	7	11	9	10		8														9
1	2	3	4	5	6	7	11	9			8	10													10
1	2	3		5	6	7	8				4	9	10	11											11
1	2			5	6	7	8		10		9		11		3	4									12
1	2			5	6	7	8		10		9		11		3	4									13
	2	3		5	6	7	8		10		9	11			4	1									14
	2	3		5	6	7	8	11	10							1	4	9							15
	2	3		5	6	7	8	11	10							1	4	9							16
	2	3		5	6	7	8	11	10		9					1	4								17
1	2	3		5	6	7	8	11	10								4	9							18
1	2	3		5	6	7		11	10		9	8						4							19
1	2	3		5	6	7		11	9		10	8						4							20
1	2	3		5	6	7		11	9		10	8						4							21
1	2	3		5	6	7		11	9		10	8						4							22
1	2			5	6	7		11	9		10							4		3	8				23
1		3	6	4				11	8		10		7							2	9	5			24
1	2	3	6	5		7		11	9		10	8						4							25
1	2	3		5	6	7		11	9		10	8						4							26
1		3		5	6	7		11	9		10	8						4					2		27
1	2	3		5	6	7		11	9		10	8						4							28
1	2			5	6	7		11	10		9	8						4					3		29
1	2			5	6	7		11	9		10	8						4					3		30
1		3		5	6	7		11	9		10	8						4					2		31
1	2	3		5	6	7		11	9		10	8						4							32
1		3		5	6	7		11	9		10	8						4					2		33
1	2			5	6	7		11	9		10							4					3	8	34
30	29	29	19	24	32	33	33	29	28	2	21	17	3	2	2	3	4	19	3	2	2	1	6	1	
			1	2	5	11	9	8	5		5						2	1							

1 own-goal

Cup matches:

Frail J*	Dow MJ*	Ramsay A	Millar J	Higgins W*	Davidson A*	Moran M*	Wardrope W	Robertson A	Wilkie J*	Brown James*	Brown John*	McCowie A*	Eckford J*	Carrick C*	Jones J	Doig T*	Hodgson G*	Smith DW*	Gettins JH	Macfarlane T*	Thompson A*	McNally J	Cochrane M*	Brearley J*	Rd
1	2	3	4	5	6	7	11		10		9	8													Q1
1		3	4		6	7	8	9	10		5			11						2					R
1	2	3		5	6	7	8	9			4	10	11												2R
1	2	3		5	6	7	8	9			4	10	11												Q2
1	2			5	6	7	8		10		9		11		3	4									Q3
1	2	3	4		6		7	8	10		9	11							5						1
1		3			6	7		11	9		10	5	8				2	4							2
1	2	3			6	7		11	9		10	5	8					4							3
1	2	3			6	7		11	9		10	5	8					4							4
9	7	8	3	5	8	9	9	7	7		9	4	3	3	2	1	3	1	1						
			3	1	3	7	2		5			2	4												

1901-02

Manager:John Robson

#				Opponent	Result	Scorers	Att
1	Sep	7	(a)	Stockport C	W 3-1	Wardrope, Cassidy, Tennant	5,000
2		14	(h)	Newton Heath	W 5-0	Davidson, Brearley 2, Cassidy, Turner	12,000
3		21	(a)	Glossop	L 0-1		3,000
4		28	(h)	Doncaster R	W 6-0	A.Jones, Wardrope, Brearley 2, Turner, Tennant	10,638
5	Oct	5	(a)	Lincoln C	L 1-2	Tennant	4,000
6		12	(h)	West Brom A	L 1-2	D.W.Smith	15,000
7		19	(a)	W Arsenal	W 3-0	D.W.Smith (pen), Brearley, Cassidy	8,000
8		26	(h)	Barnsley	W 2-1	Brearley 2	5,000
9	Nov	2	(a)	Leicester F	W 2-0	Brearley, Tennant	6,000
10		9	(h)	Preston NE	W 2-1	Brearley, Turner	12,000
11		16	(a)	Burnley	D 2-2	Brearley, Tennant	
12		23	(h)	Port Vale	W 3-0	Turner, Cassidy, Tennant	9,000
13		30	(a)	Chesterfield	D 0-0		
14	Dec	7	(h)	Gainsborough T	W 3-1	D.W.Smith (pen), Brearley, Tennant	7,000
15		14	(a)	West Brom A	L 0-2		6,868
16		21	(a)	Bristol C	L 0-1		6,000
17		28	(h)	Blackpool	W 2-1	Thompson 2	6,000
18	Jan	1	(h)	Burton U	W 5-0	A.Jones, Cassidy 3, Turner	10,000
19		4	(h)	Stockport C	W 6-0	A.Jones, Turner, Wardrope, Brearley, Cassidy, D.W.Smith	7,000
20		18	(h)	Glossop	W 5-0	D.W.Smith, A.Jones, Wardrope 2, Cassidy	9,000
21	Feb	1	(a)	Lincoln C	D 0-0		8,000
22		15	(h)	W Arsenal	W 1-0	Cassidy	7,000
23		22	(a)	Barnsley	W 7-2	Davidson, Wardrope, Brearley 4, Leslie	2,000
24	Mar	1	(h)	Leicester F	W 5-0	D.W.Smith (pen), Cassidy 2, Leslie, Crawford	10,000
25		8	(a)	Preston NE	W 3-0	A.Jones, Brearley, Leslie	
26		15	(h)	Burnley	W 3-0	Cassidy, Brearley 2	10,000
27		22	(a)	Port Vale	D 1-1	Ramsey	
28		28	(a)	Doncaster R	D 0-0		7,000
29		29	(h)	Chesterfield	W 7-1	Wardrope, Cassidy 2, A.Robertson 3, R.Watson	7,000
30	Apr	5	(a)	Gainsborough T	W 4-1	Wardrope, Brearley, A.Robertson 2	500
31		7	(a)	Newton Heath	W 2-1	A.Jones, A.Robertson	2,000
32		12	(a)	Burton U	L 2-3	Brearley 2	3,000
33		19	(h)	Bristol C	W 2-0	Wardrope 2	12,000
34		26	(a)	Blackpool	W 2-0	A.Robertson 2	

FINAL LEAGUE POSITION: 2nd in Division Two

Appearances
Goals

FA Cup

1	Jan	25	(h)	Bristol R	D 1-1	Cassidy	13,000
R		29	(a)	Bristol R	L 0-1		7,600

Appearances
Goals

Player appearance and goalscoring grid (shirt numbers worn per match).

Frail J	Dow MJ	Ramsey A	Smith DW	Jones A*	Davidson A	Wardrope W	Brearley J	Cassidy J*	Turner P*	Tennant J*	Jones J	Leslie J*	Blackett J*	Robertson J*	Moran M	Crawford J*	Thompson A	Watson R*	Robertson A	Williamson RG*	#
1	2	3	4	5	6	7	8	9	10	11											1
1	2	3	4	5	6	7	8	9	10	11											2
1	2	3	4	5	6	7	8	9	10	11											3
1		3	4	5	6	7	8	9	10	11	2										4
1		3	4	5	6	7	8	9	10	11	2										5
1		3	4	5	6	7		9	10	11	2	8									6
1		3	4	5	6		8	9	10	11		2			7						7
1		3	4	5	6	7	8	9	10	11		2									8
1		3	4	5	6	7	8	9	10	11		2									9
1		3	4	5	6	7	8	9	10	11		2									10
1		3	4	5	6		8	9	10	11		2			7						11
1		3	4	5	6		8	9	10	11		2			7						12
1		3	4	5	6	7	8	9	10	11		2									13
1		3	4	5	6		8	9	10	11		2			7						14
1		3	4	5	6	11	8	9	10			2			7						15
1		3	4	5	6		8	11	10			2		9	7						16
1		3		5	6	4	8	10	11			2			7		9				17
1		3		5	6	11	4	8	10			2			7		9				18
1		3	4	5	6	8	11	9	10			2			7						19
1		3	4	5	6	8	11	9	10			2			7						20
1		3	4	5	6	8	11	9	10			2			7						21
1	2		4	5	6	8	9	11	10					3	7						22
1		3	4	5	6	11	9	10			8	2			7						23
1		3	4	5	6	11	9	10			8	2			7						24
1		3	4	5	6	11	9	10			8	2			7						25
1		3	4	5	6	10	9	11			8	2			7						26
1	2	3	4	5	6	10	9	11			8				7						27
1		3	4	5	6	10	9	11			8	2			7						28
1		3	4	5	6	10		11				2			7	8		9			29
1		3	4	5	6	10	8	11				2			7			9			30
1		3	4	5	6	10	8	11				2			7			9			31
1		3	4	5	6		8	10	11			2			7			9			32
		3	4	5	6	10	8		11			2			7			9	1		33
		3	4	5	6	10		11				2			7	8		9	1		34
32	5	33	32	34	27	31	32	23	17	3	7	27	2	3	20	2	2	6	2		
		1	6	6	2	10	22	15	6	7	3		1	2	1	8					

Frail J	Dow MJ	Ramsey A	Smith DW	Jones A*	Davidson A	Wardrope W	Brearley J	Cassidy J*	Turner P*	Tennant J*	Jones J	Leslie J*	Blackett J*	Robertson J*	Moran M	Crawford J*	Thompson A	Watson R*	Robertson A	Williamson RG*	
1		3	4	5	6	8	11	9	10			2			7						I
1		3	4	5	6	8	11	9	10			2			7						R
2		2	2	2	2	2	2	2	2			2			2						
						1															

1902-03

Manager: John Robson

1	Sep	1	(a)	Blackburn R	W	1-0	A.Robertson	3,000
2		6	(h)	Everton	W	1-0	A.Robertson	20,000
3		13	(a)	Sheffield W	L	0-2		20,000
4		20	(h)	West Brom A	D	1-1	Cassidy	22,420
5		27	(a)	Notts C	L	0-2		10,000
6	Oct	4	(h)	Bolton W	W	4-3	R.Watson 2, Cassidy 2	8,000
7		11	(a)	Derby C	L	2-3	A.Jones (pen), R.Watson	10,000
8		18	(a)	Newcastle U	W	1-0	Carrick	26,000
9		25	(h)	Wolves	W	2-0	Cassidy, Carrick	15,000
10	Nov	1	(a)	Liverpool	L	0-5		15,000
11		8	(h)	Sheffield U	L	0-2		14,000
12		15	(a)	Grimsby T	D	2-2	Carrick, A.Jones (pen)	5,000
13		22	(h)	Aston Villa	L	1-2	J.Robertson	15,000
14		29	(a)	Nottingham F	L	0-1		5,000
15	Dec	6	(h)	Bury	D	1-1	Carrick	18,000
16		20	(h)	Sunderland	L	0-1		15,000
17		26	(a)	Wolves	L	0-2		16,000
18		27	(a)	Stoke	W	2-0	Carrick, Goodson	7,000
19	Jan	3	(a)	Everton	L	0-3		
20		10	(h)	Sheffield W	W	2-1	D.W.Smith, R.Watson	8,000
21		17	(a)	West Brom A	L	0-1		18,033
22		24	(h)	Notts C	W	2-1	Cassidy, Thompson	10,000
23		31	(a)	Bolton W	L	1-2	A.Davidson	14,000
24	Feb	14	(h)	Newcastle U	W	1-0	Cassidy	20,000
25		28	(h)	Liverpool	L	0-2		15,000
26	Mar	7	(a)	Sheffield U	W	3-1	A.Robertson 2, Goodson	10,000
27		14	(h)	Grimsby T	W	2-0	D.W.Smith, Carrick	12,000
28		28	(h)	Nottingham F	W	2-0	A.Robertson, Goodson	10,000
29	Apr	4	(a)	Bury	L	1-3	A.Davidson	7,000
30		11	(h)	Blackburn R	W	4-0	MacAulay (pen), Cassidy, J.Robertson, A.Robertson	10,000
31		13	(h)	Derby C	W	3-1	A.Robertson, MacAulay (pen), D.W.Smith	15,000
32		18	(a†)	Sunderland	L	1-2	J.Robertson	25,000
33		25	(h)	Stoke	D	1-1	Currie	10,000
34		27	(a)	Aston Villa	L	0-5		9,000

FINAL LEAGUE POSITION: 13th in Division One Appearances

†Played at St James' Park, Newcastle. Goals

FA Cup

1	Dec	13	(a)	Bristol C	L	1-3	A.Robertson	8,000

Appearances

Goals

Appearance grid (shirt numbers by player and match). Columns are players; rows are matches (match number shown in the final column).

Macfarlane R*	Blackett J	Ramsey A	Smith DW	Jones A	Davidson A	Crawford J	MacAulay W*	Robertson A	Cassidy J	Muir J*	Robertson J	Hogg J*	Watson R	Carrick C	Muir W*	Thompson A	Millar J	Goodson L*	Godley W*	Gettins JH	Williamson RG	Piercy FR	Douglas H*	Currie R*	#
1	2	3	4	5	6	7	8	9	10	11															1
1	2	3	4	5	6		8	9	10	11	7														2
1		3	4	5	6		8	9	10	11	7	2													3
1	2	3	4	5	6		8	9	10	11	7														4
1	2	3	4	5	6		8		10		7		9	11											5
1	2	3		5	6			9	10		7		8	11	4										6
1	2	3		5	6			9	10		7		8	11	4										7
1		3	4	5	6			9	10		7	2	8	11											8
1		3	4	5	6			9	10		7	2	8	11											9
1		3	4	5	6			9	10		7	2	8	11											10
1		3	4	5	6			9	10		7	2	8	11											11
1		3	4	5	6			9	10		7	2	8	11											12
1		3	4	5	6				10		7	2	8	11		9									13
1		3	4	5				9	10		7	2	8	11			6								14
1		3	4	5	6			9	10		7	2	8	11											15
1		3	4	5	6		8				7	2		11		10		9							16
1		3	4	5	6		8			11	7	2				10		9							17
1		3	4	5	6		8				7	2		11		10		9							18
		3	4	5	6		8				7	2		11		10		9			1				19
		3	4	5	6		8				7	2		11		10		9			1				20
		3	4	5	6		8		10		7	2		11				9			1				21
		3	4	5	6		8		10		7	2		11				9			1				22
		3	4	5	6				10		7	2	8	11				9			1				23
		3	4	5	6		8		10		7	2		11				9			1				24
		3	4	5	6		8		10		7	2		11				9			1				25
		3	4	5	6				10		7	2	8	11				9			1				26
		3	4	5	6				10		7	2		11				9		8	1				27
		3	4	5	6				10		7	2	8	11				9			1				28
		3	4	5	6				10		7	2	8	11				9			1				29
		3	4	5	6		8		10		7	2		11				9			1				30
		3	4	5	6		8		10		7	2		11				9			1				31
		3	4	5	6		8				7	2		11		10		9			1				32
		3	4	5	6		8			11	7	2				10		9			1				33
		3	4	5	6		8				7	2		11		10		9			1				34
18	8	30	32	32	34	4	21	13	26	9	30	28	14	22	4	3	1	16	1	4	16	3	4	3	
		3	2	2		2	7	7		3		4	6		1			3			1				

Macfarlane R*	Blackett J	Ramsey A	Smith DW	Jones A	Davidson A	Crawford J	MacAulay W*	Robertson A	Cassidy J	Muir J*	Robertson J	Hogg J*	Watson R	Carrick C	Muir W*	Thompson A	Millar J	Goodson L*	Godley W*	Gettins JH	Williamson RG	Piercy FR	Douglas H*	Currie R*	#
1		3	4	5	6	7			10			2	8	11		9									1
1		1	1	1	1	1			1			1	1	1		1									
									1																

171

1903-04

Manager: John Robson

1	Sep	5	(a)	Sheffield W	L 1-4	A.Brown	20,000
2		12	(h)	Sunderland	L 2-3	Cassidy, A.Brown	† 30,000
3		19	(a)	West Brom A	D 0-0		14,130
4		26	(h)	Small Heath	W 3-1	Cassidy 2, A.Brown	18,000
5	Oct	3	(a)	Everton	L 0-2		15,000
6		10	(h)	Stoke	W 2-0	Cassidy, E.Gettins	15,000
7		17	(a)	Derby C	D 2-2	Cassidy, E.Gettins	7,000
8		24	(h)	Manchester C	W 6-0	Atherton 2, Cassidy, Goodson, A.Brown, D.W.Smith	15,000
9		31	(a)	Notts C	L 2-3	A.Brown, Blackett (pen)	8,000
10	Nov	7	(h)	Sheffield U	W 4-1	Goodson, A.Davidson, Atherton 2	25,000
11		14	(a)	Newcastle U	L 1-2	A.Brown	30,000
12		21	(h)	Aston Villa	W 2-1	Cassidy, Blackett (pen)	20,000
13		28	(h)	Wolves	L 1-2	Atherton	8,000
14	Dec	12	(h)	Bury	W 1-0	A.Brown	10,000
15		19	(a)	Blackburn R	D 1-1	Cassidy	15,000
16		26	(h)	Nottingham F	D 1-1	Atherton	14,000
17		28	(a)	Stoke	D 0-0		10,000
18	Jan	1	(a)	Manchester C	D 1-1	A.Brown	30,000
19		2	(h)	Sheffield W	L 0-1		
20		9	(a)	Sunderland	L 1-3	Suddick	15,000
21		16	(h)	West Brom A	D 2-2	A.Brown, Goodson	14,000
22		23	(h)	Small Heath	D 2-2	Blackett (pen), Atherton	10,000
23		30	(h)	Everton	W 3-0	A.Brown, E.Gettins, Cassidy	12,000
24	Feb	13	(h)	Derby C	D 0-0		10,000
25		22	(a)	Liverpool	L 0-1		15,000
26		27	(h)	Notts C	W 1-0	A.Brown	6,000
27	Mar	12	(h)	Newcastle U	L 1-3	Cassidy	20,000
28		19	(a)	Aston Villa	L 1-2	Atherton	10,000
29		26	(a)	Wolves	D 2-2	A.Brown, Atherton	
30		28	(a)	Sheffield U	L 0-3		
31	Apr	2	(h)	Liverpool	W 1-0	Roberts	12,000
32		9	(a)	Bury	D 1-1	Roberts	3,000
33		16	(h)	Blackburn R	L 0-2		12,000
34		23	(a)	Nottingham F	D 1-1	Cassidy	5,000

FINAL LEAGUE POSITION: 10th in Division One

†Official opening of Ayresome Park

Appearances
Goals

FA Cup

1	Feb	6	(a)	Millwall	W 2-0	A.Brown 2	12,000
2		20	(a)	Preston NE	W 3-0	A.Brown 2, Atherton	15,000
3	Mar	5	(a)	Manchester C	D 0-0		35,000
R		9	(h)	Manchester C	L 1-3	A.Brown	‡ 34,000

‡Ground attendance record

Appearances
Goals

Williamson RG	Hogg J	Ramsey A	Smith DW	Jones A	Davidson A	Gettins E*	White W*	Brown A*	Cassidy J	Atherton RH*	Blackett J	Goodson L	Carrick C	Aitken S*	Suddick J*	Muir J	McGuigan A*	Godley W	Page R	Boddington H*	Roberts RJ*	Featherstone T*	
1	2	3	4	5	6	7	8	9	10	11													1
1	2	3	4	5	6	7	8	9	10	11													2
1	2		4	5	6	7	8	9	10	11	3												3
1	2		4	5	6	7	8	9	10	11	3												4
1	2		4	5	6	7	8	9	10	11	3												5
1	2		4	5	6	7		9	10	8	3	11											6
1	2		4	5	6		7	9	10	8	3	11											7
1	2		4	5	6	7		9	10	8	3	11											8
1	2		4	5	6	7		9	10	8	3		11										9
1	2		4	5	6	7		9	10	8	3	11											10
1	2			5	6	7		9	10	8	3	11		4									11
1	2			5	6	7		9	10	8	3	11		4									12
1	2			5	6	7		9	10	8	3	11		4									13
1	2			5	6	7		9	10	8	3	11		4									14
1	2			5	6	7		9	10	8	3	11		4									15
1	2			5	6	7		9	10	8	3	11		4									16
1	2			5	6	7		9	10	8	3	11		4									17
1	2			5	6	7		9	10	8	3	11		4									18
1	2			5	6	7		9	10	8	3	11		4									19
1	2		7	5	6			9	10	8	3	11		4									20
1	2			5	6			9	10	7	3	11		4	8								21
1		3		5	6	7		9	10	8	2	11		4									22
1	2			5	6	7		9	10	8	3	11		4									23
1	2			5	6	7		9	10	8	3	11		4									24
1	2			5	6	7		9	10	8	3			4		11							25
1		3		5	6	7		9	10	8	2			4			11						26
1		3		5	6	7		9	10		2		8	4		11							27
1	2		4	5	6	7		9	10	8	3					11							28
1	2		4		6	7		9	10	8	3					11			5				29
1	2		4		6	7		9	10	8	3							5	11				30
1	2			5	6	7		9	10	8	3			4							11		31
1	2		4	5		7	8		10	6	3										11	9	32
1	2		4	5	6	7		9	10	8	3										11		33
1	2		4		6			9	10	8	3	5								7	11		34
34	31	5	17	31	33	30	7	33	34	33	32	18	2	19	1	4	1	1	2	1	4	1	
		1		1	3			12	12	9	3	3		1		2							

Williamson RG	Hogg J	Ramsey A	Smith DW	Jones A	Davidson A	Gettins E*	White W*	Brown A*	Cassidy J	Atherton RH*	Blackett J	Goodson L	Carrick C	Aitken S*	Suddick J*	Muir J	McGuigan A*	Godley W	Page R	Boddington H*	Roberts RJ*	Featherstone T*	
1	2			5	6	7		9	10	8	3	11		4									1
1	2			5	6	7		9	10	8	3			4		11							2
1	2			5	6	7		9	10	8	3	11	4										3
1	2			5	6	7		9	10	8	3	11				4							R
4	4			4	4	4		4	4	4	4	1	2	3		1	1						
										5	1												

1904-05

Manager: John Robson

1	Sep	3	(h)	Sheffield W	L 1-3	Atherton	18,000
2		10	(a)	Sunderland	D 1-1	E.Gettins	16,000
3		17	(h)	W Arsenal	W 1-0	A.Brown	15,000
4		24	(a)	Derby C	L 2-4	A.Brown, Davidson	8,000
5	Oct	1	(h)	Everton	W 1-0	E.Gettins	10,000
6		8	(a)	Small Heath	L 1-2	Atherton	12,000
7		15	(h)	Manchester C	L 0-1		20,000
8		22	(a)	Notts C	D 0-0		8,000
9		29	(h)	Sheffield U	L 0-1		14,000
10	Nov	5	(a)	Newcastle U	L 0-3		23,000
11		12	(h)	Preston NE	D 1-1	Jones	12,000
12		19	(a)	Stoke	L 1-3	A.Brown	8,000
13		26	(a)	Wolves	L 3-5	Bell, Blackett (pen), R.J.Roberts	8,000
14	Dec	3	(h)	Bury	D 2-2	Astley 2	9,000
15		10	(a)	Aston Villa	D 0-0		8,000
16		17	(h)	Blackburn R	W 2-1	Bell 2	10,000
17		24	(a)	Nottingham F	D 1-1	Astley	
18		26	(h)	Small Heath	L 0-1		20,000
19		31	(a)	Sheffield W	L 0-5		
20	Jan	7	(h)	Sunderland	L 1-3	Agnew (pen)	12,000
21		14	(a)	W Arsenal	D 1-1	Thackeray	16,000
22		21	(h)	Derby C	W 2-0	Astley, Atherton	12,000
23		28	(a)	Everton	L 0-1		20,000
24	Feb	11	(a)	Manchester C	L 2-3	Phillipson, Atherton	16,000
25		25	(h)	Sheffield U	W 1-0	Common (pen)	10,000
26	Mar	4	(h)	Nottingham F	D 0-0		12,000
27		11	(a)	Preston NE	L 0-2		5,000
28		18	(h)	Stoke	W 2-1	Common, R.J.Roberts	6,000
29		25	(h)	Wolves	W 3-1	Common, Green 2	7,000
30	Apr	1	(a)	Bury	L 0-1		5,000
31		8	(h)	Aston Villa	W 3-1	Hewitt, R.J.Roberts, Common	13,000
32		15	(a)	Blackburn R	W 2-0	Hewitt 2	4,000
33		24	(h)	Notts C	L 2-5	Green, Phillipson	10,000
34		29	(h)	Newcastle U	L 0-3		12,000

FINAL LEAGUE POSITION: 15th in Division One

Appearances
Goals

FA Cup

1	Feb	4	(h)	Tottenham H	D 1-1	Astley	20,340
R		8	(a)	Tottenham H	L 0-1		23,000

Appearances
Goals

174

Match appearance grid (shirt numbers by player). Players listed as column headers; right-hand column is the match number.

Williamson RG	Hogg J	Agnew WB*	Aitken S	Jones A	Davidson A	Astley H*	Atherton RH	Brown A	Cassidy J	Roberts RJ	Blackett J	Smith DW	Page R	Gettins E	Goodson L	Thackeray J*	Bell J*	Craig T*	McCallum D*	Davies WF*	Hewitt C*	Green T*	Phillipson T*	Frail J	Common A*	
1	2	3	4	5	6	7	8	9	10	11																1
1	2		5			9	8		10	11	3	4		6	7											2
1	2		5		6		8	9	10	11	3	4		7												3
1	2		5		6	10	8	9		11	3	4		7												4
1	2		4	5	6		8	9	10		3			7		11										5
1	2		4		6		8	9	10	11	3		5	7												6
1	2	3	4	5	6		8	10	9					7		11										7
1		3	4	5		10	9		2				6	7		11	8									8
1		3	4	5		10	9		2				6	7		11	8									9
1	2		4	5	6	9	8		10		3			7		11										10
1	2		4	5		10	9		6					7		11	8	3								11
1		3	4	5		8	9		6					7		11	10	2								12
1		3	4	5		9	6	10	2					7		11	8									13
1		3	4	5		9	6	10	2					7		11	8									14
1		3		5		9	10		6	7				4		11	8		2							15
1		3		5		9	10		6	7				4		11	8		2							16
1		3		5		9	10		6					4		11	8		2	7						17
1		3		5		9	10		6					4		11	8		2	7						18
1		3		5		9	10		6					4		11	8		2	7						19
1		3	4	5		8	9		6	11						10			2	7						20
1		3	4	5	6	8	9			11						10			2	7						21
1		3	4			9	8		6	11				5		10			2	7						22
1		3	4	5		9	8		6	11				7		10			2							23
1		3		5		8			6					4		11			2	7	9	10				24
		3	4	5		10			6							11			2	7		9		1	8	25
1		3	4	5					6							11			2	7	9	10			8	26
1		3	4	5		10			6							11			2	7		9			8	27
1		3	4	5	6				10							11			2	7		9			8	28
1		3	4	5	6				10							11			2	7		9			8	29
1		3	4	5	6				10							11			2	7		9			8	30
1		3	4	5	6				10							11			2	7		9			8	31
1		3	4	5	6				10							11			2	7		9			8	32
1	2	3	4	5	6											11				7	9	10			8	33
1		3	4	5	6				8							11			2	7		10			9	34
33	8	29	30	27	15	14	27	11	28	19	11	8	6	13	1	22	10	2	19	10	6	11	3	1	10	
	1		1	1	4	4	3		3	1				2		1	3				3	3	2		4	

Williamson RG	Hogg J	Agnew WB*	Aitken S	Jones A	Davidson A	Astley H*	Atherton RH	Brown A	Cassidy J	Roberts RJ	Blackett J	Smith DW	Page R	Gettins E	Goodson L	Thackeray J*	Bell J*	Craig T*	McCallum D*	Davies WF*	Hewitt C*	Green T*	Phillipson T*	Frail J	Common A*	
1		3	6	5		9	8	10	4							11			2	7						1
1		3	6	5		9	8		4							11	10		2	7						R
2		2	2	2		2	2	1	2							2	1		2	2						
					1																					

1905-06

Manager: Alex G.Mackie

1	Sep	2	(a)	Everton	L	1-4	Common	25,000
2		9	(h)	Derby C	L	0-1		10,000
3		16	(a)	Sheffield W	L	0-3		20,000
4		23	(h)	Nottingham F	W	2-0	Murray, Reid	15,000
5		30	(a)	Manchester C	L	0-4		15,000
6	Oct	7	(h)	Bury	W	5-1	Reid 3, Hewitt, Common	10,000
7		14	(h)	Wolves	W	3-1	Green 3	10,000
8		21	(a)	Preston NE	L	1-2	Common	10,000
9		28	(a)	Newcastle U	L	1-4	Hewitt	32,000
10	Nov	4	(a)	Aston Villa	L	1-4	Reid	15,000
11		11	(h)	Liverpool	L	1-5	Hewitt	8,000
12		18	(a)	Sheffield U	L	0-1		5,000
13		25	(h)	Notts C	W	4-1	Reid, Green 2, Hewitt	8,000
14	Dec	2	(a)	Stoke	D	1-1	Common	5,000
15		9	(h)	Bolton W	D	4-4	Hewitt, Thompson 2, Green	12,500
16		16	(a)	W Arsenal	D	2-2	Hewitt, Common	12,000
17		23	(h)	Blackburn R	D	1-1	Coxon	12,000
18		25	(h)	Birmingham	W	1-0	Common	20,000
19		26	(a)	Birmingham	L	0-7		15,000
20		30	(h)	Everton	D	0-0		15,000
21	Jan	1	(a)	Sunderland	L	1-2	Common	24,000
22		6	(a)	Derby C	D	1-1	Common	2,000
23		20	(h)	Sheffield W	D	2-2	Hewitt 2	10,000
24		27	(a)	Nottingham F	L	1-2	Common	12,000
25	Feb	10	(a)	Bury	D	1-1	Hewitt	4,000
26		17	(a)	Wolves	D	0-0		6,000
27	Mar	3	(h)	Newcastle U	W	1-0	R.H.Walker	20,000
28		10	(h)	Aston Villa	L	1-2	Common	12,000
29		14	(h)	Preston NE	L	1-2	R.H.Walker	8,000
30		17	(a)	Liverpool	L	1-6	Agnew	25,000
31		24	(h)	Sheffield U	L	0-1		12,000
32		31	(a)	Notts C	D	1-1	Common	15,000
33	Apr	7	(h)	Stoke	W	5-0	Common 3, Brawn, Bloomer	20,000
34		13	(h)	Sunderland	W	2-1	Bloomer, Common	14,000
35		14	(a)	Bolton W	L	1-2	Common	20,000
36		17	(h)	Manchester C	W	6-1	S.Aitken, Bloomer 2, Thackeray, Common 2	15,000
37		21	(h)	W Arsenal	W	2-0	Common 2	16,000
38		28	(a)	Blackburn R	D	1-1	Bloomer	

FINAL LEAGUE POSITION: 18th in Division One

Appearances
Goals

FA Cup

1	Jan	13	(h)	Bolton W	W	3-0	Common, Hewitt, Thackeray	22,000
2	Feb	3	(a)	Brighton & HA	D	1-1	Hewitt	7,462
R		7	(h)	Brighton & HA	D	1-1	Common	15,000
2R		12	(n†)	Brighton & HA	W	3-1	Common 3	11,528
3		24	(a)	Southampton	L	1-6	R.H.Walker	12,000

†Played at Bramall Lane, Sheffield.

Appearances
Goals

176

Team line-up / appearance grid. Player columns left-to-right; match numbers in the right-hand margin.

Williamson RG	McCallum D	Agnew WB	Aitken S	Jones A	Davidson A	Hewitt C	Common A	Green T	Reid GT*	Cassidy J	Hogg J	Thackeray J	Murray T*	Coxon T*	Duffy CF*	Hedley GT*	Henderson GH*	Thompson WT*	Walker RH*	Barker WC*	Trechman OL*	Hunter H*	Worrall WE*	Bloomer S*	Brawn WF*	Wilcox FJ*	Ratcliffe E*	#
1	2	3	4	5	6	7	8	9	10	11																		1
1		3	4	5	6		8	7	9	10	2	11																2
1	3		4	5	6		8	7	9	11	2		10															3
1		3	4	5	6	7	8		9	11	2		10															4
1		3	4	5	6	7	8		10		2	9	11															5
1		3	4	5	6	7	8	9	10		2						11											6
1		3	4	5	6	7	8	9	10		2						11											7
1		3	4	5	6	7	8	9	10		2						11											8
1	2	3	4	5	6	7	8	9	10								11											9
1		3		5			7	8	9	10	6			11		2	4											10
1		3	4	5			7	8	9	10	6			11		2												11
1		3	4	5	6		8	9	7	10				2		11												12
1		3	4	5	6		8	9	7	10				2		11												13
1	2	3	4	5	6			9	7	10		8		11														14
1		3	4	5	6		8	9	7					11		2	10											15
1		3	4	5	6		8	9	7					11		2	10											16
1		3		5		6	8	9	7					11		4	10											17
1		3		5		6	8	9	7					11		4	10											18
1		3		5		6		9	7	8				11		4	10											19
1	2	3		5		6	8	9	7	10				11		4												20
1	2	3		5		6	8	9	7	10				11		4												21
1		3		5		6	8	9	7				2	11		4		10										22
1		3		5		6	8	9	7				2	11		4		10										23
1		3		5		6	8	9	7	4			2	11				10										24
1		3			5		8	9	7	6			2	11				10	4									25
1		3		5		6	8			7			2	11		4		10		9								26
		3		5		6		7	9		4		2	11				10	8			1						27
		3		5		6	8	9	7	4			2	11				10				1						28
		3		5		6	8	9	7	4			2	11				10				1						29
		3		5		6	7	9		4			2	11				10					1	8				30
1		3		5		6	9				2			11		4								8	7	10		31
1		3		5		6		9						11				4						8	7	10	2	32
1		3		5		6		9						11				4						8	7	10	2	33
1		3		5		6		9						11				4						8	7	10	2	34
1		3		5		6		9	4					11										8	7	10	2	35
1		3		5		6		9						11				4						8	7	10	2	36
1		3		5		6		9						11				4						8	7	10	2	37
1		3		5		6		9						11				4						8	7	10	2	38
34	6	37	37	16	35	27	36	26	24	6	23	21	3	11	4	3	10	6	9	7	1	3	1	9	8	8	7	
	1	1				9	19	6	5		1	1	1				2	2	1					6	1			

Williamson RG	McCallum D	Agnew WB	Aitken S	Jones A	Davidson A	Hewitt C	Common A	Green T	Reid GT*	Cassidy J	Hogg J	Thackeray J	Murray T*	Coxon T*	Duffy CF*	Hedley GT*	Henderson GH*	Thompson WT*	Walker RH*	Barker WC*	Trechman OL*	Hunter H*	Worrall WE*	Bloomer S*	Brawn WF*	Wilcox FJ*	Ratcliffe E*	#
1	2	5		4	10	9	11			3	7					6		8										1
1		3	5		6	8	9	7	4		2	11					10											2
1		3	5		6	8	9	7	4		2	11					10											R
1		3	5		6	8	9	7			2	11				4	10											2R
1		3	5		6	8	9	7			2	11				4	10											3
5		5	5		5	5	5	5	2		5	5				3	5											
						2	5					1					1											

177

1906-07

Manager:

1	Sep	1	(h)	Everton	D	2-2	Wilcox, Barker	20,000
2		8	(a)	W Arsenal	L	0-2		20,000
3		15	(h)	Sheffield W	L	1-3	Thackeray	17,000
4		22	(a)	Bury	D	1-1	Bloomer	
5		29	(h)	Manchester C	L	2-3	Wilcox, O'Hagan	22,000
6	Oct	6	(a)	Derby C	L	0-1		10,000
7		13	(a)	Preston NE	L	2-4	Tucker, Brawn	
8		20	(h)	Newcastle U	L	0-3		17,000
9		27	(a)	Aston Villa	W	3-2	Bloomer 2, Common	20,000
10	Nov	3	(h)	Liverpool	L	0-1		18,000
11		10	(a)	Bristol C	L	0-3		12,000
12		17	(h)	Notts C	W	2-0	Wilcox 2	12,000
13		24	(a)	Sheffield U	D	1-1	Bloomer	
14	Dec	1	(h)	Bolton W	D	0-0		
15		8	(a)	Manchester U	L	1-3	Bloomer	12,000
16		15	(h)	Stoke	W	5-0	Wilcox, Common 2, Bloomer 2	
17		22	(a)	Blackburn R	L	1-4	Bloomer	
18		25	(h)	Sunderland	W	2-1	Wilcox, Brawn	25,000
19		26	(a)	Birmingham	D	0-0		32,000
20		29	(a)	Everton	L	1-5	Brawn	
21	Jan	1	(h)	Birmingham	W	1-0	Bloomer	16,000
22		2	(a)	Manchester C	L	1-3	Murray	7,000
23		5	(h)	W Arsenal	W	5-3	Bloomer 4, Wilcox	15,000
24		19	(a)	Sheffield W	W	2-0	Common, Wilcox	
25		26	(h)	Bury	W	3-1	Bloomer 2, Common	
26	Feb	9	(h)	Derby C	W	4-1	Brawn, Bloomer, Thackeray 2	10,000
27		16	(h)	Preston NE	W	2-1	Common 2	
28		23	(a)	Newcastle U	L	0-4		47,000
29	Mar	2	(a)	Aston Villa	W	1-0	Wilcox	20,000
30		16	(h)	Bristol C	W	1-0	Thackeray	14,000
31		30	(h)	Sheffield U	L	0-1		20,000
32	Apr	1	(a)	Sunderland	L	2-4	Bloomer, Common (pen)	30,000
33		6	(a)	Bolton W	L	0-1		
34		10	(a)	Notts C	D	2-2	Common, Wilcox	6,000
35		13	(h)	Manchester U	W	2-0	Wilcox 2	15,000
36		17	(a)	Liverpool	W	4-2	S.Aitken, Common 3	8,000
37		20	(a)	Stoke	W	2-0	S.Aitken, Bloomer	
38		27	(h)	Blackburn R	L	0-1		

FINAL LEAGUE POSITION: 11th in Division One

Appearances
Goals

FA Cup

1	Jan	12	(h)	Northampton T	W	4-2	Bloomer 2, Common, Brawn*	15,000
2	Feb	2	(a)	Brentford	L	0-1		22,000

*Some sources credit Cooch (og), but club credit Brawn.

Appearances
Goals

178

Williamson RG	Ratcliffe E	Campbell A*	Shand H*	Aitken S	Barker WC	Brawn WF	Bloomer S	Common A	Wilcox FJ	Thackeray J	Hickling W*	Hanlon E*	Priest F*	Barker FM*	Murray T	Priest AE*	Tomlin J*	O'Hagan C*	Tyldesley J*	Tucker WH*	Harkins J*	Roberts J*	Roberts WS*	Aitken A*	Cail SG*	Brown JR*	Watson J*	No.
1	2	3	4	5	6	7	8	9	10	11																		1
1	2		4	6	7	8		10	11	3	5	9																2
1		3	4	6	7	8	5	10	11					2	9													3
1		3	4	6	7	8		9		11					2	5	10											4
1		3	4	6	7	8		9		11						5	10	2										5
1		3	4	6	7	8		9		11						5	10	2										6
1		3	4	6	7	8		10		11						5		2	9									7
1		3	4	6	7	8		10							2				9	5			11					8
1		3		4	6	7	8	9	10										2		5		11					9
1		3		4		7	8	9	10										2		6		11	5				10
1		3		4		7		9	10						11			2	9		6			5				11
1				4		7		9	10	11	3					8		2			6			5				12
1		3		4			8	9	10	11						7			2		6			5				13
1		3		4		7	8	9	10	11									2		6			5				14
1		3		4		7	8	9	10	11									2		6			5				15
1		3		4		7	8	9	10						11				2		6			5				16
1		3		4		7	8	9	10						11				2		6			5				17
1		3		4		7	8	9	10						11				2		6			5				18
1				4	6	7	8	9	10						11				2		5			3				19
1				4	6	7	8			11					10				2	9	5			3				20
1		3		4		7	8	9	10						11				2		6			5				21
1		3		4		7	8		10	11					9				2		6			5				22
1		3		4		7	8	9	10	11									2		6			5				23
1		3		4		7	8	9	10	11									2		6			5				24
1		3		4		7	8	9	10	11									2		6			5				25
1		3		4		7	8	9	10	11									2		6			5				26
1		3		4		7	8	9	10	11									2		6			5				27
1				4	6	7	8	9	10	11									2					5				28
1		3		4		7	8		10	11					3				2		6			5	9			29
1		3		4		7	8	9	10	11									2		6			5				30
1		3		4		7	8	9	10										2		6		11	5				31
1		3		4		7	8	9	10										2		6		11	5				32
1			8	5	4	7			10	11					9				3		6				2			33
1				4		7	8	9	10	11	3								2		6			5				34
1		3		4		7	8	9	10	11											6			5		2	3	35
1				4		7	8	9	10	11	3										6			5		2		36
1				4		7	8	9	10	11											6			5		2	3	37
1				5	4	7	8	9	10	11											6					2	3	38
38	2	24	2	35	17	37	34	29	37	28	5	1	1	1	9	12	4	5	23	4	30	1	3	27	1	5	3	
		2	1	4	18	12	12	4						1				1			1							

Williamson RG	Ratcliffe E	Campbell A*	Shand H*	Aitken S	Barker WC	Brawn WF	Bloomer S	Common A	Wilcox FJ	Thackeray J	Hickling W*	Hanlon E*	Priest F*	Barker FM*	Murray T	Priest AE*	Tomlin J*	O'Hagan C*	Tyldesley J*	Tucker WH*	Harkins J*	Roberts J*	Roberts WS*	Aitken A*	Cail SG*	Brown JR*	Watson J*	No.
1		3		4		7	8	9	10	11									2		6			5				1
1		3		4		7	8	9	10	11									2		6			5				2
2		2		2		2	2	2	2										2		2			2				
				1		2	1																					

179

1907-08

Manager: Andy Aitken

1	Sep	4	(h)	Birmingham	W	1-0	Bloomer	20,000
2		7	(a)	Nottingham F	W	3-0	Wilcox, Common, Bloomer	12,000
3		9	(a)	Manchester U	L	1-2	Wilcox	20,000
4		14	(h)	Manchester U	W	2-1	S.Aitken, Wilcox	25,000
5		21	(a)	Blackburn R	L	0-2		20,000
6		28	(h)	Bolton W	L	0-1		18,000
7	Oct	5	(a)	Birmingham	W	4-1	Bloomer, Wilcox 2, Common	20,000
8		12	(h)	Everton	L	0-2		17,000
9		19	(a)	Sunderland	D	0-0		28,600
10		26	(h)	W Arsenal	D	0-0		15,000
11	Nov	2	(a)	Sheffield W	L	2-3	Common 2 (1 pen)	18,000
12		9	(h)	Bristol C	L	0-2		18,000
13		16	(a)	Notts C	L	0-2		8,000
14		23	(h)	Manchester C	W	2-0	Thackeray, Dixon	10,000
15		30	(a)	Preston NE	D	1-1	McCulloch	9,000
16	Dec	7	(h)	Bury	L	0-2		14,000
17		14	(a)	Aston Villa	L	0-6		10,000
18		21	(h)	Liverpool	W	3-1	Bloomer 2, Wilcox	14,000
19		25	(a)	Sheffield U	D	0-0		25,000
20		26	(a)	Chelsea	L	0-1		45,000
21		28	(h)	Newcastle U	D	1-1	Thackeray	38,000
22	Jan	1	(h)	Chelsea	W	3-1	Dixon 2, Bloomer	30,000
23		4	(h)	Nottingham F	D	1-1	Cail	15,000
24		18	(h)	Blackburn R	W	3-0	Bloomer, Common, Cail	15,000
25		25	(a)	Bolton W	D	1-1	Cail	12,000
26	Feb	1	(h)	Sheffield U	W	2-0	Cail, Common	
27		8	(a)	Everton	L	1-2	Cail	15,000
28		15	(h)	Sunderland	W	3-1	Cail, Thackeray, A.Aitken	25,000
29		22	(a)	W Arsenal	L	1-4	Cail	7,000
30	Mar	7	(a)	Bristol C	W	1-0	Bloomer	10,000
31		14	(h)	Notts C	W	3-1	Cail 2, Common	15,000
32		21	(a)	Manchester C	L	1-2	Cail	30,000
33		28	(h)	Preston NE	W	1-0	Common	20,000
34	Apr	4	(a)	Bury	W	4-1	Wilcox 2, Cail, Bloomer	11,000
35		8	(h)	Sheffield W	W	6-1	Wilcox, Bloomer 2, Common, Cail, Thackeray	
36		11	(h)	Aston Villa	L	0-1		15,000
37		18	(a)	Liverpool	W	1-0	Thackeray	8,000
38		20	(h)	Newcastle U	W	2-1	Dixon, Bloomer	20,000

FINAL LEAGUE POSITION: 6th in Division One

Appearances
Goals

FA Cup

1	Jan	11	(a)	Notts C	L	0-2		16,000

Appearances
Goals

Williamson RG	Groves JA*	Watson J	Aitken S	Aitken A	Harkins J	Roberts WS	Bloomer S	Common A	Wilcox FJ	Brawn WF	Brown JR	Thackeray J	McCulloch A*	Barker WC	Hasel AA*	Verrill E*	Dixon T*	Urquhart A*	Campbell A	Cail SG	Wilson TT*	
1	2	3	4	5	6	7	8	9	10	11												1
1		3	4	5	6	7	8	9	10		2	11										2
1		3	4	5	6		8	9	10	7	2	11										3
1		3	4	5	6	11	8	9	10	7	2											4
1		3	4	5	6	10	8		9	7	2	11										5
1		3	4	5	6		8		10	7	2	11	9									6
1		3	4	5		11	8	9	10	7	2			6								7
		3	4	5		11	8	9	10	7	2			6	1							8
1		3	4	5		11	8	9	10	7	2			6								9
1		3	4	5			8	9	10	7	2	11		6								10
1		3	4	5			8	9	10	7	2	11		6								11
1		3	4	5			8	9	10	7	2	11		6								12
1		3	4	5		7		9	10		2	11	9	6								13
1		3	4	5	6			9	10		2	11				7	8					14
1		3	4	5	6			9	11		2		10			7	8					15
1		3	4	5	6		8	9	11		2					7	10					16
1		3	4	5			8		10		2			6		11	9	7				17
1		3	4	5			8	9	10			11				6		7	2			18
1		3	4	5		11	8	9	10							6		7	2			19
1		3	4	5			8	9	10		2					6	11	7				20
1		3	4	5			8	9	10		2	11				6	7					21
1		3	4	5			8	9	10		2	11				6	7					22
1		3	4	5			8		10		2	11				6	7			9		23
1		3	4	5			7	8	10			11				6			2	9		24
1	2	3	4	5			7	8	10			11				6				9		25
1	2	3	4	5			7	8	10			11				6				9		26
1	2	3	4	5			8		10			11				6	7			9		27
1	2	3	4	5			7	8	10			11				6				9		28
1	2	3	4	5			7	8	10			11				6				9		29
1	2	3	4	5			7	8	10			11				6				9		30
1	2	3	4				7	8	10			11				6				9		31
1	2	3	4	5			7	8	10			11		5		6				9		32
1		3	4	5				9	10			11				6	7		2	8		33
1		3	4				8	7	10			11				6			2	9	5	34
1		3	4				8	7	10			11				6			2	9	5	35
1		3	4				8	7				11				6	10		2	9	5	36
1		3	4				8	5				11				6	7		2	9	10	37
1		3	4				8	5				11				6	7		2	9	10	38
37	9	38	38	32	9	9	34	34	34	11	20	28	3	9	1	25	13	4	9	16	5	
		1	1				12	9	9			5	1			4				12		

Williamson RG	Groves JA*	Watson J	Aitken S	Aitken A	Harkins J	Roberts WS	Bloomer S	Common A	Wilcox FJ	Brawn WF	Brown JR	Thackeray J	McCulloch A*	Barker WC	Hasel AA*	Verrill E*	Dixon T*	Urquhart A*	Campbell A	Cail SG	Wilson TT*	
1		3	4	5			8	9	10		2	11				6	7					1
1		1	1	1			1	1	1		1	1				1	1					

181

1908-09

Manager: Andy Aitken

1	Sep	5	(h)	Bradford C	W	1-0	Bloomer	19,000
2		9	(h)	Sunderland	L	0-3		18,000
3		12	(a)	Manchester U	L	3-6	Bloomer 2, Hall	25,000
4		19	(h)	Everton	L	2-3	Bloomer 2	18,000
5		26	(a)	Leicester F	D	1-1	Wilcox	20,000
6	Oct	3	(h)	W Arsenal	D	1-1	Cail	8,000
7		10	(a)	Notts C	L	2-3	Bloomer 2 (1 pen)	10,000
8		17	(h)	Newcastle U	D	0-0		20,000
9		24	(a)	Bristol C	D	1-1	Common	12,000
10		31	(h)	Preston NE	W	4-2	Hall 2, Bloomer, Cail	17,000
11	Nov	7	(a)	Sheffield W	L	2-3	Cail, Thackeray	15,000
12		14	(a)	Manchester C	D	0-0		15,000
13		21	(h)	Liverpool	W	1-0	Bloomer	15,000
14		28	(a)	Bury	L	1-2	Common	10,000
15	Dec	5	(h)	Sheffield U	L	1-2	Bloomer	9,000
16		12	(a)	Aston Villa	W	3-0	Hall, S.Aitken, Bloomer	20,000
17		19	(h)	Nottingham F	W	4-0	Cail, Hall 2, Common	15,000
18		25	(a)	Blackburn R	D	0-0		25,000
19		26	(a)	Sunderland	L	0-2		20,000
20	Jan	1	(h)	Chelsea	L	1-4	Common	25,000
21		2	(h)	Bradford C	W	2-0	Hall, Pentland	30,000
22		9	(h)	Manchester U	W	5-0	Cail, Common 2, Hall 2	15,000
23		23	(a)	Everton	D	1-1	Common	25,000
24		30	(h)	Leicester F	W	6-2	Hall 3, Hedley (og), Thackeray, Cail	10,000
25	Feb	13	(h)	Notts C	L	1-2	Pentland	12,000
26		27	(h)	Bristol C	W	4-0	Hall 2, Cail, Bloomer	10,000
27	Mar	6	(a)	Preston NE	D	1-1	Thackeray	6,000
28		13	(h)	Sheffield W	W	2-1	Hall, Cail	8,000
29		17	(a)	W Arsenal	D	1-1	Cail	15,000
30		20	(h)	Manchester C	W	3-0	Common 2, Bloomer	12,000
31		27	(h)	Liverpool	W	2-1	Common, Bloomer	10,000
32		31	(a)	Newcastle U	L	0-1		45,000
33	Apr	4	(h)	Bury	L	0-1		10,000
34		9	(a)	Chelsea	L	0-3		50,000
35		10	(a)	Sheffield U	L	0-2		9,000
36		12	(h)	Blackburn R	W	1-0	Hall	12,000
37		17	(h)	Aston Villa	W	1-0	Hall	8,000
38		24	(a)	Nottingham F	L	1-4	Hall	7,000

FINAL LEAGUE POSITION: 9th in Division One

Appearances
Goals

FA Cup

1	Jan	16	(a)	Preston NE	L	0-1		9,000

Appearances
Goals

Williamson RG	Groves JA	Watson J	Aitken S	Aitken A	Verrill E	Pentland FB*	Bloomer S	Hall JH*	Wilcox FJ	Thackeray J	Common A	Gordon D*	Kent H*	Cail SG	Campbell A	Wilson TT	McLeod D*	Dixon T	Young RT*	Barker WC	Jones JL*	
1	2	3	4	5	6	7	8	9	10	11												1
1	2	3	4	5	6		8	9	10	11	7											2
1	3		4	5		·7	8	9	11			2	6	10								3
1		3	4	5	6	7	8		11		9			10	2							4
1	2	3	4	5	6	7	8		10	11				9								5
1		3	4	2	6	7	8	10	11					9		5						6
1		3	4		6		8	10	11		7		5	9								7
1		3	4	5			8	10	6	11	7			9		2						8
1		3	4	5			8	10	6	11	7			9		2						9
1		3	4				8	10	5	11	7			9	6	2						10
1		3	4				8		5	11	7			9	6	2	10					11
1		3	4	5		9	8		6	11	7				2	10						12
1		3	4	5	6	7	8	10		11	9				2							13
1		3	4	5	6	7	8	10		11	9				2							14
1		3	4	5		7	8	10	6	11	9				2							15
1		3	4	5		7	8	9	6	11	10				2							16
1		3	4	5		7		9	6	11	10		8		2							17
1		3	4	5		7		9	6	11	10		8		2							18
1		3	4	5		7		9	6	11	10		8		2							19
1		3	4	5		7		9	8	11	10				2	6						20
1		3			6	7		9	5	11	10		8		2	4						21
1		3			6	7		9	5	11	10		8		2	4						22
1		3			6	7		9	5	11	10		8		2	4						23
1	3				6	7		9	5	11	10		8		2	4						24
1	3				6	7		9	5	11	10		8		2	4						25
1		3	4		6	7	8	9	5	11			10		2							26
1		3	4		6	7	8	9	5	11	10				2							27
1		3	4		6		8	9	5	11	7		10		2							28
1			4		6		8			11	10		9		2	7	5	3				29
1		3	4		6	7	8				10		5		2	9			11			30
1			4		6	7	8	9			10		5		2		3	11				31
1	3		4		6		8	9			10		5	7	2			11				32
1	3		5		6		8			11	10		9		2	7	4					33
1	3		5		6	7	8	9		11	10				2		4					34
1	3		5		6	7				11	10		9		2	8	4					35
1		3	4		6	7	8	9		11	10		5		2							36
1		3	4		6	7	8	9		11	5			10	2							37
1	3		4		6	7	8	9		11	5			10	2							38
38	12	27	33	17	26	28	28	30	26	31	33	1	6	25	1	3	32	6	10	2	3	
		1			2	14	18	1	3	10				9								

1 own-goal

1		3			6	7		9	5	11	10			8			2		4			1
1		1			1	1		1	1	1	1			1			1		1			

1909-10

Manager: Andy Walker

#	Month	Date		Opponent	Result	Scorers	Attendance
1	Sep	1	(h)	Sheffield U	L 0-2		8,000
2		4	(a)	Sheffield W	W 5-1	Dixon, S.Aitken, Hall 2, Bloomer	10,000
3		11	(h)	W Arsenal	W 5-2	Dixon 2, Bloomer (pen), Hall 2	12,000
4		18	(a)	Bristol C	L 1-4	Bloomer	10,000
5		25	(h)	Bolton W	L 1-2	Bloomer	12,000
6	Oct	2	(a)	Bury	L 1-2	Hall	10,000
7		9	(h)	Chelsea	L 0-1		12,000
8		16	(a)	Tottenham H	W 3-1	Groves 2, Common	25,000
9		23	(h)	Blackburn R	L 1-3	Bloomer	5,000
10		30	(a)	Preston NE	L 0-1		8,000
11	Nov	6	(h)	Nottingham F	W 2-1	Hall, Cail	10,000
12		13	(a)	Notts C	L 1-2	Cail	9,000
13		20	(h)	Sunderland	W 3-2	Common, Verrill, Hall	20,000
14		27	(a)	Newcastle U	L 0-2		25,000
15	Dec	4	(h)	Everton	D 1-1	Common	10,000
16		11	(a)	Liverpool	D 0-0		20,000
17		18	(h)	Manchester U	L 1-2	Hall	10,000
18		25	(h)	Bradford C	L 3-7	Hall, Bloomer 2	25,000
19		27	(a)	Bradford C	L 1-4	Bloomer (pen)	35,000
20	Jan	1	(a)	Sheffield U	L 0-2		12,000
21		8	(h)	Sheffield W	W 4-0	Elliott, Thackeray, Cail 2	10,000
22		22	(a)	W Arsenal	L 0-3		6,000
23	Feb	5	(a)	Bolton W	D 1-1	Bloomer	10,000
24		12	(h)	Bury	L 0-5		8,000
25		19	(a)	Chelsea	L 1-2	Hall	12,000
26		26	(h)	Tottenham H	W 4-3	Young, Verrill, Cail, Pentland	7,000
27	Mar	5	(a)	Blackburn R	D 1-1	Young (pen)	15,000
28		12	(h)	Preston NE	W 1-0	Verrill	8,000
29		19	(a)	Nottingham F	W 1-0	Young (pen)	5,000
30		25	(a)	Aston Villa	L 2-4	Cail, Common	30,000
31		26	(h)	Notts C	W 2-0	Hall, Pentland	12,000
32		28	(h)	Aston Villa	W 3-2	Young (pen), Cail, Elliott	20,000
33	Apr	2	(a)	Sunderland	D 2-2	Young (pen), Elliott	12,000
34		9	(h)	Newcastle U	D 1-1	Cail	12,000
35		16	(a)	Everton	D 1-1	Thackeray	15,000
36		20	(h)	Bristol C	D 0-0		12,000
37		23	(h)	Liverpool	D 2-2	Elliott, Williamson (pen)	5,000
38		30	(a)	Manchester U	L 1-4	Hall	10,000

FINAL LEAGUE POSITION: 17th in Division One

Appearances
Goals

FA Cup

#	Month	Date		Opponent	Result	Scorers	Attendance
1	Jan	15	(h)	Everton	D 1-1	Thackeray	25,000
R		19	(a)	Everton	L 3-5	Common, Cail, Bloomer	20,000

Appearances
Goals

Williamson RG	McLeod D	Watson J	Aitken S	Common A	Verrill E	Pentland FB	Elliott GW*	Hall JH	Cail SG	Thackeray J	Bloomer S	Dixon T	Jones JL	Wilcox FJ	Young RT	Groves JA	Barker WC	Wilson TT	Burton G*	Beaton S*	Flint WA*	Boardman H*	
1	2	3	4	5	6	7	8	9	10	11													1
1	2	3	4	5	6	7		9			8	10	11										2
1	2	3	4	5	6	7		9			8	10	11										3
1	2	3	4	5	6	7		9			8	10	11										4
1	2	3	4	5	6	7		9			8	10	11										5
1	2	3	4	5	6	7	10	9		11	8												6
1	2	3	4		6	7	10	9		11	8				5								7
1	2	3	4	8	6		10			11	9				5	7							8
1	2	3	4		6	7	10			11	9				5	8							9
1	2	3	5	10	6	7		9		11	8					4							10
1	2	3	4		6	7		10	9	11	8				5								11
1	2	3	4		6	7		10	9	11	8				5								12
1	2	3	4	8	6	7		10	9	11					5								13
1	2	3	4	8	6	7		10	9	11					5								14
1	2	3	4	8	6			10	9	11		7			5								15
1	2		4	8	6			10		11		7			5	3		9					16
1	2	3	4	8	6	7		10		11	9				5								17
1	2	5	4	8	6	7		10		11	9					3							18
1	2	3	5		6	7		10	8	11	9					4							19
1		3			6	7	8	10	9	11					5	2	4						20
1	2	3	4		6	7	8	10	9	11					5								21
1	2	3	4					10	9	11	8	7			5		6						22
1	2	3	4		6	7		10	9	11	8				5								23
1	2	3	4		6	7		10	9	11	8				5								24
1	2	3			6		8	10		11					5			9	4	7			25
1		3		8	6	7		10	9				11		5					4		2	26
1		3	4	8	6	7		10	9				11		5							2	27
1	2		4	8	6	7		10	9				11		5							3	28
1	2	3	4	8	6	7		10	9				11		5								29
1	2	3	4	9	6	7			10		8		11		5								30
1	2	3	4	8	6	7		9	10	11					5								31
1	2	3	4	9	6	7	8		10	11					5								32
1	2	3	4	9	6	7	8		10	11					5								33
1	2	3	4	9	6	7	8		10	11					5								34
1	2	3	4	9	6	7	8		10	11					5								35
1	2	3	4	9	6	7	8		10	11					5								36
1	2	3	5	9	6	7	8		10				11			4							37
1	2		5		6	7	8	9	10				11			4						3	38
38	35	35	35	26	37	33	15	29	25	27	20	5	11	1	24	6	5	2	2	2	1	4	—
1			1	4	3	2	4	12	8	2	9	3			5	2							—

Williamson RG	McLeod D	Watson J	Aitken S	Common A	Verrill E	Pentland FB	Elliott GW*	Hall JH	Cail SG	Thackeray J	Bloomer S	Dixon T	Jones JL	Wilcox FJ	Young RT	Groves JA	Barker WC	Wilson TT	Burton G*	Beaton S*	Flint WA*	Boardman H*	
1	2	3	4		6	7	8	10		11	9				5								1
1	2	3	4	7	6			10	9	11	8				5								R
2	2	2	2	1	2	1	1	2	1	2	2				2								
1				1				1	1	1													

185

1910-11

Manager: Andy Walker

1	Sep	3	(h)	Everton	W	1-0	McClure	17,000
2		10	(a)	Sheffield W	D	1-1	McClure	12,000
3		17	(h)	Bristol C	W	3-0	Pentland, Gibson, Williamson (pen)	20,000
4		24	(a)	Newcastle U	D	0-0		40,000
5	Oct	1	(h)	Tottenham H	W	2-0	Pentland, Elliott	24,000
6		8	(a)	Oldham A	D	1-1	Nichol	20,000
7		15	(a)	Preston NE	D	1-1	Nichol	
8		22	(h)	Notts C	W	4-1	Pentland, Cail, Nichol, Elliott	17,000
9		29	(a)	Manchester U	W	2-1	Pentland, Cail	35,000
10	Nov	5	(h)	Liverpool	D	2-2	McClure, Elliott	26,000
11		12	(a)	Bury	L	2-4	Elliott, Gibson	6,000
12		19	(h)	Sheffield U	W	3-1	Cail 2, Elliott	17,000
13		26	(a)	Aston Villa	L	0-5		15,000
14	Dec	3	(h)	Sunderland	W	1-0	Nichol	27,980
15		10	(a)	W Arsenal	W	2-0	Elliott, Nichol	8,000
16		17	(h)	Bradford C	W	3-2	Elliott, Pentland, Nichol	15,000
17		24	(a)	Blackburn R	L	1-5	Verrill	12,000
18		26	(h)	Manchester C	D	0-0		25,000
19		27	(a)	Nottingham F	D	1-1	Elliott	20,000
20		31	(a)	Everton	L	0-2		15,000
21	Jan	2	(h)	Nottingham F	D	2-2	J.Carr 2	15,000
22		7	(h)	Sheffield W	L	0-1		
23		21	(a)	Bristol C	L	2-3	Elliott, Wedlock (og)	10,000
24		28	(h)	Newcastle U	L	0-2		25,000
25	Feb	11	(a)	Oldham A	L	1-2	H.Carr	12,000
26		13	(a)	Tottenham H	L	2-6	H.Carr 2	8,000
27		18	(h)	Preston NE	W	2-0	Pentland, Elliott	7,000
28	Mar	4	(h)	Manchester U	D	2-2	Dixon, Gibson	11,000
29		11	(a)	Liverpool	L	0-3		20,000
30		18	(h)	Bury	W	2-1	Cail 2	7,000
31		27	(a)	Sheffield U	L	1-2	Best	6,000
32	Apr	1	(h)	Aston Villa	L	0-1		18,000
33		8	(a)	Sunderland	L	1-3	Pentland	
34		14	(a)	Manchester C	L	1-2	Cail	35,000
35		15	(h)	W Arsenal	D	1-1	Nichol	14,000
36		18	(a)	Notts C	L	0-1		8,000
37		27	(a)	Bradford C	L	0-1		10,000
38		29	(h)	Blackburn R	L	2-3	Leonard, Nichol	

FINAL LEAGUE POSITION: 16th in Division One

Appearances
Goals

FA Cup

1	Jan	14	(h)	Glossop	W	1-0	Cail	15,000
2		4	(h)	Leicester F	D	0-0		17,000
R		9	(a)	Leicester F	W	2-1*	Cail, Dixon	14,000
3		25	(h)	Blackburn R	L	0-3		30,369

*After extra-time

Appearances
Goals

Williamson RG	McLeod D	Weir J*	Barker WC	Jackson A*	Verrill E	Gibson RJ*	Elliott GW	Pentland FB	McClure S*	Nichol J*	Duguid W*	Cail SG	Kelly B*	Peggie J*	Wardrope A*	Davidson W*	Carr J*	Davies B	Carr H	Dixon T	Crosier J*	Best C*	Howling E*	Leonard H*	James WE*	Carr W*	
1	2	3	4	5	6	7	8	9	10	11																	1
1	2	3	4	5	6	7	8	9	10	11																	2
1	2	3	4	5	6	7	8	9	10	11																	3
1	2	3	4	5	6	7	8	9	10	11																	4
1	2	3		5	6	7	8	9	10	11	4																5
1	2	3	4	5	6	7	8	9		11		10															6
1	2	3	4	5	6	7	8			11	10	9															7
1	2	3	4	5	6	7	8	9		11		10															8
1	2	3	4	5	6	7	8	9		11		10															9
1	2	3	4	5	6	7	8	9	10	11																	10
1	2	3	4	5	6	7	8	9		11	10																11
1		3	4	5	6	7	8			11		10	2	9													12
1		3	4		6	7		9		11		10	2	8	5												13
1	2	3	4		6	7		9	8	11		10			5												14
1	2	3	4	5	6	7	8	9		11		10															15
1	2	3	4	5	6	7	8	9		10						11											16
1	2	3	4	5	6	7	8	9				10				11											17
1	2	3	4		6		8	7				10		9	5	11											18
1	2	3	4		6		8	9	10					7	5	11											19
1	2	3	4	5			8	9	10		6			7		11											20
1	2	3	4	5	6			9	10	7						11	8										21
1		3	4	5		7		9	8	10	6			2		11											22
1		3	4	5	6	7	8	9				10		2		11											23
1	2		4	5	6	7	8	9			3	10				11											24
	2	3	4			7	8			11	6	10		5				1			9						25
1	2	3	4							11	6	10		5	7						9	8					26
1	2	3	4	5	6		8	9		11		10			7												27
1	2	3		5	6	7		9		11		10									7	4					28
1	2	3		5	6	7		8	4			10			11						9						29
1	2	3		5			8	9				10	6		11					4	7						30
1	2	3	4	5	6		8	9				10			11							7					31
	2		5		6		8	7			10	3										4	1	9	11		32
1	2		4		6			7			10	3	8							5				9	11		33
1	2	3	4	5	6	7				10					11					8				9			34
1	2	3		5	6	7			11			10	4						8					9			35
1	2	3			6	7					10								5			8		9	11		36
1	2	3	4		6	7						10			11				8					9		5	37
1	2	3		5	6	7		8		11		10												9		4	38
36	**34**	**35**	**32**	**28**	**33**	**28**	**25**	**30**	**11**	**24**	**9**	**26**	**4**	**6**	**10**	**16**	**1**	**1**	**3**	**3**	**5**	**5**	**1**	**7**	**3**	**2**	
1				1	3	10	7	3	8		7				2		3	1		1		1		1			

1 own-goal

Williamson RG	McLeod D	Weir J*	Barker WC	Jackson A*	Verrill E	Gibson RJ*	Elliott GW	Pentland FB	McClure S*	Nichol J*	Duguid W*	Cail SG	Kelly B*	Peggie J*	Wardrope A*	Davidson W*	Carr J*	Davies B	Carr H	Dixon T	Crosier J*	Best C*	Howling E*	Leonard H*	James WE*	Carr W*	
		3	4	5	6	7	8	9				10				2	11										1
1	2	3	4	5		7	8		10		6	9				11											2
1	2	3	4	5	6	7	8			11	9								10								R
1	2	3	4	5	6		8	9		11		10			7												3
4	**3**	**4**	**4**	**4**	**3**	**3**	**4**	**2**	**1**	**2**	**1**	**4**		**1**	**3**				**1**			**1**					
														2								**1**					

1911-12

Manager: Tom McIntosh

1	Sep	2	(a)	Sunderland	L	0-1	30,000
2		9	(h)	Blackburn R	W	2-1 Leonard, Elliott	19,147
3		16	(a)	Sheffield W	W	2-0 Cail 2	16,000
4		23	(h)	Bury	D	1-1 Eyre	16,761
5		30	(h)	Preston NE	W	4-2 Cail, Elliott 2, Leonard	10,000
6	Oct	7	(a)	Notts C	L	1-2 Elliott	20,000
7		14	(h)	Tottenham H	W	2-0 James, Elliott	15,394
8		21	(a)	Manchester U	W	4-3 Elliott 2, Cail, Eyre	20,000
9		28	(h)	Liverpool	W	3-2 Elliott, Eyre, Stirling	13,720
10	Nov	4	(a)	Aston Villa	L	1-2 James	30,000
11		11	(h)	Newcastle U	D	1-1 Elliott	32,986
12		18	(a)	Sheffield U	D	1-1 James	
13		25	(h)	Oldham A	W	3-0 Elliott 2, James	14,527
14	Dec	2	(a)	Bolton W	L	0-1	26,000
15		9	(h)	Bradford C	W	1-0 Windridge	17,020
16		16	(a)	W Arsenal	L	1-3 James	10,000
17		23	(h)	Manchester C	W	3-1 Stirling, James 2 (1 pen)	12,000
18		25	(h)	Everton	D	0-0	22,436
19		26	(a)	Everton	L	0-1	25,000
20		30	(h)	Sunderland	D	3-3 Elliott, James, Eyre	18,750
21	Jan	6	(a)	Blackburn R	L	1-2 Elliott	8,000
22		20	(h)	Sheffield W	D	1-1 Eyre	10,887
23		27	(a)	Bury	W	2-0 Eyre 2	10,000
24	Feb	10	(h)	Notts C	W	4-0 Eyre, Cail 2, Elliott	9,714
25		17	(a)	Tottenham H	L	1-2 Elliott	22,000
26		24	(h)	W Arsenal	L	0-2	12,291
27	Mar	2	(a)	Liverpool	D	1-1 Jackson	20,000
28		9	(h)	Aston Villa	L	1-2 Windridge	13,359
29		16	(a)	Newcastle U	W	1-0 Cail	30,000
30		23	(h)	Sheffield U	D	1-1 Windridge	8,790
31		30	(a)	Oldham A	L	0-2	5,000
32	Apr	5	(h)	West Brom A	W	1-0 Cail	13,000
33		6	(h)	Bolton W	W	1-0 Cail (pen)	7,000
34		8	(a)	West Brom A	L	1-3 Elliott	25,027
35		13	(a)	Bradford C	L	1-2 J.Carr	10,000
36		17	(h)	Manchester U	W	3-0 Cail 3	5,000
37		22	(a)	Preston NE	W	3-0 Cail, Elliott, Stirling	
38		27	(a)	Manchester C	L	0-2	20,000

FINAL LEAGUE POSITION: 7th in Division One

Appearances
Goals

FA Cup

1	Jan	13	(h)	Sheffield W	D	0-0	24,700
R		25	(a)	Sheffield W	W	2-1 James, Windridge	30,468
2	Feb	3	(h)	West Ham U	D	1-1 Elliott	12,327
R		8	(a)	West Ham U	L	1-2 Elliott*	10,000

*Some sources credit Verrill, but club credits Elliott.

Appearances
Goals

Appearance and scoring grid (shirt number worn by each player per match):

Williamson RG	McLeod D	Weir J	Barker WC	Jackson A	Verrill E	Stirling J*	Elliott GW	Leonard HD	Cail SG	Eyre E*	Carr W	Duguid W	James WE	Layton AE*	Windridge JE*	Pentland FB	Crosier J	Carr J	McRobbie A*	Davies B	Hisbent JM*	Cook J*	Haworth JH*	Nichol J	Fraser A*	#
1	2	3	4	5	6	7	8	9	10	11																1
1	2	3	4	5	6	7	8	9	10	11																2
1	2	3	4		6	7	8	9	10	11	5															3
1	2	3	4		6	7	8	9	10	11	5															4
1	2	3	4		6	7	8	9	10	11	5															5
1	2	3		5	6	7	8	9	10	11	4															6
1	2	3	4		6	7	8		10	11	5	9														7
1	2	3	4		6	7	8		10	11	5	9														8
1	2	3	4		6	7	8		10	11	5	9														9
1	2		4		6	7	8		10	11	5	9	3													10
1	2	3	4	5	6	7	8		10	11		9														11
1	2	3	4	5	6	7	8		10	11		9														12
1	2	3	4	5	6	7	8		10	11		9														13
1	2	3	4	5	6	7	8			11		9			10											14
1	2	3	4	5	6	7	8			11		9			10											15
1	2	3	4	5	6	7	8						11		10	9										16
1	2	3	4	5	6	7	8			11		9			10											17
1		3	4	5	6	7	8			11		9	2		10											18
1		3	4	5	6	7	8		9	11			2		10											19
1		3	4	5	6	7	8			11		9	2		10											20
1	2	3	4	5	6	7	8		10	11		9														21
1	2	3	4		6	7	8			11	5	9			10											22
1	2					7		5	11		6	9	3		10				4	8						23
1	2		4	5	6	7	8		9	11					10		3									24
	2	3	4	5	6	7	8		9	11					10			1								25
1		3	4	5		7	8		9	11											2	10	6			26
1	2	3	4	5	6	7	8	9					10											11		27
1	2	3	4	5	6	7	8			11		9			10											28
1		3	4				8		9	11	5				10			7			2		6			29
		3	4				8		9	11	5				10			7	1		2		6			30
1		3	4			7	8		9		5	11			10						2		6			31
1		3	4			7			9		5				10						2		6	11	8	32
1		3		4		7	8		9		5										2		6	11	10	33
1		3		4		7	8		9		5										2		6	11	10	34
1						7	8		9	11	5		3		10						2		6		4	35
1			4			7	8		9	11	5		3		10						2		6			36
1		3	4		6	7	8		9	11					10						2		5			37
1		3		4		7	8		9	11	5				10			7			2		6			38
36	24	33	32	18	31	36	35	6	30	32	13	6	19	7	20	1	1	4	1	2	11	1	11	4	4	
			1		3	17	2		13	8			8		3			1								

Williamson RG	McLeod D	Weir J	Barker WC	Jackson A	Verrill E	Stirling J*	Elliott GW	Leonard HD	Cail SG	Eyre E*	Carr W	Duguid W	James WE	Layton AE*	Windridge JE*	Pentland FB	Crosier J	Carr J	McRobbie A*	Davies B	Hisbent JM*	Cook J*	Haworth JH*	Nichol J	Fraser A*	#
1	2	3	4	5	6	7	8	9	11				10													1
1	2	3	4	5	6	7	8					9	10										11			R
1	2	3	4	5	6	7	8		11			9	10													2
1	2		4	5	6	7	8		11			9	3	10												R
4	4	3	4	4	4	4	4		1	3		3	1	4									1			
							2					1	1													

1912-13

Manager: Tom McIntosh

1	Sep	4	(a)	West Brom A	L 0-2		15,085
2		7	(h)	Everton	D 0-0		17,360
3		14	(a)	Sheffield W	L 1-3	Elliott	25,000
4		21	(h)	Blackburn R	D 0-0		18,577
5		28	(a)	Derby C	W 2-0	Cail, Elliott	12,000
6	Oct	5	(h)	Tottenham H	D 1-1	Elliott	14,076
7		12	(a)	Sunderland	L 0-4		25,000
8		19	(a)	Notts C	W 3-1	Nichol, Elliott 2	10,000
9		26	(h)	Manchester U	W 3-2	J.Carr 2, Windridge	9,929
10	Nov	2	(a)	Aston Villa	L 1-5	J.Carr	20,000
11		9	(h)	Liverpool	L 3-4	J.Carr, Elliott, Nichol	11,973
12		16	(a)	Bolton W	L 2-3	Elliott, J.Carr	10,000
13		23	(h)	Sheffield U	W 4-1	Elliott 2 (1 pen), Windridge, J.Carr	10,400
14		30	(a)	Newcastle U	L 1-3	Elliott	20,000
15	Dec	7	(h)	Oldham A	D 2-2	Windridge, J.Carr	11,259
16		14	(a)	Chelsea	W 3-2	J.Carr 2, Elliott	15,000
17		21	(h)	W Arsenal	W 2-0	J.Carr, Windridge	9,568
18		26	(h)	Bradford C	D 1-1	Elliott	13,013
19		28	(a)	Everton	L 0-1		25,000
20	Jan	1	(h)	West Brom A	W 3-1	Elliott 2, Eyre	18,222
21		4	(h)	Sheffield W	L 0-2		13,575
22		25	(h)	Derby C	W 4-1	Eyre 2, Betts (og), Cail	16,021
23	Feb	4	(a)	Bradford C	W 2-1	Stirling, Elliott	12,000
24		8	(a)	Tottenham H	L 3-5	J.Carr 2, Elliott	24,000
25		10	(a)	Blackburn R	L 2-5	J.Carr (pen), Eyre	15,000
26		15	(a)	Sunderland	L 0-2		13,992
27	Mar	1	(a)	Manchester U	W 3-2	J.Cook, Elliott 2	15,000
28		15	(a)	Liverpool	L 2-4	J.Carr 2	10,000
29		21	(h)	Manchester C	D 0-0		12,026
30		22	(h)	Bolton W	W 4-0	Elliott 3, Windridge	10,165
31		24	(a)	Manchester C	L 0-3		26,000
32		31	(a)	Sheffield U	L 0-1		
33	Apr	2	(h)	Notts C	D 1-1	J.Carr (pen)	6,000
34		5	(h)	Newcastle U	D 0-0		10,370
35		9	(h)	Aston Villa	D 1-1	Cail	6,894
36		12	(a)	Oldham A	L 0-1		4,000
37		19	(h)	Chelsea	L 0-3		9,000
38		26	(a)	W Arsenal	D 1-1	Elliott (pen)	6,000

FINAL LEAGUE POSITION: 16th in Division One

Appearances
Goals

FA Cup

1	Jan	11	(a)	Millwall	D 0-0		22,000
R		15	(h)	Millwall	W 4-1	J.Carr 3 (1 pen), Elliott	12,780
2	Feb	1	(h)	Queen's Park R	W 3-2	Elliott 2, Eyre	27,774
3		22	(a)	Burnley	L 1-3	Eyre	27,824

Appearances
Goals

Williamson RG	McLeod D	Weir J	Fraser A	Carr W	Verrill E	Stirling J	Elliott GW	Brown A*	Windridge JE	Eyre E	Duguid W	Haworth JH	Hisbent JM	Cook H*	Cail SG	Crosier J	Carr J	Nichol J	McRobbie A	Barker WC	Malcolm G*	Jackson A	James WE	Davies B	Cook J	No.
1	2	3	4	5	6	7	8	9	10	11																1
1	2	3		5	6	7	8	9	10	11	4															2
1	2	3		5		7	8	9	10	11	4	6														3
1	2	3		5	6	7	8	9	10	11			4													4
1		3		5	6	7	8		10	11			2	4	9											5
1		3		5	6	7	8		10	11			2	4	9											6
1		3		5	6	7	8		10	11	4		2		9											7
1		3		5	6	7		9					2		10	4	8	11								8
1		3		5	6	7		9							10		8	11	2	4						9
1	2			5	6	7			10				3		9	8		11			4					10
1		3			6	7	9		10				2				8	11			4	5				11
1		3			6	7	9		10				2				8	11			4	5				12
1		3			6	7	9		10				2				8	11			4	5				13
1		3			6	7	9		10				2				8	11			4	5				14
1		3			6	7	9		10				2				8	11			4	5				15
1	2	3				7	9		10						4	8		11			6	5				16
1	2	3	5			7	9		10						4	8		11			6					17
1	2	3				7	9		10						4	8		11			6	5				18
1		3							9	10			2	6	8	4	7	11					5			19
1	2	3				7	9		10	11					4	8					6	5				20
1		3				7	9		10	11			2		4	8					6	5				21
1		3			6	7	9			11			2		10	8					4	5				22
1		3				7	9		10	11					4	8			2		6	5				23
1						7	9		10	11			3		4	8			2		6	5				24
1									10	11			3		8	4	7		2		6	5	9			25
	3					7			10	11			2		9	4	8		1		6	5				26
1					6	7	9			11			3		4	8			2			5		10		27
1		3			6	7	9		10	11			2			8					4	5				28
1		3			6	7	9		10	11			2			8					4	5				29
1		3			6		9		8	11			2			7					4	5			10	30
1		3			6		9		8	11			2		5	7					4				10	31
1		3					9		8	11			2		4	7					6	5			10	32
1		3		5		7			10	11			6		2	4	8						9			33
1	2			5		7			10	11			6		9	4	8								3	34
1	2			5		7	9			11			3		10	4	8				6					35
1	2	3				7	9			11			5		10	4	8				6					36
1	2	3		5	6	7	9		10	11						8					4					37
1		3				7	9		10	11			2	5	4	8					6					38
37	13	32	1	15	21	33	33	4	33	27	8	2	22	5	13	19	30	11	6	1	25	20	2	1	4	
				1	22				5	4			3			16	2				1					

1 own-goal

Williamson RG	McLeod D	Weir J	Fraser A	Carr W	Verrill E	Stirling J	Elliott GW	Brown A*	Windridge JE	Eyre E	Duguid W	Haworth JH	Hisbent JM	Cook H*	Cail SG	Crosier J	Carr J	Nichol J	McRobbie A	Barker WC	Malcolm G*	Jackson A	James WE	Davies B	Cook J	No.
1		3				7	9		10				2		4	8		11			6	5				1
1		3				7	9		10	11			2		4	8					6	5				R
1		3				7	9		10	11					4	8			2		6	5				2
1		3				7	9		10	11			2		4	8					6	5				3
4		4				4	4		4	3			3		4	4		1	1		4	4				
										3					2	3										

1913-14

Manager: Tom McIntosh

1	Sep	6	(a)	Manchester C	D	1-1	Nichol	30,000
2		10	(a)	Derby C	D	2-2	Elliott 2	5,000
3		13	(h)	Bradford C	D	1-1	Windridge	18,748
4		20	(a)	Blackburn R	L	0-6		25,000
5		27	(h)	Sunderland	L	3-4	Elliott 3	26,972
6	Oct	4	(a)	Everton	L	0-2		20,000
7		11	(h)	West Brom A	W	3-0	Stirling, Nichol, Windridge	14,197
8		18	(a)	Sheffield W	L	0-2		15,000
9		25	(h)	Bolton W	L	2-3	Eyre, J.Carr	13,633
10	Nov	1	(a)	Chelsea	L	2-3	J.Carr, Elliott	25,000
11		8	(h)	Oldham A	D	0-0		10,000
12		15	(a)	Manchester U	W	1-0	J.Carr	10,000
13		22	(h)	Burnley	W	2-1	Windridge, Elliott	15,800
14		29	(a)	Preston NE	L	1-4	Nichol	
15	Dec	6	(h)	Newcastle U	W	3-0	Elliott 2 (1 pen), Stirling	15,300
16		13	(a)	Liverpool	L	1-2	Elliott	25,000
17		20	(h)	Aston Villa	W	5-2	Tinsley 3, Elliott, J.Carr	13,411
18		25	(a)	Sheffield U	L	1-3	Elliott	30,000
19		26	(a)	Tottenham H	W	1-0	Tinsley	37,055
20		27	(h)	Manchester C	W	2-0	Tinsley, Elliott	12,000
21	Jan	1	(h)	Derby C	W	3-2	J.Carr, Tinsley, Elliott	18,341
22		3	(a)	Bradford C	W	3-2	Tinsley 2, J.Cook	20,000
23		17	(h)	Blackburn R	W	3-0	Elliott 3 (1 pen)	17,000
24		24	(a)	Sunderland	L	2-4	Elliott 2	
25	Feb	7	(h)	Everton	W	2-0	Tinsley, Elliott	13,000
26		14	(a)	West Brom A	L	1-2	J.Carr	15,692
27		21	(h)	Manchester U	W	3-1	Stirling, Elliott, Malcolm	12,000
28		28	(a)	Bolton W	D	1-1	Elliott (pen)	18,000
29	Mar	7	(h)	Chelsea	W	2-0	Elliott, J.Carr	14,000
30		14	(a)	Oldham A	L	0-3		7,000
31		18	(h)	Sheffield W	W	5-2	J.Carr, Tinsley, Elliott 3	8,000
32	Apr	4	(h)	Preston NE	W	4-1	Tinsley, Elliott 2 (1 pen), Healey	11,000
33		6	(a)	Burnley	W	2-1	J.Carr, Elliott	6,000
34		10	(h)	Sheffield U	L	2-3	Elliott, Tinsley	16,000
35		11	(a)	Newcastle U	L	0-1		25,000
36		13	(h)	Tottenham H	W	6-0	Stirling, Tinsley 2, J.Carr 2, Wynn	22,000
37		18	(h)	Liverpool	W	4-0	Davidson, Tinsley 3	13,000
38		25	(a)	Aston Villa	W	3-1	Tinsley 2, Elliott	15,000

FINAL LEAGUE POSITION: 3rd in Division One

Appearances
Goals

FA Cup

1	Jan	10	(a)	Blackburn R	L	0-3		25,395

Appearances
Goals

Appearance and scoring grid (players listed across the top; match numbers down the right-hand side):

Williamson RG	Walker J*	Weir J	Davidson S*	Jackson A	Malcolm G	Stirling J	Carr J	Elliott GW	Windridge JE	Nichol J	Verrill E	Cook J	Hisbent JM	Davies B	Cook H	Kirby F*	Carr W	Eyre E	Tinsley W*	Haworth JH	Crosier J	Storey T*	Healey R*	Stage W*	Wynn R*	#
1	2	3	4	5	6	7	8	9	10	11																1
1	2	3	4	5	6	7	8	9	10	11																2
1	2	3	4	5	6	7	8	9	10	11																3
1	2	3	4	5		7		9	10	11	6	8														4
1		3	4	5	6	7	8	9		11		10	2													5
		3	4		6	7			10	11		8	2	1	5	9										6
		3	4		9	7			10	11		8	2	1	6		5									7
		3	4		9	7			10	11		8	2	1	6	5										8
		3	4		6	7	8	9	10				2	1	5		11									9
	2	3	4		6	7	8	9	10	11				1	5											10
	2	3	4		6	7	8	9		11		10		1	5											11
		3	4	10		7	8	9		11			2	1	6		5									12
		3	4			7	8	9	10	11			2	1	6		5									13
		3			6	7	8	9	10	11			2	1	4		5									14
1	2	3		5	6	7		9				8			4				11	10						15
1	2	3		5	6	7		9				8			4				11	10						16
1		3		5	6	7	8	9				11							10	2	4					17
1		3		5	6	7	8	9				11	2						10		4					18
1		3	4	5		7	8	9			6	11							10	2						19
1		3	4	5		7	8	9			6	11							10	2						20
1		3	4	5		7	8	9			6	11							10	2						21
1		3	4	5	6		8		10			11							9	2		7				22
1		3	4	5	6	7	8	9				11							10	2						23
1		3	4	5	6	7	8	9				11							10	2						24
1		3	4	5	6	7	8	9				11							10	2						25
1		3	4	5	6	7	8				10	11							9	2						26
1		3	4		6	7	8	9	10			11					5			2						27
1		3	4	5	6	7	8	9				11							10	2						28
1		3	4	5	6	7	8	9				11							10	2						29
1		3	4	5	6	7	8	9				11							10	2						30
1		3	4	5	6		8	9				11							10	2		7				31
1		3	4	5	6	7		9				11							10	2			8			32
1		3	4	5	6	7	8	9											10	2				11		33
1		3	4	5	6	7	8	9											10	2				11		34
1			4	5	6	7	8	9				3							10	2				11		35
1		3	4	5	6	7	8	9											10	2					11	36
1		3	4	5	8	7	6	9											10	2					11	37
1		3	4	5	6	7	8	9				11							10	2						38
29	37	8	30	28	35	34	30	32	15	13	6	25	10	9	10	2	7	4	23	21	2	2	1	3	2	
	1		1	4	11	31	3	3				1						1	19			1		1		

Williamson RG	Walker J*	Weir J	Davidson S*	Jackson A	Malcolm G	Stirling J	Carr J	Elliott GW	Windridge JE	Nichol J	Verrill E	Cook J	Hisbent JM	Davies B	Cook H	Kirby F*	Carr W	Eyre E	Tinsley W*	Haworth JH	Crosier J	Storey T*	Healey R*	Stage W*	Wynn R*	#
1		3	4	5	6	7	8	9				11							10	2						1
1		1	1	1	1	1	1	1				1							1	1						

1914-15

Manager: Tom McIntosh

1	Sep	1	(a)	Sheffield W	L	1-3	Elliott (pen)	12,000
2		5	(h)	West Brom A	W	2-0	Tinsley, Jackson	12,000
3		12	(a)	Everton	W	3-2	Tinsley, J.Carr, Fleetwood (og)	14,000
4		19	(h)	Chelsea	W	3-0	Elliott, Tinsley, A.Wilson	12,000
5		26	(a)	Bradford C	D	1-1	Tinsley	20,000
6	Oct	3	(h)	Burnley	D	1-1	Elliott	15,000
7		10	(a)	Tottenham H	D	3-3	Tinsley, J.Carr 2 (1 pen)	13,000
8		17	(h)	Newcastle U	D	1-1	Tinsley	25,000
9		24	(a)	Manchester C	D	1-1	Tinsley	25,000
10		31	(a)	Sheffield U	W	1-0	Elliott	12,000
11	Nov	7	(h)	Aston Villa	D	1-1	J.Carr	15,000
12		14	(a)	Liverpool	D	1-1	Elliott	17,000
13		21	(h)	Bradford	L	1-3	Healey	9,000
14		28	(a)	Oldham A	L	1-5	J.Carr	8,300
15	Dec	5	(h)	Manchester U	D	1-1	Elliott	7,000
16		12	(a)	Bolton W	L	0-4		
17		19	(h)	Blackburn R	L	1-4	Tinsley	7,000
18		25	(h)	Notts C	W	1-0	Tinsley	9,000
19		26	(a)	Notts C	L	1-5	J.Carr	14,000
20	Jan	1	(h)	Sunderland	L	2-3	Elliott, A.Wilson	12,000
21		2	(a)	West Brom A	L	0-1		10,940
22		16	(a)	Everton	W	5-1	A.Wilson 2, J.Carr, A.N.Wilson 2	7,500
23		23	(a)	Chelsea	D	2-2	Tinsley, A.N.Wilson	9,000
24	Feb	3	(h)	Bradford C	W	3-0	A.N.Wilson, J.Cook, Tinsley	
25		6	(a)	Burnley	L	0-4		9,000
26		13	(h)	Tottenham H	W	7-5	J.Carr 2, Storey, Tinsley 3 (1 pen), Elliott	7,000
27		27	(h)	Manchester C	W	1-0	Elliott	8,000
28	Mar	10	(a)	Newcastle U	W	2-1	Elliott 2	10,000
29		13	(a)	Aston Villa	L	0-5		13,000
30		17	(h)	Sheffield U	D	2-2	Elliott 2	
31		20	(h)	Liverpool	W	3-0	Tinsley 3	6,000
32		27	(a)	Bradford	L	0-2		10,000
33	Apr	2	(a)	Sunderland	L	1-4	Elliott	18,000
34		3	(h)	Oldham A*	W	4-1	Tinsley 3 (1 pen), Urwin	5,000
35		5	(h)	Sheffield W	W	3-1	Tinsley 2, A.N.Wilson	11,000
36		10	(a)	Manchester U	D	2-2	Tinsley, Jackson	15,000
37		17	(h)	Bolton W	D	0-0		8,000
38		24	(a)	Blackburn R	L	0-4		3,000

FINAL LEAGUE POSITION: 12th in Division One   Appearances

*Abandoned, see Abandoned Games section.   Goals

FA Cup

1	Jan	9	(h)	Goole T	W	9-3	J.Carr 3, Elliott 3, Tinsley 3	8,650
2		30	(a)	Bradford C	L	0-1		26,457

Appearances

Goals

Williamson RG	Haworth JH	Walker J	Davidson S	Jackson A	Malcolm G	Wilson A*	Carr J	Elliott GW	Tinsley W	Cook J	Carr W	Davies B	Weir J	Storey T	Wynn R	Healey R	Hisbent JM	Cook H	Verrill E	Urwin T*	Davies AE*	Wilson AN*	Holmes W*	Caig H*	
1	2	3	4	5	6	7	8	9	10	11															1
1	2	3	4	5	6	7	8	9	10	11															2
1	2	3	4		6	7	8	9	10	11	5														3
1	2	3	4	5	6	7	8	9	10	11															4
1	2	3	4	5	6	7	8	9	10	11															5
1	2	3	4	5	6	7	8	9	10	11															6
1	2	3	4	5	6	7	8	9	10	11															7
	2		4	5	6		8	9	10			1	3	7	11										8
	2		4	5	6		8	9	10	11		1	3	7											9
	2		4	5	6			9	10			1	3	7	11	8									10
	2		4	5	6	7	8	9	10			1	3		11										11
	2	3	4	5	6		8	9	10			1		7	11										12
	2	3	4	5	6		8	9				1		7	11	10									13
	2		4	5	6		8	9	10	11		1	3	7											14
	2	3	4		6	7	8	9	10	11	5	1													15
	2	3	4		6	7	8	9	10	11	5	1													16
		3	4	10		7	8	9		11	5	1				2	6								17
1	2	3	4			7	8	9	10	11								5	6						18
1	2	3	4			7	8	9	10	11								5	6						19
1	2	3	4	5	6	7	8	9	10											11					20
1	2	3	4		6	7	8		10									5		11		9			21
1	2	3		5	6	7	8		10	11								4				9			22
1	2	3		5	6	7	8		10	11								4				9			23
1	2	3	4	5	6		8		10	11				7								9			24
1	2	3	4	5	6		8		10	11				7								9			25
1	2	3	4	5	6		8	9	10	11				7											26
		3	4	5	6		8	9	10	11		1		7									2		27
	2	3	4		6		8	9	10	11	5	1		7											28
		3	4				8	9	10		5	1		7				6		11			2		29
	2	3	4	5	6		8	9	10			1		7						11			2		30
		3	4	5	6		8		10			1		7						11		9	2		31
		3	4	5	6		8	9	10			1		7		8				11			2		32
		3	4	5	6		8		10			1		7						11		9	2		32
		3	4	5	6		8	9	10			1		7						11			2		33
1		3	4	5	6		8		10	11				7								9	2		34
1		3	4	5	6			9	10	11				7							8		2		35
1		3	4	5	6		8	9	10	11				7									2		36
1		3	4	5				9	10	11				7				6					2	8	37
20	27	33	36	29	34	21	33	29	37	22	6	18	5	21	5	3	1	8	2	7	1	9	10	1	38
		2		4	9	14	23	1						1	1			1				5			

1 own-goal

Williamson RG	Haworth JH	Walker J	Davidson S	Jackson A	Malcolm G	Wilson A*	Carr J	Elliott GW	Tinsley W	Cook J	Carr W	Davies B	Weir J	Storey T	Wynn R	Healey R	Hisbent JM	Cook H	Verrill E	Urwin T*	Davies AE*	Wilson AN*	Holmes W*	Caig H*	
1	2		4		6	7	8	9	10			3		5									11		1
1	2	3		5	6	7	8	9	10	11								4							2
2	2	1	1	1	2	2	2	2	2	1		1		1				2				1			
								3	3	3															

1918-19

1	Jan	11	(h)	Scotswood	D	0-0	6,000
2		18	(a)	Sunderland	L	0-2	12,000
3		25	(h)	Durham C	W	5-0 Elliott 5	
4	Feb	1	(a)	Hartlepools U	W	2-1 Elliott 2	
5		8	(h)	Newcastle U	W	3-0 Elliott 2, Forshaw	15,000
6		15	(h)	South Shields	W	2-1 W.Carr, J.Carr	10,000
7		22	(a)	Darlington Forge	W	2-0 Elliott 2	9,000
8	Mar	1	(h)	Hartlepools U	W	8-2 Elliott 6, J.Carr, Forshaw	15,000
9		8	(a)	Scotswood	W	2-1 G.Carr, Elliott	12,000
10		15	(h)	Sunderland	L	1-2 Elliott	20,000
11		22	(a)	Durham C	W	1-0 J.Carr	5,000
12		29	(a)	Newcastle U	W	1-0 Elliott	20,000
13	Apr	12	(a)	South Shields	L	1-3 Wilson	10,000
14		19	(h)	Darlington Forge	D	0-0	18,000

FINAL LEAGUE POSITION: 1st in Northern Victory League

Appearances
Goals

NB. The appearances and goals scored in the Northern Victory League do not contribute to player career records.

Williamson RG	Dixon C	Weir J	Robinson JW	Fox WV	Carr W	Storey T	Carr J	Elliott GW	Carr G	Cook J	Donaghy P	Malcolm G	Burton †	Chesser †	Forshaw R †	Gallagher J	Gascoigne †	Holmes W	Evans †	Mines †	Wilson †	Lloyd E	Stage W	
1	2	3	4	5	6	7	8	9	10	11														1
1	2	3				7		9	5	10	4	6	8	11										2
1	2	3		5		7		9	4	8		6		11	10									3
1	2			5	6	7	8	9	4	11					10	3								4
1	2			6	5	7	8	9	4			11			10	3								5
1	2			6	5	7	8	9	4						10	3	11							6
1	2			6	5	7	8	9	4			11			10	3								7
1	2			6	5		8	9	4			11			10				3	7				8
1	2			6	5	7	8	9	4			11			10	3								9
1	2			6	5	7	8	9	4			11			10	3								10
1	2			6		7	8	9	4			11			10	3					5			11
1	2			6	5		8	9	4			11			10	3					7			12
1	3	2		5	11	7	8	4				6			10			9						13
1	2			6	5	7	8	9	4							3						10	11	14
14	14	3	1	13	11	12	12	14	13	4	5	8	1	2	10	9	1	1	1	1	2	1	1	
		1				3	20	1							2						1			

†Guest players, only season with club.

1919-20

Manager: Tom McIntosh

1	Aug	30	(a)	Sheffield W	W 1-0	Tinsley	20,000
2	Sep	3	(h)	Blackburn R	D 2-2	Butler, Fox	25,000
3		6	(h)	Sheffield W	W 3-0	Elliott 2, Butler	21,000
4		13	(h)	Sheffield U	W 1-0	Butler	20,000
5		15	(a)	Blackburn R	W 2-0	Elliott 2	10,000
6		17	(h)	Bolton W	L 1-3	Butler	15,000
7		20	(a)	Sheffield U	L 1-5	Elliott (pen)	25,000
8		27	(h)	Manchester U	D 1-1	Elliott	19,300
9	Oct	4	(a)	Manchester U	D 1-1	Davidson	20,000
10		11	(h)	Oldham A	W 1-0	J.Carr (pen)	18,359
11		18	(a)	Oldham A	W 2-1	Butler 2	10,000
12		25	(h)	Aston Villa	L 1-4	Butler	10,000
13	Nov	1	(a)	Aston Villa	L 3-5	Elliott 3	45,000
14		8	(h)	Newcastle U	L 0-1		30,000
15		22	(h)	Chelsea	D 0-0		25,000
16		29	(a)	Chelsea	L 1-3	Tinsley	20,000
17	Dec	3	(a)	Newcastle U	D 0-0		40,000
18		6	(h)	Liverpool	W 3-2	Pender, Elliott, J.Carr	15,000
19		13	(a)	Liverpool	L 0-1		30,000
20		20	(h)	Bradford	L 1-2	Elliott	10,000
21		25	(a)	Burnley	L 3-5	Butler, G.Carr, Elliott	
22		27	(a)	Bradford	D 1-1	Elliott	18,000
23	Jan	1	(h)	Burnley	W 4-0	Elliott 3 (1 pen), Pender	25,000
24		3	(h)	Preston NE	W 4-1	Elliott 2, Butler, Urwin	15,000
25		17	(a)	Preston NE	L 1-3	Butler	16,000
26		24	(a)	Manchester C	L 0-1		28,000
27	Feb	7	(a)	Derby C	W 2-1	Urwin, W.Carr	15,000
28		14	(h)	Derby C	W 2-0	Pender, Elliott	25,000
29		18	(h)	Manchester C	L 0-2		15,000
30		21	(a)	West Brom A	L 1-4	Pender	24,995
31		28	(h)	West Brom A	D 0-0		30,000
32	Mar	6	(h)	Sunderland	L 0-2		21,581
33		13	(a)	Sunderland	D 1-1	Elliott	30,000
34		20	(h)	Arsenal	W 1-0	Elliott	16,000
35		27	(a)	Arsenal	L 1-2	Pender	25,000
36	Apr	2	(a)	Notts C	D 1-1	Elliott	20,000
37		3	(h)	Everton	D 1-1	Elliott	14,000
38		5	(h)	Notts C	W 5-2	Elliott 3, Urwin, G.Carr	22,000
39		10	(a)	Everton	L 2-5	Jennings, Butler	20,000
40		17	(h)	Bradford C	W 4-0	Elliott 4 (1 pen)	25,000
41		24	(a)	Bradford C	W 1-0	Jennings	13,000
42	May	1	(a)	Bolton W	L 1-2	Elliott	15,000

FINAL LEAGUE POSITION: 13th in Division One

Appearances
Goals

FA Cup

3	Jan	14	(h)	Lincoln C	W 4-1	Elliott 3, W.Carr	17,746
4		31	(a)	Notts C	L 0-1		28,000

Appearances
Goals

198

Williamson RG	Dixon C*	Walker J	Davidson S	Ellerington W*	Fox WV*	Curtis J*	Carr J	Elliott GW	Tinsley W	Urwin T	Butler R*	Holmes W	Storey T	Harrison H*	Honeyman J*	Carr G*	Robinson JW*	Marshall J*	Davison JW*	Pender R*	Lloyd EW*	Carr W	Clarke W*	Poulton A*	Jennings S*	Donaghy P*	
1	2	3	4	5	6	7	8	9	10	11																	1
1	2	3	4	5	6		7	8	10	11	9																2
1	2	3	4	5	6		7	8	10	11	9																3
1	2	3	4	5	6		7	8	10	11	9																4
1	2	3	4	5	6		7	8	10	11	9																5
1	2	3	4	5	6		7	8	10	11	9																6
1	2	3	4	5	6		7	8	10	11	9																7
1		3	4	5	6		8	9	10	11		2	7														8
	2	3	4	5			8	10		11	9		7	1	6												9
	2	3	4	5	6		8	10		11	9		7	1													10
	2	3	4	5	6		8	10		11	9		7	1													11
	2	3	4	5	6		8	10		11	9		7	1													12
1		3	4	5			8	10		11	9	2	7			6											13
1		3	4	5		7	8	10		11	9	2				6											14
1		3	4	5	6	7	8	10		11	9	2															15
1		3	4	5		7	8	9	10	11		2				6											16
1		3	4	5		7	8	9	10	11		2				6											17
1		3	4	5			8	9		11		2	7			6	10										18
1		3	4	5			8	9		11		10	7					2		6							19
1		3	4	5			8	9		11		7						2		6	10						20
1		3	4	5			8	10		11	9	7						2		6							21
1		3	4	5			8	10		11	9	7						2		6							22
1		3	4				8	9		11	10	7						2		6		5					23
1		3	4				8	10		11	9	7						2		6		5					24
1		3	4				8	9		11	10	7						2		6		5					25
1		3	4	5	6		8	9		11	10	7						2									26
1		3	4		6		8	9		11	10	7						2				5					27
1		3	4		6		8	9		11	10	7						2				5					28
1		3	4		6		8	9		11	10	7						2				5					29
1		3	4		6		8	9		11	10	7						2				5					30
1		3	4		6		8	9		11	10	7						2				5					31
1		3	4	5	6		8	9		11	10							2					7				32
1		3	4		6		8	9		11	10	7						2				5					33
1		3	4		6		8	9		11	10	7						2				5					34
1		3	4		6			9		11	10	7						2				5		8			35
1		3	4		6			9		11	10	7						2				5		8			36
1		3	4		6		8	9		11	10	7						2				5					37
1		3	4		6		8	9		11	10	7						2				5					38
1		3	4		6		8	9		11		7						2				5			10		39
1		3	4		6		8	9		11		7						2				5			10		40
1		3	4	5			8	9		11	10	7						2							6		41
1		3	4	5				9		11	10	7						2							8	6	42
38	11	34	42	31	23	5	37	38	14	39	27	15	10	4	1	15	1	24	1	23	2	16	3	2	4	2	
		1		1		2	31	2	3	11						2				5		1		2			

Williamson RG	Dixon C*	Walker J	Davidson S	Ellerington W*	Fox WV*	Curtis J*	Carr J	Elliott GW	Tinsley W	Urwin T	Butler R*	Holmes W	Storey T	Harrison H*	Honeyman J*	Carr G*	Robinson JW*	Marshall J*	Davison JW*	Pender R*	Lloyd EW*	Carr W	Clarke W*	Poulton A*	Jennings S*	Donaghy P*	
1		3	4				8	9		11	10	7						2		6		5					3
1		3	4	5	6		8	9		11	10	7						2									4
2		1	2	1	1		2	2		2	2	2						2		1		1					
								3										1									

199

1920-21

Manager: James Howie

1	Aug	28	(h)	Oldham A	L	1-2	Elliott	29,000
2		30	(h)	Preston NE	D	0-0		20,000
3	Sep	4	(a)	Oldham A	D	3-3	Elliott 2, Tinsley	19,951
4		6	(a)	Preston NE	L	0-2		20,000
5		11	(a)	Burnley	L	1-2	Elliott	
6		18	(h)	Burnley	D	0-0		
7		25	(a)	Arsenal	D	2-2	Mordue, Pender	45,000
8	Oct	2	(h)	Arsenal	W	2-1	Elliott 2	20,000
9		9	(h)	Bradford C	W	2-1	Elliott, Ellerington	20,000
10		16	(a)	Bradford C	W	1-0	Pender	30,000
11		23	(h)	Bolton W	W	4-1	J.Carr 2, Elliott 2	28,947
12		30	(a)	Bolton W	L	2-6	Elliott, Urwin	
13	Nov	6	(h)	Sunderland	W	2-0	Elliott 2	‡ 35,703
14		13	(a)	Sunderland	W	2-1	Elliott 2	40,000
15		20	(h)	Derby C	W	1-0	Elliott	28,000
16		27	(a)	Derby C	W	1-0	Poulton	12,520
17	Dec	4	(h)	Everton	W	3-1	Poulton, Elliott 2	4,000
18		11	(a)	Everton	L	1-2	Poulton	
19		18	(a)	Blackburn R	L	2-3	Poulton, Elliott	
20		25	(h)	Huddersfield T	W	2-0	J.Carr, Elliott	
21		27	(a)	Huddersfield T	W	1-0	Pender	
22	Jan	1	(h)	Blackburn R	D	1-1	Tinsley	30,000
23		15	(a)	Sheffield U	D	1-1	J.Carr	18,000
24		22	(h)	Sheffield U	D	2-2	Elliott 2 (1 pen)	25,000
25		29	(h)	West Brom A	L	0-1		28,000
26	Feb	5	(a)	West Brom A	W	1-0	Elliott	24,920
27		12	(a)	Bradford	L	0-3		15,000
28		19	(h)	Bradford	W	2-1	Birrell, Urwin	25,000
29		26	(a)	Newcastle U	L	0-2		50,000
30	Mar	5	(h)	Newcastle U	D	0-0		35,000
31		12	(a)	Liverpool	D	0-0		40,000
32		19	(h)	Liverpool	L	0-1		25,000
33		25	(a)	Manchester C	L	1-2	Poulton	25,000
34		26	(h)	Aston Villa	L	1-4	Elliott	30,000
35		28	(h)	Manchester C	W	3-1	Elliott, Dowson 2	29,000
36	Apr	2	(a)	Aston Villa	W	1-0	Elliott	35,000
37		9	(h)	Manchester U	L	2-4	W.Carr, G.Carr	15,000
38		16	(a)	Manchester U	W	1-0	Elliott	25,000
39		23	(h)	Chelsea	D	0-0		15,000
40		30	(a)	Chelsea	D	1-1	Birrell	30,000
41	May	2	(h)	Tottenham H	W	1-0	W.Carr	15,000
42		7	(a)	Tottenham H	D	2-2	Urwin, G.Carr	27,000

FINAL LEAGUE POSITION: 8th in Division One

‡Ground Record

Appearances
Goals

FA Cup

1	Jan	8	(a)	Derby C	L	0-2		23,000

Appearances
Goals

Williamson RG	Marshall J	Walker J	Davidson S	Ellerington W	Donaghy P	Hastie J*	Carr J	Elliott GW	Tinsley W	Urwin T	Holmes W	Fox WV	Jennings S	Carr W	Mordue J*	Pender R	Chipperfield F*	Poulton A	Clarke W	Carr G	Dowson F*	Birrell W*	Dixon C	Gallagher J*	Brown T*	Young EW*	
1	2	3	4	5	6	7	8	9	10	11																	1
1	3		4	5	11		8	9	10	7	2	6															2
1	2		4	5			7	9	10	11	3	6	8														3
1	2	3	4	5			7	9	10	11		6	8														4
1	2		4		6		8	9		11	3		10	5	7												5
1	2		4		6		8	9	10	11	3			5	7												6
1	2		4		6		8	9		11	3			5	7	10											7
1	2		4		6		8	9		11	3			5	7	10											8
1	2		4		6		8	9		11	3			5	7	10											9
1	2		4		6		8	9		11	3			5	7	10											10
1	2		4		6		8	9	10	11	3			5	7												11
1	2		4		6		8	9	10	11	3				7		5										12
1	2		4		6		8	9	10	11	3			5	7												13
1	2		4		6		8	9		11	3			5	7			10									14
1	2		4		6		8	9		11	3			5	7			10									15
1	2		4		6		8	9		11	3			5	7			10									16
1	2		4		6		8	9		11	3			5	7			10									17
1	2		4		6		8	9		11	3			5	7			10									18
1	2		4		6		8	9		11	3			5	7			10									19
1	2		4				8	9		11	3			5	7	6		10									20
1	2		4				8	9		11	3			5		6		10	7								21
1			4				7	9	10		3	2		5		6		8	11								22
1	2		4		6		8	9		11	3			5				10	7								23
1	2		4		6		8	9	10	11	3			5					7								24
1	2		4		6		7	9			3		8	5		10			11								25
1	2		4	5			8	9			3			10	11	6					7						26
1			4	5				9		11	3	2	10		7	6					8						27
1	2		4		6		8	9	10		3			5	11						7						28
1			4		6		8		10		3			5				9	11		7	2					29
1	2		4		6		8	9		11	3			5				10				7					30
1	2		4		6		8			11	3			5				9		10		7					31
1	2		4		6		8	9	10	11	3			5								7					32
1	2		4		6		8	9		11	3			5				10				7					33
1	2		4		6		8	9		11	3			5				10				7					34
1					6		8	9		11	3	2		5		4					10	7					35
1	2				6		8	9		11	3	5				4					10	7					36
1					6		8	9		11	2			5		4		7	10				3				37
1	2		4		6		7	9		11	3			5		10		8									38
1			4	2	6				10	11	3			5		8									7	9	39
1	2		4	5	6					11	3			8							10	9			7		40
1	2				6		8			11	3			5		4					10	9			7		41
1	2			5	6					11	3					4				8	10	9			7		42
42	36	2	37	34	10	1	38	36	12	39	40	7	6	32	19	18	1	14	5	5	7	14	1	1	4	1	
					1		4	26	2	3				2	1	3		5			2	2	2				

Williamson RG	Marshall J	Walker J	Davidson S	Ellerington W	Donaghy P	Hastie J*	Carr J	Elliott GW	Tinsley W	Urwin T	Holmes W	Fox WV	Jennings S	Carr W	Mordue J*	Pender R	Chipperfield F*	Poulton A	Clarke W	Carr G	Dowson F*	Birrell W*	Dixon C	Gallagher J*	Brown T*	Young EW*	
1	2		4		6		8	9		11	3			5				10	7								1
1	1		1		1		1	1		1	1			1				1	1								

1921-22

Manager: James Howie

#	Month	Date		Opponent	Result	Scorers	Attendance
1	Aug	27	(a)	West Brom A	D 0-0		24,880
2		29	(h)	Oldham A	D 1-1	A.N.Wilson	20,000
3	Sep	3	(h)	West Brom A	W 3-2	A.N.Wilson 3	30,000
4		5	(a)	Oldham A	W 1-0	A.N.Wilson	18,000
5		10	(a)	Tottenham H	W 4-2	G.Carr, Birrell, A.N.Wilson 2	34,882
6		17	(h)	Tottenham H	D 0-0		18,000
7		24	(a)	Cardiff C	L 1-3	Elliott (pen)	40,000
8	Oct	1	(h)	Cardiff C	D 0-0		33,000
9		8	(a)	Bradford C	W 2-0	Pender, A.N.Wilson	25,000
10		15	(h)	Bradford C	L 1-2	G.Carr	25,000
11		22	(h)	Aston Villa	W 5-0	Birrell 2, G.Carr 3	10,000
12		29	(a)	Aston Villa	L 2-6	Elliott, J.Carr	35,000
13	Nov	5	(a)	Manchester U	W 5-3	Elliott 2, A.N.Wilson, J.Carr, Urwin	30,000
14		12	(h)	Manchester U	W 2-0	A.N.Wilson, S.Davidson	18,000
15		19	(a)	Liverpool	L 0-4		40,000
16		26	(h)	Liverpool	W 3-1	Birrell 2, A.N.Wilson	24,000
17	Dec	3	(a)	Newcastle U	D 0-0		50,000
18		10	(h)	Newcastle U	D 1-1	Birrell	35,000
19		17	(h)	Burnley	W 4-1	A.N.Wilson 2, Elliott, G.Carr	25,000
20		24	(a)	Burnley	L 1-3	A.N.Wilson	25,000
21		26	(h)	Chelsea	L 0-1		35,000
22		27	(a)	Chelsea	D 1-1	A.N.Wilson (pen)	60,000
23		31	(a)	Sheffield U	L 1-6	A.N.Wilson	
24	Jan	14	(h)	Sheffield U	D 1-1	Urwin	18,000
25		21	(a)	Manchester C	D 2-2	S.Davidson, G.Carr	25,000
26	Feb	1	(h)	Manchester C	W 4-1	A.N.Wilson 3, Urwin	20,000
27		11	(h)	Everton	W 3-1	Birrell 2, G.Carr	20,000
28		18	(a)	Sunderland	D 1-1	A.N.Wilson	30,000
29		25	(h)	Sunderland	W 3-0	A.N.Wilson 2 (1 pen), G.Carr	30,000
30	Mar	1	(a)	Everton	L 1-4	G.Carr	
31		11	(h)	Huddersfield T	W 5-1	A.N.Wilson 2, Elliott 2, Urwin	26,000
32		18	(h)	Birmingham	D 1-1	A.N.Wilson	20,000
33		25	(a)	Birmingham	L 3-4	A.N.Wilson 2, Elliott	20,000
34	Apr	1	(a)	Arsenal	D 2-2	A.N.Wilson, Birrell	30,000
35		8	(h)	Arsenal	W 4-2	Elliott 3 (1 pen), Urwin	15,000
36		14	(a)	Preston NE	D 1-1	A.N.Wilson	30,000
37		15	(h)	Blackburn R	L 0-1		15,000
38		17	(h)	Preston NE	W 1-0	A.N.Wilson	20,000
39		22	(a)	Blackburn R	D 2-2	A.N.Wilson, Elliott	20,000
40		29	(h)	Bolton W	W 4-2	G.Carr 3, A.N.Wilson	16,000
41	May	1	(a)	Huddersfield T	L 1-2	G.Carr	
42		6	(a)	Bolton W	L 2-4	G.Carr, Elliott	15,000

FINAL LEAGUE POSITION: 8th in Division One

Appearances
Goals

FA Cup

#	Month	Date		Opponent	Result		Attendance
1	Jan	7	(a)	Hull C	L 0-5		25,000

Appearances
Goals

Williamson RG	Marshall J	Holmes W	Davidson S	Ellerington W	Donaghy P	Birrell W	Elliott GW	Wilson AN	Poulton A	Urwin T	Mordue J	Carr G	Fox WV	Carr J	Pender R	Davison JW	Carr W	Harrison H	Murray W*	Webster M*	No.
1	2	3	4	5	6	7	8	9	10	11											1
1	2	3	4	5	6	7	8	9	10	11											2
1	2	3	4	5	6	8		9		11	7	10									3
1	2		4	5	6	8		9		11	7	10	3								4
1	2		4	5	6	8		9		11	7	10	3								5
1	2		4	5	6		8	9		11	7	10	3								6
1	2		4	5	6	8	10	9		11			3	7							7
1	2		4	5		8	10	9		11			3	7	6						8
1	2		4	5		8		9		11		10	3	7	6						9
1	2		4	5		8		9		11	7	10	3		6						10
1	2		4	5		8		9		11	7	10	3		6						11
1	2		4	5				9		11	7	10	3	8	6						12
1	2		4	5			10	9		11	7		3	8	6						13
1	2		4	5			10	9		11	7		3	8	6						14
1		2	4	5				9		11	7	10	3	8	6						15
1	2		4	5		8		9			11	10	3	7	6						16
1	2		4	5		8	10	9		11			3	7	6						17
1		2	4	5		8	10	9		11			3	7	6						18
1		3	4			7	8	9			11	10			6	2	5				19
1		2	4		6	7	8	9			11	10	3				5				20
1			4		6	7	8	9		11		10	3			2	5				21
1			4		6	8		9		11	7	10	3			2	5				22
1			4	5	6	8		9		11	7	10	3			2					23
1	2		4					9		11	7	10	3	8	6		5				24
	2		4			8		9		11		10	3	7	6		5	1			25
	2		4			8		9		11		10	3	7	6		5	1			26
	2		4			8		9		11		10	3	7	6		5	1			27
	2		4		6	8		9		11		10	3	7			5	1			28
	2		4		6	8		9		11		10	3	7			5	1			29
		2	4		6	8		9		11		10	3	7			5	1			30
	2		4		6	8	10	9		11			3	7			5	1			31
1	2		4		6	8	10	9		11			3	7			5				32
1	2		4		6	8	10	9		11			3	7			5				33
	2		4		6	8	10	9		11			3	7			5	1			34
		3	4			8		9		11		10		7	6	2	5	1			35
	2		4		6	8	10	9		11			3	7			5	1			36
	2		4		6	8	10	9		11			3	7			5	1			37
	2				6	8		9				10	3	7	4		5	1	11		38
	2		4	5		8		9				10	3	7	6			1	11		39
	2		4	5		8		9		11		10	3	7*	6			1			40
	2		4		6	8		9		11		10	3	7				1		5	41
	2		4	5		8		9		7		10	3		6			1	11		42
26	33	9	41	33	11	35	26	35	2	37	16	28	37	28	21	5	19	16	3	1	
		2				9	13	32		5		15		2	1						

Williamson RG	Marshall J	Holmes W	Davidson S	Ellerington W	Donaghy P	Birrell W	Elliott GW	Wilson AN	Poulton A	Urwin T	Mordue J	Carr G	Fox WV	Carr J	Pender R	Davison JW	Carr W	Harrison H	Murray W*	Webster M*	No.
1	2		4	5		8	10	9		11			3	7	6						1
1	1		1	1		1	1	1		1			1	1	1						

1922-23

Manager: James Howie

1	Aug	26	(h)	Huddersfield T	D 2-2	Birrell, Elliott	20,000
2		28	(a)	Manchester C	L 1-2	Elliott	25,000
3	Sep	2	(a)	Huddersfield T	W 2-0	Birrell 2	12,000
4		4	(h)	Manchester C	W 5-0	Elliott 3, A.N.Wilson 2	15,000
5		9	(a)	Chelsea	D 1-1	A.N.Wilson	30,000
6		16	(h)	Chelsea	W 2-1	Elliott 2 (1 pen)	20,000
7		23	(a)	Aston Villa	D 2-2	Elliott, A.N.Wilson	35,000
8		30	(h)	Aston Villa	D 2-2	Elliott 2 (2 pens)	20,000
9	Oct	7	(a)	Oldham A	D 0-0		20,000
10		14	(h)	Oldham A	W 2-1	Elliott, A.N.Wilson	25,000
11		21	(h)	Birmingham	W 2-1	A.N.Wilson 2 (1 pen)	18,000
12		28	(a)	Birmingham	L 0-2		30,000
13	Nov	4	(h)	Sheffield U	W 3-2	Elliott 3	15,000
14		11	(a)	Sheffield U	L 1-4	Birrell	
15		18	(a)	Preston NE	W 2-1	G.Carr, Elliott	20,000
16		25	(h)	Preston NE	D 1-1	G.Carr	16,000
17	Dec	2	(h)	Burnley	W 4-1	J.Carr, Birrell, Elliott, Urwin	20,000
18		9	(a)	Burnley	L 0-3		15,000
19		16	(h)	Stoke	W 3-1	Elliott 2 (1 pen), J.Carr	10,000
20		23	(a)	Stoke	D 0-0		15,000
21		25	(a)	Newcastle U	D 1-1	Elliott	30,000
22		26	(h)	Newcastle U	D 1-1	Pender	30,000
23		30	(h)	Tottenham H	W 2-0	Murray, G.Carr	15,000
24	Jan	6	(a)	Tottenham H	L 0-2		30,000
25		20	(h)	Liverpool	L 0-2		25,000
26		27	(a)	Liverpool	L 0-2		42,000
27	Feb	10	(a)	Sunderland	L 1-2	Donaghy	12,000
28		17	(h)	Everton	L 2-4	Donaghy, G.Carr	12,000
29		28	(a)	Everton	L 3-5	Birrell 3	20,000
30	Mar	3	(h)	Arsenal	W 2-0	Cochrane, Elliott	20,000
31		10	(a)	Arsenal	L 0-3		25,000
32		17	(a)	Cardiff C	L 0-2		22,000
33		24	(h)	Cardiff C	L 0-1		20,000
34		30	(a)	Nottingham F	L 1-2	Urwin	18,000
35		31	(a)	Bolton W	D 1-1	A.N.Wilson	18,000
36	Apr	2	(h)	Nottingham F	W 4-0	Elliott, A.N.Wilson 2, Barrett (og)	15,000
37		7	(h)	Bolton W	L 1-2	A.N.Wilson	15,000
38		14	(a)	Blackburn R	L 0-2		15,000
39		18	(h)	Sunderland	W 2-0	Birrell, Elliott	20,000
40		21	(h)	Blackburn R	L 1-2	Elliott	12,000
41		28	(a)	West Brom A	L 0-1		10,021
42	May	5	(h)	West Brom A	L 0-1		10,000

FINAL LEAGUE POSITION: 18th in Division One

Appearances
Goals

FA Cup

1	Jan	13	(a)	Oldham A	W 1-0	Birrell	18,000
2	Feb	3	(h)	Sheffield U	D 1-1	A.N.Wilson (pen)	‡ 38,067
R		8	(a)	Sheffield U	L 0-3		38,500

‡Ground attendance record

Appearances
Goals

Match	Williamson RG	Marshall J	Fox WV	Davidson S	Ellerington W	Pender R	Carr J	Birrell W	Wilson AN	Elliott GW	Urwin T	Holmes W	Carr G	Slade CH*	Brown T	Murray W	Webster M	Bottrill WG*	Davison JW	Donaghy P	Clough J*	Harris J*	Cochrane AF*	Butler W*
1	1	2	3	4	5	6	7	8	9	10	11													
2	1	2	3	4	5	6	7	8	9	10	11													
3	1	2	3	4	5	6	7	8	9	10	11													
4	1	2	3	4	5	6	7	8	9	10	11													
5	1	2	3	4	5	6	7	8	9	10	11													
6	1	2	3	4	5	6	7	8	9	10	11													
7	1		3	4	5	6	7	8	9	10	11	2												
8	1	2	3	4	5	6	7	8	9	10	11													
9	1		3	4	5	6		7	9	10	11	2		8										
10	1	2	3	4	5	6	7	8	9	10	11													
11	1	2	3		5	6		8	9		11		10	4	7									
12	1	2	3		5	6		8	9	10	7			4		11								
13	1	2	3		5	6	7	8	9	10	11			4										
14	1	2	3		5	6	7	8		9	11		10	4										
15	1	2	3		5	6	7	8		9			10	4		11								
16	1	2	3		5	6	7	8		9			10	4		11								
17	1	2	3		5	6	7	8		9	11		10	4										
18	1	2	3	4	5	6	7	8		9	11		10											
19	1	2	3	4		6	7	8		9	11					10	5							
20	1	2	3	4		6	7	8		9	11					10	5							
21	1	2	3	4		6	7	8	9		11					10	5							
22	1	2	3	4		6		8		9	11					10	5	7						
23	1		3	4		6				9	11	2		8		10	5	7						
24	1					6		8	9		11	3	10	4			5	7	2					
25	1		3	4		6	7	8	9		11	2	10				5							
26	1		3	4	2	6	7	8	9		11						5							
27	1		3			6	7	8				2	10	4		11	5			9				
28	1		3	2		6		8					10	4		11	5	7		9				
29	1		3	4		6	7	8	9		11	2					5			10				
30			3			6	7	8	9			2				11	5				1	4	10	
31			3		5	6	7	8	9		11	2									1	4	10	
32			3				7	8			11	2				6	5	9			1	4	10	
33	1		3				7	8	9		11	2				6	5					4	10	
34		2						8	9		11	3				6	5	7			1	4	10	
35		2						8	9	10	11	3				6	5	7			1	4		
36			4	3				8	9	10	11	2				6	5	7			1			
37		2	3	4				8	9	10	11					6	5	7			1			
38			3		5			8		10	11	2				6	4			9	1	7		
39			3			6		8	9	10	11	2				4	5	7			1			
40			3			6		8	9	10	11	2				4	5	7			1			
41			3			6		8	9		11	2	10				5				1	4		7
42			3					8	9	10	11	2				6	5				1	4		7
Apps	30	23	37	22	24	33	24	38	29	33	37	19	13	20	1	12	23	8	1	7	12	8	6	2
Goals					1	2	9	11	23	2		4			1				2				1	

1 own-goal

Match	Williamson RG	Marshall J	Fox WV	Davidson S	Ellerington W	Pender R	Carr J	Birrell W	Wilson AN	Elliott GW	Urwin T	Holmes W	Carr G	Slade CH*	Brown T	Murray W	Webster M	Bottrill WG*	Davison JW	Donaghy P	Clough J*	Harris J*	Cochrane AF*	Butler W*
1	1		3	4		6	7	8	9		11	2	10				5							
2	1	2	3	4		6	7	8	9		11					10	5							
R	1		3		4	6	7	8	9		11	2				10	5							
Apps	3	1	3	2	1	3	3	3	3		3	2	1			2	3							
Goals									1	1														

205

1923-24

Manager: Herbert Bamlett

1	Aug	25	(a)	Huddersfield T	L	0-1	20,500
2		29	(h)	Notts C	L	2-3 Elliott, Wilson	10,000
3	Sep	1	(h)	Huddersfield T	W	2-0 Birrell, Cochrane	20,000
4		8	(a)	Tottenham H	L	1-2 Elliott	38,000
5		15	(h)	Tottenham H	L	0-1	25,000
6		22	(a)	West Ham U	D	1-1 Wilson	20,000
7		29	(h)	West Ham U	L	0-1	22,000
8	Oct	4	(a)	Notts C	L	0-1	12,000
9		6	(h)	Nottingham F	W	5-2 Wilson 5 (1 pen)	18,000
10		13	(a)	Nottingham F	L	1-3 Cochrane	17,000
11		20	(h)	Newcastle U	W	1-0 Elliott (pen)	25,000
12		27	(a)	Newcastle U	L	2-3 J.Carr, Cochrane	30,000
13	Nov	3	(a)	Arsenal	L	1-2 Cochrane	25,000
14		10	(h)	Arsenal	D	0-0	13,000
15		17	(h)	Chelsea	W	2-0 Wilson, Elliott	12,000
16		24	(a)	Chelsea	L	0-2	25,000
17	Dec	1	(a)	Aston Villa	D	0-0	20,000
18		8	(h)	Aston Villa	L	0-2	15,000
19		15	(a)	Preston NE	L	0-4	15,000
20		22	(h)	Preston NE	L	1-2 Wainscoat	20,000
21		25	(a)	Burnley	D	0-0	25,000
22		26	(h)	Burnley	W	3-0 Dickson 3	20,000
23		29	(a)	Sheffield U	W	1-0 Dickson	20,000
24	Jan	1	(h)	Cardiff C	L	0-1	33,000
25		5	(h)	Sheffield U	L	0-1	20,000
26		19	(a)	Everton	L	0-1	30,000
27		26	(h)	Everton	D	1-1 Dickson	15,000
28	Feb	2	(a)	Blackburn R	L	0-2	15,000
29		9	(h)	West Brom A	L	0-1	16,000
30		16	(a)	Birmingham	L	1-2 Birrell	22,000
31		23	(h)	Birmingham	L	0-1	15,000
32	Mar	1	(a)	Manchester C	L	2-3 Slade, J.Carr	20,000
33		8	(h)	Blackburn R	W	2-0 Hick, Wainscoat	14,000
34		15	(h)	Bolton W	L	1-2 Elliott	22,000
35		22	(a)	Bolton W	L	0-2	15,000
36		29	(h)	Sunderland	L	1-3 J.Carr (pen)	20,000
37	Apr	2	(h)	Manchester C	D	1-1 Slade	6,000
38		5	(a)	Sunderland	L	2-3 Hick 2	30,000
39		9	(a)	West Brom A	D	1-1 Elliott	14,473
40		12	(a)	Liverpool	L	1-3 Elliott (pen)	20,000
41		19	(h)	Liverpool	D	1-1 Hick	18,000
42		21	(a)	Cardiff C	L	0-1	35,000

FINAL LEAGUE POSITION: 22nd in Division One

Appearances
Goals

FA Cup

1	Jan	12	(h)	Watford	L	0-1	24,192

Appearances
Goals

206

Clough J	Freeman RV*	Maitland AE*	Harris J	Ellerington W	Slade CH	Bottrill WG	Birrell W	Wilson AN	Elliott GW	Urwin T	Cochrane AF	Webster M	Pender R	Carr J	Carr G	Carr W	Harrison H	Holmes W	Stevenson AB*	Fox WV	Dickson IW*	Wainscoat WR	Smith EE*	Williams O*	Hick WM*	#
1	2	3	4	5	6	7	8	9	10	11																1
1	2	3	4	5	6	7		9	8	11	10															2
1	2	3	4			7		9	8	11	10	5	6													3
1	2	3	4			7		9	8	11	10	5	6													4
1	2	3	4			7		9	8	11	10	5	6													5
1	2	3	4				8	9		11		5	6	7	10											6
1	2	3	4		6		8	9		11		5		7	10											7
1	2	3	4		6		8	9	10	11		5		7												8
	3		4		6			9		11	10	5		7	8		1	2								9
	3		4		6			9		11	10	5		7	8		1	2								10
	2	3	4				8	9	10	11		5	6	7			1									11
	2	3	4		6		8	9		11	10	5		7			1									12
1	2	3	4		6		8	9			10	5		7					11							13
1	2	3	5		7	4		9	11	10									8	6						14
1	2	3	4					9	8	11	10	5		7						6						15
1	2	3	4					9	8	11	10	5		7						6						16
1	2	3	4		6			9		11	10	5		7	8											17
1	2	3	4		6			9		11	10	5		7	8											18
1	2	3	4		6		8	9	10			5		7					11							19
1	2	3	4		6	7						5		8					11		9	10				20
1	3		4		6	7	8					5						2	11		9	10				21
1	3		4		6	7	8		10			5						2	11		9					22
1	3		4		6	7	8					5						2	11		9	10				23
1	3		4		6	7	8					5						2	11		9	10				24
1	3		4		6	7	8		11			5						2			9	10				25
1	3		4		6	7	8		11			5						2			9	10				26
1	3		4				8		7	11	6							2			9	10	5			27
1	3		4				8		7	11	6							2			9	10	5			28
1	3		4				8		7		6							2			9	10	5	11		29
1	3		4				8		7		6							2			9	10	5	11		30
1	3		4		6		8		7									2			9	10	5	11		31
	3		4		5		8		10		6			7							1	2		11	9	32
	3		4				8				6			7					10		1	2	5	11	9	33
	3		4				8				6			7					10		1	2	5	11	9	34
	3		4				8				6			7					10		1	2	5	11	9	35
	3		4				8				6			7					10		1	2	5	11	9	36
	3		4				8				6			7					10		1	2	5	11	9	37
	2	3	4				8		10		6			7							1		5	11	9	38
1	2	3	4				8		10		6			7								10	5	11		39
1	2	3	4				8				6	5		7								10		11	9	40
1	2	3	4				8		10		6	5		7										11	9	41
1	2	3	4						10		6	5		7					8		11				9	42
31	40	25	32	5	27	9	21	13	25	33	18	32	9	24	6	6	11	19	8	3	16	17	12	13	7	
					2		2	8	7		4			3							5	2		4		

Clough J	Freeman RV*	Maitland AE*	Harris J	Ellerington W	Slade CH	Bottrill WG	Birrell W	Wilson AN	Elliott GW	Urwin T	Cochrane AF	Webster M	Pender R	Carr J	Carr G	Carr W	Harrison H	Holmes W	Stevenson AB*	Fox WV	Dickson IW*	Wainscoat WR	Smith EE*	Williams O*	Hick WM*	#
1	2	3	4		6	7	8		11			5							9	10						1
1	1	1	1		1	1	1		1			1							1	1						

1924-25

Manager: Herbert Bamlett

1	Aug	30	(h)	Barnsley	W	2-0	O.Williams, Elliott	22,000
2	Sep	6	(a)	Leicester C	D	0-0		24,000
3		10	(h)	Wolves	W	2-0	Elliott 2 (1 pen)	20,000
4		13	(a)	Port Vale	L	1-2	Wainscoat	8,000
5		20	(h)	Bradford C	W	1-0	Hick	18,000
6		27	(a)	South Shields	W	1-0	Hick	10,000
7	Oct	4	(h)	Derby C	L	1-3	Wainscoat	24,000
8		11	(a)	Blackpool	D	1-1	Elliott	14,000
9		18	(h)	Hull C	L	0-1		18,000
10		25	(h)	Stoke	W	1-0	Cochrane	10,000
11	Nov	1	(a)	Coventry C	D	2-2	J.Carr, Dickinson	10,000
12		8	(h)	Oldham A	D	0-0		14,000
13		15	(a)	Sheffield W	L	0-2		13,983
14		22	(h)	Clapton O	D	1-1	Dickson	10,000
15		29	(a)	Crystal P	D	2-2	Elliott, O.Williams	15,000
16	Dec	1	(a)	Fulham	D	0-0		10,000
17		6	(h)	Southampton	D	0-0		14,000
18		13	(a)	Chelsea	L	0-2		22,000
19		20	(h)	Stockport C	D	1-1	Wainscoat	12,000
20		25	(h)	Manchester U	D	1-1	J.T.Williams	18,500
21		26	(a)	Manchester U	L	0-2		44,000
22		27	(a)	Barnsley	L	0-1		8,000
23	Jan	1	(h)	Fulham	L	1-3	Dickson	14,000
24		3	(h)	Leicester C	L	1-5	Hick (pen)	12,000
25		17	(h)	Port Vale	L	0-1		8,000
26		24	(a)	Bradford C	W	1-0	Dickson (pen)	15,000
27		31	(h)	South Shields	D	1-1	O.Williams	14,000
28	Feb	7	(a)	Derby C	L	1-3	Birrell	14,000
29		14	(h)	Blackpool	W	4-1	J.T.Williams 2, O.Williams 2	12,000
30		28	(a)	Stoke	W	1-0	Dickson	10,000
31	Mar	7	(h)	Coventry C	D	1-1	Dickson	13,000
32		14	(a)	Oldham A	D	0-0		6,000
33		19	(a)	Hull C	D	0-0		6,000
34		21	(h)	Sheffield W	W	2-0	McClelland, O.Williams	6,000
35		28	(a)	Clapton O	W	1-0	Dickson	8,000
36	Apr	4	(h)	Crystal P	D	0-0		16,000
37		10	(a)	Portsmouth	L	1-3	Dickson	20,000
38		11	(a)	Southampton	D	1-1	Birrell	10,000
39		12	(h)	Portsmouth	D	1-1	J.T.Williams	17,000
40		18	(h)	Chelsea	D	1-1	Birrell	10,000
41		20	(a)	Stockport C	D	1-1	O.Williams	12,000
42	May	2	(a)	Wolves	L	0-1		10,000

FINAL LEAGUE POSITION: 13th in Division Two

Appearances
Goals

FA Cup

1	Jan	10	(a)	Bradford	L	0-1	28,000

Appearances
Goals

208

Clough J	Bissett JT*	Freeman RV	Harris J	Webster M	Slade CH	Carr J	Cochrane AF	Elliott GW	Wainscoat WR	Williams O	Smith EE	Hick WM	Williams JT*	Birrell W	Dickinson PE*	Good H*	Ashman D*	Dickson 1W	Holmes W	French JP*	McAllister W*	Ferguson RG*	McClelland J*	Wilson J*	
1	2	3	4	5	6	7	8	9	10	11															1
1	2	3	4		6	7	8	9	10	11	5														2
1	2	3	4		6	7	8		10	11	5	9													3
1	2	3	4		6	7	8		10	11	5	9													4
1	3	2		6	4	7	8		10	11	5	9													5
1	2	3		6	4			8	10	7	5	9		11											6
1	2	3		6	4				10	7	5	9		11	8										7
1	2	3		6	4	8	10	9			7	5		11											8
1	2	3		6	4	8	10	9		5				11		7									9
1	2	3		6	4	8	11	9	10							7	5								10
1	2	3			4	8	10	9					11			7	5	6							11
1	2	3		6	4	8	10			9			11			7	5								12
1	2	3		6	4	8	10						11			7	5	9							13
1	2			6	4	8	10						11			7	5	9		3					14
1	2		4	5	6	8	10	9		11			7							3					15
1	2		4	5	6	8		9	10	11			7							3					16
1	2	3	4	5	6	8		9	10	11			7												17
1	2	3	4	5	6	8			10	11		9	7												18
1	2	3	4	5	6	8			10	11		9	7												19
1	2	3	4	5	6	8	10			9			11			7									20
1	2		4	5			10			9			11			7	8	6		3					21
1		3			6	8	11	10		9			7			4	5			2					22
1		3	5		6	7	10	9		11						4		8		2					23
1		4	5	6	7		10			11		9				8		2	3						24
1	2	3	4		6	7	10					5	11			8		9							25
1	2	3	4	5		7	10						11			8	6	9							26
1	2	3	4	5		7	10						11			8	6	9							27
1		3				7	10						11			8	6	9		2	4	5			28
1		3	5			7	10						11			8		9		2	4	6			29
1		3	5			7	8	10					11					9		2	4	6			30
1		3	5			7	10						11			8		9		2	4	6			31
1		3	5			7	10						11			8		9		2	4	6			32
1		3	5				10						11			7	6	8		2	4		9		33
1		3	5				10						11			7	6	8		2	4		9		34
1		3	5				10						11			7	6	8		2	4		9		35
1			5				10						11			7	6	8		3	4	9	2		36
1		3	5			7	10						11			8	6	9		2	4				37
1			5			10	7						11			8	6	9		3	4		2		38
1			5			7	10						11			8	6	9		3	4		2		39
1			5			7	11			10						8	6	9		3	4		2		40
1		3	5				11			10			7			8	6	9		2	4				41
1		3	5			7	10						11			8	6	9		2	4				42
42	24	33	16	37	21	31	23	17	17	30	9	9	27	6	8	13	21	22	1	15	5	4	4		
			1	1		5	3			7			3			4	3	1		7	1				

Clough J	Bissett JT*	Freeman RV	Harris J	Webster M	Slade CH	Carr J	Cochrane AF	Elliott GW	Wainscoat WR	Williams O	Smith EE	Hick WM	Williams JT*	Birrell W	Dickinson PE*	Good H*	Ashman D*	Dickson 1W	Holmes W	French JP*	McAllister W*	Ferguson RG*	McClelland J*	Wilson J*	
1		3	5		6	8	11			10			9			7	4			2					1
1		1	1		1	1	1			1			1			1	1			1					

209

1925-26

Manager: Herbert Bamlett

1	Aug	29	(a)	Portsmouth	W	5-1	Birrell, Thompson 2, O.Williams, McClelland	24,108
2	Sep	2	(h)	Blackpool	W	3-2	Thompson, Birrell 2	18,108
3		5	(h)	Wolves	W	4-1	McClelland 3, Birrell	17,414
4		7	(a)	Blackpool	W	3-2	McClelland 3	17,036
5		12	(a)	Swansea T	L	0-4		20,289
6		14	(a)	Preston NE	L	0-1		13,075
7		19	(h)	Sheffield W	W	3-0	Birrell 2 (1 pen), McClelland	13,983
8		23	(h)	Preston NE	W	5-1	Cochrane, McClelland 2, Birrell 2	14,252
9		26	(a)	Stoke C	L	0-4		9,666
10	Oct	3	(h)	Oldham A	W	2-1	Birrell, Jones	14,906
11		10	(a)	Stockport C	W	2-1	McClelland, O.Williams	11,762
12		17	(h)	Darlington	W	3-2	O.Williams, McClelland 2	31,045
13		24	(a)	Hull C	W	2-1	Birrell, McClelland	10,358
14		31	(h)	Nottingham F	W	1-0	Birrell (pen)	16,490
15	Nov	7	(a)	Southampton	L	1-3	McClelland	12,233
16		14	(h)	Barnsley	W	5-0	Cochrane, O.Williams 2, Birrell, McClelland	12,760
17		21	(a)	Port Vale	L	0-4		9,336
18		28	(h)	Bradford C	L	2-5	McClelland 2	6,672
19	Dec	5	(a)	Derby C	L	0-2		14,835
20		12	(h)	Chelsea	L	1-2	O.Williams	14,395
21		19	(a)	Clapton O	L	0-1		10,955
22		25	(a)	Fulham	L	0-2		19,616
23		26	(h)	Fulham	W	4-0	J.T.Williams 2, Birrell, McClelland	17,405
24	Jan	1	(h)	South Shields	L	1-2	J.T.Williams	19,007
25		2	(h)	Portsmouth	W	4-1	McClelland 3, J.Carr	10,028
26		16	(a)	Wolves	L	1-3	McClelland	8,888
27		23	(h)	Swansea T	L	0-3		12,134
28	Feb	6	(h)	Stoke C	W	3-0	Birrell, McClelland, J.Carr	7,462
29		13	(a)	Oldham A	L	1-4	Birrell	14,407
30		20	(h)	Stockport C	W	4-0	McClelland 2, Birrell, J.Carr	7,946
31		22	(a)	Sheffield W	L	0-2		20,684
32		27	(a)	Darlington	W	2-0	McClelland, Birrell	15,118
33	Mar	6	(h)	Hull C	D	3-3	J.Carr 2, McClelland	8,843
34		13	(a)	Nottingham F	L	0-1		10,675
35		20	(h)	Southampton	W	3-0	O.Williams 2, McClelland (pen)	8,111
36		27	(a)	Barnsley	W	1-0	Camsell	8,361
37	Apr	2	(a)	South Shields	D	2-2	Camsell 2	14,839
38		3	(h)	Port Vale	W	3-1	Webster, J.Carr, Birrell	10,231
39		10	(a)	Bradford C	L	0-2		12,581
40		17	(h)	Derby C	L	1-2	McClelland	9,462
41		24	(a)	Chelsea	W	1-0	McClelland	25,522
42	May	1	(h)	Clapton O	L	1-2	McClelland	7,788

FINAL LEAGUE POSITION: 9th in Division Two

Appearances
Goals

FA Cup

3	Jan	9	(h)	Leeds U	W	5-1	McClelland 5	29,000
4		30	(a)	Clapton O	L	2-4	McClelland, Birrell	24,247

Appearances
Goals

Appearances and goals grid. Columns are players; rows 1–42 are matches; numbers are shirt numbers worn. Totals rows follow (appearances, then goals). A separate cup table follows below.

Clough J	Holmes W	Freeman RV	McAllister W	Webster M	Ashman D	Carr J	Birrell W	McClelland J	Thompson N*	Williams O	Cochrane AF	Ferguson RG	Jones GW*	Gowland N*	Camsell GH*	Wilson J	Swales N*	Williams JT	Good H	Bissett JT	Watson A*	Cartwright P*	No.
1	2	3	4	5	6	7	8	9	10	11													1
1	2	3	4	5	6	7	8	9	10	11													2
1	2	3	4	5	6	7	8	9	10	11													3
1	2	3	4	5	6	7	8	9	10	11													4
1	2	3	4	5	6	7	8	9	10	11													5
1	2	3	4	5	6	7	8	9		11	10												6
1	2	3		5	6		8	9		11	10	4	7										7
1	2	3		5	6		8	9		11	10	4	7										8
1	2	3		5	6		8	9		11	10	4	7										9
	2	3		5	6		8	9		11	10	4	7	1									10
1	2	3		5	6		8	9		11	10	4	7										11
1	2	3	4	5			8	9		11	10	6	7										12
1	2	3	4		6		8	9		11	10	5	7										13
1	2	3	4	5			8		10	11		6	7		9								14
1	2	3	4	5			8	9		11	10	6	7										15
1	2		4	5			8	9		11	10	6	7			3							16
1	2	3	4	5			8	9	10	11		6	7										17
1	2	3	4	5			8	9		11	10	6	7										18
1	2	3	4	5		7	8	9		11	10	6											19
1		3		5	6	7	8	9	10	11		4				2							20
1		3		5	6	7	8	9	10	11						2							21
1		3		5	6	10	8	9				4	7			2		11					22
1		3		5	6	10	8	9				4	7			2		11					23
1	2	3		5	6	10	8	9				4	7			2		11					24
1	2	3		5	6	10	8	9		11		4	7										25
1	2	3	4	5	6	10	8	9					7					11					26
1	2	3	4	5	6	10	8	9		11			7										27
1	2	3		5	6	10	8	9		11		4	7										28
1	2	3		5	6	10	8			11		4			9			7					29
1		3		5	6	10	8	9		11						2		7	4				30
1		3		5	6	10	8	9		11						2		7	4				31
1		3	4		6	10	8	9		11		5				2		7					32
1		3	4		6	10	8	9		11		5				2		7					33
1		3			6	10	8	9		11		4	7							2	5		34
1		3	4		6	10	8	9		11										2	5	7	35
1		3		5	6		8			11	10				9					2	4	7	36
1		3		5	6	10	8			11					9					2	4	7	37
1		3		5	6	10	8	9		11										2	4	7	38
1		3		5	6	10	8	9		11										2	4	7	39
1		3		5	6	10	8	9		11	4									2		7	40
		3		5	6	10	8	9		11			7	1						2	4		41
		3		5	6	10	8	9		11			7	1						2	4		42
39	26	40	18	38	35	29	42	38	8	33	20	23	24	3	4	10	2	6	2	9	8	6	
	1			1		6	17	32	3	8	2		1		3			3					

Clough J	Holmes W	Freeman RV	McAllister W	Webster M	Ashman D	Carr J	Birrell W	McClelland J	Thompson N*	Williams O	Cochrane AF	Ferguson RG	Jones GW*	Gowland N*	Camsell GH*	Wilson J	Swales N*	Williams JT	Good H	Bissett JT	Watson A*	Cartwright P*	No.
1	2	3	4	5	6	10	8	9		11			7										3
1	2	3	6	5		10	8	9		11		4	7										4
2	2	2	2	2	1	2	2	2		2		1	2										
							1	6															

211

1926-27

Manager: Herbert Bamlett

1	Aug	28	(a)	Chelsea	L	0-3		29,849
2		30	(a)	Southampton	L	1-2	Birrell	9,401
3	Sep	4	(h)	Preston NE	L	0-2		13,496
4		11	(a)	South Shields	D	0-0		7,519
5		18	(h)	Hull C	W	2-0	Pease (pen), O.Williams	11,618
6		22	(h)	Bradford C	W	4-3	Pease 2, Camsell 2	11,993
7		25	(a)	Wolves	W	2-1	Camsell, J.Carr	14,434
8		29	(a)	Bradford C	W	1-0	Camsell	8,759
9	Oct	2	(h)	Notts C	W	4-2	Camsell 3, Birrell	15,386
10		9	(a)	Clapton O	W	3-2	O.Williams 2, Pease	12,034
11		16	(a)	Nottingham F	L	3-4	Camsell, Pease 2 (1 pen)	11,262
12		23	(h)	Barnsley	W	5-1	Pease 2, J.Carr 2, Camsell	12,740
13		30	(a)	Darlington	W	4-1	Pease 2, Camsell, O.Williams	17,625
14	Nov	6	(h)	Portsmouth	W	7-3	Camsell 4, Pease 2, J.Carr	8,680
15		13	(a)	Oldham A	L	1-2	Camsell	11,868
16		20	(h)	Fulham	W	6-1	Camsell 4 (1 pen), Birrell, Pease	15,752
17		27	(h)	Southampton	W	3-1	O.Williams, Camsell, Pease	19,520
18	Dec	4	(h)	Blackpool	D	4-4	Camsell 2, Pease 2	19,456
19		18	(h)	Swansea T	W	7-1	Pease, McClelland 2, Camsell 4	27,805
20		25	(a)	Manchester C	W	5-3	Camsell 5	44,077
21		27	(h)	Manchester C	W	2-1	Camsell 2	‡43,754
22	Jan	1	(h)	Port Vale	W	5-2	Camsell 3, Pease, Smith (og)	26,163
23		15	(a)	Chelsea	D	0-0		23,964
24		22	(a)	Preston NE	D	2-2	Camsell, Pease	20,122
25	Feb	5	(a)	Hull C	D	3-3	Camsell 2 (1 pen), Pease	24,110
26		8	(a)	Grimsby T	W	7-4	Camsell 3, Birrell 2, McClelland, J.T.Williams	10,288
27		12	(h)	Wolves	W	2-0	Camsell (pen), Birrell	26,974
28		23	(a)	Notts C	D	2-2	Camsell 2	12,042
29		26	(h)	Clapton O	W	6-0	Birrell 2, Camsell 2, Pease 2 (1 pen)	21,761
30	Mar	5	(h)	Nottingham F	W	1-0	Birrell	33,354
31		12	(a)	Barnsley	D	1-1	Pease	23,599
32		16	(h)	South Shields	W	5-0	O.Williams, Birrell, Camsell 3	25,322
33		19	(h)	Darlington	W	4-1	O.Williams 2, Ashman, Birrell	31,982
34		26	(a)	Portsmouth	W	1-0	Camsell	24,153
35	Apr	2	(h)	Oldham A	W	3-1	McClelland, Camsell, O.Williams	22,554
36		9	(a)	Fulham	W	3-0	Birrell 2 (1 pen), Camsell	12,178
37		15	(a)	Port Vale	L	1-3	Camsell	21,056
38		16	(h)	Grimsby T	W	3-0	Camsell, McClelland, Birrell (pen)	22,503
39		20	(a)	Reading	L	1-2	Birrell	12,836
40		23	(a)	Blackpool	D	2-2	McKay, Camsell	12,657
41		30	(h)	Reading	W	5-0	Camsell 3, J.Carr 2	23,786
42	May	7	(a)	Swansea T	W	1-0	Camsell	11,913

FINAL LEAGUE POSITION: 1st in Division Two

‡Ground attendance record

Appearances
Goals

FA Cup

3	Jan	8	(h)	Leicester C	W	5-3	O.Williams, Pease, Birrell 2, Camsell	30,000
4		29	(a)	Preston NE	W	3-0	Camsell 3	34,778
5	Feb	19	(a)	Millwall	L	2-3	O.Williams, Pease	44,250

Appearances
Goals

212

Mathieson JA*	Wilson J	Freeman RV	Miller J*	Webster M	Ashman D	Pease WH*	Birrell W	McClelland J	Carr J	Williams O	Ferguson RG	Smith J*	Holmes W	Camsell GH	Twine F*	Williams JT	McKay J*	
1	2	3	4	5	6	7	8	9	10	11								1
1	2	3	4	5	6	7	8	9	10	11								2
1	2	3	4	5		7	8	9	10	11	6							3
1		3		5	6	7	8	9	10	11	4	2						4
1		3	4		6	7	8		10	11		2	5	9				5
1		3	4		6	7	8		10	11		2	5	9				6
1		3	4		6	7	8		10	11		2	5	9				7
1		3	4		6	7	8		10	11		2	5	9				8
1	2	3	4		6	7	8		10	11			5	9				9
1		3			6	7	4	8	10	11		2	5	9				10
1		3	4		6	7	8		10	11		2	5	9				11
1		3	4		6	7	8		10	11	5	2		9				12
1		3	4		6	7	8	10		11	5			9	2			13
1		3	4		6	7	8		10	11	5	2		9				14
1		3	4		6	7	8		10	11	5	2		9				15
1		3	4		6	7	8		10	11	5	2		9				16
1		3	4		6	7	8		10	11	5			9	2			17
1		3	4		6	7	8		10	11	5	2		9				18
1		3	4		6	7		8	10	11	5	2		9				19
1		3	4		6	7	8		10	11	5	2		9				20
1		3	4		6	7	8		10	11	5	2		9				21
1		3	4		6	7	8	5	10	11		2		9				22
1			4		6	7	8		10	11	5	3		9	2			23
1			4		6	7	8		10	11	5	3		9	2			24
1		3	4		6	7	8		10		5	2		9		11		25
1		3	4		6		8	7	10		5	2		9		11		26
1		3	4		6		8	7	10		5	2		9		11		27
1		3	4		6	7	8		10	11	5			9	2			28
1		3	4		6	7	8		10	11	5			9	2			29
1		3	4		6	7	8		10	11	5			9	2			30
1		3	4	5	6	7	8		10	11		2		9				31
1			4		6	7	8		10	11	5	3		9	2			32
1			4		6		7	9	8	11	5	3			2		10	33
1			4		6		8	7	10	11	5	3		9	2			34
1			4		6		8	7	10	11	5	3		9	2			35
1			4		6		8	7			5	3		9	2	11	10	36
1			4		6		8	7		11	5	3		9	2		10	37
1			4		6		8	7		11	5	3		9	2		10	38
1			4		6		8	7		11	5	3		9	2		10	39
1			4		6		8	7		11	5	3		9	2		10	40
1			4		6		8	7	10	11	5	3		9	2			41
1			4		6		8	7		11	5	3		9	2		10	42
42	4	29	40	5	41	30	41	20	35	38	31	33	7	37	18	4	7	
					1	23	16	5	6	9				59		1	1	

l own-goal

Mathieson JA*	Wilson J	Freeman RV	Miller J*	Webster M	Ashman D	Pease WH*	Birrell W	McClelland J	Carr J	Williams O	Ferguson RG	Smith J*	Holmes W	Camsell GH	Twine F*	Williams JT	McKay J*	
1			4		6	7	8		10	11	5	3		9	2			3
1		3	4		6	7	8		10	11	5			9	2			4
1		3	4		6	7	8		10	11	5			9	2			5
3		2	3		3	3	3		3	3	3	1		3	3			
					2	2			2					4				

1927-28

Manager: Peter McWilliam

1	Aug	27	(a)	Manchester U	L 0-3	44,957
2		31	(h)	Tottenham H	W 3-1 McKay, O.Williams, Camsell	29,113
3	Sep	3	(h)	Everton	W 4-2 Camsell 4	30,299
4		10	(a)	Cardiff C	D 1-1 Pease	23,033
5		12	(a)	Tottenham H	L 2-4 J.Carr, Camsell	19,219
6		17	(h)	Blackburn R	W 2-0 Ashman, Camsell	28,300
7		24	(a)	Bolton W	D 0-0	21,720
8	Oct	1	(h)	Sheffield W	D 3-3 Camsell 2, McKay	22,230
9		8	(a)	Aston Villa	L 1-5 Birrell	38,180
10		15	(a)	Birmingham	L 2-3 Camsell, Pease	17,143
11		22	(h)	Burnley	L 2-3 Pease 2	17,803
12		29	(a)	Bury	W 4-1 Pease 3, J.Carr	18,756
13	Nov	5	(h)	Sheffield U	W 3-0 McKay, Camsell 2	22,061
14		12	(a)	Arsenal	L 1-3 Camsell	25,921
15		19	(h)	Liverpool	D 1-1 Pease	18,741
16		26	(a)	West Ham U	W 5-4 O.Williams 2, Pease, Camsell 2	14,666
17	Dec	3	(h)	Portsmouth	W 5-1 McClelland, Camsell 2, O.Williams, J.Carr	18,163
18		10	(a)	Leicester C	D 3-3 Pease, Camsell 2	26,815
19		17	(h)	Derby C	D 3-3 Camsell, McClelland, Ferguson	15,235
20		24	(a)	Sunderland	L 0-1	23,633
21		26	(h)	Newcastle U	D 1-1 Pease	37,478
22		27	(a)	Newcastle U	D 3-3 Pease 2, Camsell	40,208
23		31	(h)	Manchester U	L 1-2 McClelland	19,652
24	Jan	2	(h)	Huddersfield T	W 3-1 Camsell 2, Pease	26,032
25		7	(a)	Everton	L 1-3 Peacock	46,432
26		21	(h)	Cardiff C	L 1-2 Camsell	21,728
27	Feb	4	(h)	Bolton W	L 2-5 Camsell 2	21,109
28		11	(a)	Sheffield W	W 3-2 Camsell, J.Carr, Bruce	15,631
29		23	(a)	Blackburn R	L 0-3	12,855
30		25	(h)	Birmingham	D 1-1 McClelland	18,329
31	Mar	3	(a)	Burnley	D 1-1 Camsell	18,209
32		10	(h)	Bury	W 6-1 Camsell 4, Pease 2	13,922
33		17	(a)	Sheffield U	L 1-4 Pease	26,328
34		21	(h)	Aston Villa	D 0-0	15,698
35		31	(a)	Liverpool	D 1-1 Millar	26,840
36	Apr	7	(h)	West Ham U	D 2-2 J.Carr, Ferguson	21,860
37		10	(a)	Huddersfield T	W 4-2 Millar, Pease, Hall, Bruce	29,034
38		14	(a)	Portsmouth	L 1-4 Bruce (pen)	23,897
39		18	(h)	Arsenal	D 2-2 Bruce, Camsell	16,731
40		21	(h)	Leicester C	D 1-1 Pease	18,854
41		28	(a)	Derby C	L 1-2 J.Carr	12,017
42	May	5	(h)	Sunderland	L 0-3	41,997

FINAL LEAGUE POSITION: 22nd in Division One

Appearances
Goals

FA Cup

3	Jan	14	(h)	South Shields	W 3-0 Camsell, Peacock 2	25,000
4		28	(a)	Southport	W 3-0 Camsell 3	12,000
5	Feb	18	(a)	Huddersfield T	L 0-4	55,200

Appearances
Goals

214

Player appearance / shirt-number grid (shirt numbers per match).

Mathieson JA	Twine F	Smith J	Miller J	Ferguson RG	Ashman D	Pease WH	Birrell W	Camsell GH	Carr J	Williams O	McKay J	Kennedy F*	Webster M	Peacock J*	Freeman RV	McClelland J	Millar WM*	Bruce RF*	Jarvis S*	Hall BAC*	#
1	2	3	4	5	6	7	8	9	10	11											1
1	2	3	4	5	6	7		9	10	11	8										2
1	2	3	4	5	6	7		9	10	11	8										3
1	2	3	4	5	6	7		9	10	11	8										4
1	2	3	4	5	6	7		9	10	11	8										5
1	2	3	4	5	6	7	8	9	10		11										6
1	2	3	4		6	7	8	9		10	11	5									7
1	2	3	4	5	6	7	8	9		10	11										8
1	2	3	4	5	6	7	8	9	10	11											9
1	2	3	4	5		7	8	9	10	11				6							10
1		2	4	5		7	10	9		11				6	3	8					11
1	2	3	4			7		9	10	11		5		6		8					12
1	2	3	4			7		9	10	11		5		6		8					13
1	2	3	4	5		7		9	10	11				6		8					14
1	2	3	4	5		7		9	10	11				6		8					15
1	2	3	4	5		7		9	10	11				6		8					16
1	2	3	4	5		7		9	10	11				6		8					17
1	2	3	4	5		7		9	10	11				6		8					18
1	2		4	5		7		9			10			6	3	8	11				19
1	2	3	4	5		7		9	10	11				6		8					20
1	2	3	4	5		7		9	10	11				6		8					21
1		3	4	5		7		9		11	10			6	2	8					22
1		3	4	5		7		9		11	10			6	2	8					23
1	2	3		5	6	7		9		11	10				4	8					24
1	2	3		5	6	7		9		11	10				4	8					25
1	2	3	4	5	6	7		9	10	11						8					26
1	2	3	4	5	6	7		9	10	11						8					27
1	2	3	4	5		7		9	10	11				6		8					28
1	2	3	4		5	7		9		11	10			6		8					29
1	2	3	4		5	7		9	10	11				6		8					30
1	2	3	4	5		7		9	10	11				6		8					31
1	2	3	4			7		9	10	11		5		6		8					32
1	2	3	4			7		9		11	8	5		6				10			33
1	2	3	4	5				9	7	11	8			6				10			34
1	2	3	4	5		7		9	8					6			11	10			35
1	2	3	4	5		7		9	8					6			11	10			36
1		3	4	5		7			8					6			11	10	2	9	37
1		3	4	5		7			8					6			11	10	2	9	38
1	2	3	4	5		7		9	8					6			11	10			39
1		3	4	5		7		9	8					6			11	10	2		40
1		3	4	5		7		9	8					6			11	10	2		41
1		3	4	5		7		9	8	11				6				10	2		42
42	**34**	**41**	**40**	**35**	**15**	**41**	**7**	**40**	**32**	**31**	**9**	**8**	**5**	**32**	**4**	**19**	**8**	**12**	**5**	**2**	
		2	1	19	1	33		6	4	3				1		4	2	4		1	

Mathieson JA	Twine F	Smith J	Miller J	Ferguson RG	Ashman D	Pease WH	Birrell W	Camsell GH	Carr J	Williams O	McKay J	Kennedy F*	Webster M	Peacock J*	Freeman RV	McClelland J	Millar WM*	Bruce RF*	Jarvis S*	Hall BAC*	#
1	2	3	4	5	6			9	10	11					8	7		•			3
1	2	3	4	5	6	7		9	10	11					8						4
1	2	3	4	5		7		9	10	11				6	8						5
3	**3**	**3**	**3**	**3**	**2**	**2**		**3**	**3**	**3**				**3**	**2**						
														4	2						

1928-29

Manager: Peter McWilliam

1	Aug	25	(a)	Reading	W	3-2	Camsell 2, Peacock	20,925
2		27	(a)	Tottenham H	W	5-2	Camsell, Pease 2, O.Williams, Kennedy	23,990
3	Sep	1	(h)	Preston NE	L	2-3	Camsell 2	25,280
4		8	(a)	Chelsea	L	0-2		48,775
5		12	(h)	Hull C	D	1-1	Camsell	15,998
6		15	(a)	Oldham A	W	3-1	Camsell, Millar 2	15,819
7		22	(h)	Southampton	L	1-2	Pease	15,525
8		29	(a)	Wolves	D	3-3	Camsell, O.Williams, Bruce	16,470
9	Oct	6	(h)	Notts C	W	3-1	Pease 3	16,984
10		13	(a)	Millwall	W	3-2	Kennedy (pen), Camsell, Hill (og)	30,373
11		20	(h)	Blackpool	W	4-1	Camsell, Pease, Kennedy (pen), Williams	15,727
12		27	(a)	Swansea T	L	0-2		12,026
13	Nov	3	(h)	Bradford	W	5-3	Bruce, Kennedy 2 (1 pen), O.Williams, Pease	18,783
14		10	(a)	Barnsley	D	2-2	Millar, Pease	9,635
15		17	(h)	Stoke C	W	1-0	Camsell	15,620
16		24	(a)	Clapton O	L	0-3		9,391
17	Dec	1	(h)	West Brom A	D	1-1	Millar	15,075
18		8	(a)	Nottingham F	D	1-1	Pease	8,837
19		15	(h)	Bristol C	W	3-1	Camsell 2, Pease (pen)	9,541
20		22	(a)	Grimsby T	W	4-1	Pease, Bruce 2, Camsell	10,984
21		25	(h)	Port Vale	W	5-1	O.Williams 2, Bruce, Camsell, Pease	23,977
22		26	(a)	Port Vale	W	3-2	Camsell 2, Pease	13,988
23		29	(h)	Reading	D	0-0		16,963
24	Jan	1	(h)	Tottenham H	W	3-0	Bruce 2, Camsell	25,145
25		5	(a)	Preston NE	D	0-0		17,734
26		19	(h)	Chelsea	L	4-5	Williams, Pease 2 (1 pen), Camsell	24,768
27	Feb	2	(a)	Southampton	D	1-1	Pease	12,908
28		9	(h)	Wolves	W	8-3	Bruce, Pease 4 (2 pens), Camsell 3	14,636
29		16	(a)	Notts C	W	3-0	Camsell, Pease, Bruce	11,534
30		20	(h)	Oldham A	W	1-0	Bruce	11,754
31		23	(h)	Millwall	W	3-0	Emmerson 3	21,082
32	Mar	2	(a)	Blackpool	L	0-3		10,440
33		9	(h)	Swansea T	D	0-0		18,430
34		16	(a)	Bradford	L	2-3	Camsell, Bruce	26,109
35		23	(h)	Barnsley	W	1-0	Pease	17,050
36		30	(a)	Stoke C	L	2-3	O.Williams, Pease	19,719
37	Apr	1	(a)	Hull C	D	1-1	Camsell	19,740
38		6	(h)	Clapton O	W	4-0	Camsell 3, J.Carr	16,140
39		13	(a)	West Brom A	D	1-1	Pease	11,569
40		20	(h)	Nottingham F	W	1-0	Pease (pen)	18,220
41		27	(a)	Bristol C	W	1-0	Pease (pen)	18,234
42	May	4	(h)	Grimsby T	W	3-0	Camsell 2, O.Williams	36,503

FINAL LEAGUE POSITION: 1st in Division Two

Appearances
Goals

FA Cup

3	Jan	12	(a)	Walsall	D	1-1	Camsell	14,980
R		21	(h)	Walsall	W	5-1	Camsell 2, Williams, Pease 2	14,917
4		26	(a)	West Brom A	L	0-1		33,446

Appearances
Goals

Appearance / line-up grid (shirt numbers by match). Right-hand column = match number.

Mathieson JA	Jarvis S	Freeman RV	Miller J	Ferguson RG	Peacock J	Pease WH	Carr J	Camsell GH	Kennedy F	Millar WM	Williams O	McKay J	Webster M	Ashman D	Bruce RF	Smith J	Gowland N	Hall BAC	Emmerson GA*	Gardner JR*	#
1	2	3	4	5	6	7	8	9	10	11											1
1	2	3	4	5	6	7	8	9	10		11										2
1	2	3	4	5	6	7	8	9	10		11										3
1	2	3	4	5	6	7	8	9			11	10									4
1	2	3	4		6		8	9	7		11	10	5								5
1	2	3	4				8	9	7		11		5	6	10						6
1	2	3	4		6	7	8	9			11		5		10						7
1	2	3	4	5	6	7	8	9			11				10						8
1	2		4	5	6	7	8	9			11				10	3					9
1	2		4	5	6	7		9	8		11				10	3					10
1	2		4	5	6	7		9	8		11				10	3					11
1	2		4	5	6	7		9	8	11					10	3					12
1	2		4	5	6	7		9	8		11				10	3					13
1	2		4	5	6	7		9	8	11					10	3					14
1	2		4		6	7	8	9			11		5		10	3					15
	2		4	5	6	7		8			11				10	3	1	9			16
	2		4	5	6	7		8			11				10	3	1	9			17
1		2	4		6	7		9			11	8	5		10	3					18
1		2	4			7		9			11	8	5	6	10	3					19
1		2	4		6	7		9			11	8	5		10	3					20
1		2	4		6		8	9			11		5		10	3					21
1		2	4		6	7		9			11	8	5		10	3					22
1		2	4		6	7		9		11		8	5		10	3					23
1		2	4		6	7	8	9			11		5		10	3					24
1		2	4		6	7		9		11		8	5		10	3					25
1		2	4	5	6	7	8	9			11				10	3					26
1	2				6	7	8	9	10		11		5	4		3					27
1	2		4		6	7	8	9			11		5		10	3					28
1	2		4		6	7	8	9			11		5		10	3					29
1	2		4		6		8	9			11		5		10	3			7		30
1	2			4	6		8	9			11		5		10	3			7		31
1	2		4		6	7	8	9	10		11		5			3					32
1		2	4		6		8	9			11		5		10	3			7		33
1		2	4		6	7	8	9			11		5		10	3					34
1		2	4		6	7	8	9			11		5		10	3					35
1		2	4		6	7	8	9			11		5		10	3					36
1		2	4		6	7	8	9			11		5		10	3					37
1	3	4	2		6	7	8	9			11		5		10						38
1		2	4		6	7	8	9			11		5		10	3					39
1		2	4	5	6	7	8	9			11				10	3					40
1		2	4	5	6	7	8	9			11				10	3					41
1		2	4	5	6		8	9			11				10	3			7		42
40	22	28	40	19	40	35	29	40	15	8	33	8	25	3	35	33	2	2	4		
			1			27	1	30	5	4	9		11						3		

1 own-goal

Mathieson JA	Jarvis S	Freeman RV	Miller J	Ferguson RG	Peacock J	Pease WH	Carr J	Camsell GH	Kennedy F	Millar WM	Williams O	McKay J	Webster M	Ashman D	Bruce RF	Smith J	Gowland N	Hall BAC	Emmerson GA*	Gardner JR*	#
1		2	4		6	7	8	9			11		5		10	3					3
1		2	4		6	7	8	9			11		5		10	3					R
1	2		4			7	8	9		11	10			6		3	5				4
3	1	2	3		2	3	3	3	1		2	1	2	1	2	3	1				
			1					3			2										

217

1929-30

Manager: Peter McWilliam

1	Aug	31	(h)	Liverpool	W	5-0	Williams, Carr, Bruce 2, Camsell	28,286
2	Sep	4	(h)	Sheffield U	W	3-1	Carr, Camsell 2	25,361
3		7	(a)	West Ham U	L	3-5	Cameron 2, Camsell	22,760
4		9	(a)	Sheffield U	W	3-1	Cameron, Camsell 2	14,303
5		14	(h)	Manchester U	L	2-3	Pease, Bruce	26,428
6		18	(a)	Bolton W	D	2-2	Camsell, Cameron	13,795
7		21	(a)	Grimsby T	W	3-0	Williams, Camsell, Pease	15,863
8		28	(h)	Leicester C	L	0-2		26,851
9	Oct	5	(a)	Birmingham	D	1-1	Camsell	23,140
10		12	(h)	Huddersfield T	L	1-3	Pease (pen)	24,231
11		19	(a)	Everton	L	2-3	Pease, Cameron	30,657
12		26	(h)	Derby C	W	4-0	Camsell 3, Pease	18,409
13	Nov	2	(a)	Manchester C	L	1-3	Carr	33,302
14		9	(h)	Sunderland	W	3-0	Pease 2 (1 pen), Camsell	29,953
15		23	(h)	Aston Villa	L	2-3	Bruce, Elkes	16,051
16		27	(a)	Arsenal	W	2-1	Camsell, Muttitt	28,326
17		30	(a)	Leeds U	W	2-1	Bruce, Camsell	19,508
18	Dec	7	(h)	Sheffield W	W	4-1	Bruce, Camsell 2, Webster	21,265
19		14	(a)	Burnley	L	1-4	Bruce	8,671
20		21	(h)	Portsmouth	W	2-0	Camsell, McKay	11,391
21		25	(a)	Newcastle U	L	2-3	Pease, Bruce	38,922
22		26	(h)	Newcastle U	D	2-2	Camsell, Bruce (pen)	40,538
23		28	(a)	Liverpool	L	2-5	Elkes 2	23,982
24	Jan	1	(a)	Blackburn R	L	0-7		24,370
25		4	(h)	West Ham U	W	2-0	Camsell, Pease	17,767
26		18	(a)	Manchester U	W	3-0	Muttitt, Pease, Camsell	21,028
27	Feb	1	(a)	Leicester C	L	1-4	Camsell	19,057
28		8	(h)	Birmingham	W	5-1	Pease, Bruce, McKay, Hall, Watson	16,969
29		22	(h)	Everton	L	1-2	Jennings (pen)	17,730
30	Mar	1	(a)	Derby C	L	1-3	Warren	15,736
31		5	(h)	Grimsby T	L	1-5	Bruce (pen)	8,880
32		8	(h)	Manchester C	W	1-0	Warren	15,739
33		15	(a)	Sunderland	L	2-3	Warren, McKay	32,874
34		26	(a)	Huddersfield T	L	0-1		8,234
35		29	(a)	Aston Villa	L	2-4	Bruce, McKay	26,986
36	Apr	5	(h)	Leeds U	D	1-1	Camsell	14,136
37		9	(h)	Arsenal	D	1-1	Camsell	9,287
38		12	(a)	Sheffield W	L	0-1		23,087
39		19	(h)	Burnley	W	3-1	Camsell, McKay, Pease	5,370
40		21	(h)	Blackburn R	L	2-4	Warren, Camsell	18,146
41		26	(a)	Portsmouth	D	1-1	Camsell	16,446
42	May	3	(h)	Bolton W	W	3-1	Camsell 2, McKay	9,816

FINAL LEAGUE POSITION: 16th in Division One

Appearances

Goals

FA Cup

3	Jan	11	(a)	Chesterfield	D	1-1	Bruce (pen)	16,656
R		15	(h)	Chesterfield	W	4-3	Camsell 2, Bruce 2	18,793
4		25	(h)	Charlton A	D	1-1	Muttitt	35,707
R		29	(a)	Charlton A	D	1-1	Bruce	24,884
2R	Feb	3	(n†)	Charlton A	W	1-0*	McKay	16,676
5		15	(h)	Arsenal	L	0-2		42,073

†Played at Maine Road, Manchester.   *After extra-time.

Appearances

Goals

218

Mathieson JA	Freeman RV	Smith J	Miller J	Webster M	Macfarlane J*	Pease WH	Carr J	Camsell GH	Bruce RF	Williams O	Cameron K*	Ferguson RG	Ashman D	McKay J	Elkes JE*	Peacock J	Hall BAC	Jarvis S	Muttitt E*	Watson HL*	Emmerson GA	Forrest W*	Hillier EJG*	Jennings J*	Warren FW*	No.
1	2	3	4	5	6	7	8	9	10	11																1
1	2	3	4	5	6	7	8	9	10	11	11															2
1	2	3	4	5	6	7	8	9	10		11															3
1	2	3	4	5	6	7	8	9	10		11															4
1	2	3	4	5	6	7	8	9	10		11															5
1			4	5	6	7	8	9	10		11		2	3												6
1			4	5	6	7	8	9		11	10		2	3												7
1			4	5	6	7	8	9		11	10		2	3												8
1			4	5	6	7	8	9		11			2	3	10											9
1			4	5	6	7	8	9		11			2	3		10										10
1					6	7	8			11			2	3	10	5	4	9								11
1					6	7	8	9		11			2	3	10	5	4									12
1					6	7	8	9		11				3	10	5	4	2								13
1					6	7	8	9	10	11			2	3		5	4									14
1			4		6	7	8	9	10	11			2	3		5										15
1			4		6	7		9	10				2	3	8	5			11							16
1			4	5	6	7		9	10				2	3	8				11							17
1				5	6	7		9	10				2	3	8				11	4						18
1				5	6	7		9	10				2	3	8				11	4						19
1			4	5	6	7		9	10				2	3	8				11							20
1			4	5	6	7		9	10				2	3	8				11							21
1			4	5	6			9	10				2	3	8				11		7					22
1				5	6				10				2	3	8	9			11	4	7					23
1				5	6				10					3	8	9		2	11	4	7					24
1			4	5	6	7		9	10				2	3	8		11									25
1				5		7		9	10				2	3	8				11	4		6				26
				5		7		9	10					3	8					4		6	1	2	11	27
1						7			10					3	8	5		9		4		6		2	11	28
1				5		7		9	10					3	8					4		6		2	11	29
1			4	5	6	7		9	10					3	8									2	11	30
1		3	4	5	6	7	8	9	10															2	11	31
1				5	6	7		9	10					3	8					4				2	11	32
1				5	6	7		9	10					3	8					4				2	11	33
1				5	6	7		9						3	8	10	6			4				2	11	34
1				5	6	7		9						3	8	10	4							2	11	35
1			4			7		9	10					3	8	5	6							2	11	36
1			4			7		9	10					3	8	5						6		2	11	37
1			4			7			10					3	8	5		9				6		2	11	38
1			4			7		9	10					3	8	5						6		2	11	39
1		3	4			7		9	10						8	5						6		2	11	40
1			4			7		9	10					3	8	5						6		2	11	41
1			4			7		9	10					3	8	5						6		2	11	42
41	6	6	20	34	30	39	16	34	36	6	11	23	31	28	21	8	3	2	10	11	3	10	1	16	16	
			1			12	3	29	12	2	5	6	3	1	2	1								1	4	

Mathieson JA	Freeman RV	Smith J	Miller J	Webster M	Macfarlane J*	Pease WH	Carr J	Camsell GH	Bruce RF	Williams O	Cameron K*	Ferguson RG	Ashman D	McKay J	Elkes JE*	Peacock J	Hall BAC	Jarvis S	Muttitt E*	Watson HL*	Emmerson GA	Forrest W*	Hillier EJG*	Jennings J*	Warren FW*	No.
1			4	5	6	7		9	10	11			2	3	8											3
1			4	5	6	7	8	9	10				2	3					11							R
1			4	5	6	7	8	9	10				2	3					11							4
1	2		4	5		7		9	10					3	8				11			6				R
1	2			5		7			10					3	8	9			11	4		6				2R
1	2			5		7			10					3	8	9				4		6		11		5
6	3		4	6	3	6	2	4	6	1			3	6	3	3			4	2		3		1		
								2	4						1				1							

1930-31

Manager: Peter McWilliam

1	Aug	30	(a)	Bolton W	L 0-3		14,946
2	Sep	3	(h)	Manchester U	W 3-1	Camsell 2, Bruce	15,712
3		6	(h)	Liverpool	D 3-3	Bruce, Warren, Pease	16,816
4		8	(a)	West Ham U	W 3-0	Pease, Warren 2	13,597
5		13	(a)	Blackpool	L 2-3	Warren, Bruce	20,050
6		17	(h)	West Ham U	D 2-2	Camsell, Warren	14,748
7		20	(a)	Huddersfield T	D 2-2	Webster, Warren	17,503
8		27	(h)	Aston Villa	W 3-1	Pease, Bruce 2	19,260
9	Oct	4	(a)	Chelsea	L 0-4		48,395
10		11	(h)	Newcastle U	W 3-1	McKay, Pease, Camsell	24,827
11		18	(h)	Sunderland	W 1-0	Forrest	30,307
12		25	(a)	Leeds U	L 0-7		18,116
13	Nov	1	(h)	Portsmouth	L 0-1		13,458
14		8	(a)	Manchester C	L 2-4	Holliday 2	27,035
15		15	(h)	Birmingham	D 1-1	Pease	11,883
16		22	(a)	Arsenal	L 3-5	Bruce, Camsell, Warren	32,517
17		29	(h)	Derby C	W 4-1	Camsell 2, McKay, Pease	13,987
18	Dec	6	(a)	Leicester C	W 3-0	Warren, Cameron, Camsell	14,467
19		13	(h)	Blackburn R	W 4-1	McKay 2, Cameron, Warren	16,119
20		20	(a)	Sheffield U	L 2-4	Camsell, Warren	19,893
21		26	(h)	Sheffield W	W 2-0	McKay, Warren	23,212
22		27	(h)	Bolton W	W 3-0	Camsell 2, Waren	16,084
23		29	(a)	Sheffield W	L 2-3	McKay, Camsell	18,530
24	Jan	1	(h)	Grimsby T	W 2-1	Jennings (pen), Camsell	23,845
25		3	(a)	Liverpool	L 1-3	Pease	21,133
26		17	(h)	Blackpool	W 5-1	Jennings 2 (2 pens), Warren, Holliday, Bruce	16,060
27		24	(h)	Huddersfield T	L 2-3	Scott, Muttitt	11,015
28		31	(a)	Aston Villa	L 1-8	Camsell	15,947
29	Feb	7	(h)	Chelsea	D 2-2	Camsell 2	16,443
30		14	(a)	Newcastle U	W 5-0	Warren, Cameron, Camsell 2, McKay	31,945
31		21	(a)	Sunderland	D 1-1	Camsell	31,183
32		28	(h)	Leeds U	W 5-0	Camsell 4, Warren	15,707
33	Mar	7	(a)	Portsmouth	L 0-1		11,422
34		14	(h)	Manchester C	W 4-1	Warren 2, Pease, Cameron	12,661
35		21	(a)	Birmingham	W 2-1	Pease, Camsell	20,311
36		28	(h)	Arsenal	L 2-5	Elkes, Cameron	23,476
37	Apr	3	(a)	Grimsby T	L 1-4	Camsell	19,821
38		4	(a)	Derby C	W 2-1	Camsell, Cameron	13,871
39		11	(h)	Leicester C	D 2-2	McPhail, Cameron	10,934
40		18	(a)	Blackburn R	W 5-4	Pease 2, Warren, Camsell 2	6,917
41		25	(h)	Sheffield U	W 4-1	Pease, Bruce 2, Cameron	7,471
42	May	2	(a)	Manchester U	D 4-4	Camsell 4	3,969

FINAL LEAGUE POSITION: 7th in Division One

Appearances
Goals

FA Cup

3	Jan	14	(h)	Bradford C	D 1-1	Warren	21,698
R		19	(a)	Bradford C	L 1-2	Barkas (og)	27,532

Appearances
Goals

Football league appearances and goals grid (player columns left to right, match number at far right).

Mathieson JA	Jennings J	Ferguson RG	Macfarlane J	Webster M	Forrest W	Pease WH	Scott WR*	Camsell GH	Bruce RF	Warren FW	Freeman T*	Elkes JE	Muttitt E	McKay J	Cameron K	Carr A*	Holliday JW*	Hillier EJG	Ashman D	McPhail DD*	Jarvis S	
1	2	3	4	5	6	7	8	9	10	11												1
1	2	3	4	5	6	7	8	9	10	11												2
1	2	3	4	5	6	7	8	9	10	11												3
1	2		4		6	7	8	9	10	11	3	5										4
1	2		4		6	7	8	9	10	11	3	5										5
1	2		4		6			9	10	11	3	5	7	8								6
1	2		4	5	6	7		9	10	11	3			8								7
1	2		4		6	7		9		11	3	5		8	10							8
1	2		4		6	7		9		11	3	5		8	10							9
1	2		4	5	6	7		9	10		3		11		8							10
1	2		4	5	6	7		9	10		3		11		8							11
1	2		4	5	6	7		9	10		3			8	11							12
1	2		4		6	7		9	10		3	5		8	11							13
1	2		4		6	7					3	10		8	11	5	9					14
	2		4		6	7			10	11	3	5			8		9	1				15
	2		4		6	7		9	10	11	3	5			8			1				16
1	2		4		6	7		9		11	3	5		8	10							17
1	2		4		6	7		9		11	3	5		8	10							18
1	2		4		6	7		9		11	3	5		8	10							19
1	2		4	5	6	7		9		11	3			8	10							20
1	2		4		6	7		9		11	3	5		8	10							21
1	2		4		6	7		9		11	3	5		8	10							22
1	2		4		6	7		9		11		5		8	10					3		23
1	2		4		6	7		9		11	3	5		8	10							24
1	2		4		6	7		9		11	3	5		8	10							25
1	2		4		6				8	11	3	5			10		9		7			26
1	2		4		6	7		9	8		3	5	11		10							27
1	2		4		6			9	10		3	5	7	8	11							28
1	2		4		6	7		9		11		5		8	10						3	29
1	2		4		6	7		9		11		5		8	10						3	30
1	2		4		6			9	7	11		5		8	10						3	31
1	2		4		6	7		9		11		5		8	10						3	32
1	2		4		6	7		9		11		5		8	10						3	33
1	2		4		6	7		9	8	11		5			10						3	34
1	2		4		6	7		9	8	11		5			10						3	35
1	2		4		6	7		9	8	11		5			10						3	36
1	2		4		6			9	8	11		5			10				7		3	37
1	2		4		6			9	8	11		5			10				7		3	38
1	2		4		6			9	8	11		5			10				7		3	39
	2		4	5	6	7		9	8	11					10			1		3		40
	2		4	5	6	7		9	8	11					10			1		3		41
1	2		4	5	6	7		9		11				8	10					3		42
38	**42**	**3**	**41**	**14**	**40**	**34**	**6**	**37**	**27**	**35**	**24**	**32**	**5**	**25**	**32**	**1**	**3**	**4**	**4**	**4**	**11**	
	3		1	1	12	1		32	9	18		1	1	7	8		3				1	

Cup matches:

Mathieson JA	Jennings J	Ferguson RG	Macfarlane J	Webster M	Forrest W	Pease WH	Scott WR*	Camsell GH	Bruce RF	Warren FW	Freeman T*	Elkes JE	Muttitt E	McKay J	Cameron K	Carr A*	Holliday JW*	Hillier EJG	Ashman D	McPhail DD*	Jarvis S	
1	2		4		6	7		9	8	11	3	5			10							3
1	2		4		6			9	8		3	5	11		10				7			R
2	2		2		2	1		2	2	1	2	2	1		2				1			
								1														

1 own-goal

1931-32

Manager: Peter McWilliam

#	Month	Date		Opponent	Result	Scorers	Attendance
1	Aug	29	(h)	Chelsea	L 0-2		24,510
2		31	(a)	Leicester C	D 2-2	Pease, Warren	15,339
3	Sep	5	(a)	West Ham U	W 2-0	Camsell, Cameron	23,129
4		9	(h)	Liverpool	W 4-1	Bruce 2, Jennings (pen), Warren	15,042
5		12	(h)	Sheffield W	W 4-0	Camsell, Forrest, Warren 2	24,050
6		16	(a)	Liverpool	L 2-7	Camsell 2	20,854
7		19	(a)	Bolton W	L 2-4	Camsell, Pease	14,180
8		26	(h)	Derby C	W 5-2	Bruce 2, Scott, Camsell, Cameron	13,562
9	Oct	3	(h)	Huddersfield T	W 1-0	Camsell	16,366
10		10	(a)	Newcastle U	L 1-3	Pease	41,569
11		17	(a)	Blackpool	W 2-1	Warren, Holliday	17,481
12		24	(h)	Birmingham	W 2-0	Scott, Camsell	9,226
13		31	(a)	Sunderland	D 0-0		28,387
14	Nov	7	(h)	Manchester C	D 3-3	Cameron, Camsell, Scott	9,142
15		14	(a)	Blackburn R	L 2-4	Camsell 2	8,795
16		21	(h)	Portsmouth	L 0-1		11,136
17		28	(a)	West Brom A	D 1-1	Cameron	17,856
18	Dec	5	(h)	Sheffield U	W 4-3	Scott, Cameron 2, Bruce	11,385
19		12	(a)	Everton	L 1-5	Cameron	33,182
20		19	(h)	Arsenal	L 2-5	Pease, Bruce	17,083
21		25	(a)	Aston Villa	L 1-7	Camsell	33,774
22		26	(h)	Aston Villa	D 1-1	Cameron	28,006
23	Jan	2	(a)	Chelsea	L 0-4		25,259
24		16	(h)	West Ham U	W 3-2	Camsell, Bruce, Cameron	8,287
25		25	(a)	Sheffield W	D 1-1	Marcroft	9,525
26		30	(h)	Bolton W	W 3-1	Camsell 2, Pease	10,502
27	Feb	6	(a)	Derby C	L 2-5	Camsell 2	11,917
28		17	(a)	Huddersfield T	D 1-1	Bruce	9,491
29		20	(h)	Newcastle U	W 2-1	Bruce, McKay	18,694
30		27	(h)	Blackpool	L 0-3		11,371
31	Mar	5	(a)	Birmingham	L 0-3		18,694
32		12	(h)	Sunderland	L 0-1		21,591
33		19	(a)	Manchester C	W 2-1	Camsell, Bruce	24,114
34		25	(a)	Grimsby T	L 0-2		19,005
35		26	(h)	Blackburn R	L 0-2		9,681
36		28	(h)	Grimsby T	W 4-0	Camsell, Cameron, Bruce, McKay	8,373
37	Apr	2	(a)	Portsmouth	L 0-2		9,949
38		9	(h)	West Brom A	W 1-0	J.J.Williams	7,551
39		16	(a)	Sheffield U	L 1-2	Camsell	10,288
40		23	(h)	Everton	W 1-0	Bruce	10,728
41		30	(a)	Arsenal	L 0-5		30,714
42	May	7	(h)	Leicester C	D 1-1	Cameron	5,410

FINAL LEAGUE POSITION: 18th in Division One

Appearances
Goals

FA Cup

3	Jan	9	(h)	Portsmouth	D 1-1	Bruce	22,949
R		13	(a)	Portsmouth	L 0-3		25,000

Appearances
Goals

Player appearance and goalscoring grid.

No.	Mathieson JA	Jennings J	Jarvis S	Macfarlane J	Elkes JE	Forrest W	Pease WH	McKay J	Camsell GH	Cameron K	Warren FW	Ashman D	Freeman T	Brown WH*	Bruce RF	Scott WR	Webster M	Holliday JW	Hillier EJG	Watson HL	Surtees J*	Muttit E	Marcroft EH*	Williams JJ*	Stuart RW*	Carr A
1	1	2	3	4	5	6	7	8	9	10	11															
2	1				5	6	7	8	9	10	11	2	3	4												
3	1	2			5	6	7		9	10	11		3	4	8											
4	1	2			5	6	7		9	10	11		3	4	8											
5	1	2			5	6	7		9		11		3	4	10	8										
6	1	2			5	6	7		9		11		3	4	10	8										
7	1	2			5	6	7		9		11		3	4	10	8										
8	1	2		4	5	6	7		9		11		3		10	8										
9	1	2		4	5	6	7		9		11		3		10	8										
10	1	2		4	5	6	7			9	11		3		10	8										
11	1	2			5	6	7				11		3		10	8	4	9								
12	1				5	6		8	9		11	2	3		10	7	4									
13	1	2			5	6	7		9		11		3		10	8	4									
14	1	2			5	6	7		9		11		3		10	8	4									
15	1	2			5	6	7		9		11		3		10	8	4									
16	1				5	6	7		9		11	2	3		10	8	4									
17	1				5	6	7		9		11	2	3		10	8	4									
18	1				5	6	7		9		11	2	3		10	8	4									
19	1				5	6	7		9		11	2	3		10	8	4									
20	1	2		6	5		7		9		11		3		10	8	4									
21	1			6	5		7		9		11	2	3		10	8	4									
22						6	7		9		11	2	3		10	8	5	1	4							
23						6	7		9		11	2	3			8	5	1	4	10						
24	1		2		5	6	7		9	8			3		10		4				11					
25	1		2			6			9	8			3	4	10		5				11	7				
26	1		2			6	7		9		11		3	4	10		5				8					
27	1		2			6	7		9		11		3	4		10	5				8					
28	1		2	4		6	7	8	9		11		3		10		5									
29	1		2	4		6	7	8	9		11		3		10		5									
30	1		2	4		6	7	8	9		11		3		10		5									
31	1		2	4	10	6		8	9		11		3		7		5									
32	1		2	4		6		8	9		11		3		10		5						7			
33			2	6	5			8	9		11		3		10		4	1					7			
34			2	6	5			8	9		11		3		10		4	1					7			
35			2	6	5			8			11		3		10		4	9	1				7			
36			2	6	5			8	9		11		3		10		4		1				7			
37		2		6	5			8	9		11		3		10		4		1				7			
38		2		6	5		7	10	9	8			3				4		1				11			
39		2		4	5	6	7	10	9	8			3						1				11			
40		2		6	5		7		9	8			3		10		4		1				11			
41				6			7	10		8			3				4	9	1				11	2	5	
42										8	11		3				10		4				7	2	5	
Apps	30	18	14	20	31	32	32	16	37	38	10	18	32	9	35	20	31	3	12	2	1	5	11	2	2	
Goals		1				1	5	2	20	11	5				12	4		1					1	1		

No.	Mathieson JA	Jennings J	Jarvis S	Macfarlane J	Elkes JE	Forrest W	Pease WH	McKay J	Camsell GH	Cameron K	Warren FW	Ashman D	Freeman T	Brown WH*	Bruce RF	Scott WR	Webster M	Holliday JW	Hillier EJG	Watson HL	Surtees J*	Muttit E	Marcroft EH*	Williams JJ*	Stuart RW*	Carr A
3	1				5	6	7		9		11		3		10	8	4									
R	1		2	10	5	6	7		9		11		3			8	4									
	2		1	1	2	2	2		2	2		1	2		1	2	2									
													1													

1932-33

Manager: Peter McWilliam

#		Date		Opponent	Result	Scorers	Attendance
1	Aug	27	(h)	Aston Villa	L 0-2		18,909
2		31	(a)	Newcastle U	L 1-5	Warren	35,109
3	Sep	3	(a)	Manchester C	W 3-2	J.J.Williams, Cameron 2	20,211
4		10	(a)	Bolton W	L 3-4	Jarvis, Camsell, Cameron	12,035
5		17	(h)	Liverpool	L 0-1		11,371
6		24	(a)	Leicester C	D 1-1	Rigby	16,628
7	Oct	1	(h)	Portsmouth	W 5-4	Camsell 2, Cameron 2, J.J.Williams	8,043
8		8	(a)	Chelsea	L 1-2	Camsell	18,181
9		15	(h)	Huddersfield T	D 1-1	Camsell	11,065
10		22	(h)	Sunderland	L 1-2	J.J.Williams	14,491
11		29	(a)	Birmingham	W 4-1	Camsell 2, J.J.Williams 2	9,090
12	Nov	5	(h)	Derby C	L 0-3		11,964
13		12	(a)	Blackpool	L 1-3	Bruce	12,104
14		19	(h)	Everton	L 0-2		9,662
15		26	(a)	Arsenal	L 2-4	Camsell 2	37,748
16	Dec	3	(h)	West Brom A	W 3-1	Blackmore 3	8,276
17		10	(a)	Sheffield W	L 1-2	Blackmore	10,754
18		17	(h)	Leeds U	L 0-1		9,341
19		24	(a)	Blackburn R	L 2-4	Blackmore, Baxter	8,303
20		27	(h)	Sheffield U	D 2-2	Pease, Camsell	13,566
21		31	(a)	Aston Villa	L 1-3	Baxter	22,309
22	Jan	2	(h)	Newcastle U	L 2-3	Bruce, Baxter	20,218
23		7	(h)	Manchester C	W 2-0	Camsell, Blackmore	7,912
24		21	(h)	Bolton W	W 2-1	Blackmore 2	9,256
25	Feb	1	(a)	Liverpool	W 3-1	Camsell 2, Blackmore	9,973
26		4	(h)	Leicester C	D 1-1	J.J.Williams	11,255
27		11	(a)	Portsmouth	L 0-2		11,759
28	Mar	1	(h)	Chelsea	W 2-1	Camsell, Rigby	8,219
29		11	(h)	Birmingham	D 2-2	Morrall (og), Bruce	14,646
30		15	(a)	Huddersfield T	W 1-0	Young (og)	4,992
31		22	(a)	Sunderland	D 0-0		9,005
32		25	(h)	Blackpool	W 2-0	Baxter, Rigby	10,724
33		27	(a)	Sheffield U	L 0-2		6,404
34	Apr	1	(a)	Everton	D 0-0		21,068
35		5	(a)	Derby C	D 2-2	Jennings (pen), Griffiths	6,587
36		8	(h)	Arsenal	L 3-4	Warren 2, Cameron	22,137
37		14	(a)	Wolves	L 0-2		28,992
38		15	(a)	West Brom A	W 1-0	Warren	17,511
39		17	(h)	Wolves	W 2-1	W.H.Brown, Baxter	16,255
40		22	(h)	Sheffield W	D 1-1	Bruce	10,640
41		29	(a)	Leeds U	W 1-0	Camsell	9,006
42	May	6	(h)	Blackburn R	W 4-0	Camsell 2, Bruce, Fenton	7,340

FINAL LEAGUE POSITION: 17th in Division One

Appearances
Goals

FA Cup

#		Date		Opponent	Result	Scorers	Attendance
3	Jan	14	(a)	Manchester U	W 4-1	J.J.Williams, Blackmore, Bruce 2	39,991
4		28	(h)	Stoke C	W 4-1	Blackmore 2, Camsell, Baxter	29,457
5	Feb	18	(h)	Birmingham	D 0-0		27,705
R		22	(a)	Birmingham	L 0-3		29,191

Appearances
Goals

224

Appearances and goals grid (shirt number worn by each player in each match; final column = match number):

Mathieson JA	Jennings J	Freeman T	Webster M	Elkes JE	Macfarlane J	Pease WH	Martin GS*	Blackmore HA*	Bruce RF	Warren FW	Cameron K	Jarvis S	Forrest W	Williams JJ	Camsell GH	Brown WH	Rigby A*	McKay J	Baxter RD*	Hillier EJG	Gibson F*	Stuart RW	Carr A	Griffiths TP*	Martin J*	Fenton M*	
1	2	3	4	5	6	7	8	9	10	11																	1
1	2	3	4	5	6	7	8	9		11	10																2
1		3	4	5		10				11	8	2	6	7	9												3
1		3	4	5		10				11	8	2	6	7	9												4
1		3		5		10					8	2	6	7	9	4	11										5
1		3		5		10	4					2	6	7	9		11	8									6
1		3	4	5		10					8	2	6	7	9		11										7
1		3	4	5		10					8	2	6	7	9		11										8
1	2	3	4	5		10				11	8		6	7	9												9
1	2	3	4	5		10				11	8		6	7	9												10
1	2	3	4	5		10				11	8		6	7	9												11
1	2	3	4	5		10				11	8		6	7	9												12
	2			5	4				8	11	10	3	6	7	9					1							13
	2	3		5					4	11	10		6	7	9	8					1						14
	2	3		5				9	4	11	10		6	7	8						1						15
	2	3		5				9	4	11	10		6	7	8						1						16
	2	3		5				9	4	11	10		6	7	8						1						17
	2	3		5		7		9	4	11	10		6		8						1						18
	2			5		7		9	4	11		3	6		8				10		1						19
	2	3		5		7			4	11	8		6		9				10		1						20
	2			5					4	11			6	7	9	8			10		1	3					21
	2			5					4	11			6	7	9	8			10		1	3					22
	2			5					4	11			6	7	9	8			10		1	3					23
	2								4	11			6	7	9	8			10		1	3	5				24
	2								4	11			6	7	9	8			10		1	3	5				25
	2			5					4	11			6	7	9	8			10		1	3					26
	2			5					4	11			6	7	9	8			10		1	3					27
	2			5					4	11		3	6	7	9	8			10		1						28
	2							9	4	11		3	6	7		8			10		1			5			29
	2		7						4	11		3	6		9	8			10		1			5			30
	2							9	4	11		3	6	7		8			10		1			5			31
	2							9	4	11		3	6	7		8			10		1			5			32
	2			5				9	4	11		3	6	7		8			10		1			5			33
	2		7						4	11		3	6		9	8			10		1			5			34
	2		7						4	11		3	6		9	8			10		1			5			35
	2		7						4	11		3	6		9	8			10		1			5			36
	2		7						4	11		3	6		9	8			10		1			5			37
	2								4	11		3	6	7	9	8			10		1			5			38
	2								4	11		3	6	7	9	8			10		1			5			39
	2								4	11		3	6	7	9	8			10		1			5			40
	2								4	11		3	6	7	9	8			10		1			5			41
	2								4	11		3		7	9	8					1			5	6	10	42
12	36	18	16	21	4	10	6	19	35	25	17	23	39	30	31	30	10	1	25	1	29	7	2	13	1	1	
1					1	9		5	4	6	1		6	17	1	3			5			1		1			

2 own-goals

Mathieson JA	Jennings J	Freeman T	Webster M	Elkes JE	Macfarlane J	Pease WH	Martin GS*	Blackmore HA*	Bruce RF	Warren FW	Cameron K	Jarvis S	Forrest W	Williams JJ	Camsell GH	Brown WH	Rigby A*	McKay J	Baxter RD*	Hillier EJG	Gibson F*	Stuart RW	Carr A	Griffiths TP*	Martin J*	Fenton M*	
	2			5				9	4	11			6	7		8			10		1	3					3
	2			5				9	4	11			6	7		8			10		1	3					4
	2			5				9	4	11		3	6	7		8			10		1						5
	2			5				9	4	11		3	6	7		8			10		1						R
	4	3	1					4	3	1		2	4	4	4	4			4		4	2					
	3							2	1	1						1			1								

225

1933-34

Manager: Peter McWilliam

1	Aug	26	(h)	Derby C	W	3-1 J.J.Williams, Camsell, Warren	14,577
2		28	(a)	Leeds U	L	2-5 Camsell 2	10,896
3	Sep	2	(a)	West Brom A	L	0-3	21,152
4		9	(h)	Birmingham	L	0-3	11,501
5		16	(a)	Sheffield W	L	0-3	12,429
6		23	(h)	Manchester C	W	2-1 Bruce, Camsell	9,095
7		30	(a)	Arsenal	L	0-6	28,293
8	Oct	7	(h)	Everton	W	2-0 Warren, Bruce	10,985
9		14	(a)	Chelsea	W	3-2 Camsell 2, Ferguson	16,878
10		21	(h)	Liverpool	W	4-1 Camsell 2, Ferguson 2	10,899
11		28	(a)	Tottenham H	L	0-2	35,800
12	Nov	4	(h)	Stoke C	W	6-1 Camsell 2, Ferguson 2, Warren 2	6,969
13		11	(a)	Aston Villa	L	0-3	27,740
14		18	(h)	Sheffield U	W	10-3 Camsell 4, Ferguson, Warren, Bruce 3, Baxter	6,461
15		25	(a)	Wolves	W	1-0 Camsell	22,708
16	Dec	2	(h)	Sunderland	L	0-4	28,915
17		9	(a)	Huddersfield T	L	1-2 Camsell	9,998
18		16	(h)	Portsmouth	W	2-0 Warren, J.J.Williams	11,167
19		23	(a)	Leicester C	W	2-1 Camsell, J.J.Williams	1,980
20		25	(a)	Blackburn R	D	0-0	27,273
21		26	(h)	Blackburn R	W	3-1 Camsell, Jennings, Bruce	19,203
22		30	(a)	Derby C	L	0-2	17,387
23	Jan	1	(h)	Leeds U	W	2-1 Baxter, Jennings (pen)	16,071
24		6	(h)	West Brom A	W	3-0 Baxter, Bruce 2	13,927
25		20	(a)	Birmingham	D	0-0	20,310
26	Feb	3	(a)	Manchester C	L	2-5 Baxter 2	22,082
27		7	(h)	Sheffield W	L	2-3 Camsell, Ferguson	9,069
28		10	(h)	Arsenal	L	0-2	15,894
29		17	(a)	Everton	D	1-1 Bruce	19,105
30		24	(h)	Chelsea	D	2-2 Camsell, Jennings (pen)	12,962
31	Mar	3	(a)	Liverpool	L	2-6 Yorston 2	25,946
32		10	(h)	Tottenham H	D	1-1 Camsell	11,832
33		17	(a)	Stoke C	L	0-2	20,623
34		24	(h)	Aston Villa	L	1-2 Yorston	13,156
35		30	(a)	Newcastle U	D	1-1 Yorston	35,142
36		31	(a)	Sheffield U	L	1-3 Camsell	17,520
37	Apr	2	(h)	Newcastle U	W	1-0 Warren	17,535
38		7	(h)	Wolves	D	0-0	11,284
39		14	(a)	Sunderland	L	0-2	12,204
40		21	(h)	Huddersfield T	W	3-0 Baxter, Camsell, Yorston	11,042
41		30	(a)	Portsmouth	L	1-4 Warren	13,546
42	May	5	(h)	Leicester C	W	4-1 Yorston 2, Stuart, Warren	4,758

FINAL LEAGUE POSITION: 16th in Division One

Appearances
Goals

FA Cup

3	Jan	13	(a)	Sunderland	D	1-1 Camsell	43,600
R		17	(h)	Sunderland	L	1-2 Ferguson	40,882

Appearances
Goals

No.	Gibson F	Jennings J	Jarvis S	Brown WH	Griffiths TP	Martin J	Williams JJ	Bruce RF	Camsell GH	Baxter RD	Warren FW	Fenton M	Cameron K	Stuart RW	Webster M	Ferguson C*	McKay J	Weightman E*	Forrest W	Chadwick C*	Yorston BC*	Hillier EJG	Smith J*
1	1	2	3	4	5	6	7	8	9	10	11												
2	1	2	3	4	5	6	7	8	9			10	11										
3	1	2	3	4	5	6	7	8	9		11	10											
4	1	2		4		6		8	9		11			3	5	7		10					
5	1	2		4	5	6		8	9		11			3		7	10						
6	1	2		4	5	6	7	8	9	10	11			3									
7	1	2		4	5	6	7	8	9	10	11			3									
8	1	2		4	5	6		8	9	10	11			3			7						
9	1	2		4	5	6		8	9	10	11			3			7						
10	1	2		4	5	6		8	9	10	11			3			7						
11	1	2		4	5	6		8	9	10	11			3			7						
12	1	2		4	5	6		8	9	10	11			3			7						
13	1	2		4	5	6		8	9	10	11			3			7						
14	1	2		4	5	6		8	9	10	11			3			7						
15	1	2		4	5	6		8	9	10	11			3			7						
16	1	2		4	5			8	9	10	11			3			7		6				
17	1	2		4	5	6		8	9	10	11			3			7						
18	1	2		4	5		7	8	9	10	11			3					6				
19	1	2		4	5		7	8	9	10	11			3					6				
20	1	2		4	5	6	7	8	9	10	11			3									
21	1	2		4	5	6	7	8	9	10	11			3									
22	1	2		4	5	10	7		9		11			3		8			6				
23	1	2		4	5		7		9		11			3		8	10		6				
24	1	2		4	5	11	7	8	9					3		10			6				
25	1	2		4	5		7		9	10				3		11	8		6				
26	1	2		4	5	11			9	10		7		3		8			6				
27	1		2	4	5	11			9	10				3		7	8		6				
28	1		2	4	5	11		8	9					3		7	10		6				
29	1	2		4	5	11		8	9					3		7	10		6				
30	1	2		4	5	11		8	9	10				3					6	7			
31	1	2		4	5	11	10		9					3					6	7	8		
32	1	2		5	4				10	9	11			3					6	7	8		
33	1	2		5	4	7			10	9	11			3					6		8		
34	1	2		5	4	7	8			10	11			3					6		9		
35	1	2		4	5	6	7	8		10	11			3							9		
36	1	2		4	5	6	7	8		10	11			3							9		
37		2		4		6	7	8	9	5	11			3							10	1	
38		2		4	5	6	7		9	8	11			3							10	1	
39		2		4	5	6	7		9	8	11			3							10	1	
40		2		4	5	6		8	7	10	11			3							9	1	
41		2		4	5	6		8	7	10	11			3							9	1	
42				4	5	6	7	8			11			3					10		9	1	2
Tot	36	39	5	39	40	32	23	35	36	36	31	3	1	39	1	18	10	1	15	3	12	6	1
Gls		3				3	9	23	6	9				1		7			7				

No.	Gibson F	Jennings J	Jarvis S	Brown WH	Griffiths TP	Martin J	Williams JJ	Bruce RF	Camsell GH	Baxter RD	Warren FW	Fenton M	Cameron K	Stuart RW	Webster M	Ferguson C*	McKay J	Weightman E*	Forrest W	Chadwick C*	Yorston BC*	Hillier EJG	Smith J*
3	1	2		4	5	6	7	8	9		11			3		10							
R	1	2		4	5	7		8	9	10				3		11			6				
Tot	2	2		2	2	2	1	2	2	2	2			2		2			1				
Gls									1							1							

1934-35

Manager: Wilf Gillow

1	Aug	25	(a)	Leeds U	W	4-2	Yorston 3, Warren	15,949
2		29	(h)	Portsmouth	D	1-1	Chadwick	17,977
3	Sep	1	(h)	West Brom A	D	0-0		16,761
4		5	(a)	Portsmouth	L	0-1		16,788
5		8	(a)	Sheffield W	D	3-3	Baxter, Warren, Bruce	16,103
6		15	(h)	Birmingham	L	0-1		15,477
7		22	(a)	Stoke C	L	0-2		19,788
8		29	(h)	Manchester C	L	1-2	Yorston	9,180
9	Oct	6	(a)	Sunderland	D	1-1	Forrest	34,829
10		13	(a)	Blackburn R	L	2-3	Coleman 2	12,429
11		20	(h)	Leicester C	W	1-0	Baxter	12,363
12		27	(a)	Derby C	L	0-2		15,561
13	Nov	3	(h)	Preston NE	D	3-3	Fenton 3	6,572
14		10	(a)	Tottenham H	L	1-3	Fenton	25,761
15		17	(h)	Wolves	D	2-2	Baxter, Coleman	10,900
16		24	(a)	Huddersfield T	L	1-3	Camsell	15,790
17	Dec	1	(h)	Everton	W	3-2	Coleman 2, Fenton	12,914
18		8	(a)	Grimsby T	D	2-2	Camsell 2	12,174
19		15	(h)	Aston Villa	W	4-1	Fenton 2, Camsell 2	16,245
20		22	(a)	Chelsea	L	1-2	Coleman	23,724
21		26	(a)	Liverpool	D	2-2	Coleman, Camsell	45,936
22		29	(h)	Leeds U	D	3-3	Fenton, Warren, Stuart	15,615
23	Jan	1	(h)	Liverpool	W	2-0	Coleman 2	19,436
24		5	(a)	West Brom A	L	3-6	Camsell 2 (1 pen), Coleman	19,599
25		19	(h)	Sheffield W	W	5-3	Camsell, Warren 2, Martin, J.J.Williams	9,378
26	Feb	2	(h)	Stoke C	W	2-0	Camsell 2	12,730
27		6	(a)	Birmingham	L	2-4	Baxter, Jennings	5,729
28		9	(a)	Manchester C	L	2-6	Camsell, Bruce	29,431
29		16	(a)	Sunderland	D	0-0		17,416
30		23	(h)	Blackburn R	D	3-3	Bruce, Warren, Baxter	9,108
31	Mar	2	(a)	Leicester C	L	1-3	Chadwick	16,120
32		9	(h)	Derby C	D	1-1	Camsell	13,642
33		16	(a)	Preston NE	L	0-2		15,555
34		23	(h)	Tottenham H	W	3-1	Coleman, Birkett 2	14,625
35		30	(a)	Wolves	L	3-5	Warren, Coleman, Camsell	18,673
36	Apr	6	(h)	Huddersfield T	W	2-1	Baxter (pen), Warren	12,570
37		13	(a)	Everton	D	1-1	Birkett	15,214
38		19	(a)	Arsenal	L	0-8		45,719
39		20	(h)	Grimsby T	L	0-2		12,124
40		22	(h)	Arsenal	L	0-1		29,171
41		27	(a)	Aston Villa	W	3-0	Yorston 2, Birkett	15,685
42	May	4	(h)	Chelsea	D	2-2	Warren, Yorston	17,505

FINAL LEAGUE POSITION: 20th in Division One

Appearances

Goals

FA Cup

3	Jan	12	(h)	Blackburn R	D	1-1	J.J.Williams	34,637
R		17	(a)	Blackburn R	L	0-1		32,783

Appearances

Goals

228

Season appearance and goals grid.

Hillier EJG	Jennings J	Stuart RW	Brown WH	Griffiths TP	Martin J	Chadwick C	Bruce RF	Yorston BC	Baxter RD	Warren FW	Forrest W	Coleman E*	Fenton M	Williams JJ	Camsell GH	Bell JN*	Jarvis S	Birkett RJE*	Gibson F	No.
1	2	3	4	5	6	7	8	9	10	11										1
1	2	3	4	5	6	7	8	9	10	11										2
1	2	3	4	5		7	8	9	10	11	6									3
1	2	3	4	5		7	8	9	10	11	6									4
1	2	3	4	5		7	8	9	10	11	6									5
1	2	3	4	5		7	8	9	10	11	6									6
1	2	3	4	5			8	9	10	11	6	7								7
1	2	3	4			10	9	5	11		6	8	7							8
1	2	3	4	5		10	9	11			6	8	7							9
1	2	3	4	5		10	9		11		6	8	7							10
1	2	3	4	5			9	10	11	6	8		7							11
1	2	3	4	5			9	10	11	6	8		7							12
1	2	3	4			10	9	5	11		6	8	7							13
1	2	3	4	5				10		6	8	9		7	11					14
1	2	3	4			10		5		6	8	9		7	11					15
1	2	3	4			7		5	11	6	8	10			9					16
1	2	3	4				5	11	6	10	8	7			9					17
1	2	3		5			4	11	6	10	8	7			9					18
1	2	3		5			4	11	6	10	8	7			9					19
1	2	3		5			4	11	6	10	8	7			9					20
1	2	3		5		7	4	11	6	10	8				9					21
1	2	3		5			4	11	6	10	8	7			9					22
1	2	3		5			4	11	6	10	8	7			9					23
1	2	3		5			4	11	6	10	8	7			9					24
1	2	3	4	5	6			11		10	8	7			9					25
1	2	3	4	5	6			11		10	8	7			9					26
1	2	3	4		6	7		5	11		10	8			9					27
1	2	3	4		6	7	8	5	11		10				9					28
1	2		4		6	7	8	9	5	11	10				3					29
1	2		4		6	7	8	9	5	11	10				3					30
1		3	4	5		7	8		2	11	6	10			9					31
1		3	4	5		7			6	11		10	8		9	2				32
1		3	4		6			5	11		10	8		9	2	7				33
1		3	2	5	4		8		6	11		10			9		7			34
1		3	2	5	4		8		6	11		10			9		7			35
1		3	2	5	4		8		6	11		10			9		7			36
1		3	2	5	4		8		6	11		10			9		7			37
1	2	3	4	5			8		6	11		10		7	9					38
1	2	3	4	5				10	11	6	8			7	9					39
	2	3	4		6		8		5	11		10			9			7	1	40
	2	3	4		6			9	5	11		10			8			7	1	41
	2	3	4		6			9	5	11		10			8			7	1	42
39	35	40	35	29	16	12	22	19	39	39	24	36	21	14	26	2	4	7	3	
1	1			1	2	3	7	6	9	1	12	8	1	14				4		

Hillier EJG	Jennings J	Stuart RW	Brown WH	Griffiths TP	Martin J	Chadwick C	Bruce RF	Yorston BC	Baxter RD	Warren FW	Forrest W	Coleman E*	Fenton M	Williams JJ	Camsell GH	Bell JN*	Jarvis S	Birkett RJE*	Gibson F	No.
1	2	3		5			4	11	6	10	8	7			9					3
1	2	3	4	5			8		11	6	10			7	9					R
2	2	2	1	2			1	1	2	2	2	1	2	2				2	2	
												1								

1935-36

Manager: Wilf Gillow

1	Aug	31	(h)	Portsmouth	W 3-2	Camsell 2, Birkett	17,795
2	Sep	4	(h)	Aston Villa	L 1-2	Martin	22,421
3		7	(a)	Preston NE	W 5-0	Camsell, Chadwick, Birkett 2, Yorston	22,196
4		9	(a)	Aston Villa	W 7-2	Coleman, Camsell 5, Birkett	19,109
5		14	(h)	Brentford	D 0-0		38,107
6		18	(h)	Wolves	W 4-2	Baxter (pen), Birkett 2, Camsell	15,637
7		21	(a)	Derby C	L 2-3	Birkett, Yorston	27,170
8		28	(h)	Everton	W 6-1	Birkett 3, Yorston, Camsell 2	19,308
9	Oct	5	(a)	Bolton W	L 1-3	Birkett	29,910
10		12	(h)	Huddersfield T	W 4-2	Yorston 2, Coleman, Chadwick	25,547
11		19	(h)	Leeds U	D 1-1	Coleman	12,256
12		26	(a)	Grimsby T	L 0-1		12,108
13	Nov	2	(h)	Liverpool	D 2-2	Camsell, Birkett	18,104
14		9	(a)	Chelsea	L 1-2	Camsell	33,408
15		16	(h)	Blackburn R	W 6-1	Yorston, Camsell, Birkett 2, Chadwick, Coleman	14,945
16		23	(a)	Sunderland	L 1-2	Coleman	58,902
17		30	(h)	Manchester C	W 2-0	Camsell, Birkett	19,438
18	Dec	9	(a)	Arsenal	L 0-2		23,365
19		14	(h)	Birmingham	L 0-2		15,061
20		21	(a)	Stoke C	D 1-1	Birkett	8,486
21		26	(a)	West Brom A	L 2-5	Yorston, Camsell	25,968
22		28	(a)	Portsmouth	L 0-1		21,320
23	Jan	1	(h)	West Brom A	W 3-1	Camsell 3 (1 pen)	22,379
24		4	(h)	Preston NE	W 2-0	Chadwick, Yorston	17,245
25		18	(a)	Brentford	L 0-1		27,779
26		29	(h)	Derby C	L 0-3		7,206
27	Feb	1	(a)	Everton	L 2-5	Chadwick 2	26,602
28		8	(h)	Bolton W	D 0-0		18,377
29		19	(a)	Huddersfield T	L 1-4	Birkett	4,366
30		22	(a)	Leeds U	W 1-0	Yorston	21,055
31	Mar	4	(h)	Chelsea	W 4-1	Coleman, Cunliffe, Yorston, Camsell	7,968
32		7	(a)	Manchester C	L 0-6		20,094
33		14	(h)	Grimsby T	W 5-1	Camsell 2, Cunliffe 2, Yorston	14,174
34		21	(a)	Blackburn R	D 2-2	Birkett, Camsell	13,779
35		28	(h)	Sunderland	W 6-0	Cunliffe, Birkett 2, Camsell, Yorston (pen), Higham	29,990
36	Apr	4	(a)	Liverpool	D 2-2	Baxter, Yorston	22,223
37		11	(h)	Arsenal	D 2-2	Birkett, Coleman	31,006
38		13	(h)	Sheffield W	W 5-0	Camsell 4, Birkett	18,621
39		14	(a)	Sheffield W	D 0-0		21,157
40		18	(a)	Birmingham	L 0-1		17,072
41		25	(h)	Stoke C	D 0-0		8,613
42	May	2	(a)	Wolves	L 0-4		14,639

FINAL LEAGUE POSITION: 14th in Division One

Appearances
Goals

FA Cup

3	Jan	11	(h)	Southampton	W 1-0	Cunliffe	29,550
4		25	(h)	Clapton O	W 3-0	Camsell 2, Cunliffe	34,470
5	Feb	15	(h)	Leicester C	W 2-1	Camsell, Forrest	42,214
6		29	(a)	Grimsby T	L 1-3	Camsell	21,000

Appearances
Goals

Gibson F	Jennings J	Stuart RW	Brown WH	Baxter RD	Martin J	Birkett RJE	Yorston BC	Camsell GH	Coleman E	Warren FW	Griffiths TP	Fenton M	Chadwick C	Forrest W	Ferguson C	Cunliffe A*	Weightman E	Ross AC*	Parkin R*	Hawkins GH*	Higham N*	#
1	2	3	4	5	6	7	8	9	10	11												1
1		3	4	5	6	7	8	9	10		2	11										2
1	2	3	4	5	6	7	8	9	10					11								3
1	2	3	4	5	6	7	8	9	10					11								4
1	2	3	4	5	6	7	8	9	10					11								5
1	2	3	4	5	6	7	8	9	10					11								6
1		3	4	5	6	7	8	9	10		2			11								7
1		3	4	5		7	8	9	10	11	2			6								8
1		3	2	5	4	7	8	9	10	11				6								9
1		3	4	5	6	7	8	9	10		2		11									10
1		3	4	5	6		8	9	10	11	2	7										11
1		3	4	5	6	7	8	9	10		2		11									12
1		3	2	5	4	7	8	9				10	11	6								13
1		3	2	5	4	7	8	9	10				11	6								14
1		3	2	5	4	7	8	9	10				11	6								15
1		3	2	5	4	7	8	9	10				11	6								16
1		3	2	5	4	7	8	9	10				11	6								17
1		3	2	5	4	7	8	9	10				11	6								18
1		3	2	5	4		8	9	10				11	6	7							19
1		3	2	5	4	7	8	9	10				11	6								20
1		3	2	5	4	7	8	9	10				11	6								21
1		3	2	5	4		8	9	10				7	6		11						22
1		3	2	5	4		8	9	10				7	6		11						23
1		3	2	5	4		8	9				10	7	6		11						24
1			2	5		7	8	9				10		6		11		3	4			25
1			2	5		7	8	9	10					6		11		3	4			26
1			2	5		9	8		10				7	6		11		3	4			27
1			2	5	4	7	8	9	10					6		11		3				28
1		3	2	5	4	7		9	10					6		11	8					29
1			2	5	4	7	8	9	10					6		11		3				30
1		3	2	5	4	7	8	9	10					6		11						31
1			2	5	4	7	8	9	10					6		11		3				32
1		3	2	5	4	7	8	9	10					6		11						33
1		3	2	5	4	7		9	10					6		11					8	34
1		3	2	5	4	7		9	10					6		11					8	35
1		3	2	5	4	7		9						6		11					8	36
1		3	2	5	4	7	8	9	10					6		11						37
1		3	2	5	4	7	8	9	10					6		11						38
1		3	2	5	4	7	8	9	10					6		11						39
1	2	3	4	5		7	8	9	10					6		11						40
1	2	3	4			7	8	9	10	11			6					5				41
1	2	3	4			7		9	10	11			6					5			8	42
42	8	38	41	39	34	36	42	38	37	4	6	6	23	32	1	19	2	6	3	1	4	
			2	1	22	13	28	7					6			4				1		

Gibson F	Jennings J	Stuart RW	Brown WH	Baxter RD	Martin J	Birkett RJE	Yorston BC	Camsell GH	Coleman E	Warren FW	Griffiths TP	Fenton M	Chadwick C	Forrest W	Ferguson C	Cunliffe A*	Weightman E	Ross AC*	Parkin R*	Hawkins GH*	Higham N*	#
1			2	5	4	7	8	9				10		6		11	3					3
1			2	5	4	7	9	9	10				8	6		11	3					4
1		3	2	5	4	7	9	9	10				8	6		11						5
1		3	2	5	4	7	10	9	8					6		11						6
4		2	4	4	2	4	4	4	3				3	4		4	1	1				
									4							1	2					

1936-37

Manager: Wilf Gillow

1	Aug	29	(h)	Manchester C	W	2-0	Birkett, Yorston	23,081
2		31	(a)	Wolves	W	1-0	Chadwick	30,209
3	Sep	5	(a)	Portsmouth	L	1-2	Yorston (pen)	22,387
4		9	(h)	Wolves	W	1-0	Fenton	20,550
5		12	(h)	Chelsea	W	2-0	Birkett, Chadwick	21,278
6		19	(a)	Stoke C	L	2-6	Camsell 2	29,206
7		26	(h)	Charlton A	D	1-1	Yorston	22,795
8	Oct	3	(a)	Grimsby T	L	1-5	Cunliffe	13,073
9		10	(h)	Liverpool	D	3-3	Coleman, Cochrane, Yorston	22,858
10		17	(h)	Sunderland	D	5-5	Camsell 3, Coleman, Birkett	36,030
11		24	(a)	Huddersfield T	L	0-2		20,357
12		31	(h)	Everton	W	2-0	Fenton, Birkett	23,569
13	Nov	7	(a)	Bolton W	W	3-1	Camsell 3	18,264
14		14	(h)	Brentford	W	3-0	Yorston, James (og), Cochrane	23,064
15		21	(a)	Arsenal	L	3-5	Camsell, Birkett, Yorston	44,829
16		28	(h)	Preston NE	W	2-1	Camsell 2	20,308
17	Dec	5	(a)	Sheffield W	L	0-1		11,289
18		12	(h)	Manchester U	W	3-2	Fenton 3	11,790
19		19	(a)	Derby C	W	2-0	Fenton 2	16,155
20		25	(a)	Leeds U	L	0-5		30,647
21		26	(a)	Manchester C	L	1-2	Fenton (pen)	56,227
22		28	(h)	Leeds U	W	4-2	Camsell, Fenton (pen), Birkett 2	14,191
23	Jan	1	(h)	West Brom A	W	4-1	Chadwick 2, Higham, Fenton	28,231
24		2	(h)	Portsmouth	D	2-2	Fenton 2	25,185
25		9	(a)	Chelsea	L	0-1		30,201
26		23	(h)	Stoke C	W	1-0	Fenton	16,445
27		30	(a)	Charlton A	D	2-2	Higham, John Oakes (og)	16,559
28	Feb	6	(h)	Grimsby T	D	0-0		20,457
29		13	(a)	Liverpool	W	2-0	Fenton 2	22,459
30		24	(a)	Sunderland	L	1-4	Camsell	32,309
31		27	(h)	Huddersfield T	W	5-0	Martin, Camsell, Fenton, Chadwick 2	15,932
32	Mar	6	(a)	Everton	W	3-2	Fenton, Camsell 2	30,719
33		13	(h)	Bolton W	W	2-0	Chadwick, Camsell	20,025
34		20	(a)	Brentford	L	1-4	Fenton (pen)	23,872
35		26	(h)	Birmingham	W	3-1	Cochrane, Camsell, Fenton	24,958
36		27	(h)	Arsenal	D	1-1	Fenton	44,523
37		29	(a)	Birmingham	D	0-0		28,624
38	Apr	3	(a)	Preston NE	L	0-2		18,942
39		10	(h)	Sheffield W	W	2-0	Fenton, Cattlin (og)	16,477
40		17	(a)	Manchester U	L	1-2	Cochrane	17,656
41		24	(h)	Derby C	L	1-3	Fenton	18,447
42	May	1	(a)	West Brom A	L	1-3	Yorston	7,022

FINAL LEAGUE POSITION: 7th in Division One

Appearances
Goals

FA Cup

3	Jan	16	(a)	Wolves	L	1-6	Birkett	38,495

Appearances
Goals

232

Ferguson R*	Brown WH	Stuart RW	Martin J	Baxter RD	Forrest W	Birkett RJE	Yorston BC	Camsell GH	Coleman E	Cunliffe A	Jennings J	Chadwick C	Fenton M	Higham N	Cumming DS*	Cochrane T*	Laking GE*	Ross AC	Gibson F	Parkin R	Mannion WJ*	Bryan R*	Shepherdson H*	
1	2	3	4	5	6	7	8	9	10	11														1
1	4	3		5	6		8		10	11	2	7	9											2
1	2	3	4	5	6		8			11		7	9	10										3
1	2	3	4	5	6	7	8					11	9	10										4
1	2	3	4	5	6	7	8					11	9	10										5
1	2	3	4	5	6	7	8	9	10			11												6
1	2	3	4	5	6	7	8	9	10			11												7
1	2	3	4	5	6	7	8	9	10	11														8
	2	3	4	5	6	7	8	9	10						1	11								9
	4	3		5	6	7	8	9	10						1	11	2							10
	4	3		5	6	7	8	9	10						1	11	2							11
	4	3		5	6	7		9					8	10	1	11	2							12
	4	3		5	6	7		9					8	10	1	11	2							13
	4	3		5	6	7	10	9					8		1	11	2							14
	4	3		5	6	7	10	9					8		1	11	2							15
	4	3		5	6	7		9	10				8		1	11	2							16
	4	3		5	6	7			10				9	8	1	11	2							17
	4	3		5	6	7			10				9	8	1	11		2						18
	4	3	6	5		7			10				9	8	1	11		2						19
	4	3	6	5			10	9		7			8			11		2	1					20
	2	3	4	5	6			9		7			8	10		11			1					21
	2	3	4	5	6	7		9					8	10	1	11								22
	4	3		5	6	8						7	9	10	1	11		2						23
		3		5	6	7							9	10	1	11		2		4	8			24
	4	3		5	6	7		9					8	10	1	11	2							25
	4	3		5	6	7	10						9	8	1	11	2							26
	4	3	6	5		7	10						9	8	1	11	2							27
	4	3		5	6	7	10						9	8	1	11	2							28
	4	3	6	5	10	7							9	8	1	11	2							29
	4	3	6	5	10			7				11	9	8	1		2							30
	4	3	6	5	10			9				7	8		1	11	2							31
	4	3	6		5	7		9				11	8	10	1		2							32
	4	3	6		5			9		11		7	8	10	1		2							33
	4	3	6		5			9		11		7	8	10	1		2							34
	4	3		5	6			9				7	8	10	1	11	2							35
	4	3	6	5	10			9				7	8		1	11	2							36
		3	6	5	10								9	8	1	11	2			4		7		37
		3	6		5	7							9	10	1	11	2			4	8			38
	4	3	6	5	10	7	8						9		1	11	2							39
	4	3	6	5			10					7	9	8	1	11	2							40
	4	3		5	6		10					7	9	8	1	11	2							41
	4	3	6		10		9					7	8	1	1	11	2						5	42
8	39	42	25	37	38	28	21	23	12	8	1	17	35	26	32	30	26	5	2	3	2	1	1	
			1			7	7	18	2	1		7	22	2		4								

3 own-goals

	2	3	4	5	6	7		9					8	10	1	11								3
	1	1	1	1	1	1		1					1	1	1	1								
						1																		

1937-38

Manager: Wilf Gillow

1	Aug	28	(a)	Sunderland	L 1-3	Yorston	56,717
2	Sep	1	(a)	Birmingham	L 1-3	Yorston	19,297
3		4	(h)	Stoke C	W 2-1	Forrest, Fenton	23,652
4		8	(h)	Birmingham	D 1-1	Yorston	18,831
5		11	(a)	Portsmouth	W 2-0	Camsell 2	21,344
6		13	(a)	West Brom A	L 1-3	Yorston	8,254
7		18	(h)	Chelsea	W 4-3	Fenton, Birkett, Camsell, Chadwick	19,631
8		25	(a)	Charlton A	L 0-1		27,782
9	Oct	2	(h)	Preston NE	W 2-1	Camsell, Fenton	25,050
10		9	(a)	Grimsby T	L 1-2	Fenton	10,569
11		16	(a)	Derby C	D 1-1	Bell (og)	15,267
12		23	(h)	Manchester C	W 4-0	Cochrane, Higham, Fenton 2	18,442
13		30	(a)	Arsenal	W 2-1	Cochrane, Brown	39,066
14	Nov	6	(h)	Everton	L 1-2	Birkett	25,083
15		13	(a)	Brentford	D 3-3	Higham, Forrest, Fenton	25,682
16		20	(h)	Leicester C	W 4-2	Fenton 3, Reeday (og)	18,426
17		27	(a)	Huddersfield T	L 0-3		14,020
18	Dec	4	(h)	Blackpool	D 2-2	Fenton, Camsell	12,970
19		18	(h)	Bolton W	L 1-2	Camsell	21,407
20		25	(a)	Leeds U	L 3-5	Higham, Fenton, Camsell	37,020
21		27	(h)	Leeds U	W 2-0	Fenton (pen), Mannion	34,640
22	Jan	1	(h)	Sunderland	W 2-1	Mannion, Milne	‡ 45,854
23		15	(a)	Stoke C	L 0-3		14,103
24		26	(h)	Portsmouth	D 0-0		12,957
25		29	(a)	Chelsea	W 1-0	Mannion	27,081
26	Feb	5	(h)	Charlton A	W 3-1	Fenton, Camsell, Milne	24,687
27		16	(a)	Preston NE	W 2-0	Yorston 2	13,416
28		19	(h)	Grimsby T	W 1-0	Betmead (og)	20,156
29		26	(h)	Derby C	W 4-2	Fenton 2, Cochrane, Milne	21,863
30	Mar	9	(a)	Manchester C	W 6-1	Fenton 2, Cochrane 4	16,396
31		12	(h)	Arsenal	W 2-1	Fenton 2	‡ 46,747
32		19	(a)	Everton	D 2-2	Yorston, Higham	28,808
33		23	(a)	Wolves	W 1-0	Mannion	22,327
34		26	(h)	Brentford	L 0-1		29,339
35	Apr	2	(a)	Leicester C	W 1-0	Cochrane	17,759
36		9	(h)	Huddersfield T	L 0-1		20,901
37		15	(h)	Liverpool	D 1-1	Cochrane	29,843
38		16	(a)	Blackpool	L 2-4	Yorston, Cochrane	29,822
39		18	(a)	Liverpool	D 1-1	Forrest	32,010
40		23	(h)	Wolves	L 0-3		26,085
41		30	(a)	Bolton W	L 1-3	Camsell	12,164
42	May	7	(h)	West Brom A	W 4-1	Fenton 4	12,905

FINAL LEAGUE POSITION: 5th in Division One. Match 16: Some sources credit Chadwick, Birkett, Fenton 2 but club credit Fenton 3, Reeday (og). Match 32: Some sources credit Yorston, club credit Cochrane. ‡Ground attendance record.

Appearances
Goals

FA Cup

3	Jan	8	(h)	Stockport C	W 2-0	Fenton 2 (1 pen)	34,757
4		22	(a)	Nottingham F	W 3-1	Mannion, Camsell, Milne	39,055
5	Feb	12	(a)	York C	L 0-1		23,860

Appearances
Goals

234

Cumming DS	Laking GE	Stuart RW	Brown WH	Baxter RD	Forrest W	Birkett RJE	Fenton M	Camsell GH	Yorston BC	Cochrane T	Ferguson R	Chadwick C	Higham N	Nash FC*	Martin J	Hardwick GFM*	Milne JV*	Mannion WJ	Wardle G*	Shepherdson H	Fowler HN*	Murphy DA*	
1	2	3	4	5	6	7	8	9	10	11													1
1	2	3	4	5	6	7	8	9	10	11													2
	2	3	4	5	6		8	9	10	11	1	7											3
	2	3	4	5	6		8	9	10	11	1	7											4
1	2	3	4	5	6		8	9	10	11		7											5
1	2	3	4	5	6			9	10	11		7	8										6
1	2	3	4	5	6	7	8	9	10			11											7
1	2	3	4	5	6	7	8	9	10			11											8
	2	3	4	5	6	7	8	9	10			11		1									9
1	2	3		5	6	7	8	9	10			11			4								10
1	2	3	4	5	10	7	9					11	8		6								11
	2	3	4	5	6		8	9		11		7	10	1									12
	2	3	4	5	6		8	9		11		7	10	1									13
	2	3	4	5	6		8	9		11		7	10	1									14
	2	3	4	5	10	7	9					11	8	1	6								15
	2	3	4	5	10	7	9					11	8	1	6								16
	2	3		5	6	7	8	9				11	10	1	4								17
1	2	3		5	6	7	8	9	10			11			4								18
1	2			5	6	7	8	9					10		4	3	11						19
1	2		4	5	6	7	8	9								3	11	10					20
	2		4	5	6	7	8	9						1		3	11	10					21
	2			5	6	7	8	9						1	4	3	11	10					22
1	2		4	5	6	7	8	9				11				3	10						23
1	2		4	5	6		8	9				11				3	10	7					24
1	2			5	6			9				11	8		4	3	7	10					25
1	2	3		5	6		8	9				11			4		7	10					26
1	2	3		5	6	7		9	10						4		11	8					27
	2	3		5	6	7		9	10					1	4		11	8					28
	2	3		5	6			9	10	11				1	4		7	8					29
1	2	3	4	5	6			9	10	11							7	8					30
1	2	3		5	6			9	10	11					4		7	8					31
1	2	3			6				10	11			9		4		7	8		5			32
1	2	3	4		6			9	10	11							7	8		5			33
1	2		4		6			9	10	11						3	7	8		5			34
1	2		4	5	6			9	10	11							7	8	3				35
	2	3	4	5	6			9		11		7	10	1	8								36
1	2	3	4	5	6			9	10	11							7	8					37
1	2	3		5	6			9	10	11					4		7	8					38
1	2	3	4	5	6			9	10	11							7	8					39
1	2	3	4	5	6	7		9	10	11								8					40
1	2		4				10	9		11		7			8					5	3	6	41
1	2	3	4	5				9	10	11							7	8				6	42
28	42	32	29	38	40	22	36	24	25	26	2	19	13	12	16	8	19	22	1	4	2	2	
		1			3	2	24	9	8	10			1		4		3	4					

3 own-goals

Cumming DS	Laking GE	Stuart RW	Brown WH	Baxter RD	Forrest W	Birkett RJE	Fenton M	Camsell GH	Yorston BC	Cochrane T	Ferguson R	Chadwick C	Higham N	Nash FC*	Martin J	Hardwick GFM*	Milne JV*	Mannion WJ	Wardle G*	Shepherdson H	Fowler HN*	Murphy DA*	
1	2			5	6	7	8	9							4	3	11	10					3
1	2		4	5	6	7	8	9								3	11	10					4
1	2	3		5	6	7	8	9							4		11	10					5
3	3	1	1	3	3	3	3								2	2	3	3					
							2	1									1	1					

235

1938-39

Manager: Wilf Gillow

1	Aug	27	(h)	Manchester U	W 3-1 Fenton, Mannion, Cochrane	25,359
2		31	(h)	Aston Villa	D 1-1 Fenton	29,281
3	Sep	3	(a)	Stoke C	W 3-1 Mannion, Fenton, Yorston	23,475
4		10	(h)	Chelsea	D 1-1 Yorston	28,359
5		14	(a)	Liverpool	L 1-3 Fenton	25,535
6		17	(a)	Preston NE	L 1-3 Fenton (pen)	23,746
7		24	(h)	Charlton A	W 4-0 Laking, Milne, Fenton 2	20,227
8	Oct	1	(a)	Bolton W	L 1-4 Yorston	28,505
9		8	(h)	Leeds U	L 1-2 Fenton	23,009
10		15	(h)	Grimsby T	W 3-2 Yorston 2, Camsell	21,720
11		22	(a)	Sunderland	W 2-1 Camsell, Yorston (pen)	39,440
12		29	(h)	Wolves	W 1-0 Cochrane	24,624
13	Nov	5	(a)	Everton	L 0-4	35,683
14		12	(h)	Huddersfield T	W 4-1 Fenton 3, Yorston	19,630
15		19	(a)	Portsmouth	D 1-1 Yorston	21,463
16		26	(h)	Arsenal	D 1-1 Higham	29,047
17	Dec	3	(a)	Brentford	L 1-2 Fenton	21,746
18		10	(h)	Blackpool	W 9-2 Chadwick 2, Mannion 4, Fenton 3	17,166
19		17	(a)	Derby C	W 4-1 Fenton 2 (1 pen), Yorston, Chadwick	17,168
20		24	(a)	Manchester U	D 1-1 Chadwick	33,235
21		26	(a)	Birmingham	L 1-2 Fenton	17,953
22		27	(h)	Birmingham	D 2-2 Fenton, Yorston	33,534
23		31	(h)	Stoke C	W 5-1 Chadwick 2, Fenton, Mannion, Milne	20,092
24	Jan	2	(h)	Liverpool	W 3-0 Fenton 2, Milne	25,309
25		14	(a)	Chelsea	L 2-4 Higham, Camsell	26,750
26		25	(h)	Preston NE	D 2-2 Fenton, Higham	9,262
27		28	(a)	Charlton A	L 0-3	23,473
28	Feb	4	(h)	Bolton W	L 1-2 Fenton	16,416
29		11	(a)	Leeds U	W 1-0 Mannion	18,273
30		18	(a)	Grimsby T	W 2-0 Fenton, Chadwick	11,717
31		25	(h)	Sunderland	W 3-0 Fenton 2, Chadwick	23,882
32	Mar	8	(a)	Wolves	L 1-6 Fenton	20,938
33		11	(h)	Everton	D 4-4 Chadwick, Yorston, Milne, Fenton	20,014
34		18	(a)	Huddersfield T	W 1-0 Camsell	16,011
35		29	(h)	Portsmouth	W 8-2 Camsell 2, Chadwick, Mannion 3, Forrest, Yorston	6,116
36	Apr	1	(a)	Arsenal	W 2-1 Mannion, Camsell	34,669
37		8	(h)	Brentford	W 3-1 Camsell 2, Chadwick	18,191
38		10	(h)	Leicester C	W 3-2 Camsell, Mannion, McKenzie	19,764
39		11	(a)	Leicester C	L 3-5 Fenton 2, Mannion	12,143
40		15	(a)	Blackpool	L 0-4	13,733
41		22	(h)	Derby C	W 2-0 Fenton 2 (1 pen)	13,673
42	May	6	(a)	Aston Villa	D 1-1 Fenton (pen)	20,149

FINAL LEAGUE POSITION: 4th in Division One

Appearances
Goals

FA Cup

3	Jan	7	(h)	Bolton W	D 0-0	32,790
R		11	(a)	Bolton W	D 0-0*	16,981
2R		16	(a)	Bolton W	W 1-0 Fenton	25,577
4		21	(h)	Sunderland	L 0-2	†51,080

*After extra-time.   †Ground attendance record.

Appearances
Goals

236

Player appearance / position grid (numbers indicate shirt/position for each match).

Cumming DS	Laking GE	Stuart RW	Brown WH	Baxter RD	Forrest W	Milne JV	Mannion WJ	Fenton M	Yorston BC	Cochrane T	McKenzie D*	Fowler HN	Higham N	Martin J	Shepherdson H	Camsell GH	Scrimshaw CT*	Chadwick C	Nash FC	Murphy DA	Armes S*	Butler T*	
1	2	3	4	5	6	7	8	9	10	11													1
1	2	3		5	6	7	8	9	10	11	4												2
1	2	3		5	6	7	8	9	10	11	4												3
1	2	3		5	6	7	8	9	10	11	4												4
1	2			5	6	7		9	10	11	4	3	8										5
1	2				6	7	8	9	10	11	4	3			5								6
1	2					7	8	9	10	11	4	3			6	5							7
1	2		4	5		7	8	9	10	11		3			6								8
1	2		4	5	6	7	10	8		11		3			9								9
1		2		5	6	7	8		10	11	4					9	3						10
1		2		5	6	7	8		10	11	4					9	3						11
1		2		5	6	7	8		10	11	4					9	3						12
1		2		5	6	7		8	10	11	4					9	3						13
1		2		5	6	7	8	9	10	11	4						3						14
1		2		5	6	7	8	9	10	11	4						3						15
1		2		5	6	7		9	10	11	4			8			3						16
1		2		5	6	7	8	9	10	11	4						3						17
1	3	2		5	6	7	8	9	10		4							11					18
1	3	2		5	6	7	8	9	10		4							11					19
1	2	3	4	5	6	7	8	9	10									11					20
1	3		4	5	6	7	8	9	10						2			11					21
1	3		4	5	6	7	8	9	10						2			11					22
	3	2		5	6	7	8	9	10					4				11	1				23
	3	2		5		7	8	9	10					4				11	1	6			24
1	2		5	4	7				10						8	9	3	11		6			25
1	3	2		5	4	7	8	9		11				10						6			26
1	2	3	4		5	7	8	9		11				10						6			27
1	3		2	10	11	8	9				4				5					6	7		28
1	3		2	5	6	10	8	9			4							11			7		29
1	3		2	5	6	10	8	9		11	4							7					30
1	3		2	5	6	10	8	9		11	4							7					31
1	3		2	5	6	10	8	9		11	4							7					32
1	3		2	5	6	11	8	9	10		4							7					33
1	3		2	5	4	11	8		10							9		7		6			34
1	3		2		6	11	8		10		4				5	9		7					35
1	3		2		6	11	8		10		4				5	9		7					36
	3	2		5	6	11	8		10		4					9		7	1				37
	3	2				11	8		10		4				5	9		7	1	6			38
1	3		2			8	9	10			4				5			11		6	7		39
1	3	2			6	8	9	10	11						5			4			7		40
1		3	2	5	6	7	8	9		11	4					10							41
1		3	2	5	6	11	8	9	10		4										7		42
38	25	16	34	33	37	40	38	33	33	24	28	5	6	5	9	11	9	19	4	10	3	2	
	1				1	4	14	34	12	2	1		3			10		11					

Cumming DS	Laking GE	Stuart RW	Brown WH	Baxter RD	Forrest W	Milne JV	Mannion WJ	Fenton M	Yorston BC	Cochrane T	McKenzie D*	Fowler HN	Higham N	Martin J	Shepherdson H	Camsell GH	Scrimshaw CT*	Chadwick C	Nash FC	Murphy DA	Armes S*	Butler T*	
1		3	2	5	6	7	8	9	10		4							11					3
1		3	2	5	4	7	8	9	10									11		6			R
1		3	2	5	4	7	8	9								10		11		6			2R
1		3	2	5	4	7	8	9								10		11		6			4
4	4	4	4	4	4	4	4	2						1		2		4	3				
								1															

1939-40

Manager: Wilf Gillow

1	Aug	26	(a)	Aston Villa	L	0-2	32,427
2		30	(a)	Liverpool	L	1-4 Fenton	16,762
3	Sep	2	(h)	Stoke C‡	D	2-2 Fenton 2	12,298
						Appearances	
						Goals	

North Eastern Regional League

4	Oct	21	(a)	York C	W	3-1 Fenton 2 (1 pen), Camsell	4,500
5		28	(h)	Huddersfield T	D	2-2 Mannion, Fenton	5,000
6	Nov	11	(a)	Bradford	L	0-3	5,000
7		25	(h)	Newcastle U	L	1-2 Camsell	4,000
8	Dec	2	(a)	Hull C	L	0-3	3,000
9		9	(h)	Halifax T	W	3-1 Fenton, Forrest, Camsell	1,200
10		16	(h)	Darlington	W	8-1 Mannion 2, Camsell, Chadwick, Fenton 4	1,000
11		23	(a)	Leeds U	L	1-3 T.E.Murphy	4,500
12	Jan	6	(h)	Bradford C	W	3-0 Fenton, Mannion, Chadwick	2,000
13	Feb	24	(a)	Huddersfield T	L	2-4 McMahon, Fenton	2,835
14	Mar	2	(h)	Hartlepools U	W	2-0 Fenton, McMahon	
15		9	(h)	Bradford	D	3-3 Fenton 2, T.E.Murphy	
16		23	(a)	Newcastle U	W	5-3 Fenton 3, Forrest 2	9,410
17		25	(a)	Darlington	L	0-8	5,497
18		30	(h)	Hull C	L	2-3 Fenton 2	1,600
19	Apr	6	(h)	Halifax T	D	1-1 G.Murphy	4,000
20		13	(h)	Leeds U	D	1-1 Fenton	1,200
21	May	18	(a)	Bradford C	W	4-1 Fenton 2, Stobbart, Mannion	1,028
22		25	(a)	Hartlepools U	L	1-2 Fenton	1,000
23	Jun	5	(h)	York C	W	6-1 Stobbart 4, T.E.Murphy, Camsell	1,500
						Appearances	
						Goals	

League North Cup

24	Apr	20	(h)	Grimsby T	W	4-1 Fenton, Milne, D.A.Murphy, T.E.Murphy	7,987
25		27	(a)	Grimsby T	L	1-3 Fenton	4,000
26	May	4	(h)	Newcastle U	D	2-2 Stobbart, Fenton	10,229
27		11	(a)	Newcastle U	L	1-2 Fenton	15,300
						Appearances	
						Goals	

‡ Under normal circumstances this game would have marked Dave Miller's League debut, but with the outbreak of war on 3 September 1939, normal football was suspended for the duration. By the time the League resumed Dave had been transferred to Wolverhampton Wanderers.

Appearance and scorer grid (Middlesbrough F.C.).

Cumming DS	Laking GE	Stuart RW	McKenzie D	Baxter RD	Forrest W	Chadwick C	Yorston BC	Fenton M	Mannion WJ	Milne JV	Camsell GH	Murphy DA	Miller D	Brown WH	Martin J	Armes S	Hardwick GFM	Shepherdson H	Heywood AE*	Fowler HN	Murphy TE	Copping W*	Murphy GJ	Robinson JN	McMahon H*	Stobbart GC	Ainsworth W*	
1	2	3	4	5	6	7	8	9	10	11																		1
1	2	3	4	5	6	11		9	8	7	10																	2
1	2	3	4	5		7	10	9	8			6	11															3
3	3	3	3	3	2	3	2	3	3	2	1	1	1															
								3																				
1		3	4		5	11		9	8		10				2	6	7											4
1	2				6	11		9	8		10					4		7	3	5								5
		3			6	7		9	8					11	4	5		1	2	10								6
1		3				11						10	8	9	2	4			5		7	6						7
1	2				6	11								9	10	4	5		3		7	8						8
1		3				11						10	8	9	4	6	5				7		2					9
1		3			6	11						10	8	9	4	5					7		2					10
1		3			6	11						10	8	9	4				2		7	5						11
1		3				11		9	8			10			4	6			2		7	5						12
1		3										10	8	9	4	6			2		7	5	11					13
1		3			6			9					7		4	2				10		8	5	11				14
1		3			6			9	8	7					4	2				10		5	11					15
1		3						9	8			10			4	6			2		7	5	11					16
1								9	8			10			4	6	3		2		7	5	11					17
1		3						9	8	11		10			4	6			2		7	5						18
1		3			6			9	8	11					4				2	10	7	5						19
1		3			6			9	7						4		5		2	10			11	8	4			20
1					6		8	7							2				3	10		5	11	9	4			21
1					6		8		11	7					2	4			3	10		5			9			22
1					6		8		11	7					2	4			3	10		5			9			23
19		16	1		19	9		19	12		8	10	2	16	17	2	3	8	1	10	18	1	3	14	7	4	1	
					3	2		22	5					5	3			1			2				5			
1		3		5	6			9	8	7				11	2	4				10								24
1		3		5	6			9		7				11	2	4				10					8			25
1		3		5	6			9		7				11	2	4				10					8			26
1								9		11			10	6	2	4			3	8		5			2			27
4		3		3	4			4	1	4			1	4	4	4			1	4		1		1	2		1	
								4	1	1				1	1					1					1			

Guest players:
W.Ainsworth, W.Copping (Leeds United), A.E.Heywood (Sunderland), H.McMahon (Sunderland).

239

1940-41

Manager: Wilf Gillow

1	Aug	31	(a)	York C	L	3-4	Simpson 2, Stobbart	2,700
2	Sep	7	(h)	York C	W	2-1	Stobbart 2	2,300
3		14	(a)	Newcastle U	L	0-3		5,700
4		21	(h)	Newcastle U	W	3-2	Robinson 2 (1 pen), Stobbart	3,300
5		28	(a)	Grimsby T	W	3-1	T.E.Murphy, Stobbart 2	1,500
6	Oct	5	(h)	Sheffield W	W	5-4	Stobbart 4, Simpson	2,300
7		12	(a)	Bradford	W	2-0	Danskin (og), Stobbart	1,768
8		19	(h)	Bradford	W	6-2	Fenton 2, Stobbart 2, Simpson, Peppitt	3,000
9		26	(h)	Chesterfield	L	0-3		2,500
10	Nov	2	(a)	Sheffield W	L	3-6	Simpson, Stobbart, Shepherdson	1,500
11		9	(a)	Leeds U	L	1-2	Stobbart	1,500
12		16	(h)	York C	W	6-4	Stobbart 3, Simpson, Robinson, Clayton	1,500
13		23	(a)	Bradford C	L	2-3	Baker, Ormston	1,468
14	Dec	7	(h)	Doncaster R	D	2-2	Stobbart, Robinson	1,000
15		14	(h)	Grimsby T	W	2-1	Stobbart, Forrest	700
16		25	(a)	Newcastle U	W	3-1	Fenton 2, Stobbart	4,000
17		28	(a)	Doncaster R	L	0-5		3,313
18	Feb	1	(a)	Newcastle U	L	2-6	Stobbart, Murphy	4,000
19		8	(h)	Newcastle U	W	4-3	Forrest, Gillies, Stobbart, Busby	2,000
20	Apr	5	(a)	Hull C	W	8-0	Simpson, Cochrane, Stobbart, Camsell 5	2,000
21		19	(a)	Barnsley	L	2-3	Stobbart 2	
22		26	(h)	Barnsley	W	3-2	Simpson, Forrest, Russell	1,500
23	May	3	(a)	Halifax T	L	2-4	Camsell 2	
24		24	(a)	York C	W	4-2	Forrest 3, Cochrane	2,000

Appearances
Goals

War Cup

25	Feb	15	(a)	Huddersfield T	D	2-2	Gillies 2	3,000
26	Mar	1	(h)	Huddersfield T	W	4-2	Fenton 3, Busby (pen)	5,221
27		8	(h)	Leeds U	W	2-0	Fenton 2	5,800
28		15	(h)	Leeds U	D	2-2	Stobbart, Mannion (pen)	5,600
29		22	(h)	Newcastle U	L	0-1		12,799
30		29	(a)	Newcastle U	L	0-3		12,397

Appearances
Goals

West Riding Cup

31	Jan	11	(h)	Bradford C	W	8-2	Peppitt 4, Stobbart, Mannion, Busby, Forrest	1,000
32		18	(h)	Bradford	W	5-3	Hardisty, Busby, Simpson, Stobbart, Forrest	
33	May	17	(h)	Leeds U	W	3-2	Nevins 2, Stobbart	3,400

Appearances
Goals

240

Player appearance grid (shirt numbers worn per match). Column headers (left to right): Cumming DS, Brown WH, Wilson A*, Busby M*, Forrest W, Meek J*, Monro AD*, Robinson J*, Stobbart GC, Murphy TE, Simpson R*, Gorman J*, Martin J, Camsell GH, Mould W*, Peppitt S*, Ormston A*, Smith H, Baker F*, Fenton M, Mannion WJ, Shepherdson H, Butler F*, Hardisty JRE*, Clayton S*, Johnson A*, Hardwick GFM, Gillies J*, Murphy DA, Cochrane T*, McCabe JJ, Russell JW*, Woffinden RS*, Gilbraith RE, Bray E*, Fowler HN, Stuart RW, Hepworth AW*, McMahon H*.

Cumming DS	Brown WH	Wilson A*	Busby M*	Forrest W	Meek J*	Monro AD*	Robinson J*	Stobbart GC	Murphy TE	Simpson R*	Gorman J*	Martin J	Camsell GH	Mould W*	Peppitt S*	Ormston A*	Smith H	Baker F*	Fenton M	Mannion WJ	Shepherdson H	Butler F*	Hardisty JRE*	Clayton S*	Johnson A*	Hardwick GFM	Gillies J*	Murphy DA	Cochrane T*	McCabe JJ	Russell JW*	Woffinden RS*	Gilbraith RE	Bray E*	Fowler HN	Stuart RW	Hepworth AW*	McMahon H*	Match
1	2	3	4	5	6	7	8	9	10	11																													1
1	2		4	6		7		9	10	11	3	5	8																										2
1	2		4	6				9	10	11	3			5	7	8																							3
	2		4	6		8	9	10	7	3		5					1			11																			4
1	2		4	6		10		9	8	11	3			7	5																							5
1	2		4	10				9	8	11	3	6		5	7																							6
1	2		4	10				9	8	11	3	6		5	7																							7
	2		4	6				9		11	3	5		7			1		8	10																			8
1	2		4					9	8	11		6		5	7					10															3		10	11	9
1	2							9	8	4		6	10		3	5																					10	11	10
1	2				6			9	8	11	3			7	5														4										11
	2				6			10	9	7	3			5			1		8									4	11										12
1	2				6			9		7	3			5					10	11								4	8										13
1	2				6			10	9	11	3			7	5				8									4											14
1			6	10				9		11	3			5					8								4	2											15
1			6					8	7	11		5							9	10							4	2											16
1			6					8	7	11	2	5							9	10							4		3										17
1	6							9	10	7	3			5					8								4	2	11										18
1			6	10				9			3			5	7				8								4	2	11										19
1								8		7	3	5	9													4	2			11	6	10							20
1			6					9		7	3																2		10		8	4	5	11					21
1			4	10				9		7		6											5				2		11		8				3				22
1			4					8		7	3	6	9									10		5				2		11										23
1				10				9		7		6											4				2		11	8			5	3					24
21	**15**	**1**	**1**	**3**	**19**	**1**	**2**	**5**	**24**	**13**	**22**	**18**	**13**	**7**	**13**	**6**	**2**	**3**	**2**	**4**	**9**	**1**	**4**	**10**	**2**	**9**	**1**	**2**	**5**	**2**	**3**	**1**	**2**	**1**	**2**	**1**	**1**	**1**	
1	6				4				26	2	8			7				1	1		1	4		1				1			1	2		1					Goals

1 own-goal

Cumming DS	Brown WH	Wilson A*	Busby M*	Forrest W	Meek J*	Monro AD*	Robinson J*	Stobbart GC	Murphy TE	Simpson R*	Gorman J*	Martin J	Camsell GH	Mould W*	Peppitt S*	Ormston A*	Smith H	Baker F*	Fenton M	Mannion WJ	Shepherdson H	Butler F*	Hardisty JRE*	Clayton S*	Johnson A*	Hardwick GFM	Gillies J*	Murphy DA	Cochrane T*	McCabe JJ	Russell JW*	Woffinden RS*	Gilbraith RE	Bray E*	Fowler HN	Stuart RW	Hepworth AW*	McMahon H*	Match
			4	6				8	7	3	5						1		9	10								2			11								25
	2		6	5				8		11	3			7			1		9	10								4											26
1	2		6					8		11	3	5		7					9	10								4											27
1	2		4					8		11	3	5		7					9	10												6							28
1			6					8		7	3	5							9	10	2		4										11						29
1			4	6				8		3	5			7					9	10	2												11						30
4	**3**		**3**	**6**				**6**		**5**	**6**	**5**		**4**			**2**		**6**	**6**	**2**		**3**				**1**	**1**			**2**	**1**						
	1							**1**											**5**	**1**												**2**						Goals

Cumming DS	Brown WH	Wilson A*	Busby M*	Forrest W	Meek J*	Monro AD*	Robinson J*	Stobbart GC	Murphy TE	Simpson R*	Gorman J*	Martin J	Camsell GH	Mould W*	Peppitt S*	Ormston A*	Smith H	Baker F*	Fenton M	Mannion WJ	Shepherdson H	Butler F*	Hardisty JRE*	Clayton S*	Johnson A*	Hardwick GFM	Gillies J*	Murphy DA	Cochrane T*	McCabe JJ	Russell JW*	Woffinden RS*	Gilbraith RE	Bray E*	Fowler HN	Stuart RW	Hepworth AW*	McMahon H*	Match
1			6	10				9		11	3			5	7				8									4	2										31
1			6	10				9		11	3			5	7				8									4	2										32
1			6	10				9	7	3	5																		4	2						8				33
3			**3**	**3**				**3**	**3**	**3**	**1**			**2**	**2**				**2**									**3**	**3**						**1**				
			2	**2**				**3**	**1**						**4**				**1**									**1**											Goals

S.Pearson* played number 10 in Match 11; J.O.Spuhler* played number 7 in Match 15; H.Ferrier* played number 3 in Match 16; L.Nevins* played number 11 in Match 33 and scored twice.

Guest Players
F.Baker (Stoke C), E.Bray (Barnsley), M.Busby (Liverpool), F.Butler (Smith's Dock), S.Clayton (Notts C), T.Cochrane (Bradford C), H.Ferrier (Barnsley), J.Gillies (Clyde), J.Gorman (Sunderland), J.R.E.Hardisty (Bishop Auckland), A.Johnson (Norwich C), H.McMahon (Sunderland), J.Meek (Swansea T), A.D.Monro (Blackpool), W.Mould (Stoke C), L.Nevins (Newcastle U), A.Ormston (Stoke C), S.C.Pearson (Manchester C), S.Peppitt (Stoke C), J.Robinson (Sheffield W), J.W.Russell (Norwich C), R.Simpson (Darlington), J.O.Spuhler (Sunderland), A.Wilson (South Bank East End), R.S.Woffenden (Barnsley).

1941-42

Manager: Wilf Gillow

1	Aug	30	(h)	Huddersfield T	W 3-1	Mannion, Camsell, Robinson	3,600
2	Sep	6	(a)	Huddersfield T	W 4-2	Robinson, Cochrane, Camsell 2	2,623
3		13	(a)	York C	L 5-9	Robinson 2, Stobbart, Camsell 2	3,600
4		20	(h)	York C	W 5-2	Robinson 3, Kinnear, Camsell	4,900
5		27	(h)	Gateshead	D 1-1	Robinson	5,900
6	Oct	4	(a)	Gateshead	L 1-4	Camsell	7,000
7		11	(a)	Sunderland	D 4-4	Robinson (pen), Forrest, Stobbart 2	10,000
8		18	(h)	Sunderland	D 2-2	Stobbart, Simpson	10,000
9		25	(h)	Bradford	L 0-2		4,000
10	Nov	1	(a)	Bradford	L 0-1		4,000
11		8	(a)	Leeds U	W 3-2	Kinnear 2, Warburton	2,000
12		15	(h)	Leeds U	L 1-2	Warburton	3,300
13		22	(a)	Barnsley	L 1-3	Towers	3,000
14		29	(h)	Barnsley	W 3-2	Cochrane, Forrest, Kinnear	2,000
15	Dec	6	(h)	Newcastle U	L 0-7		3,000
16		13	(a)	Newcastle U	L 4-7	Towers, Simpson, McCabe, Reid	8,920
17		20	(a)	Bradford C	L 1-5	Towers	2,000
18		25	(h)	Bradford C	W 6-0	Dawson 4, Towers, Reid (pen)	3,000

Appearances
Goals

League Cup (Qualifying Competition)

19	Dec	27	(a)	Sunderland	L 0-6		9,000
20	Jan	3	(h)	Sunderland	W 3-0	Taylor, Stobbart 2	5,000
21		10	(a)	Bradford	D 1-1	Laking	2,000
22		17	(h)	Bradford	L 1-2	Dawson	
23		31	(h)	York C	D 3-3	Cochrane 2, Towers	2,000
24	Feb	14	(a)	Gateshead	W 3-1	Taylor 2, Dawson	2,500
25		21	(h)	Newcastle U	W 4-1	Taylor 3 (1 pen), Cochrane	2,600
26		28	(a)	Newcastle U	D 1-1	Taylor	7,400
27	Mar	14	(h)	Gateshead	W 7-1	Stobbart 4, Cochrane 2, Dawson	3,500
28		21	(a)	York C	D 1-1	Stobbart	4,000

Appearances
Goals

League North (Second Championship)

29	Mar	28	(a)	Sunderland	W 2-1	Camsell, Stobbart	3,500
30	Apr	4	(h)	Bradford	W 3-2	Taylor 3 (1 pen)	5,600
31		6	(a)	Bradford	L 0-2		6,000
32		11	(h)	Newcastle U	L 2-3	Dawson 2	3,000
33		16	(a)	York C	L 1-4	Camsell	
34		18	(a)	Newcastle U	L 1-3	Towers	4,500
35		25	(h)	Leeds U	L 2-3	Dawson (pen), Johnson	2,500
36	May	9	(a)	Leeds U	W 2-1	Forrest, Dawson	2,000

Matches 19 to 28 also included in Second Championship analysis.

Appearances
Goals

Appearance / team-selection grid (shirt numbers by player and match).

Matches 1–18

Cumming DS	Johnson A*	Ferrier H*	McCabe JJ	Martin J	Forrest W	Simpson R*	Mannion WJ	Camsell GH	Robinson J*	Cochrane T*	Fowler HN	Murphy DA	Stobbart GC	Kinnear D*	Shepherdson H	Boyes W*	Sherwood AW*	Brown WH	Stuart RW	Kirk J*	Hardisty JRE*	Warburton A*	Wright RCA*	Kelly TW*	Towers J*	Knight G*	Arran R*	Blenkinsopp TW*	Reid JDJ*	Weston RP*	Dawson T*	Match
1	2	3	4	5	6	7	8	9	10	11																						1
1	2	3	4	5	6	7	8	9	10	11																						2
1		3	4			7		9	10	11	2	6	8																			3
1	2	3	4	5	6	7		9	8	11							10															4
1	2	3	4	5	6	7	8	9	10	11																						5
1		3	4	5	6	7	8	9	10								2	11														6
1	2	3	4		6	7		8	10							9	5	11														7
1			4	5		7	8		10							9		6	11	2	3											8
1			4	5		7	8									9		10	3	2	6											9
1	2	3	4	5		7	8								6		9			11				10								10
1		3	4	5	10	7								11		2	9							8	6							11
1		3		4	10	7								11			9		5			2		8	6							12
1	5			6	10	7		9		2													4	8								13
1		3		4	6	7		9		11					10					2				8								14
1			4	3	6			9		11					8							2			5	10						15
	2			4	6		7			11												3			8	10	1	5	9			16
				4	6			8								2						3			11	10	1	5	9			17
				4			7	8														3			11	10	1	2	5	6	9	18

Appearances (totals): 15, 8, 11, 15, 14, 13, 16, 9, 9, 8, 10, 2, 3, 5, 5, 4, 2, 4, 1, 2, 6, 1, 3, 2, 2, 5, 4, 3, 3, 3, 1, 1

Goals: 1, —, 2, 2, 1, 7, 9, 2, —, —, 4, 4, —, —, —, —, —, 2, —, —, 4, —, —, —, —, 2, —, 4

Matches 19–28

Cumming DS	Johnson A*	Ferrier H*	McCabe JJ	Martin J	Forrest W	Simpson R*	Mannion WJ	Camsell GH	Robinson J*	Fowler HN	Murphy DA	Stobbart GC	Shepherdson H	Brown WH	Sherwood AW*	Kirk J*	Warburton A*	Wright RCA*	Kelly TW*	Towers J*	Knight G*	Arran R*	Blenkinsopp TW*	Reid JDJ*	Weston RP*	Dawson T*	Hardwick GFM	Taylor PT*	Laking GE	Gilbraith RE	Middleton MY*	Match
		3	4		5	7	8	9												11	10		2			6						19
1	2				6					11	4	7							10					9	3	8						20
1					6	7				11	3	9							10					8	2	4						21
			4		6					11		7		2					10	3				9	8	5						22
	2			5	6	7			3	11									10	5			9	8	4	1						23
	2			3	6	7				11		9							10	5			4	8		1						24
	2			3	6		8			11		7							10	5			4	9		1						25
				2	6	7				11		9							10				4	3	8	1	5					26
	2			4	6	7				11		9							10	5			8		2	1						27
		3		4	6	7		10		11		9							5				8	2	1							28

Appearances (totals): 3, 5, 2, 2, 6, 10, 7, 2, 2, 9, 1, 3, 8, 1, 9, 1, 6, 1, 8, 2, 7, 2, 3, 6, 1

Goals: 5, 7 … 3, 7, 1

Matches 29–36

Johnson A*	Ferrier H*	Martin J	Forrest W	Simpson R*	Mannion WJ	Camsell GH	Robinson J*	Fowler HN	Murphy DA	Stobbart GC	Brown WH	Sherwood AW*	Warburton A*	Wright RCA*	Towers J*	Knight G*	Arran R*	Blenkinsopp TW*	Reid JDJ*	Weston RP*	Hardwick GFM	Taylor PT*	Laking GE	Gilbraith RE	Middleton MY*	Baxter RD	Price WB*	Match
	3		4	6	7		10	11		9		5							8					1				29
	3	2	6	7	8			11		9					5	4		10		1				1				30
			6	10	7			11		9				4	8			2	1	5								31
	2	3	6	7		9		11						10	5	8			4	1								32
	2	5	6	7		9		11						10	8				1	4								33
			6			9		11			2	4		10	8				1	5								34
		5	6			9		11						10	8				1	3								35
	2	3	5	6	7	9		11						10	8				4	1								36

Appearances (totals): 3, 3, 7, 8, 6, 4, 8, 4, 8, 6, 1, 1, 1, 5, 3, 8, 1, 1, 2, 8, 2, 2

Goals: 1, 1 … 1, 2 … 4, 3

T.Butler played number 5 in Match 3; G.Stephenson* played number 11 in Match 9; T.Mulroy* played number 3 in Match 13; H.Gray* played number 11 in Match 13; R.B.Morris played number 5 in Match 14; J.Kirk played number 2 in Match 14; D.McKerrell* played number 7 in Match 15; J.Denmark* played number 5 in Match 20; J.Yeats* played number 5 in Match 21; H.Smith played number 1 in Match 22; G.Hepplewhite* played number 2 in Match 29; R.G.Jones* played number 3 in Match 31; D.R.Graham* played number 3 in Match 33; W.K.McLean* played number 3 in Match 34; S.Rickaby* played number 7 in Match 34; G.Hepplewhite* played number 2 in Match 35; R.J.E.Birkett* played number 7 in Match 35; T.Johnson* played number 8 in Match 35.

Guest Players
R.Arran (South Bank Juniors), R.J.E.Birkett (Newcastle United), T.W.Blenkinsopp (Grimsby Town), W.Boyes (Everton), T.Cochrane (Bradford), T.Dawson (Charlton Athletic), J.Denmark (Newcastle United), H.Ferrier (Barnsley), D.R.Graham (Leicester City), H.Gray (Barnsley), J.R.E.Hardisty (Bishop Auckland), G.Hepplewhite (Huddersfield Town), A.Johnson (Norwich City), R.G.Jones (York City), T.W.Kelly (Darlington), D.Kinnear (East Fife), J.Kirk (Clyde), G.Knight (Burnley), D.McKerrell (East Fife), W.K.McLean (South Bank Juniors), M.Y.Middleton (Plymouth Argyle), T.Mulroy (South Bank), W.B.Price (Tranmere Rovers), J.D.J.Reid (Stockport County), S.Rickaby (South Bank Juniors), J.Robinson (Sheffield Wednesday), J.W.Russell (Sunderland), H.W.Sherwood ((Reading), R.Simpson (Darlington), G.Stephenson, P.T.Taylor (Preston North End), J.Towers (Darlington), A.Warburton (Queen's Park Rangers), R.P.Weston (Plymouth Argyle), R.C.A.Wright (Charlton Athletic).

1942-43

Manager: Wilf Gillow

1	Aug	29	(a)	Leeds U	W	1-0	Simpson	3,000
2	Sep	5	(h)	Leeds U	W	2-0	Simpson, Dawson	3,500
3		12	(a)	Bradford	D	0-0		3,500
4		19	(h)	Bradford	D	2-2	Simpson, Owen	4,000
5		26	(a)	York C	D	2-2	Dawson, Stobbart	3,448
6	Oct	3	(h)	York C	L	2-3	Dawson, Kearney	
7		10	(h)	Bradford C	L	2-3	Wharton, Kearney	3,000
8		17	(a)	Bradford C	W	3-2	Dawson, Stobbart, Wharton	2,000
9		24	(h)	Huddersfield T	D	2-2	Simpson, Stobbart	2,500
10		31	(a)	Huddersfield T	L	1-4	Simpson	3,155
11	Nov	7	(a)	Sunderland	L	1-4	Wharton (pen)	8,500
12		14	(h)	Sunderland	L	3-4	Wharton 2 (1 pen), Stobbart	5,500
13		21	(a)	Newcastle U	L	0-3		7,000
14		28	(h)	Newcastle U	L	1-6	Hardisty	3,500
15	Dec	5	(a)	Gateshead	L	0-5		2,000
16		12	(h)	Gateshead	L	2-3	Stobbart 2	
17		19	(h)	Sunderland	L	2-7	Stobbart, Dawson (pen)	2,000
18		25	(a)	Sunderland	W	4-0	Harrington, Stobbart, Wilson 2	

Appearances
Goals

League North Cup (Qualifying Competition)

19	Dec	26	(a)	Newcastle U	L	2-3	Stobbart, Wilson	13,300
20	Jan	2	(h)	Newcastle U	L	3-7	Stobbart, Franklin, Dawson	2,300
21		9	(h)	Sunderland	W	4-1	Franklin, Carr 2, Stobbart	2,700
22		16	(a)	Sunderland	L	0-7		6,000
23		23	(h)	Gateshead	L	2-3	Wharton, Rudkin	3,500
24		30	(a)	Gateshead	L	0-6		3,400
25	Feb	6	(h)	Huddersfield T	L	1-2	Dawson	2,000
26		13	(a)	Huddersfield T	L	0-5		3,544
27		20	(h)	York C	L	1-5	Warburton	2,700
28		27	(a)	York C	L	0-6		4,500

Appearances
Goals

League North (Second Championship)

29	Mar	6	(a)	Leeds U	L	2-3	Franklin, Laking	2,000
30		13	(h)	Leeds U	L	2-3	Bowers, Laking	2,500
31		20	(a)	Sunderland	L	0-8		4,000
32		27	(h)	Sunderland	W	1-0	Gorman (og)	2,100
33	Apr	3	(h)	Newcastle U	W	2-1	Wharton, Towers	3,000
34		10	(a)	Newcastle U	L	0-4		7,000
35		17	(a)	Halifax T	W	4-2	Bowers 3, Dicks	3,000
36		24	(h)	Halifax T	W	7-3	Farrington 3, Johnson, Wharton, Bowers 2	2,000

Appearances
Goals

Middleton MY*	Johnson A*	Stuart RW	Hardisty JRE*	Park W*	Forrest W	Owen W*	Dawson T*	Stobbart GC	Towers J*	Simpson R*	Burchell GS*	Wharton G*	Martin J	Shepherdson H	Kearney SF*	Murphy DA	Brown WH	Brown RCA*	Wilson K	Warburton A*	Nicholson WE*	Sargent F*	Osborne F*	Douglass PG	Harrington DJA	McMahon H*	Gilbraith RE	Franklin JL	Connor J*	Rudkin TW*	Arran R*	Dent JA	Laking GE	French JW	Bowers P	Johnson T*	Cassidy W*	Farrington R*	Match
1	2	3	4	5	6	7	8	9	10	11																													1
1		3	4	5	6	7	9		10	11	2	8																											2
1	2	3		5	6		8	9	10	11	4	7																											3
1	2	3	4			7	9		10	11	8	6	5																										4
1	2	3	4	5		7	8	9	10	11	6																												5
1			4	5	6		8		10	11	2	3	7	9																									6
1		3	4	5			8		10	7	2	6			9	11																							7
1		3		5			8	9	10	11	2	6	7				4																						8
1	2				6		8	9	10	7					5			3	4	11																			9
1	2			5	6		8		10	7		4	3		9						11																		10
1	2		4	5	6		8	9	10	11		3	7																										11
1		3	4	5			8	9	10	7	2	6									11																		12
1	2		4		6		8	9	10	11					5			3	7																				13
1			4	5	6	2				7					3										8	9	10	11											14
1			6	5		4		8		7		2			3										9	10	11												15
1			4	5	6			9		7		2			3		8								10	11													16
1		3		5		4	8	9				2			6		7								10	11													17
1						2		9	6	7			3		5		11								10		4	8											18
18	**6**	**11**	**12**	**14**	**10**	**4**	**16**	**11**	**16**	**17**	**5**	**11**	**13**	**1**	**4**	**2**	**2**	**3**	**3**	**1**	**2**			**2**	**5**	**4**	**1**	**1**											
	1			**1**	**5**		**8**	**5**	**5**			**2**					**2**								**1**														
1				6		2	9	8	7				3		5	11								10	4														19
1	2			5			8	9		7	4				6									11		10													20
1		3		4	9		7			6	2				5									11	8		3												21
1			4	9	10			6			2	5				7								11	8	3													22
1			6	9		10		8	4		2	5				7									3	11													23
1			6	9		10	7	4	2		3	5												8	11														24
		3	6	8		9	4	2			5	11		7		10									1														25
1	2		3	4		7		6			11	9			10		8								1		2	6											26
		3		7	10		4	6			2		9			11								8			5												27
		3		6			10		4			11	9			8									1	5	2												28
7	**4**	**6**	**3**	**8**	**5**	**6**	**5**	**8**	**2**	**3**	**2**	**7**	**4**	**3**		**3**	**1**	**7**	**2**		**2**			**5**	**4**	**1**	**1**												
	2	**3**							**1**				**1**			**1**									**2**		**1**												
								4					11	10									8			1	2	6											29
		3						10	5				11	4									8			1	2	6	9										30
		3			7			4	2														8			1	5	6	9	10									31
1			6			11		2															4	8			3	9	5	7									32
1			6			11	10	2															4	8			3	9	5	7									33
1			6		9	11		2															4	8			10	5	7										34
1					6	8	3				11								10		4		5			3	9	10	4	7									35
1					11	8	6	2															5			3	9	10	4	7									36
5	**2**	**3**		**2**	**5**	**5**	**8**	**1**				**3**	**2**				**1**		**4**	**6**		**3**	**3**	**2**	**6**	**4**	**5**	**5**	**4**										
				1		**2**																			**1**			**2**	**6**	**1**		**3**							

1 own-goal

G.F.M.Hardwick played number 3 in Match 20; E.M.Carr* played number 10 in Match 21; R.C.R.Craddock played number 1 in Match 27; E.Goldsborough played number 7 in Match 28; H.Hirst played number 3 in Match 29; G.A.Mordue* played number 5 in Match 29; F.Buckley* played number 7 in Match 29; J.Oliver* played number 9 in Match 29; S.Rickaby* played number 7 in Match 30; T.O.Farrage* played number 11 in Match 31; J.J.Carey* played number 10 in Match 32; A.Livingstone* played number 3 in Match 34; R.W.Dicks* played number 7 in Match 35 and scored a goal.

Guest Players

R.Arran (South Bank Juniors), F.Buckley (Oldham Athletic), G.S.Burchell (Romford), J.J.Carey (Manchester United), E.M.Carr (Arsenal), W.Cassidy (Gateshead), J.Connor (Bolton Wanderers), T.Dawson (Charlton Athletic), R.W.Dicks (Dulwich Hamlet), T.O.Farrage (Birmingham), R.Farrington (Bradford City), J.R.E.Hardisty (Bishop Auckland), H.Hirst (Bradford), A.Johnson (Norwich City), T.Johnson (Gateshead), S.F.Kearney (Accrington Stanley), A.Livingstone (Gateshead), H.McMahon (Sunderland), M.Y.Middleton (Plymouth Argyle), G.A.Mordue (Tottenham Hotspur), W.E.Nicholson (Tottenham Hotspur), J.Oliver (Burnley), F.Osborne (Aston Villa), W.Owen (Everton), W.Park (Blackpool), S.Rickaby (South Bank Juniors), T.W.Rudkin (Grimsby Town), F.Sargent (Tottenham Hotspur), R.Simpson (Darlington), J.Towers (Darlington), A.Warburton (Queen's Park Rangers), G.Wharton (Portsmouth), R.C.A.Wright (Charlton Athletic).

1943-44

Manager: Wilf Gillow

1	Aug	18	(a)	Hartlepools U	L 0-1	1,500
2	Sep	4	(h)	Hartlepools U	W 3-2 Wright (pen), Skinner, Farrington	5,000
3		11	(h)	Darlington	L 2-6 Lyon 2	
4		18	(a)	Darlington	D 3-3 Lyon 3 (1 pen)	7,024
5		25	(a)	Leeds U	L 0-3	3,000
6	Oct	2	(h)	Leeds U	D 3-3 Stobbart 2, Dicks	2,500
7		9	(h)	Bradford C	L 1-8 Stobbart	3,000
8		16	(a)	Bradford C	D 1-1 Dicks	4,596
9		23	(h)	Gateshead	W 3-0 Murphy, Parlane, Stobbart	2,000
10		30	(a)	Gateshead	L 3-5 Stobbart 2, Farrington	3,000
11	Nov	6	(h)	York C	D 1-1 Parlane	3,500
12		13	(a)	York C	L 3-5 Stobbart 2, Murphy	4,000
13		20	(h)	Hartlepools U	L 1-3 Stobbart	4,000
14		27	(a)	Hartlepools U	W 4-3 Farrington 2, Forrest, Stobbart	6,000
15	Dec	4	(h)	Newcastle U	D 1-1 Parlane	3,000
16		11	(a)	Newcastle U	D 1-1 Parlane	8,000
17		18	(a)	Sunderland	L 1-6 Parlane	4,000
18		25	(h)	Sunderland	W 4-0 Hardisty, Hodgson, Stobbart 2	

Appearances
Sub Appearances
Goals

League North Cup (Qualifying Rounds)

19	Dec	27	(h)	Hartlepools U	D 1-1 Stobbart (pen)	8,500
20	Jan	1	(a)	Hartlepools U	D 1-1 Stobbart	7,000
21		8	(a)	Gateshead	L 1-2 Dicks	2,500
22		15	(h)	Gateshead	W 4-2 Oakes 2, Parlane, Brunskill	4,500
23		22	(h)	Darlington	L 0-1	6,000
24		29	(a)	Darlington	D 0-0	10,591
25	Feb	5	(h)	Newcastle U	W 2-1 Parlane, Stephens	5,000
26		12	(a)	Newcastle U	L 1-4 Stobbart	12,000
27		19	(a)	Sunderland	L 0-3	3,000
28		26	(h)	Sunderland	L 4-5 Oakes, Gallagher, Murphy, Wilson	3,000

Appearances
Sub Appearances
Goals

League North (Second Championship)

29	Mar	4	(a)	Sunderland	L 1-4 Gallagher	1,000
30		11	(h)	Sunderland	L 2-3 Oakes 2	3,000
31		18	(a)	Gateshead	L 1-2 Hodgson	2,000
32		25	(h)	Gateshead	W 4-1 Stobbart 2, Hodgson, Parlane	2,000
33		29	(a)	Sunderland	D 3-3 Wilson, Martin, J.Bell (og)	2,000
34	Apr	1	(a)	Darlington	W 3-2 Parlane 2, Oakes	6,000
35		8	(h)	Darlington	L 1-4 Parlane	3,500
36		10	(a)	Darlington	L 2-3 Martin, Stephens	5,536
37		15	(a)	Hartlepools U	W 6-2 Stobbart 5 (1 pen), Warburton	4,000
38		22	(h)	Hartlepools U	L 0-5	2,000
39	May	6	(h)	Sunderland	W 4-2 Harrington 2, Stobbart, McGorrighan	2,500

Appearances
Sub Appearances
Goals

	Cumming DS	Martin J	Stuart RW	Brunskill N*	Birse CV*	Wright RCA*	Farrington R*	Murphy TE	Lyon TK*	Barber E*	Wilson K	Dicks RW	Skinner G*	Crack FW*	Blenkinsopp TW*	Parlane J*	Laking GE	Gilbraith RE	Harrington DJA	Stobbart GC	Middleton MY*	French JW	Brown WH	Robinson JN	Forrest W	Hodgson S*	Shepherdson H	Hardisty JRE*	Oakes J*	Towers J*	Stevens RF*	Cassidy W*	Gallagher DE	Franklin JL	McGorrighan G*	Warburton G*	Davies WC	Hubble L*	Weir A*	
	1	2	3	4	5	6	7	8	9	10	11																													1
	1	2	3	4	5	6					11		9	10	7	8																								2
	1		3		4	5			9		10				7	8	11																							3
	1	6	3	4	5		7			10					11		9	2	8																					4
	1	5	3	4				8	10							6		2	7	11																				5
	1	2	3	4						10			7			11	5	8		6		9																		6
	1	2	3	4	5				7	10					11		8		6	9																				7
		5	3	8					7	10					11		2	4			1	6																		8
		5	3						7	10					11		8	4		9	1	6	2																	9
		5	3	2					7	10					8		4	11	9	1	6																			10
			3	2						10			7			11	5	8		4		9	1	6																11
		4	3	8						10				11	7			2			9	1	6		5															12
		4	3	8	5					10				11	7			4			9	1	6		2															13
		5	3	2					7	10					11		8			9	1		6																	14
			3	2					7	8				11			9		6		1			10	4	5														15
			3	2					10	8				11			5	9	6		1				4															16
		3		2			11								7		5			4	9	1		6																17
			3		2		7							11			5	10		6	9	1			4		8													18
	7	14	16	16	5	4	12	14	5	2	3	14	2	5	7	11	3	12	2	10	11	6	1	2	2	4	1	1												
		1	4	2	5				2	1			5								12					1	1	1												

	Cumming DS	Martin J	Stuart RW	Brunskill N*	Birse CV*	Wright RCA*	Farrington R*	Murphy TE	Lyon TK*	Barber E*	Wilson K	Dicks RW	Skinner G*	Crack FW*	Blenkinsopp TW*	Parlane J*	Laking GE	Gilbraith RE	Harrington DJA	Stobbart GC	Middleton MY*	French JW	Brown WH	Robinson JN	Forrest W	Hodgson S*	Shepherdson H	Hardisty JRE*	Oakes J*	Towers J*	Stevens RF*	Cassidy W*	Gallagher DE	Franklin JL	McGorrighan G*	Warburton G*	Davies WC	Hubble L*	Weir A*	
		3	2			6		7						11			5	10		4		9	1							8										19
	7	2						8			11					5	10	6		9	1	3			4															20
	7	3	2								11					5	9	6		1	8		10	4																21
	11	3	8										9	6		7	1		2		4	5		10																22
	11		2										5	8		7	1	3			4		9	10																23
	5		2						7							8	1	3		10	4			9	6	11														24
	5								7							8	1	2		10	4			9	6	11														25
	2								8		11					6	9	1	3		4			7	10		5													26
		2							8		11					6	9	1	3		4			7	10		5													27
		2						10		11			5	9		4	1	3					7	6	2	8														28
	7	4	7			1		3	2	1	7		5	8		7	6	10	8	1	3	8	1	1	7	6	1	2	1											
		1						1		1	1		2				3								3		1													

	Cumming DS	Martin J	Stuart RW	Brunskill N*	Birse CV*	Wright RCA*	Farrington R*	Murphy TE	Lyon TK*	Barber E*	Wilson K	Dicks RW	Skinner G*	Crack FW*	Blenkinsopp TW*	Parlane J*	Laking GE	Gilbraith RE	Harrington DJA	Stobbart GC	Middleton MY*	French JW	Brown WH	Robinson JN	Forrest W	Hodgson S*	Shepherdson H	Hardisty JRE*	Oakes J*	Towers J*	Stevens RF*	Cassidy W*	Gallagher DE	Franklin JL	McGorrighan G*	Warburton G*	Davies WC	Hubble L*	Weir A*	
			2		10						11					5		4		9	1	3							7	6			8							29
			2	6							11					5	9				1	3			4		10	7					8							30
	2				10						11					7		6	9	1	3				4						5	8								31
	2										11					8		6	9	1	3				4		7	10			5									32
	7		2								11					4			9	1		3					6				5		8	10						33
	3		2								11					5	8	6	9	1					4		7	10												34
	3		2								11					5	8	6	9	1					4		7	10												35
	1	4		2							11					5			9		3						7	6	10				8							36
											11					2		4	10	9						7	6				5		8	1	3					37
											11					2		4	7		3						6				5		8	10	1			9		38
			2								7					4	11	9	1			3					6				5		10	8						39
	1	6	6	2	2						10	1				7	5	9	2	10	8	6		2	5		1	7	9	1	8	2	3	4	2	1	1	1	
	2										1					4		2	8			2			3		1	1			1	1	1						

1 own-goal

F.M.Evans* played at number 2 in Match 3; R.Walton* played at number 6 in Match 3; J.F.Stephen* played at number 9 in Match 8; A.W.Kerr* played at number 7 in Match 16; R.A.Fallaize* played at number 9 in Match 5 and number 8 in Match 17; J.L.Franklin played at number 10 in Match 17; E.C.Steele* played at number 6 in Match 23; G.F.M.Hardwick played at number 3 in Match 25.

Guest Players

E.Barber (Everton), C.V.Birse (Hibs), T.W.Blenkinsopp (Grimsby T), N.Brunskill (Barnsley), W.Cassidy (Gateshead), F.W.Crack (Grimsby T), F.M.Evans (Tottenham H), R.A.Fallaize (Leeds U), R.Farrington (Bradford C), S.Hodgson (Grimsby T), L.Hubble (Newcastle U), A.W.Kerr (Aston V), T.K.Lyon (Chesterfield), M.Y.Middleton (Plymouth A), J.Oakes (Huddersfield T), J.Parlane (Rangers), G.Skinner (Tottenham H), E.C.Steele (Stockport C), J.F.Stephen (Bradford PA), R.F.Stevens, J.Towers (Darlington), R.Walton (Leicester C), G.Warburton (Chester), A.Weir (Glentoran), R.C.A.Wright (Charlton A).

1944-45

Manager: David Jack

1	Aug	26	(a)	Sunderland	D	0-0		15,000
2	Sep	2	(h)	Sunderland	L	1-5	Moody	3,000
3		9	(h)	Gateshead	W	4-1	Stuart (pen), Dixon, Long 2	4,000
4		16	(a)	Gateshead	D	5-5	Stobbart 4, Warbutton	2,000
5		23	(h)	Leeds U	W	3-2	Moody 2, Dixon	4,500
6		30	(a)	Leeds U	L	2-4	Knight (og), Moody	8,000
7	Oct	7	(a)	Newcastle U	W	1-0	Bowie	14,000
8		14	(h)	Newcastle U	L	2-8	Murphy, McGorrighan	5,000
9		21	(h)	Bradford C	L	2-3	Wilson, Stuart (pen)	3,000
10		28	(a)	Bradford C	L	0-2		4,300
11	Nov	4	(h)	Hartlepools U	W	3-2	Harrington, Stobbart 2	6,000
12		11	(h)	Hartlepools U	L	0-3		6,000
13		18	(h)	Huddersfield T	L	0-1		6,700
14		25	(a)	Huddersfield T	L	1-5	Wainwright	7,532
15	Dec	2	(a)	York C	L	1-5	Stobbart	4,941
16		9	(h)	York C	W	4-3	Dean, Nevins, Stobbart 2	4,000
17		16	(h)	Darlington	D	3-3	Fenton 2, Long	8,000
18		23	(a)	Darlington	L	2-5	Stobbart, Fenton	8,097

Appearances
Goals

League North Cup (Qualifying Competition)

19	Dec	26	(h)	Hartlepools U	D	0-0		9,600
20		30	(a)	Hartlepools U	L	4-6	Fenton, Stobbart 2, Johnson	8,000
21	Jan	6	(a)	Newcastle U	L	1-5	Rowley	20,000
22		13	(h)	Newcastle U	W	5-3	Stobbart 4, Long	5,000
23		20	(a)	Sunderland	L	3-4	Stobbart 2, Larner	5,300
24		27	(h)	Sunderland	W	2-1	Stobbart 2	
25	Feb	3	(h)	Darlington	L	0-1		8,000
26		10	(a)	Darlington	L	4-6	Stobbart 3, Wilson	7,344
27		17	(h)	Gateshead	L	2-3	Wass, Stobbart	4,000
28		24	(a)	Gateshead	W	2-1	Stobbart, Stuart (pen)	6,000

Appearances
Goals

League North (Second Championship)

29	Mar	3	(a)	Darlington	L	0-1		4,697
30		10	(h)	Newcastle U	L	1-5	Wainwright	5,000
31		17	(h)	Sunderland	W	2-1	Stobbart 2	9,000
32		24	(a)	Hartlepools U	L	0-3		
33		31	(h)	Hartlepools U	L	1-3	Stobbart (pen)	4,132
34	Apr	2	(h)	Gateshead	W	3-1	Wass, Johnson, Robinson	
35		7	(a)	Bradford	L	1-2	Stobbart	6,000
36		14	(h)	Bradford	W	1-0	Stobbart	4,000
37		21	(h)	Huddersfield T	W	2-1	Stobbart, Fenton	6,000
38		28	(a)	Huddersfield T	L	0-2		2,007
39	May	5	(h)	Newcastle U	D	1-1	Stobbart	4,000
40		12	(a)	Newcastle U	L	0-1		7,000
41		19	(h)	Hartlepools U	L	1-2	Stobbart ·	
42		21	(h)	Newcastle U	L	3-5	Bowes, Sloan, Forrest (pen)	

Matches 19 to 28 also included in Second Championship

Appearances
Goals

248

Player appearance / position grid (shirt numbers played per match). Column headers read vertically:

Middleton MY*	Hardwick GFM	Kinsell TH*	Brown WH	Shepherdson H	Gilbraith RE	Stuart RW	Dixon JT*	Stobbart GC	McGorrighan FO	Wilson K	French JW	Blenkinsopp TW*	Gallagher DE	Martin J	Moody J	Heweston K	Murphy TE	Long HR*	Harrington DJA	Warburton G*	Johnson T*	Robinson R	Bowie JD*	Franklin JL	Cumming DS	Wainwright EF*	Bell HD*	Forrest W	McArthur WJ*	Hamby DR*	Deans WHG*	Nevins L*	Fenton M	Thompson KH	Robinson JN	Wass W	Forster LJ*	Sales RD*	
1	2	3	4	5	6	7	8	9	10	11																													1
1						2	8	9	10	11	3	4	5	6	7																								2
1	2	3				6	8	9				5				7	4	10	11																				3
1						2		9	8	11	3					5	7	4			6	10																	4
1		3				2	10	9	8	11						5	7	4			6																		5
1						3	10	9	8	11		5				6	7	4																					6
1						2	8	9		11		3				7					6		4	5	10														7
1						2		9	8			3				7	4	11			6			5															8
1						2		9	8	11		3				5	7	4			6				10														9
1						2		9				3				5	7	4	11	10			6		8														10
1		2				3	8	9				6					7	4			11		10	5															11
1	3		4			2		9									7	6			11		10	5	8														12
				5		3		9							2		7				6	4	11			1	8	10											13
						3		9							2		11					5				1	8			4	6								14
				5		3		9			11										4	10	8				1	8	10										15
1					4	3		9							2								8					5		2	7	11							16
1					4	3		8				5									11							6		2	7		9						17
1						3		7															8	10							6		11		9	2	5		18
16	3	3	3	2	3	18	7	18	8	6	9	3	1	7	13	9	2	3	7	2	6	7	6	3	2	2	1	4	2	3	4	1	2	1	1				—
						2	2	10	1	1				4		1	3	1	1		1					1					1		1	1	3				

1 own-goal

Middleton MY*	Hardwick GFM	Kinsell TH*	Brown WH	Shepherdson H	Gilbraith RE	Stuart RW	Dixon JT*	Stobbart GC	McGorrighan FO	Wilson K	French JW	Blenkinsopp TW*	Gallagher DE	Martin J	Moody J	Heweston K	Murphy TE	Long HR*	Harrington DJA	Warburton G*	Johnson T*	Robinson R	Bowie JD*	Franklin JL	Cumming DS	Wainwright EF*	Bell HD*	Forrest W	McArthur WJ*	Hamby DR*	Deans WHG*	Nevins L*	Fenton M	Thompson KH	Robinson JN	Wass W	Forster LJ*	Sales RD*	
1						3		9				4				7			11				8					6		2				10		5			19
1						2		9				4	5								11						6			10	3								20
1						3		7				2								6	10	8							9										21
1						3		9				2					11			6	10	8	4											5					22
1				4		3		9				2					11			6			5														7		23
1		5				3		9		11										4	10		8	6											7				24
1	2					3		9									11			6			8	4										7					25
1						3		9		11	4									10						6	2								7	5			26
1						3		9		11					4					10			8	6	2									7	5				27
1		5				3		9		11					4					6	10					2								3	3	3	2		28
10			1	2	1	10		4	6	1		1	2		2	2	9		4	1	5	8	3		3	1	3	3	3	2									—
					1			15	1											1	1						1												

Middleton MY*	Hardwick GFM	Kinsell TH*	Brown WH	Shepherdson H	Gilbraith RE	Stuart RW	Dixon JT*	Stobbart GC	McGorrighan FO	Wilson K	French JW	Blenkinsopp TW*	Gallagher DE	Martin J	Moody J	Heweston K	Murphy TE	Long HR*	Harrington DJA	Warburton G*	Johnson T*	Robinson R	Bowie JD*	Franklin JL	Cumming DS	Wainwright EF*	Bell HD*	Forrest W	McArthur WJ*	Hamby DR*	Deans WHG*	Nevins L*	Fenton M	Thompson KH	Robinson JN	Wass W	Forster LJ*	Sales RD*	
1						3		9		11					4					6														2	7	5			29
1						3		9		11	7				4						8		5											2	7				30
1		5				3		9		11					4					10			8	6											7				31
1						3		9		11					8								4										2	7	5				32
1						2		9							8								6										3	7	5				33
1						2							4							8			6										3	7	5				34
1						3		9		11	5				4						8		6										2	7					35
		5				2		9		11					4					6			8										3	7					36
	?					3		9							6								5					9	2					7					37
	3					2		9							6					8			5					10						7					38
?		4	5			3		9							6													2											39
.			4			3		9							6						9	5						2											40
						2		9							6					1		5											3	7					41
		4				2		9							6							5						3					7						42
7	1		3	3		14		13		7	3		4		13		1		1	1	3	1	11					2	9	7	11		4						—
			8					1							1				1	1	1		1					1	1	1									

G.E.Laking played number 2 in Match 6; D.Miller played number 10 in Match 8; A.W.Kerr* played number 7 in Match 14; A.G.Sutherland* played number 10 in Match 14; I.Methley* played number 4 in Match 15; R.Bicknell* played number 5 in Match 15; L.Porter* played number 7 in Match 15; W.Adams* played number 6 in Match 16; J.D.Short* played number 10 in Match 17; J.R.E.Hardisty* played number 4 in Match 18 and number 8 in Match 20; C.Ferguson* played number 7 in Match 20 and number 4 in Match 21; T.Cross* played number 5 in Match 21; G.A.Rowley* played number 11 in Match 21; R.Simpson* played number 7 in Match 22; J.T.T.Shreeve* played number 2 in Matches 24 & 31; W.Temple played number 8 in Match 23; L.Larner* played number 10 in Matches 23 (scoring once) & 25; A.Chilton* played number 5 in Match 25; J.Lilley* played number 8 in Match 26; J.Stevenson* played number 7 in Match 28 and number 8 in Match 29; T.Stenson played number 10 in Matches 29, 30, 32, 33, 35, 36 & 42; W.Borrowman* played number 6 in Matches 30 & 32; W.H.Johnson* played number 8 in Match 32 and number 4 in Match 41; L.Mahon* played number 4 in Match 33; F.C.Nash played number 1 in Matches 38 to 42 inclusive; J.J.McCabe played number 4 in Match 37; P.C.Baines* played number 10 in Match 37; W.C.Davies played number 1 in Match 37; C.Woollett* played number 11 in Matches 34, 37, 38, 39, 40, 41 & 42; L.F.Howe* played number 4 in Match 38; J.Sinclair* played number 7 in Match 41; J.Sloan* played number 8 in Matches 41 & 42 (scoring once); J.Davison played number 10 in Match 41; W.Bowes played number 8 in Match 42.

Matches 34 to 42 inclusive — only incomplete newspaper reports on matches exist, positions listed are deduced.

1945-46

Manager: David Jack

Captain: Bobby Stuart

1	Aug	25	(a)	Manchester C	L	1-2	Stobbart	19,188
2	Sep	1	(h)	Manchester C	D	2-2	Stuart (pen), Stobbart	12,856
3		8	(h)	Newcastle U	L	0-6		16,419
4		12	(h)	Manchester U	W	2-1	Dews 2	6,506
5		15	(a)	Newcastle U	D	1-1	Stobbart	32,211
6		22	(a)	Sheffield W	L	1-2	Stuart (pen)	20,334
7		29	(h)	Sheffield W	W	2-0	Butler, Wass	12,506
8	Oct	6	(h)	Huddersfield T	L	2-8	Stobbart 2	14,654
9		13	(a)	Huddersfield T	L	0-7		10,436
10		20	(a)	Chesterfield	L	0-1		12,446
11		27	(h)	Chesterfield	L	0-4		15,368
12	Nov	3	(h)	Barnsley	L	2-5	Stuart (pen), Spuhler	10,121
13		10	(a)	Barnsley	D	2-2	Fenton 2	14,362
14		17	(a)	Everton	D	1-1	Spuhler	23,248
15		24	(h)	Everton	D	0-0		18,197
16	Dec	1	(h)	Bolton W	W	1-0	Stobbart	16,666
17		8	(a)	Bolton W	L	1-2	Spuhler	16,812
18		15	(h)	Preston NE	L	0-1		14,976
19		22	(a)	Preston NE	W	1-0	Spuhler	
20		25	(a)	Leeds U	L	0-1		12,217
21		26	(h)	Leeds U	W	4-1	Murphy, Fenton, Dews, Stobbart	23,019
22		29	(a)	Manchester U	L	1-4	Maddison	18,937
23	Jan	1	(h)	Sunderland	W	1-0	Robinson	29,157
24		12	(a)	Sheffield U	W	7-2	Fenton 5, Murphy, Maddison	18,565
25		19	(h)	Sheffield U	L	3-4	Dews, Fenton, Spuhler (pen)	23,473
26	Feb	2	(a)	Burnley	L	1-8	Stobbart	9,806
27		16	(a)	Stoke C	W	4-1	Spuhler, Murphy, Stobbart 2	9,123
28		23	(a)	Grimsby T	D	1-1	Spuhler	8,739
29	Mar	2	(h)	Grimsby T	W	3-1	Spuhler, Murphy 2	14,198
30		9	(h)	Blackpool	W	4-2	Fenton 2, Spuhler, Dews	23,000
31		16	(a)	Blackpool	L	1-3	Gordon	10,000
32		23	(a)	Liverpool	W	2-1	Fenton 2	30,000
33		30	(h)	Liverpool	L	2-5	Harley (og), Hardwick (pen)	25,000
34	Apr	6	(h)	Bury	W	3-0	Spuhler, Murphy, Fenton	20,000
35		10	(h)	Burnley	W	2-1	Murphy, Fenton	19,358
36		13	(a)	Bury	D	1-1	Fenton	10,000
37		19	(a)	Blackburn R	D	3-3	Spuhler, Gordon, Dews	
38		20	(h)	Bradford	W	3-0	Murphy, Dews 2	20,000
39		22	(h)	Blackburn R	W	5-1	Murphy 3, Fenton, Spuhler	24,000
40		27	(a)	Bradford	D	1-1	Chadwick	
41	May	1	(h)	Stoke C	W	3-1	Dews, Fenton 2	27,952
42		4	(a)	Sunderland	W	1-0	Fenton	32,000

Appearances
Goals

FA Cup

3	Jan	5	(a)	Leeds U	D	4-4	Murphy, Fenton, Dews 2	18,000
		9	(h)	Leeds U	W	7-2	Gordon, Hardwick (pen), Fenton 3, Spuhler, Douglas	24,000
4		26	(a)	Blackpool	L	2-3	Suart (og), Spuhler	17,160
		30	(h)	Blackpool	W	3-2	Fenton 2, Spuhler	46,556
R	Feb	4	(n*)	Blackpool	W	1-0	Hardwick (pen)	30,000
5		9	(a)	Bolton W	L	0-1		43,550
		13	(h)	Bolton W	D	1-1	Fenton	51,612

*Played at Elland Road, Leeds.

All FA Cup ties played on a two-legged basis.

Appearances
Goals

Cumming DS	Laking GE	Stuart RW	French JW	Jameson P	Johnson T*	Wass W	Stobbart GC	Fenton M	Dews G	Chadwick C	Hardwick GFM	Heweston K	Shepherdson H	Wainwright E*	McCabe JJ	Barclay R*	Price AJW*	Robinson R	Wharton G*	Attwell R*	Herd A*	McCormack JC*	Mullen J*	Douglas JS	Bell HD	Wilson K	Butler T	Bambrough N	Bowes W	Hepple G	Brown WH	Spuhler JO	Gordon J	Murphy TE	Maddison J	Watson R	Malan NF	Mannion WJ	#
1	2	3	4	5	6	7	8	9	10	11																													1
1	2	6			10	7	9			11	3	4	5	8																									2
1	2	3			11		7		10		6	4			5	8	9																						3
1	2		10				7								4			3	5	6	8	9	11																4
1	2				6	7	9		10		3				4									5	8	11													5
1		2		4		7	9		10		3			8										5	11														6
1	2	3				7	9		10						4									5	8		11												7
1	3	2					9		10		6														8		11	4	7										8
1		2			6		9		10		3													5	8		11	4	7										9
1	2	3			6	11	9		10						5									4	8		7												10
1	2	3				7	9		10						5									4	8	11				6									11
1	2	3				11	9		10						5										8					6	4	7							12
1	2				6	11	9		10		3				5									4	8							7							13
1	2				6	11	9		10		3				4									5	8							7							14
1	2					11	9		10		3				5									6	8						7		4						15
1	2						9		10						5		4	3						6	8					11	7								16
1	2					11	9				3				5		4							6	10						7	8							17
1	2					11	9		10		3				5									6	8						7	4							18
1	2						8	9			3				5								11	6	4						10	7							19
1	2						8	9	10		3				5								11	4							7	6							20
1	2					7	8	9			3				5								11	4								6	10						21
1	2				6		8	9	10		3													5	4						7		11						22
1	2	3					8	9	10						5								11	4							7	6							23
1		3						9	10						5			2						4							7	6	8	11					24
1		3	5					9	10									2						4							7	6	8	11					25
1	2					7	9								5			3						4							10		8	11					26
1	2	3						9	10						5								11	4							7	6	8						27
1	2							9	10				3		5									4							7	6	8	11					28
1	2							9	10				3		5									4							7	6	8	11					29
1								9	10				3					2						5	4						7	6	8	11					30
1								9	10				3					2						5	4						7	6	8	11					31
1								9	10				3					2						5	4						7	6	8	11	1				32
1								9	10		6		3					2						5	4						7	8	11	1	1				33
	3							9	10				5					2						4							7	6	11				8		34
	3							9	10		6		5					2						4							7		11				8		35
1	3							9	10									2						4							7	6	8				8		36
1								9	10				3		5			2						4							7	6	11				8		37
1								9	10				3					2						4							7	6	11				8		38
1								9	10				3		5			2						4							7	6	8	11					39
1								9	10	11			3					2						4							7	6	8						40
1								9	10	11			3					2						4							7	6	8				8		41
1								9	10	11			5					2						4							7	6	8						42
38	16	27	2	2	10	7	25	30	37	6	27	5	18	2	9	1	1	21	1	1	1	1	22	36	1	5	2	2	5	3	27	21	20	6	5	2	6		
		3			1	10	20	9	1	1			1					1							1						12	2	11	2					

1 own-goal

Cumming DS	Laking GE	Stuart RW	French JW	Jameson P	Johnson T*	Wass W	Stobbart GC	Fenton M	Dews G	Chadwick C	Hardwick GFM	Heweston K	Shepherdson H	Wainwright E*	McCabe JJ	Barclay R*	Price AJW*	Robinson R	Wharton G*	Attwell R*	Herd A*	McCormack JC*	Mullen J*	Douglas JS	Bell HD	Wilson K	Butler T	Bambrough N	Bowes W	Hepple G	Brown WH	Spuhler JO	Gordon J	Murphy TE	Maddison J	Watson R	Malan NF	Mannion WJ	#
1	2							9	10	11			5					3							6	7						7		8					3
1								9	10				5					3					11		7							2	7	6	8				
1	2							9	10				5					3					11		7								7	6	8				4
1	2					11		9	10				5					3							7								7	6	8				
1	2					11		9	10				5					3							7								7	6	8				R
1	2							9	10				5					3							7								7	6	8	11			5
1	2							9	10				5					3							7								7	6	8	11			
7	4	2						2	7	7	1		7					7							3	7						1	7	6	7	2			
								7	2		2		2												1							3	1	1					

1 own-goal

S.Jones played number 6 in Match 6; H.Wallbanks played number 6 in Match 7; R.B.Morris played number 5 in Match 8; J.Brown played number 4 in Match 12; J.N.Robinson played number 3 in Match 26; F.C.Nash played number 1 in Matches 34 & 35; H.Mattinson played number 5 in Matches 38, 40 & 41.

Guest Players

R.Attwell (West Ham U), N.Bambrough, R.Barclay (Preston NE), T.Butler (Oldham Ath), A.Herd (Manchester C), T.Johnson (Gateshead), J.C.McCormack (Gateshead), J.Mullen (Wolves), A.J.W.Price (Hartlepools U), E.Wainwright (Everton), H.Wallbanks (Fulham), G.Wharton (Portsmouth), R.Watson (Vale of Leven).

NB — Records show that both J.S.Douglas (20 games) and P.Douglass (2 games) played for Middlesbrough this season, but all reports name Douglas, and do not differentiate between the players.

251

1946-47

Manager: David Jack

1	Aug	31	(a)	Aston Villa	W 1-0	Mannion	49,246
2	Sep	4	(a)	Liverpool	W 1-0	Hughes (og)	34,140
3		7	(h)	Stoke C	W 5-4	Fenton 4, Mannion	43,685
4		14	(a*)	Manchester U	L 0-1		65,279
5		21	(h)	Preston NE	W 2-0	Hardwick (pen), Mannion	40,317
6		28	(a)	Sheffield U	L 1-2	Spuhler	36,931
7	Oct	5	(h)	Chelsea	W 3-2	Fenton, Mannion 2	44,082
8		9	(h)	Liverpool	D 2-2	Fenton, Dews	37,382
9		12	(a)	Bolton W	D 1-1	Fenton	32,000
10		19	(a)	Derby C	D 1-1	Spuhler	28,849
11		26	(h)	Huddersfield T	W 4-1	Fenton, Walker 2, Mannion	36,694
12	Nov	2	(a)	Wolves	W 4-2	Dews 2, Linacre, Walker	45,622
13		9	(h)	Sunderland	L 1-3	Walker	40,219
14		16	(a)	Blackburn R	W 2-1	Walker, Dews	23,797
15		23	(h)	Portsmouth	D 3-3	Mannion 3	31,824
16		30	(a)	Everton	L 1-2	Fenton	48,997
17	Dec	7	(h)	Arsenal	W 2-0	Fenton, Gordon	30,357
18		14	(a)	Blackpool	W 5-0	Mannion, Fenton, Spuhler 2, Murphy	14,571
19		21	(h)	Brentford	W 2-0	Spuhler 2	28,750
20		25	(a)	Leeds U	D 3-3	Spuhler 2, Fenton	28,942
21		26	(h)	Leeds U	W 3-0	Fenton 2, Walker	45,336
22		28	(h)	Aston Villa	L 1-2	Mannion	41,299
23	Jan	1	(h)	Grimsby T	W 3-0	Mannion 2, Dews	39,947
24		4	(a)	Stoke C	L 1-3	Fenton	34,057
25		18	(a)	Manchester U	L 2-4	Fenton, Mannion	37,556
26		29	(a)	Preston NE	W 1-0	Scott (og)	15,911
27	Feb	1	(h)	Sheffield U	L 2-4	Forbes (og), Dobbie	31,784
28		15	(h)	Bolton W	W 3-1	Mannion, Spuhler, Dews	31,437
29		22	(h)	Derby C	W 1-0	Mannion (pen)	32,612
30	Mar	8	(h)	Wolves	D 1-1	Dobbie	37,003
31		15	(a)	Sunderland	L 0-1		39,521
32		22	(h)	Blackburn R	L 0-1		31,001
33		29	(a)	Portsmouth	L 1-3	Fenton	30,502
34	Apr	4	(a)	Charlton A	D 3-3	Fenton, Linacre 2	38,402
35		5	(h)	Everton	W 4-0	Walker 2, Mannion 2	27,106
36		7	(h)	Charlton A	L 1-2	Dews	36,903
37		12	(a)	Arsenal	L 0-4		44,230
38		19	(h)	Blackpool	L 1-2	Spuhler	28,849
39		26	(a)	Brentford	D 0-0		19,020
40	May	3	(a)	Grimsby T	L 0-4		13,376
41		10	(a)	Chelsea	L 0-2		22,482
42		17	(a)	Huddersfield T	L 1-3	Dews	16,328

FINAL LEAGUE POSITION: 11th in Division One — Appearances

*Played at Maine Road (Old Trafford bomb-damaged) — Goals

FA Cup

3	Jan	11	(a)	Queen's Park R	D 1-1	Fenton	24,549
R		15	(h)	Queen's Park R	W 3-1	Fenton 2, Mannion	31,270
4		25	(h)	Chesterfield	W 2-1	Spuhler 2	42,250
5	Feb	8	(a)	Nottingham F	D 2-2	Mannion, Spuhler	34,000
R		12	(h)	Nottingham F	W 6-2	Spuhler, Mannion 3 (1 pen), Fenton 2	26,907
6	Mar	1	(h)	Burnley	D 1-1	Walker	52,025
R		4	(a)	Burnley	L 0-1		49,244

Appearances

Goals

Appearances and goals grid (shirt numbers by player and match):

Cumming DS	Robinson R*	Hardwick GFM	Bell HD*	Shepherdson H	Gordon H*	Spuhler JO*	Mannion WJ	Fenton M	Dews G*	Walker RG*	Stuart RW	Murphy TE*	Linwood AB*	Laking GE	Robinson JN*	McCabe JJ*	Douglas JS*	Nash FC	Mattinson H*	Dobbie H*	Maddison J*	Gallacher C*	Briggs W*	McCormack JC*	Malan NF*	Hepple G*	
1	2	3	4	5	6	7	8	9	10	11																	1
1	2	3	4	5	6	7	8	9	10	11																	2
1	2	3	4	5	6	7	8	9	10	11																	3
1	2	5	4		6	7	8	9		11	3	10															4
1	2	5	4		6		8	9		11	3	7	10														5
1	3		4		6	7		9	10	11			8	2	5												6
1	2	3	4		6	7	8	9	10	11					5												7
1	2	3	4			7	8	9	10	11					5	6											8
1	2	3	4			7	8	9	10	11					5	6											9
1	2	3	4			7	8		10	11		9			5		6										10
1	2	3	4			8	7		10	11		9			5		6										11
1	2	3	4			8	7		10	11		9			5	6											12
1	2	3	4		6	8	7		10	11		9			5												13
1	2	3	4		6	8	7		10	11		9			5												14
1	2	3	4		6	10	7	8		11		9			5												15
	2	5			6	7	10	9	8	11	3				4				1								16
1	2	5			6	7	10	9	8	11	3				4												17
1	2	5			6	7	10	9		11	3	8			4												18
1	2	5			6	7	10	9		11	3	8			4												19
1	2	5			6	7	10	9		11	3	8			4												20
1	2	5			6	7	10	9		11	3	8			4												21
1	2	5			6	7	10	9		11	3	8			4												22
1	2	3	4		6	7	10	9	8	11					5												23
1	2		4		6	7	10	9	8	11	3				5												24
1	2	5	4		6	7	10	9		11	3	8															25
1	2	3	8		6	7	10	9		11					4	5											26
1	2	3	8		6	7	10			11					4	5						9					27
1	2	3	4			7	8	9	10	11					5	6											28
1	2	3	4		6	7	8	9	10	11					5												29
1	2	3	4		6	7	10	9							5					8	11						30
1	2	3	4		6	7	10	9		11					5					8							31
1	2	3			6	7	10	8		11					4	5		9									32
1	2	3	4		6	10	7			11		9			5								8				33
1	2		4		6	10	7	8		11	3	9			5												34
1	2		4		6	10	7	8		11	3	9			5												35
1	2		4		6	10	7	8		11	3	9			5												36
1	2		4		6	8		7	10	11	3	9			5												37
1		3	4		6	7	10	9	8	11			2		5												38
	2	5	4		6	7	10	9		11	3	8							1								39
	2				6	8		9	10	11	3				5	4			1					7			40
	2				6	7		9	10	11	3				5	4								8	1		41
			4			7	8		10	11	3		2		5									9	1	6	42
37	40	33	31	3	36	32	37	40	27	41	20	8	14	1	15	27	2	2	3	4	1	1	1	3	2	1	
	1			1	10	18	18	8	8			1	3				2										

3 own-goals

Cumming DS	Robinson R*	Hardwick GFM	Bell HD*	Shepherdson H	Gordon H*	Spuhler JO*	Mannion WJ	Fenton M	Dews G*	Walker RG*	Stuart RW	Murphy TE*	Linwood AB*	Laking GE	Robinson JN*	McCabe JJ*											
1	2	5			6	7	10	9	8	11	3				4												3
1	2	5	4		6	7	10	9	8	11	3																R
1	3	5	4		8	7	10	9		11	2					6											4
1	2	5			6	7	8	9	10	11	3				4												5
1	2	5			6	7	8	9	10	11	3				4												R
1	2	3	4		6	7	8	9	10	11					5												6
1	2	3	4		6	7	8	9	11				10		5												R
7	7	7	4		7	7	7	6	6	5	5	1	1		1	5											
						4	5	5	1																		

1947-48

Manager: David Jack

1	Aug	23	(h)	Manchester U	D 2-2	Fenton 2	39,554
2		25	(a)	Sheffield U	D 1-1	Hardwick	33,274
3		30	(a)	Preston NE	L 1-2	Spuhler	31,326
4	Sep	3	(h)	Sheffield U	W 3-0	McCormack, Fenton 2	35,312
5		6	(h)	Stoke C	W 2-1	McCormack 2	38,146
6		10	(a)	Wolves	W 3-1	Fenton, Dicks, Brice (og)	49,961
7		13	(a)	Burnley	L 0-3		34,944
8		20	(h)	Portsmouth	L 1-2	Fenton	29,590
9		27	(a)	Bolton W	W 3-1	McCormack 3	30,641
10	Oct	4	(h)	Liverpool	W 3-1	Fenton 2, Spuhler	41,140
11		11	(h)	Everton	L 0-1		38,686
12		18	(a)	Chelsea	L 2-4	Walker 2	48,398
13		25	(h)	Huddersfield T	W 1-0	Fenton	36,142
14	Nov	1	(a)	Derby C	L 2-4	Fenton, Walker	32,976
15		8	(h)	Manchester C	W 2-1	Fenton 2	36,548
16		15	(a)	Grimsby T	W 5-0	Fenton, McCormack 2, Walker, Spuhler	14,812
17		22	(h)	Blackpool	W 4-0	McCormack 2, Fenton, Spuhler	38,936
18		29	(a)	Blackburn R	W 7-1	McCormack 3, Walker 2, Fenton 2	26,506
19	Dec	6	(h)	Sunderland	D 2-2	McCormack, Spuhler	45,145
20		13	(a)	Aston Villa	D 1-1	McCormack	49,188
21		20	(a*)	Manchester U	L 1-2	Fenton	47,879
22		25	(a)	Charlton A	L 0-1		25,822
23		27	(h)	Charlton A	L 1-2	Spuhler	38,454
24	Jan	1	(h)	Wolves	L 2-4	Walker, Fenton	38,150
25		3	(h)	Preston NE	D 1-1	Walker	37,375
26		17	(a)	Stoke C	W 4-2	Mannion, Spuhler, Walker, Fenton	29,436
27		31	(h)	Burnley	L 1-2	Spuhler	36,208
28	Feb	14	(h)	Bolton W	W 4-1	Fenton, Dobbie, Spuhler, Walker	24,234
29		21	(a)	Liverpool	W 1-0	Fenton	36,133
30		28	(a)	Everton	L 1-2	Spuhler	46,364
31	Mar	6	(h)	Chelsea	D 0-0		28,174
32		13	(a)	Huddersfield T	L 1-2	Fenton	23,588
33		20	(h)	Derby C	D 1-1	Fenton	24,814
34		26	(a)	Arsenal	L 0-7		57,557
35		27	(a)	Manchester C	L 0-2		42,297
36		29	(h)	Arsenal	D 1-1	Spuhler	38,249
37	Apr	3	(h)	Grimsby T	W 4-1	Walker, Fenton 3	24,130
38		10	(a)	Blackpool	L 0-1		16,330
39		14	(a)	Portsmouth	L 1-6	Fenton (pen)	23,890
40		17	(h)	Blackburn R	D 1-1	Fenton	22,033
41		24	(a)	Sunderland	L 0-3		51,581
42	May	1	(h)	Aston Villa	L 1-3	Dicks (pen)	20,892

FINAL LEAGUE POSITION: 16th in Division One   Appearances

*Played at Maine Road (Old Trafford bomb-damaged)   Goals

FA Cup

3	Jan	10	(a)	Hull C	W 3-1	Dobbie 2, Mannion	40,179
4		24	(a)	Brentford	W 2-1	Spuhler, McCormack	34,500
5	Feb	7	(h)	Derby C	L 1-2	Spuhler	43,708

Appearances

Goals

254

Player appearance and goals grid (shirt numbers worn per match). Columns are players; rows are matches.

Goodfellow DO*	Robinson R	Hardwick GFM	Bell HD	Whitaker W*	Gordon J	McCormack JC	Dews G	Fenton M	Mannion WJ	Dicks RW*	Stuart RW	Spuhler JO	Walker RG	Nash FC	McCabe JJ	Murphy TE	Briggs W	Robinson JN	Dobbie H	Hepple G	Hodgson JP*	Rickaby S*	Reagan CM*	Anderson JR*	Johnston P*	#
1	2	3	4	5	6	7	8	9	10	11																1
1		3	4	5	6		8	10	9	11	2	7														2
1		3	4	5	6		8	9	10	11	2	7														3
1		3	4	5	6		8	9	10	7	2		11													4
1		3	4	5	6		8	9	10	7	2		11													5
1		3	4	5	6		8	9	10	7	2		11													6
		3	4	5	6	7	8	9	10	11	2			1												7
1		3		5	6	8		9		11	2	7			4	10										8
		3	4	5	6	8		9	10	11	2	7			1											9
1		3	4	5	6	8		9	10		2	7	11													10
1		3	4	5	6	8		9	10		2	7	11													11
1		3	4	5	6	8		10	9		2	7	11													12
1	2	3	4	5	6	8		9	10			7	11													13
1	2	3	4	5	6	8		9	10			7	11													14
1	2	3	4	5	6	8		9	10			7	11													15
1	2	3	4	5	6	8		9	10			7	11													16
1	2	3	4	5	6	8		9	10			7	11													17
1	2	3	4	5	6	8		9	10			7	11													18
1	2	3	4	5	6	8		9	10			7	11													19
1	2	3	4	5	6	8		9	10			7	11													20
1	2	3	4	5	6	8		9	10			7	11													21
1	2	3	4	5	6	8		9	10			7	11													22
1	2	3	4	5	6	8		9	10			7	11													23
1		3	4	5	6	8		9	10			7	11		2											24
1	2	3	4	5	6	8		10				7	11					9								25
1	2	3	4		6			9	10			7	11		5				8							26
1	2	3	4		6	8		9	10			7	11		5											27
1	2	3	4		6			9	10			7	11		5				8							28
1	2	3	4		6			9	10	8		7	11		5											29
1	2	3		5	6			9	10			7	11		4				8							30
1	2	3		5	6	8		9	10			7	11		4											31
1	2		4	5	6	8		9	10			7	11						3							32
	2		4	5		8		9	10	11										6	1	3	7			33
	2	3	4	5		8		9	10	11										6			7		1	34
1	2	3	4	5		8		9	10			7	11							6						35
1	2	3	4	5				9	10	8		7	11							6						36
1	2	3	4	5				9	10	8			11							6			7			37
1	2		4	5				9	10	8		7	11							6		3				38
1	2		4	5				9	10	8		7	11							6		3				39
		3	4	5				9	10	8		7	11							6	1	2				40
1		3		5				9	10	8		7	11							6		2			4	41
		3		5					10	8			11						9	6	1	2	7	4		42
36	35	30	36	37	35	26	6	40	35	22	11	35	35	1	7	1	1	1	5	11	3	6	4	1	2	
	1			15		28	1	2		11	11									1						

1 own-goal

Goodfellow DO*	Robinson R	Hardwick GFM	Bell HD	Whitaker W*	Gordon J	McCormack JC	Dews G	Fenton M	Mannion WJ	Dicks RW*	Stuart RW	Spuhler JO	Walker RG	Nash FC	McCabe JJ	Murphy TE	Briggs W	Robinson JN	Dobbie H	Hepple G	Hodgson JP*	Rickaby S*	Reagan CM*	Anderson JR*	Johnston P*	#
1	2	3	4		6	8		10				7	11		5											3
1	2	3	4		6	8		9	10			7	11		5											4
1	2	3	4		6			9	10	8		7	11		5				9							5
3	3	3	3		3	2		2	3	1		3	3		3				1							
			1			1		2							2											

1948-49

Manager: David Jack

1	Aug	21	(a)	Chelsea	L	0-1	60,981
2		25	(a)	Birmingham C	D	0-0	37,864
3		28	(h)	Everton	W	1-0 Fenton (pen)	35,960
4	Sep	1	(h)	Birmingham C	D	1-1 Dobbie (pen)	34,016
5		4	(a)	Preston NE	L	1-6 Spuhler	36,468
6		8	(a)	Portsmouth	L	0-1	33,275
7		11	(h)	Burnley	W	4-1 Fenton, Dicks, Dobbie 2	28,903
8		15	(h)	Portsmouth	D	1-1 Fenton	33,247
9		18	(a)	Stoke C	L	0-3	28,931
10		25	(h)	Charlton A	L	2-4 Spuhler, Fenton	33,723
11	Oct	2	(a)	Manchester C	L	0-1	45,146
12		9	(a)	Wolves	W	3-0 Fenton 2, Spuhler	38,544
13		16	(h)	Bolton W	W	5-0 Fenton 3, Spuhler, Reagan	28,628
14		23	(a)	Liverpool	L	0-4	57,561
15		30	(h)	Blackpool	W	1-0 Gordon	44,780
16	Nov	6	(a)	Derby C	L	0-2	34,456
17		13	(h)	Arsenal	L	0-1	35,852
18		20	(a)	Huddersfield T	D	0-0	16,413
19		27	(h)	Manchester U	L	1-4 McCrae	31,435
20	Dec	4	(a)	Sheffield U	L	0-1	30,793
21		11	(h)	Aston Villa	W	6-0 Fenton 3, Walker 2, Dicks	21,184
22		18	(a)	Chelsea	D	1-1 Spuhler	23,464
23		25	(a)	Sunderland	L	0-1	43,692
24		26	(h)	Sunderland	D	0-0	43,455
25	Jan	1	(a)	Everton	L	1-3 Spuhler	39,445
26		15	(h)	Preston NE	W	1-0 Walker	37,702
27		22	(a)	Burnley	D	0-0	36,506
28	Feb	19	(a)	Charlton A	L	0-2	42,739
29		26	(h)	Manchester C	L	0-1	37,073
30	Mar	5	(h)	Wolves	D	4-4 Mannion 2, Hartnett, Donaldson	27,663
31		12	(a)	Bolton W	L	1-4 Mannion	28,783
32		19	(a)	Huddersfield T	W	1-0 Donaldson	33,279
33	Apr	2	(h)	Derby C	W	1-0 Donaldson	38,842
34		9	(a)	Arsenal	D	1-1 Mannion	51,540
35		15	(a)	Newcastle U	L	0-1	64,381
36		16	(h)	Liverpool	L	0-1	32,308
37		18	(h)	Newcastle U	W	3-2 McCrae, Hardwick 2 (2 pens)	44,037
38		23	(a)	Blackpool	D	1-1 Donaldson	23,128
39		27	(h)	Stoke C	D	1-1 Donaldson	40,329
40		30	(h)	Sheffield U	W	3-1 Hartnett 3	34,261
41	May	2	(a*)	Manchester U	L	0-1	22,889
42		7	(a)	Aston Villa	D	1-1 Donaldson	38,051

FINAL LEAGUE POSITION: 19th in Division One   Appearances

*Played at Maine Road (Old Trafford bomb-damaged)   Goals

FA Cup

3	Jan	8	(a)	Brentford	L	2-3 Walker, Spuhler	30,000

Appearances

Goals

Ugolini R*	Blenkinsopp TW*	Hardwick GFM	Bell HD	Whitaker W	Gordon J	Spuhler JO	Johnston CP	McCormack JC	Dicks RW	Walker RG	Robinson R	Fenton M	Dobbie H	Hepple G	Hodgson JP	Reagan CM	McCrae A*	Rickaby S	Mannion WJ	Donaldson A*	Hartnett JB*	No.
1	2	3	4	5	6	7	8	9	10	11												1
1	6	3	4	5		7		8	10	11	2	9										2
1	6	3	4	5		7		8	10	11	2	9										3
1	6	3	4	5		7		8	10	11	2		9									4
1	6	3	4	5		7		8	10	11	2		9									5
1	6			5	4	7			10	11	2	9	8	3								6
1	6			5	4	7			10	11	2	9	8	3								7
1	6	3		5	4	7			10	11	2	9	8									8
1	6	3		5	4	7			10	11	2	9	8									9
	6			5	4	7			10	11	2	9	8	3	1							10
1	10	3	4	5	6	8			7	11	2	9										11
1	10	3	4	5	6	8			7	11	2	9										12
1	10	3	4	5	6	8				11	2	9				7						13
1	10	3	4	5	6	8				11	2	9				7						14
1	10	3	4	5	6	8				11	2	9				7						15
1	8	3	4	5	6	7				11	2	9					10					16
1	8	3	4	5	6	7				11	2	9					10					17
1	8	3	4	5	6	7				11	2	9					10					18
1	4	3		5	6	8				11	2	9				7	10					19
1	4	3		5	6	8			7	11	2	9					10					20
1	4	3		5	6	8			7	11	2	9					10					21
1	4	3		5	6	8		9	7	11	2						10					22
1	4	3		5	6	8			7	11	2	9					10					23
1	10	3	4	5	6	7				11	2	9	8									24
1	2		4	5	6	7				11	3	9	8				10					25
1	6	3	4	5	10	7				11	2	9							8			26
1	6	3	4	5	10	7				11	2	9							8			27
1	6	3		5	4	7			10	11	2								8	9		28
	6	3		5	4	7				11	2	8			1				10	9		29
		3	4	5	6	7					2				1		10		8	9	11	30
1		3	4	5	6	7					2						10		8	9	11	31
1	5	3	4		6	7					2						10		8	9	11	32
1	5	3	4		6	7					2						10		8	9	11	33
1	5	3	4		6	7					2						10		8	9	11	34
1	5	3	4		6	7					2						10		8	9	11	35
1	5	3	4		6						2	9				7	10		8		11	36
1	5	3	4		6					11	2					7	10		8	9		37
1	5	3	4		6						2					7	10		8	9	11	38
1	5	3	4		6						2					7	10		8	9	11	39
1	5	3	4		6						2					7	10		8	9	11	40
1	5	3	4		6						2					7	10		8	9	11	41
1	5	3	4		6						2					7	10		8	9	11	42
39	40	39	30	30	38	31	1	8	19	30	41	24	11	3	3	11	20	1	17	14	12	
	2		1	6		2		3			12	3			1	2		4		6	4	

Ugolini R*	Blenkinsopp TW*	Hardwick GFM	Bell HD	Whitaker W	Gordon J	Spuhler JO	Johnston CP	McCormack JC	Dicks RW	Walker RG	Robinson R	Fenton M	Dobbie H	Hepple G	Hodgson JP	Reagan CM	McCrae A*	Rickaby S	Mannion WJ	Donaldson A*	Hartnett JB*	No.
1	10	3	4	5	6	8				11	2	9				7						3
1	1	1	1	1	1	1				1	1	1				1						
						1					1											

257

1949-50

Manager: David Jack

1	Aug	20	(h)	Everton	L 0-1		41,722
2		22	(a)	Blackpool	D 1-1	Bell	28,243
3		27	(a)	Huddersfield T	D 2-2	McCrae, McKennan	22,711
4		31	(h)	Blackpool	W 2-0	McKennan 2 (1 pen)	47,870
5	Sep	3	(h)	Portsmouth	L 1-5	McKennan (pen)	41,974
6		7	(h)	Fulham	L 1-2	Spuhler	36,702
7		10	(a)	Wolves	L 1-3	McCrae	50,424
8		17	(h)	Aston Villa	L 0-2		30,525
9		24	(a)	Charlton A	W 3-0	McKennan 2, McCrae	33,379
10	Oct	1	(h)	Manchester C	D 0-0		38,515
11		8	(a)	Liverpool	L 0-2		49,569
12		15	(h)	Arsenal	D 1-1	McKennan	36,221
13		22	(a)	Bolton W	W 2-1	Mannion, Woodward	30,095
14		29	(h)	Birmingham C	W 1-0	Woodward	33,214
15	Nov	5	(a)	Derby C	L 0-1		24,920
16		12	(h)	West Brom A	W 3-0	McKennan, Mannion, Woodward	28,408
17		19	(a)	Manchester U	L 0-2		44,646
18		26	(h)	Chelsea	W 2-1	McCrae, Walker	24,815
19	Dec	3	(a)	Stoke C	L 0-1		17,475
20		10	(h)	Burnley	W 4-1	Linacre, McCrae 2, Walker	26,369
21		17	(a)	Everton	L 1-3	Mannion	25,864
22		24	(h)	Huddersfield T	W 3-0	McKennan 2 (1 pen), Walker	33,424
23		26	(a)	Newcastle U	W 1-0	McCrae	61,184
24		27	(h)	Newcastle U	W 1-0	McKennan	‡ 53,802
25		31	(a)	Portsmouth	D 1-1	McKennan	32,644
26	Jan	14	(h)	Wolves	W 2-0	Walker, Spuhler	41,155
27		21	(a)	Aston Villa	L 0-4		32,387
28	Feb	4	(h)	Charlton A	W 1-0	Woodward	26,772
29		18	(a)	Manchester C	W 1-0	Woodward	59,714
30		25	(h)	Liverpool	W 4-1	McKennan 2, McCrae, Walker	31,804
31	Mar	8	(a)	Arsenal	D 1-1	McCrae	34,464
32		11	(h)	Manchester U	L 2-3	Walker, Woodward	46,702
33		25	(h)	Derby C	W 3-1	McCrae, Mannion, McKennan	30,298
34		29	(a)	Chelsea	L 1-2	Mannion	15,513
35	Apr	1	(a)	West Brom A	W 3-0	Reagan 2, McCrae	32,972
36		7	(a)	Sunderland	L 0-2		62,487
37		8	(h)	Bolton W	W 2-0	Spuhler 2	21,764
38		10	(h)	Sunderland	W 2-0	Bell, Reagan	44,260
39		15	(a)	Birmingham C	D 0-0		31,579
40		22	(h)	Stoke C	W 2-0	McCrae, Mannion (pen)	27,225
41		29	(a)	Burnley	L 2-3	McCrae, Whitaker	12,367
42	May	6	(a)	Fulham	W 2-1	Gordon, McCrae	21,031

FINAL LEAGUE POSITION: 9th in Division One

‡Ground attendance record

Appearances
Goals

FA Cup

3	Jan	7	(a)	Aston Villa	D 2-2	Linacre, McKennan	49,564
R		11	(h)	Aston Villa	D 0-0*		49,850
2R		16	(n†)	Aston Villa	W 3-0	McCrae 2, Mannion	43,011
4		28	(a)	Chesterfield	L 2-3	Walker, Spuhler	27,500

*After extra-time. †Played at Elland Road, Leeds.

Appearances
Goals

Squad appearance and goalscoring grid (shirt numbers shown per match; players as columns, matches as rows).

Ugolini R	Robinson R	Hardwick GFM	Bell HD	Blenkinsopp TW	Gordon J	Spuhler JO	McKennan PS*	McCrae A	Mannion WJ	Hartnett JB	Dicks RW	Hepple G	Walker RG	Rickaby S	Whitaker W	Brown J*	Linacre W*	Desmond P*	Dobbie H	Woodward T*	Reagan CM	Fenton M	Hodgson JP	Fitzsimons AG*	Delapenha LL*	#
1	2	3	4	5	6	7	8	9	10	11																1
1	2	3	4	5	6	7	8	9	10		11															2
1	2		4	5	6		8	9	10		7	3	11													3
1	2		4			7	8	9	10		6	3	11	5												4
1	2		4			7	8	9	10		6	3	11	5												5
1	2		4			7	8	9	10				11	2	5	6										6
1	2	3	4		6		8	9	10	11			7		5											7
1	2	3	4		6		8	9	10	11			7		5											8
1	2	3	4		6			9	11	8					5		7	10								9
1	2	3	4		6			9		8					11	5	7	10								10
1	2	3		5	4	7	8		10			6			11		9									11
1	2	3		5	4	7	8		10			6			11		9									12
1	2	3		5	4	9	8		10			6			11		7									13
1	2	3		5	4	9	8		10			6			11		7									14
1	2	3		5	4	9	8		10			6			11		7									15
1	2	3		5	4			9	10	8		6			11		7									16
1	2		4	5	6			9	10	8		3			11		7									17
1		3	4	5	6			9	10	8			2		11		7									18
1		3	4		6			9	10	8			2		11	5	7									19
1		3	4		6			9	10	8			2		11	5	7									20
1		3	4		6			9	10	8			2		11	5	7									21
1		3	4		6			9	10	8			2		11	5	7									22
1		3	4		6			9	10	8			2		11	5	7									23
1		3	4	5	6			9	10	8			2		11		7									24
1		3	4	5	6			9	10	8			2		11		7									25
1			4	3	6			9	10	8			2		11	5	7									26
1			4	3	6				10	8			2		11				9	7						27
	2		4	3	6		8		10						5		7		9	11	1					28
1	2		4	3	6			9	10	8					5		7			11						29
1	2		4	3	6			9	10	8					11				5	7						30
1	2		4	3	6			9	10	8					11				5	7						31
1	2	3	4		6			9	10	8					11				5	7						32
1		3	4		6	7		9	10	8			2		5					11						33
1		3	4	2	6	7		9	10	8					5					11						34
1			4		2			9	10	11		3			5	6				7			8			35
1			4		2			9	10	11		3			5	6				7	8					36
1	2		4		6			9	10	8		3			11	5				7						37
1	2		4		6			9	10	8		3			11	5				7						38
1	2		4		6			9	10	11		3			5					7	8					39
1	2		4					9	10	8	11	3			5	6				7						40
1	2		4					9	10	8	11	3			5	6				7						41
1	2		4		6	7		9	10	11		3			5							8				42
41	28	22	34	19	38	20	33	36	38	11	22	11	22	3	29	5	19	2	3	12	8	1	1	3	1	
		2				1	4	15	14	6					6		1			1				6	3	

Ugolini R	Robinson R	Hardwick GFM	Bell HD	Blenkinsopp TW	Gordon J	Spuhler JO	McKennan PS*	McCrae A	Mannion WJ	Hartnett JB	Dicks RW	Hepple G	Walker RG	Rickaby S	Whitaker W	Brown J*	Linacre W*	Desmond P*	Dobbie H	Woodward T*	Reagan CM	Fenton M	Hodgson JP	Fitzsimons AG*	Delapenha LL*	#
1		3	4		6			9	10	8			2		11	5	7									3
1		3	4		6			9	10	8			2		11	5	7									R
1			4	3	6	9			10	8			2		11	5	7									2R
1		3	4		6			9	8	10			2		11	5	7									4
4		3	4	1	4	2	3	4	3	4			4		4	4	4									
							1	1	2	1					1		1									

1950-51

Manager: David Jack

1	Aug	19	(a)	Portsmouth	D	1-1	Mannion	43,773
2		23	(h)	Everton	W	4-0	McCrae 3, Spuhler	41,478
3		26	(h)	Chelsea	W	3-0	McCrae, Mannion, Walker	41,573
4		30	(a)	Everton	L	2-3	Spuhler 2	43,459
5	Sep	2	(a)	Burnley	L	1-3	Hardwick	29,779
6		6	(h)	West Brom A	W	2-1	Spuhler, McCrae	28,829
7		9	(h)	Arsenal	W	2-1	Spuhler, Delapenha	46,119
8		13	(a)	West Brom A	W	3-2	Spuhler, Walker, McCrae	31,530
9		16	(a)	Sheffield W	W	1-0	Walker	46,958
10		23	(h)	Manchester U	L	1-2	Delapenha	48,051
11		30	(h)	Huddersfield T	W	8-0	Mannion 3 (1 pen), Spuhler, McCrae 3, Walker	32,401
12	Oct	7	(a)	Wolves	W	4-3	McCrae 2, Walker (pen), Spuhler	39,477
13		14	(h)	Sunderland	D	1-1	McCrae	52,764
14		21	(a)	Liverpool	D	0-0		47,426
15		28	(h)	Fulham	D	1-1	Mannion	34,117
16	Nov	4	(a)	Aston Villa	W	1-0	Bell	36,542
17		11	(h)	Derby C	D	1-1	McCrae	36,943
18		18	(a)	Bolton W	W	2-0	Spuhler, McCrae	37,296
19		25	(h)	Blackpool	W	4-3	McCrae 3, Spuhler	40,487
20	Dec	2	(a)	Tottenham H	D	3-3	Hartnett, Mannion, Delapenha	61,148
21		9	(h)	Charlton A	W	7-3	Walker, Donaldson, Opp own-goal, Mannion 2, McCrae 2	34,050
22		16	(h)	Portsmouth	W	3-1	Mannion 2 (2 pens), Delapenha	27,163
23		23	(a)	Chelsea	D	1-1	Delapenha	35,323
24		25	(h)	Newcastle U	W	2-1	Spuhler, Walker	41,318
25		30	(h)	Burnley	D	3-3	McCrae, Mannion, Delapenha	34,349
26	Jan	13	(a)	Arsenal	L	1-3	L.Compton (og)	63,038
27		20	(h)	Sheffield W	W	2-1	Dicks, Auld	34,031
28	Feb	3	(a)	Manchester U	L	0-1		46,454
29		17	(a)	Huddersfield T	W	3-2	Mannion 2, Delapenha	23,533
30	Mar	3	(a)	Sunderland	L	1-2	Spuhler	57,958
31		10	(h)	Liverpool	D	1-1	McKennan	29,247
32		17	(a)	Fulham	L	0-2		29,446
33		23	(h)	Stoke C	W	1-0	McKennan	36,200
34		24	(h)	Aston Villa	W	2-1	Linacre, Delapenha	28,580
35		26	(a)	Stoke C	L	0-2		19,000
36		31	(h)	Derby C	L	0-6		16,788
37	Apr	7	(h)	Bolton W	D	1-1	Bell	24,423
38		11	(h)	Wolves	L	1-2	McCrae	29,767
39		14	(a)	Blackpool	L	1-2	McKennan	16,300
40		21	(h)	Tottenham H	D	1-1	Spuhler	36,689
41		28	(a)	Charlton A	L	0-3		11,329
42	May	5	(a)	Newcastle U	L	0-1		35,935

FINAL LEAGUE POSITION: 6th in Division One.   Match 21: Some sources credit Delapenha, club credit own-goal;   Appearances
Match 25: Some sources credit Spuhler, club credit Mannion   Goals

FA Cup

3	Jan	6	(a)	Leeds U	L	0-1		45,483

Appearances
Goals

Ugolini R	Robinson R	Hardwick GFM	Bell HD	Whitaker W	Gordon J	Delapenha LL	Mannion WJ	Spuhler JO	McCrae A	Walker RG	Dicks RW	Woodward T	Hepple G	Reagan CM	Donaldson A	Hartnett JB	Blenkinsopp TW	Auld WB*	McKennan PS	Linacre W	Brown J	Fitzsimons AG	
1	2	3	4	5	6	7	8	9	10	11													1
1	2	3	4	5	6	7	8	9	10	11													2
1	2	3	4	5	6	7	8	9	10	11													3
1		3	4	5	6	7	8	9	10	11	2												4
1		3	4	5	6		8	9	10	11	2	7											5
1			4	5	6	7	8	9	10		2	11	3										6
1	2		4	5	6	7	8	9	10		3	11											7
1	2		4	5	6	7	8	9	10	11	3												8
1	2		4	5	6	7	8	9	10	11	3												9
1	2		4	5	6	7	8	9	10	11	3												10
1	2	3	4	5	6	7	8	9	10	11													11
1	2	3	4	5	6	8		9	10	11				7									12
1	2	3	4	5		7	8	9	10	11	6												13
1	2	3	4	5		7	8	9	10	11	6												14
1	2	3	4	5	6		8	9	10	11		7											15
1	2	3	4	5	6	7	8		10			11			9								16
1			4	5	6	8	10	7	11		2		3		9								17
1	2		4	5	6	7	8	9	10	11	3												18
1	2		4	5	6	7	8	9	10		3	11											19
1	2		4	5	6	7	8	9	10		3					11							20
1	2		4	5	6	7	8		10	11	3				9								21
1	2		4	5	6	7	8		10	11	3				9								22
1	2		4	5	6	7	8	9	10	11	3												23
1	2		4	5	6	8	10	7		11	3				9								24
1	2		4	5	6	7	8	9	10	11	3												25
1	2		4	5	6	7	8	9	10		3					11							26
1	2		4		6	8		9		7	3		10				5	11					27
1	9		4	5	6	8	10			11	2	7	3										28
1	2		4	5	6	7	8		10	11	3				9								29
1	2		4	5	6	7	10	9		11	3								8				30
1			4		6	7	10	9			2		3				5	11	8				31
1			4		6	7	10	8			2		3		9		5			11			32
1			4		6	7	8		10		2		3				5		9	11			33
1			4	5	6	7	10	8			3						2		9	11			34
1			4	5	6	7	10	9			3						2		8	11			35
1	2		4		6	7	10	9			3						5		8	11			36
1	2		4			7	8	9		11	3						5				6	10	37
1	2		4			7		9	10	11	3						5				6	8	38
1	2		4			7			10	11	3						5		9		6	8	39
1	2		4			7		9	10	11	3						5				6	8	40
1	2		4			7		9	10	11	3						5				6	8	41
1	2		4	5		7		9	10	11	3										6	8	42
42	33	11	42	32	34	40	35	35	32	29	35	7	7	1	7	2	12	2	7	5	6	6	
		1	2			8	14	13	21	7	1				1	1		1	3	1			

2 own-goals

1	2		4	5	6	7	8	9	10	11	3	3
1	1		1	1	1	1	1	1	1	1	1	

1951-52

Manager: David Jack

No	Month	Date		Opponent	Res	Score	Scorers	Attendance
1	Aug	18	(h)	Tottenham H	W	2-1	Farley (og), Bell	44,004
2		22	(a)	Manchester U	L	2-4	Mochan 2	39,176
3		25	(a)	Preston NE	W	1-0	Delapenha	37,389
4		29	(h)	Manchester U	L	1-4	Delapenha (pen)	44,434
5	Sep	1	(h)	Burnley	W	5-0	Mannion 2, Delapenha, Mochan, Walker	31,711
6		3	(a)	Bolton W	L	1-3	Mochan	33,811
7		8	(a)	Charlton A	L	3-4	Walker (pen), Mannion, Fitzsimons	26,999
8		15	(h)	Fulham	W	2-0	McCrae, Mochan	23,626
9		22	(a)	Huddersfield T	L	0-1		27,995
10		29	(a)	West Brom A	W	3-2	Delapenha (pen), Mochan 2	28,830
11	Oct	6	(h)	Chelsea	D	0-0		30,010
12		13	(a)	Portsmouth	L	4-5	Fitzsimons, Mochan, Delapenha (pen), McCrae	34,633
13		20	(h)	Liverpool	D	3-3	Mannion, Spuhler, Delapenha (pen)	26,126
14		27	(a)	Blackpool	D	2-2	Spuhler, Mochan	23,195
15	Nov	3	(h)	Arsenal	L	0-3		35,408
16		10	(a)	Manchester C	L	1-2	Fitzsimons	47,522
17		17	(h)	Derby C	D	0-0		25,656
18		24	(a)	Aston Villa	L	0-2		25,415
19	Dec	1	(h)	Sunderland	L	0-2		36,629
20		8	(a)	Wolves	L	0-4		23,800
21		15	(a)	Tottenham H	L	1-3	Delapenha (pen)	37,781
22		22	(a)	Preston NE	L	2-5	Mannion, Delapenha (pen)	16,899
23		26	(h)	Stoke C	W	3-0	Mannion, McCrae, Walker	29,515
24		29	(a)	Burnley	L	1-7	Mochan	26,057
25	Jan	5	(h)	Charlton A	W	2-1	Delapenha, Spuhler	24,672
26		19	(a)	Fulham	L	0-6		28,941
27		26	(h)	Huddersfield T	W	2-1	Spuhler, Mannion	22,876
28	Feb	9	(h)	West Brom A	L	0-1		21,604
29		16	(a)	Chelsea	L	0-5		37,805
30	Mar	1	(h)	Portsmouth	W	2-1	Mannion 2 (1 pen)	26,599
31		8	(a)	Liverpool	D	1-1	Mannion	41,945
32		15	(h)	Blackpool	W	1-0	Spuhler	35,094
33		22	(a)	Arsenal	L	1-3	Walker	50,979
34		29	(h)	Manchester C	D	2-2	Bell, McCrae	16,920
35	Apr	5	(a)	Derby C	L	1-3	Mochan	10,567
36		11	(a)	Newcastle U	W	2-0	Spuhler, McCrae	59,364
37		12	(h)	Aston Villa	W	2-0	McCrae, Delapenha	26,880
38		14	(h)	Newcastle U	W	2-1	Walker, Delapenha	36,448
39		19	(a)	Sunderland	L	1-3	Spuhler	37,670
40		23	(h)	Bolton W	W	2-0	Delapenha (pen), Mannion	23,591
41		26	(h)	Wolves	W	4-0	Walker, Delapenha 2 (1 pen), Mochan	25,577
42	May	3	(a)	Stoke C	L	2-3	Walker, Delapenha	11,554

FINAL LEAGUE POSITION: 18th in Division One

Appearances
Goals

FA Cup

Rd	Month	Date		Opponent	Res	Score	Scorers	Attendance
3	Jan	12	(h)	Derby C	D	2-2	Mannion 2	35,850
R		16	(a)	Derby C	W	2-0	Delapenha 2	30,711
4	Feb	6	(h)	Doncaster R	L	1-4	Bell	41,560

Appearances
Goals

262

Ugolini R	Robinson R	Dicks RW	Bell HD	Blenkinsopp TW	Gordon J	Linacre W	Mannion WJ	Mochan N*	McCrae A	Walker RG	Delapenha LL	Whitaker W	Fitzsimons AG	Patterson RL*	Spuhler JO	Aitken GB*	Hartnett JB	Lawrie S*	Barnard RS*	Corbett R*	Russell ET*	Mulholland FG*	Bilcliff R*	Norris OP*	Hodgson JP	
1	2	3	4	5	6	7	8	9	10	11																1
1	2	3	4	5	6	7	10	9		11	8															2
1	2	3	4		6	7	10	9		11	8	5														3
1	2	3	4		6	7	10	9		11	8	5														4
1	2	3	4		6		8	9		11	7	5	10													5
1	2	3	4		6		8	9		11	7	5	10													6
1	2	6	4				8	9		11		5	10	3	7											7
1	2	6	4		3		8	9	10	11	7	5														8
1	2	6	4		3		8	9	10	11		5			7											9
1	2	6	4		3		8	9	10		7	5			11											10
1	2		4	6	3		8	9	10		7	5			11											11
1	2	6	4	3			11	10			7	5	8		9											12
1	2	6	4	3			8	11	10		7	5			9											13
1		3	4	2	6	7	10	11				5	8		9											14
1	2	3	4		6		8	11	10		9	5			7											15
1	2	3	4	5	6		10	9		7		8				11										16
1	2	3	4	5	6		10	9		7		8				11										17
1	2	3	4	5	6		10			7		8	9			11										18
1		3	6	4	7					11	8	5	10		9				2							19
1		3	6	4	2		10	11			7	5	8		9											20
1	2	6	4				10	11			7	5	8		9					3						21
1		6	4				10	11			7	5	8		9				2	3						22
1	2	4		6			8		10	11	7	5			9					3						23
1	2			6			8	9	10	11	7	5								3	4					24
1	2	4					8		10	11	7				9					3	5	6				25
1	2	4					8			11	7		10		9					3	5	6				26
1							8		10	11	7	5			9				2	3	4	6				27
1							8	9		11	7	5	10						2	3	4	6				28
1	11						8	9			7	5	10						2	3	4	6				29
1		4	3	6			8		10	11					9	5		7	2							30
1		4	3	6			8		10	11	7				9	5			2							31
1		4	3	6		7	8		10	11					9	5			2							32
1		4	3	6		7	8		10	11					9	5			2							33
1		4	3	6			8		10	11	7				9	5			2							34
1	2	4	3	6			8	9	10	11	7	5														35
1		4		2	6		8		10	11		5			9					3		7				36
1		4		2	6		8		10	11	7	5			9					3						37
1		4		2	6		8		10	11	7	5			9					3						38
1		4		2	6		8		10	11	7	5			9					3						39
1		4		2	6		8	9	10	11	7	5								3						40
1		4		6			8	9		11	7	5	10							3		2				41
1		4		6			8	9		11	10	5								3		2	7	1		42
41	20	27	38	21	30	7	39	29	24	27	33	29	16	1	25	7	5	2	6	16	5	5	6	2	1	
		2					11	12	6	7	15		3		7											

1 own-goal

Ugolini R	Robinson R	Dicks RW	Bell HD	Blenkinsopp TW	Gordon J	Linacre W	Mannion WJ	Mochan N*	McCrae A	Walker RG	Delapenha LL	Whitaker W	Fitzsimons AG	Patterson RL*	Spuhler JO	Aitken GB*	Hartnett JB	Lawrie S*	Barnard RS*	Corbett R*	Russell ET*	Mulholland FG*	Bilcliff R*	Norris OP*	Hodgson JP	
1	2	4					8	9	10	11	7									3	5	6				3
1	2	4					8			11	7		10		9					3	5	6				R
1	11	4					8		10		7				9				2	3	5	6				4
3	3	3		3			3	1	2	2	3		1		2				1	3	3	3				
		1					2				2															

1952-53

Manager: Walter Rowley

1	Aug	23	(a)	Burnley	W	1-0	Mochan	27,386
2		27	(h)	Cardiff C	W	3-0	Bell 2, Fitzsimons	42,159
3		30	(h)	Preston NE	D	1-1	Mannion	36,412
4	Sep	3	(a)	Cardiff C	D	1-1	McCrae	51,512
5		6	(a)	Stoke C	L	0-1		32,062
6		13	(h)	Manchester C	W	5-4	Spuhler 2, Mannion, Fitzsimons, Delapenha	30,924
7		17	(a)	Sheffield W	L	0-2		41,388
8		20	(a)	Liverpool	L	1-4	Mannion	40,750
9		27	(h)	Bolton W	L	1-2	Mannion	26,679
10	Oct	4	(h)	West Brom A	W	4-2	Fitzsimons, Delapenha, McCrae, Mochan	24,420
11		11	(a)	Aston Villa	L	0-1		30,280
12		18	(h)	Sunderland	L	1-2	McCrae	38,305
13		25	(a)	Wolves	D	3-3	Edwards, Russell, Mannion	36,683
14	Nov	1	(h)	Charlton A	W	1-0	Fitzsimons	28,745
15		8	(a)	Arsenal	L	1-2	Walker	48,564
16		15	(h)	Derby C	W	1-0	Walker (pen)	14,682
17		22	(a)	Blackpool	D	1-1	Norris	19,934
18		29	(h)	Chelsea	W	4-0	Mannion 2, Lawrie, Delapenha	19,683
19	Dec	6	(a)	Manchester U	L	2-3	Mannion, Delapenha (pen)	29,619
20		13	(h)	Portsmouth	W	3-2	Walker, Mannion, Fitzsimons	22,583
21		20	(h)	Burnley	D	2-2	Mannion, Fitzsimons	19,155
22		25	(a)	Tottenham H	L	1-7	Norris	36,102
23		27	(h)	Tottenham H	L	0-4		23,265
24	Jan	1	(h)	Sheffield W	D	2-2	McCrae, Delapenha	30,632
25		3	(a)	Preston NE	L	0-3		29,139
26		17	(h)	Stoke C	D	0-0		20,861
27		24	(a)	Manchester C	L	1-5	Mannion	26,822
28	Feb	7	(h)	Liverpool	L	2-3	Delapenha 2 (1 pen)	15,445
29		18	(a)	Bolton W	L	3-5	Rayment 2, Spuhler	15,041
30		21	(a)	West Brom A	L	0-3		24,269
31	Mar	3	(h)	Aston Villa	W	1-0	Walker (pen)	13,176
32		7	(a)	Sunderland	D	1-1	Spuhler	38,237
33		14	(h)	Wolves	D	1-1	Mannion	24,454
34		21	(a)	Charlton A	L	0-2		22,204
35		28	(h)	Arsenal	W	2-0	Fitzsimons, Spuhler	25,911
36	Apr	3	(a)	Newcastle U	L	0-1		48,434
37		4	(a)	Derby C	D	3-3	Edwards, Mannion 2	17,935
38		6	(h)	Newcastle U	W	2-1	Mannion 2	37,926
39		11	(h)	Blackpool	W	5-1	Mannion, Fitzsimons 2, Spuhler 2	38,847
40		18	(a)	Chelsea	D	1-1	Fitzsimons	40,042
41		25	(h)	Manchester U	W	5-0	Mannion 2, Delapenha, Spuhler, Fitzsimons	34,344
42	May	2	(a)	Portsmouth	W	4-1	Bell, Spuhler 2, Delapenha	18,757

FINAL LEAGUE POSITION: 13th in Division One

Appearances
Goals

FA Cup

3	Jan	10	(a)	Aston Villa	L	1-3	Fitzsimons	41,557

Appearances
Goals

264

Player appearance and goals chart.

Ugolini R	Robinson R	Corbett R	Bell HD	Whitaker W	Russell ET	Delapenha LL	Mannion WJ	Mochan N	Fitzsimons AG	Walker RG	Blenkinsopp TW	McCrae A	Lawrie S	Dicks RW	Gordon J	Spuhler JO	Rayment JW*	Edwards WI*	Bilcliff R	Aitken GB	Norris OP	Mulholland FG	Hodgson JP	
1	2	3	4	5	6	7	8	9	10	11														1
1	2	3	4	5	6	7	8	9	10	11														2
1	2	3	4		6	7	8	9		11	5	10												3
1	2	3	4		6		8	9		11	5	10	7											4
1		3	4		5	8		9		11		10	7	2	6									5
1	2	3	4	5	6	7	8		10	11						9								6
1	2	3	4	5	6	7	8		10	11						9								7
1	2	3	4	5	6	11	8		10							9	7							8
1	2		4	5	6	7	8		10	11			3			9								9
1	2			5	6	7	8	9		11		3	10		4									10
1	2			5	6	7	8			11		3	10		4	9								11
1	2	3	4			7	8			11		5	10		6	9								12
1	2		4		6		8	11	10			5	7	3		9								13
1		3	4		6		8		10	11							7	9	2	5				14
1		3	4		6		8		10	11							7		2	5	9			15
1		3	4	5		8			10	11					6		7		2		9			16
1		3	4		6		8		10	11			7						2	5	9			17
1		3	4		6		8		10	11			7						2	5	9			18
1		3	4		6		8		10	11			7						2	5	9			19
1		3	4		6		8		10				7	11					2	5	9			20
1		3	4		6		8		10				7	11					2	5	9			21
1		3	4		6		8		10				7	11					2	5	9			22
1		3	4		6		8		10				7	11					2	5	9			23
1		3	4	5		7	8		10	11		9			6				2					24
1		3			6	7	8		10	11		9							2	5	4			25
1		3	11	5			8	9	10				7		6				2		4			26
1	2	3			5		8		10	11					6	9	7	4						27
		3	4	5			8		10	11					6	9	7		2				1	28
1		3	4	5			8		10	11					6	9	7		2					29
1		3	4	5			8		10	11							7	9	2			6		30
1	2		4	5			8		10	11							7	9	3			6		31
1	2		4	5					10							8	7	9	3			6		32
1	2		4	5			8		10	11							7	9	3			6		33
1	2		4	5		7	8		10	11						9			3			6		34
1	5	3	4			7	8		10	11						9			2			6		35
1		3	4			7	8		10	11				5				9	2			6		36
1		3	4			7	8		10	11				5				9	2			6		37
1		3	4			7	8		10	11				5		9			2			6		38
1		3	4			7	8		10	11				5		9			2			6		39
1		3	4			7	8		10	11				5		9			2			6		40
1		3	4			7	8		10	11				5		9			2			6		41
1		3	4			7	8		10	11				5		9			2			6		42
41	24	29	37	17	24	30	41	9	35	31	6	10	9	10	10	19	9	7	28	10	9	16	1	
		3		1	9	18	2	11	4		4	1				10	2	2				3		

Ugolini R	Robinson R	Corbett R	Bell HD	Whitaker W	Russell ET	Delapenha LL	Mannion WJ	Mochan N	Fitzsimons AG	Walker RG	Blenkinsopp TW	McCrae A	Lawrie S	Dicks RW	Gordon J	Spuhler JO	Rayment JW*	Edwards WI*	Bilcliff R	Aitken GB	Norris OP	Mulholland FG	Hodgson JP	
1		3				8	7	11	10						6				2	5	9	4		3
1		1				1	1	1	1						1				1	1	1	1		
								1																

1953-54

Manager: Walter Rowley

#	Month	Date		Opponent	Result	Score	Scorers	Attendance
1	Aug	19	(h)	Cardiff C	D	0-0		33,726
2		22	(h)	Preston NE	L	0-4		32,891
3		26	(a)	Bolton W	L	2-3	Mannion, Delapenha	29,502
4		29	(a)	Tottenham H	L	1-4	Delapenha	44,911
5	Sep	2	(h)	Bolton W	W	3-2	Delapenha 2, Mannion	25,458
6		5	(h)	Burnley	L	1-3	Edwards	32,957
7		9	(a)	Manchester U	D	2-2	Fitzsimons, Delapenha	19,893
8		12	(a)	Charlton A	L	1-8	Spuhler	23,790
9		16	(h)	Manchester U	L	1-4	Delapenha (pen)	23,791
10		19	(h)	Sheffield W	W	4-1	Mannion, Spuhler, Gannon (og), Delapenha	22,638
11		26	(a)	Huddersfield T	L	1-2	Mannion	37,054
12	Oct	3	(a)	West Brom A	L	1-2	Spuhler	36,865
13		10	(h)	Sheffield U	W	2-0	Mannion 2	26,136
14		17	(a)	Chelsea	D	1-1	Rayment	23,513
15		24	(h)	Blackpool	L	0-1		39,416
16		31	(a)	Portsmouth	W	2-0	Fitzsimons, McPherson	24,342
17	Nov	7	(h)	Wolves	D	3-3	Fitzsimons, McPherson, Hartnett	24,284
18		14	(a)	Aston Villa	L	3-5	McPherson, Delapenha, Rayment	20,735
19		21	(h)	Manchester C	L	0-1		22,099
20		28	(a)	Sunderland	W	2-0	Walker 2	41,538
21	Dec	5	(h)	Arsenal	W	2-0	Spuhler 2	30,085
22		12	(a)	Cardiff C	L	0-1		31,776
23		19	(a)	Preston NE	L	0-1		18,909
24		25	(h)	Newcastle U	L	2-3	Spuhler, Walker	28,138
25		26	(a)	Newcastle U	W	3-2	Delapenha, Lawrie, O'Connell	43,750
26	Jan	2	(h)	Tottenham H	W	3-0	Spuhler, Lawrie, O'Connell	35,141
27		16	(a)	Burnley	L	0-5		23,481
28		23	(a)	Charlton A	L	0-2		19,327
29	Feb	6	(a)	Sheffield W	L	2-4	Delapenha 2	30,856
30		13	(h)	Huddersfield T	L	0-3		18,717
31		24	(h)	West Brom A	D	1-1	Delapenha (pen)	17,144
32		27	(a)	Sheffield U	D	2-2	Delapenha, Mannion	29,029
33	Mar	6	(h)	Chelsea	D	3-3	Spuhler, Delapenha 2	27,920
34		13	(a)	Blackpool	D	0-0		20,334
35		20	(h)	Portsmouth	D	2-2	Mannion, Harris	20,743
36		27	(a)	Wolves	W	4-2	Watkin, McPherson 2, Delapenha	29,145
37	Apr	3	(h)	Aston Villa	W	2-1	Mannion, McPherson	21,142
38		10	(a)	Manchester C	L	2-5	Delapenha, Little (og)	28,445
39		16	(h)	Liverpool	L	0-1		26,882
40		17	(h)	Sunderland	D	0-0		38,762
41		19	(a)	Liverpool	L	1-4	Watkin	22,174
42		24	(a)	Arsenal	L	1-3	Delapenha	35,069

FINAL LEAGUE POSITION: 21st in Division One

Appearances
Goals

FA Cup

	Month	Date		Opponent	Result	Score	Scorers	Attendance
3	Jan	9	(h)	Leicester C	D	0-0		38,701
R		14	(a)	Leicester C	L	2-3	Spuhler, Mannion	29,736

Appearances
Goals

266

Ugolini R	Robinson R	Corbett R	McMurray J*	Dicks RW	Mulholland FG	Delapenha LL	Mannion WJ	McPherson K*	Fitzsimons AG	Walker RG	Bilcliff R	Bell HD	Edwards WI	Spuhler JO	Gordon J	Rayment JW	Hepple G	Hartnett JB	Norris OP	Birbeck J*	Lawrie S	O'Connell SPC*	Stonehouse D*	Barnard RS	Harris WC*	Watkin TWS*	Robinson JN	
1	2	3	4	5	6	7	8	9	10	11																		1
1	2	3	4	5	6	7	8	9	10	11																		2
1		3		5	6	7	8	9	10	11	2	4																3
1		3		5	6	7	8	9	10	11	2	4																4
1		3		5	6	7	8		10	11	2	4	9															5
1		3		5	6	7	8		10	11	2	4	9															6
1	2	3		5	6	7	8		10	11		4		9														7
1	2	3		5	6	7	8		10	11		4		9														8
1	5	3			6	7	8	9	10	11	2	4																9
1	5	3				8	10		11		2	4		9	6	7												10
1	5					8	10		11		2	4	9	7	6		3											11
1	5					8	10			11	2	4		9	6	7	3											12
1	5					8	10			11	2	4		9	6	7	3											13
1	5					8	10				2	4		9	6	7	3	11										14
1	5					8	10			11	2	4		9	6	7	3											15
1	5					7	8	9	10		2	4			6		3	11										16
1	5					7	8	9	10		2	4			6		3	11										17
1	5					8		9	10		2	4			6	7	3	11										18
1	5			3	4	8		9	10		2					7		11	6									19
1	5	3		2		10		9		11		4		8						6	7							20
1	5	3		2		10	8			11		4		9						6	7							21
1	5	3		2		10		9		11		4		8						6	7							22
1	5	3		2		10	8	9		11		4								6	7							23
1	5	3		2		10	8			11		4		9						6	7							24
1	5	3		2		10				11		4		9						6	7	8						25
1	5			2		7	8					4		9						6	11	10	3					26
1	5			2	4		8	9										11		6	7	10	3					27
1	5			3	4		8		10	11	2			9						6	7							28
1				5	4	10	8			11				9						6	7		3	2				29
1				5		7	8		10	11	2	4		9						6			3					30
1	5	3		6		10	8					4	9			7		11					2					31
1		3		5		8	10					4	9		6	7		11					2					32
1	5			2		10	8					4		9		7							3		6	11		33
1		3		5		10	8					4	9			7							2		6	11		34
1		3		5		10	8					4	9			7							2		6	11		35
1		3		5		10	8	9				4									7		2		6	11		36
1		3		5		10	8	9				4									7		2		6	11		37
1		3		5		10	8	9				4									7		2		6	11		38
1	5	3		6		10	8							9							7		2		4	11		39
1	5			3		10	8	9				4									7		2		6	11		40
1	5			3		10	8	9				4									7		2		6	11		41
1	5			3	6	7	10	9				4						11					2				8	42
42	30	24	2	32	14	40	37	19	17	21	17	35	7	19	10	12	8	9	1	11	16	3	16	1	9	9	1	
						18	9	6	3	3			1	8		2		1			2	2			1	2		

2 own-goals

1	5			3		7	8			11	2	4		9						6	11	10						3
1	5			3		7	8				2	4		9						6		10						R
2	2			2		2	2			1	2	2		2						2	1	2						
							1							1														

1954-55

Manager: Bob Dennison

1	Aug	21	(a)	Plymouth A	D	2-2	McPherson, Delapenha	26,484
2		25	(h)	Ipswich T	L	0-1		23,357
3		28	(h)	Stoke C	L	1-2	Hartnett	17,980
4	Sep	1	(a)	Ipswich T	L	1-6	Walker	19,830
5		4	(a)	Rotherham U	L	0-3		17,022
6		8	(h)	Nottingham F	L	1-4	McPherson	16,241
7		11	(h)	Luton T	L	0-2		16,071
8		15	(a)	Nottingham F	L	2-4	Delapenha, Edwards	11,049
9		18	(a)	Hull C	L	0-1		26,485
10		25	(h)	Lincoln C	W	2-1	Scott 2	23,706
11	Oct	2	(a)	Bury	W	1-0	Delapenha	18,522
12		9	(a)	Swansea T	L	0-2		24,399
13		16	(h)	Notts C	W	2-0	Fitzsimons, Mitchell	20,585
14		23	(a)	Derby C	W	2-1	Delapenha, Dicks	15,541
15		30	(h)	West Ham U	W	6-0	Bond (og), Wayman 4, Mitchell	25,601
16	Nov	6	(a)	Blackburn R	L	0-9		29,189
17		13	(h)	Fulham	W	4-2	Scott, Wayman 2, Delapenha	21,734
18		20	(a)	Port Vale	D	1-1	Wayman	16,753
19		27	(h)	Doncaster R	W	3-1	Scott 2, Wayman	21,373
20	Dec	4	(a)	Liverpool	L	1-3	Scott	26,750
21		11	(h)	Bristol R	W	1-0	Hartnett	20,561
22		18	(h)	Plymouth A	W	4-1	Scott 3, Delapenha	15,662
23		25	(a)	Leeds U	D	1-1	Scott	26,344
24		27	(h)	Leeds U	W	1-0	Wayman	45,271
25	Jan	1	(a)	Stoke C	W	2-1	Scott, Delapenha	19,275
26		15	(h)	Rotherham U	W	5-1	Scott, Delapenha, Mitchell 2, Wayman	12,320
27		22	(a)	Luton T	L	0-2		13,372
28	Feb	5	(h)	Hull C	L	1-2	Scott	32,619
29		12	(a)	Lincoln C	D	3-3	Wayman 2, Harris	8,368
30		26	(h)	Swansea T	W	4-2	Wayman, Kiley (og), Scott 2	20,867
31	Mar	5	(a)	Notts C	W	3-1	Fitzsimons, Scott 2	22,354
32		12	(h)	Derby C	W	3-1	Delapenha, Fitzsimons 2	20,103
33		19	(a)	West Ham U	L	1-2	Mitchell	22,313
34		26	(h)	Blackburn R	W	4-3	Wayman 2, Delapenha 2	19,426
35	Apr	2	(a)	Fulham	W	2-1	Fitzsimons, Delapenha	17,770
36		8	(h)	Birmingham C	L	2-5	Delapenha (pen), Dicks	32,519
37		9	(h)	Port Vale	W	2-0	Wayman, Delapenha	17,795
38		11	(a)	Birmingham C	L	0-3		23,657
39		16	(a)	Doncaster R	L	1-3	Robertson	9,925
40		23	(h)	Liverpool	L	1-2	McPherson	11,737
41		27	(h)	Bury	D	1-1	McPherson	7,944
42		30	(a)	Bristol R	D	2-2	McPherson, Robertson	14,553

FINAL LEAGUE POSITION: 12th in Division Two

Appearances
Goals

FA Cup

3	Jan	8	(h)	Notts C	L	1-4	Wayman	30,503

Appearances
Goals

268

Football club season appearances and goals grid.

Ugolini R	Dicks RW	Corbett R	Bell HD	Robinson R	Harris WC	Rayment JW	Delapenha LL	McPherson K	Robinson JN	Walker RG	Hodgson JP	Stonehouse D	McMurray J	Hartnett JB	Mulholland FG	Watkin TS	Fitzsimons AG	Mitchell AJ*	Barnard RS	Birbeck J	Edwards WI	Brown TE*	Scott JC*	Wayman C*	Whitaker W	Robertson WG*	Phillips BJ*	Cooper D*	#
1	2	3	4	5	6	7	8	9	10	11																			1
1	2	3	4	5	6	7	8	9	10	11																			2
		3	4	5	6		8	9		11	1	2		7		10													3
		3	5	4			8			11	1	2	7	6	9	10													4
		3	5	4		7	8				1	2		11	6	9	10												5
1		3	5	4	6		8	9		11		2		7			10												6
1		3	5	4	6		8	9		11		2		7			10												7
		3	5	4			8	9			1	2		7	6		10	11											8
1	6			5	4		7										10	11	2		9	3	8						9
1	6			5	4		7										10	11	2			3	8	9					10
1	6			5	4		7										10	11	2			3	8	9					11
1	6			5	4		7										10	11	2			3	8	9					12
1	6			5	4		7										10	11	2			3	8	9					13
1	6			5	4		7										10	11	2			3	8	9					14
1	6			5	4		7										10	11	2			3	8	9					15
1	6			5	4		7										10	11	2			3	8	9					16
1	6			5	4		7										10	11	2			3	8	9					17
1	6			5	4		7										10	11	2			3	8	9					18
1	6			5	4		7										10	11	2			3	8	9					19
1	6			5	4		7										10	11	2			3	8	9					20
1	6			5	4		7							11			10		2			3	8	9					21
1	6			5	4		7							11			10		2			3	8	9					22
1	6			5	4		7							11			10		2			3	8	9					23
1	6			5	4		7							11			10		2			3	8	9					24
1	6				4		7										10	11	2			3	8	9		5			25
1	6				4		7										10	11	2			3	8	9		5			26
1	6				4		7										10	11	2			3	8	9		5			27
1	6			5	4		7										10	11	2			3	8	9					28
1	6			5	4		7										10	11	2			3	8	9					29
1	6			5	4		7										10		2			3	8	9	11				30
1	6			5	4		7										10	11	2			3	8	9					31
1	6			5	4		7										10	11	2			3	8	9					32
1	6			5	4		7										10	11	2			3	8	9					33
1	6				4		7										10	11	2			3	8	9		5			34
1	6				4		7										10	11	2			3	8	9		5			35
1	6			5	4		7										10	11	2			3	8	9					36
1	6			5	4		7										10	11	2			3	8	9					37
1	6			5	4	7	8										10	11	2			3		9					38
1	6	3			4		8										10	11	2					9		7	5		39
1	6			5	4		8										10	11	2			3		9		7			40
1	3		5	4			8								6		10	7	2					9		11			41
1	6	3	5	4				9									10	7	2							11		8	42
38	39	10	7	33	41	3	38	9	2	4	4	4	1	9	5	2	38	31	36	2	2	31	29	32	3	5	3	1	
	2				1		15	5		1				2			5	5			1		16	16		2			

2 own-goals

Ugolini R	Dicks RW	Corbett R	Bell HD	Robinson R	Harris WC	Rayment JW	Delapenha LL	McPherson K	Robinson JN	Walker RG	Hodgson JP	Stonehouse D	McMurray J	Hartnett JB	Mulholland FG	Watkin TS	Fitzsimons AG	Mitchell AJ*	Barnard RS	Birbeck J	Edwards WI	Brown TE*	Scott JC*	Wayman C*	Whitaker W	Robertson WG*	Phillips BJ*	Cooper D*	#
1	6				4		7							11			10		2			3	8	9		5			3
1	1				1		1							1			1		1			1	1	1		1			
																										1			

1955-56

Manager: Bob Dennison

1	Aug	20	(h)	Notts C	W 3-0	Delapenha, Fitzsimons 2	20,291
2		25	(a)	Swansea T	L 1-2	Wayman	21,351
3		27	(a)	Leeds U	L 0-2		22,535
4		31	(h)	Swansea T	W 4-1	Fitzsimons 2, McPherson 2	22,417
5	Sep	3	(h)	Fulham	D 1-1	Delapenha	26,275
6		10	(a)	Bury	D 1-1	McPherson	12,278
7		17	(h)	Barnsley	D 1-1	Fitzsimons	24,960
8		24	(a)	Liverpool	D 1-1	Scott	35,213
9	Oct	1	(a)	Bristol C	L 0-2		28,788
10		8	(h)	Leicester C	W 4-3	Clough, Fitzsimons, Delapenha (pen), Harris	20,642
11		15	(a)	Lincoln C	W 2-1	Delapenha, Clough	12,532
12		22	(h)	Stoke C	L 1-3	Delapenha	22,394
13		29	(a)	Hull C	D 2-2	Fitzsimons, Day	14,013
14	Nov	5	(h)	Nottingham F	W 3-2	Wayman, Lawrie, McPherson	17,573
15		12	(a)	Sheffield W	L 1-3	Fitzsimons	24,030
16		19	(h)	Doncaster R	W 4-1	Scott, Fitzsimons 2, Wayman	15,360
17		26	(a)	Bristol R	L 2-7	Wayman, Delapenha	23,716
18	Dec	3	(h)	Blackburn R	W 1-0	Delapenha	16,827
19		10	(a)	Plymouth A	L 0-4		12,651
20		17	(a)	Notts C	L 0-5		9,693
21		24	(h)	Leeds U	W 5-3	Scott, Wayman 2, Delapenha 2	19,416
22		26	(h)	West Ham U	W 2-0	Mitchell, Wayman	22,001
23		27	(a)	West Ham U	L 0-1		21,522
24		31	(a)	Fulham	L 1-4	Wayman	18,470
25	Jan	2	(h)	Port Vale	D 1-1	Fitzsimons	21,664
26		14	(h)	Bury	L 1-3	Wayman	8,657
27		21	(a)	Barnsley	W 4-0	Wayman 3, Betts (og)	15,934
28	Feb	4	(h)	Liverpool	L 1-2	Delapenha	12,171
29		11	(h)	Bristol C	W 2-1	Delapenha, Clough	15,412
30	Mar	3	(a)	Stoke C	W 5-2	Delapenha, Scott 2, Fitzsimons, Day	20,135
31		10	(h)	Plymouth A	L 1-2	Delapenha (pen)	17,278
32		17	(a)	Nottingham F	W 4-2	Day, Peacock 2, McKinlay (og)	22,918
33		24	(h)	Sheffield W	D 2-2	Scott 2	19,026
34		31	(a)	Leicester C	D 1-1	Fitzsimons	28,450
35	Apr	2	(h)	Rotherham U	L 0-1		20,803
36		3	(a)	Rotherham U	L 1-2	Day	13,032
37		7	(h)	Bristol R	L 0-1		12,536
38		14	(a)	Blackburn R	L 1-2	Day	21,070
39		18	(h)	Lincoln C	W 4-2	McLean, Wayman, Delapenha 2	8,298
40		21	(h)	Hull C	W 5-1	Fitzsimons, Delapenha 2, Wayman, Day	11,190
41		28	(a)	Port Vale	L 2-3	Wayman, McLean	11,781
42	May	3	(a)	Doncaster R	W 1-0	Lawrie	5,670

FINAL LEAGUE POSITION: 14th in Division Two

Appearances
Goals

FA Cup

3	Jan	7	(a)	Bradford	W 4-0	Scott 2, Delapenha, Wayman	18,524
4		28	(a)	Tottenham H	L 1-3	Scott	41,895

Appearances
Goals

Football appearance and goals grid (shirt numbers by player and match).

Ugolini R	Barnard RS	Stonehouse D	Harris WC	Robinson R	Dicks RW	Delapenha LL	Scott JC	Wayman C	Fitzsimons AG	Mitchell AJ	McPherson K	Bilcliff R	Clough BH*	Day W*	Phillips BJ	Taylor PT*	Lawrie S	Peacock A*	Corbett R	Cooper D	Mulholland FG	Birbeck J	McLean JD*	
1	2	3	4	5	6	7	8	9	10	11														1
1	2	3	4	5	6	7	8	9	10	11														2
1	2	3	4	5	6	7	8	9	10	11														3
1	2	3	4	5	6	7	8		10	11	9													4
1		3	4	5	6	7	8		10	11	9	2												5
1		3	4	5	6	7	8		10	11	9	2												6
1		3	4	5	6	7	8		10	11		2	9											7
1	2	3	4	5	6	7	8		10	11			9											8
1	2	3	4	5	6	7	8		10	11			9											9
1	2	3	4	5	6	11	8		10				9	7										10
1	2	3	4	5	6	11	8		10				9	7										11
1	2	3	4		6	11	8		10				9	7	5									12
	2	3	4	5	6	11		9	10			8		7			1							13
	2	3	4	5	6			9	10			8		7		1	1	11						14
	2	3	4	5	6	11		9	10			8		7			1							15
	2	3	4		6	11		9	10			8		7	5		1							16
	2	3	4		6	11		9				8		7	5	1		10						17
1		3	4	5	6	11		9	10			8	2	7										18
1		3	4	5	6	11		9	10			8	2	7										19
1		3	4	5	6	7	8		10	11			2	9										20
1		3	4	5	6	7	8	9	10	11		2												21
1		3	4	5	6	7	8	9	10	11		2												22
1		3	4	5	6		8		10	11		2		9	7									23
1		3	4	5	6		8	9	10	11		2				7								24
1		3	4	5	6		8	9	10	11		2				7								25
1			4	5	6		8	9	10	11		2				7			3					26
1			4	5	6	7	8	9	10	11		2							3					27
1			4	5	6	7	8	9	10	11		2							3					28
1	2		4	5	6	11	8		10					7		9			3					29
1	2		4	5	6	11	8		10					7				9	3					30
1	2		4		6	11	8		10					7	5			9	3					31
1	2		4	5		11	8		10					7				9	3	6				32
1	2		4	5		11	8		10					7				9	3	6				33
1	2		4	5		11	8		10					7				9	3	6				34
1	2		4			11	8		10					7	5			9	3		6			35
1	2		4				8	9	10	11				7	5				3		6			36
1	2		4					9	10	11				7	5				3		6	8		37
1		3	4		6	11		9	10			2		7	5							8		38
1		3	4		6	11		9	10			2		7	5							8		39
1		3	4		6	11		9	10			2		7	5							8		40
1		3	4		6	11		9	10			2		7	5							8		41
		3	4		6		8	9				2		7	5		1	11					10	42
36	23	30	42	30	36	35	36	23	40	19	5	19	9	25	12	6	5	6	12	1	3	3	6	
		1				17	7	15	14	1	4		3	6			2	2					2	

2 own-goals

Ugolini R	Barnard RS	Stonehouse D	Harris WC	Robinson R	Dicks RW	Delapenha LL	Scott JC	Wayman C	Fitzsimons AG	Mitchell AJ	McPherson K	Bilcliff R	Clough BH*	Day W*	Phillips BJ	Taylor PT*	Lawrie S	Peacock A*	Corbett R	Cooper D	Mulholland FG	Birbeck J	McLean JD*	
1		3	4	5	6	7	8	9	10	11			2											3
1			4	5	6	7	8	9	10	11			2								3			4
2	1	2	2	2	2	2	2	2	2	2			2								1			
							1	3	1															

1956-57

Manager: Bob Dennison

1	Aug	18	(h)	Stoke C	D 1-1	Harris	13,413
2		21	(a)	Bury	L 2-3	Clough 2	14,979
3		25	(a)	Barnsley	W 3-1	Clough 2, Delapenha	11,651
4		29	(h)	Bury	D 2-2	Delapenha, Clough	18,344
5	Sep	1	(a)	Leicester C	D 1-1	Clough	27,227
6		4	(a)	Grimsby T	L 2-3	Clough 2	20,505
7		8	(h)	Bristol R	W 3-2	Scott, Clough, Peacock	19,149
8		12	(h)	Grimsby T	W 2-1	Delapenha (pen), Clough	15,999
9		15	(a)	Notts C	L 1-2	Harris	10,190
10		22	(h)	Liverpool	D 1-1	Clough	21,912
11		29	(a)	Leyton O	D 1-3	Clough	17,146
12	Oct	6	(h)	Port Vale	W 3-1	Delapenha 2 (2 pens), Clough	18,586
13		13	(a)	Rotherham U	W 3-2	Clough, McLean, Burbeck	13,644
14		20	(h)	Bristol C	W 4-1	Clough 2, Delapenha, Harris	23,824
15		27	(a)	Swansea T	D 2-2	Dicks, McLean	17,552
16	Nov	3	(h)	Fulham	W 3-1	McLean, Clough, Burbeck	29,201
17		10	(a)	Nottingham F	W 4-0	Clough 3, Fitzsimons	20,862
18		17	(h)	West Ham U	W 3-1	Burbeck, Fitzsimons 2	31,513
19		24	(a)	Blackburn R	L 0-1		21,066
20	Dec	1	(h)	Lincoln C	W 3-0	Delapenha 2 (1 pen), Clough	24,598
21		8	(a)	Sheffield U	L 1-2	McLean	20,479
22		15	(a)	Stoke C	L 1-3	Fitzsimons	20,689
23		22	(h)	Barnsley	L 1-2	Dicks	11,147
24		25	(h)	Doncaster R	W 3-2	Clough 2, Harris	16,515
25		26	(a)	Doncaster R	L 1-2	Robinson	8,975
26		29	(h)	Leicester C	L 1-3	Fitzsimons	29,704
27	Jan	12	(a)	Bristol R	W 2-0	Scott, Clough	24,015
28		19	(h)	Notts C	D 0-0		23,085
29	Feb	2	(a)	Liverpool	W 2-1	Fitzsimons, Burbeck	38,890
30		9	(h)	Leyton O	L 1-2	Clough	27,315
31		16	(a)	Port Vale	L 1-2	Clough	12,064
32		23	(h)	Rotherham U	L 0-1		14,829
33	Mar	2	(a)	Bristol C	L 1-2	McLean	22,402
34		9	(h)	Swansea T	W 6-2	Fitzsimons, Day, Harris, McLean, Clough 2	17,072
35		16	(a)	Fulham	W 2-1	Clough, McLean	20,450
36		23	(h)	Nottingham F	D 2-2	McLean, Clough	25,009
37		30	(a)	West Ham U	D 1-1	Clough	15,166
38	Apr	6	(h)	Blackburn R	W 2-1	Clough 2	20,716
39		13	(a)	Lincoln C	D 1-1	McLean	8,601
40		20	(h)	Sheffield U	W 3-1	Harris 2 (2 pens), Clough	21,075
41		22	(h)	Huddersfield T	W 7-2	Clough 4, McLean, Fitzsimons, Harris (pen)	20,651
42		23	(a)	Huddersfield T	W 1-0	Fitzsimons	13,818

FINAL LEAGUE POSITION: 6th in Division Two

Appearances
Goals

FA Cup

3	Jan	5	(h)	Charlton A	D 1-1	Scott	32,863
R		10	(a)	Charlton A	W 3-2	Day, Clough, Fitzsimons	22,613
4		26	(h)	Aston Villa	L 2-3	Clough, Harris	42,396

Appearances
Goals

Taylor PT	Bilcliff R	Stonehouse D	Harris WC	Robinson R	Dicks RW	Day W	Scott JC	Cooper D	Fitzsimons AG	Delapenha LL	Lawrie S	Clough BH	Barnard RS	McLean JD	Peacock A	Corbett R	Million E*	Burbeck RT*	Mulholland FG	Brown TE	Phillips BJ	
1	2	3	4	5	6	7	8	9	10	11												1
1	2	3	4	5	6		8		10	11	7	9										2
1	2		4	5	6		8		10	11	7	9	3									3
1	2		4	5	6		8		10	11	7	9	3									4
1		3	4	5	6		8		10	11		9	2	7								5
1		3	4	5	6		8		10	11	7	9	2									6
1		3	4	5	6		7		8	11		9	2		10							7
1		3	4	5	6		7		8	11		9	2		10							8
1			4	5	6		7		8	11		9	2		10	3						9
1	3		4	5	6	7	8			11		9	2	10								10
1	3		4	5	6		8		7	11		9	2	10								11
		3	4	5	6				10	7		9	2	8			1	11				12
		3	4	5	6				10	7		9	2	8			1	11				13
		3	4	5	6				10	7		9	2	8			1	11				14
1		3	4	5	6				10	7		9	2	8				11				15
1		3	4	5	6				10	7		9	2	8				11				16
1		3	4	5	6				10	7		9	2	8				11				17
1		3	4	5	6				10	7		9	2	8				11				18
1	3		4	5	6		10			7		9	2	8				11				19
1		3	4	5	6				10	7		9	2	8				11				20
1	3		4	5	6				10	7		9	2	8				11				21
1	3		4	5	6		8		10	7		9	2					11				22
	3		4	5	6				10	7		9	2	8			1	11				23
1		3	4	5	6				10	7		9	2	8				11				24
1		3	4	5		7			10	8		9	2					11	6			25
1	3		4	5	6		8		10	7		9	2					11				26
1			4	5	6	7	8		10			9	2					11		3		27
1		3	4	5	6	7	8		10			9	2					11				28
1		3	4	5	6		8		10			9	2	7				11				29
1		3	4	5	6	7	8					9	2	10				11				30
1		3	4	5	6		8	10				9	2	7				11				31
1			4	5	6	7						9	2	8	10			11		3		32
1	2		4		6	7		10				9		8				11		3	5	33
1	2	3	4		6	7			10			9		8				11			5	34
1	2	3	4		6	7			10			9		8				11			5	35
1	2		4	3	6	7			10			9		8				11			5	36
1	2		4	3	6	7			10			9		8				11			5	37
1	2		4	3	6	7			10			9		8				11			5	38
1	2		4	3	6	7			10			9		8				11			5	39
1	2		4	3	6	7			10			9		8				11			5	40
1	2		4	3	6	7			10			9		8				11			5	41
1	2		4	3	6	7			10			9		8				11			5	42
38	21	22	42	39	41	17	19	3	36	26	4	41	30	29	4	1	4	31	1	3	10	
			8	1	2	1	2		9	8		38		10	1			4				

Taylor PT	Bilcliff R	Stonehouse D	Harris WC	Robinson R	Dicks RW	Day W	Scott JC	Cooper D	Fitzsimons AG	Delapenha LL	Lawrie S	Clough BH	Barnard RS	McLean JD	Peacock A	Corbett R	Million E*	Burbeck RT*	Mulholland FG	Brown TE	Phillips BJ	
1		3	4	5	6	7	8		10			9	2					11				3
1		3	4	5	6	7	8		10			9	2					11				R
1		3	4	5	6		8		10	7		9	2					11				4
3		3	3	3	3	2	3		3	1		3	3					3				
			1			1	1		1			2										

1957-58

Manager: Bob Dennison

1	Aug	24	(a)	Stoke C	L	1-4	Clough	23,398
2		28	(h)	Rotherham U	D	2-2	Dicks, Burbeck	28,696
3		31	(h)	Bristol C	D	0-0		21,834
4	Sep	5	(a)	Rotherham U	W	4-1	Clough 2, McLean, Fitzsimons	13,195
5		7	(a)	Cardiff C	W	2-0	Clough 2	14,013
6		11	(h)	Doncaster R	W	5-0	Burbeck, Clough 4	24,758
7		14	(h)	Liverpool	D	2-2	Peacock, McLean	30,645
8		18	(a)	Doncaster R	L	2-3	McLean, Peacock	9,237
9		21	(a)	Barnsley	D	1-1	Peacock	11,577
10		28	(a)	Leyton O	L	0-4		18,487
11	Oct	5	(h)	Charlton A	W	2-0	Clough, Fitzsimons	28,123
12		12	(h)	Fulham	W	2-0	Clough 2	31,752
13		19	(a)	Swansea T	W	4-1	McLean 2, Burbeck, Clough	8,905
14		26	(h)	Derby C	W	3-2	Clough, Fitzsimons, McLean	30,531
15	Nov	2	(a)	Bristol R	L	0-5		20,390
16		9	(h)	Lincoln C	W	3-1	Clough 2, Burbeck	20,705
17		16	(a)	Notts C	L	0-2		13,800
18		23	(h)	Ipswich T	W	5-2	Clough 4, Day	20,522
19		30	(a)	Blackburn R	D	3-3	Woods (og), Day, Burbeck	29,248
20	Dec	7	(h)	Sheffield U	L	1-2	Henderson	22,207
21		14	(a)	West Ham U	L	1-2	Cantwell (og)	20,737
22		21	(h)	Stoke C	L	1-3	Clough	22,354
23		25	(a)	Huddersfield T	L	0-1		16,281
24		26	(h)	Huddersfield T	L	0-1		22,964
25		28	(a)	Bristol C	D	0-0		23,124
26	Jan	11	(h)	Cardiff C	W	4-1	Peacock 3, Harris (pen)	23,115
27		18	(a)	Liverpool	W	2-0	Clough, Burbeck	39,246
28	Feb	1	(h)	Barnsley	W	3-1	Clough, Peacock 2	19,498
29		15	(a)	Charlton A	L	2-6	Clough 2	26,198
30		22	(a)	Ipswich T	D	1-1	Clough	17,768
31	Mar	1	(h)	Swansea T	W	2-1	Clough 2	23,312
32		8	(a)	Derby C	L	1-2	Clough	17,419
33		15	(h)	Bristol R	W	4-3	Peacock 2, Clough 2	21,274
34		19	(a)	Leyton O	W	2-0	Peacock 2	20,346
35		22	(a)	Lincoln C	W	3-2	Holliday, McLean, Clough	8,901
36		29	(h)	Notts C	W	3-1	Clough 2, Peacock	14,879
37	Apr	4	(a)	Grimsby T	L	1-4	Harris (pen)	17,579
38		7	(h)	Grimsby T	W	5-1	Clough 3, Peacock, Harris (pen)	22,546
39		12	(h)	Blackburn R	L	2-3	Clough 2	31,771
40		19	(a)	Sheffield U	L	2-3	C.Taylor, Peacock	20,967
41		21	(a)	Fulham	W	1-0	Clough	26,148
42		26	(h)	West Ham U	L	1-3	Fitzsimons	30,526

FINAL LEAGUE POSITION: 7th in Division Two

Appearances
Goals

FA Cup

3	Jan	4	(h)	Derby C	W	5-0	Day, Holliday, Peacock 2, Clough	29,530
4		25	(a)	Stoke C	L	1-3	Clough	43,756

Appearances
Goals

274

Taylor PT	Bilcliff R	Robinson R	Harris WC	Phillips BJ	Dicks RW	Day W	McLean JD	Clough BH	Fitzsimons AG	Burbeck RT	Peacock A	Delapenha LL	Mulholland FG	Stonehouse D	Scott JC	Taylor CW*	Henderson R*	Holliday E*	Brown TE	Birbeck J	Million E	
1	2	3	4	5	6	7	8	9	10	11												1
1	2	3	4	5	6	7	8	9	10	11												2
1	2	3	4	5	6	7	8	9		11	10											3
1	2	3	4	5	6		8	9	10	11		7										4
1	2	3	4	5	6		8	9	10	11		7										5
1	2	3	4	5	6		8	9	10	11		7										6
1	2	3	4	5	6		8	9		11	10	7										7
1	2	3	4	5	6	7	8			11	9	10										8
1	2	3		5	6		8		10	11	9	7	4									9
1	2	3	4	5	6		8	9	10	11		7										10
1	2		4	5	6		8	9	10	11		7		3								11
1	2		4	5	6		8	9	10	11		7		3								12
1	2			5	6		8	9	10	11		7	4	3								13
1	2		4	5	6		8	9	10	11		7		3								14
1	2		4	5	6			9	10	11		7		3	8							15
1	2		4	5	6		8	9	10	11		7		3								16
1	2		4	5	6		8	9	10	11				3		7						17
1	2		4	5	6	7	8	9	10	11				3								18
1	2	3	4	5	6	7	8	9		11							10					19
1	2	3	4	5	6		8	9		11		7					10					20
1	2	3	4	5	6	7		9	10						8			11				21
1	2		4	5	6	7		9	10					3	8			11				22
1	2		4	5		7	10	9										11	3	6		23
1	2			5	4	7	8	9	10									11	3	6		24
1	2		4	5		7	8	9			10							11	3	6		25
1	2		4	5		7	8	9			10							11	3	6		26
1	2		4	5			8	9			10	7						11	3	6		27
1	2		4	5			8	9			10	7						11	3	6		28
1	2		4	5		7	8	9			10							11	3	6		29
1	2		4	5			8	9			10	7						11	3	6		30
	2		4	5		7	8	9			10							11	3	6	1	31
	2		4	5		7	8	9			10							11	3	6	1	32
	2	3	4	5		7	8	9			10							11		6	1	33
	2	3	4	5			8	9			10	7						11		6	1	34
	2	3	4	5			8	9			10	7						11		6	1	35
	2	3	4	5		7	8	9			10							11		6	1	36
	2	3	4	5		7	8	9			10							11		6	1	37
	2	3	4	5		7	8	9			10							11		6	1	38
	2	3	4	5			8	9			10	7						11		6	1	39
	2	3	4	5			8	9			10					7		11		6	1	40
1		3	4		5		8	9			10				2	7		11		6		41
1		3	4		5		8	9			10				2	7		11		6		42
32	40	23	39	40	25	18	34	40	22	24	22	17	2	11	5	4	2	22	10	20	10	
		3			1	2	7	40	4	6	15				1	1		1				

2 own-goals

Taylor PT	Bilcliff R	Robinson R	Harris WC	Phillips BJ	Dicks RW	Day W	McLean JD	Clough BH	Fitzsimons AG	Burbeck RT	Peacock A	Delapenha LL	Mulholland FG	Stonehouse D	Scott JC	Taylor CW*	Henderson R*	Holliday E*	Brown TE	Birbeck J	Million E	
1	2		4	5		7	8	9			10							11	3	6		3
1	2		4	5		7	8	9			10							11	3	6		4
2	2		2	2		2	2	2			2							2	2	2		
							1	2										2		1		

1958-59

Manager: Bob Dennison

1	Aug	23	(h)	Brighton & HA	W	9-0	Harris 2 (2 pens), Clough 5, Peacock 2	32,367
2		25	(a)	Sheffield U	W	1-0	Clough	25,666
3		30	(a)	Grimsby T	L	2-3	Clough, Day	21,327
4	Sep	3	(h)	Sheffield U	D	0-0		42,866
5		6	(h)	Liverpool	W	2-1	Clough 2	34,714
6		11	(a)	Rotherham U	W	4-1	Rodgerson 2, Clough 2	12,089
7		13	(a)	Stoke C	L	1-3	Clough	24,866
8		17	(h)	Rotherham U	L	1-2	Clough	34,231
9		20	(a)	Charlton A	L	0-1		19,407
10		27	(h)	Bristol C	D	0-0		29,498
11	Oct	4	(a)	Cardiff C	L	2-3	Phillips, Peacock	20,560
12		11	(h)	Sunderland	D	0-0		37,223
13		18	(a)	Lincoln C	D	1-1	Peacock	10,803
14		25	(h)	Fulham	L	2-3	Clough 2	31,973
15	Nov	1	(a)	Swansea T	L	2-5	Peacock, Holliday	15,741
16		8	(h)	Scunthorpe U	W	6-1	Peacock 3, Clough 3	23,020
17		15	(a)	Leyton O	L	2-5	Peacock 2	10,234
18		22	(h)	Derby C	W	5-0	Holliday, Harris, Peacock, Scott, Davies (og)	16,773
19		29	(a)	Bristol R	L	1-3	Clough	15,767
20	Dec	6	(h)	Ipswich T	L	2-3	Clough, Burbeck	25,946
21		13	(a)	Sheffield W	L	0-2		25,127
22		20	(a)	Brighton & HA	W	6-4	Peacock 2, Clough 3, Bertolini (og)	21,063
23		26	(h)	Barnsley	W	3-1	Clough 2, Peacock	31,720
24		27	(a)	Barnsley	L	0-1		14,917
25	Jan	1	(h)	Huddersfield T	W	3-1	Clough 2, Fernie	28,154
26		31	(h)	Stoke C	D	0-0		19,077
27	Feb	7	(h)	Charlton A	L	1-3	Peacock	16,210
28		14	(a)	Bristol C	D	2-2	Harris (pen), Clough	18,336
29		21	(h)	Cardiff C	D	1-1	Peacock	12,986
30		28	(a)	Scunthorpe U	W	3-0	Clough 3	11,171
31	Mar	7	(h)	Lincoln C	L	1-2	Peacock	14,396
32		11	(h)	Grimsby T	W	1-0	Clough	12,019
33		14	(a)	Fulham	L	2-3	Clough, Harris	26,800
34		21	(h)	Swansea T	W	6-2	Clough 4, Fernie, Harris (pen)	15,272
35		28	(a)	Sunderland	D	0-0		45,954
36		30	(a)	Huddersfield T	L	1-5	Clough	14,671
37	Apr	4	(h)	Leyton O	W	4-2	Peacock 2, Harris, Clough	20,683
38		8	(a)	Liverpool	W	2-1	Holliday, Clough	36,288
39		11	(a)	Derby C	W	3-0	Clough 2, Burbeck	19,911
40		18	(h)	Bristol R	D	2-2	Burbeck, Clough	17,451
41		22	(h)	Sheffield W	D	2-2	Holliay, Rodgerson	25,822
42		25	(a)	Ipswich T	L	1-2	Burbeck	11,927

FINAL LEAGUE POSITION: 13th in Division Two

Appearances
Goals

FA Cup

3	Jan	24	(h)	Birmingham C	L	0-1		36,587

Appearances
Goals

276

Taylor PT	Bilcliff R	Robinson R	Harris WC	Phillips BJ	Walley E*	Day W	McLean JD	Clough BH	Peacock A	Holliday E	Stonehouse D	Burbeck RT	Rodgerson AR*	Dicks RW	Scott JC	Fitzsimons AG	Taylor CW	Jordon BA*	Million E	Fernie DW*	Yeoman RI*	McNeil M*	Barnard RS	Birbeck J	#
1	2	3	4	5	6	7	8	9	10	11															1
1		3	4	5	6		8	9	10	11	2	7													2
1		3	4	5	6	7	8	9	10	11	2														3
1		3	4	5	6		8	9	10	11	2	7													4
1		3	4	5	6		8	9	10	11	2	7													5
1		3	4	5	6	7		9	10	11	2		8												6
1		3	4	5	6	7		9	10	11	2		8												7
1		3	4	5	6	7		9	10	11	2		8												8
1	2		4	5		7		9	10	11	3		8	6											9
1	2		4	5		7		9			3	11		6	8	10									10
1	2		4	5			8	9	10		3	11		6		7									11
1	2		4	5				9	10		3	11	8	6		7									12
1	2		4	5				9	10		3	11		6	8	7									13
1	2	5	4			7	8	9	10		3	11		6											14
1	2	5	4			7	8	9	10	11	3			6											15
1		3	4	5			8	9	10	11	2	7		6											16
1		3	4	5				9	10	11	2	7	8	6											17
	2		4	5				9	10	11	3	7	8	6					1						18
	2		4	5				9	10	11	3	7	8	6					1						19
	2		4	5				9	10		3	11		6	7				1	8					20
	2			5		7		9	10		3	11		6					1	8	4				21
	2	3		5		7		9	10			11							1	8	4	6			22
	2			5		7		9	10		3	11							1	8	4	6			23
	2			5		7		9	10		3	11							1	8	4	6			24
	2		6	5		7		9	10		3	11							1	8	4				25
	2		6	5				9	10	11	3			4		7			1	8	4				26
	2		6	5				9	10		3	11				7			1	8	4				27
1			6	5				9	10	11	3	7								8	4		2		28
1			6	5				9	10	11	3	7								8	4		2		29
1				5				9	10	11	3	7								8	4	6	2		30
1				5				9	10	11	3	7								8	4	6	2		31
1			4	5		7		9		11	3					10				8	6	3	2		32
1			4	5				9	10	11	3	7								8	6	3	2		33
1	2		4	5				9	10	11	3	7								8	6				34
1	2		4	5		7		9	10	11	3									8	6				35
1	2	5	4					9		11	3	7				10				8	6				36
1			4	5				9	10	11	3	7								8	6	2			37
1			4	5				9		11	3	7				10				8	6	2			38
1			4	5				9		11	3	7				10				8	6	2			39
1			4	5				9		11	3	7				10				8	6	2			40
			4					9		11	3	7				10			1	8		6	5	2	41
			4					9		11	3	7				10			1	8		6	5	2	42
30	21	14	36	37	8	14	11	42	34	29	39	26	11	8	4	10	6	5	12	23	22	7	11	2	
	7	1		1				43	19	4		4	3		1				2						

2 own-goals

Taylor PT	Bilcliff R	Robinson R	Harris WC	Phillips BJ	Walley E*	Day W	McLean JD	Clough BH	Peacock A	Holliday E	Stonehouse D	Burbeck RT	Rodgerson AR*	Dicks RW	Scott JC	Fitzsimons AG	Taylor CW	Jordon BA*	Million E	Fernie DW*	Yeoman RI*	McNeil M*	Barnard RS	Birbeck J	#
	2		6	5		7		9	10		3	11							1	8	4				3
	1		1	1		1		1	1		1	1							1	1	1				

1959-60

Manager: Bob Dennison

1	Aug	22	(h)	Portsmouth	D	0-0	26,122
2		26	(a)	Cardiff C	L	0-2	23,052
3		29	(a)	Derby C	W	7-1	Peacock 4, Day, Holliday, Harris	19,537
4	Sep	2	(h)	Cardiff C	D	1-1	Harris (pen)	29,122
5		5	(h)	Plymouth A	W	6-2	Clough 4, Peacock 2	22,562
6		9	(h)	Hull C	W	4-0	Clough, Harris (pen), Yeoman, Day	28,368
7		12	(a)	Liverpool	W	2-1	Phillips, Harris	39,000
8		14	(a)	Hull C	D	3-3	Peacock 2, Clough	22,024
9		19	(h)	Charlton A	W	3-0	Clough 3	30,918
10		26	(a)	Bristol C	L	0-2		21,640
11	Oct	3	(h)	Scunthorpe U	W	3-1	Fernie, Clough 2	27,979
12		10	(h)	Sunderland	D	1-1	Holliday	47,297
13		17	(a)	Aston Villa	L	0-1		35,362
14		24	(h)	Lincoln C	W	3-2	McLean 2, Clough	24,007
15		31	(a)	Leyton O	L	0-5		15,600
16	Nov	7	(h)	Huddersfield T	W	1-0	Holliday	23,077
17		14	(a)	Ipswich T	L	0-1		12,975
18		21	(h)	Bristol R	W	5-1	Clough 3, Day, Harris	24,357
19		28	(a)	Swansea T	L	1-3	Holliday	13,889
20	Dec	5	(h)	Brighton & HA	W	4-1	Harris (pen), Clough 2, Holliday	19,677
21		12	(a)	Stoke C	W	5-2	Holliday, Day, Clough 3	15,195
22		19	(a)	Portsmouth	L	3-6	Clough, Harris (pen), Day	9,912
23		26	(a)	Rotherham U	W	2-0	Peacock, McLean	19,980
24		28	(h)	Rotherham U	W	3-0	Holliday, Harris (pen), Clough	36,184
25	Jan	2	(h)	Derby C	W	3-0	McLean, Clough 2	32,575
26		16	(a)	Plymouth A	D	2-2	Peacock, Clough	20,854
27		23	(h)	Liverpool	D	3-3	Clough 2, Harris (pen)	28,800
28	Feb	6	(a)	Charlton A	L	0-1		16,487
29		13	(h)	Bristol C	W	6-3	Clough 3, Harris (pen), McLean 2	17,871
30		20	(a)	Scunthorpe U	D	1-1	Haig (og)	10,817
31		27	(a)	Sunderland	D	2-2	Waldock, Harris (pen)	37,059
32	Mar	5	(h)	Aston Villa	L	0-1		39,432
33		12	(a)	Lincoln C	L	2-5	Clough 2	9,780
34		19	(h)	Swansea T	W	2-0	Waldock, Clough	15,719
35		26	(a)	Huddersfield T	L	0-2		13,887
36	Apr	2	(h)	Ipswich T	W	4-1	Peacock, Holliday, Clough 2	13,336
37		9	(a)	Bristol R	W	2-0	Clough, Holliday	15,847
38		16	(h)	Stoke C	W	1-0	Clough	17,394
39		18	(h)	Sheffield U	L	1-2	Clough	18,713
40		19	(a)	Sheffield U	D	0-0		13,667
41		23	(a)	Brighton & HA	L	2-3	Jennings (og), Clough	17,526
42		30	(h)	Leyton O	D	2-2	Peacock 2	13,044

FINAL LEAGUE POSITION: 5th in Division Two

Appearances
Goals

FA Cup

3	Jan	9	(a)	Sheffield W	L	1-2	Clough	49,586

Appearances
Goals

278

Taylor PT	Barnard RS	McNeil M	Harris WC	Phillips BJ	Yeoman RI	Day W	Fernie DW	Clough BH	Peacock A	Holliday E	Bilcliff R	McLean JD	Windross D*	Burbeck RT	Wilkie D*	Thomson KG*	Million E	Waldock R*	Stonehouse D	Taylor CW	Walker DH*	Rodgerson AR	Appleby R*	
1	2	3	4	5	6	7	8	9	10	11														1
1	2	3	4	5	6	7	8	9	10	11														2
1	2	3	4	5	6	7	8	9	10	11														3
1	2	3	4	5	6	7	8	9	10	11														4
1		3	4	5	6	7	8	9	10	11	2													5
1		3	4	5	6	7		9	10	11	2	8												6
1		3	4	5	6	7	8	9	10	11	2													7
1		3	4	5	6	7	8	9	10	11	2													8
1	2	3	4	5	6	7	8	9	10	11														9
1	2	3	4	5	6	7	8	9	10	11														10
1		3	4	5	6	7	8	9	10	11	2													11
1		3	4	5	6	7	8	9	10	11	2													12
1		3	4	5	6	7	8				2	10	9	11										13
1		3	4	5	6	7	8	9		11	2	10												14
1		3	4	5	6	7	8	9	10	11	2													15
1		3	4		6		8	9	10	11	2			7	5									16
1		3	4		6		8	9	10	11	2			7	5									17
1		3	4		6	7	8	9	5	11	2	10												18
1		3	4		6		8	9	5	11	2	10		7										19
1		3	4		6	7	8	9	5	11	2	10												20
1		3	4	5	6	7	8	9	10	11	2													21
1		3	4		6	7	8	9	10	11	2					5								22
1		3	4		6		8	9	10	11	2			7		5								23
1		3	4		6		8	9	10	11	2			7		5								24
1		3	4		6		8	9	10	11	2			7		5								25
1		3	4		6		8	9	10	11	2			7		5								26
		3	4		6		8	9	10	11	2			7		5	1							27
1		3	4		6		8	9		11	2			7		5		10						28
1		3	4		6		8	9		11				7		5		10	2					29
1		3	4		6		8	9		11				7		5		10	2					30
1		3	4		6		8	9		11				7		5		10	2					31
1		3	4		6		8	9		11				7		5		10	2					32
1		3	4		6		8	9	10	11						5			2	7				33
1		3	4		7		8	9	10	11						5			2		6			34
1		3	4		7		8	9	10	11						5			2		6			35
		3	4		7			9	10	11						5	1		2		6	8		36
		3	4		7		8	9	10	11						5	1		2		6			37
		3	4		7		8	9	10	11						5			2		6		1	38
		3	4	5	7		8	9	10	11									2		6		1	39
		3	4	5	7		8	9	10	11									2		6		1	40
		3	4	5	7		8	9	10	11									2		6		1	41
		3	4		7		8	9	10	11						5			2		6		1	42
34	6	42	35	19	42	19	39	41	35	41	22	16	1	9	2	18	3	8	14	1	9	1	5	
		11	1	1		5	1	39	13	8		6						2						

2 own-goals

Taylor PT	Barnard RS	McNeil M	Harris WC	Phillips BJ	Yeoman RI	Day W	Fernie DW	Clough BH	Peacock A	Holliday E	Bilcliff R	McLean JD	Windross D*	Burbeck RT	Wilkie D*	Thomson KG*	Million E	Waldock R*	Stonehouse D	Taylor CW	Walker DH*	Rodgerson AR	Appleby R*	
1		3	4		6		8	9	10	11				7		5			2					3
1		1	1		1		1	1	1	1				1		1			1					
							1																	

1960-61

Manager: Bob Dennison

1	Aug	20	(a)	Bristol R	W 3-2	Peacock 2, Holliday	20,093
2		24	(h)	Derby C	L 1-2	McLean	18,348
3		27	(h)	Liverpool	D 1-1	Peacock	21,236
4		31	(a)	Derby C	L 0-1		19,019
5	Sep	3	(a)	Rotherham U	W 2-1	Clough, Peacock	10,568
6		10	(h)	Southampton	W 5-0	Windross, Clough 2, Peacock, Harris	16,760
7		15	(a)	Scunthorpe U	D 1-1	Clough	13,852
8		17	(a)	Leeds U	D 4-4	Henderson, Clough 2, McLean	17,799
9		21	(h)	Scunthorpe U	L 1-3	Henderson	19,744
10		24	(h)	Sunderland	W 1-0	Clough	27,458
11	Oct	1	(h)	Brighton & HA	D 2-2	Clough, Henderson	15,700
12		8	(a)	Plymouth A	D 3-3	Burbeck, Clough 2	19,894
13		15	(h)	Norwich C	W 2-0	Henderson, Clough	14,737
14		22	(a)	Charlton A	D 6-6	Clough 3, Burbeck 2, McLean	10,064
15		29	(h)	Sheffield U	W 3-1	Harris (pen), Clough, McLean	23,070
16	Nov	5	(a)	Stoke C	D 1-1	Harris (pen)	9,019
17		12	(h)	Swansea T	W 3-1	Clough, Peacock 2	17,178
18		19	(a)	Luton T	L 1-6	Waldock	12,579
19		26	(h)	Lincoln C	D 1-1	Harris	13,053
20	Dec	10	(h)	Huddersfield T	W 2-1	Harris (pen), Clough	9,948
21		17	(h)	Bristol R	D 1-1	Kaye	11,759
22		26	(h)	Leyton O	W 2-0	Clough, Kaye	15,996
23		31	(a)	Liverpool	W 4-3	Molyneux (og), Peacock, Clough 2	34,645
24	Jan	14	(h)	Rotherham U	D 2-2	Morgan (og), Clough	15,638
25		21	(a)	Southampton	L 2-3	Harris (pen), Peacock	18,560
26		28	(a)	Portsmouth	W 3-0	Clough 3	7,272
27	Feb	4	(h)	Leeds U	W 3-0	Peacock, Clough 2	16,593
28		11	(a)	Sunderland	L 0-2		53,254
29		18	(a)	Brighton & HA	W 1-0	Peacock	16,286
30		23	(h)	Plymouth A	W 3-1	Hamilton, Yeoman, Walker (pen)	16,606
31	Mar	4	(a)	Norwich C	L 1-4	Kaye	25,610
32		11	(h)	Charlton A	D 2-2	Peacock, McNeil	15,126
33		14	(a)	Leyton O	D 1-1	Clough	11,658
34		18	(a)	Huddersfield T	L 0-1		11,788
35		25	(h)	Stoke C	W 1-0	Clough	8,736
36		31	(a)	Ipswich T	L 1-3	Peacock	22,239
37	Apr	1	(a)	Lincoln C	L 2-5	Clough, Peacock	5,115
38		3	(h)	Ipswich T	W 3-1	Yeoman, Harris (pen), Clough	12,996
39		8	(h)	Luton T	W 2-1	Clough 2	13,017
40		15	(a)	Swansea T	L 2-3	Peacock, Clough	15,335
41		22	(h)	Portsmouth	W 3-0	Waldock 2, Clough	9,339
42		29	(a)	Sheffield U	L 1-4	McLean	18,868

FINAL LEAGUE POSITION: 5th in Division Two

Appearances
Goals

FA Cup

3	Jan	7	(a)	Manchester U	L 0-3		49,184

Appearances
Goals

League Cup

1	Oct	3	(h)	Cardiff C	L 3-4	Clough 2, Peacock	15,695

Appearances
Goals

Player appearance grid (shirt numbers worn per match).

Appleby R	Stonehouse D	McNeil M	Harris WC	Thomson KG	Yeoman RI	McLean JD	Fernie DW	Livingstone J*	Peacock A	Holliday E	Clough BH	Waldock R*	Windross D	Burbeck RT	Henderson R	Bilcliff R	Million E	Wilkie D	Walker DH	Rodgerson AR	Kaye A*	Jones GE*	Day W	Hamilton W*	Horner W*	
1	2	3	4	5	6	7	8	9	10	11																1
1	2	3	4	5	6	7	8	9	10	11																2
1	2	3	4	5	6	7	8		10	11	9															3
1	2	3	4	5	6		8		10	11	9	7														4
1	2	3	4	5	6	7			10		9	11	8													5
1	2	3	4	5	6	7			10		9		8	11												6
1	2	3	4	5	6	7			10		9	11	8													7
1	2	3	4	5	6	7			10		9		11	8												8
1		3	4	5	6	7			10		9		11	8	2											9
		3	4	5	6	7			10	11	9			8		1	2									10
		3	4	5	6	7			10	11	9			8		1	2									11
1			4	5	6				10		9	7	11	8	2						3					12
1			4	5	6				10		9	7	11	8	2											13
1		3	4	5	6		8		10		9	7		11	2											14
1		3	4	5	6		8		10		9	7		11	2											15
1		3	4	5	6				10		9	7		11	2						8					16
1		3	4	5	6		8		10		9	7		11	2											17
1		3	4	5	6		8		10		9	7		11	2											18
1	2	3	4	5	6				10	11	9	8									7					19
1	2	3	4	5	6				10		9	8		11							7					20
1	2	3	4	5	6						9	8		11	10						7					21
1	2	3		5	4				10		9	8		11				6			7					22
1	2	3		5	4				10		9	8		11				6			7					23
	2	3		5	4				10		9	8		11			1		6		7					24
		3	8	5	4				10		9			11			1		6		7	2				25
		3	8	5	4				10		9			11			1		6		7	2				26
		3	8	5	4				10		9			11			1		6		7	2				27
		3	8	5	4				10		9			11			1		6		7	2				28
		3	8	5	4				10		9						1		6		11	2	7			29
		3		5	4				10		9			11			1		6			2	7	8		30
		3		5	4				10		9						1		6		11	2	7	8		31
		3		5	4				10		9						1		6		11	2	7	8		32
		3		5	4					11	9						1				8	2	7	10	6	33
		3		5	4					11	9						1				8	2	7	10	6	34
		3		5	4				10	11	9						1				7	2		8	6	35
		3		5	4				10	11	9						1				7	2		8	6	36
	2	3		5	4				10	11	9						1		6		7			8		37
	2			5	4				10	11	9						1		6			3	7	8		38
	2			5	4				10	11	9						1		6			3	7	8		39
	2		4	5	6				10	11	9						1					3	7	8		40
1	2			5	4				10	11	9								6		7	3		8		41
1	2			5	4				10	11	9								6		7	3		8		42
23	21	39	31	38	42	20	3	2	34	17	40	22	3	20	7	8	19	2	12	1	20	17	9	8	4	
	1	7		2	5				15	1	34	3		1	3	4		1			3		1			

2 own-goals

Appleby R	Stonehouse D	McNeil M	Harris WC	Thomson KG	Yeoman RI	McLean JD	Fernie DW	Livingstone J*	Peacock A	Holliday E	Clough BH	Waldock R*	Windross D	Burbeck RT	Henderson R	Bilcliff R	Million E	Wilkie D	Walker DH	Rodgerson AR	Kaye A*	Jones GE*	Day W	Hamilton W*	Horner W*	
1	2	3		5	4				10		9	8		11					6		7					3
1	1	1		1	1				1		1	1		1					1		1					

Appleby R	Stonehouse D	McNeil M	Harris WC	Thomson KG	Yeoman RI	McLean JD	Fernie DW	Livingstone J*	Peacock A	Holliday E	Clough BH	Waldock R*	Windross D	Burbeck RT	Henderson R	Bilcliff R	Million E	Wilkie D	Walker DH	Rodgerson AR	Kaye A*	Jones GE*	Day W	Hamilton W*	Horner W*	
1		3	4	5	6		8		10	11	9			7							2					1
1		1	1	1	1		1		1	1	1			1							1					
											1										2					

1961-62

Manager: Bob Dennison

1	Aug	19	(h)	Derby C	L	3-4	Livingstone, Waldock 2	15,462
2		26	(a)	Leyton O	L	0-2		9,269
3		30	(h)	Rotherham U	W	5-1	Holliday, Peacock 4	11,919
4	Sep	2	(h)	Preston NE	W	1-0	McNeil	16,100
5		9	(a)	Plymouth A	D	1-1	Day	16,213
6		16	(h)	Huddersfield T	W	1-0	Peacock	14,003
7		20	(h)	Luton T	L	2-4	Peacock, Kaye	15,878
8		23	(a)	Swansea T	D	3-3	Livingstone 2, Kaye	14,730
9		27	(a)	Luton T	L	2-3	Peacock 2	11,276
10		30	(h)	Southampton	D	1-1	Kaye	13,880
11	Oct	7	(h)	Liverpool	W	2-0	White 2 (2 og's)	24,123
12		14	(a)	Charlton A	L	0-1		12,156
13		21	(h)	Bury	W	2-1	Peacock, Harris	15,188
14		28	(a)	Brighton & HA	L	0-2		13,387
15	Nov	4	(h)	Scunthorpe U	L	1-2	Peacock	12,142
16		11	(a)	Sunderland	L	1-2	Kaye (pen)	48,428
17		18	(h)	Leeds U	L	1-3	Day	10,758
18		25	(a)	Bristol R	W	2-0	Peacock, Harris	9,504
19	Dec	2	(h)	Stoke C	D	2-2	Peacock, Harris	21,066
20		9	(a)	Norwich C	L	4-5	Peacock 3, Neal	14,928
21		16	(a)	Derby C	L	2-3	Kaye, Neal	15,838
22		23	(h)	Leyton O	L	2-3	Harris 2 (2 pens)	9,955
23		26	(a)	Newcastle U	W	4-3	Peacock, Harris 3	21,038
24	Jan	13	(a)	Preston NE	L	3-4	Holliday 2, Peacock	10,912
25		20	(h)	Plymouth A	D	1-1	Day	11,156
26	Feb	3	(a)	Huddersfield T	D	0-0		11,619
27		10	(h)	Swansea T	L	1-3	Livingstone	11,220
28		21	(a)	Southampton	W	3-1	Peacock, Burbeck, Weddle	13,535
29		24	(a)	Liverpool	L	1-5	Livingstone	37,629
30	Mar	3	(h)	Charlton A	W	3-2	Thomson, Harris 2	13,193
31		7	(h)	Newcastle U	W	3-0	Orritt 2, Harris	21,296
32		10	(a)	Bury	L	1-2	Harris	9,418
33		16	(h)	Brighton & HA	W	4-0	Burbeck 2, Orritt, Peacock	17,465
34		23	(a)	Scunthorpe U	D	1-1	Harris	8,149
35		31	(h)	Sunderland	L	0-1		35,666
36	Apr	3	(a)	Rotherham U	W	1-0	Gibson	6,037
37		7	(a)	Leeds U	L	0-2		16,116
38		14	(h)	Bristol R	W	5-0	Gibson 2, Burbeck, Harris (pen), Kaye	10,599
39		21	(a)	Stoke C	L	0-2		8,379
40		23	(a)	Walsall	W	2-1	Peacock 2	9,664
41		24	(h)	Walsall	W	3-0	Peacock 2, Livingstone	18,238
42		28	(h)	Norwich C	W	2-1	Kaye, Peacock	12,704

FINAL LEAGUE POSITION: 12th in Division Two

Appearances
Goals

FA Cup

3	Jan	10	(h)	Cardiff C	W	1-0	Peacock	29,260
4		27	(a)	Shrewsbury T	D	2-2	Peacock 2	14,534
R		31	(h)	Shrewsbury T	W	5-1	Harris, Holliday 2, Peacock, Kaye	34,751
5	Feb	17	(a)	Blackburn R	L	1-2	Burbeck	32,714

Appearances
Goals

League Cup

1	Sep	13	(a)	Tranmere R	W	6-3	Day, Peacock 3, Burbeck 2	9,077
2	Oct	4	(h)	Crewe A	W	3-1	Kaye 2, Peacock	9,830
3	Nov	15	(a)	Norwich C	L	2-3	Holliday, Allcock (og)	15,242

Appearances
Goals

Appearance grid (player names as column headers, running vertically):

Columns: Appleby R · Jones GE · McNeil M · Yeoman RI · Thomson KG · Horner W · Day W · Harris WC · Livingstone J · Waldock R · Holliday E · Peacock A · McLean JD · Kaye A · Burbeck RT · Stonehouse D · Gates WL* · Neal RM* · Walker DH · Weddle DK* · Hamilton W · Million E · Chapman N* · Orritt B* · Gibson IS*

No.	Appleby R	Jones GE	McNeil M	Yeoman RI	Thomson KG	Horner W	Day W	Harris WC	Livingstone J	Waldock R	Holliday E	Peacock A	McLean JD	Kaye A	Burbeck RT	Stonehouse D	Gates WL*	Neal RM*	Walker DH	Weddle DK*	Hamilton W	Million E	Chapman N*	Orritt B*	Gibson IS*
1	1	2	3	4	5	6	7	8	9	10	11														
2	1	2	3	4	5	6	7	8	9		11	10													
3	1	2	3	4	5	6	7	8		10	11	9													
4	1	2	3	4	5	6	7	8		10	11	9													
5	1	2	3	4	5	6	7			10	11	9	8												
6	1	2	3	4	5	6	7				9	8	10	11											
7	1	2	3	4	5	6					11	9	8	10	7										
8	1	3	5	4		6				10	11	9		8	7	2									
9	1	3		4		6				10	11	9		8	7	2	5								
10	1		3	4		6				10	11	9		8	7	2	5								
11	1		3	4	10		7				11	9		8	2	5	6								
12	1	3		4	10		7				11	9		8	2	5	6								
13	1	3		4			7				11	9		8	2	5	6	10							
14	1	3		4			7				11	9		8	2	5	6	10							
15	1	3	10	4								8	7	11	2	5	6	9							
16	1	3	5	4			7				11	9		8	2	6			10						
17	1	3	2	4			7				11	9		8		5	6		10						
18		2	3	4	5		7	10			11	9		8		6				1					
19		2	3	4	5		7	10			11	9		8		6				1					
20		2	3	4	5		7	10	8		11	9				6				1					
21			3	4	5		7	10			11	9		8	2	6				1					
22	1		3	4	5		7	10			11	9		8	2	6									
23	1	3	6	4			7	10			11	9		8	2	5									
24	1	3	6	4	5		7	10			11	9		8	2										
25	1	3	6	4	5		7	10			11	9		8	2										
26	1	3	6	4	5		7	10			11	9		8									2		
27	1	3	6	4	5		7	10	9		11			8									2		
28	1	3	6	4	5				10			9	7	11	2			8							
29	1	3	6	4	5				10	9			7	11	2			8							
30	1	3	6	4	5				10			7		11									2	8	
31	1	3	6	4	5				10		9	7		11									2	8	
32	1	3	6	4	5				10		9	7		11									2	8	
33	1	3	6	4	5				10		9	7		11									2	8	
34	1	3	6	4	5				10		9	7		11									2		8
35	1	3	6	4					10		9	7		11		5							2	8	
36	1	3	6	4					10	11		7				5							2	9	8
37	1	3	6	4					10	9		7				5							2	11	8
38	1	3	6	4					10			7		11		5							2	9	8
39	1	3	6	4					10			7		11		5							2	9	8
40	1	3	6	4	5						11	9		7									2	10	8
41	1	3	6	4						11		9		7		5							2	10	8
42	1	3	6	4	5					11		9		7									2	10	8
Apps	38	38	38	42	25	12	18	30	14	4	25	34	3	36	16	17	14	13	2	3	2	4	14	12	8
Goals		1		1		3	14	6	2	3		24		7	4			2		1				3	3

2 own-goals

No.	Appleby R	Jones GE	McNeil M	Yeoman RI	Thomson KG	Horner W	Day W	Harris WC	Livingstone J	Waldock R	Holliday E	Peacock A	McLean JD	Kaye A	Burbeck RT	Stonehouse D	Gates WL*	Neal RM*	Walker DH	Weddle DK*	Hamilton W	Million E	Chapman N*	Orritt B*	Gibson IS*
3	1	3	6	4	5		7	10			11	9		8	2										
4	1	3	6	4			7	10			11	9		8	2	5									
R	1	3	6	4			7	10			11	9		8	2	5									
5	1	3	6	4	5		7	10				9		8	11	2									
Apps	4	4	4	4	2		4	4			3	4		4	1	4	2								
Goals							1				2	4		1	1										

No.	Appleby R	Jones GE	McNeil M	Yeoman RI	Thomson KG	Horner W	Day W	Harris WC	Livingstone J	Waldock R	Holliday E	Peacock A	McLean JD	Kaye A	Burbeck RT	Stonehouse D	Gates WL*	Neal RM*	Walker DH	Weddle DK*	Hamilton W	Million E	Chapman N*	Orritt B*	Gibson IS*
1	1	2	3	4	5	6	7			9	8	10	11												
2	1		3	4		6		7			11	9		8		2	5		10						
3	1	3	5	4		6	7				11	9		8		2			10						
Apps	3	2	3	3	1	3	2	1		1	2	3	1	3	1	2	1		2						
Goals							1				1	4		2	2										

1 own-goal

283

1962-63

Manager: Bob Dennison

#	Month		Date		Opponent	Result	Scorers	Attendance
1	Aug		18	(a)	Sunderland	L 1-3	Burbeck	48,106
2			22	(h)	Newcastle U	W 4-2	Peacock, Gibson, Kaye (pen), Burbeck	30,841
3			25	(h)	Huddersfield T	L 0-5		18,470
4			29	(a)	Newcastle U	L 1-6	Gibson	41,550
5	Sep		1	(a)	Cardiff C	W 2-1	Kaye 2 (1 pen)	18,940
6			4	(a)	Walsall	L 0-1		10,691
7			7	(h)	Portsmouth	W 4-2	Peacock, Gibson 2, McNeil	15,958
8			12	(h)	Walsall	L 2-3	Kaye (pen), Livingstone	18,436
9			15	(a)	Preston NE	W 1-0	Peacock	14,070
10			22	(h)	Plymouth A	W 3-0	Peacock 2, Kaye	17,812
11			29	(a)	Grimsby T	W 4-3	Orritt, Peacock 2, Kaye (pen)	11,857
12	Oct		6	(a)	Leeds U	W 3-2	Gibson, Hume, Peacock	28,222
13			13	(h)	Swansea T	D 2-2	Neal, Hume	19,718
14			20	(a)	Chelsea	L 2-3	Orritt, Kaye (pen)	32,551
15			27	(h)	Luton T	L 0-2		13,835
16	Nov		3	(a)	Southampton	L 0-6		14,956
17			10	(h)	Scunthorpe U	W 4-3	Peacock 2, Burbeck, Hume	10,738
18			17	(a)	Bury	L 0-1		10.131
19			24	(h)	Rotherham U	W 2-1	Neal, Hume	12,478
20	Dec		1	(a)	Charlton A	W 4-3	Peacock 3, Gibson	12,562
21			8	(h)	Stoke C	D 2-2	Peacock, Hume	12,004
22			15	(h)	Sunderland	D 3-3	Horner, Kaye, Orritt	43,509
23			29	(a)	Norwich C	W 4-3	Gibson 2, Orritt, Peacock	13,039
24	Feb		9	(a)	Plymouth A	W 5-4	Kaye, Reeves (og), Peacock 2, Gibson	12,612
25			16	(h)	Grimsby T	L 0-1		17,804
26	Mar		2	(a)	Swansea T	D 1-1	Peacock	9,686
27			9	(h)	Chelsea	W 1-0	Kaye (pen)	24,781
28			23	(h)	Southampton	L 1-2	Peacock	15,416
29			25	(a)	Luton T	L 3-4	Peacock 2, Orritt	6,431
30			29	(a)	Scunthorpe U	D 1-1	Kaye (pen)	7,474
31	Apr		6	(h)	Bury	D 0-0		8,888
32			12	(h)	Derby C	W 5-1	Harris 2, Peacock 2, Gibson	11,116
33			13	(a)	Rotherham U	L 1-4	Horner	8,059
34			15	(a)	Derby C	D 3-3	Orritt, Moore (og), Gibson	13,253
35			20	(h)	Charlton A	W 2-1	Peacock, Wakeham (og)	9,223
36			27	(a)	Stoke C	W 1-0	Peacock	25,746
37			29	(a)	Huddersfield T	D 0-0		14,000
38	May		6	(h)	Leeds U	W 2-1	Peacock, Orritt	17,465
39			11	(h)	Cardiff C	W 3-2	Peacock 2, Horner	9,423
40			15	(h)	Preston NE	W 2-0	Peacock, Kaye	11,553
41			18	(a)	Portsmouth	D 1-1	Kaye (pen)	11,605
42			21	(h)	Norwich C	W 6-2	Metcalfe (og), Gibson, Kaye (pen), Orritt, Peacock 2	7,626

FINAL LEAGUE POSITION: 4th in Division Two

Appearances
Goals

FA Cup

#	Month		Date		Opponent	Result	Scorers	Attendance
3	Mar		5	(a)	Blackburn R	D 1-1	Orritt	16,375
R			11	(h)	Blackburn R	W 3-1	Peacock 2, Kaye (pen)	39,595
4			16	(h)	Leeds U	L 0-2		39,672

Appearances
Goals

League Cup

#	Month		Date		Opponent	Result	Scorers	Attendance
2	Sep		24	(a)	Hull C	D 2-2	Burbeck 2	10,640
R	Oct		8	(h)	Hull C	D 1-1*	Gibson	15,612
2R			10	(a)	Hull C	L 0-3		11,960

*After extra-time

Appearances
Goals

This was the severest winter in living memory with snow and ice causing many postponements. From 26 December 1962 until 16 February 1963 only one game was played at Ayresome Park before the weather closed in again for almost another month. The League was extended until the end of May 1963 to cope with the huge backlog of fixtures.

Appleby R	Chapman N	Jones GE	Yeoman RI	Thomson KG	Neal RM	Kaye A	Gibson IS	Peacock A	Orritt B	Burbeck RT	Harris WC	Lightening AD*	Horner W	McNeil M	Livingstone J	Gates WL	Hume RM*	Nurse MTG*	Emmerson M*	Povey W*	Knowles CB*	Bryan PA*	Stonehouse D	Walker DH	No.
1	2	3	4	5	6	7	8	9	10	11															1
1	2	3	4	5	6	7	8	9	10	11															2
1	2	3	4	5	6	7	8	9			11	10													3
		3	4		5	7	8	9		11	10	1	6	2											4
1		3	4		5	7	8	9	10				6	2			11								5
1		3	4		5	7	8	9	10				6	2			11								6
1		3	4		5	7	8	9	10				6	2			11								7
1		3	4			7	8	9	10				6	2			11	5							8
	6	3	4		5	7		9	10			1	8	2			11								9
		3	4		5	7	8	9	10			1	6	2			11								10
	2		4			7	8	9	10			1	6	3			11	5							11
		3	4		6	7	8	9	10			1		2			11	5							12
1		3	4		6	7	8	9	10					2			11	5							13
		3	4		6	7	8	9	10			1		2			11	5							14
	2	3	4		6	7	8	9	10			1					11	5							15
		3	4		6	7	8	9		10		1		2			11	5							16
		3	4		6	7	8	9		10		1		2			11	5							17
		3	4		6	7	8	9	10					2			11	5	1						18
		3	4		6	7	8	9	10					2			11	5	1						19
		3	4		6	7	8	9		10				2			11	5	1						20
		3	4		6	7		9	8	10				2			11	5	1						21
		3	4			7	8	9	10				6	2			11	5	1						22
		3	4			7	8	9		10			6	2				5	1	11					23
		3	4			7	8	9					6	2			11	5	1	10					24
		3	4			7	8	9	10				6	2				5	1	11					25
		3	4		6	7	8	9	10	11				2				5	1						26
		3	4			7	8	9	10	11			6	2				5	1						27
		3	4			7	8	9		11	10	1	6	2				5							28
	2	3	4			7		9	10			8	1	6				5		11					29
	2	3	4			7	8		9		10	1		6				5		11					30
		3	4			7	8	9	11		10	1	6	2				5							31
		3	2			7	8	9	6		10	1			4		11	5							32
		3	2				8	9	6	7	10	1			4		11	5							33
1		3	4				8	9	10				6				11	5		7	2				34
1		3	4				8	9	10				6				11	5			2				35
1		3	4			7	8	9	11		10		6					5			2				36
1		3	4			7	8	9	11		10		6					5			2				37
1			4			7	8	9	11		10		6	3				5			2				38
1			4			7	8	9	11		10		6	3				5			2				39
1			4			7	8	9	11		10		6	3				5			2				40
1			4			7	8	9	11		10		6	3				5			2				41
1			4			7	8	9	11		10		6	3				5			2				42
17	8	36	42	3	20	40	39	40	35	13	15	15	25	32	4	2	19	32	10	6	9				
					2	14	12	31	8	3	2		3	1	1		5								

4 own-goals

Appleby R	Chapman N	Jones GE	Yeoman RI	Thomson KG	Neal RM	Kaye A	Gibson IS	Peacock A	Orritt B	Burbeck RT	Harris WC	Lightening AD*	Horner W	McNeil M	Livingstone J	Gates WL	Hume RM*	Nurse MTG*	Emmerson M*	Povey W*	Knowles CB*	Bryan PA*	Stonehouse D	Walker DH	No.
		3	4			7	8	9	10	11			6	2				5	1						3
		3	4			7	8	9	10	11			6	2				5	1						R
		3	4			7	8	9	10	11			6	2				5	1						4
		3	3			3	3	3	3	3			3	3				3	3						
							1		2	1															

Appleby R	Chapman N	Jones GE	Yeoman RI	Thomson KG	Neal RM	Kaye A	Gibson IS	Peacock A	Orritt B	Burbeck RT	Harris WC	Lightening AD*	Horner W	McNeil M	Livingstone J	Gates WL	Hume RM*	Nurse MTG*	Emmerson M*	Povey W*	Knowles CB*	Bryan PA*	Stonehouse D	Walker DH	No.
		3	4	5		7	8	9	10	11		1	6	2											2
	2	3	4		6	7	8		10			1					9	5	11						R
	2		4		6					7	8	1						5	11		9	3	10		2R
	2	2	3		2	2	1	2	2	1	3	1	1	1			2	2			1	1	1		
									1			2													

1963-64

Manager: Raich Carter

1	Aug	24	(h)	Plymouth A	W	5-0	Gibson, Horner, Peacock 2, Harris	18,744
2		26	(h)	Newcastle U	W	3-0	Gibson, Kaye 2	37,803
3		31	(a)	Charlton A	W	4-2	Braithwaite 2, Kaye, Gibson	13,345
4	Sep	4	(a)	Newcastle U	L	0-2		56,918
5		7	(h)	Grimsby T	W	6-0	Harris 2, Gibson 2, Kaye, Horsfield	22,458
6		9	(h)	Rotherham U	D	2-2	Kaye (pen), Harris	30,013
7		14	(a)	Preston NE	D	2-2	Jones, Gibson	15,499
8		17	(a)	Rotherham U	L	1-2	Gibson	12,572
9		21	(h)	Leyton O	W	2-0	Gibson 2	23,282
10		28	(a)	Swansea T	L	1-2	Harris	10,519
11	Oct	5	(h)	Southampton	W	1-0	Peacock	19,892
12		9	(a)	Leeds U	L	0-2		37,019
13		12	(h)	Portsmouth	W	3-1	Harris, Orritt, Gibson	17,388
14		19	(a)	Scunthorpe U	L	0-1		7,347
15		26	(h)	Sunderland	W	2-0	Orritt 2	43,905
16	Nov	2	(a)	Cardiff C	D	1-1	Orritt	13,455
17		9	(h)	Swindon T	D	1-1	Harris	26,476
18		23	(h)	Bury	W	2-0	Gibson, Orritt	15,815
19		30	(a)	Northampton T	L	2-3	Kaye, Gibson	10,346
20	Dec	7	(h)	Norwich C	L	0-1		15,592
21		14	(a)	Plymouth A	L	0-2		8,559
22		21	(h)	Charlton A	L	2-3	Nurse, Braithwaite	11,917
23		26	(h)	Derby C	W	3-0	Orritt, Braithwaite, Ratcliffe	18,422
24		28	(a)	Derby C	D	2-2	Ratcliffe, Horsfield	11,506
25	Jan	11	(a)	Grimsby T	L	1-3	Peacock	6,681
26		18	(h)	Preston NE	W	3-0	Peacock, Kaye, Harris	14,985
27	Feb	1	(a)	Leyton O	L	2-3	Horsfield 2	8,367
28		8	(h)	Swansea T	W	2-1	Horsfield, Kaye	12,668
29		15	(a)	Southampton	D	2-2	Harris, Braithwaite	14,978
30		22	(a)	Portsmouth	L	0-1		12,081
31		29	(h)	Manchester C	D	2-2	Gates, Harris	12,763
32	Mar	7	(a)	Sunderland	D	0-0		46,855
33		14	(a)	Leeds U	L	1-3	Horsfield	15,987
34		17	(a)	Manchester C	L	0-1		8,053
35		21	(a)	Swindon T	L	0-2		13,810
36		28	(h)	Scunthorpe U	W	2-0	Harris, Gates	8,839
37		30	(h)	Huddersfield T	D	1-1	Gates	9,871
38		31	(a)	Huddersfield T	L	0-1		10,964
39	Apr	4	(a)	Bury	D	1-1	Gibson	6,148
40		10	(h)	Northampton T	W	1-0	Branston (og)	9,220
41		15	(a)	Norwich C	D	1-1	Braithwaite	13,135
42		24	(h)	Cardiff C	W	3-1	Gibson, Horsfield 2	8,472

FINAL LEAGUE POSITION: 10th in Division Two

Match 1: Some sources credit Williams (og), club credit Horner.

Appearances
Goals

FA Cup

3	Jan	4	(a)	Brentford	L	1-2	Kaye	16,070

Appearances
Goals

League Cup

2	Sep	25	(a)	Bradford	D	2-2	Peacock 2	9,273
R	Oct	2	(h)	Bradford	L	2-3	Peacock, Harris	11,991

Appearances
Goals

	Connachan ED*	Knowles CB	Jones GE	Orritt B	Nurse MTG	Horner W	Kaye A	Gibson IS	Peacock A	Harris WC	Braithwaite RM*	Yeoman RI	Horsfield A*	Kirk H*	McNeil M	Gates WL	Ratcliffe D*	Chapman N	Townsend J	Appleby R	Spraggon F*	Rodgerson AR
1	1	2	3	4	5	6	7	8	9	10	11											
2	1	2	3	4	5	6	7	8	9	10	11											
3	1	2	3	4	5	6	7	8	9	10	11											
4	1	2	3	4	5	6	7	8	9	10	11											
5	1	2	3	11	5	6	7	8		10			4	9								
6	1	2	3	9	5	6	7	8		10			4		11							
7	1	2	11	4	5	6	7	8		10				9		3						
8	1	2	11	4	5	6	7	8		10						3	9					
9	1	2	11	4	5	6	7	8	9	10						3						
10	1	2	3	4	5	6	7	8	9	10							11					
11	1	2	3	4	5	6	7	8	9	10							11					
12	1	2	3	9	5	6	7	8		10			4				11					
13	1	2	3	9	5	6	7	8		10			4				11					
14	1	2	3	9	5	6	7	8		10			4				11					
15	1	2	3	9	5	6	7	8		10			4				11					
16	1	2	3	9	5	6	7	8		10			4				11					
17	1	2	3	9	5	6	7	8		10			4				11					
18	1	2	3	9		6	7	8		10			4			5	11					
19	1	2	3	9		6	7	8		10			4			5	11					
20	1		3	9	5	6	7	8		10			4				11	2				
21	1	2	3	9	5	4	7	8		10					6		11					
22	1	2	3	4	5	6	7	8			11		9			10						
23	1	2	3	4	5	6	10	8			11		9			7						
24	1	2	3	4	5	6		8		10	11		9			7						
25	1	2	3	4	5	6	10	8	9		11					7						
26	1			6	5		7	8	9	10	11	4			3		2					
27	1			6	5		7	8		10	11	4	9		3		2					
28	1			6			7	8			11	4	9		3	5	10	2				
29	1			9	5		7	8		10	11	6			3		2	4				
30	1			9	5		10	8			11	6			3		7	2	4			
31	1			6	5		7	8		10	11				3	9	2	4				
32	1	2		6	5		7	8			11	4			3	9	10					
33	1	2		6	5		7	8			11	4	9		3		10					
34		2			6		7			10	11	4			3	5	9	8	1			
35	1	2		6			7	10			11	4	9		3	5	8					
36	1			6	5	4		8			10	11			3	9	7	2				
37	1			6	5			8			10	11			3	9	7	2	4			
38	1		3		5		7	8			10				2	9	11	4	6			
39	1		3		5		7	8			10				2	9	11	4	6			
40	1		3		5		7	8			10		9		2		11	4	6			
41	1		3		5			8			10	11	9			2	7	4	6			
42	1			7	5			8			10	11	9		3	2		4	6			
	41	28	29	37	37	27	36	42	9	34	22	20	12	1	20	14	25	9	13	1	5	
		1	6	1	1	8	14	5	11	6		8			3	2						

1 own-goal

	Connachan ED*	Knowles CB	Jones GE	Orritt B	Nurse MTG	Horner W	Kaye A	Gibson IS	Peacock A	Harris WC	Braithwaite RM*	Yeoman RI	Horsfield A*	Kirk H*	McNeil M	Gates WL	Ratcliffe D*	Chapman N	Townsend J	Appleby R	Spraggon F*	Rodgerson AR	
	1	2	3	4	5	6	8	10	9		11					7							3
	1	1	1	1	1	1	1	1	1		1					1							
						1																	

	Connachan ED*	Knowles CB	Jones GE	Orritt B	Nurse MTG	Horner W	Kaye A	Gibson IS	Peacock A	Harris WC	Braithwaite RM*	Yeoman RI	Horsfield A*	Kirk H*	McNeil M	Gates WL	Ratcliffe D*	Chapman N	Townsend J	Appleby R	Spraggon F*	Rodgerson AR	
	1	2	11	4	5	6	7	8	9				3							10			2
	1		3	4	5		7	8	9	10			11			2		6					R
	2	1	2	2	2	1	2	2	2	1			1	1		1		1	1				
									3	1													

287

1964-65

Manager: Raich Carter

1	Aug	22	(a)	Southampton	W 3-0	Braithwaite 2, Horsfield	18,855
2		24	(h)	Northampton T	W 1-0	Horsfield	27,122
3		29	(h)	Huddersfield T	D 0-0		23,152
4	Sep	1	(a)	Northampton T	D 1-1	Horsfield	17,028
5		5	(a)	Coventry C	L 0-3		36,086
6		7	(h)	Bolton W	W 5-2	Harris 2, Kaye (pen), Townsend, Irvine	22,670
7		12	(h)	Cardiff C	D 0-0		22,770
8		16	(a)	Bolton W	L 2-4	Harris, Gibson	13,912
9		19	(a)	Preston NE	L 3-4	Kaye (pen), Irvine 2	15,726
10		26	(h)	Ipswich T	L 2-4	Bolton (og), Horsfield	15,593
11	Oct	3	(a)	Plymouth A	L 0-1		18,382
12		6	(a)	Charlton A	W 2-0	Irvine, Horner (pen)	11,837
13		10	(h)	Bury	D 3-3	Irvine, Bunner (og), Nurse	11,772
14		17	(a)	Crystal P	L 1-3	Irvine	18,055
15		24	(h)	Norwich C	W 2-0	Kaye, Irvine	10,061
16		31	(a)	Rotherham U	W 3-2	Braithwaite 2, Irvine	10,552
17	Nov	7	(h)	Swansea T	W 4-0	Masson, Townsend 2, Kaye	11,855
18		14	(a)	Derby C	D 3-3	Horner, Gibson, Irvine	11,933
19		21	(h)	Swindon T	W 4-1	Nurse, Gibson, Masson 2	14,948
20		28	(a)	Portsmouth	L 1-2	Irvine	10,653
21	Dec	5	(h)	Manchester C	L 0-1		13,873
22		12	(h)	Southampton	W 4-1	Irvine, Masson, Kaye (pen), Townsend	12,499
23		26	(h)	Newcastle U	L 0-2		38,194
24		28	(a)	Newcastle U	L 1-2	Kaye	54,750
25	Jan	2	(h)	Coventry C	L 2-3	Gibson, Nurse	15,714
26		15	(a)	Cardiff C	L 1-6	Irvine	9,490
27		23	(h)	Preston NE	D 1-1	Townsend	12,466
28	Feb	6	(a)	Ipswich T	L 2-5	Irvine, Nurse	11,071
29		13	(h)	Plymouth A	L 1-3	Irvine	10,165
30		23	(a)	Bury	L 2-3	Gibson, Horsfield	6,143
31		27	(h)	Crystal P	D 0-0		12,071
32	Mar	6	(a)	Manchester C	D 1-1	Irvine	14,231
33		13	(h)	Rotherham U	L 3-5	Nurse (pen), Le Flem, Irvine	10,972
34		20	(a)	Swansea T	W 2-1	Irvine, Nurse	9,366
35		27	(h)	Derby C	L 1-2	Gibson	12,719
36		30	(a)	Huddersfield T	L 0-1		13,215
37	Apr	3	(a)	Swindon T	W 1-0	Jones	13,862
38		9	(h)	Portsmouth	W 4-1	Orritt, Gibson, Irvine 2	10,533
39		16	(a)	Leyton O	D 1-1	Gibson	11,200
40		17	(a)	Norwich C	L 0-2		12,228
41		19	(h)	Leyton O	W 2-0	Horner, Irvine	11,749
42		24	(h)	Charlton A	L 1-2	Nurse	8,627

FINAL LEAGUE POSITION: 17th in Division Two

Appearances
Goals

FA Cup

3	Jan	9	(h)	Oldham A	W 6-2	Horsfield 2, Irvine 3, Kaye	17,178
4		30	(a)	Charlton A	D 1-1	Nurse	17,982
R	Feb	1	(h)	Charlton A	W 2-1	Gibson, Masson	30,460
5		20	(h)	Leicester C	L 0-3		31,099

Appearances
Goals

League Cup

2	Sep	23	(a)	Charlton A	L 1-2	Irvine	8,625

Appearances
Goals

Connachan ED	Gates WL	Jones GE	Townsend J	Nurse MTG	Orritt B	Kaye A	Gibson IS	Horsfield A	Irvine JD*	Braithwaite RM	Harris WC	Ratcliffe D	Horner W	Bryan PA	Spraggon F	Masson DS*	Chapman N	Appleby R	Davidson I*	Le Flem RP*	No.
1	2	3	4	5	6	7	8	9	10	11											1
1	2	3	4	5	6	7	8	9	10	11											2
1	2	3	4	5	6	7	8	9	10	11											3
1	2	3	4	5	6	7	8	9	10	11											4
1	2	3	4	5	6	7	8	9	10	11											5
1	2	3	4	5	6	7	8		9		10	11									6
1	2	3	4	5	6	7	8		9		10	11									7
1		3	4	5	6	7	8		9		10	11	2								8
1	2	3	4	5	6	7	8	9	10	11											9
1		3	4	5	6	7	8	9	10	11				2							10
1		3	10	5		7	8		9		11		4	2	6						11
1		3	10	5			8		9		11	7	4	2	6						12
1		3	10	5			8		9		11	7	4	2	6						13
1	2	3		5	10		8		9		11	7	4		6						14
1	2	3	6	5		7	8		9		11		4			10					15
1	2	3	6		5	7	8		9		11		4			10					16
1	2	3	6	5		7			9	8	11		4			10					17
1	2	3	6	5		7	8		9		11		4			10					18
1		3	6	5	4	7	8		9		11					10	2				19
1		3	6	5	4	7	8		9		11		2			10					20
1		3	6	5	4	7	8		9		11		2			10					21
1			4	5	3	7	8		9		11		2		6	10					22
1		3	4	5	6	7	8		9		11		2			10					23
1		3	4	5		7	8		9		11	10	2		6						24
1		3	4	5		7	8				11				6	10	2				25
1		3	4	5		7	8	9	10		11		2		6						26
1	2	3	4	5		7	8		9		11				6	10					27
1	2	3	4	5			8		9		11	7			6	10					28
1	2	3	6	5		7	8		9	10	11		4								29
	2	3	7	5			8	9	10		11		4					1	6		30
	2	3		5			8	9	10		11		4					1	6	7	31
	2	3	10	5			8		9		11		4					1	6	7	32
	2	3	10	5			8		9		11		4					1	6	7	33
1	2	3	4	5	9		8		10		11								6	7	34
1	2	3	4	5	9		8		10		11								6	7	35
1	2	3	10	5		7	8		9		11		4						6		36
1	2	3		5	9	7	8		10		11		4						6		37
1	2	3		5	9	7	8		10		11		4						6		38
1	2	3		5	9	7	8		10		11		4						6		39
1	2	3	4	5		7	8	9	10		11								6		40
1	2	3	6	5		7	8		9		11		4			10					41
1	2	3	6	5		7	8		9		11		4			10					42
38	29	41	37	41	22	32	41	11	42	26	6	26	23	4	7	14	2	4	11	5	
	1	5	6	2	6	8	5	20	4	3		3		3		4			1		

2 own-goals

Connachan ED	Gates WL	Jones GE	Townsend J	Nurse MTG	Orritt B	Kaye A	Gibson IS	Horsfield A	Irvine JD*	Braithwaite RM	Harris WC	Ratcliffe D	Horner W	Bryan PA	Spraggon F	Masson DS*	Chapman N	Appleby R	Davidson I*	Le Flem RP*	No.
1		3	4	5		7	8	9	10		11		6			2					3
1	2	3	4	5		7	8		9		11		6			10					4
1	2	3	4	5		7	8		9		11		6			10					R
	2	3	6	5		7	8	9	10		11		4					1			5
3	3	4	4	4		4	4	2	4		4		4			2		1	1		
			1			1	1	2	3				1								

Connachan ED	Gates WL	Jones GE	Townsend J	Nurse MTG	Orritt B	Kaye A	Gibson IS	Horsfield A	Irvine JD*	Braithwaite RM	Harris WC	Ratcliffe D	Horner W	Bryan PA	Spraggon F	Masson DS*	Chapman N	Appleby R	Davidson I*	Le Flem RP*	No.
1		3	4	5	6	7		9		11	8		2			10					2
1		1	1	1	1	1		1		1	1		1			1					
								1													

1965-66

Manager: Raich Carter

1	Aug	21	(h)	Manchester C	D	1-1	Nurse	17,982
2		25	(a)	Birmingham C	D	1-1	Orritt	16,772
3		28	(a)	Huddersfield T	L	0-6		14,772
4		31	(h)	Birmingham C	D	1-1	Orritt	17,300
5	Sep	4	(h)	Crystal P	D	2-2	Irvine, Rooks	10,269
6		7	(a)	Ipswich T	L	1-2	Gibson	15,478
7		11	(a)	Preston NE	D	1-1	Irvine	15,024
8		14	(h)	Ipswich T	W	3-2	Ratcliffe, Garbett, Irvine	15,221
9		18	(h)	Charlton A	D	2-2	Braithwaite, Horner	13,476
10		25	(a)	Plymouth A	D	2-2	Orritt, Holliday	11,955
11	Oct	9	(h)	Rotherham U	W	4-0	Horner, McMordie, Gibson, Irvine	13,152
12		16	(a)	Wolves	L	0-3		20,927
13		22	(h)	Norwich C	L	0-1		10,897
14		26	(h)	Portsmouth	W	5-2	Harris (og), Rooks (pen), Horsfield, Holliday, Irvine	9,582
15		30	(a)	Bury	L	0-2		8,070
16	Nov	6	(h)	Southampton	D	0-0		11,555
17		13	(a)	Derby C	L	0-5		12,019
18		20	(h)	Cardiff C	L	3-4	McMordie, Holliday, Anderson	11,898
19	Dec	4	(h)	Coventry C	D	1-1	Irvine	12,024
20		11	(a)	Bristol C	D	2-2	Irvine, Holliday	16,086
21		18	(h)	Wolves	W	3-1	Rooks, Gibson, Horsfield	13,419
22		27	(h)	Leyton O	W	2-1	McMordie, Horsfield	21,107
23	Jan	1	(a)	Rotherham U	L	1-4	Anderson	10,922
24		8	(h)	Derby C	D	0-0		11,897
25		29	(a)	Manchester C	L	1-3	Townsend	25,278
26	Feb	5	(h)	Huddersfield T	L	1-3	Downing	13,485
27		19	(a)	Crystal P	D	1-1	Irvine	13,902
28		26	(h)	Preston NE	W	2-1	Singleton (og), Irvine	13,229
29	Mar	5	(h)	Bristol C	W	4-2	Irvine 2, Gibson, Rooks	13,744
30		8	(a)	Carlisle U	L	1-2	Irvine	13,459
31		12	(a)	Charlton A	L	0-1		11,482
32		19	(a)	Plymouth A	L	0-1		12,284
33		25	(a)	Portsmouth	L	1-4	Gibson	10,640
34	Apr	2	(a)	Southampton	L	1-3	Irvine	13,687
35		9	(h)	Bury	W	1-0	Braithwaite	12,983
36		11	(a)	Bolton W	L	0-6		11,948
37		12	(h)	Bolton W	D	1-1	Gibson	11,384
38		18	(a)	Leyton O	W	3-2	Irvine 2, Rooks (pen)	2,286
39		23	(h)	Carlisle U	L	0-2		15,564
40		27	(a)	Norwich C	W	2-1	McMordie, Downing	7,849
41		30	(a)	Coventry C	L	1-2	Gibson	19,747
42	May	3	(a)	Cardiff C	L	3-5	Rooks 3 (1 pen)	12,935

FINAL LEAGUE POSITION: 21st in Division Two

Appearances
Sub Appearances
Goals

FA Cup

3	Jan	22	(a)	Tottenham H	L	0-4		37,349

Appearances
Goals

League Cup

2	Sep	22	(a)	Colchester U	W	4-2	Horner, Irvine 2, McMordie	7,777
3	Oct	13	(h)	Millwall	D	0-0		12,927
R		18	(a)	Millwall	L	1-3*	Gibson	12,888

*After extra-time

Appearances
Goals

Player appearance and goals grid. Columns (left to right): Connachan ED, Gates WL, Jones GE, Horner W, Nurse MTG, Davidson I, Holliday E*, Gibson IS, Horsfield A, Ratcliffe D, Braithwaite RM, Orritt B, Le Flem RP, Rooks R*, Townsend J, Irvine JD, Chapman N, Garbett TG*, Appleby R, McMordie A*, Downing DG*, Marshall SK*, Spraggon F, Masson DS, Anderson S*, McPartland D*, Smith RA*, Butler G*, Lawson J*.

Connachan ED	Gates WL	Jones GE	Horner W	Nurse MTG	Davidson I	Holliday E*	Gibson IS	Horsfield A	Ratcliffe D	Braithwaite RM	Orritt B	Le Flem RP	Rooks R*	Townsend J	Irvine JD	Chapman N	Garbett TG*	Appleby R	McMordie A*	Downing DG*	Marshall SK*	Spraggon F	Masson DS	Anderson S*	McPartland D*	Smith RA*	Butler G*	Lawson J*	#
1	2	3	4	5	6	7	8	9	10	11																			1
1	2	3	4	5	6	7	8	9			10	11																	2
1	2	3	4	10	6	7	8	9				11	5																3
1	2	3			6	7	8				9	11	5	4	10														4
1	2	3			6	7	8				9	11	5	4	10														5
1		3	4		6		8		7	11			5		10	2		9											6
		3	4		6		8		7	11	12		5		10	2*		9	1										7
	2	3	4		6		8		7	11			5		10			9	1										8
	2	3	4		6		8		7	11	12		5		10			9	1*										9
1	2	3	4		6	7	8			11	9		5		10														10
1	2	3	4		6	7	8			11			5		9				10										11
1	2	3	4		6	7	8			11			5		10	9													12
1	2	3	4		6	11	8*						5		9				7	10		12							13
1	2	3			11		8	7				4	5		9				10			6							14
1	2	3			6	11	8	7				4	5		10							12		9*					15
1		3			6	11	9	7				4	5		10	2						8							16
1	2	3			6	11	9	7				4	5		10							8							17
1	2	3			6	11	10	7					5		9							8			4				18
1*	2	3				11	10	7			12		5		9							8		6	4				19
	2	3			6	11	10	7*					5	12	9							8		4	1				20
	2	3			6	11	10	9					5		7							8		4	1				21
	2	3			6	11	10	9					5		7							8		4	1				22
	2	3	12		6	11*	10	9					5		7							8		4	1				23
	2	3					10	9	11				5		7							8	6	4	1				24
	2	3			6		8						5		7			9		11	10			4	1				25
	2	3			6		7						5	4	9				10	11		8			1				26
	5	3	4				8				11		9		10	2			7					6	1				27
	5	3	4				8				11		9		10	2			7					6	1				28
	5	3	4*				8				11		9		10	2			7					6	1	12			29
	5	3					8				11		9		10	2			7					6	1	4			30
	5*	3					8				11		9	12	10	2			7					6	1	4			31
		3	2				8		11				5	4	10				7			6			1				32
		3	4	6			8			11			9	7	10	2									1	5			33
		3	4		6		8			11			9	7	10	2								6	1	5			34
		3	4				8			11			9	7	10									6	1	5	2		35
		3	4			7	8						5	10	9				1					6		2		11	36
		3	4			7	8						5	10	9				1					6		2		11	37
		3	4			7	8						5	10	9				1					6		2		11	38
		3	4	6			8							9				1	10	7						5	2	11	39
		3	4	6			8							9				1	10	7						5	2	11	40
		3	4	6			8						5	9				1	10	7	3					2			41
	11	4		6			8						5		9			1	10	7						3		2	42
16	28	42	24	3	27	23	38	12	14	16	9	4	37	15	31	11	7	9	17	13	2	5	1	21	17	9	6	5	
				1								3		2							1	1		1						
		2	1		4	7	3	1	2	3			8	11	15		1		4	2				2					

2 own-goals

Connachan ED	Gates WL	Jones GE	Horner W	Nurse MTG	Davidson I	Holliday E*	Gibson IS	Horsfield A	Ratcliffe D	Braithwaite RM	Orritt B	Le Flem RP	Rooks R*	Townsend J	Irvine JD	Chapman N	Garbett TG*	Appleby R	McMordie A*	Downing DG*	Marshall SK*	Spraggon F	Masson DS	Anderson S*	McPartland D*	Smith RA*	Butler G*	Lawson J*	#
	2	3			6		10	9	7			11	5					8						4	1				3
	1	1			1		1	1	1			1	1					1						1	1				

Connachan ED	Gates WL	Jones GE	Horner W	Nurse MTG	Davidson I	Holliday E*	Gibson IS	Horsfield A	Ratcliffe D	Braithwaite RM	Orritt B	Le Flem RP	Rooks R*	Townsend J	Irvine JD	Chapman N	Garbett TG*	Appleby R	McMordie A*	Downing DG*	Marshall SK*	Spraggon F	Masson DS	Anderson S*	McPartland D*	Smith RA*	Butler G*	Lawson J*	#
1	2	3	4		6	7	8			11			5		9				10										2
1	2	3	4		6	7	8			11			5		9				10										3
1	2	3	4		6	7	8		9			5	11		10														R
3	3	3	3		3	3	3		2	1			3		3				3										
			1			1							2		1														

1966-67

Manager: Stan Anderson

1	Aug	20	(a)	Colchester U	W	3-2	Lawson, O'Rourke 2	4,382
2		27	(h)	Bristol R	L	1-2	Irvine	10,658
3	Sep	3	(a)	Oxford U	D	1-1	Masson (pen)	6,668
4		6	(a)	Queen's Park R	L	0-4		8,807
5		10	(h)	Oldham A	L	0-2		8,932
6		17	(a)	Scunthorpe U	L	2-3	Horsfield 2	4,053
7		24	(h)	Workington	W	3-2	Hickton (pen), Horsfield 2	8,813
8		26	(h)	Queen's Park R	D	2-2	Horsfield, O'Rourke	13,091
9	Oct	1	(a)	Gillingham	L	1-5	Horsfield	5,789
10		8	(a)	Watford	L	0-2		6,677
11		15	(h)	Swindon T	W	4-0	O'Rourke 3, Irvine	8,126
12		17	(h)	Swansea T	W	4-1	Horner, O'Rourke, Horsfield, Downing	12,471
13		22	(a)	Reading	D	0-0		6,485
14		29	(h)	Doncaster R	W	2-0	Horner, Horsfield	12,082
15	Nov	5	(a)	Mansfield T	W	5-4	O'Rourke 2, Downing 2, Hickton	6,379
16		12	(h)	Grimsby T	L	0-1		14,164
17		15	(a)	Swansea T	D	4-4	O'Rourke 2, Downing, Hickton	4,297
18		19	(a)	Walsall	L	1-2	Horsfield	8,967
19	Dec	3	(a)	Torquay U	L	1-2	Hickton	4,701
20		10	(h)	Brighton & HA	W	1-0	O'Rourke	9,585
21		17	(h)	Colchester U	W	4-0	O'Rourke 2, Horsfield 2	8,819
22		26	(a)	Darlington	W	3-0	Downing, O'Rourke, Chadwick	18,144
23		27	(h)	Darlington	W	4-0	Hickton (pen), Horsfield 2, Lawson	25,213
24		31	(a)	Bristol R	D	2-2	Horsfield, Chadwick	10,645
25	Jan	14	(a)	Oldham A	W	1-0	Horsfield	12,659
26		21	(h)	Scunthorpe U	W	2-1	Gates, Horsfield	19,005
27	Feb	4	(a)	Workington	W	2-1	Hickton, Lugg	4,246
28		11	(h)	Gillingham	D	1-1	Horsfield	18,945
29		18	(a)	Bournemouth	D	1-1	Butler	5,479
30		25	(h)	Watford	W	3-0	Downing 2, Horsfield	22,059
31	Mar	4	(a)	Swindon T	L	1-4	O'Rourke	14,370
32		11	(h)	Bournemouth	W	3-1	Hickton, Jones, Downing	15,644
33		18	(h)	Reading	D	2-2	O'Rourke, Horsfield	17,569
34		25	(a)	Doncaster R	W	4-0	O'Rourke, Horsfield 3	9,628
35		27	(h)	Shrewsbury T	W	1-0	Hickton	23,452
36		29	(a)	Shrewsbury T	L	0-1		6,497
37	Apr	1	(h)	Mansfield T	W	1-0	Edwards (og)	23,226
38		8	(a)	Grimsby T	L	1-2	O'Rourke	4,905
39		10	(a)	Leyton O	L	0-2		5,772
40		15	(h)	Walsall	L	0-2		18,090
41		22	(a)	Peterborough U	W	2-1	O'Rourke, Rooks	6,458
42		24	(h)	Leyton O	W	3-1	O'Rourke 2, Hickton (pen)	15,184
43		29	(h)	Torquay U	W	4-0	Hickton 3, O'Rourke	27,160
44	May	6	(a)	Brighton & HA	D	1-1	O'Rourke	12,692
45		13	(h)	Peterborough U	W	2-1	Hickton 2	32,503
46		16	(h)	Oxford U	W	4-1	O'Rourke 3, Hickton	39,683

FINAL LEAGUE POSITION: 2nd in Division Three

Appearances
Sub Appearances
Goals

FA Cup

1	Nov	26	(a)	Chester	W	5-2	O'Rourke 3, Downing, Hickton	7,607
2	Jan	7	(h)	York C	D	1-1	Hickton	20,573
R		11	(a)	York C	D	0-0*		14,531
2R		16	(n†)	York C	W	4-1	Lawson, Jackson (og), Lugg, Horsfield	21,347
3		28	(a)	Mansfield T	L	0-2		17,332

†Played at St James' Park, Newcastle. *After extra-time.

Appearances
Sub Appearances
Goals

League Cup

1	Aug	24	(h)	York C	D	0-0		9,758
R		29	(a)	York C	L	1-2	Chadwick	4,970

Appearances
Sub Appearances
Goals

292

Player appearance and goals grid.

Appleby R	Gates WL	Jones GE	Davidson I	Rooks R	Horner W	Chadwick DE*	Masson DS	O'Rourke J*	Irvine JD	Lawson J	Chapman N	McPartland D	Braithwaite RM	McMordie A	Butler G	Horsfield A	Smith RA	Hickton J*	Lugg R*	Whigham W*	Downing DG	Spraggon F	
1	2	3	4	5*	6	7	8	9	10	11	12												1
1	5	3	4		6	7	8	9	10	11	2												2
	5	3	4		6	7	8	9	10		2	1	11										3
	5	3	4		6	7	8	9	10		2	1	11										4
	2	3	4	5	6	7		9*	10			1	11	8	12								5
	9	3	4	5*	6	7			10	11		1		2	8	12							6
		3	4		6	7			10	11		1		2	8	5							7
		3			6			9	10	11		1	7	2	8	4	5						8
		3	9		6				10	11*		1	7	2	8	4	5	12					9
	5*	6	4	9		7		11	10		12				3	8		2	1				10
	6		5	4	7			9	10						3	8		2		1	11		11
	6		5	4	7			9	10						3	8		2		1	11		12
	6		5	4	7			9	10						3	8		2		1	11		13
	12	6	5	4	7			9	10*						3	8		2		1	11		14
	6		5	4	7			9	10						3	8		2		1	11		15
	6		5	4	7			9	8						3	10		2		1	11		16
	6		5	4	7			9		2					3	8		10		1	11		17
	6		5	4	7			9		2					3	8		10		1	11		18
	6		5	4	7			9		2					3	8		10		1	11		19
	6		5	4	7			9		2					3			10		1	11	8	20
	6		5	4	7			9	10						3	8		2		1	11		21
	12	6	5*	4	7			9	10						3	8		2		1	11		22
	5	6		4	7			9*	12	10					3	8		2		1	11		23
	6		5	4	7			9		10					3	8		2		1	11		24
	2	6		5	4	7					1			9	3	8		10	11				25
	5	6			4	7			10		1			9	3	8		2	11				26
	2	6		5*	4	7			12					9	3	8		10	11	1			27
	5	6			4	7			10					9	3	8		2		1	11		28
	5	6			4	7		9							3	8		2		1	11		29
	5	6			7	4		9						10	3	8		2		1	11		30
	5	6			7	4		9						10	3	8		2		1	11		31
	5	6			4	7		9	10						3			2	8	1	11		32
	5	6			4	7		9	8						3	10		2		1	11		33
	5				6	7	4	9	8						3	10		2		1	11		34
	5				6	7	4	9	8*	12					3	10		2		1	11		35
	5				6	7	4	9	10*	12					3	8		2		1	11		36
	5				6	7	4	9	10						3	8		2		1	11		37
	5	12			6	7	4	9	10*						3	8		2		1	11		38
	5	6			4	7		8						9	3	10		2		1	11		39
	5	6			7	4	9		10						3	8		2		1	11		40
2*	12		5	6	7	4	9							8	3			10		1	11		41
	3		5	6	7	4	9							10	2			8		1	11		42
	3		5	6	7	4	9							10	2			8		1	11		43
	3		5	6	7	4	9							10	2*	12		8		1	11		44
	3		5	6	7	4	9							10	2			8		1	11		45
	3		5	6	7	4	9							10	2			8		1	11		46
2	25	40	8	26	42	44	19	39	17	17	7	9	3	19	41	33	2	40	4	35	33	1	
	2	2							1	2	2		1			1	1	1		1			
1	1		1	2	2	1	27	2	2					1	22			15	1		8		

1 own-goal

Appleby R	Gates WL	Jones GE	Davidson I	Rooks R	Horner W	Chadwick DE*	Masson DS	O'Rourke J*	Irvine JD	Lawson J	Chapman N	McPartland D	Braithwaite RM	McMordie A	Butler G	Horsfield A	Smith RA	Hickton J*	Lugg R*	Whigham W*	Downing DG	Spraggon F	
	6		5	4	7			9				2			3	8		10		1	11		1
	12	6		5	4	7		9*		10					3	8		2		1	11		2
	6		5	4	7				10					9	3	8		2		1	11		R
	5	6			4	7			10		1			9	3	8	2	11					2R
	2	6		5	4	7			11					9	3	8		10	1				3
	2	5		4	5	5		2		4	1	1		3	5	5		5	1	4	3		
	1																						
					3			1						1		2	1		1				

1 own-goal

Appleby R	Gates WL	Jones GE	Davidson I	Rooks R	Horner W	Chadwick DE*	Masson DS	O'Rourke J*	Irvine JD	Lawson J	Chapman N	McPartland D	Braithwaite RM	McMordie A	Butler G	Horsfield A	Smith RA	Hickton J*	Lugg R*	Whigham W*	Downing DG	Spraggon F	
1	5	3	4		6	7	8	9	10	11	2												1
	5	3	4			7	8	9		11	2	1		10	6								R
1	2	2	2		1	2	2	2	1	2	2	1			1	1							
					1																		

293

1967-68

Manager: Stan Anderson

#	Month	Date		Opponent	Result	Scorers	Attendance
1	Aug	19	(h)	Ipswich T	L 0-2		25,916
2		26	(a)	Carlisle U	D 2-2	Jones, O'Rourke	12,389
3		29	(h)	Birmingham C	D 1-1	Rooks	25,814
4	Sep	2	(h)	Blackburn R	D 0-0		23,757
5		5	(a)	Bristol C	D 0-0		13,216
6		9	(a)	Blackpool	L 0-3		24,346
7		16	(h)	Millwall	L 0-1		23,446
8		23	(a)	Hull C	W 2-0	Lawson, O'Rourke	17,727
9		26	(a)	Birmingham C	L 1-6	Crossan	28,885
10		30	(h)	Aston Villa	D 1-1	Hickton	20,534
11	Oct	7	(a)	Charlton A	D 2-2	Kear, O'Rourke	14,798
12		14	(h)	Plymouth A	W 5-0	Hickton 3, Kear, O'Rourke	18,025
13		24	(a)	Cardiff C	L 0-3		10,441
14		28	(h)	Portsmouth	W 1-0	Hickton	18,180
15	Nov	4	(a)	Norwich C	L 1-2	Horsfield	12,429
16		11	(h)	Rotherham U	D 1-1	Hickton (pen)	16,519
17		18	(a)	Queen's Park R	D 1-1	Hickton	17,557
18		25	(h)	Preston NE	W 5-0	Hickton, O'Rourke, Masson, Rooks, Kear	14,359
19	Dec	2	(a)	Derby C	W 4-2	O'Rourke 3, Hickton	20,381
20		9	(h)	Crystal P	W 3-0	Kear, McMordie, Crossan	16,654
21		16	(a)	Ipswich T	W 2-1	Hickton 2 (1 pen)	12,724
22		23	(h)	Carlisle U	W 4-0	O'Rourke 3, Kear	27,952
23		26	(a)	Bolton W	L 0-2		16,076
24		30	(h)	Bolton W	L 1-2	Hickton	29,217
25	Jan	6	(a)	Blackburn R	L 0-3		14,420
26		13	(h)	Blackpool	D 0-0		19,728
27		20	(a)	Millwall	L 0-4		12,139
28	Feb	3	(h)	Hull C	W 2-1	Hickton 2 (1 pen)	16,028
29		10	(a)	Aston Villa	W 1-0	Horsfield	22,724
30		24	(h)	Charlton A	D 1-1	Hickton	13,414
31	Mar	2	(a)	Plymouth A	W 1-0	Horsfield	9,040
32		9	(h)	Cardiff C	L 2-3	Crossan, Hickton	15,582
33		23	(a)	Portsmouth	L 0-2		18,197
34		30	(h)	Norwich C	W 2-0	Kear, Hickton	10,181
35	Apr	6	(a)	Rotherham U	W 1-0	Rooks	15,399
36		13	(h)	Queen's Park R	W 3-1	Hickton 2, Horsfield	20,849
37		15	(h)	Huddersfield T	W 3-2	Hickton 2 (1 pen), Horsfield	15,065
38		16	(a)	Huddersfield T	L 0-1		12,709
39		20	(a)	Preston NE	D 0-0		15,229
40		27	(h)	Derby C	D 2-2	Hickton 2	13,123
41	May	4	(a)	Crystal P	W 3-1	Hickton, Crossan, Horsfield	9,679
42		11	(h)	Bristol C	W 2-1	Webb 2	12,684

FINAL LEAGUE POSITION: 6th in Division Two

Appearances
Sub Appearances
Goals

FA Cup

Round	Month	Date		Opponent	Result	Scorers	Attendance
3	Jan	27	(h)	Hull C	D 1-1	Crossan	28,509
R		31	(a)	Hull C	D 2-2*	Horsfield 2	33,916
2R	Feb	7	(n†)	Hull C	W 1-0	Downing	16,524
4		17	(h)	Bristol C	D 1-1	Parr (og)	29,086
R		20	(a)	Bristol C	L 1-2	Hickton	21,771

*After extra-time.   †Played at Bootham Crescent, York.

Appearances
Sub Appearances
Goals

League Cup

#	Month	Date		Opponent	Result	Scorers	Attendance
1	Aug	22	(h)	Barnsley	W 4-1	Hickton 3, Smith	15,968
2	Sep	13	(h)	Chelsea	W 2-1	McMordie, Smith	30,417
3	Oct	11	(a)	Blackburn R	L 2-3	Hickton (pen), O'Rourke	10,442

Appearances
Sub Appearances
Goals

McPartland D	Butler G	Jones GE	Masson DS	Rooks R	Horner W	Chadwick DE	Hickton J	O'Rourke J	McMordie A	Downing DG	Gates WL	Spraggon F	Crossan JA*	Lugg R	Smith D*	Lawson J	Horsfield A	Worthington PR	Kear MP*	Whigham W	Allen M*	McNeill AA*	Wilson FP*	Laidlaw JD*	Smith RA	Short M*	Webb SJ*	
1	2	3	4	5	6	7	8	9	10	11																		1
1	2	3		5		7	8	9				4	6	10	11													2
1	2	3	4	5		7	8	9		11*	6		10	12														3
1	2	3	4		6	7	8	9	12		5		10	11*														4
1	2	3	7	5	6	11	8	9				4	10															5
1	2	3	7	5	6	11	8	9				4	10															6
1	3	6	4	5		7	2	9	8				10		11*	12												7
1	6		5*	4			2	12	8		3		10	7	11	9												8
1		6				2	9	8		5		4				11	10	3	7									9
	3	4	5	6	11*	9		8		2		10		12					7	1								10
	3		5	4		8	9	10		2	6		11						7	1								11
	3	12	5	4*	11	8	9		2	6	10								7	1								12
	3		5	4	11	8	9		2	6	10								7	1								13
	3	4	5		11	8		2	6	9		10							7	1								14
	3	4	5		11	8	9		2*	6	10		12						7	1								15
	3	4	5		11	2	9		6	10		8							7	1								16
	3		5	4	11	2	9	8		6	10								7	1								17
	3	8	5	4	11	2	9		6	10									7	1								18
	3		5	4	11	2	9	8		6	10								7	1								19
	3		5	4	11	2	9	8		6	10		12						7*	1								20
	3		4	11	2	9	8		5	6	10								7	1								21
	3		5	4	11	2	9	8		6	10								7	1								22
	3		5	4	11	2	9	8		6*	10		12						7	1								23
	3		5	4	11	2	9	8		10									7	1		6						24
	3		5	4	11*	2	9	8		6	10		12						7	1								25
	3	12	5	4	11	2	9	8		6	10*								7	1								26
	3		4	11*	2	9	8		5	6	10	12							7	1								27
	3	4		2		9		10	11	5	6								8	7	1							28
	2	4			9		5	6	10		8	3	7		1		11											29
	3	4			10	9		11	5	6		7	1		8	2												30
	3		4	12	2		8	11*	5	6	10		9						7	1								31
	3		4	12	2		8		5	6	11		10						7	1			9*					32
	3	4*	5	12	7	2		8	11		6	10		9						1								33
	3	4*	5		8	9		11	2		6	10		12					7	1								34
	3		5		11	9		8		6		10							7	1	4				2			35
	3		5		11	9		8		6		10							7	1					2			36
	3		5		11	9		8		6		10							7	1	4				2			37
	3		5	4		9		8		6		11	10						7	1					2			38
	3		5	12	11	9		8		6		10							7	1	4*				2			39
	3		5	4	11	9		8		6		10							7						2	1		40
	3*		5		11	9		4		6	8		10						7	1	12				2			41
	3		5		7	10		8		6	4	11		1						2	9							42
9	7	41	16	33	26	34	42	24	29	7	20	32	32	5	1	3	16	2	32	32	5	2	1	1	8	1	1	
			2		2	2			1	1					1	1	4	3	1									
	1	1	3				24	11	1				4			1	6		6						2			

		3	4		2		8	9*			5	6	10			11	12		7	1								3
		3	4		2		9		12	11*	5	6	10			8			7	1								R
		3	4		2		9			11	5	6	10			8			7	1								2R
		3	4*		2		9			11	5	6	10			8			7	1	12							4
		3	4			12	10			11	5	6	8*			9	2		7	1								R
		5	5		4		5	1		4	5	5	5			1	4		1	5	5							
					1					1			1			1												
					1					1			1			2												

1 own-goal

1	2	3		5	4	7	8	9			6		10	11														1
1	3	6	4	5	12	7	2	9	8*			10	11															2
		3		5	4	11*	8	9		2	6	10	12			7	1											3
2	2	3	1	3	2	3	3	3	1	1	2	2	1	2		1	1											
		1						1																				
			4	1	1					2																		

295

1968-69

Manager: Stan Anderson

1	Aug	10	(h)	Preston NE	W 2-1	Hickton 2 (1 pen)	19,014
2		14	(a)	Norwich C	W 2-0	Horsfield, Downing	19,431
3		17	(a)	Portsmouth	L 0-3		24,273
4		20	(h)	Crystal P	W 4-0	Horsfield 2, Crossan, Lugg	21,622
5		24	(h)	Carlisle U	W 1-0	Hickton	22,392
6		27	(h)	Huddersfield T	D 1-1	McMordie	25,422
7		31	(a)	Hull C	L 0-3		16,838
8	Sep	7	(a)	Cardiff C	L 0-2		14,225
9		14	(h)	Birmingham C	W 3-1	Hickton, Gates 2	17,398
10		21	(a)	Bury	W 3-2	Horsfield 2, Webb	7,471
11		28	(h)	Charlton A	W 1-0	Downing	21,628
12	Oct	5	(h)	Derby C	D 0-0		28,636
13		8	(a)	Huddersfield T	L 0-3		14,799
14		12	(a)	Sheffield U	W 3-1	Chadwick, Kear, Downing	18,334
15		19	(h)	Fulham	W 2-0	McMordie, Downing	23,238
16		26	(a)	Oxford U	W 4-2	Downing, Horsfield 2, Rooks (pen)	11,209
17	Nov	9	(a)	Millwall	L 0-2		22,019
18		16	(h)	Bolton W	D 0-0		18,458
19		23	(a)	Aston Villa	L 0-1		15,281
20		30	(h)	Blackburn R	W 2-0	Coddington (og), Downing	16,423
21	Dec	3	(h)	Bristol C	W 4-1	Hickton 2 (1 pen), Downing, McMordie	18,038
22		7	(a)	Blackpool	D 1-1	Rooks	13,356
23		21	(a)	Fulham	W 3-0	Downing, Hickton 2	13,333
24		26	(a)	Derby C	L 2-3	Hickton 2 (1 pen)	34,481
25	Jan	11	(a)	Bristol C	L 0-3		13,696
26		18	(h)	Millwall	D 1-1	Kinnell	17,153
27		24	(h)	Oxford U	W 2-0	Crossan, Hickton	23,030
28		28	(h)	Sheffield U	W 3-1	Hickton, Webb 2	24,784
29	Feb	1	(a)	Bolton W	D 0-0		7,658
30		22	(h)	Blackpool	W 2-1	Hickton (pen), Webb	18,707
31	Mar	1	(a)	Preston NE	W 2-1	Hickton, Lugg	12,520
32		4	(h)	Aston Villa	D 0-0		29,824
33		8	(h)	Portsmouth	W 1-0	Crossan	23,982
34		15	(a)	Carlisle U	L 0-3		13,920
35		22	(h)	Hull C	W 5-3	Hickton 4, McMordie	18,330
36		25	(a)	Blackburn R	D 1-1	Downing	7,193
37		29	(h)	Cardiff C	D 0-0		24,470
38	Apr	4	(a)	Crystal P	D 0-0		43,781
39		5	(a)	Charlton A	L 0-2		23,930
40		8	(h)	Norwich C	D 0-0		19,366
41		12	(h)	Bury	L 2-3	Maddren, McMordie	10,417
42		19	(a)	Birmingham C	L 1-3	McMordie	25,899

FINAL LEAGUE POSITION: 4th in Division Two

Appearances
Sub Appearances
Goals

FA Cup

3	Jan	4	(h)	Millwall	D 1-1	Allen	26,960
R		6	(a)	Millwall	L 0-1		22,230

Appearances
Sub Appearances
Goals

League Cup

2	Sep	4	(a)	Bristol C	L 0-1	14,218

Appearances
Sub Appearances
Goals

Football appearances and goals grid.

Whigham W	Smith RA	Jones GE	McNeill AA	Rooks R	Spragon F	Kear MP	McMordie A	Hickton J	Horsfield A	Crossan JA	Downing DG	Lugg R	Horner W	Gates WL	Myton B*	Webb SJ	Chadwick DE	Kinnell G*	Short M	Allen M	Moody A*	Smith G*	Laidlaw JD	Maddren WD*	Mills DJ*	
1	2	3	4*	5	6	7	8	9	10	11	12															1
1	2	3		5	6	7	8	9	10	11	4															2
1	2	3		5	6	7	8	9	10	11	4															3
1	2	3		5	6		8	9	10	11	4	7														4
1	2	3		5	6		8	9	10	11	4	7														5
1	2	3		5	6		8	9	10	11	4	7														6
1	2	3		5	6	7	8	9	10		4	11														7
1	2	3		5		7	8	9	10			11		4	6											8
1	2	3		5			8	10	9	6	11	7		4												9
1	2	3		5	6		8		10		11	7		4		9										10
1	2	3		5	6		8		10		11	7		4		9										11
1	2	3		5	6		8		10		11	7		4		9										12
1	2	3		5	6			9	10	8*	11	7		4		12										13
1	2	3		5	6	7		12	9		11	8		4			10*									14
1	2	3		5				10	12	9	11*	8		4		7	6									15
1	2	3		5				12	10	9	11	8				7*	6									16
1		3		5	2	7	10		9		11	8		4			6									17
1	2	3		5	4	7	10	12	9		11	8*					6									18
1	2	3		5	4	12	10*	8	9		11					7	6									19
1	2	3		5	4		10	8	9		11					7	6									20
1	2	3		5	4		10	8	9		11					7	6									21
		3		5	4		10		9		11				2	7	6		1	8						22
1		3		5	4		10	8	9*		11				2	7	6						12			23
1		3		5	4		10	8			11				2	9	6			7						24
1		3		5	4*		10	8	9		11				2	7	6					12				25
1		3		5	4	7	10		9	8	11						6				2					26
1		3		5	6	7	10		9	8	11*				12						2	4				27
1		3		5	6	7	11	10		8						9					2	4				28
1		3		5	6	7	11	10		8						9					2	4				29
1		3		5	6	7	10	8			11					9					2	4				30
1		3		5	6	7	10	8			11					9					2	4				31
1		3		5	6	7*	10	8			12	11				9					2	4				32
1		3		5	6		10	8			11					9	7				2	4				33
1				5	6	7*	9	8	10		11				12					3	2	4				34
1	2	3		5	6			9	10	8	11			4		7										35
1	2	3		5	6			9	10	8	11			7		4										36
1	2	3		5	6			9	10	8*	11				12	7						4				37
1	2	3		5	6*			9	10	8	11				12	7						4				38
1				5	6			10		8*	11					7				2	3	9	4	12		39
1	2*	3		5	6			10		8	11				12	7					9	4				40
1					6		8				11			7			5	3			2	4	9	10		41
1	2	3		5		7		10			4	11			8*		6	9					12			42
41	27	38	1	40	38	16	39	34	23	22	30	21	1	17	3	11	15	12	1	3	10	15	3	1		
					2	1	6	18	7	3	9	2		2		4	1	1				1				

1 own-goal

Whigham W	Smith RA	Jones GE	McNeill AA	Rooks R	Spragon F	Kear MP	McMordie A	Hickton J	Horsfield A	Crossan JA	Downing DG	Lugg R	Horner W	Gates WL	Myton B*	Webb SJ	Chadwick DE	Kinnell G*	Short M	Allen M	Moody A*	Smith G*	Laidlaw JD	Maddren WD*	Mills DJ*	
		3		5	4		10	8	12		11			2		7	6	1	9*							3
	2	3		5	6		10	8		12	11			4		7		1	9*							R
	1	2		2	2		2	2		2	2			1		2	1	2	2							
								1		1																
																	1									

Whigham W	Smith RA	Jones GE	McNeill AA	Rooks R	Spragon F	Kear MP	McMordie A	Hickton J	Horsfield A	Crossan JA	Downing DG	Lugg R	Horner W	Gates WL	Myton B*	Webb SJ	Chadwick DE	Kinnell G*	Short M	Allen M	Moody A*	Smith G*	Laidlaw JD	Maddren WD*	Mills DJ*	
1	2	3		5		7	8	9	10*		11	12		4	6											2
1	1	1		1		1	1	1	1		1			1	1											
									1																	

1969-70

Manager: Stan Anderson

1	Aug	9	(a)	Sheffield U	L 0-3		14,707
2		12	(h)	Millwall	W 3-1	Hickton, McMordie, Laidlaw	16,221
3		16	(h)	Leicester C	W 2-1	Laidlaw, Hickton	22,159
4		18	(a)	Millwall	D 1-1	Hickton	12,641
5		23	(a)	Carlisle U	L 0-1		12,578
6		27	(a)	Cardiff C	L 0-1		21,623
7		30	(h)	Aston Villa	W 1-0	Hickton	19,438
8	Sep	6	(a)	Blackburn R	L 0-4		12,120
9		13	(h)	Bristol C	W 2-0	Downing, R.A.Smith	14,513
10		16	(h)	Swindon T	D 0-0		15,632
11		20	(a)	Oxford U	D 1-1	McMordie	9,496
12		27	(h)	Blackpool	L 0-2		20,268
13	Oct	4	(a)	Queen's Park R	L 0-4		21,421
14		8	(a)	Leicester C	L 1-2	Downing	26,528
15		11	(h)	Bolton W	W 4-0	Hickton 2, McIlmoyle 2	14,020
16		18	(a)	Huddersfield T	D 0-0		12,269
17		25	(h)	Watford	W 3-1	Hickton, McIlmoyle, Laidlaw	15,402
18	Nov	1	(a)	Preston NE	W 1-0	Hickton (pen)	13,075
19		8	(h)	Charlton A	W 2-0	Hickton, Downing	15,196
20		15	(h)	Hull C	W 1-0	Hickton	14,235
21		22	(a)	Portsmouth	W 3-2	Hickton, McIlmoyle, Laidlaw	15,621
22	Dec	13	(a)	Bristol C	D 0-0		15,290
23		16	(h)	Birmingham C	W 4-2	Hickton 2, Laidlaw, Spraggon	17,020
24		26	(h)	Carlisle U	L 0-2		29,703
25	Jan	10	(a)	Oxford U	W 2-0	Hickton 2	16,922
26		13	(h)	Blackburn R	W 4-1	Gates, Mills, Murray, Downing	21,950
27		17	(a)	Blackpool	D 1-1	Laidlaw	15,154
28		31	(h)	Queen's Park R	W 1-0	Downing	25,821
29	Feb	11	(a)	Bolton W	L 1-2	Laidlaw	9,928
30		28	(h)	Preston NE	D 1-1	Hickton	25,050
31	Mar	3	(a)	Charlton A	W 2-0	Laidlaw, Hickton	9,805
32		7	(h)	Portsmouth	W 2-1	Laidlaw, Hickton (pen)	22,498
33		11	(a)	Norwich C	L 0-2		10,390
34		14	(a)	Birmingham C	D 0-0		17,974
35		17	(h)	Sheffield U	W 1-0	Hickton	25,026
36		21	(h)	Norwich C	D 0-0		24,514
37		27	(a)	Watford	W 3-2	Hickton 2, McMordie	22,486
38		28	(a)	Hull C	L 2-3	Laidlaw, Hickton	17,434
39		31	(h)	Huddersfield T	D 1-1	Hickton (pen)	27,519
40	Apr	4	(h)	Cardiff C	W 2-1	McIlmoyle, Laidlaw	13,859
41		8	(a)	Aston Villa	L 0-2		22,805
42		14	(a)	Swindon T	W 3-0	McIlmoyle, Mills, Hickton	16,668

FINAL LEAGUE POSITION: 4th in Division Two

Appearances
Sub Appearances
Goals

FA Cup

3	Jan	3	(h)	West Ham U	W 2-1	McIlmoyle, Downing	32,585
4		24	(h)	York C	W 4-1	McMordie, G.Smith, Hickton (pen), Laidlaw	32,283
5	Feb	7	(a)	Carlisle U	W 2-1	Hickton, Downing	27,599
6		21	(h)	Manchester U	D 1-1	Hickton	40,040
R		25	(a)	Manchester U	L 1-2	Hickton	63,418

Appearances
Sub Appearances
Goals

League Cup

2	Sep	3	(a)	Manchester U	L 0-1	38,939

Appearances
Sub Appearances
Goals

298

Player appearance grid (shirt numbers by match). Columns are players; the final column is the match number.

Short M	Moody A	Jones GE	Smith G	Gates WL	Spraggon F	McMordie A	Kear MP	Laidlaw JD	Hickton J	Chadwick DE	Smith RA	Downing DG	Lugg R	Webb SJ	Mills DJ*	Myton B	McIlmoyle H*	Allen M	Whigham W	Murray A*	Crossan JA	Maddren WD	#
1	2	3	4	5	6	7	8	9	10	11													1
1		3	4	5	6	7	8	9	10	11	2												2
1		3	4	5	6	7	8	9	10	11	2												3
1		3	4*	5	6	7	8	9	10		2	11	12										4
1		3	4	5	6	7	8	9	10	11	2												5
1		3	4	5	6	7	8	9	10	11	2												6
1	2	3	4	5	6	7	8*	9	10	11		12											7
1		3	4	5	6	7	8	9	10		2	11											8
1		3	4	5	6			8	10		2	11	7	9									9
1		3	4	5	6			8*	10		2	11	7	9	12								10
1		3	4	5	6			8	10		2	12	7	9*		11							11
1		3	4	5	6			8	10	7	2	11				9							12
1		3	4	5	6	8		9	10		2	7					11						13
1		3	4	5	6			8	10		2	7					9	11					14
		3	4	5	6			8	10		2	7					9	11	1				15
		3	4	5	6			8	10		2	7					9	11	1				16
		3	4	5	6			8	10		2	7					9	11*	1	12			17
		3	4	5	6			8	10		2	7					9	11	1				18
		3	4	5	6	12		8	10		2	7					9	11*	1				19
		3	4	5	6	12		8	10		2	7*					9	11	1				20
		3	4	5	6	12		8	10		2	7					9	11*	1				21
		3	4	5	6			8	10		2	7					9	11	1				22
		3	4	5	6			8	10*		2	7					9	11	1	12			23
	2	3	4	5	6			8	10			7					9	11*	1	12			24
		3	4	5	6	11*		8	10		2	7					9		1	12			25
		3	4	5	6	11*			10		2	7				12	9	8	1				26
		3	4	5	6	12		11	10		2	7					9	8*	1				27
		3	4	5	6	8		11	10		2	7					9		1				28
		3	4	5	6	8		11	10		2	7					9		1				29
		3	4		6	8		11	10		2	7*				12	9		1			5	30
		3	4		6	8		11	10		2	7		9					1			5	31
		3	4		6	8*		11	10		2	7				12	9		1			5	32
		3	4		6	8		11	10		2	7					9		1			5	33
		3	4		6			11	10		2	8					9		1	7		5	34
		3	4		6			11	10		2	8					9		1	7		5	35
		3	4		6*			11	10		2	8				12	9		1	7		5	36
		3	4			8		11	10		2	7					9	6	1			5	37
		3	4			8		11	10		2	7				12	9	6	1			5*	38
		3	4*			8		11	10		2	7				12	9	6	1			5	39
		3	4	5		8		11	10		2	7					9	6	1				40
		3	4	5		8		11*	10		2	7				12	9	6	1				41
		3	4	5	6			8	10		2	7					9	11	1				42
14	5	42	41	31	37	28	8	35	42	7	39	32	4	5	1	4	29	15	28	5		10	
					4								2	1	4	4			2	2			
			1	1	3			11	24		1	5				2	6		1				

Cup matches:

Short M	Moody A	Jones GE	Smith G	Gates WL	Spraggon F	McMordie A	Kear MP	Laidlaw JD	Hickton J	Chadwick DE	Smith RA	Downing DG	Lugg R	Webb SJ	Mills DJ*	Myton B	McIlmoyle H*	Allen M	Whigham W	Murray A*	Crossan JA	Maddren WD	#
		3	4	5	6			8	10		2	7					9	11	1				3
		3	4	5	6	8		11	10		2	7					9		1				R
		3	4	5	6	8		11	10		2	7					9		1				4
		3	4	5	6	8		11	10		2	7					9		1				5
		3	4	5	6	8		11	10		2	7					9		1				R
		5	5	5	5	4		5	5		5	5					5	5	1				
		1			1			1	4			2					1						

Short M	Moody A	Jones GE	Smith G	Gates WL	Spraggon F	McMordie A	Kear MP	Laidlaw JD	Hickton J	Chadwick DE	Smith RA	Downing DG	Lugg R	Webb SJ	Mills DJ*	Myton B	McIlmoyle H*	Allen M	Whigham W	Murray A*	Crossan JA	Maddren WD	#
1		3	4	5	6	7	8	9	10	11	2												2
1		1	1	1	1	1	1	1	1	1	1												

1970-71

Manager: Stan Anderson

1	Aug	15	(h)	Carlisle U	W	2-1	Laidlaw, Hickton	21,228
2		22	(a)	Hull C	L	0-1		20,929
3		29	(h)	Oxford U	L	0-2		17,548
4	Sep	1	(a)	Birmingham C	W	1-0	Hickton	27,769
5		5	(a)	Luton T	L	0-1		16,018
6		12	(h)	Blackburn R	D	1-1	McIlmoyle	15,083
7		19	(a)	Sheffield U	D	1-1	Hickton	19,780
8		26	(h)	Queen's Park R	W	6-2	Hickton 3 (1 pen), McIlmoyle 2, Downing	16,788
9		30	(a)	Leicester C	L	2-3	Hickton 2	26,260
10	Oct	3	(a)	Cardiff C	W	4-3	Hickton, McIlmoyle, Laidlaw, Maddren	20,925
11		10	(h)	Portsmouth	W	3-2	McIlmoyle 2, Hickton	18,775
12		17	(a)	Carlisle U	L	0-1		15,863
13		20	(h)	Bristol C	W	1-0	Hickton	16,651
14		24	(a)	Swindon T	L	0-3		15,434
15		31	(h)	Watford	D	2-2	Laidlaw, Downing	16,018
16	Nov	7	(a)	Orient	D	0-0		6,690
17		14	(h)	Charlton A	W	3-0	Hickton, Downing, McIlmoyle	14,247
18		21	(a)	Sheffield W	L	2-3	Downing, McIlmoyle	15,421
19		28	(h)	Millwall	W	1-0	Hickton	13,036
20	Dec	5	(a)	Norwich C	D	1-1	Downing	13,073
21		12	(h)	Bolton W	W	1-0	Hickton	12,873
22		19	(h)	Hull C	W	1-0	Hickton	17,957
23		26	(a)	Sunderland	D	2-2	Hickton 2	42,617
24	Jan	9	(h)	Leicester C	W	1-0	Hickton	30,682
25		16	(a)	Bristol C	W	2-0	Hickton, Downing	10,535
26		30	(a)	Millwall	L	0-1		10,180
27	Feb	6	(h)	Norwich C	W	5-0	Downing, Hickton 2, McIlmoyle, Laidlaw	19,106
28		13	(a)	Bolton W	W	3-0	Laidlaw, Downing 2	9,877
29		20	(h)	Sheffield W	W	1-0	Hickton	25,916
30		26	(a)	Watford	L	0-1		14,112
31	Mar	6	(h)	Swindon T	W	3-0	McIlmoyle, Maddren, Downing	20,813
32		13	(a)	Charlton A	L	0-1		9,420
33		20	(h)	Orient	L	0-1		17,132
34		27	(h)	Luton T	W	2-1	McIlmoyle 2	19,585
35	Apr	3	(a)	Oxford U	D	2-2	Hickton, Downing	7,517
36		9	(a)	Blackburn R	D	1-1	Laidlaw	11,210
37		10	(h)	Sunderland	D	2-2	Laidlaw, Hickton	26,479
38		13	(h)	Cardiff C	D	1-1	Downing	19,559
39		17	(a)	Portsmouth	D	1-1	McIlmoyle	8,193
40		24	(h)	Sheffield U	D	1-1	Hickton	16,946
41		27	(h)	Birmingham C	D	0-0		12,802
42	May	1	(a)	Queen's Park R	D	1-1	Mills	10,390

FINAL LEAGUE POSITION: 7th in Division Two

Appearances
Sub Appearances
Goals

FA Cup

3	Jan	2	(a)	Manchester U	D	0-0		47,024
R		5	(h)	Manchester U	W	2-1	McIlmoyle, Downing	40,040
4		23	(a)	Everton	L	0-3		54,875

Appearances
Sub Appearances
Goals

League Cup

2	Sep	8	(a)	Oldham A	W	4-2	Laidlaw, McIlmoyle, Downing, Hickton	9,539
3	Oct	7	(a)	Chelsea	L	2-3	Hickton, Jones	28,597

Appearances
Sub Appearances
Goals

Whigham W	Smith RA	Jones GE	Smith G	Gates WL	Spraggon F	Mills DJ	McMordie A	Maddren WD	Hickton J	Laidlaw JD	Downing DG	McIlmoyle H	Allen M	Myton B	Moody A	Webb SJ	Charlton H*	Vincent JV*	Burluraux D*	Murray A	
1	2	3	4	5	6	7	8	9*	10	11	12										1
1	2	3	4	5	6	7	8		10	11		9									2
1	2*	3	4	5	6	7	8		10	11	12	9									3
1			4		6		12	5	10	11*		9	2	3	7	8					4
1		3		12	6			5	10	7		9*	2	11	4	8					5
1		3	4		6			5	10	8	7	9	2	11							6
1		3	4	5	6		8	2	10	11	7	9									7
1		3	4	5	6	12	8	2	10	11	7	9*									8
1		3	4	5	6		8	2	10	11	7	9									9
1		3	4	5	6		8	2	10	11	7	9									10
1		3	4	5	6	7	8	2	10	11		9									11
1		3	4	5	6	12	8	2	10	11		9	7*								12
1		3	4	5	6	7	8*	2	10	11		9			12						13
1		3	4	5	6	7		2	10			9	11		8						14
1	2	3	4		6			5	10	11	7	9				8					15
1	2	3		4	6			5	10	11	7	9				8					16
1	2*	3		4	6	12		5	10	11	7	9				8					17
1	2	3		4	6	12		5	10	11	7	9					8*				18
1	2	3		4	6	8	12	5*	10	11	7	9									19
1	2	3	8	5	6				10	11	7	9			4						20
1	2	3	8	5	6	12			10	11	7	9			4*						21
1	2	3	4	5	6	12	8		10	11	7*	9									22
1	2	3	4	5	6		8		10	11	7	9									23
1	2	3		5	6		8		10	11	7	9			4						24
1	2	3		5	6		8		10	11	7	9			4						25
1	2	3		5			8	6	10	11	7	9			4						26
1	2	3		5			8	6	10	11	7	9			4						27
1	2	3		5			8	6	10	11	7	9			4						28
1	2	3		5			8	6	10	11	7	9			4						29
1	2	3		5		12	8	6	10	11	7	9			4*						30
1	2	3		5			8	6	10	11	7	9			4						31
1	2	3		5			8*	6	10	11	7	9			4		12				32
1	2	3		5	4	12		6	10	11	7	9*					8				33
1	2	3		5			8	6	9	4	7*	12					10	11			34
1	2	3		5			7	6	9	4		8					10	11			35
1	2	3		5		12	7	6	9	4	11	8					10*				36
1	2	3		5			7	6	9	10	11	8			4						37
1	2	3		5			7	6	9	10	11	8			4						38
1	2	3		5		12	7	6	9	4	11*	8							10		39
1	2	3		5		10*	7	6	9	4	11	8							12		40
1		3		5		10*	8	6		4	11	9						7	12		41
42	30	41	18	38	26	10	30	34	41	40	32	40	6	3	16	3	4	4	3	1	
			1		9	3						2	1				1	1		2	
					1	1	2	25	7	11	13										

Whigham W	Smith RA	Jones GE	Smith G	Gates WL	Spraggon F	Mills DJ	McMordie A	Maddren WD	Hickton J	Laidlaw JD	Downing DG	McIlmoyle H	Allen M	Myton B	Moody A	Webb SJ	Charlton H*	Vincent JV*	Burluraux D*	Murray A	
1	2	3		5	6		8		10	11	7	9			4						3
1	2	3		5	6		8		10	11	7	9			4						R
1	2	3		5	6		8		10	11	7	9			4						4
3	3	3		3	3		3		3	3	3	3			3						
											1	1									

Whigham W	Smith RA	Jones GE	Smith G	Gates WL	Spraggon F	Mills DJ	McMordie A	Maddren WD	Hickton J	Laidlaw JD	Downing DG	McIlmoyle H	Allen M	Myton B	Moody A	Webb SJ	Charlton H*	Vincent JV*	Burluraux D*	Murray A	
1		3	4		6			5	10	8	7	9	2	11							2
1		3	4	5	6	12	8	2	10	11	7*	9									3
2		2	2	1	2	1	2	2	2	2	2	2	1	1							
		1						2	1	1	1										

1971-72

Manager: Stan Anderson

1	Aug	14	(a)	Portsmouth	L	1-2	Vincent	15,649
2		21	(h)	Queen's Park R	W	3-2	Hickton, Mills, Vincent	20,547
3		28	(a)	Bristol C	L	1-2	Maddren	16,474
4		31	(h)	Sheffield W	W	2-1	Maddren, Hickton	23,963
5	Sep	4	(h)	Fulham	W	2-0	Vincent, Maddren	20,228
6		11	(a)	Charlton A	W	2-0	Maddren 2	11,167
7		18	(h)	Cardiff C	W	1-0	Gates	18,288
8		25	(a)	Luton T	L	2-3	Hickton, Maddren	13,001
9		29	(a)	Sunderland	L	1-4	Vincent	28,129
10	Oct	2	(h)	Blackpool	W	1-0	Gates	18,671
11		9	(a)	Oxford U	D	0-0		9,925
12		16	(h)	Portsmouth	W	2-1	Hickton, Vincent	16,296
13		19	(h)	Millwall	W	1-0	Hickton	20,383
14		23	(h)	Watford	W	2-1	Craggs, Laidlaw	19,947
15		30	(a)	Swindon T	W	1-0	Maddren	13,782
16	Nov	6	(h)	Preston NE	L	0-1		21,907
17		13	(a)	Burnley	L	2-5	Laidlaw, Downing	15,720
18		20	(h)	Orient	W	1-0	Hickton	13,288
19		27	(a)	Norwich C	L	0-2		21,303
20	Dec	4	(h)	Birmingham C	D	0-0		15,671
21		11	(a)	Hull C	L	3-4	Mills 2, Craggs	13,532
22		18	(a)	Fulham	D	2-2	Stiles, Hickton	7,571
23		27	(h)	Carlisle U	D	2-2	Mills, Downing	24,796
24	Jan	1	(a)	Cardiff C	L	0-1		12,758
25		8	(h)	Bristol C	W	1-0	Downing	13,117
26		22	(h)	Sunderland	W	2-0	Hickton 2	34,446
27		29	(a)	Millwall	L	0-1		14,127
28	Feb	12	(a)	Watford	W	1-0	Hickton	8,109
29		19	(h)	Swindon T	W	2-0	Downing, Mills	18,205
30	Mar	4	(h)	Burnley	W	1-0	Dobson (og)	17,069
31		11	(h)	Oxford U	W	2-1	Mills 2	13,334
32		14	(a)	Carlisle U	L	0-3		10,313
33		18	(a)	Queen's Park R	L	0-1		11,467
34		25	(h)	Charlton A	D	2-2	Hickton, McMordie	11,100
35		31	(h)	Luton T	D	0-0		11,720
36	Apr	3	(h)	Blackpool	L	1-3	Vincent	13,726
37		8	(a)	Orient	D	1-1	McMordie	7,372
38		15	(h)	Norwich C	W	1-0	Spraggon	14,279
39		17	(a)	Preston NE	L	0-1		11,388
40		22	(a)	Birmingham C	D	1-1	Hickton	37,202
41		26	(a)	Sheffield W	L	0-1		13,936
42		29	(h)	Hull C	W	3-0	McMordie, Vincent, Mills	9,539

FINAL LEAGUE POSITION: 9th in Division Two

Appearances
Sub Appearances
Goals

FA Cup

3	Jan	15	(a)	Manchester C	D	1-1	Mills	42,620
R		18	(h)	Manchester C	W	1-0	Hickton	39,917
4	Feb	5	(a)	Millwall	D	2-2	Hickton, Downing	23,579
R		8	(h)	Millwall	W	2-1	Downing, Hickton (pen)	36,489
5		26	(a)	Manchester U	D	0-0		53,850
R		29	(h)	Manchester U	L	0-3		39,671

Appearances
Sub Appearances
Goals

League Cup

2	Sep	8	(a)	York C	D	2-2	Downing, Hickton	11,041
R		14	(h)	York C	L	1-2	Craggs	21,021

Appearances
Sub Appearances
Goals

Player appearance and goals grid.

Whigham W	Maddren WD	Jones GE	Stiles NP*	Boam SW*	Spraggon F	Downing DG	Mills DJ	Hickton J	Vincent JV	Laidlaw JD	McMordie A	Craggs JE*	Allen M	Gates WL	Burluraux D	Platt JA*	Moody A	Smith RA	Stone JG*	Lynch P*	Armstrong D*	Smith M	No.
1	2	3	4	5	6	7	8	9	10	11													1
1	2	3	4	5	6	7	8	9	10			11											2
1	2	3	4	5	6	7	12	8	10	11*	9												3
1	9	3		5	6	11	7	10	8			2	4										4
1	9	3		5		11	7*	10	8			2	4	6	12								5
1	9	3	4	5		7		10	8	11		2		6									6
1	9	3		5		7		10	8*	11	12	2	4	6									7
1	9	3	4*	5		7		10	11	12	8	2		6									8
1	9	3	4	5		7		10	11		8	2		6									9
	9	3						10	11		8	2		6	7	1	4	5					10
	9	3						10	11	7	8	2		6		1	4	5					11
	9	3		5				10	11	7	8	2		6		1	4						12
	9	3		5				10	11	7	8	2		6		1	4						13
	9	3		5				10	11	7	8	2		6		1		4					14
	9	3		5				10	11	7	8	2		6		1	4						15
	9	3		5			12	10	11	7	8	2				1	4*	6					16
	9	3		5			10		2	11	7	8			6		1	4					17
	9	3		5				10	11	7	8*	2		6		1	4						18
	12	3	7	5				10	11	9*	8	2		6		1	4						19
	12	3	7	5		11		10		9	8	2		6		1	4*						20
	4	3	7	5		11	9	10			8	2		6		1							21
	4	3	7*	5		11	9	10		12	8	2		6		1							22
	4	3		5		11	9	10	7		8	2		6		1							23
	4			5		11	9	10		7	8	2		6		1		3					24
	4			5		11	9	10		7	8	2		6		1		3					25
	4	3	7*	5		11	9	10		12	8	2		6		1							26
	4	3	7	5		11	9	10			8	2		6		1							27
	6	3	4	5		11	9	10		7	8	2				1							28
	4	3	7	5		11	9	10			8	2		6		1							29
	4	3	7	5		11	9	10	12		8	2		6*		1							30
	4	3	7	5			9	10	11		8	2		6		1							31
	6	3	7		4	9	10	11	12	8	2		5*			1							32
	5	3	4		6	7	9*	10			11	8	2			1			12				33
	4	3	7	5	6	11	9	10			8	2				1							34
	4	3	7*	5	6	12		10	11	9	8	2				1							35
	6	3		5	4	12	9*		10	7	8	2				1			11				36
	6		4	5	3		9	12	11*	7	8	2				1			10				37
	6		4*	5	3		9	10	12	7	8	2				1			11				38
	6			5	3	12	9	10	8	4	7*	2				1			11				39
	6		4	5	3		9	10	11	7	8	2				1			12				40
	6		4	5	3	11	9	10*	8	7		2				1	4		11	12			41
	6		7*	5	3		9		10		8	2				1	4		11	12			42
9	40	34	25	38	14	25	25	39	29	25	36	38	3	26	1	33	11	4	2	5			
2				3	2	1	2	4		1				1				1	1	1			
7		1		1	4	8	12	7	2	3	2		2										

1 own-goal

Whigham W	Maddren WD	Jones GE	Stiles NP*	Boam SW*	Spraggon F	Downing DG	Mills DJ	Hickton J	Vincent JV	Laidlaw JD	McMordie A	Craggs JE*	Allen M	Gates WL	Burluraux D	Platt JA*	Moody A	Smith RA	Stone JG*	Lynch P*	Armstrong D*	Smith M	No.
	4	3	7	5		11	9	10			8	2		6		1							3
	4	3	7*	5		11	9	10		12	8	2		6		1							R
	4	3	7*	5		11	9	10		12	8	2		6		1							4
	6	3	4	5		11	9	10		7	8	2		6		1							R
	4	3	7	5		11	9	10			8	2		6		1							5
	4	3	7	5		11	9	10			8	2		6		1							R
	6	6	6	6		6	6	6		1	6	6		5		6							
									2														
				2		1	3																

Whigham W	Maddren WD	Jones GE	Stiles NP*	Boam SW*	Spraggon F	Downing DG	Mills DJ	Hickton J	Vincent JV	Laidlaw JD	McMordie A	Craggs JE*	Allen M	Gates WL	Burluraux D	Platt JA*	Moody A	Smith RA	Stone JG*	Lynch P*	Armstrong D*	Smith M	No.
1	9	3	4	5		7		10	8	11		2		6									2
1	9	3	4	5		7		10	8	11		2		6									R
2	2	2	2	2		2		2	2	2		2		2									
						1		1				1											

303

1972-73

Manager: Stan Anderson

1	Aug	12	(h)	Sunderland	W 2-1	M.Smith 2	24,145
2		19	(a)	Oxford U	L 0-4		8,651
3		26	(h)	Fulham	L 1-2	McMordie	11,410
4		28	(a)	Orient	L 0-2		5,130
5	Sep	2	(a)	Queen's Park R	D 2-2	M.Smith, Hickton	10,601
6		9	(h)	Carlisle U	W 1-0	Mills	9,799
7		16	(a)	Bristol C	D 1-1	McMordie	12,185
8		19	(h)	Preston NE	D 0-0		9,679
9		23	(h)	Hull C	W 1-0	Mills	9,180
10		26	(a)	Burnley	D 0-0		12,398
11		30	(a)	Blackpool	W 1-0	Boam	14,714
12	Oct	7	(h)	Millwall	W 1-0	Maddren	10,863
13		14	(a)	Cardiff C	L 0-2		10,407
14		21	(h)	Huddersfield T	W 2-1	Craggs, Gates	9,907
15		28	(a)	Aston Villa	D 1-1	Armstrong	30,345
16	Nov	4	(h)	Burnley	D 3-3	Mills, McMordie, Hickton	18,127
17		11	(a)	Preston NE	W 1-0	Hickton	10,015
18		18	(a)	Sheffield W	L 1-2	Hickton (pen)	15,874
19		25	(h)	Swindon T	L 0-2		11,418
20	Dec	2	(a)	Brighton & HA	W 2-0	M.Smith, Hickton	11,116
21		9	(h)	Nottingham F	D 0-0		10,326
22		16	(a)	Portsmouth	D 0-0		4,688
23		23	(h)	Luton T	L 0-1		10,122
24		26	(a)	Hull C	L 1-3	McMordie	13,580
25		30	(h)	Oxford U	W 1-0	Foggon	9,069
26	Jan	6	(a)	Fulham	L 1-2	M.Smith	9,693
27		20	(h)	Queen's Park R	D 0-0		8,398
28		27	(a)	Carlisle U	D 1-1	Gates	7,653
29	Feb	2	(h)	Blackpool	W 2-0	Mills 2	10,446
30		10	(h)	Bristol C	W 2-1	Hickton, Boam	8,511
31		17	(a)	Sunderland	L 0-4		26,040
32		24	(h)	Portsmouth	W 3-0	Foggon, Stiles, Hickton	7,038
33	Mar	2	(a)	Millwall	L 0-1		11,473
34		10	(h)	Cardiff C	W 2-0	Brine, Foggon	7,686
35		17	(a)	Huddersfield T	D 1-1	M.Smith	7,193
36		24	(h)	Aston Villa	D 1-1	Hickton	9,776
37		31	(a)	Swindon T	L 0-1		7,278
38	Apr	7	(h)	Brighton & HA	D 1-1	Foggon	6,816
39		14	(a)	Nottingham F	W 3-1	Foggon 2, Hickton (pen)	9,258
40		21	(h)	Sheffield W	W 3-0	Gates, Hickton, Foggon	8,119
41		23	(a)	Luton T	W 1-0	Maddren	6,177
42		28	(h)	Orient	W 3-2	Hickton 3	7,939

FINAL LEAGUE POSITION: 4th in Division Two

Appearances
Sub Appearances
Goals

FA Cup

3	Jan	13	(a)	Plymouth A	L 0-1		15,361

Appearances
Sub Appearances
Goals

League Cup

2	Sep	5	(h)	Wrexham	W 2-0	Mills 2	5,808
3	Oct	3	(h)	Tottenham H	D 1-1	Hickton	23,822
R		11	(a)	Tottenham H	D 0-0*		19,256
2R		30	(a)	Tottenham H	L 1-2*	Hickton	19,287

*After extra-time

Appearances
Sub Appearances
Goals

Platt JA	Craggs JE	Spraggon F	Stiles NP	Boam SW	Maddren WD	McMordie A	Mills DJ	Smith M*	Charlton H	Vincent JV	Moody A	Creamer PA*	Jones GE	Hickton J	Armstrong D	Gates WL	Brine PK*	Foggon A*	Taylor B*	Souness GJ*	
1	2*	3	4	5	6	7	8	9	10	11	12										1
1	2	3	4	5	6	7*	8	9	10	11	12										2
1	2			5	6	7	8	9*	10	11	4	3	12								3
1	2		4	5	6		8	9		11	7*	3	12	10							4
1	2	12	4	5	6	7	8	9				3*	11	10							5
1	2	3	4	5	6	7	8	9					11	10							6
1	2	3	4	5	6	7	8	9					11	10							7
1	2	3	4	5	6	7	8	9						10	11						8
1	2	3	4	5	6	7	8	9					11	10							9
1	2	3	4	5	6	7		9					11	10	8						10
1	2	3	4	5	6	7		9					11	10	8						11
1	2	3	4	5	6	7		9					11*	10	8	12					12
1	2	3		5	6	7*		9				4	11	10	8	12					13
1	2	3	4	5	6			9					11	8	10	7					14
1	2	3	4	5	6			9					11	8	10	7					15
1	2	3	4	5	6		8	9						10	11	7					16
1	2	3	4	5	6		11	9						8	10	7					17
1		3	4*	5	6		11	9		2			12	8	10	7					18
1	2	3	4	5	6		11*	9						8	10	7	12				19
1	2		4	5	6		10	9					3	8	11	7					20
1	2	4		5	6		10*	9					3	8	11	7					21
1	2			5	7	8	9						3	10	11	4	6				22
1	2		4	5	11	9	12						3	8	10	7*	6				23
1	2		4	9	5	10	7*						3	8	11	12	6				24
1	2		4*	5	6	8	9	12					3	10		7	11				25
1	2		4	5	6		9	12					3	8		7	11	10*			26
1	2	3		5	6	7	9						10		4	8		11			27
1	2	3		5	6	7	8						11	10	12	4	9*				28
1	2	3		5	6	7	8	9*						10		4	12	11			29
1	2*	3		5	6	7	8	9						10		4	12	11			30
1	2	3		5	6	7	8	9						10		4		11			31
1	2	3	4	5	6		10*	8						9		7	12	11			32
1	2	3	4	5	6			8						9		7	10	11			33
1	2	3	4	5	6			9						7	8	10		11			34
1	2	3	4	5	6*			9					12		8	10		11			35
1	2	3	4	5				9*					12	8	6	7	11		10		36
1	2	3	4	5									9	8	7		10	6	11		37
1	2	3	4	5	6		8						9	10	7		11				38
1	2	3	4	5	6		8	12					9*	10	7		11				39
1	2	3	4	5	6		8						9	10	7		11				40
1	4	3		5	6		8				2		9	10	7		11				41
1	2	3	4	5	6		8*	12					9	10	7		11				42
42	41	33	32	40	40	26	37	19	3	4	2	6	18	36	19	32	5	12	4	11	
	1							5			2		3	2	1	1	4	3			
	1		1	2	2	4	5	6					13	1	3	1	7				

Platt JA	Craggs JE	Spraggon F	Stiles NP	Boam SW	Maddren WD	McMordie A	Mills DJ	Smith M*	Charlton H	Vincent JV	Moody A	Creamer PA*	Jones GE	Hickton J	Armstrong D	Gates WL	Brine PK*	Foggon A*	Taylor B*	Souness GJ*	
1	2			4	5	6	7	9	12				3	8			11*		10		3
1	1			1	1	1	1	1					1	1			1		1		
								1													

Platt JA	Craggs JE	Spraggon F	Stiles NP	Boam SW	Maddren WD	McMordie A	Mills DJ	Smith M*	Charlton H	Vincent JV	Moody A	Creamer PA*	Jones GE	Hickton J	Armstrong D	Gates WL	Brine PK*	Foggon A*	Taylor B*	Souness GJ*	
1	2	3	4*	5	6	7	8	9					11	10	12						2
1	2	3	4	5	6	7*	9		12				11	10		8					3
1	2	3	4*	5	6	7	9						11	10		8	12				R
1	2	3		5	6	7*	9						12	11	8	10	4				2R
4	4	4	3	4	4	4	4	1					4	4	1	3					
									1			1			1	1					
								2					2								

305

1973-74

Manager: Jack Charlton

1	Aug	25	(a)	Portsmouth	W 1-0	Foggon	19,799
2	Sep	1	(h)	Fulham	L 0-2		14,977
3		8	(a)	Crystal P	W 3-2	Hickton, Mills, Taylor	17,554
4		11	(h)	Carlisle U	W 1-0	Craggs	16,837
5		15	(h)	Aston Villa	D 0-0		14,742
6		17	(a)	Orient	D 0-0		9,744
7		22	(a)	Blackpool	D 0-0		14,784
8		29	(h)	Bristol C	W 2-0	Murdoch, Armstrong	17,069
9	Oct	2	(h)	Orient	W 3-2	Foggon, Hickton 2 (1 pen)	22,164
10		6	(a)	Swindon T	W 1-0	Murdoch	6,958
11		13	(h)	Hull C	W 1-0	M.Smith	22,135
12		20	(h)	West Brom A	D 0-0		18,997
13		23	(a)	Carlisle U	D 1-1	Foggon	11,152
14		27	(a)	Millwall	W 1-0	M.Smith	13,253
15	Nov	3	(h)	Luton T	W 2-1	Foggon, Armstrong	22,590
16		10	(a)	Oxford U	W 2-0	Foggon, Murdoch	8,983
17		17	(h)	Cardiff C	W 3-0	Mills, Craggs, M.Smith	18,034
18		24	(a)	Notts C	D 2-2	Hickton, Mills	16,314
19	Dec	8	(a)	Sheffield W	D 2-2	Foggon, Mills	11,968
20		11	(h)	Preston NE	W 3-0	Mills, Murdoch, Souness	23,980
21		15	(h)	Nottingham F	W 1-0	Boam	16,764
22		22	(a)	Bristol C	D 1-1	Mills	13,116
23		26	(h)	Sunderland	W 2-1	Foggon, Boam	37,030
24		29	(h)	Crystal P	W 2-0	Foggon, Armstrong	26,115
25	Jan	12	(a)	Aston Villa	D 1-1	Craggs	26,906
26		19	(h)	Portsmouth	W 3-0	Foggon, M.Smith, Souness	22,134
27	Feb	2	(a)	Nottingham F	L 1-5	Foggon	18,799
28		9	(h)	Blackpool	D 0-0		21,913
29		16	(a)	Hull C	W 3-1	Hickton, Mills, Foggon	15,287
30		23	(h)	Swindon T	W 2-1	Hickton, Foggon	23,194
31	Mar	2	(a)	Sunderland	W 2-0	Mills, Foggon	41,658
32		9	(h)	Millwall	W 2-1	Mills, Spraggon	20,740
33		16	(a)	West Brom A	W 4-0	Foggon, Hickton 2 (1 pen), Souness	24,178
34		19	(a)	Fulham	W 4-0	Maddren 2, Souness, Boam	18,114
35		23	(h)	Oxford U	W 1-0	Armstrong	26,877
36		30	(a)	Luton T	W 1-0	Mills	19,812
37	Apr	6	(h)	Notts C	W 4-0	Hickton, Needham (og), Armstrong, Foggon	27,823
38		9	(h)	Bolton W	D 0-0		28,143
39		13	(a)	Cardiff C	L 2-3	Maddren, Foggon	12,861
40		15	(a)	Bolton W	L 1-2	Boam	22,545
41		20	(h)	Sheffield W	W 8-0	Hickton, Mills, Murdoch, Souness 3, Foggon 2	25,287
42		27	(a)	Preston NE	W 4-2	Brine 2, Foggon, Hickton	16,177

FINAL LEAGUE POSITION: 1st in Division Two

Appearances
Sub Appearances
Goals

FA Cup

3	Jan	5	(a)	Grantham	W 2-0	Mills, Armstrong	6,573
4		26	(a)	Wrexham	L 0-1		20,612

Appearances
Sub Appearances
Goals

League Cup

2	Oct	8	(a)	Manchester U	W 1-0	M.Smith	23,906
3		31	(a)	Stoke C	D 1-1	Brine	19,194
R	Nov	6	(h)	Stoke C	L 1-2	Foggon	26,068

Appearances
Sub Appearances
Goals

306

Player appearance / goals grid (shirt numbers by match).

Platt JA	Craggs JE	Spragon F	Boam SW	Taylor B	Maddren WD	McMordie A	Mills DJ	Hickton J	Foggon A	Armstrong D	Smith M	Souness GJ	Murdoch RW*	Charlton H	Poskett M*	McAndrew A*	Gates WL	Brine PK	Cochrane JK*	Creamer PA	Cuff PJ*	#
1	2	3	4	5	6	7	8	9*	10	11	12											1
1	2	3	4	5	6	7*	8	9	10	11	12											2
1	2	3	4	5	6	7	8	9	10	11												3
1	2	3	5	4*	6	7	8	9	10	11			12									4
1	2	3	5		6	7	8	9	10	11		4										5
1	2	3	5		6	7	8	9	10	11		4										6
1	2	3	5		6		8	9	10	11		4	7									7
1	2	3	5		6		8	9	10	11		4	7									8
1	2	3	5		6		8*	9	10	11		4	7	12								9
1	2	3	5		6			9	10	11	8	4	7									10
1	2	3	5		6			9	10	11	8*	4	7	12								11
1	2	3	5		6		8	9*	10	11	12	4	7									12
1	2	3	5		6		8	9	10	11		4	7									13
1	2	3	5		6			9	10	11	8	4	7									14
1	2	3	5*		6		12	9	10	11	8	7	4									15
1	2	3	5		6		8	9	10	11		4	7									16
1	2	3	5		6	7	8	9	10*	11	12	4										17
1	2	3	5		6		8	9		11		4	7				10					18
1	2		5		6		8	9	10	11		4	7					3				19
1	2	3	5		6		8	9	10	11		4	7									20
1	2	3	5		6		8	9	10	11		4	7									21
1		3	5		6		8	9	10	11		4	7						2			22
1		3	5		6		8	9*	10	11	12	4	7						2			23
1	2	3	5		6		8	9*	10	11	12	4	7									24
1	2	3	5		6		8	9*	10	11		4	7		12							25
1	2	3	5		6		8	9*	10	11	12	4	7									26
1	2	3	5		6		8	9*	10	11	12	4	7									27
1	2	3	5		6		8	9	10	11	12	4	7*									28
1	2	3	5		6*		8	9	10	11		4	7		12							29
1	2	3	5		6		8	9	10	11		4	7*		12							30
1	2	3	5		6		8	9*	10	11		4	7		12							31
1	2	3	5		6		8	9	10	11		4	7									32
1	2	3	5		6		8	9	10	11		4	7									33
1	2	3	5		6		8	9	10	11	12	4	7*									34
1	2	3	5		6		8	9	10	11		4	7*		12							35
1	2		5		6		8	9	10	11		4	7					3				36
1	2	3	5		6		12	9	10	11	8	7				4*						37
	2		5		6		8	9	10*	11		4	7		12			3			1	38
1	2	3	5		6		8		10	11		9	4	7*	12							39
		3	5		6		8	9*	10	11		4	7		12					2	1	40
1	2	3	5		6		8	9	10	11		4	7*	12								41
1	2	3	5		6		8	9	10	11		4	7									42
40	39	39	42	4	42	7	38	40	41	42	6	34	33			1	1	5	3	3	2	
						1	1				10	1	1	2	1			1	6			
	3	1	4	1	3		11	11	19	5	4	7	5	2								

1 own-goal

Platt JA	Craggs JE	Spragon F	Boam SW	Taylor B	Maddren WD	McMordie A	Mills DJ	Hickton J	Foggon A	Armstrong D	Smith M	Souness GJ	Murdoch RW*	Charlton H	Poskett M*	McAndrew A*	Gates WL	Brine PK	Cochrane JK*	Creamer PA	Cuff PJ*	#
1	2	3	5		6		8	9*	10	11		4	7			12						3
1	2	3	5		6		8	9*	10	11	12	4	7									4
2	2	2	2		2		2	2	2	2	2	2	2									
												1				1						
								1		1												

Platt JA	Craggs JE	Spragon F	Boam SW	Taylor B	Maddren WD	McMordie A	Mills DJ	Hickton J	Foggon A	Armstrong D	Smith M	Souness GJ	Murdoch RW*	Charlton H	Poskett M*	McAndrew A*	Gates WL	Brine PK	Cochrane JK*	Creamer PA	Cuff PJ*	#
1	2	3	5		6			9	10	11	8	4	7									2
1	2	3	5		6				10	11	8	4	7				9					3
1	2	3	5		6		8	9	10	11			7			4						R
3	3	3	3		3		1	2	3	3	2	2	3			1	1					
								1		1						1						

1974-75

Manager: Jack Charlton OBE

1	Aug	17	(a)	Birmingham C	W	3-0	Hickton, Foggon 2	32,105
2		20	(h)	Carlisle U	L	0-2		28,719
3		24	(h)	Luton T	D	1-1	Mills	21,478
4		27	(a)	Carlisle U	W	1-0	Armstrong	18,473
5		31	(a)	Stoke C	D	1-1	Souness	23,475
6	Sep	7	(h)	Chelsea	D	1-1	Maddren	25,480
7		14	(a)	Sheffield U	L	0-1		22,519
8		21	(h)	Manchester C	W	3-0	Mills, Foggon 2	30,256
9		28	(a)	Tottenham H	W	2-1	Armstrong, Mills	23,282
10	Oct	5	(h)	Wolves	W	2-1	Hickton, Willey	27,443
11		12	(a)	Liverpool	L	0-2		52,590
12		16	(a)	Luton T	W	1-0	Foggon	10,464
13		19	(h)	Coventry C	D	4-4	Souness 2, Mills, Foggon	25,499
14		26	(a)	Derby C	W	3-2	Hickton, Foggon, Mills	24,036
15	Nov	2	(a)	West Ham U	L	0-3		28,915
16		9	(h)	Newcastle U	D	0-0		38,380
17		16	(a)	Leeds U	D	2-2	Boam, M.Smith	45,488
18		23	(h)	Queen's Park R	L	1-3	Foggon	27,530
19		30	(a)	Arsenal	L	0-2		25,283
20	Dec	7	(h)	Ipswich T	W	3-0	Souness 2, Foggon	23,735
21		10	(h)	Leicester C	W	3-0	Foggon 2, Willey	22,699
22		14	(h)	Birmingham C	W	3-0	Foggon, Hickton (pen), Page (og)	23,737
23		21	(a)	Burnley	D	1-1	Armstrong	17,637
24		26	(h)	Sheffield U	W	1-0	Armstrong	31,879
25		28	(a)	Everton	D	1-1	Maddren	41,105
26	Jan	11	(a)	Ipswich T	L	0-2		24,720
27		18	(h)	Arsenal	D	0-0		27,996
28	Feb	1	(a)	Newcastle U	L	1-2	Hickton	42,514
29		8	(h)	West Ham U	D	0-0		29,179
30		22	(h)	Leeds U	L	0-1		39,500
31		25	(a)	Queen's Park R	D	0-0		18,487
32	Mar	1	(h)	Stoke C	W	2-0	Hickton, Foggon	25,766
33		15	(h)	Tottenham H	W	3-0	Hickton, Souness 2	25,637
34		18	(h)	Everton	W	2-0	Mills, Armstrong	32,813
35		22	(a)	Chelsea	W	2-1	Willey, Craggs	22,240
36		28	(a)	Manchester C	L	1-2	Mills	37,772
37		29	(h)	Burnley	W	2-0	Murdoch, Foggon	28,922
38	Apr	5	(h)	Derby C	D	1-1	Mills	30,066
39		9	(a)	Leicester C	L	0-1		24,531
40		12	(a)	Wolves	L	0-2		21,066
41		19	(h)	Liverpool	W	1-0	Foggon	33,982
42		26	(a)	Coventry C	W	2-0	Foggon, Hickton	18,121

FINAL LEAGUE POSITION: 7th in Division One

Appearances
Sub Appearances
Goals

FA Cup

3	Jan	4	(a)	Wycombe W	D	0-0		12,200
R		7	(h)	Wycombe W	W	1-0	Armstrong (pen)	30,128
4		25	(h)	Sunderland	W	3-1	Murdoch, Hickton 2 (2 pens)	39,400
5	Feb	15	(a)	Peterborough U	D	1-1	Mills	25,742
R		18	(h)	Peterborough U	W	2-0	Foggon 2	34,303
6	Mar	8	(a)	Birmingham C	L	0-1		47,260

Appearances
Sub Appearances
Goals

League Cup

2	Sep	11	(a)	Tottenham H	W	4-0	M.Smith, Mills, Hickton (pen), Armstrong	15,216
3	Oct	8	(h)	Leicester C	W	1-0	Mills	23,901
4	Nov	12	(a)	Liverpool	W	1-0	Maddren	24,906
5	Dec	4	(h)	Manchester U	D	0-0		36,005
R		18	(a)	Manchester U	L	0-3		49,501

Appearances
Sub Appearances
Goals

Platt JA	Craggs JE	Spraggon F	Maddren WD	Boam SW	Taylor B	Murdoch RW	Mills DJ	Hickton J	Foggon A	Armstrong D	Souness GJ	Smith M	Brine PK	Willey AS*	Woof W*	Charlton H	McAndrew A	Paterson T*	Cooper T*	Creamer PA	
1	2	3	4	5	6	7	8	9	10	11											1
1	2	3	6	5		7	8	9*	10	11	4	12									2
1	2	3	6	5		7	8	9	10	11	4										3
1	2	3	6	5		7	8	9	10	11	4										4
1	2	3	6	5		7	8	9	10	11	4*		12								5
1	2	3	4	5	6	7	8	9	10*	11		12									6
1	2		4	5	6	7	8	9	10	11		3									7
1	2		6	5	12	7	8	3	10	11	4*		9								8
1	2	3	6	5		7	8		10	11	4		9								9
1	2	3	6	5		7*	8	9	10	11	4		12								10
1	2	3	6	5		7	8	9	10	11	4										11
1	2	3	6	5		7	8	9*	10	11	4		12								12
1	2	3	6	5		7	8	9*	10	11	4		12								13
1	2	3	6	5		7	8	9	10	11	4										14
1	2	3	6	5		7	8*	9	10	11	4		12								15
1	2	3	6	5		7	8*	9	10	11	4	12									16
1	2	3	6	5		7		9	10	11	4	8									17
1	2	3	6	5		7*		9	10	11	4	8		12							18
1	2	3	6	5	12			9	10	11	4	8*		7							19
1	2		6*	5				8	10	11	4	12	7	9		10					20
1	2	3	6*	5	12			8	10	11	4		7	9							21
1	2	3	6	5		7		8	10	11	4	12					9*				22
1	2	3	6	5		7	8	9	10*	11	4		12								23
1	2	3	6	5		7	9	8	10*	11	4	12									24
1	2	3	6	5		7	9	8	10	11	4										25
1	2	3	6	5		7	8	9	10*	11	4		12								26
1	2	3	6	5		7	8*	9	10	11	4		12								27
1	2	3	6	5		7	8	9	10*	11	4		12								28
1	2	3	6	5	12	4	8	9		11*				7		10					29
1	2	3	6	5		7*	9	8	10	11	4		12								30
1	2	3	6	5		7	9	8	10	11	4										31
1	2	3	6	5		7	9	8	10	11	4										32
1	2		6	5		7	9	8	10	11	4								3		33
1	2		6	5		7	8		10	11	4			9					3		34
1	2		6	5		7	8		10	11	4			9					3		35
1	2		6	5		7	8	9	10	11	4								3		36
1	2	3	6	5		7	8	9	10	11	4										37
1	2		6	5		7	8	9*	10	11	4	12							3		38
1	2		6	5		7*	8	9	10	11	4	12							3		39
1	2		6	5		7	8	9*	10	11	4		12						3		40
1	2		6	5		7	8	9	10	11	4								3		41
1	2		6	5		7	8	9	10	11	4								3		42
42	41	31	42	42	3	39	36	39	41	42	38	4	3	7		1	1	1	9		
					4							6	4	9	1						
	1		2	1		1	8	8	16	5	7	1		3							

1 own-goal

Platt JA	Craggs JE	Spraggon F	Maddren WD	Boam SW	Taylor B	Murdoch RW	Mills DJ	Hickton J	Foggon A	Armstrong D	Souness GJ	Smith M	Brine PK	Willey AS*	Woof W*	Charlton H	McAndrew A	Paterson T*	Cooper T*	Creamer PA	
1	2	3	6	5			9	8	10*	11	4		7	12							3
1	2	3	6	5			9	8	10*	11	4		12			7					R
1	2	3	6	5		7	9	8	10	11		12	8*								4
1	2	3	6	5			4	9	7	10	11			12							5
1	2	3	6	5		7	9	8*	10	11	4		12								R
1	2	3	6	5		7	9	8	10	11	4										6
6	6	6	6	6		4	6	6	6	6	5	1	1	1							
												2	2								
			1	1		2	2	1													

Platt JA	Craggs JE	Spraggon F	Maddren WD	Boam SW	Taylor B	Murdoch RW	Mills DJ	Hickton J	Foggon A	Armstrong D	Souness GJ	Smith M	Brine PK	Willey AS*	Woof W*	Charlton H	McAndrew A	Paterson T*	Cooper T*	Creamer PA	
1	2		4	5	6	7	8	3	10	11		9									2
1	2	3	6	5		7	8	9	10*	11	4		12								3
1	2	3	6	5	12	7*		9	10	11	4	8									4
1		3	6	5			8	10	11	4	12		9			7		2*			5
1	2	3	6	5		7	9	8	10	11	4										R
5	4	4	5	5	1	4	3	5	5	5	4	2		1		1		1			
					1							1	1								
		1				2	1			1		1									

309

1975-76

Manager: Jack Charlton OBE

1	Aug	16	(a)	Tottenham H	L	0-1	25,502
2		20	(a)	Newcastle U	D	1-1 Gowling (og)	41,417
3		23	(h)	Wolves	W	1-0 Hickton	22,639
4		26	(h)	Birmingham C	W	2-0 Hickton, Mills	22,423
5		30	(a)	Burnley	L	1-4 Armstrong	17,066
6	Sep	6	(h)	Stoke C	W	3-0 Hickton, Mills 2	21,975
7		13	(a)	Manchester C	L	0-4	30,353
8		20	(h)	Queen's Park R	D	0-0	24,867
9		23	(a)	Coventry C	W	1-0 Mills	15,132
10		27	(a)	Ipswich T	W	3-0 Foggon, Armstrong, Hickton (pen)	22,321
11	Oct	4	(h)	Aston Villa	D	0-0	24,102
12		11	(a)	Leicester C	D	0-0	19,095
13		18	(h)	West Ham U	W	3-0 Souness, Armstrong, Foggon	25,831
14		25	(a)	Arsenal	L	1-2 Mills	23,606
15	Nov	1	(h)	Liverpool	L	0-1	30,952
16		8	(a)	Norwich C	W	1-0 Souness	19,286
17		15	(h)	Leeds U	D	0-0	32,959
18		22	(a)	West Ham U	L	1-2 Mills	26,944
19		29	(a)	Derby C	L	2-3 Boam, Craggs	27,745
20	Dec	6	(h)	Manchester U	D	0-0	32,454
21		13	(a)	Wolves	W	2-1 Armstrong, Mills	13,548
22		20	(h)	Tottenham H	W	1-0 Hickton (pen)	22,046
23		26	(a)	Sheffield U	D	1-1 Foggon	28,593
24		27	(h)	Everton	D	1-1 Maddren	29,275
25	Jan	10	(h)	Manchester C	W	1-0 Armstrong	22,358
26		17	(a†)	Stoke C	L	0-1	21,049
27		31	(h)	Newcastle U	D	3-3 Mills, Keeley (og), Maddren	30,365
28	Feb	7	(a)	Birmingham C	L	1-2 Mills	18,599
29		14	(h)	Burnley	D	1-1 Boam	17,856
30		21	(a)	Leeds U	W	2-0 Hickton 2	32,993
31		24	(h)	Coventry C	W	2-0 Boam, Souness	18,553
32		28	(h)	Arsenal	L	0-1	19,857
33	Mar	6	(a)	Liverpool	W	2-0 Cooper, Hickton	41,391
34		13	(h)	Leicester C	L	0-1	17,634
35		20	(h)	Derby C	L	0-2	24,120
36		27	(a)	Manchester U	L	0-3	58,527
37	Apr	3	(h)	Ipswich T	W	2-0 Mills, Armstrong	14,764
38		6	(h)	Norwich C	L	0-1	15,768
39		10	(a)	Queen's Park R	L	2-4 Boersma, Brine	24,342
40		17	(h)	Sheffield U	W	3-0 McAndrew 3	16,889
41		19	(a)	Everton	L	1-3 Woof	18,204
42		24	(a)	Aston Villa	L	1-2 Hickton	33,241

FINAL LEAGUE POSITION: 13th in Division One
†Played at Vale Park, Burslem. Stoke's ground storm-damaged.

Appearances
Sub Appearances
Goals

FA Cup

3	Jan	3	(h)	Bury	D	0-0	20,728
R		6	(a)	Bury	L	2-3 Brine, Hickton (pen)	11,488

Appearances
Sub Appearances
Goals

League Cup

2	Sep	9	(a)	Bury	W	2-1 Hickton, Mills	9,121
3	Oct	7	(h)	Derby C	W	1-0 Foggon	25,740
4	Nov	11	(h)	Peterborough U	W	3-0 Boam, Hickton (pen), Armstrong	17,749
5	Dec	3	(a)	Burnley	W	2-0 Mills, Maddren	15,509
SF	Jan	13	(h)	Manchester C	W	1-0 Armstrong	34,579
		21	(a)	Manchester C	L	0-4	44,246

Appearances
Sub Appearances
Goals

Appearance and scoring grid (players listed across the top, match numbers down the right).

Platt JA	Craggs JE	Cooper T	Souness GJ	Boam SW	Maddren WD	Murdoch RW	Mills DJ	Hickton J	Willey AS	Armstrong D	Brine PK	Taylor B	Foggon A	Spraggon F	Boersma P*	Bailey IC*	McAndrew A	Woof W*	Smith M	Cuff PJ	Coleman EP*	Ramage A*	#
1	2	3	4	5	6	7	8	9	10	11													1
1	2	3	4	5	6	7	8	9		11	10												2
1	2	3	4		6	7	8	9*	12	11	10	5											3
1	2	3	4		6*	7	8	9	12	11	10	5											4
1	2	3	4		6	7	8	9*	12	11	10	5											5
1	2	3	4	5	6	7	8	9	10*	11			12										6
1	2	3	4	5	6	7	8	9	10*	11			12										7
1	2	3	4	5	6		8	9		11		7	10										8
1	2		4	5	6		8	9		11		7	10	3									9
1	2	3	4	5	6		8	9		11		7	10										10
1		3	4	5	6	12	8	9		11		7*	10	2									11
1	2	3	4	5	6		8	9		11		7	10										12
1	2	3	4	5	6	7	8	9		11			10							.			13
1	2	3	4	5	6		8	9		11		7	10										14
1	2	3	4	5	6	7	8	9		11			10*	12									15
1	2	10	4	5	6		8	9		11		7		3									16
1	2	10	4*	5	6	7	8	9		11			12	3									17
1	2	10		5	6	4	8	9*		11		7	12	3									18
1	2	3		5	6	4	8	10		11		7	9										19
1	2	3		5	6	7	8	10	9	11				4									20
1	2	3		5	6	7	8	10	9	11				4									21
1	2	10		5	6	7		8	9	11			12	4	3*								22
1	2	3		5	6	7	8	10		11	12	9*		4									23
1	2	3		5	6	7	8	10		11		9		4									24
1	2	10	12	5	6	7	8		9*	11				4	3								25
1	2	3	4	5	6			10	9	11	7			8									26
1		10	4	5	6	7	8			11				2	9	3							27
1	2	10	4	5	6	7*	8	12		11				9	3								28
1		10	4	5	6		8*	9	12	11				2	7	3							29
1	2	3	4	5	10		8	9		11					7*		6	12					30
1	2	3	4	5	10		8	9		11					7*		6	12					31
1	2	3	4	5	10		8	9		11					7*		6	12					32
1	2	3	4	5	10		8	9		11					7		6						33
1		3	4	5	10		8	9*	12	11				2	7		6						34
1		3	4	5	10		8	9		11			12	2*	7		6						35
1	2		4	5	10		8	3		11	12			7*	6		9						36
	2	3	4	5			8			11	7				6		9	10	1				37
1	2	3	4	5	10*		8			11			12	7	6		9						38
1		3	4	5	10		8	2		11	7			9	6								39
1	2	3	4	5	6	7	8*			11							10	9	12				40
1	2	3	4	5	6			8	11*	7							10	9	12				41
1	2	10	4	5	6		8			11	7					3		9*	12				42
41	36	40	34	39	41	21	38	35	9	42	18	3	11	9	19	6	12	3	3	1	1	1	
	1					1		1		5		2		7	1		3	2			1		
	1	1	3	3	2		10	9		6	1		3		1		3	1					

2 own-goals

Platt JA	Craggs JE	Cooper T	Souness GJ	Boam SW	Maddren WD	Murdoch RW	Mills DJ	Hickton J	Willey AS	Armstrong D	Brine PK	Taylor B	Foggon A	Spraggon F	Boersma P*	Bailey IC*	McAndrew A	Woof W*	Smith M	#
1	2	3		5	7		8	9*		11			10		4	12	6			3
1	2	9		5	6	7	8	10		11	4		12		3*					R
2	2	2		2	2	1	2	2		2	1		1		1	1	1			
										1					1					
								1			1									

Platt JA	Craggs JE	Cooper T	Souness GJ	Boam SW	Maddren WD	Murdoch RW	Mills DJ	Hickton J	Willey AS	Armstrong D	Brine PK	Taylor B	Foggon A	Spraggon F	Boersma P*	Bailey IC*	McAndrew A	#
1	2	3	4	5	6	7	8	9	10	11								2
1	2	3	4	5	6	7	8	9*		11			10	12				3
1	2	10	4	5	6	7	8	9		11			12	3				4
1	2	3		5	6	4	8	9	10	11*	7						12	5
1	2	10	4	5	6	7	8	9*		11			12		3			SF
1	2	3	4	5	6	7*	10	9		11	8						12	
6	6	6	5	6	6	6	6	6	2	6	2		1	1	1			
								1	1							2		
			1	1		2	3		1				1					

1976-77

Manager: Jack Charlton OBE

1	Aug	21	(h)	Coventry C	W 1-0	McAndrew		17,694
2		25	(a)	Derby C	D 0-0			23,344
3		28	(a)	Tottenham H	D 0-0			21,721
4	Sep	4	(h)	Newcastle U	W 1-0	Mills		26,014
5		11	(h)	Sunderland	W 2-1	Willey 2		28,329
6		18	(a)	Manchester U	L 0-2			56,712
7		25	(h)	Leeds U	W 1-0	Willey		24,671
8	Oct	2	(a)	Liverpool	D 0-0			45,107
9		9	(h)	Norwich C	W 1-0	Souness		21,998
10		16	(a)	Birmingham C	L 1-3	Boersma		27,740
11		23	(h)	West Brom A	W 1-0	Mills		22,643
12		30	(h)	Leicester C	L 0-1			24,288
13	Nov	6	(a)	Stoke C	L 1-3	Armstrong		16,068
14		20	(a)	Queen's Park R	L 0-3			16,037
15		27	(h)	Ipswich T	L 0-2			20,070
16	Dec	4	(a)	West Ham U	W 1-0	Boersma		20,453
17		7	(h)	Manchester C	D 0-0			18,484
18		18	(a)	Bristol C	W 2-1	Armstrong (pen), Brine		15,145
19		27	(h)	Aston Villa	W 3-2	Mills 3		31,451
20		29	(a)	Everton	D 2-2	Armstrong 2		28,169
21	Jan	1	(h)	Stoke C	D 0-0			20,987
22		15	(h)	Derby C	W 2-0	George (og), Mills		17,914
23		22	(a)	Coventry C	D 1-1	Mills		12,893
24	Feb	5	(h)	Tottenham H	W 2-0	Mills 2		21,231
25		15	(h)	Arsenal	W 3-0	Brine, Armstrong, Mills		26,083
26		19	(a)	Sunderland	L 0-4			33,226
27	Mar	5	(a)	Leeds U	L 1-2	Wood		32,125
28		9	(a)	Norwich C	L 0-1			16,625
29		12	(h)	Liverpool	L 0-1			29,166
30		16	(a)	Leicester C	D 3-3	Craggs, Mills, Wood		13,483
31		22	(h)	Birmingham C	D 2-2	Willey, Boam		16,439
32		26	(a)	Newcastle U	L 0-1			33,643
33	Apr	2	(a)	West Brom A	L 1-2	Mills		18,519
34		5	(a)	Aston Villa	L 0-1			32,646
35		9	(h)	Everton	D 2-2	Hedley, Mills		16,159
36		11	(a)	Manchester C	L 0-1			37,735
37		16	(h)	Queen's Park R	L 0-2			14,500
38		23	(a)	Ipswich T	W 1-0	Armstrong		23,348
39		26	(h)	Manchester U	W 3-0	Armstrong 2, Mills		21,744
40		30	(h)	West Ham U	D 1-1	Mills		16,360
41	May	7	(a)	Arsenal	D 1-1	Souness		23,911
42		14	(h)	Bristol C	D 0-0			14,849

FINAL LEAGUE POSITION: 12th in Division One

Appearances
Sub Appearances
Goals

FA Cup

3	Jan	8	(a)	Wimbledon	D 0-0			8,750
R		11	(h)	Wimbledon	W 1-0	Armstrong (pen)		22,485
4		29	(h)	Hereford U	W 4-0	Souness, Armstrong 2 (1 pen), Willey		25,163
5	Feb	26	(h)	Arsenal	W 4-1	Mills 3, Armstrong		35,208
6	Mar	19	(a)	Liverpool	L 0-2			55,881

Appearances
Sub Appearances
Goals

League Cup

2	Aug	31	(h)	Tottenham H	L 1-2	McAndrew		19,042

Appearances
Sub Appearances
Goals

Player appearance grid (shirt numbers worn in each match; `*` denotes substitute).

Platt JA	Craggs JE	Cooper T	Souness GJ	Boam SW	Maddren WD	McAndrew A	Mills DJ	Hedley G*	Boersma P	Armstrong D	Hickton J	Woof W	Willey AS	Brine PK	Wood AEH*	Cummins S*	Cuff PJ	Ramage A*	Bailey IC	
1	2	3	4	5	6	7	8	9	10	11										1
1	2	3	4	5	6	7	8		10	11	9									2
1	2	3	4	5	6	7	8		10	11	9*	12								3
1	2	3	4	5	6	7	8		10*	11				9	12					4
1	2	3	4	5	6	7	8		10*	11				9	12					5
1	2	3	4	5	6	7	8		12	11				9	10*					6
1	2	3	4	5	6	7	8		10	11	12		9*							7
1	2	3	4	5	6	7	8		10	11	9*		12							8
1	2	3	4	5	6	7	8		10	11			9*	12						9
1	2	3	4	5	6	7	8		10	11				9						10
1	2	3	4	5	6	7	8		10*	11			12	9						11
1	2	3	4	5	6	7	8			11			10*	12	9					12
1	2	3	4	5	6	7	8			11	12			10*	9					13
1	2	3	4	5	6	7	8		10	11	12			9*						14
1	2	3	4	5	6	7	12		10	11	9				8*					15
1	2	3	4	5	6	7	8		10*	11	12			9						16
1	2	3	4	5	6	7	8			11			10*	9	12					17
1	2	3	4	5	6	7	8		12	11				9	10*					18
1	2	3	4	5	6*	7	8			11	12			9	10					19
	2	3	4	5	6	7	8		12	11				9	10*		1			20
	2	3	4	5	6	7	8			11				9	10		1			21
	2	3	4	5	6	7*	8			11	12			9	10		1			22
	2	3	4	5	6		8		7	11				9	10		1			23
	2	3	4	5	6		8	9	7	11					10		1			24
	2	3	4	5	6		8		7	11	12			9	10*		1			25
	2	3	4	5	6	12	8		7*	11				9	10		1			26
	2	3		5		4	8		7	11			12	9*	10		1	6		27
	2	3	4	5	6	7	8		12	11				9*	10		1			28
	2	3	4	5		7	8	9		11			12		10*		1	6		29
	2	3	4	5		7	8			11				9	10		1	6		30
	2	3	4	5	6	7	8			11			12	10	9*		1			31
	2	3	4	5	6	7	8			11				9	10		1			32
	2	3		5	6	7	8	4*		11				9	10		1		12	33
	2	3		5	6	7	8			11				10	9		1		4	34
	2	10		5	6	7	8	4		11			9*			12	1		3	35
2*	3	4	5	6	7	8		10	11				9				1		12	36
	2	3	4	5	6	9	8	7	10	11							1			37
1	2	3	4	5	6	7	8			11				9	10					38
1	2	3	4	5	6	7	8			11				10	9					39
1	2	3	4	5	6	7	8		12	11				10*	9					40
1	2		4	5	6	7	8	10		11				9				3		41
1	2		4	5	6	7	8	10	12	11				9*				3		42
24	42	40	38	42	39	38	41	6	22	42	4		11	25	22	1	18	3	4	
			1	1		6		5	1		7	4	1	1			2			
	1		2	1		1	15	1	2	8		4	2	2						

I own-goal

Platt JA	Craggs JE	Cooper T	Souness GJ	Boam SW	Maddren WD	McAndrew A	Mills DJ	Hedley G*	Boersma P	Armstrong D	Hickton J	Woof W	Willey AS	Brine PK	Wood AEH*	Cummins S*	Cuff PJ	Ramage A*	Bailey IC	
	2	3	4	5	6	7	8			11				9	10		1			3
	2	3	4	5	6	7	8			11				9	10		1			R
	2	3	4	5	6		8		7	11			12	9	10*		1			4
	2	3	4*	5	6	12	8		7	11				9	10		1			5
	2	3	4	5	6	7	8		12	11				9	10*		1			6
	5	5	5	5	5	3	5		2	5				5	5		5			
						1		1					1							
	1						3		1				4				1			

Platt JA	Craggs JE	Cooper T	Souness GJ	Boam SW	Maddren WD	McAndrew A	Mills DJ	Hedley G*	Boersma P	Armstrong D	Hickton J	Woof W	Willey AS	Brine PK	Wood AEH*	Cummins S*	Cuff PJ	Ramage A*	Bailey IC	
1	2	3	4	5	6	7	8	9*	10	11	12									2
1	1	1	1	1	1	1	1	1	1	1	1									
											1									
		1																		

1977-78

Manager: John Neal

1	Aug	20	(h)	Liverpool	D	1-1	Armstrong	30,805
2		24	(a)	Norwich C	D	1-1	Souness	14,245
3		27	(h)	Newcastle U	W	2-0	Armstrong 2	26,902
4	Sep	3	(a)	West Brom A	L	1-2	Mills	19,044
5		10	(h)	Birmingham C	L	1-2	Ashcroft	19,240
6		17	(a)	Coventry C	L	1-2	Mills	13,910
7		24	(h)	Ipswich T	D	1-1	Mills	19,843
8	Oct	1	(a)	Derby C	L	1-4	Armstrong	21,040
9		3	(a)	West Ham U	W	2-0	Mills 2	26,508
10		8	(h)	Manchester U	W	2-1	Mills, Ashcroft	26,822
11		15	(a)	Chelsea	D	0-0		21,091
12		22	(h)	Leeds U	W	2-1	Souness 2	27,493
13		29	(a)	Nottingham F	L	0-4		27,373
14	Nov	5	(h)	Queen's Park R	D	1-1	Hedley	18,215
15		12	(a)	Aston Villa	W	1-0	Cummins	31,837
16		19	(h)	Wolves	D	0-0		18,464
17		26	(a)	Bristol C	L	1-4	Mills	20,536
18	Dec	3	(h)	Arsenal	L	0-1		17,412
19		10	(a)	Everton	L	0-3		38,647
20		17	(h)	Aston Villa	W	1-0	Hedley (pen)	14,999
21		26	(a)	Leicester C	D	0-0		18,476
22		27	(h)	Manchester C	L	0-2		27,319
23		31	(h)	Norwich C	D	2-2	Cummins, Armstrong	15,646
24	Jan	2	(a)	Liverpool	L	0-2		49,305
25		14	(a)	Newcastle U	W	4-2	Boam, Ashcroft 2, Cummins	34,460
26		21	(h)	West Brom A	W	1-0	Boam	19,172
27	Feb	4	(a)	Birmingham C	W	2-1	Craggs, Mills	14,302
28		25	(h)	Derby C	W	3-1	Mills, Craggs, Mahoney	20,703
29	Mar	4	(a)	Manchester U	D	0-0		46,332
30		18	(a)	Leeds U	L	0-5		25,158
31		21	(a)	Ipswich T	D	1-1	Ashcroft	17,759
32		25	(h)	Manchester C	D	2-2	Cummins, Ashcroft	37,944
33		27	(h)	Leicester C	L	0-1		15,534
34		29	(h)	Nottingham F	D	2-2	Mills, Cummins	25,445
35	Apr	1	(a)	Queen's Park R	L	0-1		12,925
36		4	(h)	Chelsea	W	2-0	Shearer 2	15,268
37		8	(h)	Bristol C	W	2-0	Ramage, Cummins	14,667
38		11	(h)	Coventry C	D	1-1	Armstrong	14,184
39		15	(a)	Wolves	D	0-0		15,466
40		22	(h)	Everton	D	0-0		15,969
41		25	(h)	West Ham U	L	1-2	Johnston	13,247
42		29	(a)	Arsenal	L	0-1		32,138

FINAL LEAGUE POSITION: 14th in Division One

Appearances
Sub Appearances
Goals

FA Cup

3	Jan	7	(h)	Coventry C	W	3-0	Mills 2, McAndrew	18,015
4		28	(h)	Everton	W	3-2	Mahoney, Mills 2	33,652
5	Feb	27	(h)	Bolton W	W	2-0	Ashcroft, Cummins	36,662
6	Mar	11	(h)	Orient	D	0-0		33,426
R		14	(a)	Orient	L	1-2	Armstrong	18,051

Appearances
Sub Appearances
Goals

League Cup

2	Aug	30	(a)	Sunderland	D	2-2	Armstrong 2 (1 pen)	26,597
R	Sep	13	(h)	Sunderland	W	1-0	Boam	29,572
3	Oct	25	(a)	Everton	D	2-2	Woof, Mills	32,766
R		31	(h)	Everton	L	1-2	Mills	28,409

Appearances
Sub Appearances
Goals

Player appearance grid (player columns left to right, match number in right-hand column).

Platt JA	Craggs JE	Cooper T	Souness GJ	Boam SW	Maddren WD	Mahoney JF*	Mills DJ	Woof W	McAndrew A	Armstrong D	Hickton J	Brine PK	Ashcroft W*	Hedley G	Bailey IC	Ramage A	Willey AS	Cuff PJ	Cummins S	Johnston CP*	Brown DJ*	Walsh A*	Johnson PE*	Shearer DJ*	Bell IC*	#
1	2	3	4	5	6	7	8	9*	10	11	12															1
1	2	3	4*	5	6	7	8	9	10	11	12															2
1	2	3		5	6	7	8	9	10	11		4														3
1	2	3		5	6	7	8		10	11		4*	9	12												4
1	2	3	4	5		7	8		6	11		10*	9	12												5
1	2		4	5		7	8		10	11			9		3	6										6
1	2*		4	5		7	8		10	11			9		3	6		12								7
1	2	3	4	5		7	8		10	11			9		3	6										8
1	2	3	4	5		7	8		10	11			9		3	6										9
1	2	3	4	5		7	8		10	11			9		3	6										10
1		3	4	5		7	8		10	11			9		2	6										11
1		3	4	5		7	8		10	11			9		2	6										12
1	2		4	5		7	8		10	11	12		9*		3	6										13
		3	4	5		7	8		10*	11			9	12	2	6		1								14
		3	4	5		7			10	11			9		2	6	1	8								15
	2	3	4	5		7*	8		10	11			9	12		6	1									16
	2	3	4	5		7	8		10	11*			9			6	1	12								17
	2*	3		5		7	8		10	11			9	4		6	1	12								18
	2	3*	4	5		7	8		10	11	12		9			6	1									19
	2			5		7			10	11			9	4	3	6	1	8								20
	2		4						10	11	5		9	7	3	6	1	8								21
	2		4				12		10	11	5		9*	7	3	6	1	8								22
	2		4			7			10	11	5		9		3	6	1	8								23
1	2			5		4	7		10	11			9		3	6		8								24
1	2			5		4	7		10	11	12		9*		3	6		8								25
1	2			5		4	7		10	11			9		3	6		8								26
1	2			5		4	7	12		11			9		3	6		8		10*						27
1	2			5		4	7		10	11			9		3	6		8								28
1	2			5		4	7	12	10	11			9*		3	6		8								29
1	2			5		4	7		10	11			9		3	6		8								30
1	2			5		4			10	11	12		9		3	6		8		7*						31
1	2			5		4	7		10	11			9		3	6		8								32
	2			5		4	7		10	11			9*		3	6		8	12	1						33
	2			5		4	7		10	11			9		3	6		8		1						34
	2			5		4	7		10*	11			9		3	6		8		1	12					35
				5		4	7		10	11					2	6		8*		1	12	3	9			36
	2			5		4	7		10	11					3	6		8	7	1		9				37
	2			5		4			10	11					3	6		8	7	1		9				38
	2			5		4			10	11			9		3					1	12	6	8*	7		39
	2			5		4			10	11	12		9*	7	3			8		1	6					40
	2			5			7		10	11	12		9		3*	6		8	4	1						41
	2			5		4	7	12	10	11			9			6		8*		1		3				42
22	37	16	19	39	4	37	35	3	41	42	3	3	36	5	29	35	10	23	4	10	4	4	1			
								4				8			3	1		2	1		3					
	2		3	2		1	10		6		6	2		1		6	1		2							

Platt JA	Craggs JE	Cooper T	Souness GJ	Boam SW	Maddren WD	Mahoney JF*	Mills DJ	Woof W	McAndrew A	Armstrong D	Hickton J	Brine PK	Ashcroft W*	Hedley G	Bailey IC	Ramage A	Willey AS	Cuff PJ	Cummins S	Johnston CP*	Brown DJ*	Walsh A*	Johnson PE*	Shearer DJ*	Bell IC*	#
1	2			5		4	7		10	11			9		3	6		8								3
1	2			5		4	7		10	11			9		3	6		8								4
1	2			5		4	7			11			9		3	6		8	10							5
1	2			5		4	7		10*	11			9		3	6		8	12							6
1	2			5		4	7		10	11			9		3	6		8*	12							R
5	5			5		5	5		4	5			5		5	5		5	1							
																			2							
						1	4		1	1			1			1			1							

Platt JA	Craggs JE	Cooper T	Souness GJ	Boam SW	Maddren WD	Mahoney JF*	Mills DJ	Woof W	McAndrew A	Armstrong D	Hickton J	Brine PK	Ashcroft W*	Hedley G	Bailey IC	Ramage A	Willey AS	Cuff PJ	Cummins S	Johnston CP*	Brown DJ*	Walsh A*	Johnson PE*	Shearer DJ*	Bell IC*	#
1*	2	3		5	6	7	8	9	10	11	12	4														2
1	2	3*	4	5		7	8	9	10	11				12		6										R
1		3	4	5		7	8	9	10	11	12				2*	6										3
1		3	4	5		7	8	9	10*	11	12				2	6										R
4	2	4	3	4	1	4	4	4	4	4					2	3										
																			3							
			1			2	1		2						1											

315

1978-79

Manager: John Neal

1	Aug	19	(h)	Coventry C	L	1-2	Woof	17,918
2		22	(a)	Birmingham C	W	3-1	Armstrong, Ashcroft, Mills	24,409
3		26	(a)	Southampton	L	1-2	Armstrong	20,691
4	Sep	2	(h)	Ipswich T	D	0-0		14,427
5		9	(a)	Everton	L	0-2		36,191
6		16	(h)	Queen's Park R	L	0-2		12,822
7		23	(a)	Nottingham F	D	2-2	Mills, Armstrong	26,287
8		30	(h)	Arsenal	L	2-3	Ashcroft, Mills	14,511
9	Oct	7	(a)	Manchester U	L	2-3	Mills, Burns	45,402
10		14	(h)	Norwich C	W	2-0	Peters (og), Mills	18,286
11		21	(h)	Wolves	W	2-0	Burns, Armstrong	19,029
12		27	(a)	Aston Villa	W	2-0	Burns, Cochrane	32,614
13	Nov	4	(h)	Bristol C	D	0-0		20,461
14		11	(a)	Coventry C	L	1-2	Burns	18,636
15		18	(h)	Southampton	W	2-0	Burns, Mills	17,169
16		21	(a)	Ipswich T	L	1-2	Armstrong	17,818
17		25	(a)	Liverpool	L	0-2		39,812
18	Dec	9	(a)	West Brom A	L	0-2		19,865
19		16	(h)	Chelsea	W	7-2	Proctor, Burns 4, Armstrong, Cochrane	15,107
20		23	(a)	Leeds U	L	1-3	Proctor	27,146
21		26	(h)	Bolton W	D	1-1	Cummins	20,125
22	Jan	20	(a)	Queen's Park R	D	1-1	Hodgson	9,899
23	Feb	3	(h)	Nottingham F	L	1-3	Proctor	21,330
24		10	(a)	Arsenal	D	0-0		28,371
25		24	(a)	Norwich C	L	0-1		12,914
26	Mar	3	(a)	Wolves	W	3-1	Ashcroft, McAndrew, Shearer	18,782
27		6	(h)	Everton	L	1-2	Armstrong (pen)	16,084
28		10	(a)	Aston Villa	W	2-0	Proctor, Burns	16,558
29		13	(h)	Derby C	W	3-1	Boam, Armstrong, Burns	16,286
30		17	(a)	Bristol C	D	1-1	Armstrong	13,559
31		24	(h)	Birmingham C	W	2-1	Burns, Ashcroft	15,013
32		27	(a)	Manchester U	D	2-2	Armstrong (pen), Proctor	20,138
33		31	(h)	Tottenham H	W	1-0	Proctor	19,172
34	Apr	7	(a)	Tottenham H	W	2-1	Proctor, Ashcroft	21,580
35		10	(a)	Leeds U	W	1-0	Ashcroft	23,260
36		14	(a)	Bolton W	D	0-0		22,621
37		17	(h)	Manchester C	W	2-0	Proctor, Burns	19,676
38		21	(a)	Chelsea	L	1-2	Armstrong	13,413
39		24	(a)	Manchester C	L	0-1		28,264
40		28	(h)	West Brom A	D	1-1	Burns	18,063
41	May	5	(a)	Derby C	W	3-0	Cochrane, Proctor, Jankovic	18,151
42		11	(h)	Liverpool	L	0-1		32,214

FINAL LEAGUE POSITION: 12th in Division One

Appearances
Sub Appearances
Goals

FA Cup

3	Jan	9	(h)	Crystal P	D	1-1	Ashcroft	21,447
R		15	(a)	Crystal P	L	0-1		23,361

Appearances
Sub Appearances
Goals

League Cup

2	Aug	29	(h)	Peterborough U	D	0-0	12,510
R	Sep	5	(a)	Peterborough U	L	0-1*	8,093

*After extra-time

Appearances
Sub Appearances
Goals

316

Squad appearance and scoring grid (shirt numbers per match; * denotes substituted/substitute).

Stewart J*	Craggs JE	Bailey IC	Mahoney JF	Boam SW	Ramage A	Mills DJ	McAndrew A	Ashcroft W	Woof W	Armstrong D	Hedley G	Proctor MG*	Johnson PE	Johnston CP	Cummins S	Hodgson DJ*	Burns ME*	Cochrane GT*	Shearer DJ	Platt JA	Jankovic B*	Bell IC	
1	2	3	4	5	6	7	8	9	10	11*	12												1
1	2	3	4	5	6		8	9	10	11		7											2
1	2	3	4	5	6		8	9*	10	11		7		12									3
1	2	3	4	5	6		8	9	10	11		7											4
1	2	3	4	5	6		8	10	9	11		7											5
1	2			5	6	9	8	12		11		7*	3	4	10								6
1	2		4	5	6	7	8*	9		11			3		10	12							7
1	2		4	5	6	7	8	9*		11			3		10	12							8
1	2	3	4	5	6	7	8	9		11					10								9
1	2	3	4	5		8	6	9		11							10	7					10
1	2	3	4*	5		8	6	9		11						12	10	7					11
1	2	3	4	5		8	6	9		11							10	7					12
1	2	3	4	5		8	6			11		7			9		10						13
1	2	3	4	5		8	6	9*		11			12				10	7					14
1	2	3	4	5		8	6			11					9		10	7					15
1	2	3	4*	5		8	6	9		11			12				10	7					16
1	2	3	4	5		8	6*	12		11					9		10	7					17
1	2	3	4	5			6	12		11		8*			9		10	7					18
1	2		4	5	6			9		11		8	3				10	7					19
1	2		4*	5	6			9		11		8	3	12			10	7					20
1	2		4	5	6			9		11		8	3				10	7					21
1	2*	3	4	5			6	9		11		8			12		10						22
1	2		4	5			6			11		8	3		12	7	10	9*					23
1	2		4	5			6			11		8	3		12	7*	10	9					24
1	2		4	5			6*	9		11		8	3		12	7	10						25
1	2		4	5			6	9*		11		8	3			7	10	12					26
1	2		4	5			6	9		11		8	3			7	10*	12					27
	2		4	5			6	9		11		8	3			7	10			1			28
	2		4	5			6	9		11		8	3			7	10			1			29
	2		4	5			6	9		11		8	3			7	10*			1	12		30
	2		4	5			6	9		11		8	3			7	10*			1	12		31
	2		4	5			6	9*		11		8	3			7	10	12		1			32
	2		4	5			6	9		11		8	3			7	10			1			33
	2		4	5			6	9		11		8	3			7	10			1			34
	2		4	5			6	9*		11		8	3			7	10			1	12		35
	2		4	5			6	9		11		8	3			7	10			1			36
	2	12	4	5			6			11		8	3				10	7		1	9*		37
	2		4	5	6			9		11		8	3		12		10*	7		1			38
	2			5			6	9	12	11		8	3				10*	7		1	4		39
	2		4	5			6	9		11		8	3*				10	7		1	12		40
	2	3	4	5			6			11		8					10	7		1	9		41
	2	3	4	5			6	9		11		8						7		1		10	42
27	41	18	40	40	14	17	38	33	4	42		31	21	1	11	13	31	18	2	15	4	1	
	1									4	1		1	2		1	6		1	3		4	
	1					6	1	6	1	11		9			1	1	14	3	1			1	

1 own-goal

Stewart J*	Craggs JE	Bailey IC	Mahoney JF	Boam SW	Ramage A	Mills DJ	McAndrew A	Ashcroft W	Woof W	Armstrong D	Hedley G	Proctor MG*	Johnson PE	Johnston CP	Cummins S	Hodgson DJ*	Burns ME*	Cochrane GT*	Shearer DJ	Platt JA	Jankovic B*	Bell IC	
1	2	3*	4	5			6	12		11		8				7	10	9					3
1	2	3	4	5			6	12		11		8				7	10	9*					R
2	2	2	2				2			2		2				2	2	2					
								2															
								1															

Stewart J*	Craggs JE	Bailey IC	Mahoney JF	Boam SW	Ramage A	Mills DJ	McAndrew A	Ashcroft W	Woof W	Armstrong D	Hedley G	Proctor MG*	Johnson PE	Johnston CP	Cummins S	Hodgson DJ*	Burns ME*	Cochrane GT*	Shearer DJ	Platt JA	Jankovic B*	Bell IC	
1	2	3	4	5	6	8		9	10*	11		7		12									2
1	2	3	4*	5	6	8	10	9		11		7		12									R
2	2	2	2	2	2	2	1	2	1	2		2											
									2														

1979-80

Manager: John Neal

1	Aug	18	(a)	Tottenham H	W 3-1	Armstrong, Burns, Jankovic	32,743
2		21	(h)	Manchester C	W 3-0	Johnston, Burns, Cummins	24,002
3		25	(h)	Crystal P	D 1-1	Cummins	24,506
4	Sep	1	(a)	Manchester U	L 1-2	Johnston	51,015
5		8	(h)	Norwich C	W 1-0	Proctor	19,575
6		15	(a)	Arsenal	L 0-2		30,341
7		22	(a)	Derby C	L 0-1		18,620
8		29	(h)	Aston Villa	D 0-0		16,017
9	Oct	6	(h)	West Brom A	W 2-1	Burns, Armstrong (pen)	16,312
10		10	(a)	Manchester C	L 0-1		29,384
11		13	(a)	Stoke C	D 0-0		18,406
12		20	(h)	Wolves	W 1-0	Proctor	18,393
13		27	(a)	Ipswich T	L 0-1		18,343
14	Nov	3	(h)	Tottenham H	D 0-0		19,557
15		10	(a)	Everton	W 2-0	Johnston 2	25,155
16		17	(h)	Bristol C	W 1-0	Armstrong	14,517
17		24	(h)	Brighton & HA	D 1-1	Burns	16,010
18	Dec	1	(a)	Liverpool	L 0-4		39,885
19		8	(h)	Southampton	L 0-1		15,469
20		21	(h)	Bolton W	W 3-1	Armstrong, Craggs, Cochrane	11,789
21		26	(h)	Leeds U	W 3-1	Jankovic 2, Armstrong	26,655
22		29	(a)	Crystal P	W 2-1	Hedley, Hodgson	25,272
23	Jan	1	(a)	Coventry C	L 0-2		17,081
24		12	(h)	Manchester U	D 1-1	Armstrong	30,587
25	Feb	9	(h)	Derby C	W 3-0	Burns, Ashcroft, Armstrong	15,587
26		16	(a)	Nottingham F	D 2-2	Burns 2	23,889
27		23	(h)	Stoke C	L 1-3	Burns	15,953
28		27	(a)	Norwich C	D 0-0		13,666
29	Mar	1	(a)	Wolves	W 2-0	Hodgson 2	21,820
30		11	(h)	Ipswich T	D 1-1	Ashcroft	18,690
31		14	(a)	West Brom A	D 0-0		15,875
32		19	(a)	Aston Villa	W 2-0	Ashcroft, Armstrong	15,319
33		22	(h)	Everton	W 2-1	Hodgson, McAndrew	17,587
34	Apr	2	(a)	Leeds U	L 0-2		17,906
35		5	(h)	Coventry C	L 1-2	Hodgson	15,258
36		8	(h)	Bolton W	D 2-2	Hodgson, Burns	10,613
37		19	(a)	Brighton & HA	L 1-2	Burns	20,394
38		22	(a)	Bristol C	L 1-3	Armstrong	12,013
39		26	(h)	Nottingham F	D 0-0		17,021
40	May	3	(a)	Southampton	L 1-4	Ramage	18,476
41		6	(h)	Liverpool	W 1-0	Shearer	24,458
42		19	(h)	Arsenal	W 5-0	Johnston, Hodgson, Shearer, Armstrong 2	15,579

FINAL LEAGUE POSITION: 9th in Division One

Appearances
Sub Appearances
Goals

FA Cup

3	Jan	9	(a)	Portsmouth	D 1-1	Cochrane	31,743
R		14	(h)	Portsmouth	W 3-0	Cochrane, Johnson, Armstrong	22,551
4		26	(a)	Birmingham C	L 1-2	Hodgson	29,152

Appearances
Sub Appearances
Goals

League Cup

2	Aug	29	(a)	Derby C	W 1-0	Armstrong (pen)	15,205
2	Sep	4	(h)	Derby C	D 1-1	Jankovic	19,466
3		25	(h)	Nottingham F	L 1-3	Armstrong	29,869

Appearances
Sub Appearances
Goals

Appearance grid (player codes across the top; right-hand column = match number):

Platt JA	Craggs JE	Bailey IC	Johnston CP	Ashcroft W	McAndrew A	Hodgson DJ	Proctor MG	Jankovic B	Burns ME	Armstrong D	Johnson PE	Cummins S	Hedley G	Nattrass I*	Ramage A	Shearer DJ	Cochrane GT	Peters J*	Bell IC	Woof W	Stewart J	Angus MA	Askew W*	No.
1	2*	3	4	5	6	7	8	9	10	11	12													1
1	2	3	4	5	6	7	8	9	10*	11		12												2
1	2	3	4	5	6	7	8		10	11		9												3
1	2	3	4	5	6	7	8*	9	10	11	12													4
1	2	3	4	5	6	7	8	9		11	10													5
1	2	3	4	5	6	7	8*	9	12	11			10											6
1	2	3	4	5*	6		8	9	7	11	10	12												7
1	2	3	4		6	7	8		11	10				5	9*	12								8
1	2	3	4	5	6	7	8	9*	10	11						12								9
1	2	3	4	5	6		8		10	11					9	7								10
1	2	3	4	5*	6	9	8		10	11						7								11
1	2	3	4	5	6	9*	8		10	11	12					7								12
1	2	3	4	5	6	9	8	12	10	11						7*								13
1	2		4	5	6	9	8	10	7*	11			12	3										14
1	2		5	6	9			10	11				8	3	7									15
1	2		5	6	9			10	11				4	7	3	8								16
1	2	7	5	6	9			10	11				4	12	3	8*								17
1	2	4*	5	6	7	8	10		11				9	12	3									18
1	2	5*	6	9	8	10		11				12	4	7	3									19
1	2	5	6	9	8	10		11	3		4				7									20
1	2	5	6	9	8	10		11	3		4				7									21
1	2	5	6	9	8	10	11*	3		4	12				7									22
1	2	5	6	9	8	10		11	3		4	12				7*								23
1	2		6	9	8	10		11	3		4	5			7									24
1	2	5	6	9	8	10*	11	3		4	12				7									25
1	2	5	6	9	8	10	11	3		4					7									26
1	2	5	6	9	8	10	11	3	4*	12					7									27
1	2	5	6	9		10	11	3	4	8					7									28
1	2	4		9	8	10*	11	3	12	6	5				7									29
1	2	4	12	6	9	8		11	3*	10			5		7									30
1	2	4	10	6	9	8		11	3				5		7									31
1	2	4	10	6	9	8		11	3				5		7									32
1	2	4	9	6	10	8		11	3				5		7									33
1	2	4	9	6	10	8		11	3				5		7									34
1	2	4	10*		9	8	12		11	3			6	5	7									35
1	2	4		6	9	8		10	11	3				5	7									36
	2	4	5	6	9	8		10	11		12	3*			7		1							37
	2	3	4	5*		9	8	10		11			12			7	1	6						38
	2	3		6	9	8		10	11			4		5	7	1								39
	2	3	12		6	9	8	7*	10	11			4	5	7	1								40
1	2	3	7		6	9	8		11			4	5	10			1	12						41
	2	3	7*	5	6	9	8		11			4		10			1		12					42
37	42	18	29	34	39	40	38	17	23	42	17	4	14	10	13	4	25	6	3	1	5	1		
		1	1					2	1		1	6	3	3	1	4					1			
	1		5	3	1	7	2	3	10	11		2	2			1	1	1						

Platt JA	Craggs JE	Bailey IC	Johnston CP	Ashcroft W	McAndrew A	Hodgson DJ	Proctor MG	Jankovic B	Burns ME	Armstrong D	Johnson PE	Cummins S	Hedley G	Nattrass I*	Ramage A	Shearer DJ	Cochrane GT	Peters J*						No.
1	2		5	6	9	8	10		11	3		4				7								3
1	2		6	9	8	10		11	3		4	5				7								R
1	2		5	6	9	8	10*	12	11	3		4				7								4
3	3		2	3	3	3	3		3	3		3	1			3								
						1																		
			1			1	1					2												

Platt JA	Craggs JE	Bailey IC	Johnston CP	Ashcroft W	McAndrew A	Hodgson DJ	Proctor MG	Jankovic B	Burns ME	Armstrong D	Johnson PE	Cummins S												No.
1	2	3	4	5	6	7	8	9	10	11														2
1	2	3	4	5	6	7		9	10	11	12	8*												
1	2	3	4		5	7	8	9*	10	11	6	12												3
3	3	3	3	2	3	3	2	3	3	3	1	1												
								1	1															
											1													

1980-81

Manager: John Neal

1	Aug	16	(a)	Manchester U	L 0-3		54,394
2		19	(h)	Leeds U	W 3-0	Johnston, Nattrass, Armstrong	19,468
3		23	(a)	Crystal P	L 2-5	Ashcroft, Johnston	17,192
4		30	(h)	Manchester C	D 2-2	Mackenzie (og), Jankovic	15,761
5	Sep	6	(h)	Nottingham F	D 0-0		17,119
6		13	(a)	Sunderland	W 1-0	Jankovic	32,745
7		20	(h)	Arsenal	W 2-1	Proctor, Armstrong	14,860
8		27	(a)	Stoke C	L 0-1		11,847
9	Oct	4	(h)	Norwich C	W 6-1	McAndrew, Jankovic 2, Armstrong, Woods (og), Johnston	12,958
10		7	(a)	Liverpool	L 2-4	Johnston, Jankovic	28,204
11		11	(a)	Tottenham H	L 2-3	Hodgson, Johnston	27,380
12		18	(h)	Southampton	D 1-1	Jankovic	15,858
13		21	(h)	Leicester C	W 1-0	Armstrong	13,114
14		25	(a)	West Brom A	L 0-3		15,907
15	Nov	1	(h)	Birmingham C	L 1-2	Jankovic	13,292
16		8	(a)	Brighton & HA	W 1-0	Johnston	12,117
17		12	(a)	Leeds U	L 1-2	Jankovic	17,382
18		15	(h)	Manchester U	D 1-1	Johnston	20,606
19		22	(h)	Wolves	W 2-0	Johnston, Shearer	13,562
20	Dec	6	(h)	Aston Villa	W 2-1	Johnston, Shearer	15,721
21		13	(a)	Leicester C	L 0-1		13,998
22		20	(h)	Tottenham H	W 4-1	Hodgson 3, Johnston	15,990
23		26	(a)	Coventry C	L 0-1		16,106
24		27	(h)	Everton	W 1-0	Ashcroft	20,181
25	Jan	10	(a)	Wolves	L 0-3		16,253
26		17	(a)	Manchester C	L 2-3	Hodgson, McAndrew	30,774
27		31	(h)	Crystal P	W 2-0	Armstrong, McAndrew (pen)	16,099
28	Feb	7	(h)	Sunderland	W 1-0	Hedley	35,065
29		17	(a)	Ipswich T	L 0-1		24,772
30		21	(h)	Stoke C	W 3-1	Jankovic 2 (1 pen), Cochrane	15,142
31		28	(a)	Arsenal	D 2-2	Armstrong, Shearer	24,504
32	Mar	3	(a)	Nottingham F	L 0-1		19,690
33		17	(a)	Norwich C	L 0-2		13,561
34		21	(a)	Southampton	L 0-1		20,651
35		28	(h)	West Brom A	W 2-1	Batson (og), Shearer	13,228
36	Apr	4	(a)	Birmingham C	L 1-2	C.Bell	12,472
37		11	(h)	Brighton & HA	W 1-0	Shearer	11,076
38		18	(a)	Everton	L 1-4	Shearer	15,709
39		21	(h)	Coventry C	L 0-1		11,371
40		25	(a)	Aston Villa	L 0-3		38,018
41	May	2	(h)	Ipswich T	W 2-1	Jankovic 2	15,503
42		5	(h)	Liverpool	L 1-2	Shearer	19,102

FINAL LEAGUE POSITION: 14th in Division One

Appearances
Sub Appearances
Goals

FA Cup

3	Jan	3	(a)	Swansea C	W 5-0	Hodgson 2, Ashcroft, Angus, Cochrane	18,015
4		24	(h)	West Brom A	W 1-0	Bailey	28,285
5	Feb	14	(a)	Barnsley	W 2-1	Proctor, Jankovic	37,557
6	Mar	7	(h)	Wolves	D 1-1	Cochrane	36,382
R		10	(a)	Wolves	L 1-3*	Hodgson	40,524

*After extra-time

Appearances
Sub Appearances
Goals

League Cup

2	Aug	26	(h)	Ipswich T	W 3-1	Shearer 2, Proctor	14,430
	Sep	2	(a)	Ipswich T	L 0-3		15,027

Appearances
Sub Appearances
Goals

Platt JA	Craggs JE	Bailey IC	Johnston CP	Ashcroft W	McAndrew A	Shearer DJ	Hedley G	Hodgson DJ	Nattrass I	Armstrong D	Burns ME	Proctor MG	Jankovic B	Cochrane GT	Askew W*	Angus MA	Stewart J	Macdonald G*	Bell IC	Blackburn C*	Ross C*	Woof W	Nobbs KA*	
1	2	3	4	5	6	7	8*	9	10	11	12													1
1	2	3	4	5	6	10	8	9	7	11														2
1	2	3	4*	5	6	7	8	9	10	11	12													3
1	2	3	4*	5		10	8	9	6		11			7	12									4
1	2	3	4	5*	6		12	9			8	10	7	11										5
1	2	3	4		6			9			8	10	7	11	5									6
	2	3	4		6			9	12	11	8	10	7*			5	1							7
	2	3	4		6		12	9	7*	11	8	10				5	1							8
1	2	3	4		6	9		7		11	8	10				5								9
1	2	3	4	12	6	9		7*		11	8	10				5								10
1	2	3	4	12	6	9*		7		11	8	10				5								11
1	2	3	4		6			9	12	11	8	10	7*			5								12
1	2		4*	12	6			9	3	11	7	8	10			5								13
1	2	3	4	12	6			9		11	7*	8	10			5								14
1	2	3	4		6		7	9		11	8	10				5								15
1	2		4	5	6			9	3	11	8	10					7							16
1	2		4	5	6		12	9	3	11	8	10					7*							17
1		3	4	5*	6	10	12	9	2	11	8		7											18
1		3	4	5	6	10		9	2	11	8		7											19
1	2	3	4	5		10		9	6	11	8		7											20
1	2	3	4	5		10		9	6	11	8		7											21
1	2	3	4	5		10		9	6	11	8		7											22
1	2	3	4*	5	12	10		9	6	11	8		7											23
1	2	3		5	4	10		9	6	11	8		7											24
1	2	3		5*	4	10		9	6	11	8		7	12										25
1		3			4	10*		9	2	11	8	12	7	5		6								26
1		3		5*	6	12	4	9	2	11	8	10	7											27
1		3		5	6		4	9	2	11	8	10	7											28
1	7	3	4	5	6	10		9	2	11	8													29
1		3	4	5	6		9	2	11	8	10	7												30
1	12	3	4	5*	6	9		2	11	8	10	7												31
1	2	3		9	4		5	11	8	10*		6	12	7										32
1		3	4	5	6*	10		9	2	11	8		7	12										33
1		3	12	6	10		2		8	7*	11	5	9	4										34
1		3	12	6	10		9	2*	11	8	7	5	4											35
1		3	12	6	10		2	11		4	5	9*	8	7										36
1		3		6	10		2	11	8	5	9	4	7											37
1		3	12	6	10		2*	11	7	4	5	9	8											38
1		3		6	10		11	9*	8	7	12	5	4	2										39
1	2	3	5	6	9		11	8	10	7		4												40
1	2	3	6	9		11	8	10	7	5		4												41
1	2	3	6	9		11	8	10	7	5		4												42
40	28	39	27	22	36	29	8	32	29	39	4	38	21	24	4	20	2	6	5	1	5	2	1	
	1			8	1	1	4		2		2		2	1	2		1							
		10	2	3	7	1	5	1	6		1	12	1			1								

3 own-goals

Platt JA	Craggs JE	Bailey IC	Johnston CP	Ashcroft W	McAndrew A	Shearer DJ	Hedley G	Hodgson DJ	Nattrass I	Armstrong D	Burns ME	Proctor MG	Jankovic B	Cochrane GT	Askew W*	Angus MA	Stewart J	Macdonald G*	Bell IC	Blackburn C*	Ross C*	Woof W	Nobbs KA*	
1	2	3		5	11	10		9	6		8		7	4										3
1		3	4*	5	6	9		2	11	8	10	7	12											4
1		3	4	5	6		9	2	11	8	10	7	5											5
1		3	4	5	6	12	9	2	11	8	10*	7												6
1		3	4	5	6	12	9	2	11	8	10	7*												R
5	1	5	4	5	5	2		4	5	4	5	4	5	1										
						2							1											
	1		1			3					1	1	2		1									

Platt JA	Craggs JE	Bailey IC	Johnston CP	Ashcroft W	McAndrew A	Shearer DJ	Hedley G	Hodgson DJ	Nattrass I	Armstrong D	Burns ME	Proctor MG	Jankovic B	Cochrane GT	Askew W*	Angus MA	Stewart J	Macdonald G*	Bell IC	Blackburn C*	Ross C*	Woof W	Nobbs KA*	
1	2	3	4*	5		10	8	9	6	11		7	12											2
1	2	3		6	10	8	9	5	11		7	12		4										
2	2	2	1	1	1	2	2	2	2	2	2	2		1										
													2											
				2								1												

1981-82

Manager: Bobby Murdoch

1	Aug	29	(h)	Tottenham H	L	1-3	Otto	20,490
2	Sep	1	(a)	Liverpool	D	1-1	Shearer	31,963
3		5	(a)	Brighton & HA	L	0-2		13,383
4		12	(h)	Birmingham C	W	2-1	Otto, Hodgson	13,167
5		19	(a)	Southampton	L	0-2		20,105
6		22	(h)	Manchester U	L	0-2		19,895
7		26	(h)	Stoke C	W	3-2	Cochrane, Woof, Shearer	11,604
8	Oct	3	(a)	West Brom A	L	0-2		12,977
9		10	(h)	Nottingham F	D	1-1	Gunn (og)	15,043
10		17	(a)	Wolves	D	0-0		12,061
11		21	(a)	Manchester U	L	0-1		38,342
12		24	(h)	Everton	L	0-2		13,423
13		31	(a)	West Ham U	L	2-3	Woof, Thomson	27,604
14	Nov	7	(a)	Manchester C	L	2-3	Angus, Thomson	32,025
15		14	(h)	Sunderland	D	0-0		21,019
16		21	(h)	Aston Villa	D	3-3	McAndrew (pen), Ashcroft 2	12,522
17		28	(a)	Coventry C	D	1-1	Woof	10,403
18	Dec	5	(h)	Ipswich T	L	0-1		13,577
19	Jan	27	(a)	Tottenham H	L	0-1		22,819
20		30	(h)	Southampton	L	0-1		12,693
21	Feb	6	(a)	Birmingham C	D	0-0		10,715
22		13	(h)	Swansea C	D	1-1	McAndrew (pen)	11,209
23		16	(a)	Arsenal	L	0-1		13,738
24		20	(a)	Stoke C	L	0-2		10,683
25		27	(a)	Nottingham F	D	1-1	Hodgson	16,464
26	Mar	6	(h)	Wolves	D	0-0		10,155
27		9	(h)	West Brom A	W	1-0	Hodgson	9,403
28		13	(a)	Everton	L	0-2		15,328
29		20	(h)	West Ham U	L	2-3	McAndrew (pen), Ashcroft	12,134
30		27	(h)	Manchester C	D	0-0		11,709
31	Apr	3	(a)	Sunderland	W	2-0	Ashcroft, Baxter	19,006
32		6	(h)	Leeds U	D	0-0		15,471
33		10	(h)	Notts C	W	3-0	Woods, Bolton, Bailey	10,402
34		13	(a)	Leeds U	D	1-1	Shearer	20,458
35		17	(a)	Aston Villa	L	0-1		21,098
36		20	(h)	Brighton & HA	W	2-1	Otto, McAndrew	9,788
37		24	(h)	Coventry C	D	0-0		10,968
38	May	1	(a)	Ipswich T	L	1-3	Thomas	17,924
39		8	(h)	Arsenal	L	1-3	Baxter	9,565
40		11	(a)	Notts C	W	1-0	Macdonald	6,707
41		15	(a)	Swansea C	W	2-1	Otto, Stanley (og)	12,961
42		18	(h)	Liverpool	D	0-0		17,431

FINAL LEAGUE POSITION: 22nd in Division One

Appearances
Sub Appearances
Goals

FA Cup

3	Jan	2	(a)	Queen's Park R	D	1-1	Thomson	12,100
R		18	(h)	Queen's Park R	L	2-3§	Otto, Thomson	14,819

§After extra-time

Appearances
Sub Appearances
Goals

League Cup

2	Oct	6	(h)	Plymouth A	W	2-1	Ashcroft, Thomson	8,201
		27	(a)	Plymouth A	D	0-0		6,402
3	Nov	10	(a)	Liverpool	L	1-4	Shearer	16,145

Appearances
Sub Appearances
Goals

322

Season appearance and scorer grid.

No.	Platt JA	Craggs JE	Bolton J*	Hedley G	Baxter MJ*	Nattrass I	Woof W	Otto HM*	Macdonald G	Shearer DJ	McAndrew A	Hodgson DJ	McCreesh A*	Angus MA	Cochrane GT	Ross C	Bailey IC	Wood DT*	Ashcroft W	Askew W	Thomson R*	Bell S*	Thomas D*	Currie DN*
1	1	2	3	4	5	6	7	8	9	10*	11	12												
2	1		3	4	5		7	8		10*	6	9	2	11	12									
3	1		3	4	5		7*			10	6	9	2	11	12									
4	1	2	3		5			8	12	10*	6	9			7	4	11							
5	1	2	3		5		9	8			6				7	4	11*	10	12					
6	1	2	3		5		7	8		10	6	9				4			11					
7	1	2	3		5		10	8	9		6				7	4*			11	12				
8	1	2	3		5		9*	8		10	6				7			12	11	4				
9	1	2	3		5		12	8		10	6			4	7			9	11*					
10	1	2	3		5		12	8		10	6			4	7			9*	11					
11	1	2	3		5		9	8		10	6			4	7				11					
12	1	2	3		5		9	8		10*	6	12		4	7				11					
13	1		3		5	2	9	8		12	6*	10		4	7				11					
14	1	2			5	3	9	8		10	6			4	7				11					
15	1		3		5	2	9	8*		10	6	12			7	4			11					
16	1		3		5	2	9*	8		11	6	10			7	4		12						
17	1		3		5	2	9*	8		11	6	10			7	4		12						
18	1		3		5	2	9*	8			6	10			7	4		12	11					
19	1	2			5			8	12	10*	6	9			7	4	3		11					
20	1	2			5			8			6	9			7	4	3		11	10				
21	1	2			5	6		8		11		9			7	4	3		10					
22	1	2			5	6		8		11		10			7	4	3	9						
23	1	2			5	6		8		11*		10		4	7		3	9	12					
24	1	2			5	6	12	8		11				4	7		3	10	9*					
25	1				5	2	10	7		6	9	8			4	3			11					
26	1				5	2	10*	7		6	9	8	12	4	3				11					
27	1				5	2	12	8		6	9			7*	4	3		10	11					
28	1	8			5	2				6	9				7	4	3	10	11					
29	1	2			5	8				6	9				7	4	3	10	11					
30	1				5	2	12	8		10		7			4	3	6	9			11*			
31	1	7			5	2	12	8		9				4	3	6	10*				11			
32	1	7			5	2		8						4	9	3	6	10			11			
33	1	7			5	2		8				12		4	9*	3	6	10			11			
34	1	7			5	2		8		10				4	9	3	6				11			
35	1	7*			5	2		8		10		12		4	9	3	6				11			
36	1				5	2		8				12		4	9	7	3	6	10		11*			
37	1	2			5	6		8		10		12		4	9	7	3				11*			
38	1	2			5	6		8		10		7			4	3		12			11			
39	1	2	4*		5			8				12		7	9		3	6	10		11			
40	1		3		5			8	10			4		9	2	6		7			11			
41	1	2	6		5			8	10					9	3		4		7		11*	12		
42	1	2	6		5			8	10			4	9		3			12	7*		11			
Apps	42	23	27	3	40	27	17	40	4	20	39	31	2	14	22	22	26	11	14	6	18	1	13	
Goals			1		2		3	4	1	3	4	3		1	1		1	1	4		2		1	

2 own-goals

No.	Platt JA	Craggs JE	Bolton J*	Hedley G	Baxter MJ*	Nattrass I	Woof W	Otto HM*	Macdonald G	Shearer DJ	McAndrew A	Hodgson DJ	McCreesh A*	Angus MA	Cochrane GT	Ross C	Bailey IC	Wood DT*	Ashcroft W	Askew W	Thomson R*	Bell S*	Thomas D*	Currie DN*
3	1		3		5	2		8		10	6	9			7	4			11					
R	1		3		5	2	12	8	10*		6	9			7	4			11					
Apps	2		2		2	2		2	1	1	1	2		2	2				2					
Goals					1														2					

No.	Platt JA	Craggs JE	Bolton J*	Hedley G	Baxter MJ*	Nattrass I	Woof W	Otto HM*	Macdonald G	Shearer DJ	McAndrew A	Hodgson DJ	McCreesh A*	Angus MA	Cochrane GT	Ross C	Bailey IC	Wood DT*	Ashcroft W	Askew W	Thomson R*	Bell S*	Thomas D*	Currie DN*
2	1	2	3		5		12	8		10	6			4	7			9	11*					
	1		3		5	2	9*	8		12	6	10		4	7				11					
3	1	2	11		5	3	9	8		10	6			4	7				3					
Apps	3	2	3		3	2	2	3		2	3	1		3	3			1	2					
Goals					1													1	1					

1982-83

Manager: Bobby Murdoch

1	Aug	28	(a)	Sheffield W	L 1-3	Shearer	18,881
2	Sep	4	(h)	Burnley	L 1-4	Shearer	8,036
3		8	(a)	Newcastle U	D 1-1	Wood	27,984
4		11	(a)	Derby C	D 1-1	S.Bell	9,050
5		18	(h)	Fulham	L 1-4	Shearer	6,427
6		25	(a)	Crystal P	L 0-3		7,530
7		27	(h)	Grimsby T	L 1-4	Shearer	5,927
8	Oct	2	(h)	Oldham A	D 1-1	Otto	5,615
9		9	(a)	Shrewsbury T	D 2-2	S.Bell, Otto	3,620
10		16	(h)	Bolton W	W 1-0	Macdonald	5,521
11		23	(h)	Queen's Park R	W 2-1	Nattrass (pen), Otto	7,892
12		30	(a)	Rotherham U	D 1-1	Otto	8,135
13	Nov	6	(h)	Barnsley	W 2-0	Shearer, Wood	11,787
14		13	(a)	Charlton A	W 3-2	Shearer 2, Kennedy	10,807
15		20	(a)	Leeds U	D 0-0		18,482
16		27	(h)	Blackburn R	L 1-5	Cochrane	10,821
17	Dec	4	(a)	Wolves	L 0-4		11,856
18		11	(h)	Chelsea	W 3-1	Otto, Wood, Shearer	8,836
19		17	(a)	Cambridge U	L 0-2		2,533
20		27	(h)	Leicester C	D 1-1	S.Bell (pen)	12,665
21		28	(a)	Carlisle U	W 3-1	Bell 2, Sugrue	8,181
22	Jan	1	(h)	Leeds U	D 0-0		17,057
23		3	(a)	Burnley	D 1-1	Shearer	9,205
24		15	(h)	Sheffield W	D 1-1	S.Bell	11,863
25		22	(a)	Fulham	L 0-1		8,431
26	Feb	5	(h)	Newcastle U	D 1-1	Baxter	25,184
27		12	(a)	Oldham A	L 0-3		6,002
28		26	(a)	Bolton W	L 1-3	Otto	5,598
29	Mar	5	(a)	Queen's Park R	L 1-6	Kennedy (pen)	9,596
30		8	(h)	Shrewsbury T	W 2-1	Kennedy, Hankin	7,496
31		12	(h)	Rotherham U	D 1-1	Sugrue	8,875
32		19	(a)	Barnsley	L 0-2		10,681
33		26	(h)	Charlton A	W 3-0	S.Bell, Baxter 2	7,057
34	Apr	2	(h)	Carlisle U	W 1-0	S.Bell	9,965
35		5	(a)	Leicester C	L 0-1		12,025
36		9	(h)	Derby C	L 2-3	Kennedy 2 (1 pen)	9,078
37		16	(a)	Grimsby T	W 3-0	Sugrue, Hamilton, Otto	5,985
38		23	(h)	Wolves	D 0-0		10,315
39		30	(a)	Blackburn R	D 1-1	Otto	4,803
40	May	7	(h)	Cambridge U	L 0-1		9,949
41		10	(h)	Crystal P	W 2-0	Hamilton, Otto (pen)	10,014
42		14	(a)	Chelsea	D 0-0		19,341

FINAL LEAGUE POSITION: 16th in Division Two

Appearances
Sub Appearances
Goals

FA Cup

3	Jan	8	(h)	Bishop's Stortford	D 2-2	S.Bell 2	13,207
R		11	(a)	Bishop's Stortford	W 2-1	Shearer 2	6,000
4		29	(h)	Notts C	W 2-0	Hankin, Beattie (pen)	17,114
5	Feb	19	(h)	Arsenal	D 1-1	Otto	20,790
R		28	(a)	Arsenal	L 2-3	Shearer 2	28,689

Appearances
Sub Appearances
Goals

League Cup

2	Oct	5	(a)	Burnley	L 2-3	Otto, Cochrane	3,926
		26	(h)	Burnley	D 1-1	Hankin	10,389

Appearances
Sub Appearances
Goals

Platt JA	Ross C	Bolton J	Otto HM	Baxter MJ	Wood DT	Cochrane GT	Currie DN*	Shearer DJ	Kennedy MF*	Bell S	Macdonald G	Brownlie J*	Mowbray AM*	Ward PT*	Hankin R*	Nattrass I	Roberts A*	Beattie TK*	Sugrue P*	O'Hanlon KG*	Hamilton GJ*	
1	2	3	4	5	6	7	8*	9	10	11	12											1
1	4	3	12	5	6	7*		9	8	11	10	2										2
1	4	3	12	5	6			9	10	11		2	7	8*								3
1	4	3	8	5	6		9*	10	11			2	7	12								4
1	4	3	8	5	6		12	9	10	11		2*	7									5
1	4	3	8	5	6			9	10	11*		2	7	12								6
1	2	3	4*	5	6	12		8	10	11			7		9							7
1		3	4	5	6	8		10	11	12	2*	7				9						8
1		3	4	5	6	8		10	11		2		7			9						9
1		3	4	5	6	8			11	9	2		7			10						10
1		3	4	5	6	8			11	9	2		7			10						11
1		3	4	5	6	8			10	11	2		7*	9		12						12
1		3	9	4	6			11	7	10			2	8		5						13
1	12	3	9	4	6			11	7	10			2	8			5*					14
1	5	3	9	4	6			11	7	10			2	8								15
1	5*	3	9	4	6	12		11	7	10			2	8								16
1		3	9	4	6		7	2	10	11					8	5						17
1		3	9	4	6	12		7	10	11			2	8*	5							18
1		3*	6	5	5	12		9	11				2	10	4			8				19
1		3	6	5	5			9	11				2	10	4			8				20
1		3	6	4	5	12		9	11				2	10*	5			8				21
1		3	6	4	5	12	10*	9	11				2		5			8				22
1		3	6	4	5	12	10	9	11				2*		5			8				23
		3	6*	4	5			9	10	11			2		12		5	8	1			24
		3	6		5			9	4	11			2		10		5	8	1			25
		3	7	5	4			12	10	11					9		4*	8	1			26
		3	7	4	4			9	2	11				12	10	5*		8	1			27
		3*	7	4	4	10		8	11				2		5			9	1		12	28
			6	4	5			10	8	11			5		9	2		3	1			29
			6	4	3			10	8	11			5		9	2		7	1			30
			6	4	3			10	8	11			5		9	2		7	1			31
			6	4	9			10	8	11			5			2		7	1	3		32
		3	6*	4	9	12		10	8	11			5			2		7	1			33
		3	6	4	9			10	8	11			5			2		7	1			34
		3	6*	4	9			8	11				5	12		2		7	1	10		35
		3*	6	4	9			10	8	11			5			2	12	7	1			36
			6	4	9			10	8	11			5			2		7	1	3		37
			6	4	9	12		10*	8	11			5			2		7	1	3		38
	7		6	4	9			10*	8	11	12		5			2			1	3		39
			6	4	9			8	11	10			5		12	2*		7	1	3		40
			6	4	9			8	11	10			5		12	2		7*	1	3		41
			6	4	9			8	11	10			5	7		2			1	3		42
23	10	32	40	41	42	7	4	29	38	42	6	12	25	11	19	29	3	22	19	8		
	1		2			7	4				3		1	4	2		1	1		1		
		9	3	3	1		9	5	8	1				1	1			3		2		

Platt JA	Ross C	Bolton J	Otto HM	Baxter MJ	Wood DT	Cochrane GT	Currie DN*	Shearer DJ	Kennedy MF*	Bell S	Macdonald G	Brownlie J*	Mowbray AM*	Ward PT*	Hankin R*	Nattrass I	Roberts A*	Beattie TK*	Sugrue P*	O'Hanlon KG*	Hamilton GJ*	
1		3	6	4	7			9	2	11			10		5			8				3
1			6	4	7			9	10	11			2	3	5			8				R
		3	6		7			10		11			2		9	4	5	8	1			4
	5*	6	4	7			10	8	11	12			3			2		9	1			5
		6	4	7			10	8	11				5		9	2		3	1			R
2		3	5	4	5		1	4	4	5		1	3	1	3	5	1	5	3			
									1													
			1				4		2				1			1						

Platt JA	Ross C	Bolton J	Otto HM	Baxter MJ	Wood DT	Cochrane GT	Currie DN*	Shearer DJ	Kennedy MF*	Bell S	Macdonald G	Brownlie J*	Mowbray AM*	Ward PT*	Hankin R*	Nattrass I	Roberts A*	Beattie TK*	Sugrue P*	O'Hanlon KG*	Hamilton GJ*	
1		3	4*	5	6	8		10	11			2	7		9	12						2
1		3	4	5	6	8		11			12	2	7		9	10*						
2		2	2	2	2	2		2	1		2	2		2	1							
						1							1									
		1		1								1										

1983-84

Manager: Malcolm Allison

1	Aug	27	(a)	Portsmouth	W	1-0	Otto	17,817
2	Sep	3	(h)	Leeds U	D	2-2	Currie 2	12,773
3		6	(h)	Newcastle U	W	3-2	Currie 2, Hamilton	19,807
4		10	(a)	Barnsley	W	2-0	Wood, Otto	10,039
5		17	(h)	Grimsby T	D	1-1	Baxter	10,248
6		24	(a)	Chelsea	D	0-0		15,822
7		27	(a)	Fulham	L	1-2	Currie	6,452
8	Oct	1	(h)	Crystal P	L	1-3	Macdonald	8,925
9		8	(h)	Blackburn R	L	1-2	Currie	7,062
10		15	(a)	Oldham A	L	1-2	Macdonald	3,965
11		22	(a)	Manchester C	L	1-2	Roberts	24,466
12		29	(h)	Shrewsbury T	W	4-0	Otto, Currie 2, Ward	6,372
13	Nov	5	(h)	Cardiff C	W	2-0	Currie, Crawford	7,686
14		12	(a)	Derby C	L	0-1		12,683
15		19	(a)	Cambridge U	D	0-0		2,819
16		26	(h)	Swansea C	W	1-0	Otto	6,804
17	Dec	3	(a)	Charlton A	L	0-2		5,053
18		10	(h)	Brighton & HA	D	0-0		6,037
19		17	(a)	Huddersfield T	D	2-2	Baxter, Sugrue	7,889
20		26	(h)	Carlisle U	L	0-1		11,147
21		27	(a)	Sheffield W	W	2-0	Sugrue, Currie (pen)	25,188
22		31	(a)	Leeds U	L	1-4	Currie (pen)	14,148
23	Jan	2	(h)	Chelsea	W	2-1	Hamilton, Currie	11,620
24		14	(h)	Portsmouth	D	0-0		7,971
25		21	(a)	Grimsby T	D	0-0		7,342
26	Feb	4	(a)	Crystal P	L	0-1		5,819
27		11	(h)	Barnsley	W	2-1	Currie 2 (1 pen)	7,480
28		25	(h)	Manchester C	D	0-0		9,343
29		28	(a)	Shrewsbury T	L	0-1		3,043
30	Mar	3	(a)	Cardiff C	L	1-2	Macdonald	4,422
31		17	(a)	Newcastle U	L	1-3	Bell	30,421
32		20	(h)	Derby C	D	0-0		5,735
33		24	(h)	Fulham	L	0-2		5,415
34		31	(h)	Oldham A	W	3-2	Bell, Sugrue, Otto	5,615
35	Apr	7	(a)	Blackburn R	L	0-1		4,914
36		14	(h)	Cambridge U	D	1-1	Otto	5,121
37		21	(a)	Carlisle U	D	1-1	Mowbray	5,674
38		25	(h)	Sheffield W	W	2-0	Hamilton, Currie	12,362
39		27	(a)	Swansea C	L	1-2	Wood	3,632
40	May	5	(h)	Charlton A	W	1-0	Otto	4,720
41		7	(a)	Brighton & HA	L	0-3		9,168
42		12	(h)	Huddersfield T	D	0-0		5,687

FINAL LEAGUE POSITION: 17th in Division Two

Appearances
Sub Appearances
Goals

FA Cup

3	Jan	7	(h)	Arsenal	W	3-2	Macdonald, Sugrue, Baxter	17,813
4		31	(h)	Bournemouth	W	2-0	Sugrue 2	20,175
5	Feb	18	(a)	Notts C	L	0-1		17,487

Appearances
Sub Appearances
Goals

League Cup

1	Aug	30	(h)	Chesterfield	L	0-1		7,163
	Sep	13	(a)	Chesterfield	W	1-0§	Otto	3,980

§After extra-time.   Lost 3-5 on penalties.

Appearances
Sub Appearances
Goals

Appearance / shirt-number grid

O'Hanlon KG	Wood DT	Ward PF	Otto HM	Baxter MJ	Nattrass I	Roberts A	Macdonald G	Currie DN	Sugrue P	Bell S	Mowbray AM	Kennedy MF	Hamilton GJ	Crawford A*	Pears S*	Gill G*	Match
1	2	3	4	5	6	7	8	9	10*	11	12						1
1	2	3	4	5	6	7	11	9	10			8					2
1	2	3	4*	5	6	7	11	9	10			8	12				3
1	2	3	9	5	6	7	11		10			8	4				4
1	2	3	4	5	6	7*	11	9	10			8	12				5
1	2	3	4	5	6		11	9	10	7		8*	12				6
1	2	3	4	5	6		11	9	10*	7	12		3				7
1	2	3	4	5	6	7	11	9	10	8							8
1	2	8	4	5	6		11	9	10	7*	3		12				9
1	2	3	4	5	6		11	9	10	7	8						10
1	2		4	5	6	7	11	9	10		3			8			11
1	2	7	4	5	6			9	10		3	8	11				12
	2	7	4	5	6			9	10		3	8	11	1			13
	2	7	4	5	6			9	12	11*	3	8	10	1			14
	2	7*	4	5	6			9	10		3	8	12	11	1		15
	2		4	9	5	6			10	7		8	3	11	1		16
	2		9	5	6		11	10	7	3	8	4		1			17
	2		9	5	6	12	11	10*	7	3	8	4		1			18
1	2		9	5	6		11	10	7	3	8	4					19
1	2		9	5	6	12	11	10	7	3	8	4*					20
1	2	4	9	5	6		7	11	10		3	8					21
1	2	7	4	5	6		9	11	10	12	3*		8				22
1	2	7	4	5	6		9	11	10		3		8				23
1	2	12	4	5	6		9	11*	10		3	8	7				24
	2	12	4	5	6		9		10	11	3	8	7*		1		25
	2		4	5	6		9	11	10		3	8	7		1		26
	2		4	5	6		9	11	10	12	3	8	7*		1		27
	2		4	5	6		9	11	10	12	3	8	7*		1		28
	2		4	5	6		9	11	10		3	8	7				29
	2		4	5	6		9	11	10	8	3		7*		1	12	30
1	2		4	5	6		9	11	10	8	3		7*			12	31
1	2	11	4	5	6		9	12	10*	7	3	8					32
1	2		4	5	6		9	12	10	7*	3	8	11				33
1	2	4	9	5	6			12	10*	7	3	8	11				34
1	2	4	9	5	6		12	11		7	3	8	10*				35
1	2	4	9	5	6		12	10	7*	3	8	11					36
1	2	4	9	5	6		11	10		3	8	7*	12				37
1	2	4	8	5	6		12	10	9	3		11*	7				38
1	2	4	8	5	6		10	9	12	3		7*		11			39
1	2		9	5	6		11	10		3	8	4		7			40
1	2		9	5	6		11	10		3	8	4		7			41
1	2	11	9		6		12	5*	10		3	8	4		7		42
30	42	26	42	41	42	7	24	35	39	21	33	30	26	8	12	4	
	2						5	4	1	4	2		5	1	2		
2	1	7	2		1	3	15	3	2	1		3	1				

O'Hanlon KG	Wood DT	Ward PF	Otto HM	Baxter MJ	Nattrass I	Roberts A	Macdonald G	Currie DN	Sugrue P	Bell S	Mowbray AM	Kennedy MF	Hamilton GJ	Crawford A*	Pears S*	Gill G*	Match
1	2		4	5	6		9	11	10		3	8	7				3
	2		4	5	6		9		10	11	3	8	7		1		4
	2	12	4	5	6		9	11	10*		3	8	7		1		5
1	3		3	3	3		3	2	3	1	3	3	3		2		
	1																
			1			1		3									

O'Hanlon KG	Wood DT	Ward PF	Otto HM	Baxter MJ	Nattrass I	Roberts A	Macdonald G	Currie DN	Sugrue P	Bell S	Mowbray AM	Kennedy MF	Hamilton GJ	Crawford A*	Pears S*	Gill G*	Match
1	2	3	4	5	6	12	7	9	10	11*		8					1
1	2	3*	4	5	6	7	11	9	10			12	8				
2	2	2	2	2	2	1	2	2	2	1		2					
			1			1											
		1															

1984-85

Manager: Willie Maddren

1	Aug	25	(a)	Portsmouth	L	0-1		13,070
2	Sep	1	(h)	Grimsby T	L	1-5	Currie	5,252
3		8	(a)	Notts C	L	2-3	Otto, Mills	4,911
4		15	(h)	Wolves	D	1-1	Mowbray	4,688
5		18	(h)	Wimbledon	L	2-4	Mills, Currie	4,277
6		22	(a)	Fulham	L	1-2	Mills (pen)	4,736
7		29	(h)	Cardiff C	W	3-2	Currie 2, Mills	4,259
8	Oct	2	(a)	Oldham A	L	0-2		2,815
9		6	(h)	Charlton A	W	1-0	Currie (pen)	4,172
10		13	(a)	Sheffield U	W	3-0	Currie (pen), Bell, Mills	10,733
11		20	(h)	Manchester C	W	2-1	Mills 2	7,735
12		27	(a)	Leeds U	L	0-2		14,824
13	Nov	3	(a)	Huddersfield T	L	1-3	Currie	5,811
14		10	(h)	Barnsley	D	0-0		5,231
15		17	(h)	Blackburn R	L	1-2	Mills	4,815
16		24	(a)	Brighton & HA	W	2-1	Mills 2	9,089
17	Dec	1	(h)	Crystal P	D	1-1	Mills	4,681
18		8	(a)	Birmingham C	L	2-3	Currie (pen), Mills	8,004
19		14	(h)	Shrewsbury T	D	1-1	MacLaren (og)	4,044
20		22	(a)	Grimsby T	L	1-3	Otto	5,760
21		26	(a)	Carlisle U	W	3-0	Currie, Mills, Mowbray	4,423
22	Jan	1	(h)	Oxford U	L	0-1		6,760
23		12	(a)	Wolves	D	0-0		6,152
24		19	(h)	Portsmouth	D	0-0		4,622
25	Feb	2	(a)	Cardiff C	L	1-2	Currie	2,564
26		5	(h)	Oldham A	L	1-2	Mowbray	3,477
27		9	(h)	Notts C	L	0-1		3,364
28		23	(h)	Huddersfield T	D	2-2	Otto, Mills	4,453
29		26	(a)	Barnsley	L	0-1		6,866
30	Mar	2	(h)	Leeds U	D	0-0		8,817
31		9	(a)	Manchester C	L	0-1		22,399
32		16	(h)	Sheffield U	W	1-0	Kernaghan	5,204
33		22	(a)	Charlton A	L	0-1		3,741
34		30	(a)	Wimbledon	D	1-1	Stephens	2,338
35	Apr	6	(h)	Carlisle U	L	1-2	Roberts	5,278
36		8	(a)	Oxford U	L	0-1		11,108
37		13	(h)	Fulham	W	2-0	Stephens, Bell	4,443
38		20	(a)	Blackburn R	L	0-3		8,216
39		27	(h)	Brighton & HA	W	2-1	Otto, Currie	4,415
40	May	4	(a)	Crystal P	L	0-1		4,900
41		6	(h)	Birmingham C	D	0-0		7,840
42		11	(a)	Shrewsbury T	W	2-0	Laws, Beagrie	5,348

FINAL LEAGUE POSITION: 19th in Division Two

Appearances
Sub Appearances
Goals

FA Cup

3	Jan	5	(h)	Darlington	D	0-0		19,084
R		8	(a)	Darlington	L	1-2	McAndrew	14,237

Appearances
Sub Appearances
Goals

League Cup

1	Aug	29	(a)	Bradford C	L	0-2		4,788
	Sep	4	(h)	Bradford C	D	2-2	Buckley, Sugrue	3,980

Appearances
Sub Appearances
Goals

Player appearance / shirt-number grid (numbers indicate shirt worn; * indicates substitute).

O'Hanlon KG	Wood DT	Ward PT	Buckley MJ*	Mowbray AM	Nattrass I	Mills DJ*	Hamilton GJ	Otto HM	Sugrue P	Currie DN	Gill G	Scott G*	Bell S	Roberts A	McAndrew A*	Saxby MW*	Beagrie PS*	Thomas MR*	Kay J*	Ripley SE*	Kernaghan AN*	Strong A*	Laws B*	Stephens A*	
1	2	3	4	5	6	7	8	9	10	11															1
1	2		4	5	6	7	8	9	10*	11		3	12												2
1	2		4	5	6*	7	8	9	10	11		3		12											3
1	2	12	4	5	6*		8		9		10	3		11	7										4
1	2	3	4	5			8		9	12	10*	6		11	7										5
1	2	3	4	5			8		9	10	6			11	7										6
1		3	4	5			8	12	9	10	2		11	7	6*										7
1		3	4	5			8		9	10	2		11	7*	6	12									8
1		3	4	5			8	2	9	10	7		11		6										9
1		3	4	5			8	2	9	10	7		11		6										10
1		3	4	5			8	12	9	10	2*		11	7	6										11
		3	4	5			8	2*	9	12	10	7	11		6	1									12
		3	4	5		2	9		10	7	8*	12	11	6	1										13
		3	4		6	8	2	9	10	11	7	5	1												14
		4	5	6	8	3	9	10	2	7	11	1													15
1		4	5	6	8	3	9	10	2	7	11														16
1		4	5	6	8	3	9	10		2	7	11													17
1		4	5	6	8	2	9	10		7	11	3*	12												18
1	3	4	5	6	8	2	9	10*		7	11		12												19
1	10	4	2	8	3	12	9*		7	6	5	11													20
1	11	4*	7	2	8	3	9		10		12	6	5												21
1	11	4	7	2	8	3*	9		10		12	6	5												22
1	6	4	7		8	3	9		10		11	5		2											23
1	7	4	5	6	8	3*	9		10		12	11		2											24
1	7*	4	5	6	8	3	9		10		12	11		2											25
1		3	4	5	6*	8		9		10			11	7		2	12								26
1		3	4	6		8		10		11		12	7	5		2*		9							27
1		3		5	6	8	7	9		11*	12		4			2	10								28
1		3		5		8	7	9		12	11*		6	4		2	10								29
1			5	6		7	9	8		11			4			2	10	3							30
1			5	6	12	2	9	8		11*	7	4					10	3							31
1			5	6	8	11	9		12	7	4						10	3*	2						32
1			5	6		11	9		12	7	4						10*	3	2	8					33
1			5	6	8	7	9		11		4							3	2	10					34
1			5	6	8*	7	9		11		12	4						3	2	10					35
1	3*		5	6	8	9		12		11	7	4							2	10					36
1	3		5	6		7	9			11	8	4							2	10					37
1	3		5	6*		7	9		12	11	8	4					10		2						38
1	3		5	6		7	9			11	8	4							2	10					39
1	3		5	6		7	9			11	8	4*	12						2	10					40
1	3*		5	6		7	9			11	12	4	8						2	10					41
1	3		5	6		7	9			11		4	8						2	10					42
38	6	29	27	40	30	31	34	41	5	34	14	2	15	20	32	15	3	4	8	8	6	11	9		
	1			1	2	1	2	5			2	9			4			1							
		3		14		4		11			2	1			1			1	1	2					

1 own-goal

1		6	4	7	2	8	3	9		10				11	5										3
1		6	4	7	2	8	3*	9		10			12	11	5										R
2		2	2	2	2	2	2	2		2				2	2										
														1											
														1											

1	2	8	4	5	6	7	3	9	10*	11	12														1
1	2	4*	5	6	7	8	9	10	11			3	12												
2	2	1	2	2	2	2	2	2	2	2	1	1													
												1	1												
		1					1																		

329

1985-86

Manager: Willie Maddren

1	Aug	17	(a)	Wimbledon	L 0-3		2,844
2		24	(h)	Fulham	W 1-0	Stephens	5,368
3		27	(a)	Charlton A	L 0-2		4,045
4		31	(h)	Brighton & HA	L 0-1		5,520
5	Sep	7	(a)	Hull C	D 0-0		7,710
6		10	(h)	Stoke C	D 1-1	Rowell	4,189
7		14	(h)	Norwich C	D 1-1	Rowell (pen)	5,462
8		21	(a)	Sheffield U	W 1-0	Rowell	10,535
9		28	(h)	Barnsley	D 0-0		5,572
10	Oct	5	(h)	Crystal P	L 0-2		4,991
11		12	(a)	Leeds U	L 0-1		14,095
12		19	(h)	Bradford C	D 1-1	Slaven	6,130
13		22	(a)	Sunderland	L 0-1		20,541
14		26	(a)	Grimsby T	L 2-3	Stephens, Laws	4,378
15	Nov	2	(h)	Blackburn R	D 0-0		5,140
16		16	(h)	Oldham A	W 3-2	Currie, Heard, Rowell	4,234
17		23	(a)	Millwall	L 0-3		3,188
18		30	(h)	Shrewsbury T	W 3-1	Rowell, Heard, McAndrew	4,061
19	Dec	7	(a)	Stoke C	L 2-3	Stephens, O'Riordan	7,646
20		14	(h)	Wimbledon	W 1-0	Mowbray	4,531
21		21	(a)	Fulham	W 3-0	Slaven, Rowell 2	3,513
22		26	(a)	Carlisle U	L 0-1		4,238
23		28	(h)	Sunderland	W 2-0	Mowbray, McAndrew	19,701
24	Jan	1	(h)	Huddersfield T	L 0-1		8,487
25		11	(a)	Norwich C	L 0-2		13,050
26		18	(a)	Brighton & HA	D 3-3	Rowell 2, Slaven	10,098
27		25	(a)	Portsmouth	L 0-1		10,768
28	Feb	1	(h)	Charlton A	L 1-3	Rowell (pen)	4,465
29	Mar	5	(h)	Grimsby T	W 3-1	Slaven 2, Mowbray	4,412
30		8	(a)	Crystal P	L 1-2	Slaven	4,863
31		15	(h)	Leeds U	D 2-2	Currie 2	6,899
32		18	(h)	Sheffield U	L 1-2	O'Riordan	5,736
33		22	(h)	Hull C	L 1-2	Currie	6,227
34		25	(a)	Barnsley	D 0-0		3,827
35		29	(a)	Huddersfield T	W 3-0	Hamilton 2, Slaven	5,585
36		31	(h)	Carlisle U	L 1-3	Hamilton	7,603
37	Apr	5	(a)	Blackburn R	W 1-0	Hamilton	4,049
38		12	(h)	Portsmouth	W 1-0	Mowbray	7,188
39		19	(a)	Oldham A	L 0-1		4,193
40		23	(a)	Bradford C	L 1-2	Oliver (og)	3,426
41		26	(h)	Millwall	W 3-0	Beagrie, Slaven (pen), Laws	5,484
42	May	3	(a)	Shrewsbury T	L 1-2	Stephens	6,695

FINAL LEAGUE POSITION: 21st in Division Two

Appearances
Sub Appearances
Goals

FA Cup

3	Jan	13	(h)	Southampton	L 1-3	O'Riordan	12,703

Appearances
Sub Appearances
Goals

League Cup

1	Aug	20	(a)	Mansfield T	L 0-2		3,179
	Sep	3	(h)	Mansfield T	D 4-4	Pollard (og), Currie, Rowell 2 (1 pen)	4,051

Appearances
Sub Appearances
Goals

Career record grid — appearances and goals.

Pears S	Laws B	Corden S*	Pallister GA*	Mowbray AM	Nattrass I	Roberts A	O'Riordan DJ*	Stephens A	McAndrew A	Rowell G*	Currie DN	Ward PT	Beagrie PS	Hamilton GJ	Kernaghan AN	Heard TP*	Gill G	Cook M*	Slaven BJ*	McManus CE*	Cooper CT*	Ripley SE	Kite PD*	Turnbull LM*	No.
1	2	3*	4	5	6	7	8	9	10	11	12														1
1	2			5			8	9	4	10	11*	3	6	7	12										2
1	2			5			8	9	4	10	12	3	6	7	11*										3
1	2			5			8	9	4	10		3*	11	7	12	6									4
1	2			5			8	9	4	10	11*		6		12	3	7								5
1	2			5			8	9	4	10	11		6			3	7								6
1	2			5	6		8	9	4	10			11			3	7*	12							7
1	2			5	6		8	9	4	10			11	7		3									8
1	2			5	6		8	9	4	10			11*	7		3	12								9
1	2			5*	6		8		4	10			11	7	9	3	12								10
1	2			5	6		8	10	4	12			11*	7		3			9						11
1	2		6				5		4	10			11	7		3		8	9						12
1	2		6				5	10	4	11	12			7		3		8*	9						13
1	2		6				5	10	4	11	12			7		3		8*	9						14
1	2		6				5	10	4	11			8	7		3			9						15
1	2		6		4		5	10	3				11	7		8			9						16
1	2		6		4		5	10	3		12		11	7*		8			9						17
1	2		6		4		5	10	3				11	7		8			9						18
1	2		6		4		5	10	3				11*	7	12	8			9						19
1	2		6		4		5	10	3				11	7		8			9						20
1	2		6		4		5	10	3				11	7		8			9						21
1	2		6		4		5	10	3				11	7		8			9						22
1	2		6		4		5	10	3				11	7		8			9						23
1	2		6		4		5	10	3				11	7		8			9						24
1	2		6		4		5	10	3				11	7		8			9						25
	2		6		4		5	10	3				11	7		8			9	1					26
	2		6		4		5	10	3				11	7		8			9	1					27
1	2		6*		4		5	10	3				11	7	12	8			9						28
1	2		6		4	3		5					10	9		11					8	7			29
1	2		6		4	3		5*					10	9		11					8	7	12		30
1	2		6		4	3		5					10	9		11					8	7			31
1	2		6		4	3		5					10	9		11					8*	7	12		32
1	2		6		4	3		5					9	11		8			7		10*	12			33
1	2		6		4	3		5					9	11		7					10	8			34
1	2		6		4	3		5					9	10		7					8	11			35
1	2		6		4	3		5					9	12	10	7*					8	11			36
1	2		6		4	5		3					9	11		7					10	8			37
1	2		6		4	5		3					10	11		9					8	7			38
	2		6		4	5*		3					10	11	12	9					8	7	1		39
	2		6		4			3			12	3	10		11	9			5		7	8	11*	1	40
1	2		6		4	5		9	3				11	10		7					8*		12		41
1	2		6		4	5		9	3		12		11	10		7					8*				42
38	42	1	28	35	19	1	41	26	34	27	21	3	21	33	2	25	9	3	32	2	9	7	2	1	
								2			5	4	4			3			8						
	2		4			2	4	2	10	4		1	4			2			8						

1 own-goal

Pears S	Laws B	Corden S*	Pallister GA*	Mowbray AM	Nattrass I	Roberts A	O'Riordan DJ*	Stephens A	McAndrew A	Rowell G*	Currie DN	Ward PT	Beagrie PS	Hamilton GJ	Kernaghan AN	Heard TP*	Gill G	Cook M*	Slaven BJ*	McManus CE*	Cooper CT*	Ripley SE	Kite PD*	Turnbull LM*	No.
1	2		6		4		5	10*	3	11	12		7			8			9						3
1	1		1		1		1	1	1	1	1		1			1			1						
									1																

1 own-goal

Pears S	Laws B	Corden S*	Pallister GA*	Mowbray AM	Nattrass I	Roberts A	O'Riordan DJ*	Stephens A	McAndrew A	Rowell G*	Currie DN	Ward PT	Beagrie PS	Hamilton GJ	Kernaghan AN	Heard TP*	Gill G	Cook M*	Slaven BJ*	McManus CE*	Cooper CT*	Ripley SE	Kite PD*	Turnbull LM*	No.
1	2		6	5		7*	8	9	4	10	11	3			12										1
1	2			5			8	12	4	10	11	3	6	7*		9									
2	2		1	2		1	2	1	2	2	2	2	1	1	1										
									1							1									
									2	1															

1 own-goal

1986-87

Manager: Bruce Rioch

1	Aug	23	(h†)	Port Vale	D	2-2	Stephens 2	3,690
2		30	(a)	Wigan A	W	2-0	Turnbull, Mowbray	2,904
3	Sep	6	(h)	Bury	W	3-1	Stephens 2, Slaven	6,499
4		13	(a)	Gillingham	D	0-0		4,888
5		17	(a)	Bristol R	W	2-1	Slaven 2	3,768
6		20	(h)	Chesterfield	W	2-0	Mowbray, Laws	7,633
7		27	(a)	Fulham	D	2-2	Laws, Hamilton	3,852
8		30	(h)	Swindon T	W	1-0	Laws	9,221
9	Oct	4	(a)	Rotherham U	W	4-1	Stephens 2, Laws 2	4,321
10		11	(h)	Blackpool	L	1-3	Stephens	11,470
11		18	(h)	Walsall	W	3-1	Stephens 2, Laws	8,349
12		21	(a)	Notts C	L	0-1		4,405
13		25	(a)	Bristol C	D	2-2	Slaven, Laws	8,800
14	Nov	1	(h)	Bournemouth	W	4-0	Stephens, Slaven, Hamilton, Ripley	10,702
15		4	(h)	Bolton W	D	0-0		10,092
16		8	(a)	Darlington	W	1-0	Stephens	9,947
17		22	(a)	Newport C	W	1-0	Mowbray	2,788
18		29	(h)	Chester C	L	1-2	Slaven	9,376
19	Dec	13	(h)	Doncaster R	W	1-0	Mowbray	8,100
20		21	(a)	Brentford	W	1-0	Slaven	5,504
21		26	(h)	Carlisle U	W	1-0	Gill	14,216
22		27	(a)	Mansfield T	D	1-1	Proudlock	5,042
23	Jan	1	(a)	York C	L	1-3	Mowbray	8,611
24		3	(h)	Newport C	W	2-0	Gill, Stephens	9,595
25		24	(a)	Bury	W	3-0	Slaven 2, Laws (pen)	3,485
26	Feb	7	(h)	Bristol R	W	1-0	Ripley	9,610
27		14	(a)	Chesterfield	L	1-2	Slaven	4,085
28		17	(a)	Port Vale	D	0-0		3,263
29		21	(h)	Fulham	W	3-0	Slaven, Hamilton 2	9,361
30		28	(a)	Swindon T	L	0-1		11,341
31	Mar	3	(a)	Bournemouth	L	1-3	Slaven	13,835
32		7	(h)	Bristol C	W	1-0	Mowbray	10,220
33		14	(a)	Walsall	L	0-1		7,332
34		17	(h)	Notts C	W	2-0	Stephens, Slaven	9,845
35		21	(a)	Blackpool	W	1-0	Stephens	7,132
36		28	(h)	Rotherham U	D	0-0		9,569
37	Apr	5	(h)	Darlington	D	1-1	Slaven	11,969
38		11	(a)	Bolton W	W	1-0	Slaven	5,858
39		18	(h)	York C	W	3-1	Ripley, Stephens, Turnbull	10,546
40		20	(a)	Carlisle U	W	1-0	Pallister	5,993
41		25	(h)	Brentford	W	2-0	Slaven, Turnbull	9,942
42		28	(h)	Gillingham	W	3-0	Stephens, Slaven, Turnbull	11,937
43	May	2	(a)	Chester C	W	2-1	Mowbray, Hamilton	3,788
44		4	(h)	Mansfield T	W	1-0	Hamilton (pen)	13,545
45		6	(h)	Wigan A	D	0-0		18,523
46		9	(a)	Doncaster R	W	2-0	Hamilton, Ripley	3,556

FINAL LEAGUE POSITION: 2nd in Division Three — Appearances
†Played at the Victoria Ground, Hartlepool. — Sub Appearances
Goals

FA Cup

1	Nov	15	(h)	Blackpool	W	3-0	Slaven 3	11,205
2	Dec	7	(a)	Notts C	W	1-0	Hamilton	7,415
3	Jan	10	(h)	Preston NE	L	0-1		15,458

Appearances
Sub Appearances
Goals

League Cup

1	Aug	26	(a)	Hartlepool U	D	1-1	Slaven	2,356
	Sep	2	(h)	Hartlepool U	W	2-0	Ripley, Hamilton	7,735
2		23	(h)	Birmingham C	D	2-2	Stephens, Ripley	9,412
	Oct	7	(a)	Birmingham C	L	2-3*	Laws 2 (1 pen)	4,978

*After extra-time

Appearances
Sub Appearances
Goals

Appearance grid (shirt numbers; * = substitute appearance). Players left to right: Pears S, Laws B, Cooper CT, Mowbray AM, Gill G, Parkinson GA*, Slaven BJ, Stephens A, Hamilton GJ, Kernaghan AN, Ripley SE, Turnbull LM, Pallister GA, Proudlock P*, Coyle RP*, Kerr PA*, Hodgson DJ*, Spriggs S*, Rowell G.

Pears S	Laws B	Cooper CT	Mowbray AM	Gill G	Parkinson GA*	Slaven BJ	Stephens A	Hamilton GJ	Kernaghan AN	Ripley SE	Turnbull LM	Pallister GA	Proudlock P*	Coyle RP*	Kerr PA*	Hodgson DJ*	Spriggs S*	Rowell G	
1	2	3	4	5	6	7	8	9	10*	11	12								1
1	2	3	4	10	5	7		9		11	8	6							2
1	2	3	4	10	5	7	8	9		11		6							3
1	2	3	4	10	5	7	8	9		11		6							4
1	2	3	4	10	5	7	8	9		11		6							5
1	2	3	4	10	5	7*	8	9		11	12	6							6
1	2	3	4	10	5	7	8	9		11		6							7
1	2	3	4	10	5	7	8	9		11		6							8
1	2	3	4	10	5	7	8	9		11		6							9
1	2	3	4	10	5	7*	8	9	12	11		6							10
1	2	3	4	10	5	7	8	9		11		6							11
1	2	3	4	10	5	7	8	9		11*	12	6							12
1	2	3	4	10	5	7	8	9		11		6							13
1	2	3	4	10*	5	7	8	9		11	12	6							14
1	2	3	4	10	5	7	8	9*		11	12	6							15
1	2	3	4	10	5	7	8		9	11		6							16
1	2	3	4	10	5	7	8	12	9*	11		6							17
1	2	3	4	10*	5	7	8	12	9	11		6							18
1	2	3	4	10	5	7	8	9				6	11						19
1	2	3	4	10	5	7	8*	9		11		6	12						20
1	2	3	4	10	5	7	8	9		11		6							21
1	2	3	4	10	5	7		9		11		6	8*	12					22
1	2	3	4	10	5	7	8	9		11		6							23
1	2	3	4	10	5	7	8	9		11		6							24
1	2	3	4	10	5	7	8			11		6			9				25
1	2*	3	4	10	5	7	8	12		11		6			9				26
1		3	4	10	5	7	8	2		11		6			9				27
1		3	4	10	5	7	8	2		11		6			9				28
1		3	4	10	5	7	8	2		11		6			9				29
1		3	4		5	7	8	2	10	11		6			9				30
1		3	4		5	7	8	2	10	12		6*			9	11			31
1		3	4	10	5	7	8	9	6				2		11				32
1		3	4	10	5	7	8*	2	12	11		6			9				33
1		3	4		5	7	8	2	10	11		6			9				34
1		3	4	12	5	7	8	2*	10	11		6			9				35
1		3	4	12	5	7	8	2*	10	11		6			9				36
1		3	4	10	5	7	8	9		11		6					2		37
1		3	4		5	7	8	9		11		6			10		2		38
1		3	4		5	7	8	9		11	12	6			10		2*		39
1		3	4		5	7	8	2		11	9	6			10				40
1		3	4		5	7	8	2		11	9	6			10				41
1		3	4		5	7*	8	2		11	9	6		12	10				42
1		3	4		5	7	8	2		11	9	6			10				43
1		3	4	12	5	7	8	2		11	9*	6			10				44
1		3	4		5	7	8	2		11	9	6			10				45
1		3	4	2	5	7	8	9*		11	12	6			10				46
46	26	46	46	33	46	46	44	41	10	43	7	44	2	1	20	2	3		
											3		2	3	1	7	1	2	
	8		7	2		17	16	7		4	4	1	1						

Pears S	Laws B	Cooper CT	Mowbray AM	Gill G	Parkinson GA*	Slaven BJ	Stephens A	Hamilton GJ	Kernaghan AN	Ripley SE	Turnbull LM	Pallister GA	Proudlock P*	Coyle RP*	Kerr PA*	Hodgson DJ*	Spriggs S*	Rowell G	
1	2	3	4	10	5	7	8		9	11		6							1
1	2	3	4	10	5	7	8	9		11		6							2
1	2*	3	4	10	5	7		9	14	11		6		12	9†				3
3	3	3	3	3	3	3	2	2	1	3		3		1					
	+												1		1				
				3									1						

Pears S	Laws B	Cooper CT	Mowbray AM	Gill G	Parkinson GA*	Slaven BJ	Stephens A	Hamilton GJ	Kernaghan AN	Ripley SE	Turnbull LM	Pallister GA	Proudlock P*	Coyle RP*	Kerr PA*	Hodgson DJ*	Spriggs S*	Rowell G	
1	2	3	4	6	5	7	8	9	12	11								10*	1
1	2	3	4	10	5	7	8*	9		11	12	6							
1	2	3	4	10	5	7	8	9		11		6							
1	2	3	4	10*	5	7	8	9	12	11		6							2
4	4	4	4	4	4	4	4	4		4	3							1	
									2				1						
	2							1		1	1							2	

333

1987-88

Manager: Bruce Rioch

1	Aug	15	(h)	Millwall	D	1-1	Stephens	11,471
2		22	(a)	Stoke C	L	0-1		9,345
3		29	(h)	Oldham A	W	1-0	Slaven	10,551
4	Sep	1	(a)	Crystal P	L	1-3	Slaven	6,671
5		5	(h)	Swindon T	L	2-3	Stephens, Slaven	9,344
6		8	(a)	Aston Villa	W	1-0	Kerr	12,665
7		15	(h)	Bournemouth	W	3-0	Hamilton 2, Slaven	9,660
8		19	(h)	Leeds U	W	2-0	Pallister, Kerr	12,051
9		26	(a)	Blackburn R	W	2-0	Kernaghan, Kerr	6,879
10		29	(h)	Reading	D	0-0		10,093
11	Oct	3	(a)	Bradford C	L	0-2		14,114
12		10	(a)	Huddersfield T	W	4-1	Slaven 3, Laws	6,169
13		17	(h)	West Brom A	W	2-1	Slaven, Cooper	10,684
14		20	(h)	Ipswich T	W	3-1	Pallister, Slaven, Kernaghan	10,491
15		24	(a)	Birmingham C	D	0-0		7,404
16		31	(h)	Shrewsbury T	W	4-0	Slaven 3, Kernaghan	10,183
17	Nov	4	(a)	Manchester C	D	1-1	Glover	18,434
18		7	(a)	Sheffield U	W	2-0	Slaven, Ripley	11,278
19		14	(h)	Hull C	W	1-0	Ripley	15,709
20		21	(a)	Plymouth A	W	1-0	Hamilton	9,428
21		28	(h)	Barnsley	W	2-0	Slaven, Kernaghan	12,732
22	Dec	5	(a)	Leicester C	D	0-0		9,411
23		12	(h)	Stoke C	W	2-0	Hamilton, Slaven	12,289
24		19	(a)	Bournemouth	D	0-0		6,792
25		26	(h)	Blackburn R	D	1-1	Slaven	23,536
26		28	(a)	Leeds U	L	0-2		34,186
27	Jan	1	(a)	Oldham A	L	1-3	Kerr	8,181
28		16	(a)	Millwall	L	1-2	Slaven	8,617
29		23	(h)	Crystal P	W	2-1	Mowbray, Glover (pen)	12,597
30	Feb	6	(a)	Swindon T	D	1-1	Mowbray	9,941
31		14	(h)	Aston Villa	W	2-1	Kernaghan, Mowbray	16,957
32		20	(a)	Reading	D	0-0		6,446
33		27	(h)	Bradford C	L	1-2	Cooper	21,079
34	Mar	5	(a)	West Brom A	D	0-0		8,316
35		12	(h)	Huddersfield T	W	2-0	Glover (pen), Kerr	13,866
36		19	(a)	Shrewsbury T	W	1-0	Glover (pen)	5,603
37		26	(h)	Birmingham C	D	1-1	Pallister	15,465
38	Apr	2	(a)	Sheffield U	W	6-0	Senior 2, Ripley 3, Slaven	17,340
39		4	(a)	Hull C	D	0-0		10,758
40		9	(h)	Manchester C	W	2-1	Ripley, Hamilton	19,443
41		23	(a)	Ipswich T	L	0-4		12,773
42		30	(h)	Plymouth A	W	3-1	Ripley, Kernaghan, Hamilton	16,615
43	May	2	(a)	Barnsley	W	3-0	Ripley, Slaven 2	13,240
44		7	(h)	Leicester C	L	1-2	Slaven	27,645

FINAL LEAGUE POSITION: 3rd in Division Two

Appearances
Sub Appearances
Goals

Play-offs

SF	May	15	(a)	Bradford C	L	1-2	Senior	16,017
		18	(h)	Bradford C	W	2-0*	Slaven, Hamilton	25,868
F		25	(h)	Chelsea	W	2-0	Senior, Slaven	25,531
		28	(a)	Chelsea	L	0-1		40,550

*After extra-time

Appearances
Sub Appearances
Goals

FA Cup

3	Jan	9	(a)	Sutton U	D	1-1	Pallister	5,600
R		12	(h)	Sutton U	W	1-0*	Kerr	17,932
4		30	(a)	Everton	D	1-1	Kerr	36,564
R	Feb	3	(h)	Everton	D	2-2*	Mowbray, Kernaghan	25,235
2R		9	(a)	Everton	L	1-2	Ripley	32,222

*After extra-time

Appearances
Sub Appearances
Goals

League Cup

1	Aug	18	(a)	Sunderland	L	0-1		15,770
		25	(h)	Sunderland	W	2-0	Slaven, Mowbray	15,570
2	Sep	23	(h)	Aston Villa	L	0-1		11,424
	Oct	7	(a)	Aston Villa	L	0-1		11,702

Appearances
Sub Appearances
Goals

Pears S	Glover DV*	Cooper CT	Mowbray AM	Gill G	Parkinson GA	Slaven BJ	Stephens A	Hamilton GJ	Kerr PA	Ripley SE	Pallister GA	Kernaghan AN	Proudlock P	Laws B	Burke MS*	Poole K*	Senior TJ*	
1	2	3	4		5	7	8	9	10	11	6							1
1	2	3	4		5	7	8	9*	10	11	6	12						2
1	2	3	4		5	7	8	9	10	11*	6	12						3
1		3	4	2	5	7	8	9	10	11	6							4
1		3	4	2*	5	7	8	9	10	11†	6	12	14					5
1	2	3	4		5	7	8	9	10	11	6							6
1	2	3	4		5	7	8*	9	10	11	6	12						7
1	2	3	4		5	7	8*	9	10	11	6	12						8
1	2	3	4		5	7		9	10	11	6	8						9
1	2	3	4		5	7		9	10	11	6	8						10
1	2	3	4		5	7	12	9*	10	11	6	8						11
1	2	3	4		5	7		9	10	12	6	8*		11				12
1	2	3	4		5	7		9	10	12	6	8*		11				13
1	2	3	4		5	7		9	10	12	6	8		11*				14
1	2	3	4		5	7		9	10	11	6	8*		12				15
1	2	3	4		5*	7		9	10	11	6	8		12				16
1	2	3	4		5*	7		9	10	11	6	8		12				17
1	2	3	4		5	7		9	10	11	6	8						18
1	2	3	4		5	7	12	9	10	11	6	8*						19
1	2	3	4		5	7		9	10	11	6	8						20
1	2	3	4		5*	7		9	10	11	6	8		12				21
1	2	3	4			7	12	9	10	11	6	8*		5				22
1	2	3	4		12	7		9	10	11*	6	8		5				23
1	2	3	4			7*		9	10	11	6	8		5	12			24
1	2*	3	4		12	7		9	10	11	6	8		5†	14			25
1		3	4		12	7		9	10	11	6	8		5*	2			26
1		3	4	12	5	7		9	10	11†	6	8		2*	14			27
	2	3	4		5	7		9	10		6	8		11		1		28
1	2	3	4		5	7		9	10		6	8		11				29
1	2	3	4		5	7*		9	10	8	6	12		11				30
1	2	3	4		5	7		9	10†	8*	6	14		11	12			31
1	2	3	4		5	7		9	10†	8*	6	14		11	12			32
1	2	3	4		5	7*		9	10†	8	6	12		11	14			33
1	2	3	4		5*	7		9	10	8†	6	11		12	14			34
1	2	3	4		5	7			10	8	6			11	9			35
1	2	3	4		5	7		9	10	8	6	12		11				36
1	2	3	4		5	7			10	8	6	12		11*			9	37
1	2	3	4			7			10	8	6	12		5	11		9	38
1	2	3	4			7			10	8	6			5	11		9	39
1		3	4			7	2		10	8	6			5	11		9	40
1	2*	3	4			7	12		10	8	6			5	11		9	41
1	12	3	4	2		7	5		10	8	6	9		11*				42
1		3	4	2		7	5		10	8*	6	9		11	12			43
1	12		4	2		7	5		10	8*	6	9†	3	11	14			44
43	36	43	44	2	35	44	8	40	43	40	44	24		24	8	1	5	—
	2			1	3		3	1	1	3		11	1	5	8	1		—
	4	2	3		21	2	6	5	8	3	6		1		2			—

Pears S	Glover DV*	Cooper CT	Mowbray AM	Gill G	Parkinson GA	Slaven BJ	Stephens A	Hamilton GJ	Kerr PA	Ripley SE	Pallister GA	Kernaghan AN	Proudlock P	Laws B	Burke MS*	Poole K*	Senior TJ*	
1	11		4	2		7	5		10	8	6			3			9	
1	11		4	2		7	5		10	8*	6	12			14		9†	SF
1	11		4	2		7	5		10	8	6						9	
1	11		4	2		7	5		10	8	6						9	F
4	4		3	4		4	4		4	4	4	1		1			4	—
												1		1				—
							2		1						2			—

Pears S	Glover DV*	Cooper CT	Mowbray AM	Gill G	Parkinson GA	Slaven BJ	Stephens A	Hamilton GJ	Kerr PA	Ripley SE	Pallister GA	Kernaghan AN	Proudlock P	Laws B	Burke MS*	Poole K*	Senior TJ*	
1		3	4	8	5	7		9	10	11	6			2				3
	2	3	4	14	5	7		9*	10†		6	8	12	11		1		R
1	2	3	4		5	7		9	10	8	6			11				4
1	2	3	4		5	7		9	10	8	6*	12		11				R
1	2†	3	4		5	7*		9	10	8	6	12		11	4			2R
4	4	5	5	1	5	5		5	5	4	5	1		4	1	1		—
	1											2		1	1			—
		1						2	1	1	1							—

Pears S	Glover DV*	Cooper CT	Mowbray AM	Gill G	Parkinson GA	Slaven BJ	Stephens A	Hamilton GJ	Kerr PA	Ripley SE	Pallister GA	Kernaghan AN	Proudlock P	Laws B	Burke MS*	Poole K*	Senior TJ*	
1	2	3	4		5	7	8	9	10	11	6*	12						1
1	2	3	4	12	5	7	8	9	10*	11	6							
1	2	3	4		5	7	8*	9	10	11	6	12						2
1	2	3	4		5	7		9	10	11	6	8*		12				
4	4	4	4		4	4	3	4	4	4	4	1						—
				1								2		1				—
		1			1													—

1988-89

Manager: Bruce Rioch

1	Aug	27	(a)	Derby C	L	0-1		19,432
2	Sep	3	(h)	Norwich C	L	2-3	Mowbray, Burke	18,595
3		10	(a)	Manchester U	L	0-1		40,442
4		17	(h)	Wimbledon	W	1-0	Hamilton	17,709
5		24	(a)	Tottenham H	L	2-3	Slaven, Mowbray	23,427
6	Oct	1	(a)	Coventry C	W	4-3	Slaven 3, Burke	14,527
7		8	(h)	West Ham U	W	1-0	Pallister	19,608
8		22	(h)	Luton T	W	2-1	Slaven, Cooper	17,792
9		26	(a)	Newcastle U	L	0-3		23,927
10		29	(h)	Millwall	W	4-2	Slaven, Ripley, Burke, Parkinson (pen)	19,788
11	Nov	5	(a)	Liverpool	L	0-3		39,489
12		12	(h)	Queen's Park R	W	1-0	Brennan	20,565
13		19	(a)	Arsenal	L	0-3		32,294
14		26	(h)	Sheffield W	L	0-1		19,310
15	Dec	3	(a)	Nottingham F	D	2-2	Brennan, Ripley	17,742
16		10	(h)	Aston Villa	D	3-3	Brennan, Hamilton, Mowbray	18,096
17		17	(h)	Charlton A	D	0-0		16,065
18		26	(a)	Everton	L	1-2	Glover (pen)	32,651
19		31	(h)	Norwich C	D	0-0		16,021
20	Jan	2	(h)	Manchester U	W	1-0	Davenport	24,411
21		14	(a)	Southampton	W	3-1	Kerr, Slaven, Burke	13,157
22		21	(h)	Tottenham H	D	2-2	Cooper, Ripley	23,692
23	Feb	4	(h)	Coventry C	D	1-1	Slaven	17,352
24		18	(a)	Luton T	L	0-1		8,187
25		21	(a)	Millwall	L	0-2		11,396
26		26	(h)	Newcastle U	D	1-1	Slaven	24,385
27	Mar	11	(h)	Liverpool	L	0-4		25,197
28		18	(h)	Derby C	L	0-1		16,580
29		25	(a)	Wimbledon	D	1-1	Slaven	5,275
30		27	(h)	Everton	D	3-3	Slaven, Parkinson (pen), Davenport	23,151
31	Apr	1	(a)	Charlton A	L	0-2		6,696
32		8	(h)	Southampton	D	3-3	Hamilton, Slaven, Burke	16,983
33		11	(a)	West Ham U	W	2-1	Slaven 2	16,217
34		15	(a)	Queen's Park R	D	0-0		10,347
35		22	(h)	Nottingham F	L	3-4	Hamilton, Slaven, Davenport	20,778
36		29	(a)	Aston Villa	D	1-1	Davenport	18,590
37	May	6	(h)	Arsenal	L	0-1		21,803
38		13	(a)	Sheffield W	L	0-1		20,582

FINAL LEAGUE POSITION: 18th in Division One

Appearances
Sub Appearances
Goals

FA Cup

3	Jan	7	(h)	Grimsby T	L	1-2	Slaven	19,190

Appearances
Sub Appearances
Goals

League Cup

2	Sep	28	(h)	Tranmere R	D	0-0		12,084
	Oct	11	(a)	Tranmere R	L	0-1		8,617

Appearances
Sub Appearances
Goals

Pears S	Parkinson GA	Cooper CT	Mowbray AM	Hamilton GJ	Kernaghan AN	Slaven BJ	Brennan MR*	Senior TJ	Ripley SE	Glover DV	Gill G	Burke MS	Pallister GA	Kerr PA	Davenport P*	Mohan N*	Poole K	Proudlock P	Proctor MG*	Barham MF*	#
1	2	3	4	5*	6	7	8	9†	10	11	12	14									1
1	2	3	4	5	12	7	8	9*	10			11	6								2
1	2	3	4	5	12	7	8		9			11	6	10*							3
1	2	3	4	5		7	8	9	11				6	10							4
1	2	3	4	5		7	8	9	11				6	10							5
1	2	3		5	4	7	8		11			9	6	10							6
1	2	3	4	5	12	7	8	11	14			9*	6	10†							7
1	2	3	4	5	12	7	8	11				9*	6	10							8
1	2	3	4	5	12	7	8	11†	14			9	6	10*							9
1	2	3	4	5	12	7	8	11				9	6	10*							10
1	2	3	4	5		7	8	11				9	6		10						11
1	2	3	4	5	12	7	8	11	14			9†	6		10*						12
1	2	3	4	5†	12	7	8	11	14			9*	6		10						13
1	2	3	4	5*		7	8	11	9			12	6		10						14
1	2	3	4	5			8	7	9			11	6		10						15
1	2	3	4	5	14	12	8	7*	9			11†	6		10						16
1	2	3	4	5	12	7	8		9			11	6		10*						17
1	2	3	4	5	12	7	8	11*	9†				6	14	10						18
1	2	3	4	5		7	8	11	9				6		10						19
1	2*	3	4	5		7	8	11	9			12	6		10						20
1		3	4	5		7		11		8*		12	6	9	10	2					21
1	2	3	4	5		7	8*	11				12	6	9	10						22
		3	4	5		7	8	11			12	9	6	10*		2	1				23
	2	3	4	5	14	7	8*	11		9†	12	6		10			1				24
	2	3	4	5	9	7		11				6	8	10			1				25
	2	3	4	5		7	8	11				12	6	9*	10		1				26
1	2	3	4	5		7	8*	9				6	11	10				12			27
1	2	3	4	5		7		9				11	6	8	10						28
1	2	3	4			7		9			8		6		10			5	11		29
1	2	3	4		12	7		9*			8		6		10			5	11		30
	2	3	4	14	12	7*		9			8		6		10		1	5	11†		31
	2	3	4		9	12	7		11			8*	14	6	10†		1	5			32
	2	3	4	11	8	7		9*				10	6	12			1	5			33
	2	3	4	11	8	7		9				10	6				1	5			34
	2	3*	4	11†		7		9				10	6	8	12	14	1	5			35
	2		4		9	12	7				8	11*	6		10	3	1	5			36
	2		4		9	12	7	8*				11†	6		10	3	1	5	14		37
	2		4		9	12	7					11*	6	8	10	3	1	5			38
26	36	35	37	35	5	36	25	4	36	8	6	21	37	18	23	5	12	10	3		
			1	18	1				4	2	8			2	1	1		1		1	
	2	2	3	4		15	3		3	1			5	1	1	4					

Pears S	Parkinson GA	Cooper CT	Mowbray AM	Hamilton GJ	Kernaghan AN	Slaven BJ	Brennan MR*	Senior TJ	Ripley SE	Glover DV	Gill G	Burke MS	Pallister GA	Kerr PA	Davenport P*	Mohan N*	Poole K	Proudlock P	Proctor MG*	Barham MF*	#
1		3	4	5		7*	8		11	9		2	6		10	12					3
1		1	1	1		1	1		1	1		1	1		1	1					
				1																	

Pears S	Parkinson GA	Cooper CT	Mowbray AM	Hamilton GJ	Kernaghan AN	Slaven BJ	Brennan MR*	Senior TJ	Ripley SE	Glover DV	Gill G	Burke MS	Pallister GA	Kerr PA	Davenport P*	Mohan N*	Poole K	Proudlock P	Proctor MG*	Barham MF*	#
1	2	3	4	5	12	7	8	9*	11			6	10								2
1	2	3	4	5	12	7	8	11*			9	6	10								
2	2	2	2	2		2	2	1	2		1	2	2								
			2																		

Against Other League Clubs

Since September 1899 Middlesbrough have played 89 other Football League clubs. Some clubs, like Bradford, New Brighton Tower and Glossop North End have dropped out of the League. Some clubs, like Leicester Fosse, Woolwich Arsenal and Burslem Port Vale have modified their names. Some clubs have totally changed their names from the original choice registered with the Football League. For example, Small Heath became Birmingham and then Birmingham City, Newton Heath became Manchester United etc. The names listed here are the names by which the clubs are currently known. Three points for a win started in 1981-2. League positions of clubs sharing the same number of points was originally decided on goal average, but since season 1977 the League positions are determined by goal difference. Play-off games in 1987-8 against Bradford City and Chelsea are not included.

| | | HOME | | | | | AWAY | | | | |
	P	W	D	L	F	A	W	D	L	F	A	Pts
AFC Bournemouth	6	3	0	0	10	1	0	2	1	2	4	10
Arsenal	90	19	13	13	68	55	5	11	29	43	111	72
Aston Villa	100	20	14	16	76	63	13	9	28	58	115	91
Barnsley	32	12	3	1	35	8	6	4	6	27	20	48
Birmingham City	78	15	14	10	54	44	7	12	20	44	72	71
Blackburn Rovers	82	17	10	14	71	55	8	11	22	49	98	74
Blackpool	52	17	4	5	62	31	6	10	10	31	42	61
Bolton Wanderers	86	21	10	12	82	52	6	10	27	52	97	76
Bradford	8	2	0	2	9	9	0	1	3	3	9	5
Bradford City	30	8	3	4	29	25	8	1	6	17	17	36
Brentford	12	4	1	1	10	2	1	2	3	6	10	15
Brighton & HA	24	7	4	1	27	8	5	2	5	19	21	33
Bristol City	50	19	5	1	47	13	4	10	11	23	40	62
Bristol Rovers	20	6	2	2	23	12	5	2	3	18	22	28
Burnley	46	12	7	4	54	28	2	7	14	21	59	42
Burton Swifts	6	3	0	0	16	2	0	1	2	2	8	7
Bury	42	9	7	5	38	30	6	5	10	32	32	44
Cambridge United	4	0	1	1	1	2	0	1	1	0	2	2
Cardiff City	42	9	7	5	32	19	3	3	15	21	44	35
Carlisle United	28	7	1	6	15	15	4	4	6	14	17	32
Charlton Athletic	60	16	6	8	56	37	7	4	19	39	64	60
Chelsea	76	18	13	7	70	45	5	10	23	33	72	71
Chester City	2	0	0	1	1	2	1	0	0	2	1	3
Chesterfield	8	3	0	1	11	2	1	1	2	5	11	10
Colchester United	2	1	0	0	4	0	1	0	0	3	2	4
Coventry City	24	2	6	4	15	16	3	3	6	14	19	20
Crystal Palace	26	6	5	2	20	10	3	3	7	16	25	28
Darlington	8	3	1	0	12	4	4	0	0	10	1	16
Derby County	100	27	11	12	99	56	12	11	27	78	100	101
Doncaster Rovers	14	7	0	0	24	4	3	1	3	11	8	23
Everton	84	20	12	10	73	45	3	8	31	42	102	66
Fulham	40	11	2	7	39	24	8	3	9	30	31	47
Gainsborough Trinity	6	2	1	0	12	3	1	1	1	5	7	8
Gillingham	4	1	1	0	4	1	0	1	1	1	5	5
Glossop	4	1	1	0	7	2	0	0	2	0	3	3
Grimsby Town	50	16	3	6	52	27	7	3	15	45	55	54

		HOME					AWAY					
	P	W	D	L	F	A	W	D	L	F	A	Pts
Huddersfield Town	80	24	8	8	83	43	9	9	22	37	63	86
Hull City	32	11	2	3	32	14	3	7	6	22	26	38
Ipswich Town	34	8	3	6	31	23	3	2	12	16	35	28
Leeds United	58	15	9	5	51	28	7	6	16	34	67	60
Leicester City	50	12	5	8	45	34	4	11	10	29	38	48
Leyton Orient	36	12	2	4	41	19	3	6	9	15	35	38
Lincoln City	20	6	3	1	20	10	3	3	4	17	24	24
Liverpool	106	19	17	17	90	74	13	13	27	58	115	94
Loughborough Town	2	1	0	0	3	0	0	1	0	1	1	3
Luton Town	22	4	3	4	11	14	3	1	7	12	21	19
Manchester City	92	26	12	8	88	38	5	8	33	54	106	83
Manchester United	74	16	9	12	73	56	8	6	23	47	77	64
Mansfield Town	4	2	0	0	2	0	1	1	0	6	5	8
Millwall	22	8	2	1	20	7	2	1	8	6	19	25
New Brighton	4	2	0	0	7	3	0	1	1	2	4	5
Newcastle United	82	19	14	8	58	45	9	9	23	44	74	80
Newport County	2	1	0	0	2	0	1	0	0	1	0	6
Northampton Town	4	2	0	0	2	0	0	1	1	3	4	5
Norwich City	38	11	4	4	35	13	4	5	10	18	30	39
Nottingham Forest	48	11	10	3	40	25	5	8	11	36	45	50
Notts County	48	18	2	4	58	22	4	6	14	28	44	55
Oldham Athletic	38	10	5	4	30	20	4	4	11	16	34	40
Oxford United	16	6	0	2	12	5	2	4	2	10	11	20
Peterborough United	2	1	0	0	2	1	1	0	0	2	1	4
Plymouth Argyle	22	7	1	3	32	12	3	5	3	17	21	28
Portsmouth	76	24	10	4	91	46	9	7	22	44	67	85
Port Vale	22	8	2	1	29	9	2	3	6	13	21	25
Preston North End	80	23	10	7	74	43	12	9	19	49	64	89
Queen's Park Rangers	26	6	4	3	20	16	0	6	7	8	28	24
Reading	8	1	3	0	7	2	1	2	1	4	4	9
Rotherham United	30	5	6	4	32	20	9	1	5	29	24	36
Scunthorpe United	14	5	0	2	19	11	1	4	2	9	8	16
Sheffield United	82	22	7	12	87	49	10	9	22	42	71	85
Sheffield Wednesday	76	22	8	8	93	43	7	5	26	40	76	73
Shrewsbury Town	12	5	1	0	15	3	2	1	3	6	6	22
South Shields	6	1	1	1	7	3	1	2	0	3	2	7
Southampton	30	6	5	4	25	13	3	3	9	20	32	27
Stockport County	8	3	1	0	13	1	3	1	0	7	3	14
Stoke City	78	25	10	4	78	32	9	7	23	43	71	87
Sunderland	102	22	12	17	78	68	6	14	31	45	95	84
Swansea City	34	12	3	2	49	21	4	4	9	27	38	41
Swindon Town	20	6	2	2	19	8	4	1	5	8	12	24
Torquay United	2	1	0	0	4	0	0	0	1	1	2	2
Tottenham Hotspur	52	17	6	3	55	25	7	4	15	45	64	58
Walsall	12	3	1	2	11	8	1	2	3	4	6	12
Watford	8	3	1	0	10	4	2	0	2	4	5	11
West Bromwich Albion	66	20	8	5	55	25	6	7	20	31	59	69
West Ham United	30	7	4	4	29	17	6	2	7	25	25	34
Wigan Athletic	2	0	1	0	0	0	1	0	0	2	0	4
Wimbledon	6	2	0	1	4	4	0	2	1	2	5	8
Wolves	66	19	10	4	65	34	12	7	14	47	66	79
Workington	2	1	0	0	3	2	1	0	0	2	1	4
York City	2	1	0	0	3	1	0	0	1	1	3	3

Middlesbrough have yet to play the following teams in the Football League: Aldershot, Crewe Alexandra, Exeter City, Halifax Town, Hartlepool United, Hereford United, Maidstone United, Rochdale, Scarborough, Southend, Tranmere Rovers and Wrexham.

FA Cup (1883-1899)

THE first FA Cup Final was between Wanderers and Royal Engineers in 1872 and took place at Kennington Oval. Wanderers became the first team to lift the famous Cup, winning 1-0.

Middlesbrough entered the competition in 1883 and Archie Pringle is credited with scoring the Club's first FA Cup goal, against Staveley, a Derbyshire mining side, in a physical game which saw several Middlesbrough men require subsequent hospital treatment.

Contemporary newspapers covered the games but the paucity of available information regarding such vital elements as team line-ups, goalscorers, attendances etc, was not always recorded and has now been lost to history — a football historian's nightmare.

1883-4
Round 1
Nov 10 v Staveley (h) 1-5
Pringle

1884-5
Round 2
Dec 6 v Newark (h) 4-1
Pringle 2, Borrie, Hardwick
Att: 2,000
Round 3
Bye
Round 4
Jan 24 v Old Etonians (a) 2-5
Borrie, Pringle

1885-6
Round 2
Nov 21 v Gainsborough Trinity (a) 2-1
Thompson, Wilson
Round 3
Dec 19 v Grimsby Town (h) 2-1
Pickstock, Borrie
Round 4
Bye
Round 5
Jan 23 v Redcar* (a) 1-2
Pickstock

1886-87
Qualifying Round
Oct 30 v Bishop Auckland CI (a) 1-0
Borrie
Att: 3,000

Qualifying Round
Nov 20 v Lincoln City (h) 1-1
Borrie
Qualifying Round Replay
Nov 27 v Lincoln City (a) 0-2

1887-8
Qualifying Round
Oct 8 v Hallam (h) 6-0
Scorers unknown
Round 1
Oct 15 v Whitburn (h) 4-0
Borrie, Other scorers unknown
Round 2
Nov 5 v South Bank (h) 4-1
Borrie 2, E.J.Wilson, Dennis
Round 3
Nov 26 v Sunderland (h) 2-2
McCrie, Dennis
Round 3 Replay
Dec 3 v Sunderland (a) 2-4
Cochrane, Unknown
Tie awarded to Middlesbrough, Sunderland disqualified because of veiled professionalism.
Round 1
Jan 7 v Old Foresters (h) 4-0
Dennis, Borrie, Fox, E.J.Wilson
Meeting held in London on 14 January to hear Old Foresters' complaint that the ground conditions affected the result of the game. Mr Jope, the referee reported that in places the ground was covered in 'tan and sand', and therefore the conditions did

not allow a 'fair battle to be waged'. The Association ruled that a replay was necessary and was to be played on 21 January at Middlesbrough and, if the ground was still unfit, the tie would be switched to Sheffield. On hearing that the replayed tie was scheduled for Middlesbrough, the Old Foresters scratched from the competition.

Round 1
Jan 21 v Old Foresters (h) 2-1
Round 2
Jan 28 v Crewe Alexandra (h) 0-2

1888-9
Qualifying Round
Oct 6 v Ecclesfield (h) 0-1

1889-90
Round 1
Sep 21 v Ecclesfield (h) 3-1
Taylor, Garland, Unknown
Round 2
Oct 5 v South Bank (h) 3-4
Dennis, Other scorers unknown
Att: 6,000

1890-91
Qualifying Round
Oct 4 v Scarborough† (h) 11-0
Johnston 3, Wilson, Allen, Petrie 2, Dennis 3, Stevenson
Qualifying Round
Oct 25 v St Augustines (a) 4-1
Kay (og), Allan 2, Unknown
Att: 2,000
South Bank protested on eligibility of some of 'Boro's players, who had played in some Scottish games during the close season. The Association ruled that the relevant players could still play in the English Cup.
Qualifying Round
Nov 15 v Darlington (h) 2-0
Allan, Theakston (og)
Darlington protested over Bell's registration, alleging that he had played in a Scottish five-a-side competition in June, the day after signing as a professional with Middlesbrough. The player, supported by an affidavit signed by the referee, claimed that the game had been played the week before his signing. Despite this the protest was upheld and the tie was awarded to Darlington.

1891-2
Round 1
Jan 16 v Luton Town (a) 3-0
Campbell, Bell, Black
Round 2
Jan 30 v Preston North End (h) 1-2
Scorer unknown

1892-3
Round 1
Jan 1 v Newcastle United (a) 3-2
Black, Blyth, McKnight
Round 2
Feb 4 v Wolves (a) 1-2 (aet)
Black

1893-4
Qualifying Round
Oct 14 v Leadgate Exiles (a) 4-2
Qualifying Round
Nov 4 v Gateshead NER (h) 2-1
Qualifying Round
Nov 25 v Tow Law (h) 3-0
Qualifying Round
Dec 16 v Willington Athletic (a) 4-1
Stewart, Dunkerley 2, Unknown
Round 1
Jan 27 v Newton Heath (a) 0-4

1894-5
Qualifying Round
Oct 6 v Rendel (h) 4-0
Qualifying Round
Oct 13 v Willington Athletic (h) 2-1
Davison, T.Morren
Att: 1,500
Qualifying Round
Nov 3 v Howden Rangers (h) 4-1
Bach, Other scorers unknown
Qualifying Round
Nov 24 v Darlington (a) 1-0
Qualifying Round
Dec 15 v Bishop Auckland (a) 3-1
Round 1
Feb 2 v Chesterfield (h) 4-0
Davison 2, Roger, Mullen

Round 2
Feb 16 v Sheffield Wednesday (a) 1-6
Nelmes

1895-6
Qualifying Round
Oct 12 v Jarrow (a) 3-0
A.Johnson, Adams, Mullen
Qualifying round
Nov 2 v Newcastle United (a) 1-4
Scorer unknown

1896-7
Qualifying Round
Dec 12 v Hebburn Argyle (a) 1-8
Scorer unknown
1897-8
Qualifying Round
Sep 25 v South Bank (a) 3-2
Scorers unknown

Qualifying Round
Oct 16 v Rendel (a) 1-0
Purvis
Qualifying Round
Oct 30 v Bishop Auckland (h) 3-1
Scorers unknown
Qualifying Round
Nov 20 v Hebburn Argyle (h) 2-0
Scorers unknown
Qualifying Round
Dec 11 v Newcastle United (h) 0-2

1898-9
Qualifying Round
Oct 29 v Hebburn Argyle (h) 0-1

	P	W	D	L	F	A
Summary						
Home	26	17	2	7	70	29
Away	21	12	0	9	40	46
	47	29	2	16	110	75

*Redcar lost 2-0 (a) to Small Heath in the 6th round.
†The 11-0 victory over Scarborough obviously betters the 10-3 win over Sheffield United in November 1933 and now stands as Middlesbrough's record score.

Other Competitions

Anglo-Italian Cup

1969-70
May 2 v AC Roma (h) 1-0
Hickton
Whigham; R.A.Smith, Jones, G.Smith, Gates, Spraggon, McMordie, Laidlaw, McIlmoyle, Hickton, Mills.
Att: 14,196
May 8 v Lanerossi Vicenza (h) 2-0
Laidlaw, Hickton (pen)
Whigham; R.A.Smith(Webb), Jones, G.Smith, Gates, Spraggon, Downing, McMordie(Moody), McIlmoyle, Hickton, Laidlaw.
Att: 6,656
May 10 v AC Roma (a) 1-1
Downing
Whigham; R.A.Smith(Moody), Jones, G.Smith, Gates, Spraggon, Downing, Laidlaw, Webb, Hickton, McMordie.
May 24 v Lanerossi Vicenza (a) 2-2
Gates, McMordie
Whigham; R.A.Smith, Jones, G.Smith, Gates, Spraggon, Downing, McMordie, Hickton, Laidlaw, Mills.
Att: 2,000

	Apps	Subs	Gls	Summary	Pld	W	D	L	F	A	Pts
Downing DG	3	0	1	Home	2	2	0	0	3	0	7
Gates WL	4	0	1	Away	2	0	2	0	3	3	5
Hickton J	4	0	2								
Jones GE	4	0	0		4	2	2	0	6	3	12
Laidlaw JD	4	0	1								
McIlmoyle H	2	0	0								
McMordie A	4	0	1								
Mills DJ	2	0	0								
Moody A	0	2	0								
Smith G	4	0	0								
Smith RA	4	0	0								
Spraggon F	4	0	0								
Webb SJ	1	1	0								
Whigham W	4	0	0								
	44	3	6								

Anglo-Scottish Cup

Qualifying Rounds
1975-76
Aug 2 v Sunderland (h) 3-2
Souness, Craggs, Murdoch
Platt; Craggs, Bailey, Souness, Boam, Maddren, Murdoch, Mills, Hickton(Brine), Cooper, Armstrong.
Att: 12,849

Aug 5 v Carlisle United (h) 4-1
Willey 2, Hickton (pen), Bailey
Platt; Craggs, Bailey, Souness, Boam, Maddren, Murdoch, Mills, Hickton, Willey, Armstrong.
Att: 8,737
Aug 9 v Newcastle United (a) 2-2
Willey, Armstrong
Cuff; Craggs, Bailey, Souness, Boam, McAndrew, Brine, Mills(M.Smith), Willey, H.Charlton, Armstrong.
Att: 12,362
Quarter-final (lst leg)
Sep 16 v Aberdeen (h) 2-0
Hickton (pen), Mills
Platt; Craggs, Cooper, Souness, Boam, McAndrew, Murdoch(H.Charlton), Mills, Hickton, Foggon, Armstrong.
Att: 13,965
Quarter-final (2nd leg)
Oct 1 v Aberdeen (a) 5-2
Hickton 2, Mills 2, Foggon
Platt(Cuff); Craggs, Cooper, Souness, Boam, Maddren, Brine, Mills, Hickton, Foggon(Murdoch), Armstrong.
Att: 9,200
Middlesbrough won 7-2 on aggregate.
Semi-final (1st leg)
Oct 21 v Mansfield Town (h) 3-0
Armstrong 2, Hickton
Platt; Craggs, Cooper, Souness, Boam, Maddren, Murdoch, Mills, Hickton, Foggon(Spraggon), Armstrong.
Att: 14,929
Semi-final (2nd leg)
Nov 3 v Mansfield Town (a) 2-0
Murdoch, Souness
Platt; Craggs, Spraggon, Souness, Boam, Maddren, Murdoch(Brine), Mills, Hickton, Cooper, Armstrong.
Att: 7,110
Middlesbrough won 5-0 on aggregate.
Final (1st leg)
Nov 26 v Fulham (h) 1-0
Strong (og)
Platt; Craggs, Spraggon, Murdoch(Foggon), Boam, Maddren, Brine, Mills, Hickton, Cooper, Armstrong.
Att: 14,700
Final (2nd leg)
Dec 9 v Fulham (a) 0-0
Platt; Craggs, Cooper, Boersma, Boam, Maddren, Murdoch, Mills, Willey, Hickton, Armstrong.
Att: 13,723
Middlesbrough won 1-0 on aggregate.

1976-77
Qualifying Rounds
Aug 7 v Hull City (a) 2-0
Souness, Boersma
Platt; Craggs, Bailey, Souness, Boam, Maddren, Boersma(Hickton), Mills, Hedley, Armstrong, Cooper.
Att: 6,837
Aug 10 v Sheffield United (a) 1-0
Souness
Cuff; Craggs, Bailey, Souness, Boam, Ramage, Boersma, Mills, Hedley, Armstrong, Cooper.
Att: 4,043

Aug 14 v Newcastle United (a) 0-3
Platt; Craggs, Bailey, Souness, Boam, Maddren, Brine, Mills, Hedley(Hickton), Armstrong, Cooper.
Att: 14,708

	Apps	Subs	Gls	Summary	Pld	W	D	L	F	A
Armstrong D	12	0	3	Home	5	5	0	0	13	3
Bailey IC	6	0	1	Away	7	4	2	1	12	4
Boam SW	12	0	0		12	9	2	1	25	7
Boersma P	3	0	1							
Brine PK	4	2	0							
Charlton H	1	1	0							
Cooper T	10	0	0							
Craggs JE	12	0	1							
Cuff PJ	2	1	0							
Foggon A	3	1	1							
Hedley G	3	0	0							
Hickton J	8	2	5							
McAndrew A	2	0	0							
Maddren WD	9	0	0							
Mills DJ	12	0	3							
Murdoch RW	7	1	2							
Platt JA	10	0	0							
Ramage A	1	0	0							
Smith M	0	1	0							
Souness GJ	10	0	4							
Spraggon F	2	1	0							
Willey AS	3	0	3							
Strong (Fulham)	0	0	1(og)							
	132	10	25							

Stuart Boam

Freight/Rover Trophy

1986-87
Preliminary Round
Nov 24 v Doncaster Rovers (h) 3-0
Proudlock 2, Turnbull
Pears; Laws, Cooper, Mowbray, Parkinson, Pallister, Slaven(Turnbull), Proudlock, Hamilton(Kernaghan), Gill, Ripley.
Att: 3,977
Preliminary Round
Dec 2 v Chesterfield (a) 1-2
Stephens
Pears; Laws, Cooper, Mowbray, Parkinson, Pallister, Slaven, Stephens, Hamilton, Gill, Ripley.
Att: 1,764
Round 1
Jan 21 v Halifax Town (a) 2-1
Kernaghan, Ripley
Pears; Kernaghan, Cooper, Mowbray, Parkinson, Pallister, Slaven, Kerr, Hamilton, Gill, Ripley.
Att: 1,411
Round 2
Feb 10 v Rochdale (a) 0-0
Pears; Kernaghan(Coyle), Cooper, Mowbray, Parkinson, Pallister, Slaven, Stephens, Kerr, Gill, Ripley(Hamilton).
Att: 2,615
(Middlesbrough won 4-3 with penalties from *Stephens, Cooper, Slaven and Hamilton*)

Area semi-final
Mar 10 v Mansfield Town (h) 0-1
Pears; Coyle(Kerr), Cooper, Mowbray, Parkinson, Kernaghan, Slaven, Stephens, Hamilton, Gill, Hodgson(Ripley).
Att: 11,754

	Apps	Subs	Gls
Cooper CT	5	0	1
Coyle RP	1	1	0
Gill G	5	0	0
Hamilton GJ	4	1	1
Hodgson DJ	1	0	0
Kernaghan AN	3	1	1
Kerr PA	2	1	0
Laws B	2	0	0
Mowbray AM	5	0	0
Pallister GA	4	0	0
Parkinson GA	5	0	0
Pears S	5	0	0
Proudlock P	1	0	2
Ripley SE	4	1	1
Slaven BJ	5	0	1
Stephens A	3	0	2
Turnbull LM	0	1	1
	55	6	10

Summary	Pld	W	D	L	F	A
Home	2	1	0	1	3	1
Away	3	2	0	1	7	6
	5	3	0	2	10	7

Gary Gill

Full Members Cup

1985-86
Oct 8 v Carlisle United (h) 2-0
O'Riordan, Saunders (og)
Pears; Laws, Heard, McAndrew, Mowbray, Nattrass, Hamilton, O'Riordan, Currie, Rowell(Cook), Beagrie.
Att: 2,177
Northern Area semi-final
Nov 5 v Hull City (a) 1-3 (aet; 90 mins: 1-1)
Slaven
Pears; Laws, Heard, McAndrew(Cooper), O'Riordan, Hamilton, Turnbull(Beagrie), Currie, Slaven, Kernaghan, Cook.
Att: 3,637

	Apps	Subs	Gls
Beagrie PS	1	1	0
Cook M	1	1	0
Cooper CT	0	1	0
Currie DN	2	0	0
Hamilton GJ	2	0	0
Heard TP	2	0	0
Kernaghan AN	1	0	0
Laws B	2	0	0
McAndrew A	2	0	0
Mowbray AM	1	0	0
Nattrass I	1	0	0
O'Riordan DJ	2	0	1
Pears S	2	0	0
Rowell G	1	0	0
Slaven BJ	1	0	1
Turnbull LM	1	0	0
Saunders	0	0	1(og)
	22	3	3

Summary	Pld	W	D	L	F	A
Home	2	2	0	0	3	0
Away	2	0	2	0	3	3
	4	2	2	0	6	3

Alan Kernaghan

Simod Cup

1987-88
Round 1
Nov 10 v Ipswich Town (a) 0-1
Poole; Glover, Laws, Mowbray, Parkinson, Pallister, Slaven(Proudlock), Kernaghan(Gill), Hamilton, Kerr, Ripley.
Att: 6,108

1988-89
Round 1
Dec 14 v Oldham Athletic (h) 1-0
Glover (pen)
Pears; Parkinson, Cooper, Mowbray, Hamilton, Pallister, Slaven, Brennan, Glover, Davenport, Burke.
Att: 7,439
Round 2
Dec 21 v Portsmouth (h) 2-1 (aet)
Slaven
Pears; Parkinson, Cooper, Mowbray, Hamilton, Pallister, Slaven, Brennan, Glover, Davenport, Ripley(Kerr).
Att: 6,853
Round 3
Jan 11 v Coventry City (h) 1-0
Davenport
Pears; Mohan, Cooper, Mowbray, Hamilton, Pallister, Slaven, Gill, Kerr, Davenport, Ripley.
Att: 9,910
Round 4
Jan 28 v Crystal Palace (h) 2-3
Slaven, Cooper
Pears; Parkinson, Cooper, Mowbray, Hamilton, Pallister, Slaven, Brennan, Burke, Kernaghan, Ripley.
Att: 16,314

	Apps	Subs	Gls
Brennan MR	3	0	0
Burke MS	2	0	0
Cooper CT	4	0	1
Davenport P	3	0	1
Gill G	1	1	0
Glover DV	3	0	2
Hamilton GJ	5	0	0
Kernaghan AN	2	0	0
Kerr PA	2	1	0
Laws B	1	0	0
Mohan N	1	0	0
Mowbray AM	5	0	0
Pallister GA	5	0	0
Parkinson GA	4	0	0
Pears S	4	0	0
Poole K	1	0	0
Proudlock P	0	1	0
Ripley SE	4	0	0
Slaven BJ	5	0	2
	55	3	6

Summary	Pld	W	D	L	F	A
Home	4	3	0	1	5	3
Away	1	0	0	1	0	1
	5	3	0	2	5	4

Kevin Poole

347

Texaco Cup

Qualifying Rounds
1974-75
Aug 3 v Carlisle United (h) 0-1
Platt; Craggs, Spraggon, Souness, Boam, Maddren, Murdoch, Mills(M.Smith), Hickton, Foggon, Armstrong.
Att: 10,692
Aug 6 v Sunderland (a) 1-0
Armstrong
Platt; Craggs, Spraggon, Souness, Boam, Taylor, Brine(H.Charlton), Mills, Hickton, M.Smith, Armstrong.
Att: 22,828
Aug 10 v Newcastle United (a) 0-4
Platt; Craggs, J.Cochrane, Brine, Boam, Maddren, Murdoch, Mills, Hickton, M.Smith, Armstrong.
Att: 11,575

	Apps	Subs	Gls
Armstrong D	3	0	1
Boam SW	3	0	0
Brine PK	2	0	0
Charlton H	0	1	0
Cochrane JK	1	0	0
Craggs JE	3	0	0
Foggon A	1	0	0
Hickton J	3	0	0
Maddren WD	2	0	0
Mills DJ	3	0	0
Murdoch RW	2	0	0
Platt JA	3	0	0
Smith M	2	1	0
Souness GJ	2	0	0
Spraggon F	2	0	0
Taylor B	1	0	0
	33	2	1

Summary	Pld	W	D	L	F	A
Home	1	0	0	1	0	1
Away	2	1	0	1	1	4
	3	1	0	2	1	5

David Mills, one of several ever-presents in Middlesbrough's Texaco Cup campaign.

Middlesbrough In The
Northern League
1889-1899

THE Football League was formed in 1888 and, within a year, football in the North-East adopted the same rigid format as its parent body with the birth of the Northern League.

The founder members of the Northern League were Birtley, Bishop Auckland (then called Auckland Town), Darlington, Darlington St Augustine's, Elswick Rangers, Middlesbrough, Newcastle East End, Newcastle West End, South Bank and Stockton.

The first games in the League took place on Saturday, 7 September 1889, although Middlesbrough's first fixture was the following Saturday with a home game against Elswick Rangers.

Undoubtedly, the most dominant team of the Northern League's early days was Ironopolis of Middlesbrough. The infant club, formed in 1889, joined in the League's second season and won three consecutive championships, dropping only 12 points in three seasons.

In 1893, the Football League Second Division came into being and Ironopolis sought and gained entry — along with Liverpool — into the new League, leaving the door open for the other clubs in the Northern League to fight it out amongst themselves. Middlesbrough, with Ironopolis out of the way, came into prominence.

In May 1899 Middlesbrough followed the path of the now defunct Ironopolis and successfully gained entry into the Second Division, having spent ten seasons in the Northern League. All home games took place on the Linthorpe Road ground.

1889-1890	18	4	3	2	26	15	4	0	5	16	22	19	6th
1890-1891	14	6	1	0	21	4	2	2	3	12	13	19	2nd
1891-1892	16	6	0	2	18	10	7	0	1	15	3	26	2nd
1892-1893	10	4	0	1	12	5	0	0	5	5	12	8	4th
1893-1894	14	6	1	0	21	6	5	0	2	30	10	23	1st
1894-1895	18	7	2	0	39	5	5	3	1	19	12	29	1st
1895-1896	16	6	2	0	23	7	2	2	4	5	15	20	3rd
1896-1897	16	8	0	0	21	4	3	4	1	15	11	26	1st
1897-1898	16	5	2	1	28	10	4	2	2	14	12	22	2nd
1898-1899	16	5	1	2	21	10	2	3	3	8	17	18	3rd
	184	57	12	8	230	76	34	16	27	139	127	210	

Abandoned Games

25 Dec 1912 v Bradford C (a) 0-1 (abandoned after 84 minutes – fading light).
Williamson; McLeod, Weir, Crosier, W.Carr, Malcolm, Stirling, J.Carr, Elliott, Windridge, Nichol.
(Replayed on 4 February 1913).

3 Apr 1915 v Oldham A (a) 4-1 (abandoned after 56 mins)
Tinsley 2 (1 pen), Urwin 2
Davies; Holmes, Walker, Davidson, Jackson, Malcolm, Storey, Carr, A.N.Wilson, Tinsley, Urwin.
Match abandoned when Billy Cook, the Oldham Athletic full-back, refused to leave the field after being sent off. The result was ordered to stand.

4 Feb 1922 v Everton (a) 0-1 (abandoned after 57 mins – snowstorm).
Harrison; Holmes, Fox, S.Davidson, Ellerington, Pender, Mordue, Birrell, Elliott, G.Carr, Urwin.
(Replayed on 1 March 1922).

16 Nov 1929 v Arsenal (a) 0-1 (abandoned after 55 minutes – fog).
Mathieson; Ferguson, Ashman, Miller, Elkes, Macfarlane, Pease, J.Carr, Camsell, Bruce, O.Williams.
Att: 30,000

10 Jan 1959 v Birmingham C (h) 1-1 (abandoned after 60 minutes – icy pitch).
Clough
Million; Bilcliff, Stonehouse, Yeoman, Phillips, Harris, Day, Fernie, Clough, Peacock, Burbeck.
Att: 34,079
(Replayed on 24 January 1959).

24 Sep 1974 v Leicester C (h) 1-0 (abandoned after 29 minutes – floodlight failure).
Souness
Platt; Craggs, Hickton, Souness, Boam, Maddren, Murdoch, Mills, Willey, Foggon, Armstrong.
(Replayed on 12 December 1974).

Middlesbrough line-up in 1922. Back row (left to right): W.Birrell, J.Carr. Second row: P.Donaghy, R.Pender, V.Fox, R.G.Williamson, W.Carr, G.Carr. Seated: J.Marshall, A.N.Wilson, S.Davidson, G.W.Elliott, W.Ellerington. On ground: T.Urwin, W.Murray.

Friendly Matches
(1899-1989)

Listed below are all games played by Middlesbrough under the general heading of Friendlies. Included in this list are testimonial games, which are awarded to players who reach ten years service with one club, and are usually played at the end of a season. In days gone by these games were called benefit games but instead of playing an additional match outside the normal boundary of the League season, the club sanctioned a specific home League game and the net receipts were handed to the beneficiary. These games are not included in this list. Pre-season friendlies are used by a manager to assess the playing strengths and weaknesses of his playing squad in a competitive environment against other clubs but this was not always the case. For many years the pre-season games, usually two or three in number, took place within the confines of the club and the Reds, the probables, played the Whites, the reserve side. More often than not the paying public witnessed these games with the turnstile money being donated to local charities. These matches are also excluded from this list. Goalscorers and attendances are given where known.

1899-1900
Sep 7 v Kaffirs (h) 8-2
Att: 3,000
Dec 25 v Edinburgh St Bernards (h)
Dec 26 v Hibernian (h) 3-4
Att: 4,000
Jan 1 v Tottenham H (h) 2-2
Jan 2 v Glossop NE (h) 1-2
Att: 3,000
Jan 3 v London Casuals (h) 2-4
Att: 1,000
Apr 13 v Sunderland (h) 0-1
Att: 4,000
Apr 16 v Clyde (h) 0-1
Att: 4,000

1900-01
Sep 5 v Newcastle United (h) 1-2
Att: 4,000
Jan 2 v Everton (h) 1-6
Att: 5,000
Apr 8 v Clyde (h) -
Att: 2,000
Apr 30 v Sunderland (h) -

1901-02
Sep 2 v Newcastle United (h) 2-1
Sep 9 v Sunderland (h) 1-1
Wardrope
Oct 23 v Newcastle United (a) 1-4
Turner
Att: 3,000
Dec 25 v Edinburgh St Bernard's (h) 3-2
Att: 5,000
Dec 26 v Dundee (h) 3-0
Att: 5,000
Jan 2 v Third Lanark (h) 3-2

Feb 7 v Chesterfield (h) 1-2
Douglas
Apr 23 v Newcastle United (a)
(In Aid of Ibrox Disaster Fund)

1902-03
Sep 5 v Newcastle United (h) 1-2
Millar
Att: 4,000
Sep 8 v Hearts (h) 3-1
J.Muir, Turner, J.Robertson
Dec 30 v Corinthians (h) 6-4
Godley, Macaulay, R.Watson, J.H.Gettins, Carrick 2
Jan 1 v Manchester C (h) 0-1
Att: 5,000
Feb 7 v Chesterfield (h) 1-2
Feb 21 v Rangers (h) 1-1
Currie

1903-04
Sep 1 v Celtic (h) 1-0
White (pen)
Att: 7,000
Oct 12 v Dundee (a) 2-2
Blackett, Cassidy
Att: 5,000
Dec 1 v Manchester United (h) 0-1
Dec 25 v Leith Athletic (h) 5-1
Millward 3, Carrick, Unknown 1
Att: 2,000
Apr 4 v Dundee (h) 2-0
Brown, E.Gettins
Apr 27 v Darlington (a) 4-4
Brown, Cassidy 2, McGuigan

1904-05
Feb 18 v Sunderland (h) 1-2
Phillipson
Att: 1,000
Apr 3 v Newcastle United (h) 1-1
Phillipson
Att: 1,000
Apr 21 v Dundee (h)
Brown
Att: 1,000
Apr 22 v Third Lanark (h) 1-1
Murray
Att: 1,000
Apr 30 v Newcastle United (h) 1-1
Phillipson
Att: 1,000

1905-06
Sep 6 v Sunderland (h) 4-0
Murray, Reid 3
Att: 1,000
Jan 2 v Darlington (a) 6-2
J.Bell 3, Walker, Barker, Reid

1906-07
Apr 3 v Airdrieonians (h)
 Danish Tour
May 8 v Danish University (a) 5-3
May 9 v Danish XI (a) 2-2

1907-08
Apr 29 v North Inverness XI (a) 5-0
 Danish Tour
Jun v Denmark XI (a) 5-2
Bloomer 2, Hall 2, Cail

1908-09
Dec 16 v Newcastle United (h) 1-2
Cail
Feb 16 v Oldham Athletic (h) 1-4
Feb 20 v Edinburgh St Bernard's (h) 4-0
Hall 2, Common, Verrill
Att: 2,000

1912-13
Mar 8 v Bradford City (h) 5-1
Carr (pen), Nichol, J.Cook 2, Elliott
Att: 4,000
Apr 28 v Norwich City (a) 1-1

1913-14
Mar 21 v Celtic (a) 3-1
Tinsley 2, Elliott
Att: 10,000

1918-19
Dec 14 v Rendel (a) 1-5
Dec 26 v South Shields (a) 4-2
Dec 27 v Rendel (h) 2-2

Jan 1 v Sunderland (a) 3-1
Apr 5 v Newcastle United (h) 4-1
Apr 18 v Hartlepools United (h) 0-2
Apr 21 v Rendel (h) 1-0
Apr 26 v Hartlepools United (a) 1-1
May 3 v Newcastle United (a) 2-2

1920-21
Apr 4 v Raith Rovers (a) 0-3
Att: 9,000

1926-27
May 3 v Newcastle United (h) 0-0
(Charlie Cole's Benefit)
 Danish Tour
May 21 v Danish XI (a) 2-4
Camsell 2
May 25 v Danish XI (a) 8-2
Camsell 5, Unknown 3

1929-30
Dec 29 v Corinthians (h) 1-0
Att: 500

1930-31
Apr 27 v Hearts (a) 5-1
Camsell 4, Cameron
(Bill Murray's Testimonial)

1934-35
Oct 16 v Army XI (a) 2-4
Camsell, Warren
Jan 27 v Army XI (h) 2-2
Fenton 2

1935-36
Oct 17 v Newcastle United (a) 2-3
Camsell, Warren
(Gresford Colliery Fund)
May 4 v Norwich City (a) 3-1
Birkett, Coleman, Chadwick
 Norwegian Tour
May 12 v Oslo (a) 2-1
Cunliffe, Yorston
May 14 v Fredrikstad (a) 1-1
Camsell
May 15 v Dammen (a) 3-2
Yorston 2, Birkett

1938-39
Aug 20 v Sunderland (a) 2-4
Yorston, Fenton
Att: 10,871
(FA Jubilee Fund)
Nov 14 v Army XI (a) 9-0
Higham 4, Camsell 2, Chadwick 2, Cochrane
Mar 25 v Hearts (h) 1-4
Camsell
Att: 15,500

Apr 26 v Scarborough (h) 2-3
Fenton, Unknown 1
May 2 v South Bank (a) 6-1
Higham 3, Armes 2, Fenton
May 4 v Hartlepools United (a) 5-4
Fenton 2, Miller 2, T.E.Murphy
May 8 v Norwich City (a) 0-3
Att: 4,000

1939-40
Oct 7 v Newcastle United (a) 2-3
Fenton 2
Oct 14 v Hartlepools United (h) 3-2
Camsell, Chadwick, Fenton
Nov 4 v Hartlepools United (a) 5-4
Fenton 2, Miller 2, Murphy
Nov 18 v Stockton (h) 6-3
Camsell 3, Fenton 2, Chadwick
Dec 25 v Darlington (a) 5-1
Murphy, Camsell, Fenton 3
Dec 26 v Newcastle United (a) 1-1
Chadwick
Dec 30 v Barnsley (h) 4-2
Fenton 4
Jan 1 v Newcastle United (h) 5-2
Fenton 3, Stobbart, Mannion
Apr 11 v Stockton (a) 1-2
Fenton

1940-41
Apr 12 v Army XI (a) 8-1
McCabe 3, Camsell 2, Mannion 2, Fenton

1948-49
Jan 29 v Tottenham Hotspur (a) 1-4
McCrae
Att: 40,000
Feb 5 v Bolton Wanderers (h) 1-1
Donaldson
Att: 35,000
Feb 12 v Newcastle United (h) 3-3
Donaldson 2, Dicks
Att: 38,000
Mar 26 v Hearts (h) 4-0
Hardwick, Spuhler 2, Hartnett

1949-50
Feb 11 v Newcastle United (a) 2-3
Woodward 2
Att: 17,000
Mar 4 v Blackburn Rovers (h) 5-0
Walker, Spuhler 3, Reagan
Att: 10,000

1950-51
Jan 27 v Barnsley (h) 2-1
Mannion, Delapenha
Att: 15,000

Feb 10 v Southampton (a) 1-1
Mannion
Att: 16,000
Festival of Britain
May 12 v Partizan Belgrade (h) 2-3
Walker, Mochan
Att: 20,000

1951-52
Feb 23 v Notts County (h) 2-1
Bell, Mannion
Att: 12,000
Irish Tour
May 8 v Glentoran (a) 3-0
McCrae, Mannion, Delapenha
May 9 v Glenavon (a) 3-0
Dicks, Delapenha, McCrae
May 11 v Cork (a) 5-1
Noonan 2 (2 ogs), McCrae, Mannion, Delapenha
May 14 v Drumcondra (a) 6-1
Delapenha 2, Fitzsimons, McCrae 2, Spuhler

1952-53
Jan 31 v Aberdeen (h) 6-3
Mannion, Spuhler 4, Fitzsimons
Att: 5,000
Feb 28 v Notts C (a) 1-4
Fitzsimons
Att: 7,095
Coronation Match
May 6 v Sunderland (a) 4-3
Fitzsimons 2, Walker, Edwards
Att: 5,896
Dutch Tour
May 14 v Dutch XI (a) 2-2
Delapenha 2
Att: 35,000
May 20 v Dutch National Reserve (a) 3-1
Fitzsimons 2, Delapenha
Att: 20,000

1953-54
Feb 19 v Watford (a) 1-3
Rayment
Mar 16 v Falkirk (a) 1-2
Lawrie
(Floodlit friendly, second half televised)

1954-55
Jan 29 v Sheffield U (h) 4-1
Scott, Mitchell 2, J.Shaw (og)

1955-56
Nov 28 v Torquay U (a) 1-1
Delapenha

Floodlit Friendlies

1957-58
Oct 16 v Sunderland (h) 2-0
Fitzsimons, Clough
Att: 27,273
Oct 30 v Newcastle United (h) 3-0
Fitzsimons, McLean, Peacock
Att: 27,056
Nov 13 v Cologne (h) 1-2
Clough
Att: 31,923
Nov 27 v Hibernian (h) 0-5
Att: 26,981
Dec 11 v Celtic (h) 6-1
Clough 4, Delapenha (pen), Scott
Att: 14,062
Mar 27 v PSV Eindhoven (h) 3-3
Clough 3
Att: 12,285
Apr 28 v Hull City (a) 3-1
Clough 2, Stonehouse
Att: 5,172

1958-59
Oct 6 v Bela Vista (h) 4-0
Peacock 2, Scott 2
Att: 15,944
Oct 22 v Munich 1860 (h) 2-2
Peacock, Burbeck
Att: 17,016
Dec 3 v Nimes Olympique (h) 3-0
Clough 2, Peacock
Att: 21,166
Feb 16 v First Vienna (h) 4-1
Holliday 2, Clough 2
Att: 12,904

1959-60
Nov 2 v Hibernian (a) 6-6
Peacock 2, Fernie 2, Clough, Harris
Att: 15,000
Nov 9 v Hull City (h) 4-0
Yeoman, Clough, Day, Harris (pen)
Nov 23 v Army XI (h) 3-3
Fernie, Harris (pen), Clough
Att: 9,191
Mar 14 v Peterborough United (a) 2-3
Peacock, Clough
Att: 10,002
Mar 28 v Saarbrucken (h) 4-0
Holliday, Clough, Peacock, Rodgerson
Att: 7,849
May 2 v Fluminense (h) 2-3
Harris (pen), Clough
Att: 14,432

Switzerland/Germany Tour
May 8 v Bienne FC (a) 3-1
Peacock, Waldock, Alleman (og)
Att: 4,000
May 10 v Swiss 'B' (a) 2-0
Peacock, Fernie
May 12 v Bonn (a) 1-1
Rodgerson
(Abandoned after 74 minutes — thunderstorm)
May 14 v Fortuna Düsseldorf (a) 4-3
Waldock, Yeoman, Clough, Rodgerson
Att: 3,000

Friendship Cup
1960-61
Oct 12 v Lille Olympique (h) 4-1
Waldock, Harris, Clough 2
Att: 7,594
Nov 16 v Bonn (h) 5-0
Clough 3, Peacock 2
Att: 7,863
Dec 7 v Army XI (h) 2-1
Burbeck, Kaye
Att: 2,865

1961-62
Aug 5 v Arsenal (h) 2-1
Peacock 2
Att: 8,865
Cock O' The North
Oct 11 v Sunderland (h) 2-0
Kaye, Holliday
Att: 24,733
Oct 16 v Newcastle United (a) 3-2
Peacock 2, Neal
Att: 10,150
Nov 1 v Sunderland (a) 2-2
Weddle, Peacock
Nov 8 v Newcastle United (h) 4-3
Peacock 2, Burbeck 2
Att: 5,386
(Middlesbrough champions)

1962-63
Aug 11 v Bolton Wanderers (h) 0-2
Att: 5,360

1963-64
Aug 14 v Mansfield Town (h) 4-0
Peacock 3, Gibson
Att: 8,300
Aug 17 v Peterborough United (a) 0-1
Att: 8,364
Jan 25 v Newcastle United (a) 3-4
Gibson 2, Peacock
Att: 10,000

1964-65
Aug 12 v Sunderland (h) 2-1
Garbett, Irvine
Att: 16,451

1965-66
Aug 10 v Newcastle United (h) 2-0
Irvine, Horsfield
Att: 12,590
Aug 14 v Newcastle United (a) 2-3
Holliday 2
Att: 15,000

1966-67
Aug 9 v FC Sparta (h) 2-0
O'Rourke, Eijkenbroeg (og)
Att: 5,765
Aug 10 v Whitby (a) 4-2
Lugg, D.Smith, Horsfield 2
Aug 13 v Scarborough (a) 2-2
Horsfield, O'Rourke
Mar 4 v Hartlepools United (a) 1-0
Chadwick
Att: 2,926

1967-68
Aug 5 v Sunderland (a) 0-1
Aug 8 v Newcastle United (h) 3-2
Hickton 3
Att: 14,708
Aug 12 v Newcastle United (a) 0-2
Att: 14,000
Apr 8 v Go Ahead Deventer (h) 1-3
Hickton
Att: 6,004
           Holland/Germany Tour
May 16 v Leeuwarden (a) 2-0
Hickton, Masson
Att: 2,000
May 18 v Bremerhaven (a) 1-0
Horsfield
Att: 1,000

1968-69
Jul 30 v Sunderland (h) 0-1
Att: 13,502
Aug 3 v Hearts (h) 4-3
Rooks, Hickton (pen), McMordie, Horsfield
Att: 7,150

1969-70
Oct 20 v SC Cambuur (h) 3-0
Mills, McIlmoyle, Hickton
Att: 4,209
Nov 11 v All-Stars XI (h) 3-4
Hickton 2, Chadwick
Att: 7,650
(Gordon Jones' Testimonial)

Nov 25 v VFR Neuess (h) 7-1
Hickton 3, Mills 3, Murray
Att: 1,177

1970-71
Aug 1 v Burnley (h) 2-2
McMordie, Maddren
Att: 8,333
Aug 5 v York City (a) 0-1
Att: 2,949
Aug 7 v Liverpool (h) 3-1
Mills 2, Laidlaw
Att: 13,120
Aug 8 v Mansfield Town (a) 0-3
Att: 4,000

1971-72
Jul 31 v Hibernian (a) 2-0
Laidlaw, Hickton
Att: 15,000
Aug 4 v Hartlepools United (a) 2-2
Mills, Allen
Att: 1,560
Aug 7 v Hibernian (h) 4-2
Hickton 3, Laidlaw
Att: 8,061
Aug 10 v Benfica (h) 1-1
Hickton
Att: 21,101

1972-73
Jul 31 v Groningen (h) 4-0
Mills 2, Hickton (pen), Smith (pen)
Att: 3,700
Aug 2 v Mansfield Town (a) 3-0
Mills, McMordie, Vincent
Aug 7 v Barnsley (a) 0-1
May 7 v England XI (h) 7-5
Hickton 3, Foggon 2, Peters (og), Mills
Att: 10,674
(Harold Shepherdson's Testimonial)

1973-74
Jul 28 v Morton (a) 2-0
Mills 2
Jul 30 v Hamilton Academical (a) 3-1
Craggs, Armstrong, Hickton
Att: 3,500
Aug 1 v Partick Thistle (a) 2-0
McMordie, Brine
Aug 11 v Newcastle United (h) 1-3
Mills
Att: 12,272
Aug 16 v Shildon (a) 4-1
McGivern, M.Smith 2, Poskett
Aug 18 v York City (a) 1-2
Mills

Aug 20 v Grimsby Town (a) 2-1
Foggon, Hickton
Att: 5,042
Mar 26 v Darlington (a) 4-0
Foggon 2, Mills, Boam
Att: 5,000
(Alan Sproates' Testimonial)
May 1 v Aldershot (a) 0-1
Att: 5,027
(Richard Walden Testimonial)
May 7 v Leeds U (h) 4-4
Mills, Foggon 3
Att: 31,643
(Billy Gates' Testimonial)
May 10 v Newcastle United (a) 3-5
Hickton, Foggon, M.Smith
Att: 27,938
(Tony Green Testimonial)
Norway Tour
May 17 v Stavanger Vikings (a) 3-1
M.Smith, Foggon, Boam
May 19 v Vard (a) 4-0
M.Smith 2, Hickton, Platt (pen)

1974-75
Jul 27 v Dunfermline Athletic (a) 1-2
Armstrong
Att: 3,000
Australia/New Zealand Tour
May 4 v Western Australia (a) 1-1
Mills
Att: 6,000
May 7 v South Australia (a) 1-1
Mills
Att: 6,000
May 11 v Queensland (a) 4-0
Maddren, Mills, Armstrong, J.Charlton
Att: 7,000
May 14 v Balgownie (a) 5-3
Murdoch 3 (2 pens), Boam, Souness
May 18 v Northern NSW (a) 8-0
Mills 2, J.Charlton 2, Armstrong, Murdoch, Brine
Att: 10,500
May 20 v Auckland (a) 5-1
Mills 3, Armstrong, Willey
May 26 v Tahiti Select XI (a) 6-0
Mills 2, Craggs, Willey, Cooper, J.Charlton

1975-76
Oct 28 v Dinamo Zagreb (h) 2-2
Spraggon (pen), Hickton (pen)
Att: 9,393
(Frank Spraggon's Testimonial)
Finnish Tour
1976-77
Aug 3 v Kuopion Palloseura (a) 2-1
Boersma, Craggs

Aug 4 v HJK Helsinki (a) 1-1
Hickton
Aug 6 v Lahden Reipas (a) 3-0
Armstrong, Boersma, Maddren

Nov 13 v Hearts (h) 3-0
Brine, Cummins, Hickton
Att: 8,000
Apr 19 v Sunderland (h) 6-1
Hickton 3, Charlton, Hedley, Cummins
Att: 10,500
(John Hickton's Testimonial)

1977-78
Aug 6 v Wrexham (a) 0-3
Att: 3,000
Aug 9 v Hearts (a) 0-1
Att: 8,000
May 9 v Scottish XI (h) 5-5
Ashcroft 3, Cummins, Armstrong (pen)
Att: 18,000
(Willie Maddren's Testimonial)

1978-79
Aug 5 v Inverness Clach'ddin (a) 4-0
Hedley 2, Armstrong (pen), McCrae (og)
Aug 7 v Aberdeen (a) 2-3
Cummins, Hedley
Aug 8 v Hearts (a) 0-3
Aug 11 v AFC Ajax (h) 1-0
Woof
Att: 9,527
Aug 16 v Huracán (h) 2-1
Woof, Ashcroft
Att: 9,672

1979-80
Aug 4 v China (h) 2-0
Armstrong (pen), Ashcroft
Att: 8,605
Oct 16 v Tulsa Roughnecks (h) 4-0
Burns 3, Proctor
Att: 4,114
Dec 12 v Army XI (a) 3-1
Hodgson, Woof 2
World Tour
May 27 v Japan XI (a) 2-1
Hodgson 2
May 29 v Argentinos Juniors (a) 4-0
Hodgson, Ashcroft, Jankovic, Woof
May 31 v China (a) 3-1
Proctor, Shearer, Hedley
Jun 3 v RCD Español (a) 1-1
Johnston
(Won 4-3 on penalties)
Jul 27 v WAC Casablanca (a) 2-2
Shearer 2
Jul 29 v Tetouan (a) 2-1
Shearer, Armstrong

1980-81
Aug 6 v Panathinaikos (a) 0-4
Att: 25,000
Aug 7 v Olympiakos (a) 2-2
Woof, Johnston
Aug 9 v Olimpija Ljubljana (h) 4-1
Armstrong, Jankovic, Johnston, Hodgson
Att: 2,339
Oct 1 v Middlesbrough XI (h) 1-1
Jankovic
Att: 7,611
(David Armstrong's Testimonial)

1981-82
Aug 11 v Japan XI (h) 0-0
Att: 4,200
Aug 17 v Shildon (a) 4-2
Shearer, Askew, Macdonald, McMahon
Aug 19 v Spennymoor United (a) 4-0
Hedley 2, Askew, Macdonald
Aug 22 v Sheffield Wednesday (a) 3-0
Macdonald, Cochrane, Holton (og)
Att: 4,139
Aug 24 v Queen of the South (a) 1-0
Nattrass (pen)
Sep 8 v Sunderland (h) 1-2
Hodgson
Att: 7,425
(Jim Platt's Testimonial)
Nov 17 v Morton (a) 1-2
Hedley
Dec 2 v Combined Services (a) 3-1
Hodgson, Ashcroft 2
Att: 2,854
Jan 23 v Sheffield Wednesday (a) 2-1
Thomson (pen), Hedley
May 20 v Cliftonville (a) 2-2
Largey (og), Armstrong
(John Platt's Testimonial)

1982-83
Aug 9 v Berwick Rangers (a) 0-0
Aug 12 v Linfield (a) 2-0
Ross, Shearer
Aug 18 v Spennymoor United (a) 4-0
Bell, Otto, Cochrane, Macdonald
Nov 16 v Newcastle United (h) 3-3
Hodgson 3
Att: 3,573
(John Craggs' Testimonial)
May 17 v England XI (h) 1-2
Sugrue
Att: 13,710
(George Hardwick/Wilf Mannion Testimonial)

1983-84
Aug 3 v Horden (a) 3-3
Martin, Angus, McMahon

Aug 8 v North Shields (a) 1-2
Gill
Aug 10 v Spennymoor United (a) 6-0
Currie 3, Hankin, Roberts, Hamilton
Aug 12 v Darlington (a) 2-0
Wood, Currie
Att: 1,623
Aug 15 v Hull City (a) 2-2
Currie 2
Aug 19 v Sunderland (a) 0-4
Att: 5,006

1984-85
Aug 2 v Motherwell (a) 2-0
Mills 2
Aug 4 v Morton (a) 1-2
Currie
Aug 7 v Hibernian (a) 0-0
Aug 14 v Sunderland (h) 0-1
Att: 2,595
Aug 18 v Newcastle United (a) 2-2
Sugrue, Gill
Att: 6,867

1985-86
Aug 3 v Lincoln City (a) 2-1
Rowell, Stephens
Att: 641
Aug 5 v Guisborough (a) 4-2
Corden, Roberts, Kernaghan, Hamilton
Aug 10 v Scarborough (a) 1-1
O'Riordan
Apr 28 v Newcastle United (h) 2-1
Duffield 2
Att: 3,500
(David Mills' Testimonial)

1987-88
Jul 21 v Norton/Stockton Ancients (a) 11-0
Kerr 4, Stephens, Slaven 2, Hamilton,
Glover 2, Kernaghan
Att: 1,500
Jul 23 v South Bank (a) 0-0
Jul 27 v Seattle Storm (h) 2-1
Kerr, Slaven
Att: 4,858
Apr 15 v Rochdale (a) 3-0
Senior, Slaven 2
Att: 843
North American Tour
Jun 3 v San Jose Earthquakes (a) 2-1
Kernaghan 2
Jun 8 v Calgary Kickers (a) 2-0
Kerr, Hamilton
Att: 2,700
Jun 11 v Seattle Storm (a) 1-2
Kernaghan
Jun 14 v Albany Capitals (a) 1-1
Burke

Swedish Tour

1988-89
Jul 30 v Saro (a) 2-1
Slaven, Brennan
Aug 1 v Munkedal (a) 4-1
Gill, Senior, Glover, Kernaghan
Aug 2 v Alingas (a) 2-0
Gill, Glover
Aug 4 v Skara (a) 4-0
Cooper, Gill, Kernaghan 2
Aug 6 v Sodravingsif (a) 3-0
Slaven, Burke, Ripley

Aug 10 v Seattle Storm (h) 3-0
Slaven, Senior 2
Att: 7,065

Aug 12 v Norton/Stockton Ancients (a) 5-1
Kernaghan 2, Hamilton, L.Tucker, Burke
Att: 1,500
Aug 17 v Hull City (a) 2-2
Ripley, Burke
Att: 1,214
Aug 20 v Shrewsbury Town (a) 1-0
Slaven
Att: 1,379

Bermudan Tour
Mar 3 v Coventry City (a) 1-2
Davenport
Mar 7 v Bermudan XI (a) 3-0
Proudlock 2, Burke

Middlesbrough legend Wilf Mannion meets the England XI before his joint testimonial match with another 'Boro great, George Hardwick.

Internationals

Appearances given here refer to caps won while with Middlesbrough. The number of caps won is shown in brackets after each players' name. The figures in brackets after results are goals scored by the player in that match. Before 1924 there was only one Ireland team, then the Republic of Ireland began separate matches. WCQ = World Cup Qualifier. WCF = World Cup Finals. ENC = Europe Nations' Cup. ‡ Cap awarded to player when Middlesbrough were in the Second Division. † Cap awarded to player when Middlesbrough were in the Third Division. *Another Middlesbrough player in same match.

ENGLAND

Armstrong, David (1)
| 31 May 1980 | Australia | Sydney | 2-1 | |

Birkett, Ralph (1)
| 19 Oct 1935 | Northern Ireland | Belfast | 3-1 | |

Bloomer, Steve (2)
| 18 Mar 1907 | *Wales | Fulham | 1-1 | |
| 6 Apr 1907 | *Scotland | Newcastle | 1-1 | (1) |

Camsell, George (9)
9 May 1929	*France‡	Paris	4-1	(2)
11 May 1929	*Belgium‡	Brussels	5-1	(4)
19 Oct 1929	*Northern Ireland	Belfast	3-0	(2)
20 Nov 1929	Wales	Chelsea	6-0	(3)
6 Dec 1934	France	Tottenham	4-1	(2)
4 Dec 1935	Germany	Tottenham	3-0	(2)
4 Apr 1936	Scotland	Wembley	1-1	(1)
6 May 1936	Austria	Vienna	1-2	(1)
9 May 1936	Belgium	Brussels	2-3	(1)

[handwritten in margin: 18 goals / 9 games / Av. 2]

Carr, Jackie (2)
| 25 Oct 1919 | Ireland | Belfast | 1-1 | |
| 5 Mar 1923 | Wales | Cardiff | 2-2 | |

Clough, Brian (2)
| 17 Oct 1959 | *Wales‡ | Cardiff | 2-1 | |
| 28 Oct 1959 | *Sweden‡ | Wembley | 2-3 | |

Common, Alf (1)
| 19 Mar 1906 | Wales | Cardiff | 1-0 | |

Elliott, George (3)
15 Feb 1913	*Ireland	Belfast	1-2	
14 Feb 1914	Ireland	Middlesbrough	0-3	
15 Mar 1920	Wales	Highbury	1-2	

Fenton, Micky (1)
| 9 Apr 1938 | *Scotland | Wembley | 0-1 | |

Hardwick, George (13)
28 Sep 1946	*Northern Ireland	Belfast	7-2	
30 Sep 1946	*Republic of Ireland	Dublin	1-0	
19 Oct 1946	*Wales	Maine Road	3-0	
27 Nov 1946	*Holland	Huddersfield	8-2	
12 Apr 1947	*Scotland	Wembley	1-1	
3 May 1947	*France	Highbury	3-0	
18 May 1947	*Switzerland	Zurich	0-1	

Above: George Hardwick leads out the Great Britain team which met the Rest of Europe in 1947. Below: Wilf Mannion (second left) clips the ball home to help Great Britain to a 6-1 victory at Hampden Park.

27 May 1947	*Portugal	Lisbon	10-0	
21 Sep 1947	*Belgium	Brussels	5-2	
18 Oct 1947	*Wales	Cardiff	3-0	
5 Nov 1947	*Northern Ireland	Goodison Park, Liverpool	2-2	
19 Nov 1947	*Sweden	Highbury	4-2	
10 Apr 1948	Scotland	Glasgow	2-0	

Holliday, Eddie (3)

17 Oct 1959	*Wales‡	Cardiff	2-1	
28 Oct 1959	*Sweden‡	Wembley	2-3	
18 Nov 1959	Northern Ireland‡	Wembley	2-1	

Mannion, Wilf (26)

28 Sep 1946	*Northern Ireland	Belfast	7-2	(3)
30 Sep 1946	*Republic of Ireland	Dublin	1-0	
19 Oct 1946	*Wales	Maine Road	3-0	(2)
27 Nov 1946	*Holland	Huddersfield	8-2	(1)
12 Apr 1947	*Scotland	Wembley	1-1	
3 May 1947	*France	Highbury	3-0	(1)
18 May 1947	*Switzerland	Zurich	0-1	
27 May 1947	*Portugal	Lisbon	10-0	
21 Sep 1947	*Belgium	Brussels	5-2	
18 Oct 1947	*Wales	Cardiff	3-0	
5 Nov 1947	*Northern Ireland	Goodison Park, Liverpool	2-2	(1)
19 Nov 1947	*Sweden	Highbury	4-2	
16 May 1948	Italy	Turin	4-0	
18 May 1949	Norway	Oslo	4-1	
22 May 1949	France	Paris	3-1	
21 Sep 1949	*Republic of Ireland	Goodison Park, Liverpool	0-2	
15 Apr 1950	WCQ Scotland	Glasgow	1-0	
14 May 1950	Portugal	Lisbon	5-3	
18 May 1950	Belgium	Brussels	4-1	(1)
25 Jun 1950	WCF Chile	Rio de Janeiro	2-0	(1)
29 Jun 1950	WCF USA	Belo Horizonte	0-1	
7 Oct 1950	Northern Ireland	Belfast	4-1	
15 Nov 1950	Wales	Sunderland	4-2	(1)
22 Nov 1950	Yugoslavia	Highbury	2-2	
14 Apr 1951	Scotland	Wembley	2-3	
3 Oct 1951	France	Highbury	2-2	

McNeil, Mick (9)

8 Oct 1960	Northern Ireland‡	Belfast	5-2	
19 Oct 1960	Luxembourg‡	Luxembourg	9-0	
26 Oct 1960	Spain‡	Wembley	4-2	
23 Nov 1960	Wales‡	Wembley	5-1	
15 Apr 1961	Scotland‡	Wembley	9-3	
10 May 1961	Mexico‡	Wembley	8-0	
21 May 1961	Portugal‡	Lisbon	1-1	
24 May 1961	Italy‡	Rome	3-2	
28 Sep 1961	WCQ Luxembourg‡	Highbury	4-1	

Pallister, Gary (2)

27 Apr 1988	Hungary‡	Budapest	0-0	
16 Nov 1988	Saudi Arabia	Riyadh	1-1	

Peacock, Alan (4)

2 Jun 1962	WCF Argentina‡	Rancagua	3-1	

361 (continued on P363)

Davidson, Stewart (1)
    9 Apr 1921 *England   Glasgow 3-1
Marshall, Jock (6)
    12 Feb 1921 Wales   Aberdeen 2-1
    26 Feb 1921 Ireland   Belfast 2-0
    9 Apr 1921 *England   Glasgow 3-1
    4 Feb 1922 Wales   Wrexham 1-2
    4 Mar 1922 Ireland   Glasgow 2-1
    8 Apr 1922 *England   Villa Park................ 1-0
Milne, Jacky (2)
    9 Apr 1938 *England   Wembley 1-0
    15 Apr 1939 *England   Glasgow 1-2
Souness, Graeme (3)
    30 Oct 1974 East Germany   Glasgow 3-0
    20 Nov 1974 ENC Spain   Glasgow 1-2
    16 Apr 1975 Sweden   Gothenburg.............. 1-1 (1)
Stewart, Jim (1)
    7 Jun 1979 Norway   Oslo 0-4
Watson, Jimmy (2)
    15 Mar 1909 Ireland   Glasgow 5-0
    3 Apr 1909 England   Crystal Palace............ 0-2
Wilson, Andy (6)
    4 Feb 1922 Wales   Wrexham 1-2
    4 Mar 1922 Ireland   Glasgow 2-1 (2)
    8 Apr 1922 *England   Villa Park................ 1-0 (1)
    3 Mar 1923 Ireland   Belfast 1-0 (1)
    16 Mar 1923 Wales   Glasgow 2-2 (2)
    14 Apr 1923 England   Glasgow 2-2 (1)

WALES

Atherton, Bob (4)
    29 Feb 1904 England   Wrexham 2-2
    12 Mar 1904 Scotland   Dundee 1-1 (1)
    21 Mar 1904 Ireland   Bangor 0-1
    8 Apr 1905 Ireland   Belfast 2-2 (1)
Davies, A (1)
    6 Mar 1905 Scotland   Wrexham 3-1
Griffiths, Tom (6)
    25 May 1933 France   Paris..................... 1-1 (1)
    4 Oct 1933 Scotland   Cardiff................... 3-2
    15 Nov 1933 England   Newcastle 2-1
    29 Sep 1934 England   Cardiff................... 0-4
    27 Mar 1935 Northern Ireland Wrexham 3-1
    5 Oct 1935 England   Cardiff................... 1-1
Harris, Bill (6)
    6 May 1954 Austria   Vienna................... 0-2
    19 May 1957 WCQ East Germany‡ Leipzig 1-2
    26 May 1957 Czechoslovakia‡   Prague................... 0-2
    25 Sep 1957 WCQ East Germany‡ Cardiff................. 4-1
    19 Oct 1957 England‡   Cardiff................... 0-4
    13 Nov 1957 Scotland‡   Hampden Park............ 1-1

7 Jun 1962	WCF Bulgaria‡	Rancagua	0-0
20 Oct 1962	Northern Ireland‡	Belfast	3-1
21 Nov 1962	*Wales‡	Wembley	4-0 (2)

Peacock, Joe (3)

9 May 1929	*France‡	Paris.....................	4-1
11 May 1929	*Belgium‡	Brussels..................	5-1
15 May 1929	Spain‡	Madrid	3-4

Pease, Billy (1)

12 Feb 1927	Wales‡	Wrexham	3-3

Pentland, Fred (5)

15 Mar 1909	Wales	City Ground, Nottingham	2-0
3 Apr 1909	Scotland	Crystal Palace............	2-0
29 May 1909	Hungary	Budapest..................	4-2
31 May 1909	Hungary	Budapest..................	8-2
1 Jun 1909	Austria	Vienna....................	8-1

Urwin, Tom (2)

21 May 1923	Sweden	Stockholm	4-2
24 May 1923	Sweden	Stockholm	3-1

Webster, Maurice (3)

5 Apr 1930	Scotland	Glasgow	5-2
10 May 1930	Germany	Berlin.....................	3-3
14 May 1930	Austria	Vienna....................	0-0

Williamson, Tim (7)

25 Feb 1905	Ireland	Middlesbrough............	1-1
11 Feb 1911	Ireland	Baseball Ground, Derby ...	2-1
13 Mar 1911	Wales	Millwall	3-0
1 Apr 1911	Scotland	Goodison Park............	1-1
11 Mar 1912	Wales	Wrexham	2-0
23 Mar 1912	Scotland	Glasgow	1-1
15 Feb 1913	*Ireland	Belfast	1-2

SCOTLAND

Aitken, Andy (3)

4 Mar 1907	Wales	Wrexham	0-1
18 Mar 1907	*England	Fulham	1-1
4 Apr 1908	England	Glasgow	1-1

Baxter, Bob (3)

9 Nov 1938	Wales	Edinburgh	3-2
7 Dec 1938	Hungary	Glasgow	3-1
15 Apr 1939	*England	Glasgow	1-2

Brown, Sandy (1)

9 Apr 1904	England	Glasgow	0-1

Bruce, Bobby (1)

29 Nov 1933	Austria	Glasgow	2-2

Connachan, Eddie (2)

29 Nov 1961	WCQ Czechoslovakia‡	Brussels..................	2-4
2 May 1962	Uruguay‡	Glasgow	2-3

Cumming, Dave (1)

9 Apr 1938	*England	Wembley	1-0

363

continued on P 362

Jones, Love (1)

11 Apr 1910	Ireland	Wrexham	4-1	

Mahoney, John (13)

6 Sep 1977	Kuwait	Wrexham	0-0	
20 Sep 1977	Kuwait	Kuwait	0-0	
12 Oct 1977	Scotland	Liverpool	0-2	
16 Nov 1977	Czechoslovakia	Prague...................	0-1	
18 Apr 1978	Iran	Tehran...................	1-0	
13 May 1978	England (Sub)	Cardiff...................	1-3	
17 May 1978	Scotland	Glasgow	1-1	
19 May 1978	*Northern Ireland	Wrexham	1-0	
2 May 1979	ENC West Germany	Wrexham	0-2	
19 May 1979	Scotland	Cardiff...................	3-0	
23 May 1979	England	Wembley	0-0	
25 May 1979	Northern Ireland	Belfast	1-1	
2 Jun 1979	ENC Malta	Valletta	2-0	

Nurse, Mel (3)

7 Nov 1962	ENC Hungary‡	Budapest.................	1-3	
21 Nov 1962	*England‡	Wembley	0-4	
20 Nov 1963	Scotland‡	Hampden Park...........	1-2	

Warren, Freddy (3)

22 Apr 1931	Northern Ireland	Wrexham	3-2	(1)
16 Nov 1932	England	Wrexham	0-0	

NORTHERN IRELAND

Braithwaite, Bobby (7)

15 Apr 1964	Wales	Swansea	3-2	
29 Apr 1964	Uruguay‡	Belfast	3-0	
3 Oct 1964	England‡	Belfast	3-4	
14 Oct 1964	Switzerland‡	Belfast	1-0	
14 Nov 1964	WCQ Switzerland‡	Lausanne	1-2	
25 Nov 1964	Scotland‡	Glasgow	2-3	
7 Apr 1965	Holland‡	Rotterdam	0-0	

Cochrane, Terry (19)

29 Nov 1978	ENC Bulgaria	Sofia	2-0	
7 Feb 1979	England	Wembley	0-4	
2 May 1979	Bulgaria	Belfast	2-0	
19 May 1979	England	Belfast	0-2	
6 Jun 1979	ENC Denmark	Copenhagen	0-4	
17 Oct 1979	ENC England	Belfast	1-5	
26 Mar 1980	WCQ Israel	Tel Aviv	0-0	
20 May 1980	England (Sub)	Wembley	1-1	(1)
23 May 1980	*Wales (Sub)	Cardiff...................	1-0	
15 Jun 1980	*Australia (Sub)	Melbourne	1-1	
28 Jun 1980	*Australia	Adelaide	2-1	
19 Nov 1980	WCQ*Portugal (Sub)	Lisbon	0-1	
25 Mar 1981	WCQ Scotland	Glasgow	1-1	
29 Apr 1981	WCQ Portugal	Belfast	1-0	
19 May 1981	Scotland	Glasgow	0-2	
3 Jun 1981	WCQ*Sweden	Stockholm	0-1	
23 Feb 1982	England (Sub)	Wembley	0-4	

Jim Platt (left) and Terry Cochrane proudly show off their international caps.

24 Mar 1982	*France	Paris	0-4
4 Jul 1982	WCF*France	Madrid	1-4

Crossan, Johnny (1)

21 Oct 1967	Scotland‡	Belfast	1-0

McMordie, Eric (21)

10 Sep 1968	Israel‡	Jaffa	3-2	
23 Oct 1968	WCQ Turkey‡	Belfast	4-1	(1)
11 Dec 1968	Turkey‡	Istanbul	3-0	
3 May 1969	England‡	Belfast	1-3	
6 May 1969	Scotland‡	Glasgow	1-1	(1)
10 May 1969	Wales‡	Belfast	0-0	
10 Sep 1969	WCQ USSR‡	Belfast	0-0	
18 Apr 1970	Scotland‡	Belfast	0-1	
21 Apr 1970	England‡	Wembley	1-3	
25 Apr 1970	Wales‡	Swansea	0-1	
3 Feb 1971	ENC Cyprus‡	Nicosia	3-0	
21 Apr 1971	ENC Cyprus‡	Belfast	5-0	
15 May 1971	England	Belfast	0-1	
18 May 1971	Scotland‡	Glasgow	1-0	
22 May 1971	Wales‡	Belfast	1-0	
13 Oct 1971	ENC USSR‡	Belfast	1-1	
16 Feb 1972	Spain‡	Hull	1-1	
20 May 1972	Scotland‡	Glasgow	0-2	
23 May 1972	England‡	Wembley	1-0	
27 May 1972	Wales‡	Wrexham	1-0	
18 Oct 1972	Bulgaria‡	Sofia	0-3	

Miller, Joe (3)

2 Feb 1929	Wales‡	Wrexham	2-2
23 Feb 1929	Scotland ‡	Belfast	3-7
19 Oct 1929	*England	Belfast	0-3

Platt, Jim (20)

24 Mar 1976	Israel (Sub)	Tel Aviv	1-1
13 May 1978	Scotland	Glasgow	1-1
16 May 1978	England	Wembley	0-1
19 May 1978	*Wales	Wrexham	0-1
16 May 1980	Scotland	Belfast	1-0
20 May 1980	England	Wembley	1-1
23 May 1980	*Wales	Cardiff	1-0
11 Jun 1980	Australia	Sydney	2-1
15 Jun 1980	*Australia	Melbourne	1-1
18 Jun 1980	*Australia	Adelaide	2-1
15 Oct 1980	WCQ Sweden	Belfast	3-0
19 Nov 1980	WCQ *Portugal	Lisbon	0-1
24 Mar 1982	*France	Paris	0-4
28 Apr 1982	Scotland	Belfast	1-1
27 May 1982	Wales (Sub)	Wrexham	0-3
11 Jul 1982	WCF Austria	Madrid	2-2
13 Oct 1982	ENC Austria‡	Vienna	0-2
17 Nov 1982	West Germany‡	Belfast	1-0
15 Dec 1982	Albania‡	Tiranë	0-0
30 Mar 1983	Turkey‡	Belfast	2-1

REPUBLIC OF IRELAND

Desmond, Peter (4)

8 Sep 1949	WCQ*Finland	Dublin	3-0
21 Sep 1949	*England	Goodison Park	2-0
9 Oct 1949	WCQ Finland	Helsinki	1-1
13 Nov 1949	Sweden	Dublin	1-3

Fitzsimons, Arthur (25)

8 Sep 1949	WCQ*Finland	Dublin	3-0	
10 May 1950	Belgium	Brussels	1-5	
17 Oct 1951	West Germany	Dublin	3-2	
4 May 1952	West Germany	Cologne	0-3	
7 May 1952	Austria	Vienna	0-6	
1 Jun 1952	Spain	Madrid	0-6	
16 Nov 1952	France	Dublin	1-1	
25 Mar 1953	Austria	Dublin	4-0	
4 Oct 1953	WCQ France	Dublin	3-5	
28 Oct 1953	Luxembourg	Dublin	4-0	(2)
25 Nov 1953	WCQ France	Paris	0-1	
1 May 1955	Holland‡	Dublin	1-0	
25 May 1955	Norway‡	Oslo	3-1	
28 May 1955	West Germany‡	Hamburg	1-2	
19 Oct 1955	Yugoslavia‡	Dublin	1-4	(1)
27 Nov 1955	Spain‡	Dublin	2-2	
10 May 1956	Holland‡	Rotterdam	4-1	
3 Oct 1956	WCQ Denmark‡	Dublin	2-1	
25 Nov 1956	West Germany‡	Dublin	3-0	
8 May 1957	WCQ England	Wembley	1-5	
19 May 1957	WCQ England‡	Dublin	1-1	
2 Oct 1957	WCQ Denmark‡	Copenhagen	2-0	
11 May 1958	Poland‡	Katowice	2-2	
14 May 1958	Austria‡	Vienna	1-3	
5 Oct 1958	Poland‡	Dublin	2-2	

Hartnett, Jimmy (2)

12 Jun 1949	Spain	Dublin	1-4
7 Mar 1954	WCQ Luxembourg	Luxembourg	0-1

UNDER-23 INTERNATIONALS
ENGLAND

Armstrong, David (4)

19 Nov 1974	Portugal	Lisbon	3-2
21 Jan 1975	Wales	Wrexham	2-0
28 Oct 1975	*Czechoslovakia	Selhurst Park	1-1
18 Nov 1975	*Portugal	Selhurst Park	2-0

Clough, Brian (3)

26 Feb 1957	Scotland‡	Glasgow	1-1	
19 May 1957	Bulgaria‡	Sofia	1-2	(1)
23 Apr 1958	Wales‡	Wrexham	1-2	(1)

Holliday, Eddie (5)

23 Sep 1959	Hungary‡	Anfield, Liverpool	0-1
16 Mar 1960	*Holland‡	Hillsborough, Sheffield	5-2

15 May 1960	*East Germany‡	Berlin.....................	4-1	(2)
18 May 1960	*Poland‡	Warsaw...................	3-2	
22 May 1960	Israel‡	Tel Aviv	0-4	

Jones, Gordon (9)

9 Nov 1961	Israel‡	Elland Road, Leeds	7-1	
29 Nov 1961	Holland‡	Rotterdam	5-2	
28 Feb 1962	Scotland‡	Aberdeen	4-2	
2 May 1962	Turkey‡	Southampton	4-1	
7 Nov 1962	*Belgium‡	Plymouth	6-1	
28 Nov 1962	*Greece‡	St Andrew's, Birmingham	5-0	
21 Mar 1963	Yugoslavia‡	Manchester	0-0	
13 Nov 1963	Wales‡	Bristol	1-1	
27 Nov 1963	West Germany‡	Liverpool	4-1	

McNeil, Mick (9)

11 Nov 1959	France‡	Sunderland	2-0	
16 Mar 1960	*Holland‡	Hillsborough..............	5-2	
15 May 1960	*East Germany‡	Berlin.....................	4-1	
18 May 1960	*Poland‡	Warsaw...................	3-2	
22 May 1960	*Israel‡	Tel Aviv	0-4	
2 Nov 1960	Italy‡	Newcastle.................	1-1	
28 Feb 1962	Scotland‡	Aberdeen	4-2	
7 Nov 1962	*Belgium‡	Plymouth	6-1	
28 Nov 1962	*Greece‡	St Andrew's, Birmingham	5-0	

Maddren, Willie (5)

7 Mar 1973	Czechoslovakia‡	Villa Park.................	1-0	
13 Nov 1973	Denmark‡	Portsmouth	1-1	
13 Mar 1974	*Scotland‡	Newcastle	2-1	
15 May 1974	*Yugoslavia (Sub)‡	Zrenjanin	0-1	
19 May 1974	*France‡	Valence	2-2	

Mills, David (8)

| 13 Mar 1974 | *Scotland‡ | Newcastle .... | 2-1 | (1) |
| 11 May 1974 | Turkey‡ | Ankara .... | 0-0 | |

(abandoned at half-time, rain)

15 May 1974	*Yugoslavia‡	Zrenjanin	0-1	
19 May 1974	*France‡	Valence	2-2	
29 Oct 1974	Czechoslovakia	Selhurst Park	3-1	(1)
28 Oct 1975	*Czechoslovakia	Trnava....................	1-1	
18 Nov 1975	Portugal (Sub)	Selhurst Park	2-0	(1)
10 Mar 1976	Hungary (Sub)	Budapest..................	0-3	

O'Rourke, John (1)

| 7 Jun 1967 | Turkey† | Ankara .... | 3-0 | (1) |

SCOTLAND

Gibson, Ian (2)

| 4 Dec 1963 | Wales‡ | Wrexham .... | 1-3 | |
| 24 May 1964 | France‡ | Nantes.................... | 2-0 | |

Souness, Graeme (2)

| 13 Mar 1974 | *England‡ | Newcastle .... | 0-2 | |
| 18 Feb 1976 | Holland | Breda..................... | 0-2 | |

Willie Maddren (left) and Ian Gibson (right) were capped by England and Scotland Under-23s respectively.

Two men with Middlesbrough connections, who made major contributions to England winning the World Cup in 1966. Harold Shepherdson (left) was trainer to the team. Nobby Stiles (right), who was then with Manchester United, gave a great display in midfield when West Germany were beaten in the Final.

NORTHERN IRELAND

McMordie, Eric (1)

22 Feb 1967 Wales‡   Belfast 2-1

(abandoned after 73 minutes, waterlogged pitch)

McNeill, Allan (1)

20 Mar 1968 Wales‡   Cardiff.................... 1-0

FOOTBALL LEAGUE REPRESENTATIVES

Birkett, Ralph

| 30 Oct 1935 | *Scottish League | Glasgow .... | 2-2 | |
| 23 Sep 1936 | Irish League | Belfast .... | 2-3 | |

Blenkinsopp, Tom

| 20 Sep 1948 | *Irish League | Anfield .... | 5-1 | |

Camsell, George

| 30 Oct 1935 | *Scottish League | Ibrox .... | 2-2 | (1) |

Carr, Jacky

4 Oct 1922	Irish League	Bolton	5-1	
17 Feb 1923	Scottish League	Newcastle	2-1	
21 Sep 1927	Irish League	Newcastle	9-1	

Clough, Brian

| 8 Oct 1958 | Scottish League | Ibrox .... | 1-1 | (1) |
| 23 Sep 1959 | Irish League | Windsor Park, Belfast ..... | 5-0 | (5) |

Common, Alf

| 24 Mar 1906 | Scottish League | Chelsea .... | 6-2 | (1) |

Elliott, George

9 Feb 1914	Southern League	Millwall	3-1	
24 Mar 1915	Scottish League	Glasgow	4-0	(1)
5 Apr 1919	Scottish League	Glasgow	2-3	(1)

Hardwick, George

19 Feb 1947	*Irish League	Goodison Park	4-2	
12 Mar 1947	*Scottish League	Glasgow	3-1	
17 Mar 1948	*Scottish League	Newcastle	1-1	

Holliday, Eddie

| 4 Nov 1959 | League of Ireland | Ewood Park .... | 2-0 | |

Mannion, Wilf

19 Feb 1947	*Irish League	Goodison Park	4-2	
12 Mar 1947	*Scottish League	Glasgow	3-1	(2)
17 Mar 1948	*Scottish League	Newcastle	1-1	
23 Mar 1949	Scottish League	Ibrox	3-0	
15 Feb 1950	League of Ireland	Molineux	7-0	(3)
22 Mar 1950	Scottish League	Middlesbrough	3-1	
4 Apr 1951	League of Ireland	Dublin....................	1-0	

McNeil, Mick

| 22 Mar 1961 | Scottish League | Ibrox .... | 2-3 | |
| 10 Oct 1961 | League of Ireland | Goodison Park .... | 9-1 | |

Robinson, Dicky

30 Apr 1947	League of Ireland	Dublin....................	3-1	
22 Oct 1947	Irish League	Windsor Park, Belfast	4-3	
20 Sep 1948	*Irish League	Anfield	5-1	

| 29 Nov 1950 | Scottish League | Ibrox .... | 0-1 |
| 10 Oct 1951 | League of Ireland | Goodison .... | 9-1 |

Webster, Maurice

| 24 Sep 1930 | Irish League | Belfast .... | 2-2 |

Whitaker, Bill

| 26 Apr 1950 | Irish League | Belfast .... | 3-1 |

Williamson, Tim

12 Oct 1907	Irish League	Sunderland	6-3
8 Oct 1910	Irish League	Belfast	6-2
17 Feb 1912	Scottish League	Middlesbrough	2-0
30 Sep 1912	Southern League	Manchester	2-1
23 Oct 1912	Irish League	Belfast	0-0

WARTIME INTERNATIONALS

No caps were awarded to players who appeared for their countries in the unofficial wartime and Victory internationals.

ENGLAND

Fenton, Micky (1)

| 20 Oct 1945 | Wales | West Bromwich .... | 0-1 |

Hardwick, George (17)

16 Apr 1941	Wales	City Ground, Nottingham	4-1
24 Oct 1942	Wales	Molineux	1-2
17 Apr 1943	Scotland	Hampden Park............	4-0
8 May 1943	Wales	Cardiff....................	1-1
25 Sep 1943	Wales	Wembley	8-3
16 Oct 1943	Scotland	Manchester	8-0
19 Feb 1944	Scotland	Wembley	6-2
16 Sep 1944	Wales	Anfield	2-2
14 Oct 1944	*Scotland	Wembley	6-2
3 Feb 1945	Scotland	Villa Park.................	3-2
14 Apr 1945	Scotland	Hampden Park............	6-1
5 May 1945	Wales	Cardiff....................	3-2
26 May 1945	France	Wembley	2-2
19 Jan 1946	Belgium	Wembley	2-0
13 Apr 1946	Scotland	Hampden Park............	0-1
11 May 1946	Switzerland	Chelsea	4-1
19 May 1946	France	Paris......................	1-2

Mannion, Wilf (4)

8 Feb 1941	*Scotland	Newcastle	2-3
3 May 1941	Scotland	Hampden Park............	3-1
4 Oct 1941	Scotland	Wembley	2-0
17 Jan 1942	Scotland	Wembley	3-0

SCOTLAND

Baxter, Bob (4)

2 Dec 1939	England	Newcastle	1-2
11 May 1940	§England	Hampden Park............	1-1
22 Apr 1944	England	Hampden Park............	2-3
14 Oct 1944	*England	Wembley	2-6

Cumming, Dave (1)
14 Oct 1944 *England   Wembley 2-6
Milne, Jacky (1)
8 Feb 1941 *England   Newcastle 3-2
§Listed as a Hearts player

ENGLAND TRIAL GAMES

Birkett, Ralph
25 Mar 1936 *Possibles v Probables   Old Trafford 0-3
Camsell, George
17 Jan 1927 *Rest v England   Stamford Bridge 3-7 (1)
7 Feb 1927 *Rest v England   Bolton 3-2 (2)
23 Jan 1928 *Rest v England   West Bromwich 1-5
8 Feb 1928 England v Rest   Middlesbrough 3-8 (1)
12 Mar 1930 *England v Rest   Anfield 1-6
Carr, Jackie
23 Jan 1928 *England v Rest   West Bromwich 5-1
8 Feb 1928 England v Rest   Middlesbrough 3-8
12 Feb 1923 England v South   Millwall 1-0
Cunliffe, Arthur
25 Mar 1936 *Possibles v Probables   Old Trafford 0-3
McNeil, Mick
5 May 1961 England v Young England   Stamford Bridge 1-1
Pease, Billy
17 Jan 1927 *England v Rest   Stamford Bridge 7-3
7 Feb 1927 *England v Rest   Bolton 2-3
Stuart, Bobby
25 Mar 1936 *Possibles v Probables   Old Trafford 0-3
13 Oct 1937 Possibles v Probables   Goodison Park 1-1
Webster, Maurice
12 Mar 1930 *Rest v England   Anfield 6-1
Williams, Owen
11 Feb 1924 Rest v England   Tottenham 0-1
Williamson, Tim
23 Jan 1911 Whites v Stripes   Tottenham 4-1
The first named side is the team the player turned out for.

ENGLAND 'B' PLAYERS

Armstrong, David (2)
26 Mar 1980 Spain   Roker Park, Sunderland ... 1-0
14 Oct 1980 USA   Old Trafford, Manchester 1-0
Clough, Brian(1)
6 Feb 1957 Scotland   St Andrew's, Birmingham   4-1 (1)
Mannion, Wilf (2)
15 May 1949 Finland   Helsinki 4-0
22 Feb 1950 Holland   St James' Park, Newcastle 1-0

Two great Middlesbrough servants from different eras. Wilf Mannion (right), arguably 'Boro's greatest-ever player. David Armstrong (left) made a tremendous contribution in later years. Both men were capped by England.

Mowbray, Tony (2)
  16 May 1989 *Switzerland   Winterthur 2-0
  22 May 1989 *Norway   Stavanger 1-0
Pallister, Gary (3)
  16 May 1989 *Switzerland   Winterthur 2-0
  19 May 1989 Iceland   Reykjavik 2-0
  22 May 1989 *Norway (Sub)   Stavanger 1-0

Under 21 Internationals
England

Cooper, Colin (8)
  13 Apr 1988 EC France   Besancon 2-4
  5 Jun 1988   Mexico   Toulon 2-1
  7 Jun 1988   *Russia   Toulon 1-0
  9 Jun 1988   Morocco   Toulon 1-0
  12 Jun 1988 *France   Toulon 2-4
  13 Sep 1988 *Denmark   Vicarage Road, Watford . . . 0-0
  18 Oct 1988 EC Sweden   Highfield Road, Coventry   1-1
  7 Feb 1989   *Greece   Patras 0-1
Hodgson, David (6)
  9 Sep 1980   *Norway   The Dell, Southampton. . . . 3-0
  14 Oct 1980 EC Romania (Sub)   Ploieşti. 0-4
  18 Nov 1980 EC Switzerland   Ipswich 5-0 (1)
  25 Feb 1981 *Republic of Ireland Anfield, Liverpool. 1-0
  17 Mar 1982 EC Poland   Warsaw. 2-1 (1)
  21 Sep 1982 EC West Germany   Bramall Lane, Sheffield. . . . 3-1
Johnston, Craig (2)
  25 Feb 1981 *Republic of Ireland Anfield, Liverpool. 1-0
  9 Sep 1980   *Norway   The Dell, Southampton. . . . 3-0
Proctor, Mark (2)
  25 Feb 1981 *Republic of Ireland (Sub) Anfield, Liverpool. 1-0
  31 May 1981 EC Switzerland   Neuenburg 0-0
Ripley, Stuart (7)
  7 Jun 1988   *Russia   Toulon 0-0
  12 Jun 1988 *France (Sub)   Toulon 2-4
  13 Sep 1988 *Denmark (Sub)   Vicarage Road, Watford . . . 0-0
  18 Oct 1988 EC Sweden (Sub)   Highfield Road, Coventry   1-1
  7 Feb 1989   *Greece   Patras 0-1
  7 Mar 1989   EC Albania   Shkoder 2-1 (1)
  25 Apr 1989 EC Albania   Portman Road, Ipswich . . . 2-0

Scotland

Stewart, Jim (1)
  28 Nov 1978 Portugal   Lisbon 3-0

FA Tour to South Africa (Test Matches)

Fenton, Micky
  27 May 1939 Western Province   6-1 (2)
  10 Jun 1939 South Africa   6-1 (2)
  1 Jul 1939   South Africa   Johannesburg 2-1

Three men who won England honours whilst with 'Boro. Above: Craig Johnston shows off his Under-21 cap. Below: Stuart Ripley (left) and Mark Proctor (right) also appeared in the Under-21 side.

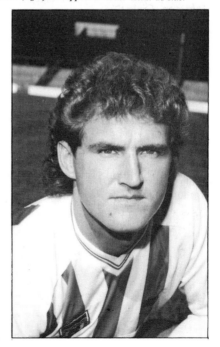

Miscellaneous Representative Games Involving Middlesbrough Players

Birrell, Billy
22 Mar 1922 Home Scots v Anglo Scots Glasgow 1-1
20 Mar 1923 Home Scots v Anglo Scots Glasgow 1-1
Carr, Jackie
8 Mar 1922 Whites v Reds Old Trafford 1-1
(Benefit for John Robson's dependants)
Clough, Brian
30 Oct 1957 FA XI v Army 6-3 (5)
Griffiths, Tom
11 May 1935 Wales XI v Ireland XI Wrexham 10-2
Jennings, Jack
28 Sep 1931 FA XI v Sheffield XI Hillsborough 0-1
(Marsden Benefit Fund)
McMordie, A
Oct 1974 Sheffield W v England XI Hillsborough 5-0
(Testimonial for late Eric Taylor)
Maddren, Willie
Oct 1974 Sheffield W v England XI Hillsborough 5-0
(Testimonial for late Eric Taylor)
Mannion, Wilf
11 Oct 1941 Football Lge v Scottish Lge Bloomfield Road 3-2 (1)
19 May 1948 England XI v Switzerland 'B' Zurich 5-1
18 May 1950 England 'A' v Belgium Brussels 4-1 (2)
Smith, Jock
13 Jan 1928 Home Scots v Anglo Scots Firhill Park, Glasgow 1-1
Webster, Maurice
27 Apr 1925 Lancashire v Yorkshire Turf Moor 3-4
First team is the team the listed player turned out for

Youth Internationals

England	Scotland

Stephen Bell 1983   **Tony McAndrew** 1974
Steve Fenton 1969
Arthur Horsfield 1964
Gordon Jones 1960
Des McPartland 1966
Len Mole 1964
Alan Peacock 1956

Players who have scored

50 or more Goals

Listed here are all players who have scored 50 or more goals in their Middlesbrough playing career. Only goals scored in the Football League, FA Cup and League/Littlewoods Cup are included in this analysis.

Player	Pos	Seasons	Lge	FA	LC	Total
George Camsell	CF	1925-39	325	20	0	345
George Elliott	CF	1909-25	203	10	0	213
Brian Clough	CF	1955-61	197	5	2	204
John Hickton	F	1966-77	159	13	13	185
Micky Fenton	F	1932-50	147	15	0	162
Alan Peacock	CF	1955-64	125	8	8	141
Wilf Mannion	IF	1936-54	99	11	0	110
David Mills	IF	1969-85	90	10	8	108
Billy Pease	OR	1926-33	99	3	0	102
Lindy Delapenha	F	1949-58	90	3	0	93
Johnny Spuhler	CF	1946-54	69	12	0	81
Jackie Carr	IF	1910-30	75	6	0	81
David Armstrong	OL	1970-81	59	8	6	73
Bill Harris	WH	1953-65	69	2	1	72
Bobby Bruce	IF	1927-35	64	7	0	71
Bernie Slaven*	F	1985-89	61	4	2	67
Alf Common	CF	1905-10	58	7	0	65
Billy Birrell	IF	1920-28	59	4	0	63
Steve Bloomer	IF	1905-09	59	3	0	62
Andy Wilson	CF	1914-24	56	1	0	57
Arthur Horsfield	F	1963-69	51	5	0	56
Sammy Cail	IF	1906-13	52	3	0	55
Benny Yorston	F	1933-39	54	0	0	54
Geoff Walker	OL	1946-55	50	3	0	53
Arthur Fitzsimons	IF	1949-59	49	2	0	51
Freddy Warren	OL	1929-36	49	1	0	50

*Still with the club at the end of 1988-9 season.

Leading
Goalscorers
(1899-1989)

Listed below are the club's leading goalscorers. League, FA Cup and Football League/ Littlewoods' Cup games are included in the analysis. *First Division leading goalscorer. †Second Division leading goalscorer.

Season	Leading goalscorer	Goals	Runner-up	Goals
Division Two				
1899-1900	Eddie Pugh	7	Tom Lamb	6
1900-01	Sandy Robertson	16	Willie Wardrope	14
1901-02	Jack Brearley	23	Joe Cassidy	16
Division One				
1902-03	Sandy Robertson	8	Joe Cassidy	7
1903-04	Alex Brown	17	Joe Cassidy	12
1904-05	Harry Astley	5	Bob Atherton	4
			Alf Common	4
1905-06	Alf Common	24	Charlie Hewitt	11
1906-07	Steve Bloomer	20	Alf Common	13
1907-08	Steve Bloomer	12	Alf Common	9
	Sammy Cail	12	Freddy Wilcox	9
1908-09	John Hall	18	Steve Bloomer	14
1909-10	John Hall	12	Steve Bloomer	10
1910-11	George Elliott	10	Sammy Cail	9
1911-12	George Elliott	19	Sammy Cail	13
1912-13	George Elliott	25	Jackie Carr	19
1913-14	George Elliott	*31	Walter Tinsley	19
1914-15	Walter Tinsley	26	George Elliott	17
1919-20	George Elliott	34	Reuben Butler	11
1920-21	George Elliott	26	Alonzo Poulton	5
1921-22	Andy Wilson	32	George Carr	15
1922-23	George Elliott	23	Andy Wilson	12
1923-24	Andy Wilson	8	George Elliott	7
Division Two				
1924-25	Ian Dickson	7	George Elliott	5
	Owen Williams	7		
1925-26	Jimmy McClelland	38	Billy Birrell	18
1926-27	George Camsell	†63	Billy Pease	25
(59 League goals — Division Two record)				
Division One				
1927-28	George Camsell	37	Billy Pease	19
Division Two				
1928-29	George Camsell	33	Billy Pease	28
Division One				
1929-30	George Camsell	31	Bobby Bruce	16
1930-31	George Camsell	32	Freddy Warren	19
1931-32	George Camsell	20	Bobby Bruce	13
1932-33	George Camsell	18	Harold Blackmore	12
1933-34	George Camsell	24	Freddy Warren	9
1934-35	George Camsell	14	Ernie Coleman	12
1935-36	George Camsell	32	Ralph Birkett	22
1936-37	Micky Fenton	22	George Camsell	18
1937-38	Micky Fenton	26	Tom Cochrane	10
			George Camsell	10
1938-39	Micky Fenton	35	Wilf Mannion	14

Season	Leading goalscorer	Goals	Runner-up	Goals
1946-47	Wilf Mannion	23	Johnny Spuhler	14
	Micky Fenton	23		
1947-48	Micky Fenton	29	Cec McCormack	16
1948-49	Micky Fenton	12	Johnny Spuhler	7
1949-50	Peter McKennan	16	Wilf Mannion	7
	Alex McCrae	16	Geoff Walker	7
1950-51	Alex McCrae	21	Wilf Mannion	13
1951-52	Lindy Delapenha	17	Neil Mochan	12
1952-53	Wilf Mannion	18	Arthur Fitzsimons	12
1953-54	Lindy Delapenha	18	Wilf Mannion	10

Division Two

Season	Leading goalscorer	Goals	Runner-up	Goals
1954-55	Charlie Wayman	17	Joe Scott	16
1955-56	Lindy Delapenha	18	Charlie Wayman	16
1956-57	Brian Clough	40	Derek McLean	10
1957-58	Brian Clough	42	Alan Peacock	17
1958-59	Brian Clough	43	Alan Peacock	19
1959-60	Brian Clough	40	Alan Peacock	13
1960-61	Brian Clough	36	Alan Peacock	16
1961-62	Alan Peacock	32	Bill Harris	15
1962-63	Alan Peacock	33	Arthur Kaye	15
1963-64	Ian Gibson	14	Bill Harris	12
1964-65	Jim Irvine	24	Ian Gibson	9
1965-66	Jim Irvine	17	Dicky Rooks	8

Division Three

Season	Leading goalscorer	Goals	Runner-up	Goals
1966-67	John O'Rourke	30	Arthur Horsfield	23

Division Two

Season	Leading goalscorer	Goals	Runner-up	Goals
1967-68	John Hickton	29	John O'Rourke	12
1968-69	John Hickton	18	Derrick Downing	9
1969-70	John Hickton	28	Joe Laidlaw	12
1970-71	John Hickton	27	Hugh McIlmoyle	15
1971-72	John Hickton	16	David Mills	9
1972-73	John Hickton	15	Alan Foggon	7
			David Mills	7
1973-74	Alan Foggon	20	David Mills	12

Division One

Season	Leading goalscorer	Goals	Runner-up	Goals
1974-75	Alan Foggon	18	David Mills	11
1975-76	John Hickton	13	David Mills	12
1976-77	David Mills	18	David Armstrong	12
1977-78	David Mills	16	David Armstrong	9
1978-79	Micky Burns	14	David Armstrong	11
1979-80	David Armstrong	14	Micky Burns	10
1980-81	Bosco Jankovic	13	Craig Johnston	10
1981-82	Heine Otto	5	David Shearer	4
	Billy Ashcroft	5	Tony McAndrew	4
	Bobby Thomson	5		

Division Two

Season	Leading goalscorer	Goals	Runner-up	Goals
1982-83	David Shearer	13	Heine Otto	11
1983-84	David Currie	15	Heine Otto	8
1984-85	David Mills	14	David Currie	11
1985-86	Gary Rowell	12	Bernie Slaven	8

Division Three

Season	Leading goalscorer	Goals	Runner-up	Goals
1986-87	Bernie Slaven	21	Archie Stephens	17
1987-88	Bernie Slaven	22	Stuart Ripley	9

Division One

Season	Leading goalscorer	Goals	Runner-up	Goals
1988-89	Bernie Slaven	16	Mark Burke	5

Middlesbrough players who have made

200 or more appearances

Player	Pos	Seasons	League	FA Cup	FL Cup	Total
Tim Williamson	GK	1901-23	563	39	0	602
Gordon Jones	FB	1960-73	457/5	40	26	523/5
John Craggs	FB	1971-82	408/1	33	31	472/1
Jim Platt	GK	1971-83	401	34	33	468
John Hickton	F	1966-77	395/20	37	26/4	458/24
George Camsell	CF	1925-39	418	35	0	453
Jackie Carr	IF	1910-30	421	28	0	449
Dicky Robinson	FB	1946-59	390	26	0	416
David Armstrong	OL	1970-81	357/2	29	27/1	413/3
Stuart Boam	CH	1971-79	322	29	27	378
Bill Harris	WH	1953-65	360	14	4	378
Wilf Mannion	IF	1936-54	341	27	11	368
George Elliott	CF	1909-25	344	21	0	365
David Mills	IF	1969-85	309/19	29	23/1	361/20
Tony McAndrew	D	1973-86	311/2	23/1	15/2	349/5
Willie Maddren	D	1968-77	293/3	23	24	340/3
Rolando Ugolini	GK	1948-56	320	15	0	335
Ronnie Dicks	WH	1947-58	316	18	0	334
Billy Forrest	HB	1929-39	307	26	1	333
Bill Gates	D	1961-74	277/6	26/2	18	321/8
Frank Spraggon	WH	1963-76	277/3	23	18/1	318/4
Harry Bell	WH	1946-55	290	25	0	315
Tony Mowbray*	D	1982-89	260/3	17	16/1	293/4
Maurice Webster	CH	1920-34	262	19	0	281
Billy Brown	FB	1931-46	256	18	0	274
Lindy Delapenha	F	1949-58	260	10	0	270
Micky Fenton	F	1932-50	240	29	0	269
Bobby Stuart	FB	1931-48	247	21	0	268
Bob Baxter	CH	1932-39	247	19	0	266
Jimmy Mathieson	GK	1926-33	245	19	0	264
Eric McMordie	IF	1965-74	231/10	20/1	11	262/11
Geoff Walker	OL	1946-55	240	19	3	259

John Craggs

Jim Platt

Bobby Bruce	IF	1927-35	237	16	0	253
Jimmy Gordon	WH	1946-54	231	22	0	253
Gary Hamilton*	D	1981-89	217/12	14	13	244/12
Sam Aitken	WH	1903-10	227	15	0	242
Johnny Spuhler	CF	1946-54	216	25	0	241
Billy Pease	OR	1926-33	221	17	0	238
Alan Peacock	CF	1955-64	218	13	7	238
Billy Birrell	IF	1920-28	225	10	0	235
Arthur Fitzsimons	IF	1949-59	223	8	2	231
Ray Yeoman	WH	1958-63	210	10	7	227
Brian Clough	CF	1955-61	213	8	1	222
Stewart Davidson	RH	1913-23	208	8	0	216
Irving Nattrass	FB	1979-86	186/5	18	10/1	214/6
Billy Horner	WH	1960-69	184/3	17	12/1	213/4
Willie Whigham	GK	1966-72	187	17	6	210
Jack Jennings	FB	1929-37	195	10	0	205
Andy Davidson	LH	1900-06	181	20	0	201
Derrick Downing	WF	1965-72	173/10	22/1	5	200/11

Still with the club at the end of 1988-9 season.

Middlesbrough Players'
Dismissals
(1899-1989)

League

Date	Player		Opponent
20 Mar 1915	Andy Wilson	(h)	Liverpool
17 Sep 1921	Andy Wilson	(h)	Tottenham Hotspur
7 Jan 1928	Jimmy McClelland	(a)	Everton
1 Nov 1930	John Holliday	(a)	Sunderland
29 Dec 1930	Freddy Warren	(a)	Sheffield Wednesday
7 Dec 1946	Dave Cumming	(h)	Arsenal
1 Dec 1951	Harry Bell	(h)	Sunderland
11 Nov 1961	Arthur Kaye	(a)	Sunderland
13 Oct 1962	Bryan Orritt	(h)	Swansea Town
7 Mar 1964	Jim Townsend	(a)	Sunderland
31 Mar 1964	Don Ratcliffe	(a)	Huddersfield Town
19 Apr 1965	Jim Irvine	(h)	Leyton Orient
27 Mar 1965	Don Ratcliffe	(h)	Derby County
3 Feb 1968	Bill Gates	(h)	Hull City
14 Aug 1968	John Hickton	(a)	Norwich City
14 Aug 1968	Eric McMordie	(a)	Norwich City
7 Sep 1968	Brian Myton*	(a)	Cardiff City
3 Apr 1972	John Vincent	(a)	Blackpool
23 Oct 1973	Graeme Souness	(a)	Carlisle United
22 Mar 1975	Terry Cooper	(a)	Chelsea
26 Mar 1977	Terry Cooper	(a)	Newcastle United
18 Mar 1978	David Mills	(a)	Leeds United
27 Oct 1978	Billy Ashcroft	(a)	Aston Villa
29 Dec 1979	Terry Cochrane	(a)	Crystal Palace
2 Apr 1980	Tony McAndrew	(a)	Leeds United
12 Nov 1980	John Craggs	(a)	Leeds United
22 Nov 1980	Tony McAndrew	(h)	Wolverhampton Wanderers
17 Jan 1981	David Hodgson	(a)	Manchester City
28 Sep 1982	Ray Hankin	(h)	Grimsby Town
20 Nov 1982	Paul Ward	(a)	Leeds United
5 Apr 1983	Paul Sugrue	(a)	Leicester City
12 Nov 1983	Tony Mowbray	(a)	Derby County
12 Nov 1983	David Currie	(a)	Derby County
7 May 1984	Mick Kennedy	(a)	Brighton & HA
27 Oct 1984	Tony Mowbray	(a)	Leeds United
17 Nov 1984	David Currie	(h)	Blackburn Rovers
11 May 1985	Gary Hamilton	(a)	Shrewsbury Town
11 May 1985	Peter Beagrie	(a)	Shrewsbury Town
22 Oct 1985	Archie Stephens	(a)	Sunderland
3 May 1986	Gary Pallister	(a)	Shrewsbury Town

7 Mar 1987	David Hodgson	(h)	Bristol City
2 Nov 1987	Gary Parkinson	(a)	Plymouth Argyle
28 Dec 1987	Stuart Ripley	(a)	Leeds United
14 Jan 1989	Peter Davenport	(a)	Southampton

FA Cup

16 Jan 1909	Jimmy Watson	(a)	Preston North End
29 Feb 1936	Ernie Coleman	(a)	Grimsby Town
3 Jan 1976	Phil Boersma	(h)	Bury

League Cup

| 27 Oct 1981 | Bobby Thomson | (a) | Plymouth Argyle |
| 18 Aug 1987 | Dean Glover | (a) | Sunderland |

Friendlies

| 31 Jul 1972 | John Hickton | (h) | Groningen |
| 7 Aug 1980 | Billy Ashcroft | (h) | Olympiakos |

*Also Players' League Debut

Billy Ashcroft

Tony McAndrew

Four of 'Boro's leading substitutes: Above; Terry Cochrane. Opposite: David Currie. Below: (left) Mark Burke and (right) Gary Hamilton.

The Substitutes

SUBSTITUTES were first allowed in Football League games from 1965-6 onwards but, during that first season, substitutions were permitted only for injured players. It was originally feared that the trend would spoil the game but the passing of time has proved its worth.

Bryan Orritt holds the distinction of being Middlesbrough's first 'named' substitute for a League match, on 21 August 1965 against Manchester City at Ayresome Park. He was also the first Middlesbrough player to take the field as a substitute when he replaced injured full-back Neville Chapman at Deepdale on 11 September 1965, against Preston North End, the substitution being timed at 30 minutes into the game.

Three players have appeared for the club only as substitute. The first was Pat Lynch, who substituted for David Mills after 60 minutes at Loftus Road against Queen's Park Rangers on 18 March 1972. The other was Malcolm Poskett, who replaced Malcolm Smith after 78 minutes against Hull City at Ayresome Park on 13 October 1973. Poskett was released by Jack Charlton at the end of the season. He went on to become a prolific goalscorer with Hartlepool, Brighton, Watford and Carlisle. Alan Walsh made three substitute appearances in a Middlesbrough shirt during the 1977-8 season, before his transfer to Darlington where he became that club's all-time record goalscorer.

There have been instances where players have been named as substitute for League games, but never made any first-team appearances for the club. For example, Michael Hill wore the number-12 shirt for the home game against Portsmouth on 28 October 1967 and Frank Harrison at Stamford Bridge against Chelsea on 14 May 1983. Neither made it on to the field for 'Boro.

In 1986-7, two substitutes per game were permitted in FA Cup games. The following season this was extended to Football League and other matches. The second substitute usually wears the number-14 shirt.

Listed below are all players who have made ten or more substitute appearances for the Middlesbrough club.

Player	Pos	Seasons	League	FA	LC	Total
Alan Kernaghan*	F	1984-89	36	3	7	46
Malcolm Smith	CF	1972-76	24	2	1	27
Alan Willey	F	1974-78	22	3	1	26
John Hickton	F	1966-77	20	0	4	24
Peter Brine	IF	1972-77	20	2	1	23
Billy Ashcroft	CF	1977-82	20	2	0	22
David Currie	CF	1982-86	19	1	0	20
David Mills	IF	1969-85	19	0	1	20
Billy Woof	F	1974-82	16	1	1	18
Mark Burke*	F	1987-89	16	1	0	17
Terry Cochrane	WF	1978-83	15	0	0	15
Garry Macdonald	F	1980-85	13	1	1	15
Graeme Hedley	F	1976-81	14	0	0	14
David Shearer	F	1977-83	9	2	2	13
Alan Foggon	F	1972-76	10	1	1	12
Gary Hamilton*	D	1981-89	12	0	0	12
Alan Roberts	OR	1983-84	10	1	1	12
Eric McMordie	IF	1965-74	10	1	0	11
Derrick Downing	WF	1965-72	10	1	0	11
Gary Gill*	D	1983-89	8	1	2	11
Bosco Jankovic	F	1978-81	8	0	2	10

*Player still with club at the end of 1988-9 season.

The Transfer Trail

The 588 players listed below have played for Middlesbrough in the League and FA Cup since September 1899 and the League Cup since its inception in 1960 to the end of 1988-9 season. This list does not feature any player who played for the club in the FA Cup from 1883 to May 1899 nor in the Northern Victory League covering the period November 1918 to May 1919. Also omitted are the games which took place between August 1939 and May 1946, when Middlesbrough took part in Wartime football. It must be stressed that every effort has been taken over many years of diligent research to ascertain the data listed below, but many players, especially in the early days of the Football League have scant information recorded against them, sometimes just a surname and an accompanying initial. Where exact transfer details are incomplete the year is shown to indicate the approximate date of the player's transfer. (AM) indicates player made his appearances as an amateur.

Player	Birthplace	From	To
Agnew WB	Kilmarnock, 16 Dec 1880	Newcastle U, Summer 1904	Kilmarnock, 1906
Aitken A	Ayr, 27 Apr 1877	Newcastle U, Oct 1906	Leicester F, Feb 1909
Aitken GB	Dalkeith, 13 Aug 1928	Edinburgh Thistles, Jun 1946	Workington, Jul 1953
Aitken S		Ayr U, Sep 1903	Raith R, 1910
Allen M	South Shields, 30 Mar 1949	Wallsend Boys, May 1966	Brentford T, Oct 1971
Allport HG		Ironopolis, 1894	1900
Anderson JR	Newcastle, 9 Nov 1924	Nov 1945	Blackhall CW, 1948
Anderson S	Hordern, 27 Feb 1934	Newcastle U, Nov 1965	Manager, Apr 1966
Angus MA	Middlesbrough, 28 Oct 1960	Professional, Aug 1978	Released, Southend, Aug 1983
Appleby R	Warkworth, 15 Jan 1940	Amble Welfare, May 1957	Carlisle U, Sep 1966
Armes S	New Seaham, 30 Mar 1908	Leeds U, Feb 1939	Released, Apr 1946
Armstrong D	Durham, 26 Dec 1954	Professional, Dec 1971	Southampton, Aug 1981
Ashcroft W	Liverpool, 1 Oct 1952	Wrexham, Aug 1977	Released, May 1982 Twente Enschede
Ashman D	Staindrop	Cockfield Alb, May 1924	Queen's Park R, May 1932
Askew W	Lumley 2 Oct 1959	Professional, Oct 1977	Released, May 1982 Gateshead
Astley H		Millwall, Summer 1904	Crystal P, 1905
Atherton RH	Wales	Hibs, May 1903	Chelsea, May 1906
Auld WB	Bellshill, 9 Jul 1929	Bellshill Ath, Dec 1950	Berwick R, Jun 1952
Bailey IC	Middlesbrough, 20 Oct 1956	Professional, Oct 1974	Sheffield W, Jul 1982
Barham MF	Folkestone, 12 Jul 1962	Huddersfield T, Nov 1988	Released, Summer 1989
Barker FM		South Bank, Summer 1906	1907
Barker WC	Linthorpe	South Bank, Jul 1905	Became Assistant trainer, 1919
Barnard RS	Middlesbrough, 16 Apr 1933	Professional, Apr 1950	Lincoln C, Jun 1960
Baxter MJ	Birmingham, 30 Dec 1956	Preston NE, Aug 1981	Rejected Contract, Portsmouth, May 1984
Baxter RD	Gilmerton, 23 Jan 1911	Bruntonian Jrs, May 1931	Hearts, Aug 1945
Beagrie PS	North Ormesby, 28 Nov 1965	Local, Summer 1984	Sheffield U, Aug 1986
Beaton S		Feb 1910	Huddersfield T, 1910
Beattie TK	Carlisle, 18 Dec 1953	Carlisle U, Nov 1982	Dispute, Aug 1983
Bell FW		Sep 1899	Released, 1900
Bell HD	Sunderland, 14 Oct 1924	Sunderland, Oct 1945	Darlington, Sep 1955
Bell IC	Middlesbrough, 14 Nov 1958	Professional, Dec 1976	Mansfield T, Jul 1981
Bell, James		Grangetown, Sep 1904	Eston Utd, 1905
Bell, Joseph N	30 Aug 1912	Amateur, Sep 1934 Professional, Oct 1934	West Ham U, May 1935
Bell S	Middlesbrough, 13 Mar 1965	May 1982	Contract cancelled, 1985 Portsmouth
Best C	Boosbeck, 1888	Eston U, 1910 (AM)	Hull C, 1911
Bilcliff R	Blaydon, 24 May 1931	Spennymoor Jrs, May 1949	Hartlepools U, Jan 1961

Player	Birthplace	From	To
Birbeck J	Gateshead, 15 Apr 1932	Evenwood T, Apr 1953	Grimsby T, Jun 1959
Birkett RJE	Ashford, 9 Jan 1913	Arsenal, Mar 1935	Newcastle U, Jul 1938
Birrell W	Anstruther, 13 Mar 1897	Raith R, Jan 1921	Raith R, Nov 1927
Bissett JT	Dundee	Rochdale, May 1924	Lincoln C, Jul 1926
Blackburn C	Dalton, 16 Jan 1961	Professional, Dec 1979	Released, 1981
Blackett J	1875	Sunderland, Oct 1901	Luton T, Jun 1905
Blackmore HA	Silverton, 13 May 1904	Bolton W, Jun 1932	Bradford, May 1933
Blenkinsopp TW	Whitton Park, 13 May 1920	Grimsby T, May 1948	Barnsley, Nov 1952
Bloomer S	Cradley Heath, 20 Jan 1875	Derby C, Apr 1906	Derby C, Sep 1910
Boam SW	Kirkby-in-Stephen, 20 Jan 1948	Mansfield T, Jun 1971	Newcastle U, Aug 1979
Boardman H		Grangetown, Feb 1910	1910
Boddington H		Mar 1904	1904
Boersma P	Liverpool, 24 Sep 1949	Liverpool, Dec 1975	Luton T, Aug 1977
Bolton J	Barley Mow, 9 Feb 1955	Sunderland, Jul 1981	Sheffield U, Aug 1983
Bottrill WG	South Bank, 8 Jan 1903	Professional, Oct 1921	Nelson, Jun 1924
Braithwaite RM	Belfast, 24 Feb 1937	Linfield, Jun 1963	Durban SA, Dec 1967
Brawn WF	Wellingborough, 1 Aug 1878	Aston V, Mar 1906	Chelsea, Nov 1907
Brearley J	Liverpool	Notts C, Summer 1901	Everton, 1902
Brennan MR	Rossendale, 4 Oct 1965	Ipswich T, Summer 1988	
Briggs W	Middlesbrough, 29 Nov 1923	Cochranes, Apr 1947 (AM) Professional, Jun 1947	Southport, Jun 1948
Brine PK	London, 18 Jul 1953	Winns W, Jul 1968	Retired, 1978
Brown Alexander	Beith, 7 Apr 1879	Portsmouth, Aug 1900	1905
Brown Arthur S	Gainsborough, 6 Apr 1885	Fulham, Apr 1912	1912
Brown DJ	Hartlepool, 28 Jan 1957	Horden CW, Feb 1977	Oxford U, Oct 1979
Brown James	Luton, 1880	Luton T, Summer 1900	1901
Brown John	Motherwell, 1876	Portsmouth, Summer 1900	1901
Brown John R	1885	South Bank, Mar 1907	Bristol C, 1908
Brown Joseph	Cramlington, 26 Apr 1929	Juniors, Apr 1946	Burnley, Aug 1952
Brown Thomas	Middlesbrough	Apr 1921	Accrington S, May 1922
Brown Thomas E	Throckley, 8 Sep 1935	Apr 1953	Released, Jun 1959
Brown WH	Choppington, 11 Mar 1909	West Stanley, Dec 1928	Hartlepools U, Jun 1946
Brownlie J	Calder Cruix, 11 Mar 1952	Newcastle U, Aug 1982	Released, May 1984 Hartlepool U
Bruce RF	Paisley, 20 Jan 1906	Aberdeen, Jan 1928	Sheffield W, Oct 1935
Bryan PA	Birmingham, 22 Jun 1943	Aug 1961	Oldham A, Jul 1965
Bryan R	26 Jul 1916	Bishop Auckland, May 1935	Released, Sep 1938
Buckley MJ	Manchester, 4 Nov 1953	Carlisle U, Aug 1984	Released, May 1985
Buckley S		Haverton Hill, Aug 1899	1900
Burbeck RT	Leicester, 27 Feb 1934	Leicester C, Oct 1956	Darlington, Jul 1963
Burke MS	Solihull, 12 Feb 1969	Aston V, Dec 1987	
Burluraux D	Skelton, 8 Jun 1951	Juniors, Jul 1968	Darlington, Jul 1972
Burns ME	Preston, 8 Dec 1946	Cardiff C, Oct 1978	Joined Club staff, 1981
Burton G		Grangetown, Dec 1909	Cardiff C, 1910
Butler G	Middlesbrough, 29 Sep 1946	Professional, May 1964	Chelsea, Sep 1967
Butler R	Stillington	Hartlepools U, 1919	Oldham A, 1920
Butler T	Atherton, 28 Apr 1918	Oldham A, Mar 1939	Released, 1946 Accrington S
Butler W		Darlington, Apr 1923	1923
Caig H	Dalry 1894	Kilwinning, Jul 1913	1915
Cail SG	1888	Army, Mar 1907	Stalybridge Cel, Jul 1913
Callaghan J		South Bank, Summer 1899	Released, 1900
Cameron K	Hamilton, 1905	Preston NE, Mar 1929	Bolton W, Oct 1933
Campbell A		Aug 1906	Broke leg, 1908
Camsell GH	Framwelgate Moor, 27 Nov 1902	Durham C, Oct 1925	Joined Club staff, 1946
Carr A	Burradon	Percy Main, May 1929	Mansfield T, Jun 1934
Carr G	South Bank, 19 Jan 1899	Bradford, Jun 1919	Leicester C, Mar 1924
Carr H	South Bank	Feb 1911 (AM)	
Carr J	South Bank, 26 Nov 1891	South Bank, Dec 1910	Blackpool, May 1930
Carr W	South Bank	South Bank, Apr 1911	1925

Peter Beagrie

Stephen Bell

Billy Brawn

Alan Comfort

Player	Birthplace	From	To
Carrick C	Stockton	Local, Summer 1900	West Ham U, 1904
Cartwright P	Scarborough, 8 Feb 1908	March 1925	Bradford, Mar 1926
Cassidy J	Motherwell	Manchester C, May 1901	1906
Chadwick C	Bolton, 26 Jun 1914	Oldham A, Feb 1934	Hull C, Feb 1946
Chadwick DC	Ooctamund, 19 Aug 1943	Southampton, Jul 1966	Halifax T, Jan 1970
Chapman N	Cockfield, 15 Sep 1941	Juniors, Sep 1958	Darlington, Sep 1967
Charlton H	Gateshead, 22 Jun 1951	Redheugh BC, Jul 1968	Chesterfield, Mar 1976
Chipperfield F	Shiremoor	Lincoln C, Jun 1920	Released, Jun 1923 Ashington
Clark E		Nov 1899	Released 1900
Clark J	Dundee	Apr 1900	Scotland 1900
Clarke W	Jarrow, 14 Jul 1896	Durham C, Summer 1919	Leeds U, May 1921
Clough BH	Middlesbrough, 21 Mar 1935	Amateur, Nov 1951	Sunderland, Jul 1961
Clough J	Murton, 13 May	Fatfield Alb, Sep 1922	Bradford, Jul 1926
Cochrane AF	Glasgow	Alloa Ath, Feb 1923	Darlington, Jul 1926
Cochrane GT	Killyleagh, 23 Jan 1953	Burnley, Oct 1978	Gillingham, Oct 1983
Cochrane JK	Glasgow, 14 Jan 1954	Drumchapel Amateurs, May 1971	Darlington, Feb 1975
Cochrane M	Ireland	Leicester F, Mar 1901	Distillery, Summer 1901
Cochrane T	Newcastle, 7 Oct 1908	Leeds U, Oct 1936	Bradford, May 1939
Coleman, Edward P	Middlesbrough, 23 Sep 1957	Professional, Sep 1975	Workington, Mar 1977
Coleman, Ernest	Hucknall, 4 Jan 1908	Arsenal, Aug 1934	Norwich C, Feb 1937
Common A	Millfield, 1880	Sunderland, Feb 1905	Preston NE, 1910
Connachan ED	Preston Pans, 27 Aug 1935	Dunfermline, Aug 1963	Falkirk, Nov 1966
Cook H	Middlesbrough	Local, Oct 1912	Killed in War
Cook J	Sunderland	South Bank, Aug 1911	Notts C 1919
Cook M	Scarborough, 15 Oct 1961	Darlington, Sep 1985	Scarborough, 1986
Cooper CT	Sedgefield, 28 Feb 1967	Mar 1986	
Cooper D	Middlesbrough, 18 Oct 1936	Grangetown BC, Oct 1953	Rotherham U, Jan 1959
Cooper T	Castleford, 12 Jul 1944	Leeds U, Mar 1975	Bristol C, Jul 1978
Corbett R	North Warbottle, 26 Mar 1922	Newcastle U, Dec 1951	Northampton T, Aug 1957
Corden S	Eston, 9 Jan 1967	Professional, Jun 1983	Broke leg, Aug 1985
Cowan J		Nov 1899	Released, 1900
Coxon T	Hanley, 10 Jun 1883	Stoke C, Sep 1905	Southampton, May 1906
Coyle RP	Glasgow, 19 Aug 1961	Celtic, Mar 1987	Rochdale, Aug 1987
Craggs JE	Flinthill, 31 Oct 1948	Newcastle U, Aug 1971	Released, May 1982
			Newcastle U, Aug 1982
Craig T		Nov 1904	Falkirk 1905
Crawford A	Filey, 30 Jan 1959	AFC Bournemouth, Oct 1983	Released, May 1984
Crawford J	Leith	Derby C, Nov 1901	Sunderland, 1903
Creamer PA	Hartlepool, 20 Sep 1953	Professional, Oct 1970	Doncaster R, Dec 1975
Crosier J	Middlesbrough, 4 Dec 1889	Mar 1911	Bradford
Crossan JA	Londonderry, 29 Nov 1938	Manchester C, Aug 1967	Tongren, Belgium 1970
Cuff PJ	Middlesbrough, 19 Mar 1952	Professional, Oct 1969	Millwall, Aug 1978
Cumming DS	Aberdeen, 6 May 1910	Arbroath, Oct 1936	Retired, 1947
Cummins S	Sedgefield, 6 Dec 1958	Professional, Dec 1976	Sunderland, Nov 1979
Cunliffe A	Blackrod, 5 Feb 1909	Aston Villa, Dec 1935	Burnley, Apr 1937
Currie DN	Stockton, 27 Nov 1962	Professional, Feb 1982	Darlington, Jun 1986
Currie R		Arthurlie, Feb 1903	1903
Curtis J	South Bank	Tottenham H, Aug 1919	1920
Davenport P	Birkenhead, 24 Mar 1961	Manchester U, Nov 1988	
Davidson A	Ayr, 1878	Ayr U, Summer 1900	Bury, 1906
Davidson I	East Lothian, 8 Sep 1937	Preston NE, Feb 1965	Darlington, Sep 1967
Davidson S	Aberdeen, 1 Jun 1889	Aberdeen, Apr 1913	Aberdeen, May 1923
Davidson W		Dec 1910	Queen's Park, 1910-11
Davies AE		West Brom A, Dec 1914	Swindon T, 1914-15
Davies B	Middlesbrough	Local, Feb 1911	Cardiff C, 1919
Davies WF		Dec 1904	1905
Davison JW	Byers Green	Local, Oct 1919	Portsmouth, May 1923
Day W	South Bank, 27 Dec 1936	South Bank Jrs, May 1955	Newcastle U, Mar 1962
Delapenha LL	Kingston, 20 May 1927	Portsmouth, Apr 1948	Mansfield T, Jun 1958

Player	Birthplace	From	To
Desmond P	Cork, 23 Nov 1926	Shelbourne, May 1949	Southport, Jul 1950
Dews G	Ossett, 5 Jun 1921	Summer 1946	Plymouth A, Oct 1947
Dickinson PE		Willington Ath, Oct 1924	Annfield Pl, May 1925
Dicks RW	London, 13 Apr 1924	Dulwich Hamlet, May 1943	Retired 1958
Dickson, IW	Maxwelltown	Aston Villa, Dec 1923	Released, May 1926
Dixon C	Middlesbrough	Darlington, Feb 1915	Hartlepools U, 1923
Dixon T		Bedlington U, Nov 1907	Watford, 1911
Dobbie H	Binchester, 20 Feb 1923	South Bank SP, Oct 1946	Plymouth A, Mar 1950
Doig T		Nov 1900	1901
Donaghy P	Grangetown	GT St Mary's, Aug 1919	Bradford C, May 1923
Donaldson A	Newcastle, 22 Mar 1925	Newcastle U, Jan 1949	Exeter C, Sep 1953
Douglas H	Hartlepools	South Bank, Jan 1903	1903
Douglas JS	W/Hartlepool, 1 Dec 1917	Hartlepools U, Sep 1945	Hartlepools U, Nov 1948
Dow MJ	Dundee 1873	Luton T, Summer 1900	1902
Downing DG	Doncaster, 3 Nov 1945	Frickley Colliery, Feb 1965	Orient, May 1972
Dowson F	North Ormesby	May 1920	Released, May 1922
			Hartlepools U
Duffy CF	Jarrow, 1885	Jarrow, Oct 1905	Newcastle U, 1906
Duguid W	Wishaw	Albion R, Sep 1910	1913
Eckford J	Kilcaldy, 1876	Luton T, Summer 1900	Raith R, Dec 1900
Edwards WI	Bowburn, 10 Dec 1933	Bowburn, Mar 1952	Released, 1955
Eglington R		Thornaby, Sep 1899	Released, 1900
Elkes AJ	Wellington St George's, 31 Dec 1895	Tottenham H, Aug 1929	Watford, Aug 1933
Ellerington W	Sunderland	Darlington, May 1919	Nelson, Jun 1924
Elliott GW	Sunderland, 7 Jan 1889	South Bank, May 1910	Retired, May 1925
Emmerson GA	Bishop Auckland, 1900	Jarrow, Jan 1927	Cardiff C, Jun 1930
Emmerson M	Sunniside, 23 Oct 1942	Juniors, Nov 1959	Peterborough U, Jul 1963
Evans RW		Bury, 1900	Released, 1900
Eyre E	Worksop	Aston Villa, Aug 1911	Birmingham, 1914
Featherstone T	Darlington	Local, Apr 1904	Bolton W, Summer 1904
Fenton M	Stockton, 30 Oct 1913	South Bank EE, Mar 1933	Joined Club staff, 1948
Ferguson C	Dunfermline, 22 Nov 1910	Glasgow Benburb, May 1932	Notts C, May 1936
Ferguson R	Darlington, 25 Jul 1917	Sunderland, Aug 1935	York C, May 1939
Ferguson RG	Glasgow	Sunderland, Jan 1925	Crystal P, Sep 1932
Fernie DW	Kinglassie, 22 Nov 1930	Celtic, Dec 1958	Celtic, Oct 1960
Fitzsimons AG	Dublin, 16 Dec 1929	Shelbourne, May 1949	Lincoln C, Mar 1959
Flint WA	Eastwood, 21 Mar 1890	Hebburn Argyle, 1908	Notts C, 1910
Foggon A	West Pelton, 23 Feb 1950	Cardiff C, Aug 1971	Manchester U, Jul 1976
Forrest W	Tranent, 28 Feb 1908	Edinburgh St Bernard's Mar 1929	Darlington Manager, 1946
Fowler HN	Stockton, 3 Sep 1919	South Bank, Jun 1934	Hull C, Sep 1946
Fox WV	Middlesbrough, 8 Jan 1898	Professional, May 1919	Wolves, Oct 1924
Frail J	Burslem, 1873	Chatham, May 1900	Stockport C, Nov 1905
Fraser A		Darlington, Apr 1911	Darlington 1913
Freeman RV	Birkenhead 1893	Oldham A, May 1923	Rotherham U, May 1930
Freeman T	Brandon, 26 Jan 1907	Durham C, Oct 1929	Chester, Jun 1933
French JP		Professional, Feb 1924	Southend, May 1926
Gallacher C	Derry, 25 Apr 1922	Lochee Harps, Jan 1947	Hull C, May 1947
Gallagher J	Dipton, 17 Feb 1897	Oldham A, 1921	Millwall, Summer 1921
Garbett TG	Malton, 9 Sep 1945	Stockton, Nov 1963	Watford, Sep 1971
Gardner JR	Hartlepool	Hartlepools U, Jun 1927	Aldershot, May 1929
Gates WL	Ferryhill, 8 May 1944	Amateur, Sep 1961 Professional, Oct 1961	Retired, Jul 1974
Gettins E		Gainsborough Tr, May 1903	Released, 1905
Gettins JH		1899 (AM)	
Gibson FW	Summerscoat, 18 Jun 1902	Hull C, Nov 1932	Bradford C, May 1937
Gibson IS	Newton Stewart, 30 Mar 1943	Bradford, Mar 1962	Coventry C, Jul 1966
Gibson RJ		Sep 1910	Newcastle U, 1911
Gill G	Middlesbrough, 28 Nov 1964	Professional, Dec 1982	
Glover DV	Birmingham, 29 Dec 1963	Aston Villa, Summer 1987	Port Vale, Feb 1989

390

Player	Birthplace	From	To
Godley W		Local, Dec 1902	Stoke, Apr 1904
Good H	Motherwell	Wishaw YMCA, May 1924	Exeter C, May 1926
Goodfellow DO	Shilbottle, 26 Jun 1917	Sheffield W, Jun 1947	Exeter C, 1948
Goodson L		Doncaster R, Dec 1902	1905
Gordon D	West Calder, 1885	St Mirren, May 1908	1908
Gordon J	Fauldhouse, 23 Oct 1915	Newcastle U, Nov 1945	Joined Club staff, 1953
Gowland N	Butterknowle, 1902	Chilton Colliery, May 1924	Released, Stockport C, 1930
Gray RSM	Stirling, 27 Feb 1872	Bristol R, Oct 1899	Luton T, 1900
Green T	Rockferry, 25 Nov 1883	Stockport C, Feb 1905	Queen's Park R, May 1906
Griffiths TP	Wrexham, 21 Feb 1906	Bolton W, Mar 1933	Aston V, Nov 1935
Groves JA	South Bank, July 1883	Sheffield U, Aug 1907	Wingate Alb, 1912
Hall BAC	Sheffield, 29 Mar 1908	Doncaster R, Mar 1928	Bradford C, Jun 1930
Hall JH		Brighton, May 1908	Birmingham, 1910
Hamilton GJ	Glasgow, 27 Dec 1965	Professional, May 1983	
Hamilton WM	Airdrie, 16 Feb 1938	Sheffield U, Feb 1961	Hibs, 1961
Hankin R	Wallsend, 2 Feb 1956	Vancouver Whitecaps, Sep 1982	Peterborough U, Sep 1983
Hanlon E	Dundee	Darlington, Sep 1906	Barnsley 1907
Hardwick GFM	Saltburn, 2 Feb 1920	South Bank EE, May 1937	Oldham A, Nov 1950
Harkins J	Scotland	Sep 1906	Leeds C, 1907
Harris J	Glasgow, 19 Mar 1896	Partick Th, Mar 1923	Newcastle U, Sep 1925
Harris WC	Swansea, 31 Oct 1928	Hull C, Mar 1954	Bradford C, Mar 1965 (Player-manager)
Harrison H	Redcar, 21 Nov 1893	Grangetown, May 1913	Darlington, 1924
Hartnett JB	Dublin, 21 Mar 1927	Dundalk, Jun 1948	Hartlepools, Sep 1957
Hasell AA	Bristol	Bolton W, Oct 1907	Swindon T, 1907
Hastie J		Plymouth A, Sep 1919	Dundee
Hawkins GH	24 Nov 1915	Feb 1935	Watford, Jun 1937
Haworth JH	Turton	Brighton, Feb 1912	1915
Healey R	Darlington 1890	Bishop Auck, (AM) Apr 1914	
Heard TP	Hull, 17 Mar 1960	Newcastle U, Sep 1985	Hull C, May 1986
Hedley, George T	County Durham, 1882	West Stanley, Oct 1905	Hearts, Jan 1906
Hedley, Graeme	Easington, 1 Mar 1957	Professional, Mar 1975	Contract cancelled, Mar 1982
Henderson GH	Ladhope, 2 May 1880	Rangers, Jun 1905	Chelsea, Apr 1906
Henderson R	Wallsend, 31 Mar 1937	Ashington, May 1957	Hull C, Jun 1961
Hepple G	Sunderland, 16 Sep 1925	North Sands, May 1947	Norwich C, Jun 1954
Hewitt C	Oldham, 1885	West Hartlepool, 1905	Tottenham H, May 1906
Hick WM	Beamish	South Shields, Feb 1924	Southend, Mar 1925
Hickling W		Derby C, Sep 1906	Tottenham H, 1907
Hickton J	Brimington, 24 Sep 1944	Sheffield W, Sep 1966	Contract cancelled, Fort Lauderdale, Apr 1978
Higgins W	Smethwick, 1874	Newcastle U, Summer 1900	Manchester U, Sep 1901
Higham N	Chorley, 14 Feb 1912	Everton, May 1925	Southampton, May 1939
Hillier EJG	Eastleigh, 10 Apr 1907	Cardiff C, Jan 1930	Newport C, Jun 1936
Hisbent JM	Plymouth	Feb 1912	1915
Hodgson DJ	Gateshead, 1 Nov 1960	Professional, Aug 1978 Norwich C, Mar 1987 (Loan)	Liverpool, Aug 1982
Hodgson G		Summer 1900	1901
Hodgson JP	Dawdon, 10 May 1922	Leeds U, Mar 1948	Released, 1955
Hogg J		Hearts, Sep 1902	Luton T, Jun 1906
Holliday E	Barnsley, 17 Jun 1939	Juniors, Aug 1956 Sheffield W, Jun 1965	Sheffield W, Mar 1962 Hereford U, 1966
Holliday JW	Cockfield, 19 Dec 1908	Cockfield, 1930	Brentford, May 1932
Holmes, W	Willington, 9 May	Willington Ath, Apr 1914	Released, 1928 Darlington
Honeyman JW	Middlesbrough, 29 Dec 1893	Local, Oct 1919	Dundee, Sep 1920
Horner W	Cassop, 7 Sep 1942	Professional, Sep 1959	Darlington, Jun 1969
Horsfield A	Newcastle, 5 Jul 1946	Professional, Jul 1963	Newcastle U, Jan 1969
Howling E		South Bank, Apr 1911 (AM)	Bristol C
Hughes M	Fauldhouse	Scotland, Jun 1899	1900
Hume RM	Kirkintilloch, 18 Mar 1941	Rangers, Sep 1962	Aberdeen, Jul 1963
Hunter H		Mar 1906	Apr 1906

Player	Birthplace	From	To
Irvine JD	Whitburn, 17 Aug 1940	Dundee U, May 1964	Hearts, May 1967
Jackson A	Cambose Mount	Scotland, Aug 19!0	Killed in Action
James WE		Mar 1911	Portsmouth, 1912-13
Jankovic B	Sarajevo, 22 May 1951	Zeljeznicar, Feb 1979	Released, Summer 1981
Jarvis S	Sheffield,1905	Raith R, Nov 1927	Darlington, Jul 1936
Jennings J	Platt Bridge, 27 Aug 1902	Cardiff C, Jan 1930	Preston NE, Sep 1936
Jennings S	Cinderhill	Norwich C, Apr 1920	Reading, Jun 1921
Johnson PE	Harrogate, 5 Oct 1958	Professional, Oct 1976	Newcastle U, Oct 1980
Johnston Craig P	Johannesburg, 8 Dec 1960	Professional, Feb 1978	Liverpool, Apr 1981
Johnston C Patrick	Dublin, 16 Jul 1924	Shelbourne, Dec 1947	Grimsby T, Feb 1949
Jones A		West Brom Alb, Summer 1901	Luton T, 1906
Jones GW	Crook, 28 Jun	Everton, Jun 1925	Southend, Jul 1926
Jones GE	Sedgefield, 6 Mar 1943	Professional, Mar 1960	Darlington, Feb 1973
Jones James		Dec 1899	1905
Jones J Love		Stoke C, Mar 1909	Portsmouth, 1910
Jordon BA	Bentley, 31 Jan 1933	Rotherham U, Nov 1958	York C, Jul 1960
Kay J	Sunderland, 29 Jan 1964	Wimbledon (Loan), Jan 1985	
Kaye A	Barnsley, 9 May 1933	Blackpool, Nov 1960	Colchester U, Jun 1965
Kear MP	Coleford, 27 May 1943	Nottingham F, Sep 1967	Contract cancelled, Apr 1970
Kelly B		Ashfield, Nov 1911	1911
Kennedy F	Radcliffe, 1904	Everton, May 1927	Reading, May 1929
Kennedy MF	Salford, 9 Apr 1961	Huddersfield T, Aug 1982	Portsmouth, Jun 1984
Kent H		Brighton, May 1908	Watford, Aug 1909
Kernaghan AN	Otley, 25 Apr 1967	Mar 1985	
Kerr PA	Portsmouth, 9 Jun 1964	Aston Villa, Jan 1987	
Kinnell G	Cowdenbeath, 22 Dec 1937	Sunderland, Oct 1968	Juventus, Australia 1969
Kirby F	Durham County	Durham C, Oct 1913	Bradford, 1914
Kirk H	Saltcoats, 25 Aug 1944	Ardeer Ath, May 1963	Third Lanark, Summer 1964
Kite PD	Bristol, 26 Oct 1962	Southampton (Loan), Apr 1986	
Knowles CB	Fitzwilliam, 13 Jul 1944	Monckton CW, Oct 1962	Tottenham H, May 1964
Laidlaw JD	Swalwell, 12 Jul 1950	Professional, Aug 1967	Carlisle U, Jul 1972
Laking GE	Harthill, 17 Mar 1913	Wolves, Oct 1936	1946-47
Lamb TJ		Newcastle U, Sep 1899	Willington Ath, 1900
Lawrie S	Dinnistown, 15 Dec 1934	Bedlay Jrs, Feb 1952	Charlton Ath, Nov 1956
Laws B	Wallsend, 14 Oct 1961	Huddersfield T, Mar 1985	Nottingham F, Jun 1988
Lawson J	Middlesbrough, 11 Dec 1947	South Bank, Dec 1964	Huddersfield T, Jul 1968
Layton AE		Nov 1911	1912
Le Flem RP	Bradford on Avon, 12 Jul 1942	Wolves, Feb 1965	Leyton O, Mar 1966
Leonard HD	Sunderland, 1886	Grimsby T, Nov 1911	Newcastle U, Nov 1911
Leslie J		Sunderland, Oct 1901	Clyde, 1902
Lightening AD	Durban SA, 1 Aug 1936	Coventry C, Aug 1962	Released, May 1963
Linacre W	Chesterfield, 10 Aug 1924	Manchester C, Sep 1949	Hartlepools U, Aug 1953
Linton T		Stockton, Feb 1900	Released, 1900
Linwood AB	Drumsmudden, 13 Mar 1920	St Mirren, Jun 1946	Hibs, Jun 1947
Livingstone J	Middlesbrough, 18 Jun 1942	Professional Jan 1960	Carlisle U, Nov 1962
Lloyd, E	Middlesbrough	Dec 1919	Bradford, 1920
Longstaffe G		Jun 1899	Released, 1900
Lugg R	Jarrow, 18 Jul 1948	Primrose FC, Jul 1965	Watford, Nov 1969
Lynch P	Belfast, 22 Jan 1950	Cliftonville, Jun 1970	Released, 1972
McAllister W	Glasgow	Brighton, Jul 1924	Queen's Park R, Oct 1926
McAndrew A	Lanark, 11 Apr 1956	Professional, Aug 1973	Chelsea, Sep 1982
		Chelsea, Sep 1984	Released, May 1986
Macaulay W		Summer 1902	Portsmouth, 1903
McCabe JJ	Draperstown, 17 Sep 1918	South Bank EE, May 1937	Leeds U, Mar 1948
McCallum D		Sunderland, Dec 1904	1905
McClelland J	Dysart	Southend, Mar 1925	Bolton W, Mar 1928
McClure S		Grangetown, Sep 1910	Aston Villa, 1911
McCormack JC	Newcastle, 15 Feb 1922	Gateshead, Apr 1947	Barnsley, Jul 1950

John Mahoney

Player	Birthplace	From	To
McCorquodale D		Scotland, Dec 1899	Returned to Scotland, Dec 1899
McCowie A		Arsenal, Nov 1900	1901
McCracken JP	1868	Nottingham F, 1899	Chesterfield, 1900
McCrae A	Stoneburn, 2 Jan 1920	Charlton Ath, Oct 1948	Falkirk, Mar 1953
McCreesh A	Billingham, 8 Sep 1962	Professional, Sep 1980	Contract cancelled, Mar 1982
McCulloch A	Scotland	Leith Ath, Feb 1907	Newcastle U, 1908
Macfarlane J	Bathgate	Celtic, Jun 1929	Dunfermline, 1933
Macfarlane R	Greenock, 1875	Grimsby T, 1902	Aberdeen, 1908
Macfarlane T		Mar 1901	1901
Macdonald G	Middlesbrough, 26 Mar 1962	Professional, March 1980	Released, Jul 1984 Carlisle U
McGuigan A		Aug 1902	Southport Cent., Jun 1905
McIlmoyle H	Cambuslang, 29 Jan 1940	Carlisle U, Sep 1969	Preston NE, Jul 1971
McKay J	Glasgow, 1 Nov 1898	Blackburn R, Mar 1927	Bolton W, Jun 1936
McKennan PS	Airdrie, 16 Jul 1918	Brentford T, May 1949	Oldham A, Jul 1951
McKenzie D	Glasgow, 10 Aug 1912	Brentford T, May 1938	Released, 1945
McLean JD	Brotton, 21 Dec 1932	Professional, Oct 1952	Hartlepools U, Oct 1961
McLeod D	Stenhousemuir, Jun 1883	Celtic, Oct 1908	Retired 1914
McManus CE	Limavady, 14 Nov 1950	Bradford C, Jan 1986 (Loan)	
McMordie A	East Belfast, 12 Apr 1946	Professional, Sep 1964	York C, May 1975
McMurray, J	Billingham, 5 Oct 1931	Local, May 1949	Aug 1956
McNally J		Thornaby, Aug 1899	1900
McNeil M	Middlesbrough, 7 Feb 1940	Cargo Fleet Jrs, Jun 1954	Ipswich T, Jul 1964
McNeill AA	Belfast, 16 Aug 1945	Belfast Crusaders, Aug 1967	Huddersfield T, Nov 1968
McPartland D	Middlesbrough, 15 Oct 1947	Professional, Oct 1964	Carlisle U, Jan 1968
McPhail DD	Dumbarton, 17 Feb 1911	Dumbarton, Apr 1928	Released, Apr 1932
McPherson K	Hartlepool, 25 Mar 1929	Notts C, Aug 1953	Coventry C, Dec 1955
McRobbie A		Feb 1912	Swindon T, Apr 1913
Madden G	Loftus	Haverton Hill, Jan 1900	Released, 1900
Maddison J	South Shields, 9 Nov 1924	Professional, Dec 1945	Darlington, Aug 1949
Maddren WD	Billingham, 11 Jan 1951	Port Clarence, Jun 1968	Retired, 1978
Mahoney JF	Cardiff, 20 Sep 1946	Stoke C, Aug 1977	Swansea C, Jul 1979
Maitland AE	Leith, 8 Oct 1896	South Shields, Jun 1923	Newcastle U, Oct 1924
Malan NF	South Africa, 23 Nov 1923	Defos FC, Oct 1945	Darlington, Jul 1948
Malcolm G	Thornaby	Plymouth A, Oct 1912	Darlington, 1915
Mannion WJ	South Bank, 16 May 1918	South Bank SP, Sep 1936	Hull C, Dec 1954
Marcroft EH	Rochdale	Great Harwood, Dec 1931	Queen's Park R, May 1932
Marshall J	Saltcoats	St Mirren, Nov 1919	Llanelly, 1923
Marshall SK	Goole, 20 Apr 1946	Goole T, Jul 1963	Notts C, Jun 1966
Martin GS	Bathgate, 14 Jul 1899	Everton, May 1932	Luton T, Aug 1933
Martin J	Sunderland, 6 Oct 1912	Horden CW, Jan 1932	Released, 1946 Huddersfield T, Trainer
Masson DS	Banchory, 26 Aug 1946	Juniors, Sep 1963	Notts C, Sep 1968
Mathieson JA	Methil, 10 May	Raith R, Jun 1926	Brentford T, May 1934
Mattinson H	Ireby, 20 Jul 1925	Professional, Nov 1945	Preston NE, Mar 1949
Millar J	1877	Rangers, May 1900	Bradford C, Summer 1903
Millar WM	Glasgow, 1902	Rhyl Ath, Dec 1927	York C, Summer 1929
Miller J	Belfast, 27 Apr	Aberdare Ath, Apr 1926	Hibs, Nov 1930
Million E	Ashington, 15 Mar 1938	Amble Jrs, May 1956	Bristol R, Jun 1962
Mills DJ	Whitby, 6 Dec 1951	Professional, Dec 1968	West Bromwich A, Jan 1979
		Newcastle U, Aug 1984	Released, Summer 1985
Milne JV	Stirling, 25 Mar 1911	Arsenal, Dec 1937	Dumbarton, 1941
Mitchell AJ	Stoke, 22 Jan 1922	Luton T, Jul 1951	Southport, Aug 1956
Mochan N	Larbert, 6 Apr 1927	Morton, May 1951	Celtic, May 1953
Mohan N	Middlesbrough, 6 Oct 1960	Professional, Nov 1987	
Moody A	Middlesbrough, 18 Jan 1951	Professional, Jan 1968	Southend, Oct 1972
Moran M	Glasgow, 1878	Sheffield U, Summer 1900	1901
Mordue J	Edmondsley	Sunderland, May 1920	Hartlepools U, May 1922
Mowbray AM	Saltburn, 22 Nov 1963	Professional, Nov 1981	
Muir J		Leith Ath, Aug 1902	Summer 1903
Muir W		Hamilton A, Sep 1902	Bradford C, Summer 1903

Player	Birthplace	From	To
Mulholland FG	Belfast, 28 Oct 1927	Glentoran, Oct 1951	Released, Jun 1958
Murdoch RW	Bothwell, 17 Aug 1944	Celtic, Sep 1973	Juniors Coach
Murphy DA	South Bank, 19 Jul 1917	South Bank SP, May 1935	Killed, Sep 1944
Murphy J	Ireland	Summer 1899	Released 1900
Murphy M		South Bank, 1899	Released, 1900
Murphy TE	South Bank, 25 Mar 1921	South Bank SP, May 1939	Blackburn R, Dec 1947
Murray A	Newcastle, 5 Dec 1949	Professional, Sep 1967	Brentford T, Jun 1972
Murray T		Sep 1905	Rangers, 1908
Murray W	Bishop Auckland	Derby C, Jul 1921	Hearts, Jun 1923
Muttitt E	Middlesbrough	South Bank, Apr 1929	Brentford T, Oct 1932
Myton B	Strensall, 26 Sep 1950	Juniors, Sep 1967	Southend, Nov 1971
Nash FC	South Bank, 30 Jun 1918	South Bank EE, Sep 1937	Southend U, Dec 1947
Nattrass I	Fishburn, 12 Dec 1952	Newcastle U, Jul 1979	Retired, 1986
Neal RM	Dinnington, 1 Oct 1934	Birmingham C, Oct 1961	Lincoln C, Aug 1963
Niblo, TB	Dunfermline, 24 Sep 1877	Newcastle U, 1900	Transfer cancelled by League
Nichol J	Port Glasgow	Sep 1910	Liverpool, 1913
Nobbs KA	Bishop Auckland, 19 Sep 1961	Professional, Sep 1979	Released, May 1982, Halifax T, Sep 1982
Norris OP	Londonderry, 1 Apr 1929	Juniors, Jul 1948	Bournemouth, Jul 1955
Nurse MTG	Swansea, 11 Oct 1937	Swansea T, Sep 1962	Swindon T, Aug 1965
O'Connell SCP	Carlisle, 11 Jan 1930	May 1953 (AM)	
O'Hagan C		Tottenham H, Jul 1906	Aberdeen, 1906
O'Hanlon KG	Saltburn, 16 May 1962	Professional, May 1980	Released, May 1985 Rotherham U
O'Riordan DJ	Dublin, 14 May 1957	Carlisle U, Aug 1985	Grimsby T, Summer 1986
O'Rourke J	Northampton, 11 Feb 1945	Luton T, Jul 1966	Ipswich T, Feb 1968
Orritt B	Cwm-y-Clo, 22 Feb 1937	Birmingham C, Mar 1962	South Africa, Mar 1966
Osborne F		Dykehead, Aug 1899	Released 1900
Ostler J	Scotland	Newcastle U, Apr 1900	Transfer cancelled by Football League
Otto HM	Amsterdam, 24 Aug 1954	FC Twente, Aug 1981	Den Haag, Jun 1985
Page R	1878	Grove Hill, 1898	Retired, 1906
Pallister GA	Ramsgate, 30 Jun 1965	Summer 1985	
Parkin R	Crook, 28 Jan 1911	Arsenal, Jan 1936	Southampton, Sep 1937
Parkinson GA	Thornaby, 10 Jan 1968	Professional, Summer 1986	
Paterson T	Newcastle, 30 Mar 1954	Leicester C, Sep 1974	Bournemouth, Apr 1976
Patterson RL	Gateshead, 30 Oct 1929	Whitehall Jrs, Jun 1949	Northampton T, Jun 1952
Peacock A	Middlesbrough, 29 Oct 1937	Lawson St School, Nov 1954	Leeds U, Feb 1964
Peacock J	Wigan, 15 Mar 1897	Everton, May 1927	Sheffield W, May 1930
Pears S	Brandon, 22 Jan 1962	Manchester U, (Loan) Nov 1983 (signed Jun 1985)	
Pease WH	Leeds, 30 Sep 1898	Northampton T, May 1926	Luton T, Jan 1933
Peggie J		Hibs, Oct 1910	1911
Pender R	Dumbarton	Professional, May 1919	St Johnstone, Aug 1924
Pentland FB	Wolverhampton 1883	Queen's Park R, Jun 1908	Halifax T Feb 1913
Peters J	Wide Open, 7 Mar 1961	Professional, Mar 1979	Contract cancelled, Mar 1982, Blyth Spartans
Phillips BJ	Cadishead, 9 Nov 1931	Altrincham, Jun 1954	Mansfield T, Jun 1960
Phillipson TF	Stanhope, 1886	Bishop Auckland, Feb 1905	1905
Piercy F		Jun 1899	West Ham U, 1907
Piercy HR		1899	
Platt JA	Ballymoney, 26 Jan 1952	Ballymena U, May 1970	Released, Apr 1983 Ireland
Poole K	Bromsgrove, 21 Jul 1963	Aston Villa, Aug 1987	
Poskett M	Middlesbrough, 19 Jul 1953	South Bank, Jul 1973	Hartlepools U, Jul 1974
Poulton A	Wolverhampton, 28 Mar 1890	Merthyr T, Mar 1920	Bristol C, Sep 1921
Povey W	Billingham, 11 Jan 1943	Juniors, May 1960	York C, Mar 1964
Pratt R	1876	South Bank, May 1899	Released, 1900
Priest AE	Darlington, 1875	South Bank, Sep 1906	Sheffield U, 1907
Priest F		Sep 1906	1906
Proctor MG	Middlesbrough, 30 Jan 1961	Professional, Sep 1978 Sheffield W, Mar 1989	Nottingham F, Aug 1981

Kelham O'Hanlon

Mel Nurse

Stephen Pears

Don O'Riordan

Player	Birthplace	From	To
Proudlock P	Hartlepool, 25 Oct 1965	Hartlepools U, Nov 1986	Carlisle U, Mar 1989
Pugh CE		St Augustine's 1899	1900
Raisbeck L		Third Lanark, 1900	
Ramage A	Guisborough, 29 Nov 1957	Professional, Nov 1975	Derby C, Aug 1980
Ramsay A	East Benhar, 1877	East Benhar	Leyton, Jun 1905
Ratcliffe D	Newcastle-under-Lyme, 13 Nov 1934	Stoke C, Sep 1963	Darlington, Feb 1966
Ratcliffe E	Gee Cross 1880	Derby C, Mar 1906	
Rayment JW	West Hartlepool, 25 Sep 1934	Juniors, Oct 1951	Hartlepools U, Jul 1955
Reagan CM	York, 12 May 1924	Hull C, Feb 1948	Shrewsbury T, Aug 1951
Redfern J		Sep 1899	Released, 1900
Reid, George	Kilmarnock	West Brom A, Nov 1899	Millwall, 1900
Reid, George T	Blackland Mill, 1884	St Mirren, May 1905	1906
Rickaby S	Stockton, 12 Mar 1924	South Bank, Jun 1946	West Brom A, Feb 1950
Rigby A	Manchester, 7 Jun 1900	Blackburn R, May 1932	Clapton Orient, Aug 1933
Ripley SE	Middlesbrough, 20 Nov 1967		
Roberts A	Newcastle, 8 Dec 1964	Professional, Dec 1982	Darlington, 1985
Roberts J		Oct 1906	1906
Roberts RJ	Redditch, 1878	Newcastle U, Mar 1904	Crystal P, Summer 1905
Roberts WS		Oct 1906	
Robertson A	Dundee 1878	Dundee, Summer 1900	Manchester U, 1903
Robertson J		Oct 1901	1901
Robertson WG	Glasgow, 4 Nov 1936	Juniors, Nov 1953	Released, Jun 1959
Robinson J	Middlesbrough, 10 Feb 1934	Professional, Oct 1951	Hartlepools U, Jun 1959
Robinson JN	Middlesbrough, 5 Jan 1921	South Bank SP, Jan 1946	Grimsby T, Jun 1948
Robinson JW		Aug 1919	1920
Robinson R	Whitburn, 19 Jan 1927	Professional, Apr 1945	Barrow, Jun 1959
Rodgerson AR	Easington, 19 Mar 1939	Potter's Bar, May 1956	Cambridge U, 1964
Rooks R	Sunderland, 29 May 1940	Sunderland, Aug 1965	Bristol C, Jun 1969
Ross AC	York, 7 Oct 1916	Gainsborough Tr, Feb 1935	Bradford, Mar 1937
Ross C	Dailly, 29 Aug 1962	Ayr U BC, Sep 1980	Darlington, Aug 1983
Rowell G	Seaham, 6 Jun 1957	Norwich C, Aug 1985	Released, Mar 1986 Brighton
Russell ET	Cranwell, 15 Jul 1928	Wolves, Dec 1951	Leicester C, Oct 1953
Saxby MW	Mansfield, 12 Aug 1957	Newport C, Oct 1984	Retired, Apr 1986
Scott G	Birmingham, 31 Oct 1956	Charlton Ath, Sep 1984	Monthly contract cancelled Northampton T, Sep 1984
Scott JC	Fatfield, 9 Jan 1930	Luton T, Sep 1954	Hartlepools U Jan 1959
Scott WR	Willington Quay, 6 Dec 1907	Howden B Legion, May 1927	Brentford T, May 1932
Scrimshaw CT	Heanor, 5 Apr 1911	Stoke C, Oct 1938	Released, 1945
Senior TJ	Dorchester, 28 Nov 1961	Watford, Mar 1988	Reading, Oct 1988
Shand H	Scotland	Inverness Thistle, Aug 1906	Millwall, 1908
Shaw TW		Stockton, May 1899	Released, 1900
Shearer DJ	Caol, 16 Oct 1958	Inverness Clachnacuddin, Jan 1978	Grimsby T, Jun 1983
Shepherdson H	Middlesbrough, 28 Oct 1918	South Bank EE, Dec 1934 (AM) Professional, May 1935	Southend, May 1947
Short M	Middlesbrough, 29 Dec 1949	Juniors, Feb 1967	Oldham A, Jun 1970
Slade CH	Bristol	Huddersfield T, Oct 1922	Darlington, Sep 1925
Slaven BJ	Paisley 13 Nov 1960	Albion R, Oct 1985	
Smith, David	Thornaby, 8 Dec 1947	Professional, Dec 1964	Lincoln C, Jul 1968
Smith, David W		Nottingham F, 1901	1907, Became Club Director
Smith, Edward G		Aug 1899	1900
Smith, Ernest E	Donegal	Cardiff C, Jan 1924	Watford, Sep 1925
Smith G	Newcastle, 7 Oct 1945	Portsmouth, Jan 1969	Birmingham C, Mar 1971
Smith J	Dalbeattie, 7 Dec 1898	Ayr U, Sep 1926	Cardiff C, Sep 1930
Smith J	Hurlford	1933	Queen of South, 1935
Smith M	Stockton, 21 Sep 1953	Professional, Oct 1970	Burnley, Nov 1976
Smith RA	Billingham, 6 Feb 1944	Haverton Hill, Dec 1961	Bangor C, Jun 1972
Souness GJ	Edinburgh, 6 May 1953	Tottenham H, Dec 1972	Liverpool, Jan 1978
Spraggon F	Marley Hill, 27 Oct 1945	Juniors, Nov 1962	Released, Apr 1976 Minnesota Kicks

Player	Birthplace	From	To
Spriggs S	Doncaster, 16 Feb 1956	Cambridge U, Mar 1987	Refused to sign, Apr 1987
Spuhler, JO	Sunderland, 18 Sep 1917	Sunderland, Oct 1945	Darlington, Jun 1954
Stage W		Apr 1914	Released, Apr 1914 Hibs
Stephens A	Liverpool, 19 May 1954	Bristol R, Mar 1985	Carlisle U, Dec 1987
Stevenson AB		Wigan Oct 1923	Rhondda, Summer 1924
Stewart J	Kilwinning, 10 Mar 1954	Kilmarnock, May 1978	Rangers, Mar 1981
Stiles NP	Manchester, 18 May 1942	Manchester U, May 1971	Preston NE, Aug 1973
Stirling J	Clydebank	Sep 1911	1914
Stone JG	Carlin Howe, 3 Mar 1953	South Bank Jrs, Mar 1970	York C, Jul 1972
Stonehouse D	Lingdale, 18 Nov 1932	Lingdale, May 1951	Hartlepools U, Sep 1963
Storey T	Crook	Jan 1914	Port Vale, 1920
Stott J	Middlesbrough	Newcastle U, Sep 1899	1900
Strong A	Hartlepool, 17 Sep 1966	Sep 1984	Released, Feb 1986
Stuart R W	Middlesbrough, 9 Oct 1913	South Bank Jrs, May 1928 (AM) Professional, Jan 1931	Plymouth A, Oct 1947
Suddick J		Apr 1904	Summer 1904
Sugrue P	Coventry, 6 Nov 1960	Kansas, Dec 1982	Portsmouth, Dec 1984
Surtees J	Newcastle, 1 Jul 1911	Percy Main, Mar 1930	Portsmouth, Jun 1932
Swales N	New Marske	Dec 1925	1926
Taylor B	Hodthorpe, 12 Feb 1954	Professional, Mar 1971	Doncaster R, Dec 1975
Taylor CW	Kirby Stephen, 20 Jan 1937	Penrith, Jan 1956	Aldershot, Jun 1960
Taylor PT	Nottingham, 2 Jul 1928	Coventry C, Aug 1955	Port Vale, Jun 1961
Tennant J		Arsenal, Apr 1901	Apr 1902
Thackeray J	Hebburn	Hebburn Argyle, 1904	Bradford C, 1910
Thomas D	Kirkby, 5 Oct 1950	Vancouver Whitecaps, Mar 1982	Rejected contract, Portsmouth, 1982
Thomas MR	Senghenydd, 28 Nov 1959	Newcastle U, (Loan), Oct 1984	
Thompson A		Mar 1901	Summer 1901
Thompson N	Forest Hall	South Shields, Summer 1925	Barnsley, 1925
Thompson WT		Grangetown, Oct 1905	Summer 1906
Thomson KG	Aberdeen, 25 Feb 1930	Stoke C, Dec 1959	Hartlepools U, Oct 1962
Thomson R	Glasgow, 21 Mar 1955	Morton, Sep 1981	Hibs, Jul 1982
Tinsley W		Sunderland, Dec 1913	Nottingham F, May 1921
Tomlin J		Sunderland, Sep 1906	1907
Townsend J	Greenock, 2 Feb 1945	St Johnstone, Feb 1964	St Johnstone, Aug 1966
Trechman OL		W/Hartlepool, (AM) Feb 1906	
Tucker WH		Local, Oct 1906	1907
Turnbull LM	Stockton, 27 Sep 1967	Sep 1985	Aston V, Aug 1987
Turner P		Arsenal, Apr 1901	Apr 1902
Twine FW		Army 1927	Aldershot, Summer 1928
Tyldesley J	Halesowen, 1882	Newcastle U, Sep 1906	1907
Ugolini R	Lucca, 4 Jun 1924	Celtic, May 1948	Wrexham T, Jun1957
Urquhart A		Greenock Morton, Dec 1907	1908
Urwin T	Haswell, 5 Feb 1896	Shildon, Apr 1914	Newcastle U, Aug 1924
Verrill E	Staithes	South Bank, Feb 1908	Retired, 1915
Vincent JV	West Bromwich, 8 Feb 1947	Birmingham C, Mar 1971	Cardiff C, Oct 1972
Wainscoat R W	Maltby, 28 Jul 1898	Barnsley, Dec 1923	Leeds U, Mar 1925
Waldock R	Heanor, 6 Dec 1932	Plymouth A, Jan 1960	Gillingham, Oct 1961
Walker DH	Edinburgh, 10 Sep 1935	Leicester C, Oct 1959	Grimsby T, Sep 1963
Walker J	Beith	Swindon T, Sep 1913	Reading T, 1921
Walker RG	Bradford, 29 Sep 1926	Bradford, Jun 1946	Doncaster R, Dec 1954
Walker RH		Hearts, Jan 1906	Tottenham H, May 1906
Walley E	Caernarfon, 19 Apr 1934	Tottenham H, May 1958	Released, May 1960 Crystal Pal
Walsh A	Hartlepool, 9 Dec 1956	Horden CW, Dec 1976	Darlington, Oct 1978
Wanless R	Middlesbrough, 19 Jul 1876	Jun 1899	Released, 1900
Ward PT	Wedgefield, 15 Sep 1963	Professional, Nov 1982	Darlington, Sep 1985
Wardle G	Kimbleworth, 24 Sep 1919	Durham BC, 1937	Exeter C, Summer 1946
Wardrope A	1887	Airdrie, Nov 1910	1911

Player	Birthplace	From	To
Wardrope W	Motherwell, 1875	Newcastle U, Summer 1900	1902
Warren FW	Cardiff, 23 Dec 1909	Cardiff C, Jan 1930	Hearts, May 1936
Watkin TWS	Grimsby, 21 Sep 1932	Gateshead, Mar 1954	Mansfield T, Jun 1955
Watson A	Ferryhill, 26 Dec 1903	Chilton, May 1925	1926
Watson HL	Springwell	Pelton Fell, May 1926	Brentford T, May 1932
Watson J	Motherwell, 4 Oct 1877	Sunderland, Apr 1907	Retired, 1910
Watson R		South Bank, Sep 1902	Woolwich Ars, Summer 1903
Wayman C	Bishop Auckland, 16 May 1921	Preston NE, Sep 1954	Darlington, Dec 1956
Webb SJ	Middlesbrough, 6 Dec 1947	Juniors, Jul 1967	Carlisle U, Feb 1971
Webster, M	Blackpool, Nov 1899	Stalybridge Celtic, Mar 1922	Carlisle U, Jun 1935
Weddle DK	Newcastle, 27 Dec 1935	Cambridge U, Aug 1961	Darlington, Jun 1962
Weightman E	York, 4 May 1910	Scarborough, Mar 1933	Chesterfield, Oct 1936
Weir J	Benfoot Hill	Celtic, Sep 1910	Retired, 1920
Whigham W	Airdrie, 9 Oct 1939	Falkirk, Oct 1966	Dumbarton, Aug 1974
Whitaker W	Chesterfield, 7 Oct 1923	Chesterfield, Jun 1947	Retired, Summer 1955
White W	Braxburn	Dundee, Sep 1903	1904
Wilcox FJ	St Worburgh's	Birmingham, Mar 1906	Plymouth A, 1909
Wilkie D	Browney, 27 Jul 1939	Browney Jrs, Sep 1956	Hartlepools U, Sep 1961
Wilkie J	Govan	Rangers, Aug 1900	Rangers, 1901
Willey AS	Houghton-le-Spring, 18 Oct 1956	Professional, Sep 1974	Contract cancelled, Feb 1978
Williams JJ	Rotherham, Jun 1902	Arsenal, Mar 1932	Carlisle U, Aug 1935
Williams, JT		Wrexham, May 1924	Clapton O, Jul 1928
Williams O	Ryhope, 23 Sep 1895	Clapton O, Feb 1924	Southend, Aug 1930
Williamson RG	North Ormesby, 6 Jun 1884	Redcar Crusaders, Apr 1902	Retired, Apr 1923
Wilson Andrew N	New Mains, 14 Feb 1896	Cambuslang, Feb 1914	Chelsea, Nov 1923
Wilson Archibald		Southend, Jul 1914	Killed in action
Wilson FP	Newcastle, 15 Sep 1947	Professional, Apr 1966	Gateshead, 1967
Wilson J	Chilton	Chilton CW, May 1924	Southend 1927
Wilson TT		Morpeth Harriers, Apr 1908	Hearts, 1909
Windridge JE	Birmingham, 21 Oct 1883	Chelsea, Dec 1911	1913
Windross D	Dunsdale, 12 May 1938	Blackett Hutton, May 1956	Brighton, Nov 1960
Wood AEH	Macclesfield, 25 Oct 1945	Hull C, Oct 1976	Walsall, Jul 1977
Wood DT	Scarborough, 9 Jun 1964	Professional, Jul 1981	Chelsea, Sep 1984
Woodward T	West Houghton, 8 Dec 1918	Bolton W, Oct 1949	1951
Woof W	Gateshead, 16 Aug 1956	Professional, Aug 1974	Released, May 1982
Worrall WE	Shildon 1886	South Bank, 1905-06 (AM)	Sunderland, Nov 1905
Worthington PR	Halifax, 22 Apr 1947	Halifax T, Aug 1966	Notts C, Sep 1968
Wynn R		Chester, Feb 1914	1914
Yeoman RI	Perth, 13 May 1934	Northampton T, Nov 1958	Darlington, Jun 1964
Yorston BC	Aberdeen, 14 Oct 1905	Sunderland, Mar 1934	Released, 1945
Young EW		Apr 1921	Darlington, Summer 1921
Young RT	Swinehill, 1886	West Ham U, Oct 1908	Everton, Jan 1910

Middlesbrough Career Records

The following is a full schedule of all players to have appeared in Football League, FA Cup and League Cup games for Middlesbrough. Excluded are wartime fixtures, abandoned matches, friendlies, tour games and testimonials, etc. An asterisk (*) denotes the player appeared in the 1987-8 play-off games, details of which can be found in the seasonal statistics. The years given are the first and last of the seasons played, irrespective of how many spells the player had with Middlesbrough. i.e. 1926-36 is 1926-7 to 1935-6. The position given indicates that player's preferred role with the club (G — Goalkeeper, WH — Wing-half etc).

Player	Pos	Seasons	League App	League Gls	FA Cup App	FA Cup Gls	FL Cup App	FL Cup Gls	TOTAL App	TOTAL Gls
Agnew, William Barbour	LB	1904-06	66	2	7	0	0	0	73	2
Aitken, Andrew	CH	1906-09	76	1	3	0	0	0	79	1
Aitken, George Bruce	CH	1951-53	17	0	1	0	0	0	18	0
Aitken, Samuel	WH	1903-10	227	6	15	0	0	0	242	6
Allen, Michael	HB	1967-72	32/2	0	2	1	1	0	35/2	1
Allport, Henry George	RH	1899-1900	31	0	1	0	0	0	32	0
Anderson, John Robert	G	1947-48	1	0	0	0	0	0	1	0
Anderson, Stanley	WH	1965-66	21	2	1	0	0	0	22	2
Angus, Michael A	LH	1979-82	35/2	1	1/1	0	4	0	40/3	2
Appleby, Robert	G	1959-67	99	0	6	0	5	0	110	0
Armes, Samuel	OR	1938-39	3	0	0	0	0	0	3	0
Armstrong, David	OL	1970-81	357/2	59	29	8	27/1	6	413/3	73
Ashcroft, William	CF	1977-82	139/20	21	12/2	3	6	1	157/22	25
Ashman, Donald	WH	1924-32	160	2	14	0	0	0	174	2
Askew, William	WF	1980-82	10/2	0	0	0	0	0	10/2	0
Astley, Harry	CF	1904-05	14	4	2	1	0	0	16	5
Atherton, Robert H	WF	1903-05	60	13	6	1	0	0	66	14
Auld, Walter Bottomley	OL	1950-51	2	1	0	0	0	0	2	1
Bailey, Ian Craig	FB	1975-82	140/4	1	13/1	1	10/1	0	163/6	2
Barham, Mark Francis	IF	1988-89	3/1	0	0	0	0	0	3/1	0
Barker, Frederick Malcolm	RB	1906-07	1	0	0	0	0	0	1	0
Barker, William Charles	HB	1905-13	105	2	8	0	0	0	113	2
Barnard, Raymond Scholey	RB	1951-60	113	0	5	0	0	0	118	0
Baxter, Michael John	CH	1981-84	122	7	9	1	7	0	138	8
Baxter, Robert Denholm	CH	1932-39	247	19	19	1	0	0	266	20
Beagrie, Peter Sydney	WF	1984-86	24/8	2	0	0	1	0	25/8	2
Beaton, Samuel	RH	1909-10	2	0	0	0	0	0	2	0
Beattie, T Kevin	HB	1982-83	3/1	0	1	1	0	0	4/1	1
Bell, F William	LH	1899-1900	1	0	0	0	0	0	1	0
Bell, Henry Davey	WH	1946-55	290	9	25	1	0	0	315	10
Bell, Ian Charles	IF	1977-81	10	1	0	0	0	0	10	1
Bell, James	IR	1904-05	10	3	1	0	0	0	11	3
Bell, Joseph Nicholson	OL	1934-35	2	0	0	0	0	0	2	0
Bell, Stephen	IF	1981-85	79/6	12	6	2	2/1	0	87/7	14
Best, Charles	IF	1910-11	5	1	0	0	0	0	5	1
Bilcliff, Raymond	RB	1951-61	182	0	8	0	0	0	190	0
Birbeck, Joseph	LH	1953-59	38	0	4	0	0	0	42	0
Birkett, Ralph James Evans	WF	1934-38	93	35	8	1	0	0	101	36
Birrell, William	IF	1920-28	225	59	10	4	0	0	235	63
Bissett, James Thompson	D	1924-26	33	0	0	0	0	0	33	0
Blackburn, Colin	OR	1980-81	1	0	0	0	0	0	1	0
Blackett, Joseph	FB	1901-05	78	4	6	0	0	0	84	4
Blackmore, Harold Alfred	CF	1932-33	19	9	4	3	0	0	23	12
Blenkinsopp, Thomas William	D	1948-52	98	0	2	0	0	0	100	0
Bloomer, Stephen	IF	1905-10	125	59	5	3	0	0	130	62
Boam, Stuart William	CH	1971-79	322	14	29	0	27	2	378	16
Boardman, Harry	FB	1909-10	4	0	0	0	0	0	4	0
Boddington, Harold	OL	1903-04	1	0	0	0	0	0	1	0
Boersma, Philip	F	1975-77	41/6	3	3/1	0	1	0	45/7	3
Bolton, Joseph	FB	1981-83	59	1	5	0	5	0	69	1
Bottrill, Walter Gibson	OR	1922-24	17	0	1	0	0	0	18	0
Braithwaite, Robert Munn	F	1963-67	67/1	12	1	0	3	0	71/1	12
Brawn, William Frederick	OR	1905-08	56	5	2	1	0	0	58	6

Player	Pos	Seasons	League App	Gls	FA Cup App	Gls	FL Cup App	Gls	TOTAL App	Gls
Brearley, John	IF	1900-02	32	22	2	1	0	0	34	23
Brennan, Mark Robert	IR	1988-89	25	3	1	0	2	0	28	3
Briggs, Walter	G	1946-48	2	0	0	0	0	0	2	0
Brine, Peter Kenneth	IF	1972-77	59/20	6	7/2	1	4/1	1	70/23	8
Brown, Alexander	CF	1903-05	44	15	5	5	0	0	49	20
Brown, Arthur Samuel	CF	1912-13	4	0	0	0	0	0	4	0
Brown, David J	G	1977-78	10	0	0	0	0	0	10	0
Brown, James	CH	1900-01	4	0	0	0	0	0	4	0
Brown, John	F	1900-01	19	5	9	5	0	0	28	10
Brown, John Robert	FB	1906-08	25	0	1	0	0	0	26	0
Brown, Joseph	LH	1949-51	11	0	0	0	0	0	11	0
Brown, Thomas	OR	1920-23	5	0	0	0	0	0	5	0
Brown, Thomas Edward	FB	1954-58	44	0	3	0	0	0	47	0
Brown, William Hutchinson	FB	1931-46	256	2	18	0	0	0	274	2
Brownlie, John	FB	1982-83	12	0	1	0	2	0	15	0
Bruce, Robert Frederick	IF	1927-35	237	64	16	7	0	0	253	71
Bryan, Peter Anthony	FB	1962-65	4	0	0	0	1	0	5	0
Bryan, Raymond	OR	1936-37	1	0	0	0	0	0	1	0
Buckley, Michael J	RH	1984-85	27	0	2	0	2	1	31	1
Buckley, Seth	CF	1899-1900	1	0	0	0	0	0	1	0
Burbeck, Ronald Thomas	WF	1956-63	139	24	9	1	4	4	152	29
Burke, Mark Stephen	F	1987-89	29/16	5	2/1	0	1	0	32/17	5
Burluraux, Donald	WF	1970-72	4/1	0	0	0	0	0	4/1	0
Burns, Michael Edward	F	1978-81	58/3	24	2/1	0	3	0	63/4	24
Burton, George	CF	1909-10	2	0	0	0	0	0	2	0
Butler, Geoffrey	FB	1965-67	54/1	1	5	0	2	0	61/1	1
Butler, Reuben	F	1919-20	27	11	1	0	0	0	28	11
Butler, Thomas	OR	1938-39	2	0	0	0	0	0	2	0
Butler, William	OR	1922-23	2	0	0	0	0	0	2	0
Caig, Hugh	IR	1914-15	1	0	0	0	0	0	1	0
Cail, Samuel George	IF	1906-13	136	52	7	3	0	0	143	55
Callaghan, James	IR	1899-1900	2	0	0	0	0	0	2	0
Cameron, Kenneth	WF	1929-34	99	30	6	0	0	0	105	30
Campbell, Alexander	FB	1906-09	34	0	2	0	0	0	36	0
Camsell, George Henry	CF	1925-39	418	325	35	20	0	0	453	345
Carr, Andrew	CH	1930-33	5	0	0	0	0	0	5	0
Carr, George	IF	1919-24	67	23	3	0	0	0	70	23
Carr, Henry	CF	1910-11	3	3	0	0	0	0	3	3
Carr, John	IF	1910-30	421	75	28	6	0	0	449	81
Carr, William	D	1910-24	116	3	2	1	0	0	118	4
Carrick, Christopher	F	1900-04	26	6	6	4	0	0	32	10
Cartwright, Phillip	OR	1925-26	6	0	0	0	0	0	6	0
Cassidy, Joseph	F	1901-06	126	34	9	0	0	0	135	34
Chadwick, Clifton	WF	1933-39	93	27	4	0	0	0	97	27
Chadwick, David E	WF	1966-70	100/2	3	7/1	0	6	1	113/3	4
Chapman, Neville	FB	1961-67	51/2	0	2	0	5	0	58/2	0
Charlton, Harry	WF	1970-75	8/2	0	1	0	1	0	10/2	0
Chipperfield, Francis	CH	1919-20	1	0	0	0	0	0	1	0
Clark, Ernest	RB	1899-1900	1	0	0	0	0	0	1	0
Clark, Joseph	IR	1899-1900	1	0	0	0	0	0	1	0
Clarke, Wallace	IF	1919-21	8	0	1	0	0	0	9	0
Clough, Brian Howard	CF	1955-61	213	197	8	5	1	2	222	204
Clough, John	G	1922-26	124	0	4	0	0	0	128	0
Cochrane, Alexander Fraser	IF	1922-26	67	8	1	0	0	0	68	8
Cochrane, George Terence	WF	1978-83	96/15	7	12	4	5	1	113/15	12
Cochrane, James Kyle	LB	1973-74	3	0	0	0	0	0	3	0
Cochrane, Michael	FB	1900-01	6	0	0	0	0	0	6	0
Cochrane, Thomas	OL	1936-39	80	16	1	0	0	0	81	16
Coleman, Edward P	CF	1975-76	1	0	0	0	0	0	1	0
Coleman, Ernest	WF	1934-37	85	21	5	0	0	0	90	21
Common, Alfred	CF	1905-10	168	58	10	7	0	0	178	65
Connachan, Edward Devlin	G	1963-66	95	0	4	0	6	0	105	0
Cook, Henry	HB	1912-15	23	0	2	0	0	0	25	0
Cook, John	F	1911-15	52	3	2	0	0	0	54	3
Cook, Mitchell	IR	1985-86	3/3	0	0	0	0	0	3/3	0
Cooper, Colin Terence*	FB	1985-89	133/2	4	9	0	10	0	152/2	4
Cooper, Douglas	F	1955-57	5	0	0	0	0	0	5	0
Cooper, Terence	FB	1974-78	105	1	7	0	11	0	123	1
Corbett, Robert	FB	1951-57	92	0	5	0	0	0	97	0

Colin Cooper with his
Middlesbrough Young
Player of the Year award
which he won in 1988.

Player	Pos	Seasons	League App	League Gls	FA Cup App	FA Cup Gls	FL Cup App	FL Cup Gls	TOTAL App	TOTAL Gls
Corden, Stephen	FB	1985-86	1	0	0	0	0	0	1	0
Cowan, James	FB	1899-1900	17	0	0	0	0	0	17	0
Coxon, Thomas	OL	1905-06	11	1	0	0	0	0	11	1
Coyle, Ronald Paul	FB	1986-87	1/2	0	0/1	0	0	0	1/3	0
Craggs, John Edward	FB	1971-82	408/1	12	33	0	31	1	472/1	13
Craig, Thomas	FB	1904-05	2	0	0	0	0	0	2	0
Crawford, Andrew	F	1983-84	8/1	1	0	0	0	0	8/1	1
Crawford, James	OR	1901-03	24	1	2	0	0	0	26	1
Creamer, Peter Anthony	FB	1972-75	9	0	0	0	1/1	0	10/1	0
Crosier, Joseph	RH	1910-14	27	0	4	0	0	0	31	0
Crossan, John Anthony	IF	1967-70	54/2	7	5	1	2	0	61/2	8
Cuff, Patrick Joseph	G	1973-78	31	0	5	0	0	0	36	0
Cumming, David Scott	G	1936-47	135	0	22	0	0	0	157	0
Cummins, Stanley	F	1976-80	39/4	9	7	1	0/1	0	46/5	10
Cunliffe, Arthur	OL	1935-37	27	5	4	2	0	0	31	7
Currie, David Norman	CF	1982-86	94/19	30	5/1	0	6	1	105/20	31
Currie, Robert	CF	1902-03	3	1	0	0	0	0	3	1
Curtis, John	OR	1919-20	5	0	0	0	0	0	5	0
Davenport, Peter	IL	1988-89	23/1	4	1	0	0	0	24/1	4
Davidson, Andrew	LH	1900-06	181	8	20	0	0	0	201	8
Davidson, Ian	LH	1964-67	46	0	1	0	5	0	52	0
Davidson, Stewart	RH	1913-23	208	4	8	0	0	0	216	4
Davidson, William	OL	1910-11	16	0	3	0	0	0	19	0
Davies, Albert E	OL	1914-15	1	0	1	0	0	0	2	0
Davies, Benjamin	G	1910-15	31	0	0	0	0	0	31	0
Davies, William F	OR	1904-05	10	0	2	0	0	0	12	0
Davison, John W	LH	1919-20	1	0	0	0	0	0	1	0
Day, William	F	1955-62	120	18	9	2	2	1	131	21
Delapenha, Lloyd Lindbergh	F	1949-58	260	90	10	3	0	0	270	93
Desmond, Peter	IL	1949-50	2	0	0	0	0	0	2	0
Dews, George	F	1946-48	33	8	6	0	0	0	39	8
Dickinson, Peter E	OR	1924-25	6	1	0	0	0	0	6	1
Dicks, Ronald William	WH	1947-58	316	10	18	0	0	0	334	10
Dickson, Ian W	CF	1923-25	37	12	1	0	0	0	38	12
Dixon, Charles	RB	1919-21	12	0	0	0	0	0	12	0
Dixon, Thomas	IR	1907-11	27	8	2	1	0	0	29	9
Dobbie, Harold	CF	1946-50	23	6	1	2	0	0	24	8
Doig, Thomas	RH	1900-01	3	0	1	0	0	0	4	0
Donaghy, Peter	HB	1919-23	30	2	0	0	0	0	30	2
Donaldson, Andrew	CF	1948-51	21	7	0	0	0	0	21	7
Douglas, Harry	OR	1902-03	4	0	0	0	0	0	4	0
Douglas, John Stuart	LH	1946-47	2	0	0	0	0	0	2	0
Dow, M John	FB	1900-02	34	0	7	0	0	0	41	0
Downing, Derrick George	WF	1965-72	173/10	39	22/1	7	5	2	200/11	48
Dowson, Francis	IL	1920-21	7	2	0	0	0	0	7	2
Duffy, Christopher Francis	OL	1905-06	4	0	0	0	0	0	4	0
Duguid, William	HB	1910-13	23	0	1	0	0	0	24	0
Eckford, John	IF	1900-01	4	0	3	0	0	0	7	0
Edwards, William Inman	CF	1952-55	16	4	0	0	0	0	16	4
Eglington, Robert	IL	1899-1900	5	2	1	1	0	0	6	3
Elkes, John E	F	1929-33	105	4	8	0	0	0	113	4
Ellerington, William	HB	1919-24	127	0	4	0	0	0	131	0
Elliott, George Washington	CF	1909-25	344	203	21	10	0	0	365	213
Emmerson, George Arthur	OR	1928-30	7	3	0	0	0	0	7	3
Emmerson, Morris	G	1962-63	10	0	3	0	0	0	13	0
Evans, R W	IL	1899-1900	2	0	0	0	0	0	2	0
Eyre, Edmund 'Ninty'	OL	1911-14	63	13	6	2	0	0	69	15
Featherstone, Thomas	CF	1903-04	1	0	0	0	0	0	1	0
Fenton, Michael	F	1932-50	240	147	29	15	0	0	269	162
Ferguson, Charles	OR	1933-36	19	7	1	1	0	0	20	8
Ferguson, Robert	G	1936-38	10	0	0	0	0	0	10	0
Ferguson, Robert G	HB	1924-31	149	2	10	0	0	0	159	2
Fernie, D William	IR	1958-61	65	3	2	0	1	0	68	3
Fitzsimons, Arthur Gerard	IF	1949-59	223	49	8	2	0	0	231	51
Flint, William Arthur	OR	1909-10	1	0	0	0	0	0	1	0
Foggon, Alan	F	1972-76	105/10	45	10/1	2	9/1	2	124/12	49
Forrest, William	HB	1929-39	307	7	26	1	0	0	333	8
Fowler, Henry Norman	LB	1937-39	7	0	0	0	0	0	7	0
Fox, William Victor	FB	1919-24	107	1	5	0	0	0	112	1

Player	Pos	Seasons	League App	League Gls	FA Cup App	FA Cup Gls	FL Cup App	FL Cup Gls	TOTAL App	TOTAL Gls
Frail, Joseph	G	1900-05	63	0	11	0	0	0	74	0
Fraser, Alexander	FB	1911-13	5	0	0	0	0	0	5	0
Freeman, Reginald Victor	FB	1923-30	179	0	8	0	0	0	187	0
Freeman, Thomas	FB	1930-33	74	0	4	0	0	0	78	0
French, John Proctor	LB	1924-25	1	0	0	0	0	0	1	0
Gallacher, Connor	IR	1946-47	1	0	0	0	0	0	1	0
Gallagher, James	LB	1920-21	1	0	0	0	0	0	1	0
Garbett, Terence G	CF	1965-66	7	1	0	0	0	0	7	1
Gardner, John Robert	CH	1928-29	0	0	1	0	0	0	1	0
Gates, William Lazenby	D	1961-74	277/6	12	26/2	0	18	0	321/8	12
Gettins, Edward	OR	1903-05	43	5	4	0	0	0	47	5
Gettins, Joseph H	CF	1899-1903	10	1	0	0	0	0	10	1
Gibson, Frederick William	G	1932-36	110	0	10	0	0	0	120	0
Gibson, Ian Stewart	F	1961-66	168	44	9	1	7	2	184	47
Gibson, Robert J	OR	1910-11	28	3	3	0	0	0	31	3
Gill, Gary	D	1983-89	68/8	2	4/1	0	4/2	0	76/11	2
Glover, Dean Victor*	FB	1987-89	44/6	5	5	0	4	0	53/6	5
Godley, William	F	1902-04	2	0	0	0	0	0	2	0
Good, Hugh	HB	1924-26	10	0	0	0	0	0	10	0
Goodfellow, Derek Ormond	G	1947-48	36	0	3	0	0	0	39	0
Goodson, Leonard	OL	1902-05	35	6	1	0	0	0	36	6
Gordon, David	RB	1908-09	1	0	0	0	0	0	1	0
Gordon, James	WH	1946-54	231	3	22	1	0	0	253	4
Gowland, Norman	G	1925-29	5	0	0	0	0	0	5	0
Gray, Robert SM	IF	1899-1900	3	0	0	0	0	0	3	0
Green, Thomas	F	1904-06	37	9	5	0	0	0	42	9
Griffiths, Thomas Percival	CH	1932-35	88	1	4	0	0	0	92	1
Groves, James Albert	FB	1907-10	27	2	0	0	0	0	27	2
Hall, Bertram Allan Couldwell	CF	1927-30	7	2	0	0	0	0	7	2
Hall, John H	F	1908-10	59	30	3	0	0	0	62	30
Hamilton, Gary James*	D	1981-89	217/12	25	14	1	13	1	244/12	27
Hamilton, William Murdoch	IF	1960-62	10	1	0	0	2	0	12	1
Hankin, Raymond	F	1982-83	19/2	1	3	1	2	1	24/2	3
Hanlon, Edward	CH	1906-07	1	0	0	0	0	0	1	0
Hardwick, George Francis Moutrey	FB	1937-50	143	5	23	2	0	0	166	7
Harkins, John	LH	1906-07	39	0	2	0	0	0	41	0
Harris, Joseph	WH	1922-25	56	0	2	0	0	0	58	0
Harris, William Charles	WH	1953-65	360	69	14	2	4	1	378	72
Harrison, Henry	G	1919-22	20	0	0	0	0	0	20	0
Hartnett, James Benedict	WF	1948-55	48	8	1	0	0	0	49	8
Hasell, Albert A	G	1907-08	1	0	0	0	0	0	1	0
Hastie, John	OR	1920-21	1	0	0	0	0	0	1	0
Hawkins, George Henry	IR	1935-36	1	0	0	0	0	0	1	0
Haworth, John Houghton	LH	1911-15	61	0	3	0	0	0	64	0
Healey, Richard	IF	1913-15	4	2	0	0	0	0	4	2
Heard, Timothy Patrick	IF	1985-86	25	2	1	0	0	0	26	2
Hedley, George Thomas	RB	1905-06	3	0	0	0	0	0	3	0
Hedley, Graeme	F	1976-81	36/14	6	3	0	4	0	43/14	6
Henderson, George Hunter	RH	1905-06	10	0	3	0	0	0	13	0
Henderson, Raymond	IF	1957-61	9	5	0	0	0	0	9	5
Hepple, Gordon	FB	1946-54	41	0	0	0	0	0	41	0
Hewitt, Charles	F	1904-06	33	12	5	2	0	0	38	14
Hick, William Morris	F	1923-25	16	7	1	0	0	0	17	7
Hickling, William	LB	1906-07	5	0	0	0	0	0	5	0
Hickton, John	F	1966-77	395/20	159	37	13	26/4	13	458/24	185
Higgins, William	CH	1900-01	24	1	5	3	0	0	29	4
Higham, Norman	IF	1935-39	49	10	1	0	0	0	50	10
Hillier, Ernest John Guy 'Joe'	G	1929-35	63	0	2	0	0	0	65	0
Hisbent, Joseph M	FB	1911-15	44	0	3	0	0	0	47	0
Hodgson, David James	F	1978-86	118/9	16	9	4	6	0	133/9	20
Hodgson, George	G	1900-01	4	0	0	0	0	0	4	0
Hodgson, John Percival	G	1947-55	13	0	0	0	0	0	13	0
Hogg, John	FB	1902-06	90	0	10	0	0	0	100	0
Holliday, Edwin	WF	1957-66	157	21	6	3	6	1	169	25
Holliday, John William	CF	1930-32	6	4	0	0	0	0	6	4
Holmes, Walter	FB	1914-27	167	1	7	0	0	0	174	1
Honeyand, John William	LH	1919-20	1	0	0	0	0	0	1	0
Horner, William	WH	1960-69	184/3	11	17	0	12/1	1	213/4	12
Horsfield, Arthur	F	1963-69	107/4	51	12/2	5	2	0	121/6	56

404

Arthur Horsfield

Mick Kennedy

Tony Mowbray

Brian Laws

Player	Pos	Seasons	League App	League Gls	FA Cup App	FA Cup Gls	FL Cup App	FL Cup Gls	TOTAL App	TOTAL Gls
Howling, Edward	G	1910-11	1	0	0	0	0	0	1	0
Hughes, Martin	G	1899-1900	24	0	1	0	0	0	25	0
Hume, Robert Morgan	OL	1962-63	19	5	0	0	2	0	21	5
Hunter, Herbert	G	1905-06	3	0	0	0	0	0	3	0
Irvine, James D	F	1964-67	90/1	37	4	3	5	3	99/1	43
Jackson, Andrew	CH	1910-15	123	3	14	0	0	0	137	3
James, William E	F	1910-13	24	8	3	1	0	0	27	9
Jankovic, Bosko	F	1978-81	42/8	16	7	1	3/2	1	52/10	18
Jarvis, Sydney	FB	1927-35	86	1	4	0	0	0	90	1
Jennings, John	FB	1929-37	195	10	10	0	0	0	205	10
Jennings, Samuel	F	1919-20	10	2	0	0	0	0	10	2
Johnson, Peter E	FB	1977-80	42/1	0	3	1	0	0	45/1	1
Johnston, Christopher Patrick	RH	1947-48	2	0	0	0	0	0	2	0
Johnston, Craig Peter	F	1977-81	61/3	16	5/2	0	4/2	0	70/7	16
Jones, Abraham	CH	1901-06	140	9	9	0	0	0	149	9
Jones, George Wilfred	OR	1925-26	24	1	2	0	0	0	26	1
Jones, Gordon Edward	FB	1960-73	457/5	4	40	0	26	1	523/5	5
Jones, John Love	OL	1908-10	14	0	0	0	0	0	14	0
Jones, James	FB	1899-1905	7	0	2	0	0	0	9	0
Jordan, Brian Athol	LH	1958-59	5	0	0	0	0	0	5	0
Kay, John	FB	1984-85	8	0	0	0	0	0	8	0
Kaye, Arthur	WF	1960-65	164	38	13	4	8	2	185	44
Kear, Michael P	WF	1967-70	56/2	7	5	0	3	0	64/2	7
Kelly, B	FB	1910-11	4	0	0	0	0	0	4	0
Kennedy, Frederick	IF	1927-29	23	5	1	0	0	0	24	5
Kennedy, Michael F	IF	1982-84	68	5	7	0	4	0	79	5
Kent, Henry	HB	1908-09	6	0	0	0	0	0	6	0
Kernaghan, Alan Nigel*	F	1984-89	49/36	7	3/3	1	2/7	0	54/46	8
Kerr, Paul Andrew*	F	1986-89	81/3	6	6	2	6	0	93/3	8
Kinnell, George	LH	1968-69	12/1	1	1	0	0	0	13/1	1
Kirby, Frederick	CF	1913-14	2	0	0	0	0	0	2	0
Kirk, Harry	OL	1963-64	1	0	0	0	1	0	2	0
Kite, Philip D	G	1985-86	2	0	0	0	0	0	2	0
Knowles, Cyril Barry	FB	1962-64	37	0	1	0	1	0	39	0
Laidlaw, Joseph Dennis	F	1967-72	103/5	20	9/2	1	5	1	117/7	22
Laking, George Edward	FB	1936-47	94	1	3	0	0	0	97	1
Lamb, Thomas John	IR	1899-1900	23	6	1	0	0	0	24	6
Lawrie, Samuel	IF	1951-57	36	5	1	0	0	0	37	5
Laws, Brian*	FB	1984-87	103/5	12	8/1	0	6/1	2	117/7	14
Lawson, James	WF	1965-68	25/6	3	4	1	2	0	31/6	4
Layton, Arthur E	FB	1911-12	7	0	1	0	0	0	8	0
Le Flem, Richard Peter	WF	1964-66	9	1	1	0	0	0	10	1
Leonard, Henry Droxford 'Harry'	CF	1910-12	13	3	0	0	0	0	13	3
Leslie, James	IR	1901-02	7	3	0	0	0	0	7	3
Lightening, Arthur Douglas	G	1962-63	15	0	0	0	3	0	18	0
Linacre, William	WF	1949-50	31	2	4	1	0	0	35	3
Linton, Thomas	CF	1899-1900	4	0	0	0	0	0	4	0
Linwood, Alexander Bryce	CF	1946-47	14	3	1	0	0	0	15	3
Livingstone, Joseph	CF	1960-63	20	7	0	0	2	0	22	7
Lloyd, Evan	IL	1919-20	2	0	0	0	0	0	2	0
Longstaffe, Geoffrey	OR	1899-1900	19	3	1	0	0	0	20	3
Lugg, Raymond	F	1966-70	34/3	3	2	1	1/2	0	37/5	4
Lynch, Patrick	D	1971-72	0/1	0	0	0	0	0	0/1	0
McAllister, William	RH	1924-26	19	0	2	0	0	0	21	0
McAndrew, Anthony	D	1973-86	311/2	15	23/1	2	15/2	1	349/5	18
Macaulay, W	IF	1902-03	21	2	0	0	0	0	21	2
McCabe, James Joseph	CH	1946-48	34	0	8	0	0	0	42	0
McCallum, Donald	FB	1904-06	25	0	2	0	0	0	27	0
McClelland, James	CF	1924-28	81	42	4	6	0	0	85	48
McClure, Samuel	IL	1910-11	11	3	1	0	0	0	12	3
McCormack, James Cecil	F	1946-49	37	15	2	1	0	0	39	16
McCorquodale, Douglas	CF	1899-1900	2	0	0	0	0	0	2	0
McCowie, Alexander	IF	1900-01	16	5	4	2	0	0	20	7
McCracken, James Peter	HB	1899-1900	33	0	1	0	0	0	34	0
McCrae, Alexander	F	1948-53	122	47	8	2	0	0	130	49
McCreesh, Andrew	FB	1981-82	2	0	0	0	0	0	2	0
McCulloch, James	CF	1907-08	3	1	0	0	0	0	3	1
Macdonald, Garry	F	1980-85	40/13	5	4/1	1	2/1	0	46/15	6
Macfarlane, John	HB	1929-33	95	0	6	0	0	0	101	0

Player	Pos	Seasons	League App	League Gls	FA Cup App	FA Cup Gls	FL Cup App	FL Cup Gls	TOTAL App	TOTAL Gls
Macfarlane, Robert	G	1902-03	18	0	1	0	0	0	19	0
Macfarlane, Thomas	FB	1901-02	2	0	1	0	0	0	3	0
McGuigan, Andrew	OR	1902-04	1	0	0	0	0	0	1	0
McIlmoyle, Hugh	CF	1969-71	69/1	19	8	2	2	1	79/1	22
McKay, John	IF	1926-34	104	19	5	1	0	0	109	20
McKennan, Peter Stewart	F	1949-51	40	18	3	1	0	0	43	19
McKenzie, Duncan	WH	1938-39	28	1	0	0	0	0	28	1
McLean, James Derek	IF	1955-62	119	30	3	0	1	0	123	30
McLeod, Donald	FB	1908-13	138	0	10	0	0	0	148	0
McManus, Charles Eric	G	1985-86	2	0	0	0	0	0	2	0
McMordie, Alexander 'Eric'	IF	1965-74	231/10	22	20/1	1	11	2	262/11	25
McMurray, John	WH	1953-55	3	0	0	0	0	0	3	0
McNally, John	CH	1899-1901	3	0	1	0	0	0	4	0
McNeil, Michael	FB	1958-64	178	3	9	0	6	0	193	3
McNeill, Allan A	F	1967-69	3	0	0/1	0	0	0	3/1	0
McPartland, Desmond	G	1965-68	35	0	2	0	3	0	40	0
McPhail, Donald Douglas	OR	1930-31	4	1	1	0	0	0	5	1
McPherson, Kenneth	CF	1953-56	33	15	0	0	0	0	33	15
McRobbie, Alan	LB	1911-12	1	0	0	0	0	0	1	0
Madden, George	IF	1899-1900	3	0	0	0	0	0	3	0
Maddison, James	OL	1946-47	1	0	0	0	0	0	1	0
Maddren, William Dixon	D	1968-77	293/3	19	23	0	24	2	340/3	21
Mahoney, John F	WH	1977-79	77	1	7	1	6	0	90	2
Maitland, Alfred Edward	LB	1923-24	25	0	1	0	0	0	26	0
Malan, Norman Frederick	G	1946-47	2	0	0	0	0	0	2	0
Malcolm, George	LH	1912-15	94	1	7	0	0	0	101	1
Mannion, Wilfred James	IF	1936-54	341	99	27	11	0	0	368	110
Marcroft, Edward Hallows	OR	1931-32	1	1	0	0	0	0	1	1
Marshall, John	FB	1919-23	116	0	5	0	0	0	121	0
Marshall, Stanley Kenneth	IL	1965-66	2	0	0	0	0	0	2	0
Martin, George Scott	IF	1932-33	6	0	0	0	0	0	6	0
Martin, John	WH	1932-39	129	3	8	0	0	0	137	3
Masson, Donald Sanderson	IF	1964-68	50/3	6	7	1	4	0	61/3	7
Mathieson, James Adamson	G	1926-33	245	0	19	0	0	0	264	0
Mattinson, Harry	CH	1946-47	3	0	0	0	0	0	3	0
Millar, James	HB	1900-03	19	0	3	0	0	0	22	0
Millar, William M	OL	1927-29	16	6	0	0	0	0	16	6
Miller, Joseph	WH	1926-30	140	0	13	0	0	0	153	0
Million, Esmond	G	1956-62	52	0	1	0	0	0	53	0
Mills, David John	IF	1969-85	309/19	90	29	10	23/1	8	361/20	108
Milne, John Vance	WF	1937-39	59	7	7	0	0	0	66	7
Mitchell, Albert James	OL	1954-56	50	6	2	0	0	0	52	6
Mochan Neil	F	1951-53	38	14	1	0	0	0	39	14
Moody, Alan	RB	1968-73	44/2	0	3	0	0	0	47/2	0
Moran, Martin	F	1900-02	36	5	9	1	0	0	45	6
Mordue, John	WF	1920-22	35	1	0	0	0	0	35	1
Mowbray, Anthony Mark*	D	1982-89	260/3	21	17	1	16/1	1	293/4	23
Muir, John	OL	1902-04	13	0	0	0	0	0	13	0
Muir, William	HB	1902-04	4	0	0	0	0	0	4	0
Mulholland, Francis Gerard	LH	1951-58	46	0	4	0	0	0	50	0
Murdoch, Robert White	WH	1973-76	93/2	6	7	1	13	0	113/2	7
Murphy, David Anthony	LH	1937-38	12	0	3	0	0	0	15	0
Murphy, Joseph	IL	1899-1900	6	5	0	0	0	0	6	5
Murphy, Michael	IL	1899-1900	2	2	0	0	0	0	2	2
Murphy, Thomas Edwin	IL	1946-48	9	1	0	0	0	0	9	1
Murray, Alan	IR	1969-71	6/4	1	0	0	0	0	6/4	1
Murray, Thomas	IF	1905-07	12	2	0	0	0	0	12	2
Murray, William	OL	1921-23	15	1	2	0	0	0	17	1
Muttitt, Ernest	OL	1929-32	20	3	5	1	0	0	25	4
Myton, Brian	LH	1968-71	10	0	0	0	2	0	12	0
Nash, Frank Cooper	G	1937-48	19	0	0	0	0	0	19	0
Nattrass, Irving	FB	1979-86	186/5	2	18	0	10/1	0	214/6	2
Neal, Richard M	LH	1961-63	33	4	2	0	3	0	38	4
Niblo, Thomas Bruce	CF	1899-1900	3	2	0	0	0	0	3	2
Nichol, James	WF	1910-14	52	13	4	0	0	0	56	13
Nobbs, Keith Alan	FB	1980-81	1	0	0	0	0	0	1	0
Norris, Oliver Plunkett	OR	1951-54	12	3	1	0	0	0	13	3
Nurse, Melvyn Tudor George	CH	1962-66	113	8	8	1	3	0	124	9
O'Connell, Seamus Cyril Patrick	IL	1953-54	3	2	2	0	0	0	5	2

Ken McPherson

Bernie Slaven

Trevor Senior

Trevor Putney

Player	Pos	Seasons	League App	League Gls	FA Cup App	FA Cup Gls	FL Cup App	FL Cup Gls	TOTAL App	TOTAL Gls
O'Hagan, Charles	IF	1906-07	5	1	0	0	0	0	5	1
O'Hanlon, Kelham Gerrard	G	1982-85	87	0	6	0	4	0	97	0
O'Riordan, Donal J	CH	1985-86	41	2	1	1	2	0	44	3
O'Rourke, John	CF	1966-68	63/1	38	3	3	5	1	71/1	42
Orritt, Bryan	F	1961-66	115/3	22	4	1	6	0	125/3	23
Osborne, Fergus	IF	1899-1900	12	2	0	0	0	0	12	2
Ostler, John	CH	1899-1900	3	0	0	0	0	0	3	0
Otto, Heine M	IF	1981-85	163/4	24	12	2	9	2	184/3	28
Page, Robert	HB	1899-1904	22	4	1	0	0	0	23	4
Pallister, Gary Andrew*	LH	1985-89	153	5	10	1	10	1	173	6
Parkin, Raymond	RH	1935-37	6	0	0	0	0	0	6	0
Parkinson, Gary Anthony*	D	1986-89	117/3	2	8	0	10	0	135/3	2
Paterson, Thomas	CF	1974-75	1	0	0	0	0	0	1	0
Patterson, Ronald Lindsay	LB	1951-52	1	0	0	0	0	0	1	0
Peacock, Alan	CF	1955-64	218	125	13	8	7	8	238	141
Peacock, Joseph	LH	1927-30	80	2	5	2	0	0	85	4
Pears, Stephen*	G	1983-89	165	0	11	0	12	0	188	0
Pease, William Harold	OR	1926-33	221	99	17	3	0	0	238	102
Peggie, James	F	1910-11	6	0	0	0	0	0	6	0
Pender, Robert	HB	1919-24	104	10	6	0	0	0	110	10
Pentland, Frederick Beaconsfield	F	1908-11	92	11	4	0	0	0	96	11
Peters, Jeffrey	LB	1979-80	6	0	0	0	0	0	6	0
Phillips, Bryan John	D	1954-60	121	2	3	0	0	0	124	2
Phillipson, Thomas F	IL	1904-05	3	2	0	0	0	0	3	2
Piercy, Frank R	LH	1899-1903	4	0	1	0	0	0	5	0
Piercy, Henry Robert	WH	1899-1900	8	1	0	0	0	0	8	1
Platt, James Archibald	G	1971-83	401	0	34	0	33	0	468	0
Poole, Kevin	G	1987-89	13	0	1	0	0	0	14	0
Poskett, Malcolm	F	1973-74	0/1	0	0	0	0	0	0/1	0
Poulton, Alonzo	F	1919-22	18	5	1	0	0	0	19	5
Povey, William	IF	1962-63	6	0	0	0	0	0	6	0
Pratt, Richard	IF	1899-1900	16	1	1	0	0	0	17	1
Priest, Alfred Ernest	FB	1906-07	12	0	0	0	0	0	12	0
Priest, F	CF	1906-07	1	0	0	0	0	0	1	0
Proctor, Mark Gerard	HB	1978-89	117/2	12	10	1	6	1	133/2	14
Proudlock, Paul	F	1986-89	2/2	1	0	0	0	0	2/2	1
Pugh, Charles Edwin	OL	1899-1900	31	7	1	0	0	0	32	7
Raisbeck, Luke	CH	1899-1900	19	1	0	0	0	0	19	1
Ramage, Alan	HB	1975-80	65/4	2	6	0	5	0	76/4	2
Ramsay, Andrew	FB	1899-1904	124	1	12	0	0	0	136	1
Ratcliffe, Donald	WH	1963-66	65	3	6	0	0	0	71	3
Ratcliffe, Ernest	FB	1905-07	9	0	0	0	0	0	9	0
Rayment, Joseph Watson	WF	1952-55	24	4	0	0	0	0	24	4
Reagan, Charles Martin	OR	1947-51	24	4	1	0	0	0	25	1
Redfern J	LH	1899-1900	3	0	0	0	0	0	3	0
Reid, George	CF	1899-1900	15	5	0	0	0	0	15	5
Reid, George T	F	1905-06	24	5	2	0	0	0	26	5
Rickaby, Stanley	FB	1947-50	10	0	0	0	0	0	10	0
Rigby, Arthur	OL	1932-33	10	3	0	0	0	0	10	3
Ripley, Stuart Edward*	F	1984-89	126/6	15	8	1	10	2	144/6	18
Roberts, Alan	OR	1983-84	28/10	2	0/1	0	2/1	0	30/12	2
Roberts, J	OL	1906-07	1	0	0	0	0	0	1	0
Roberts, Richard James	OL	1903-05	23	5	0	0	0	0	23	5
Roberts, William S	OL	1906-08	12	0	0	0	0	0	12	0
Robertson, Alexander	CF	1900-03	48	24	8	8	0	0	56	32
Robertson, James	OR	1901-03	32	3	0	0	0	0	32	3
Robertson, William George	OL	1954-55	5	2	0	0	0	0	5	2
Robinson, John	IR	1953-55	3	0	0	0	0	0	3	0
Robinson, Joseph Norman	CH	1946-48	16	0	1	0	0	0	17	0
Robinson, John W	LH	1919-20	1	0	0	0	0	0	1	0
Robinson, Richard	FB	1946-59	390	1	26	0	0	0	416	1
Rodgerson, Alan Ralph	IF	1958-64	13	3	0	0	1	0	14	3
Rooks, Richard	CH	1965-69	136	14	7	0	7	0	150	14
Ross, Albert Cyril	FB	1935-37	11	0	1	0	0	0	12	0
Ross, Colin	WH	1980-83	37/1	0	2	0	0	0	39/1	0
Rowell, Gary	IF	1985-87	27	10	1	0	2	2	30	12
Russell, Edward Thomas	HB	1951-53	29	1	3	0	0	0	32	1
Saxby, Michael W	HB	1984-85	15	0	2	0	0	0	17	0
Scott, Geoffrey	LB	1984-85	2	0	0	0	1	0	3	0

Player	Pos	Seasons	League		FA Cup		FL Cup		TOTAL	
			App	Gls	App	Gls	App	Gls	App	Gls
Scott, Joseph Cumpson	IF	1954-58	93	26	6	4	0	0	99	30
Scott, William Reed	IF	1930-32	26	5	2	0	0	0	28	5
Scrimshaw, Charles Thomas	LB	1938-39	9	0	0	0	0	0	9	0
Senior, Trevor John*	F	1987-89	9/1	2	0	0	1	0	10/1	2
Shand, Hector	WH	1906-07	2	0	0	0	0	0	2	0
Shaw, Thomas William	FB	1899-1900	12	0	1	0	0	0	13	0
Shearer, David John	F	1977-83	88/9	23	10/2	4	4/2	3	102/13	30
Shepherdson, Harold	CH	1936-47	17	0	0	0	0	0	17	0
Short, Maurice	G	1967-70	16	0	2	0	1	0	19	0
Slade, Charles Howard	WH	1922-25	68	2	2	0	0	0	70	2
Slaven, Bernard Joseph*	F	1985-89	158/1	61	10	4	10	2	178/1	67
Smith, David	OL	1967-68	1/1	0	1	0	2	2	4/1	2
Smith, David W	WH	1900-05	108	12	6	0	0	0	114	12
Smith, Edward George	G	1899-1900	10	0	0	0	0	0	10	0
Smith, Ernest Edwin	CH	1923-25	21	0	0	0	0	0	21	0
Smith, George	WH	1968-71	74	0	5	1	3	0	82	1
Smith, John	FB	1926-30	113	0	10	0	0	0	123	0
Smith, John	RB	1933-34	1	0	0	0	0	0	1	0
Smith, Malcolm	CF	1972-76	32/24	11	0/2	0	5/1	2	37/27	13
Smith, Robert Alexander	FB	1965-72	119/2	1	9	0	3	0	131/2	1
Souness, Graeme James	WH	1972-78	174/2	22	13	1	15	0	202/2	23
Spraggon, Frank	WH	1963-76	277/3	3	23	0	18/1	0	318/4	3
Spriggs, Stephen	RB	1986-87	3	0	0	0	0	0	3	0
Spuhler, John Oswald	CF	1946-54	216	69	25	12	0	0	241	81
Stage, William	OL	1913-14	3	0	0	0	0	0	3	0
Stephens, Arthur 'Archie'	IF	1984-88	87/5	24	3	0	8/1	1	98/6	25
Stevenson, Arthur Brown	OL	1923-24	8	0	0	0	0	0	8	0
Stewart, James	G	1978-80	34	0	2	0	2	0	38	0
Stiles, Norbert Peter	WH	1971-73	57	2	7	0	5	0	69	2
Stirling, John	WF	1911-14	103	8	9	0	0	0	112	8
Stone, John G	LB	1971-72	2	0	0	0	0	0	2	0
Stonehouse, Derek	FB	1953-61	174	0	11	0	2	0	187	0
Storey, Thomas	OR	1913-20	33	1	0	0	0	0	33	1
Stott, James	LH	1899-1900	1	0	0	0	0	0	1	0
Strong, Andrew	FB	1984-85	6	0	0	0	0	0	6	0
Stuart, Robert William	FB	1931-48	247	2	21	0	0	0	268	2
Suddick, James	IR	1903-04	1	1	0	0	0	0	1	1
Sugrue, Paul	IF	1982-85	66/3	6	8	3	4	1	78/3	10
Surtees, John	IL	1931-32	1	0	0	0	0	0	1	0
Swales, Norman	RH	1925-26	2	0	0	0	0	0	2	0
Taylor, Brian	HB	1972-76	14/4	1	0	0	1/1	0	15/5	1
Taylor, Carl Wilson	OR	1957-60	11	1	0	0	0	0	11	1
Taylor, Peter Thomas	G	1955-61	140	0	6	0	0	0	146	0
Tennant, James	OL	1901-02	17	7	0	0	0	0	17	7
Thackeray, James	OL	1904-10	157	16	13	2	0	0	170	18
Thomas, David	OL	1981-82	13	1	0	0	0	0	13	1
Thomas, Martin R	G	1984-85	4	0	0	0	0	0	4	0
Thompson, A	CF	1900-03	7	3	1	0	0	0	8	3
Thompson, Norman	IL	1925-26	8	3	0	0	0	0	8	3
Thompson, William T	IL	1905-06	6	2	0	0	0	0	6	2
Thomson, Kenneth Gordon	CH	1959-63	84	1	4	0	2	0	90	1
Thomson, Robert	OL	1981-82	18/2	2	2	2	2	1	22/2	5
Tinsley, Walter	IL	1913-21	86	46	3	3	0	0	89	49
Tomlin, John	CH	1906-07	4	0	0	0	0	0	4	0
Townsend, James	WH	1963-66	65/2	6	4	0	1	0	70/2	6
Trechman, Otto L	CF	1905-06	1	0	0	0	0	0	1	0
Tucker, William Henry	CF	1906-07	4	1	0	0	0	0	4	1
Turnbull, Lee Mark	F	1985-87	8/8	4	0	0	0/1	0	8/9	4
Turner, Peter	IL	1901-02	23	6	2	0	0	0	25	6
Tyldesley, James	RB	1906-07	23	0	2	0	0	0	25	0
Ugolini, Rolando	G	1948-56	320	0	15	0	0	0	335	0
Urquhart, A	OR	1907-08	4	0	0	0	0	0	4	0
Urwin, Thomas	WF	1914-24	192	14	8	0	0	0	200	14
Verrill, Edward	HB	1907-15	181	4	11	0	0	0	192	4
Vincent, John Victor	WF	1970-72	37/3	7	0	0	2/1	0	39/4	7
Wainscoat, William Russell	IF	1923-25	34	5	2	0	0	0	36	5
Waldock, Ronald	WF	1959-62	34	7	1	0	0	0	35	7
Walker, Donald Hunter	LH	1959-62	23	1	1	0	0	0	24	1
Walker, John	LB	1913-21	106	0	3	0	0	0	109	0

Player	Pos	Seasons	League App	League Gls	FA Cup App	FA Cup Gls	FL Cup App	FL Cup Gls	TOTAL App	TOTAL Gls
Walker, Robert Geoffrey	OL	1946-55	240	50	19	3	0	0	259	53
Walker, Robert H	IL	1905-06	9	2	5	1	0	0	14	3
Walley, Ernest	LH	1958-59	8	0	0	0	0	0	8	0
Walsh, Alan	F	1977-78	0/3	0	0	0	0	0	0/3	0
Wanless, Robert	OR	1899-1900	10	0	0	0	0	0	10	0
Ward, Paul Terence	D	1982-86	69/7	1	3/1	0	5	0	77/8	1
Wardle, George	OR	1937-38	1	0	0	0	0	0	1	0
Wardrope, Alexander	CH	1910-11	10	0	1	0	0	0	11	0
Wardrope, William	F	1899-1902	62	21	11	3	0	0	73	24
Warren, Frederick Windsor	OL	1929-36	160	49	4	1	0	0	164	50
Watkin, Thomas William Steel	OL	1953-55	11	2	0	0	0	0	11	2
Watson, Arnold	WH	1925-26	8	0	0	0	0	0	8	0
Watson, Herbert Leonard	RH	1929-32	13	1	2	0	0	0	15	1
Watson, James	LB	1906-10	103	0	4	0	0	0	107	0
Watson, Robert	IR	1901-03	16	5	1	0	0	0	17	5
Wayman, Charles	CF	1954-56	55	31	3	2	0	0	58	33
Webb, Stanley J	CF	1967-71	20/9	6	0	0	0	0	20/9	6
Webster, Maurice	CH	1920-34	262	3	19	0	0	0	281	3
Weddle, Derek Keith	CH	1961-62	3	1	0	0	0	0	3	1
Weightman, Eric	D	1935-36	2	0	1	0	0	0	3	0
Weir, James	LB	1910-15	113	0	12	0	0	0	125	0
Whigham, William	G	1966-72	187	0	17	0	6	0	210	0
Whitaker, William	CH	1947-55	177	1	7	0	0	0	184	1
White, William	IR	1903-04	7	0	0	0	0	0	7	0
Wilcox, Frederick J	OR	1905-10	106	12	4	0	0	0	110	12
Wilkie, Derrick	CH	1959-61	4	0	0	0	0	0	4	0
Wilkie, John	IL	1900-01	28	8	7	2	0	0	35	10
Willey, Alan S	F	1974-78	27/22	7	1/3	1	3/1	0	31/26	8
Williams, Jesse T	OL	1924-28	37	8	1	0	0	0	38	8
Williams, Joseph Joshua	F	1931-35	78	11	7	2	0	0	85	13
Williams, Owen	OL	1923-30	184	40	10	4	0	0	194	44
Williamson, Reginald Garnet	G	1901-23	563	2	39	0	0	0	602	2
Wilson, Andrew Nesbit	CF	1914-24	86	56	4	1	0	0	90	57
Wilson, Archibald	WF	1914-15	21	4	2	0	0	0	23	4
Wilson, F Peter	RB	1967-68	1	0	0	0	0	0	1	0
Wilson, John	RB	1924-27	18	0	0	0	0	0	18	0
Wilson, Thomas T	F	1907-10	10	0	0	0	0	0	10	0
Windridge, James Edward	IF	1911-14	68	11	8	1	0	0	76	12
Windross, Dennis	IR	1959-61	4	1	0	0	0	0	4	1
Wood, Alfred E H	IF	1976-77	22/1	2	5	0	0	0	27/1	2
Wood, Darren Terence	D	1981-84	101	6	8	0	6	0	115	6
Woodward, Thomas	OL	1949-51	19	6	0	0	0	0	19	6
Woof, William	F	1974-82	30/16	5	0/1	0	7/1	1	37/18	6
Worrall, William Edward	G	1905-06	1	0	0	0	0	0	1	0
Worthington, Peter Robert	FB	1967-68	2	0	1	0	0	0	3	0
Wynn, Richard	OL	1913-15	7	1	0	0	0	0	7	1
Yeoman, Ramon Irvine	WH	1958-63	210	3	10	0	7	0	227	3
Yorston, Benjamin Collard	F	1933-39	152	54	7	0	0	0	159	54
Young, Ernest Wilson	CF	1920-21	1	0	0	0	0	0	1	0
Young, Robert T	CH	1908-10	34	5	3	0	0	0	37	5

SUBSCRIBERS

Presentation Copies
1 Middlesbrough Football Club
2 The Football League • 3 The Football Association

4 Harry Glasper
5 Wilf Mannion
6 George Hardwick
7 Alan Murray
8 Ian Yates
9 Wayne Britton
10 Alan Holmes
11 Simon Ditchburn
12 Philip King
13 William Steven Byrne
14 Simon Park
15 Alan Maloney
16 Alastair Brownlee
17 Trevor Glasper
18 Richard Barnes
19 J M Sinton
20 Robert Homer
21 G E Glasper
22 P Sutcliffe
23 Michael Charlton
24 C P Fletcher
25 Allan & Jonathan
   Woodgate
26 Jeff Myers
27 Sonny Alder
28 Derek Ferguson
29 M D Clarke
30 Stuart Ferguson Lillie
31 Martin James Milburn
32 Mark Carman
33 Victor S W Farrow
34 Bryan Rodgerson
35 George Robert Conroy
36 Nigel Bailey
37 W M Martin
38 Mark John Lythe
39 Nigel Gibb
40 Leslie Fegan
41 Keith M Johnson
42 Martin Wood

43 John Mitchell
44 Michael Bentley
45 G Dixon
46 Darren W Milburn
47 Gordon William Holt
48 Gary Smith
49 Robert James
   McCallion
50 Carl Erik Lindberg
51 Ronald Hartas
52 Mark Simpson
53 B Day
54 Colin Galloway
55 Raymond James
   Murphy
56 John Davis
57 Andrew Davis
58 J M Ingledew
59 P Shipton
60 N Bannister
61 Nigel Ball
62 Ian Brickman
63 Peter Jackson
64 Alan Maude
65 David Simpson
66 Simon Dale
67 G W Taylor
68 Ian Webb
69 Graham Warr
70 Geoffrey Coppack
71 David J Walton
72 Lennie Downs
73 Timothy John
   Donaldson
74 D Milsom
75 S W Cockerill
76 Geoffrey Grainger
77 John Henry Barker
78 Kevin Newbury
79 Gary Alan Blakemore

80 Geoff Wilson
81 Jane K Souter
82 John Armstrong
83 Peter Boland
84 Christopher Alan
   Jones
85 R Smith
86 A P R Whitehead
87 Christopher John
   Michael Davey
88 Ray Dales
89 Allan Roberts
90 Derek Allen
91 Jason Speck
92 Paul Jackson
93 G N Smith
94 D P Mahoney Snr
95 Steven Wilkinson
96 J I Veacock
97 Christopher James
   Cocks
98 Robert C D Storey
99 Geoffrey Alan Hope
100 K Laing
101 John Anthony Stone
102 Dave McCullagh
103 M F Carling
104 Thomas Edward
   Brown
105 Kevin Roy
106 David Griffiths
107 Michael Baty
108 William Colgan
109 Andrew Trenholm
   Richards
110 Leigh Sayers
111 Sheila Neal
112 A Laity
113 Joe Hodgson
114 Robert M Buckley

115 Gary H Sillett
116 John Watts
117 J A Smithard
118 Jack Marshall
119 Derek Hall
120 Philip Wilkinson
121 David Vickers
122 K Jeffels
123 Thomas Edward Griffiths
124 W G Davenport
125 David Hand
126 Denis Barry
127 Barry Paterson
128 Michael W Weatherill
129 J R Keeley
130 H Innes
131 Mark Taylor
132 Andrew Sinclair
133 John Edward Leyshon
134 Ian Davison
135 Stephen Mark Kernan
136 Raymond Henry Watton
137 Trevor C Walker
138 Brian H Douglass
139 Paul Radics
140 Stephen Garbutt
141 John Whittingham
142 Paul Whittingham
143 R W Gibbs
144 Jonathan D Bell
145 Colin Butterworth
146 David Scott
147 Patrick J J Murray
148 Malcolm Danby
149 P Kelleher
150 Wallie Davies
151 Iain Thomson
152 Karen Wallis
153 Neil Andrew Williams
154 B Fairweather
155 Lee Midgley
156 Gizzard (Plastic Geordie)
157 Trevor Pattison

158 Brian Brown
159 Sean Tranter
160 Alan J Gregory
161 Stephen Dent
162 David Edward South
163 Thomas Henry Taylor
164 Adam John Taylor
165 Leonard James Smith
166 Anthony Harris
167 D J Killington
168 S D Killington
169 Norman Beall
170 Vince Leonard
171 A Underwood
172 Sheila Kettlewell
173 Derek Taylor
174 John Smitheringale
175 Mark E McNeill
176 Gary Hodgson
177 Ian M Wilson
178 Mark Smith
179 Anthony Farrell
180 John Robertson
181 Jim Richardson
182 Ashley Young
183 Keith Watson
184 Adam E Robinson
185 Mark & Louise Armitstead
186 M Teague
187 Peter Stockdale
188 W A Marsay
189 I P Broom
190 K Williams
191 John George Skinn
192 Richard Dargue
193 Ross Code
194 John R Pearson
195 J T Myers
196 Bryn T Roberts
197 Billy Simpson
198 Gordon R Henderson
199 L J Ward
200 Anthony McCormick
201 P C Stephenson

202 Royal Air Force Topcliffe Supporters
203 Buff Harding
204 R W Rix
205 Philip Robinson
206 Denis H Phillips
207 Michael Jones
208 Maureen Boyle
209 Peter Boyle
210 Alan Stangoe
211 Harold Welsh
212 Carl Carvello
213 Simon R Smith
214 Gerald Lister
215 Andrew Gough
216 Michael Smith
217 Roger Clews
218 Raymond Smith
219 Gareth Aungiers
220 Cheryl Clarke
221 T Mason
222 T Mason
223 T Mason
224 T Mason
225 T Mason
226 Malcolm Baldwin
227 Christopher Best
228 R A Atkinson
229 Mark Antony Robinson
230 Keith Atkinson
231 A W Slingsby
232 Mike Millett
233 Michael Dallin
234 Paul Gotheridge
235 John Appleby
236 Paul A Griffiths
237 Brian Appleton
238 C Swain
239 Edward Leeson
240 Peter Wilson
241 John & Richard Bartle
242 Duncan Watt
243 D T Bryant
244 Stephen Cooper
245 J A Harris

246 John Treleven
247 J S Pyke
248 Gerald Hill
249 A P J M Otten
250 Christopher Minchin
251 Esa Kautonen
252 Geir Juva
253 W F Pratt
254 Lars-Olof Wendler
255 P W Stevenson
256 Simons Martin
257 Rudolf Iseli
258 Harald Lohr
259 Surapot Saengchote
260 Kåre M Torgrimsen
261 David J Godfrey
262 M Swart
263 A Young
264 Keith Lowe
265 R G Woolman
266 Richard Stocken
267 Gordon Small
268 A L Tweddell
269 John Motson
270 S P Tomlin
271 P H Whitehead
272 Phil Soar
273 G D Painter
274 Mrs L Ford
275 Paul Flintoft
276 J F Taylor
277 Simon Longworth
278 Wilfred Cook
279 David J Graham
280 Bob Brown
281 Steven Williams
282 Graham Alderson
283 Jim Skeen
284 David Woodgate
285 Kevin McPartland
286 Des Hudson
287 Claire Owen
288 Denis Poole
289 Ian Turner Wallis
290 D G McLay
291 L J Garrett

292 Geoff Flintoff
293 C J Lackenby
294 Mary Hide
295 Martin Baines
296 Mark S Baines
297 B E Sellers
298 Michael G Holtom
299 Harry Kay
300 Derek Hyde
301 Geoff Allman
302 R J Gamble
303 B H Standish
304 David Keats
305 Moira & Frederick
     Furness
306 Fred Lee
307 Donald Noble
308 Graham & Janet
     Carter
309 Peter Lunn
310 D A R H Webster
311 R D N Wells
312 David Robert
     Earnshaw
313 Dave Hillam
314 Colin Cameron
315 Gary Wynne
316 John Qvarnberg
317 R A Kelly
318 Andrew Siddaway
319 Graham R Bunn
320 Martin Hargan
321 A G Galloway
322 Andrew Hyams
323 Dave Palmer
324 Paul Hancock
325 Anthony Ian Parsons
326 Mark & Anne Green
327 Sir Owen Green
328 Sonya Louise Whem
329 Michael David Harvey
330 Kevin Cuthbert
331 David Higgins
332 Nicky Reidy
333 Gary Phillips
334 Ian Phillips

335 Peter Holton
336 Richard Emms
337 Peter Pickup
338 Malcolm Hartley
339 Ian Willott
340 Ken Wiles
341 C Emmerson
342 Graham Richards
343 S M Smith
344 G Wm Smith
345 Peter Jackson
346 Peter Jackson
347 John Byrne
348 Derek E Johnstone
349 David Shane Berriman
350 Graeme Beales
351 Darren Beales
352 Steven Whelerton
353 Sundeep 'Sunny'
     Basson
354 S G Waites
355 David Blain
356 R T Postlethwaite
357 A J Hindley
358 Eric Heesom
359 Anders Johansson
360 J Gardiner
361 Ian Griffiths
362 Ake Axelsson
363 W D Phillips
364 Ian Green
365 Derek Jones
366 Harry Thompson
367 Dave Helliwell
368 Angus W Rodger
369 Svend Madsen
370 Brian Vickers
371 Gordon Scott
372 Peter Collins
373 Gerald Neil Gallagher
374 David C Davies
375 Andrew Anderson
376 Dominic Hartford
377 Paul Mewse
378 Simon Oliver
379 Richard F Sanderson

380 Raymond Shaw	425 Andy Smith	468 David & Simon Curtis
381 David Gregg	426 R H Motson	469 D K Rickards
382 Neil Rogers	427 Graham Fitzgerald	470 K G Rickards
383 Paul Sisson	428 Tony Colliver	471 Michael Gowland
384 Les Gold	429 Roger Wash	472 John Robert Hoggarth
385 A Bare	430 Glyn Jones	473 Malcolm France
386 J Ringrose	431 Brian Tabner	474 W K Wilde
387 Alex W Brown	432 Haji Mohammed	475 David J Horner
388 Ronald Ford	Boota	476 Anthony G Horner
389 Stewart Fell	433 Kenneth Seaman	477 Mark Smith
390 Douglas Lamming	434 Barry Lister	478 Christopher Grieveson
391 Andrew G McAuliffe	435 Michael B Rooney	479 George Woods
392 Malcolm Ferguson	436 R Peachey	480 Paul Hannah
393 C Swain	437 Dr C J Morton	481 Des McMann
394 John D Landreth	438 Maurice Golesworthy	482 Norman Hardy
395 Mike Purkiss	439 Peter Baxter	483 David Smith
396 Mike Fenton	440 Stanley A Robinson	484 Laurie Nelson
397 Trond Isaksen	441 F Beale	485 M G Phillips
398 Mark J Nelson	442 Craig Walker	486 Alexander Reid
399 Christopher J Nelson	443 Andrea Emma Sophie	487 Ian Garbutt
400 Paul Whitfield	Dodds	488 G Staton
401 Henry McWilliam	444 Nathan Donovan	489 G Growe
402 Andrew Warwick	445 David Downs	490 Robert Neeve
403 A E Honeyman	446 Norman Green	491 John Henry List
404 Steven F Thomas	447 Brian Rees	492 Mr Brine
405 D G Coates	448 D M Seymour	493 Neal Andrew Bullock
406 A W Palmer	449 J W Seymour	494 Ken Moore
407 Adam Pallagi	450 K Manvel	495 L Smith
408 Bernie Haw	451 Craig Pletts	496 John Harrison
409 Andrew Carbert	452 Jon Hunt	497 Steven Westcough
410 Robert Page	453 Anthony Jones	498 Paul Birch
411 Sports Marketing	454 Peter Sutherland	499 Chris Ingoe
(Australia)	455 Jake Bell	500 Sean Anthony
412 Geoffrey Wright	456 Craig Andrew Watson	Harrison
413 Tim Kirton	457 Steven Bateman	501 Thomas Ian Webster
414 David Taylor	458 D R Harvey	502 Domenico Polimeno
415 Ruth Taylor	459 Bernie Hamilton	503 Alan Nudd
416 Graham Lister	460 Paul Jerome	504 Andrew J Grainger
417 Stewart John Cope	461 Andrew John Park	505 Mathew Rice
418 Colin Cope	462 Richard Bayles	506 E R Barnes
419 Ian Gamble	463 David Graeme	507 Kenneth Howell
420 John Burton	Mackenzie	508 Keith Buxton
421 Stephen Canney	464 Martyn Pilley	509 John David Thompson
422 Christopher Risbrough	465 R A Peacock	510 D Matterson
423 L A Zammit	466 Stephen Peacock	511 A Jones
424 Mark White	467 Richard Peacock	512 K G Nudd

513 Tasos D Botsis	546 Andrew D McLeod	579 Mark Jones
514 Mioche Serge	547 Graham Crowe	580 R P Swatman
515 J C Cunningham	548 Phil Armstrong	581 Dave & Sandie
516 Ronnie Lane	549 Michael Richard Blyth	Hartley
517 Colin Paul Fairlamb	550 Doug Clements	582 Derren Wicks
518 G N Lewin	551 Tamla Veejay Benson	583 Martin Sydney
519 John A Mitchell	552 John Michael Sweeney	Willoughby
520 Michael R Carter	553 Brian Bailey	584 Ashley J Harvey
521 R N Smith	554 J Bailey	585 Francis Paul Watson
522 Frank Kay	555 J W Lyth	586 Philip John Carter
523 Derek Nisbet	556 Alan G Story	587 George Brendan Quinn
524 EDC (North-East) Ltd	557 Mulholland Family	588 M C Fisher
525 Keith Nudd	558 David Cope	589 Tony Hunt
526 L A Henwood	559 David John Solly	590 Ian Fox
527 Tanya Russell	560 Lindsey H Kitching	591 C A Hepworth
528 Brian S Cowen	561 K H Jones	592 Oliver J F Amsden
529 Graham Clarke	562 Edward James Yare	593 Mark C Richmond
530 Brian G Hurst	563 Kevin Towse	594 James Kevin Alderton
531 John Gibson	564 Andrew Allen	595 Peter Lynch
532 D J Harper	565 Chris Clark Solicitor	596 J A Wright
533 David R Smith	566 Gordon Rees	597 Clark Gibson
534 Paul Hudson	567 Ian Connorton	598 Steven Hurst
535 Paul Coles	568 Simon O'Connor	599 Simon Callaghan
536 David Tomasetti	569 Sean Gilgallon	600 David Higgett
537 J C Ryan	570 Thomas Michael Rea	601 Kenneth James Quinn
538 C J A Foxton	571 John Williams	602 Alan Bestford
539 Ernest Burniston	572 John Wilson	603 Tom Havelock
540 Keith Gibson	573 D R Waddleton	604 Simon R S Fletcher
541 Kenneth Stockill	574 David Neil McConville	605 Brian H Hobbs
542 P R Dewey	575 Colin Mendum	606 Malcolm Phillips
543 Neil McCabe	576 Grahame Bandeira	607 L Bone
544 M V McCabe	577 James Robert Bridge	608 Kenneth R Dutton
545 Keith Lavender	578 Ian R Garbutt	609 Guy Brian Young